6th Workshop on Online Abuse and Harms (WOAH 2022)

Online
14 July 2022

ISBN: 978-1-7138-5646-7

Printed from e-media with permission by:

Curran Associates, Inc.
57 Morehouse Lane
Red Hook, NY 12571

CURRAN ASSOCIATES INC. proceedings .com

Some format issues inherent in the e-media version may also appear in this print version.

Association for Computational Linguistics
209 N. Eighth Street
Stroudsburg, Pennsylvania 18360

Phone: 1-570-476-8006
Fax: 1-570-476-0860

acl@aclweb.org

Additional copies of this publication are available from:

Curran Associates, Inc.
57 Morehouse Lane
Red Hook, NY 12571 USA
Phone: 845-758-0400
Fax: 845-758-2633
Email: curran@proceedings.com
Web: www.proceedings.com

WOAH 2022

The Sixth Workshop on Online Abuse and Harms

Proceedings of the Workshop

July 14, 2022

The WOAH organizers gratefully acknowledge the support from the following sponsors.

Gold

Silver

Order copies of this and other ACL proceedings from:

Association for Computational Linguistics (ACL)
209 N. Eighth Street
Stroudsburg, PA 18360
USA
Tel: +1-570-476-8006
Fax: +1-570-476-0860
acl@aclweb.org

Introduction

Digital technologies have brought myriad benefits for society, transforming how people connect, communicate and interact with each other. However, they have also enabled harmful and abusive behaviors to reach large audiences and for their negative effects to be amplified, including interpersonal aggression, bullying and hate speech. Work on online abuse and harms has traditionally centred on abuse in English and other Western European languages, further widening the resource gap between Western European languages and all other languages.

As academics, civil society, policymakers and tech companies devote more resources and effort to tackling online abuse, there is a pressing need for scientific research that critically and rigorously investigates how it is defined, detected and countered. Technical disciplines such as machine learning (ML), natural language processing (NLP) and statistics have made substantial advances in this field. However, concerns have been raised about the differences in attention given to different languages and geographies. For example, English, particularly dominant forms of American English, are overrepresented in most NLP resources. Technological solutions can be developed for speakers of other dialects and languages. On the other hand, languages such as Yuruba, Urdu, Amharic, and many other languages have few to no resources available, thus providing significant challenges in developing technological systems for the detection of abuse and other harms.

For this sixth edition of the Workshop on Online Abuse and Harms (6th WOAH!) we advance research in online abuse through our theme: **On Developing Resources and Technologies for low resource Online Abuse and Harms**. We continue to emphasize the need for inter-, cross- and anti- disciplinary work on online abuse and harms. These include but are not limited to: NLP, machine learning, computational social sciences, law, politics, psychology, network analysis, sociology and cultural studies. Continuing the tradition started in WOAH 4, we invite civil society, in particular individuals and organisations working with women and marginalised communities who are often disproportionately affected by online abuse, to submit reports, case studies, findings, data, and to record their lived experiences. We hope that through these engagements WOAH can directly address the issues faced by those on the front-lines of tackling online abuse.

Speaking to the complex nature of the issue of online abuse, we are pleased to invite Mona Diab, Murali Shanmugavelan, Gebre Gebremeske, Daniel Borkan, Lucas Dos Santos, Alyssa Lees, and Rachel Rosen to deliver keynotes. In addition to our invited keynotes, we received 47 submissions out of which 24 were accepted. Of the accepted papers, 20 were long papers and 4 were short papers. These papers will be presented in our poster session. We thank the reviewers for their dedication and efforts in providing in-depth and timely reviews.

With this, we welcome you to the Sixth Workshop on Online Abuse and Harms. We look forward to a day filled with spirited discussion and thought provoking research!

Aida, Bertie, Kanika, Lambert, and Zeerak.

Organizing Committee

Organizer

Kanika Narang, Meta AI
Aida Mostafazadeh Davani, University of Southern California
Lambert Mathias, Meta AI
Bertie Vidgen, The Alan Turing Institute
Zeerak Talat, Simon Fraser University

Program Committee

Chairs

Kanika Narang, Meta AI
Aida Mostafazadeh Davani, University of Southern California
Lambert Mathias, Meta AI
Bertie Vidgen, Alan Turing Institute
Zeerak Talat, Simon Fraser University

Emergency Reviewers

Francielle Vargas, University of São Paulo
Alon Halevy, Facebook AI
Qifan Wang, Meta AI
Shaoliang Nie, Facebook Inc
Yi-ling Chung, The Alan Turing Institute
Sheikh Sarwar, Amazon.com

Program Committee

Piush Aggarwal, FernUniversität in Hagen, Computational Linguistics
Khalid Alnajjar, University of Helsinki
Nikolay Babakov, Skoltech Institute of Science and Technology
Xingjian Bai, University of Oxford
Dan Bateyko, Georgetown University Law Center
Thales Bertaglia, Maastricht University
Noah Broestl, University of Oxford
Tommaso Caselli, Rijksuniversiteit Groningen
Yung-sung Chuang, Massachusetts Institute of Technology
Leon Derczynski, IT University of Copenhagen
Nemanja Djuric, Aurora Innovation
Lucie Flek, CAISA Lab, Faculty of Mathematics and Informatics, Philipps University of Marburg
Paula Fortuna, TALN, Pompeu Fabra University
Simona Frenda, Università degli Studi di Torino and Universitat Politècnica de València
Sara E. Garza, FIME-UANL
Shlok Gilda, University of Florida
Lee Gillam, University of Surrey
Darina Gold, University of Duisburg-Essen
Udo Hahn, Friedrich-Schiller-Universität Jena
Adeep Hande, Indian Institute of Information Technology,Tiruchirappalli
Alex Hanna, Google
Christopher Homan, Rochester Institute of Technology
Ruihong Huang, Texas A&M University
Pica Johansson, Alan Turing Institute
Srecko Joksimovic, University of South Australia
David Jurgens, University of Michigan
Brendan Kennedy, University of Southern California
Ashiqur Khudabukhsh, Carnegie Mellon University

Thomas Kleinbauer, Saarland University
Vasiliki Kougia, University of Vienna
Ralf Krestel, ZBW & Kiel University
Sheng Li, University of Georgia
Zi Lin, University of California, San Diego
Jeremiah Liu, Google Research
Hongyin Luo, MIT
Diana Maynard, University of Sheffield
Mainak Mondal, Institute of Engineering and Management
Smruthi Mukund, Amazon
Isar Nejadgholi, National Research Council Canada
Debora Nozza, Bocconi University
Ali Omrani, University of Southern California
Alexander Panchenko, Skolkovo Institue of Science and Technology
Kartikey Pant, Salesforce
Viviana Patti, University of Turin, Dipartimento di Informatica
John Pavlopoulos, Athens University of Economics and Business
Matúš Pikuliak, Kempelen Institute of Intelligent Technologies
Vinodkumar Prabhakaran, Google
Michal Ptaszynski, Kitami Institute of Technology
Masoumeh Razzaghi, Texas A&M University-Commerce
Georg Rehm, DFKI
Björn Ross, University of Edinburgh
Paolo Rosso, Universitat Politècnica de València
Dana Ruiter, Saarland University
Paul Röttger, University of Oxford
Nazanin Sabri, University of Tehran
Qinlan Shen, Oracle
Karthik Shivaram, Tulane University
Marian Simko, Kempelen Institute of Intelligent Technologies
Jeffrey Sorensen, Google Jigsaw
Gerasimos Spanakis, Maastricht University
Arjun Subramonian, University of California, Los Angeles
Sajedul Talukder, Southern Illinois University
Tristan Thrush, Hugging Face
Sara Tonelli, FBK
Dimitrios Tsarapatsanis, University of York
Gareth Tyson, QMUL
Avijit Vajpayee, Amazon
Ingmar Weber, Qatar Computing Research Institute
Jing Xu, Facebook AI
Fan Yang, Nuance Communications
Seunghyun Yoon, Adobe Research
Samira Zad, Florida International University
Aleš Završnik, Institute of criminology at the Faculty of Law Ljubljana
Torsten Zesch, Computational Linguistics, FernUniversität in Hagen

Keynote Talk: Multilingual hate speech detection: From labeling to systems, challenges and opportunities

Mona Diab
George Washington University - Facebook AI

Abstract: Assessing social media content is quite challenging due to the subjective nature of the material where context plays a pivotal role. In this talk, I highlight the challenges of dealing with nuanced language due to inherent characteristics of dialects as manifested in the Arabic language as well as in English. I will talk about challenges in labeling and building systems where the amount of labeled data is on the low. However such challenges can be mitigated with smart designs while also heeding diversity and inclusion in the process.

Bio: Mona Talat Diab is a computer science professor at George Washington University and a research scientist with Facebook AI. Her research focuses on natural language processing, computational linguistics, cross lingual/multilingual processing, computational socio-pragmatics, and applied machine learning. Besides this, she also has special interests in Arabic NLP and low resource scenarios. Diab completed her Ph.D. in computational linguistics at the University of Maryland, Linguistics Department and University of Maryland Institute for Advanced Computer Studies (UMIACS) in 2003, under the supervision of Philip Resnik. She was also a postdoctoral research scientist at Stanford University (2003–2005) under the mentorship of Dan Jurafsky, where she was a part of the Stanford NLP Group. After her postdoc at Stanford, Diab took a position as principal investigator at the Center for Computational Learning Systems (CCLS) in Columbia University, where she was also adjunct professor in the computer science department. In 2013 she joined the George Washington University as an associate professor, where she was promoted to full professor in 2017. Diab is the founder and director of the GW NLP lab CARE4Lang.

Keynote Talk: Keynote by Murali Shanmugavelan

Murali Shanmugavelan
Oxford Internet Institute - Data and Society, NYC

Bio: Murali Shanmugavelan researches caste in media and communication studies and digital cultures. His PhD from the School of Oriental and African Studies (SOAS) University of London was focused on everyday communicative practices of caste. He has over 15 years of experience developing, managing and implementing projects focused on developing media and ICT policies and practice; outreach and strategic communications; and innovations in mobile applications in multi-disciplinary and cross-cultural settings.

Keynote Talk: Social media and hate speech in time of war: The case of Tigray

Gebre Gebremeskel
The Centre for Mathematics and Computer Science (CWI), Netherlands

Abstract: Hate Speech has been around in Ethiopia before social media, but with very limited reach. With the coming of social media companies that have no or little business interest to lose in low-resourced languages such as those in Ethiopia, diaspora activists that have nothing or little to lose from engaging in online hate speech, and several technical and institutional challenges, hate speech on social media slowly became mainstream in Ethiopia, tearing societies apart and eventually serving as an animating force for a genocidal war on Tigrayans. In this speech, I will briefly assess the normalization of hate speech in Ethiopia, the factors that led to this, and the role hate speech and social media played during the Tigray war, social media hate speech detection and monitoring, and what should be done going forward.

Bio: Gebrekirstos G. Gebremeskel is the founder and chief editor of Tghat.com, founder of mermru.com, and a PhD candidate at Radboud University Nijmegen, Netherlands. He has a double masters degree: MSc in Human Language Science and Technology from the University of Malta and MA/MSc in Linguistics (research) from the University of Groningen. Tghat was founded in November 2020 following the start of the war on Tigray in response to the Ethiopian government's imposition of media and telecommunications blackout as part of the war on Tigray. Tghat has been engaged in documenting, researching and writing about the Tigray war. Merrmru.com, is a website dedicated to collecting and developing Natural Language Processing tools and resources for the learning and the computational processing of Geez-based languages such as Tigrinya, Geez and Amharic. The website has an extensive capability to take any Tigrinya verb and provide tens of thousands of inflections. His PhD research focuses on the intersection of Information Retrieval, Recommender Systems, NLP and their impacts on society. Some of his academic publications can be found in Google Scholar.
He has previously worked as a researcher at the CWI Amsterdam, interned at Yahoo! And worked for other companies. Gebrekirstos also writes for other outlets, speaks in different platforms and events, and appears on local and international media including Al Jazeera and the BBC to offer analysis and views on the Tigray war, Ethiopia and the Horn of Africa. He tweets at @gebrekirstosG. His more extended bio can be found at https://www.tghat.com/gebrekirstos-gebreselassie-gebremeskel/

Keynote Talk: Next generation of perspective: Multilingual large language models and combating online harassment

Daniel Borkan, Lucas Dos Santos, Alyssa Lees, and Rachel Rosen
Google Jigsaw

Abstract: We explore two developments in Google Jigsaw's Perspective API. First, we describe a new multilingual, token-free, Charformer model infrastructure that is applicable across a range of languages, domains, and tasks. This architecture was extensively evaluated on an array of tasks and enabled Perspective API launches in 10 new languages, including Arabic, Chinese, Indonesian, Korean, and Japanese. We also discuss how we leveraged Perspective API to create Harassment Manager, an open-source web application that enables users to document and take action on abuse targeted at them on online platforms. The tool allows users to consolidate their experiences of online harassment into a story, complete with context and examples.

Bio:

- Daniel Borkan attended UCSC where he graduated with a BSc in computer science. He joined Jigsaw in 2014 to build the Outline tool to bypass repressive censorship. Daniel now works on the Perspective API to combat online toxicity, where he focuses on internationalization, bias mitigation, and new model development.
- Lucas Dos Santos attended Pomona College where he graduated with a BA in computer science. He joined the Conversation AI team at Jigsaw in 2018 and focuses on efforts around combatting online harassment, machine learning model development, and API infrastructure.
- Alyssa Lees attended Brown University and NYU where she received BSc/MS/PhD degrees in statistics and computer science while cultivating interests in AI, cooking, architecture and fine art. Alyssa has worked in various capacities at Google Jigsaw including developing the next generation of the Perspective API and currently as lead combatting disinformation. Her research interests include ML Fairness, NLP and Knowledge Acquisition.
- Rachel Rosen attended NYU where she graduated with a BA for a joint computer science and math major. She completed two Google internships while studying at NYU and began working for Google full time after graduating in 2014. She joined the ConversationAI team at Jigsaw in 2016 where she began working on solutions for countering toxic speech and online harassment.

Table of Contents

Program

Thursday, July 14, 2022

08:40 - 08:30	*Welcome + Opening Remarks*
09:25 - 08:40	*Keynote 1 - Mona Diab*
10:10 - 09:25	*Keynote 2 - Murali Shanmugavalan*
10:30 - 10:10	*Morning Break*
11:15 - 10:30	*Keynote 3 - Gebre Gebremeskel*
12:00 - 11:15	*Poster Session (1)*
13:30 - 12:00	*Lunch Break*
14:15 - 13:30	*Poster Session (2)*
15:00 - 14:15	*Keynote 4 - Daniel Borkan, Lucas Dos Santos, Alyssa Lees, and Rachel Rosen*
15:05 - 15:00	*Closing Remarks*

Separating Hate Speech and Offensive Language Classes via Adversarial Debiasing

Shuzhou Yuan *
Karlsruhe Institute of Technology
shuzhou.yuan@kit.edu

Antonis Maronikolakis
CIS, LMU Munich
antmarakis@cis.lmu.de

Hinrich Schütze
CIS, LMU Munich

Abstract

Research to tackle hate speech plaguing online media has made strides in providing solutions, analyzing bias and curating data. A challenging problem is ambiguity between hate speech and offensive language, causing low performance both overall and specifically for the hate speech class. It can be argued that misclassifying actual hate speech content as merely offensive can lead to further harm against targeted groups. In our work, we mitigate this potentially harmful phenomenon by proposing an adversarial debiasing method to separate the two classes. We show that our method works for English, Arabic German and Hindi, plus in a multilingual setting, improving performance over baselines.

1 Introduction

Online hate speech has become a pernicious phenomenon of modern society and a lot of effort is being expended in tackling this challenge. While there has been plenty of work to develop automatic methods for hate speech detection (Schmidt and Wiegand, 2017), this has proven to be a difficult challenge to tackle with impractically poor performance.

In the NLP community, a prevailing convention is to frame this problem as a three-way classification: between *hate speech*, *offensive language* and *neither* (Davidson et al., 2017; Mulki et al., 2019; Founta et al., 2018; Mubarak et al., 2017; Mathur et al., 2018). While this convention allows for the application of more traditional NLP pipelines, performance has been low (Mozafari et al., 2019; Davidson et al., 2017) especially when it comes to generalization to unseen data (Swamy et al., 2019), with even humans struggling to distinguish hate speech (Chatzakou et al., 2017; Waseem, 2016).

In our work we also adopt the wide-spread 3-class definition of hate speech, where *hate speech* is defined as language used to express hatred towards a targeted group/individual based on protected attributes such as race or religion, *offensive language* contains offensive terms but is not targeting any group in particular, while *neither* is the case where none of the other two classes are present. As an example, in Table 1 we present the tweets that are annotated as hate speech and offensive language respectively, from Davidson et al. (2017), alongside DistilBERT predictions.

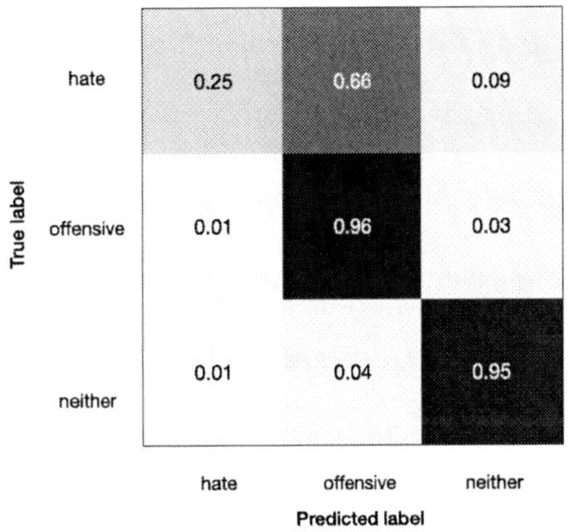

Figure 1: Performance of BERT on Davidson et al. (2017). We see the confusion between hate speech and offensive language, with numerous False Negatives. We argue that these are very insidious mistakes that could lead to further harm against target groups. With our adversarial debiasing method, we can separate these two classes further and thus minimize this type of error as well as increase overall performance.

An observation that can be made from the way classifiers operate is that oftentimes hate speech is misclassified as offensive language and vice-versa (Davidson et al., 2017; Mozafari et al., 2019). We showcase this in Figure 1. We argue that for hate speech detection models to be trustworthy, we need to work along two axes: increasing overall efficiency while keeping false negatives (i.e., hate speech marked as offensive language) to a mini-

* The work was done while at LMU Munich.

Proceedings of the Sixth Workshop on Online Abuse and Harms (WOAH), pages 1 - 10
July 14, 2022

tweet	class	prediction
bitch get off my twitter hoe	offensive	offensive
You ain't gunna do shit spear chucker	hateful	offensive
LMFAO I HATE BLACK PEOPLE	hateful	hateful

Table 1: Labeled tweets (from Davidson et al. (2017)) alongside model prediction.

mum, and that we cannot have one if it comes at the expense of the other. Thus, models should be able to tackle both challenges simultaneously. If models have low accuracy, they will not find application in real-world settings, and if there is too much hate speech content slipping through the cracks, targeted communities will experience increased harm online.

With that goal in mind, we propose a novel method to separate the two classes (*hate speech* and *offensive language*) via adapting adversarial debiasing methods to the problem at hand. This model stabilizes and improves classifier behavior and performance, increasing metrics across all classes, while at the same time keeping performance for hate speech content stable (or improving upon it). We thus strike a balance between performance overall and specifically for hate speech.

We experiment with different architectures for the classifier (BERT (Devlin et al., 2019), DistilBERT (Sanh et al., 2020)) and the adversary (BERT, DistilBERT and LSTMs (Hochreiter and Schmidhuber, 1997)). We perform hyperparameter tuning on English data before applying our findings on several languages (German, Arabic and Hindi) diverse in script, typography and grammar, as well as on a multilingual task setting using mBERT. To more objectively frame the benefit of our method, we compare against a battery of baselines, while we also perform error analysis to identify patterns where our method helps.

In summary, our contributions[1] are: **i)** Employing adversarial debiasing to separate hate speech and offensive language **ii)** Showing that our method works in keeping false negatives to a minimum and increasing F1-scores on multiple English datasets **iii)** Generalizing our findings to other languages, including a multilingual setting.

[1]Code available at https://github.com/ShuzhouYuan/hate_speech_adversarial_debiasing

2 Related Work

For hate speech detection, supervised learning approaches are often used. Schmidt and Wiegand (2017) provide a comprehensive survey on the earlier research of hate speech detection. In more recent work, focus has been placed on various classification methods and curation of datasets (Davidson et al., 2017; Wulczyn et al., 2017; Zhang et al., 2018; Mozafari et al., 2019; Qian et al., 2021).

In Davidson et al. (2017), the prevailing definition of the task as a three-way classification was formulated concretely. In their work, despite the high overall accuracy, over 30% of hate speech was misclassified as offensive language, which saliently sheds light on this pervasive challenge in hate speech detection. This finding was corroborated more recently in Mozafari et al. (2019), where the state-of-the-art BERT model (Devlin et al., 2019) was applied on a hate speech detection task, with over 60% of hate speech misclassified as offensive language. In the other direction, efforts have also been made to tackle false positives (Markov and Daelemans, 2021).

Further, recent efforts in hate speech detection have increased language coverage from English to multiple languages around the globe, including Hindi (Mathur et al., 2018), Arabic (Mubarak et al., 2017), Levantine (Mulki et al., 2019), Indonesian (Ibrohim and Budi, 2019), Danish (Sigurbergsson and Derczynski, 2020) as well as more general multilingual data (Ousidhoum et al., 2019; Ranasinghe and Zampieri, 2020; Basile et al., 2019) and code-mixing (Bohra et al., 2018).

A similar methodology to adversarial debiasing was applied to recidivism prediction (Wadsworth et al., 2018). There, racial biases existing in criminal history datasets were mitigated through adversarial training. This method was also applied in hate speech research to minimize bias against AAE text (Xia et al., 2020). In this case, adversarial debiasing was employed to counteract the disproportionate labeling of AAE text as offensive or hate speech. These works have shown the potential of adversarial debiasing methods in training fairer models.

3 Data

Since we wanted to evaluate the 3-class setting (*hate speech*, *offensive language* and *neither*), we either used datasets that already utilized these classes or equivalent ones (for example, in Founta et al. (2018) *offensive language* is called *abusive language*). Overall, we made use of seven datasets. A summary of each dataset is presented in Table 2.

3.1 English

Davidson17. Davidson et al. (2017) is a well-studied English hate speech dataset collected from Twitter. It contains 25K tweets that are annotated as hate speech, offensive (but not hate) speech, or neither hate speech nor offensive language. The definition of hate speech and offensive language is the same as in §1. We utilize this dataset's development set for the early phase of experimentation to make design decisions, e.g. selecting model architectures, hyperparameters, baselines, etc.

Founta18. Founta et al. (2018) contains 100K English samples collected from Twitter. The definition of hate speech is the usual definition (as described in §1), while the *abusive language* class is defined as any impolite content using profanity, which is equivalent to the definition of offensive language. Thus, we regard it as offensive language for our experiments.

HasocEn19. Mandl et al. (2019) is an English hate speech dataset of 6K samples from Twitter and Facebook. The samples were labeled into four categories: *hate speech*, *offensive language*, *profanity*, and *normal*. *Offensive language* is defined as unacceptable language in the absence of insults and abuse. The *profanity* class expands on this definition to include swear words. We merged the two classes, because both classes meet our definition.

3.2 German

GermEval18. Wiegand et al. (2018) is a Twitter dataset containing 5K German tweets annotated as abuse, insult, profanity, and other/normal. The authors define the class *abusive* as behaviour that promotes dehumanization towards a target societal group or individual. Since it is as same as the aforementioned definition of hate speech, we rename it as hate speech in our research. *Profanity* is defined as text containing profane words and the class *insult* expresses a clear intention to insult or offend somebody. The two categories are merged into one class, *offensive language*.

HasocDe19. Mandl et al. (2019) is a 4K German dataset collected from Twitter and Facebook. The classes of *HasocDe19* are the same as *HasocEn19*: hate speech, offensive language, profanity, and normal. Similarly, the class *profanity* and *offensive language* are merged in our work.

3.3 Arabic

L-HSAB19. Mulki et al. (2019) contains 5K Arabic tweets. They were annotated as hate tweets, abusive tweets, and normal tweets. The definition of hate tweets is the same as our definition of hate speech in §1. The abusive tweets are defined as including offensive, aggressive or insulting language, which is equivalent to our definition of offensive language. We rename the class *abusive* as *offensive language* in our work.

3.4 Hindi

HasocHin19. Mandl et al. (2019) is a dataset of 5k samples written in Hindi. This dataset also comes from the *Hasoc* family of data, and therefore has the same classes: hate speech, offensive language, profanity and normal. As with the other two *Hasoc* datasets, the classes *offensive language* and *profanity* are merged into *offensive language*.

4 Adversarial Debiasing

In this section, we detail our adversarial debiasing scheme. In this setup two models are trained in conjunction: the classifier (predictor) and the adversary. The classifier is predicting the actual class of an example, while the adversary learns to predict a protected variable.

For the classifier, we compare the performance of three different models. And for the adversary, we investigate three different architectures, loss functions and protected variables[2]. In a first step, the models are trained and evaluated with *Davidson17*, *Founta18* and *HasocEn19* (the English datasets in our experiments).

4.1 Classifier

In the adversarial debiasing setting, the classifier is the component making predictions for the given task. The goal is to use the adversarial component to "debias" the classifier in order to achieve a desired result. In our case, our goal is to separate the *hate speech* from the *offensive language* class. We hypothesize this is going to improve performance. Here we explored `BERT`, `DistilBERT` and LSTM models for the classifier.

In our preliminary experiments (without adversarial debiasing), we found that LSTMs performed poorly in classifying hate speech. `BERT` and `DistilBERT` fared much better. All models, though, made a lot of false positive predic-

[2] In some papers it is called "protected attribute/label".

Language	Dataset	Domain	Classes: size	Source
English	Davidson17	Twitter	hate speech: 1431	Davidson et al. 2017
			offensive language: 19190	
			neither: 4163	
	Founta18	Twitter	hate speech: 4065	Founta et al. 2018
			abusive (OFF): 17150	
			normal (NEI): 53851	
	HasocEn19	Twitter, Facebook	hate speech: 1143	Mandl et al. 2019
			offensive ∪ profanity (OFF): 1118	
			none (NEI): 3591	
German	GermEval18	Twitter	abuse (HAT): 1022	Wiegand et al. 2018
			insult ∪ profanity (OFF): 19190	
			Other(NEI): 3321	
	HasocDe19	Twitter, Facebook	hate speech: 111	Mandl et al. 2019
			offensive ∪ profanity (OFF): 296	
			none(NEI): 3412	
Arabic	L-HSAB19	Twitter	hate speech: 417	Mulki et al. 2019
			abusive (OFF): 1559	
			normal (NEI): 3285	
Hindi	HasocHin19	Twitter, Facebook	hate speech: 556	Mandl et al. 2019
			offensive ∪ profanity (OFF): 1913	
			none (NEI): 2197	

Table 2: Summary of the datasets used in our research. HAT: hate speech, OFF: offensive language, NEI: neither

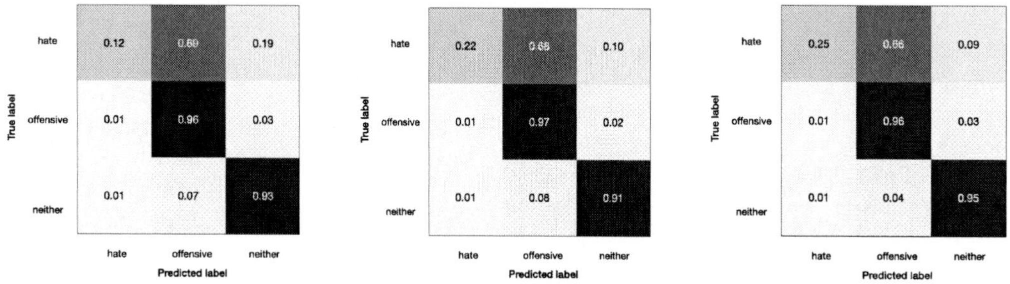

(a) LSTM (b) DistilBERT (c) BERT

Figure 2: Confusion matrices for different classifier models

tions, classifying hate speech as offensive language. Since BERT and DistilBERT had the highest true positive rate and both had similar performance, we chose to continue experimentation with DistilBERT to save on computational resources without a large performance drop. Confusion matrices for all three models are shown in Figure 2.

4.2 Adversary

The adversary in the setup is used to debias the classifier, learning to predict a particular attribute given the representations learned by the classifier. Then, via joint updating of weights, the classifier learns to generate representations that are not useful to the adversary, i.e., the goal is for the adversary to be unable to complete its task. We experiment with various protected variables, loss functions and architectures.

4.2.1 Adversary Architecture

The classifier we used in our final experiments was DistilBERT. Given some textual input, DistilBERT computes its internal representation which is then given as input to the adversary to predict the corresponding target. We experimented with two architectures for the adversary: Feed Forward Neural Networks (FFNs) and LSTMs. Accuracy for both adversaries was on average similar, plateauing around 75%. Since there is little difference in accuracy, we chose the FFN as our adversary since it requires fewer computational resources.

4.2.2 Protected variable and loss function

While in other research with adversarial debiasing (Xia et al., 2020; Sap et al., 2019; Han et al., 2021) has focused on debiasing for a protected variable (for example African American English), we instead propose a novel objective. In our experiments the adversary learns to predict the offensiveness of a sample, either by separating it from hate speech or merging it (and thus separating *hate speech* and *offensive language* in the classifier).

Adversary predicts *hate speech* ∪ *offensive language* jointly ($\texttt{Adversary}_{joint}$).[3] Here the adversary is trying to jointly predict the *hate speech* and *offensive language* classes. Thus, we merge the two classes for the adversary's task, by labeling both classes as *offensive*. *Neither* is relabeled as *not-offensive*. In this case, the adversary learns to predict all hate speech and offensive language examples as one class from the representation of the classifier. Thus, since the goal is for the adversary to be unable to do so, the classifier learns how to *separate* these two classes. The loss function is defined as

$$loss_{total} = loss_{classifier} - \alpha * loss_{adversary}.$$

The loss function is the same as in Wadsworth et al. (2018); Xia et al. (2020), with $loss_{adversary}$ being the loss of the adversary for its task, $loss_{classifier}$ the loss of the classifier for the original task (hate speech vs. offensive language vs. neither) and α being a parameter to regulate the effect of $loss_{adversary}$. Xia et al. (2020) found that the value should be neither too large nor too small. Empirically, they set α=0.05. After some hyperparameter tuning, we found that in this setup an α value of 0.05 was the best-performing. Under $loss_{total}$, the classifier minimizes its original loss while maximizing the adversary's loss. As a result, the classifier is encouraged to actively develop diverging representations for the two classes.

Adversary discriminates between hate speech and offensive language ($\texttt{Adversary}_{sep}$). We also experiment with another adversarial setup: the adversary acts like "support", actively aiding the classifier in separating hate speech from offensive language. This is accomplished by employing an adversary that learns to model the "offensiveness" property, by discriminating between the *hate speech/neither* classes and *offensive language*. Since this method is aimed at directly helping the classifier, instead of subtracting this adversary loss, we *add* it instead:

$$loss_{total} = loss_{classifier} + \alpha * loss_{adversary}.$$

For this setup, we set the α hyperparameter to 2. The value of α was tuned on the development set of *Davidson17*, achieving the highest true positive rate for hate speech.

This "supportive" setup (discriminating between *hate speech* ∪ *neither* and *offensive*) was the best performing, so for the majority of our experiments we are using $\texttt{Adversary}_{sep}$.

Adversary predicts whether text contains swear words ($\texttt{Adversary}_{swear}$).[4] We also evaluated an adversary that predicts whether swear words are present in the text or not. We measured the proportion of *hate speech* and *offensive language* examples that contain a word from a dictionary of swear words[5] and found that in both classes more than 90% of examples contain at least one swear word. A lot of hate speech is labeled by annotators as such because of the presence of swear words in the text even when that should not be an indicator of hatefulness (Sap et al., 2019).

So, in this instance we train the adversary to predict whether swear words are present in text and then subtract this loss from the classifier's loss function. This forces the classifier to base its decisions on features other than the presence of swear words. The loss function is then

$$loss_{total} = loss_{classifier} - \alpha * loss_{adversary}.$$

4.3 Class Rebalancing

One thing to note is that data is heavily imbalanced against hate speech across all datasets (Table 2). For example, the number of offensive samples in *Davidson17* is 15 times higher than the number of hate speech samples. Before our adversarial debiasing experiments, we perform a study on the effect of imbalance on the training set of *Davidson17*. To compare against the original training set (denoted with *original dataset*), we sampled equally-sized sets from each class. Henceforth, we call this new, balanced dataset *uniform dataset*. Note that the development and testing sets remained unchanged for fair comparison: only the training sets were rebalanced. In Table 3 we see that the improvement of the true positive rate of hate speech is significant, from 22.0% to 81.8%. Although the overall accuracy drops by 16%, we believe this model would be more applicable in a real world scenario. If we build hate speech de-

[3]Even though this method did not work consistently, we mention it as a good starting point of discussion.

[4]This can only be applied in settings where swearword dictionaries are available, in our case we only applied it on the English datasets.

[5]`https://www.cs.cmu.edu/~biglou/resources/bad-words.txt`

tection models, we should be aiming for acceptable accuracy for the problematic class. Since we see that the uniform training set helps the model achieve acceptable performance for hate speech, we continue further experimentation using the uniform dataset.

Data	Best TPH	Accuracy
Original dataset	22.0%	91.2%
Uniform dataset	81.8%	75.2%

Table 3: Comparison of original and uniform dataset with *Davidson17*, evaluated on the same test set

5 Experimental Setup

For each dataset, we either use the provided training, development and testing set splits, or we sample them at 80:10:10 rates randomly. Then, we further downsample (to the number of examples in the smallest class according to each dataset) the training set classes to generate a uniform training set.

For *HasocEn19*, *HasocDe19*, *HasocHin19* and *GermEval18*, the dataset was already split in training and test sets. The original rates are presented in Table 4. In these cases, we keep the test set invariant and take 10% samples from the training set to form our development set.

Dataset	training:test
HasocEn19	84:16
HasocDe19	82:18
HasocHin19	78:22
GermEval18	59:41

Table 4: Original split distributions

For each experiment, we train for five epochs and keep the best-performing model across the epochs as evaluated on the development set. Then, we compute this model's performance on the held-out test set. We repeat this process three times and average the results.

Adversarial debiasing setup. The main setup we examine is $\texttt{Adversary}_{sep}$ where the adversary actively supports the classifier in separating the *hate speech* from the *offensive language* class, as defined in Section 4.2.2.

Multilingual dataset. To obtain a multilingual hate speech dataset, we combine all the datasets in Table 2 together. This new multilingual hate speech dataset contains 110k samples with the distribution of the three classes presented in Table 5.

Baselines. To evaluate the benefits of our method, we compare against vanilla finetuning with `DistilBERT` on each hate speech dataset as well as a simple class weighting baseline. We experimented with different weights and found that the best performing one (on the *Davidson17* dataset which served as an overall development set for design decisions) was $[1, 0.5, 1]$[6]. That is, we halve the weight of the *offensive* class.

6 Results

Results are summarized in Table 6. All the experiments are conducted on the uniform dataset, since the goal is to achieve an acceptable true positive rate (**TPH**: **T**rue **P**ositive rate for **H**ate speech) and this is a more solid starting point than the original distributions. We provide both macro and weighted F1 to show a more complete picture. Since our dataset is imbalanced, we focus on macro F1 for a more representative picture.

For *Davidson17* and *Founta18*, our method does not provide positive findings. In *Davidson17* both TPH and overall performance are lower, while in *Founta18*, adversarial debiasing does provide a performance boost, but it comes at the expense of TPH. For these two datasets, $\texttt{Adversary}_{swear}$ was applied as well, improving the TPH for *Davidson17* but not for *Founta18*.

Results are better for the final English dataset, *HasocEn19*. There, even though TPH drops substantially (10%), overall performance increases by more than 0.2 F1 points. Without an adversary, accuracy and F1-scores suffer, making for sub-par classifiers biased heavily towards hate speech. Instead, with our method, more separation is achieved and the model manages to separate the two contentious classes (*hate speech* and *offensive language*) with greater efficiency. Whereas before the classifier would not be practical due to low accuracy, with our method F1-scores and accuracy increase to acceptable levels.

HasocDe19 follows the same pattern, with the vanilla model being unable to provide strong overall results, instead becoming biased towards hate speech and dropping the rest of the classes. With our method, better balance is struck and we see an improvement of 0.15 F1-score over the vanilla model.

In *GermEval18*, we see stronger performance gains both for the TPH (+5.7% over the non-adversary model) and overall (+0.02 in F1-score). Even though the class-weighting baseline does

[6] [hate speech, offensive language, neither]

	Hate		Offensive		Neither	
	total	%	total	%	total	%
training set	8,042	7.3%	42,037	38.0%	60,604	54.8%
dev set	946	7.1%	5,204	38.3%	7,446	54.8%
test set	1,835	9.9%	5,925	32%	10,754	58.1%
uniform training set	8,042	33.3%	8,042	33.3%	8,042	33.3%

Table 5: Class distribution in the training, development and testing sets of the multilingual dataset

score higher in TPH, we note a drop in F1-scores and accuracy.

For *HasocHin19*, we observe the same pattern as the other *Hasoc* family of datasets, although to a lesser extent. In *L-HSAB19*, we show that the simple class-weighting baselines is better than both the vanilla and adversary models.

Finally, in the multilingual setting, we get mixed results. Compared to the vanilla model, adversarial debiasing offers a better TPH score with minimal drop in performance (while macro F1 increases by 0.02 too). Against the baseline model, while the baseline has a higher TPH, in all the other metrics performance is worse.

In synopsis, apart from *L-HSAB19*, performance is better when using the adversarial debiasing method, either for the TPH or the overall F1-score metrics. For the multilingual dataset, performance of our method is mixed, improving upon the vanilla model on the TPH and upon the baseline model on the other metrics.

All in all, our method manages to strike a better balance between TPH and overall performance and we thus believe these models are more applicable to a real-world scenario where both axes need to be taken into consideration.

7 Error Analysis

We observe that a few samples of hate speech are misclassified as offensive language by the vanilla model without the adversary, but correctly predicted by the adversarial model. In Table 7, we show six examples which indicate the significant improvement of adversarial models.

In English, we see that hateful speech was marked as merely offensive by the vanilla model, potentially because no slur was used, but only some offensive language ('c*nt', 'ass' and 'bad ass'). The model failed to take into account the context in which these words were used, or failed to pick up innocuous words used here as slurs (for example, 'orangutan'). The adversarial model was able to make correct predictions, potentially because it is not putting as much weight on individual words, but the combinations between them.

In German, the vanilla model's shortcomings are again centered around a lack of slurs. In both examples, there are no direct slurs so the model interprets it as offensive because of the overall negative sentiment (created through phrases such as 'böse Männer', meaning 'evil men' and 'sexuelle Gewalt', meaning 'sexual violence'). In one of the examples, the model misses that 'Froschfresser' (meaning 'frog eaters') is used as a slur. The adversarial model again shows an ability to expand from keyword-based predictions to a better understanding of context.

In Hindi, while the example is merely offensive, the vanilla model has marked it as hateful, potentially because of the politically heavy 'terrorist' term. The adversarial model has not put as much weight on the word and thus made a correct prediction. In Arabic, the vanilla model again misses that innocuous words are used as slurs (eg., 'dogs'), marking the text as offensive instead of hateful.

8 Conclusion

In hate speech detection efforts, it can be observed that a lot of classifiers struggle with the *hate speech* and *offensive language* classes. A lot of models trained on current datasets misclassify hate speech as offensive language. We argue that this type of error is particularly insidious, since it can lead to targeted groups getting exposed to harmful content more often. Further, a lot of hate speech classifiers are impractical, either having a low true positive rate for hate speech or low performance overall.

We propose a method to both increase the true positive rate for hate speech and to stabilize the classifiers in general. We base our method on the adversarial debiasing setup, where in our instance we are trying to support the classifier in separating the *hate speech* and *offensive language* classes.

We evaluate on seven hate speech datasets spanning four languages, plus a multilingual set we create by combining all data. Our method is at best performing just as well for all datasets ex-

Dataset	Experiment	Best TPH %	Overall Accuracy%	Macro F1	Weighted F1
Davidson17	Without adversary	77.96	**77.81**	**0.67**	**0.83**
	Adversary$_{sep}$	76.88	76.88	0.66	0.82
	Adversary$_{swear}$	**80.38**	75.1	0.66	0.81
	Baseline	78.77	72.64	0.64	0.79
Founta18	Without adversary	74.37	78.22	0.67	0.83
	Adversary$_{sep}$	68.74	**80.79**	**0.69**	**0.84**
	Adversary$_{swear}$	73.24	77.82	0.67	0.82
	Baseline	**77.57**	78.58	0.68	0.83
HasocEn19	Without adversary	82.53	39.99	0.37	0.32
	Adversary$_{sep}$	72.58	**47.53**	**0.47**	**0.54**
	Baseline	**86.83**	38.51	0.42	0.43
GermEval18	Without adversary	50.41	63.66	0.53	0.65
	Adversary$_{sep}$	56.11	**65.71**	**0.56**	**0.67**
	Baseline	**63.86**	64.45	0.53	0.65
HasocDe19	Without adversary	75.00	31.11	0.25	0.39
	Adversary$_{sep}$	65.04	**41.02**	**0.47**	**0.54**
	Baseline	**92.68**	38.67	0.42	0.43
HasocHin19	Without adversary	**79.90**	58.67	0.56	0.63
	Adversary$_{sep}$	68.95	61.84	**0.59**	**0.66**
	Baseline	73.08	**62.92**	0.58	0.66
L-HSAB19	Without adversary	79.08	53.84	0.48	0.58
	Adversary$_{sep}$	77.78	54.93	0.49	0.59
	Adversary$_{joint}$	81.04	54.64	0.50	0.58
	Baseline	**81.71**	**59.03**	**0.52**	**0.62**
Multilingual	Without adversary	77.04	**72.37**	0.63	**0.76**
	Adversary$_{sep}$	79.45	70.03	**0.65**	0.74
	Baseline	**81.85**	68.41	0.63	0.73

Table 6: Summary of the results

Language	Text	True Label	Vanilla	Adversary
en	I can't stress how much I hate these liberal Muslims that bend over backwards for these cunts and these Uncle Tom ass middle eastern / south Asian /Asian / african peoples who sell out like this	hate	offensive	hate
en	RT @user: This is one bad ass orangutan @emoji; @url	hate	offensive	hate
de	@user @user Glaubte Du echt, eine Frau mit befriedigendem Sexleben rennt durch die Welt und sieht überall böse Männer und sexuelle Gewalt? *(@user @user Did you really believe that a woman with a satisfying sex life runs through the world and sees evil men and sexual violence everywhere?)*	hate	offensive	hate
de	@user Genau. Die Froschfresser haben nichts gelernt! Ihr Untergang ist selbstverschuldet. *(@user Exactly. The frog eaters haven't learned anything! Your downfall is self-inflicted.)*	hate	offensive	hate
hindi	झोंपड़ी के, कुछ दिन पहले तक तो तू उस आदतन 'बाइक चोर' तबरेज के लिये छाती पीट रहा था। हर चैनल पर रंडी रोना मचा रखा था। अब सेक्युलरिज्म का 'अखरोट' अपने पिछवाड़े से तोड़ने की कोशिश कर रहा है। आतंकी साला *(Of the hut, till a few days ago, you were habitually beating your chest for that 'bike thief' Tabrez. Randi was crying on every channel. Now the 'nut' of secularism is trying to break from its backyard. terrorist brother)*	offensive	hate	offensive
arabic	ma fy ay shk bs aldrwz klab w khwnh[7] *(True, there is no doubt, but the Druze are dogs and traitors)*	hate	offensive	hate

Table 7: Error analysis on `DistilBERT` predictions versus actual labels for the examined languages.

cept *L-HSAB19*, while also outperforming baseline models on multiple occasions. Error analysis reveals that the debiased model moves past keyword-based predictions, taking into account the context as well. Both the true positive rate for hate speech and overall performance are improved, showcasing the stabilizing capabilities of our novel methodology on hate speech detection.

[7]Example transliterated.

9 Ethical Considerations

In our work we deal with hate speech, which could potentially cause harm (directly or indirectly) to vulnerable social groups. We do not support the views expressed in these hateful posts, we merely venture to analyze and provide solutions to mitigate this online phenomenon.

Further, we could only examine a specific problem (neutral vs. offensive vs. hateful language) in specific languages. This is a non-exhaustive list and there is a lot we did not cover. Care should be taken to use these methods only in the examined languages since generalization may not be feasible (in fact, we show there are issues with our method in Arabic).

10 Acknowledgments

This work has been funded by the German Federal Ministry of Education and Research (BMBF) under Grant No. 01IS18036A. The second author was partly supported by the European Research Council (#740516). The authors of this work take full responsibility for its content.

References

Valerio Basile, Cristina Bosco, Elisabetta Fersini, Debora Nozza, Viviana Patti, Francisco Manuel Rangel Pardo, Paolo Rosso, and Manuela Sanguinetti. 2019. SemEval-2019 task 5: Multilingual detection of hate speech against immigrants and women in Twitter. In *Proceedings of the 13th International Workshop on Semantic Evaluation*, pages 54–63, Minneapolis, Minnesota, USA. Association for Computational Linguistics.

Aditya Bohra, Deepanshu Vijay, Vinay Singh, Syed Sarfaraz Akhtar, and Manish Shrivastava. 2018. A dataset of Hindi-English code-mixed social media text for hate speech detection. In *Proceedings of the Second Workshop on Computational Modeling of People's Opinions, Personality, and Emotions in Social Media*, pages 36–41, New Orleans, Louisiana, USA. Association for Computational Linguistics.

Despoina Chatzakou, Nicolas Kourtellis, Jeremy Blackburn, Emiliano De Cristofaro, Gianluca Stringhini, and Athena Vakali. 2017. Mean birds: Detecting aggression and bullying on twitter. In *Proceedings of the 2017 ACM on web science conference*, pages 13–22.

Thomas Davidson, Dana Warmsley, Michael Macy, and Ingmar Weber. 2017. Automated hate speech detection and the problem of offensive language. In *International AAAI Conference on Web and Social Media*.

Jacob Devlin, Ming-Wei Chang, Kenton Lee, and Kristina Toutanova. 2019. Bert: Pre-training of deep bidirectional transformers for language understanding.

Antigoni-Maria Founta, Constantinos Djouvas, Despoina Chatzakou, Ilias Leontiadis, Jeremy Blackburn, Gianluca Stringhini, Athena Vakali, Michael Sirivianos, and Nicolas Kourtellis. 2018. Large scale crowdsourcing and characterization of twitter abusive behavior. In *11th International Conference on Web and Social Media, ICWSM 2018*. AAAI Press.

Xudong Han, Timothy Baldwin, and Trevor Cohn. 2021. Diverse adversaries for mitigating bias in training. In *Proceedings of the 16th Conference of the European Chapter of the Association for Computational Linguistics: Main Volume*, pages 2760–2765, Online. Association for Computational Linguistics.

Sepp Hochreiter and Jürgen Schmidhuber. 1997. Long short-term memory. *Neural Comput.*, 9(8):1735–1780.

Muhammad Okky Ibrohim and Indra Budi. 2019. Multi-label hate speech and abusive language detection in Indonesian Twitter. In *Proceedings of the Third Workshop on Abusive Language Online*, pages 46–57, Florence, Italy. Association for Computational Linguistics.

Thomas Mandl, Sandip Modha, Prasenjit Majumder, Daksh Patel, Mohana Dave, Chintak Mandlia, and Aditya Patel. 2019. Overview of the hasoc track at fire 2019: Hate speech and offensive content identification in indo-european languages. In *Proceedings of the 11th forum for information retrieval evaluation*, pages 14–17.

Ilia Markov and Walter Daelemans. 2021. Improving cross-domain hate speech detection by reducing the false positive rate. In *Proceedings of the Fourth Workshop on NLP for Internet Freedom: Censorship, Disinformation, and Propaganda*, pages 17–22, Online. Association for Computational Linguistics.

Puneet Mathur, Ramit Sawhney, Meghna Ayyar, and Rajiv Shah. 2018. Did you offend me? classification of offensive tweets in Hinglish language. In *Proceedings of the 2nd Workshop on Abusive Language Online (ALW2)*, pages 138–148, Brussels, Belgium. Association for Computational Linguistics.

Marzieh Mozafari, Reza Farahbakhsh, and Noel Crespi. 2019. A bert-based transfer learning approach for hate speech detection in online social media. In *International Conference on Complex Networks and Their Applications*, pages 928–940. Springer.

Hamdy Mubarak, Kareem Darwish, and Walid Magdy. 2017. Abusive language detection on Arabic social media. In *Proceedings of the First Workshop on*

Abusive Language Online, pages 52–56, Vancouver, BC, Canada. Association for Computational Linguistics.

Hala Mulki, Hatem Haddad, Chedi Bechikh Ali, and Halima Alshabani. 2019. L-HSAB: A Levantine Twitter dataset for hate speech and abusive language. In *Proceedings of the Third Workshop on Abusive Language Online*, pages 111–118, Florence, Italy. Association for Computational Linguistics.

Nedjma Ousidhoum, Zizheng Lin, Hongming Zhang, Yangqiu Song, and Dit-Yan Yeung. 2019. Multilingual and multi-aspect hate speech analysis. In *Proceedings of the 2019 Conference on Empirical Methods in Natural Language Processing and the 9th International Joint Conference on Natural Language Processing (EMNLP-IJCNLP)*, pages 4675–4684, Hong Kong, China. Association for Computational Linguistics.

Jing Qian, Hong Wang, Mai ElSherief, and Xifeng Yan. 2021. Lifelong learning of hate speech classification on social media. In *Proceedings of the 2021 Conference of the North American Chapter of the Association for Computational Linguistics: Human Language Technologies*, pages 2304–2314, Online. Association for Computational Linguistics.

Tharindu Ranasinghe and Marcos Zampieri. 2020. Multilingual offensive language identification with cross-lingual embeddings. In *Proceedings of the 2020 Conference on Empirical Methods in Natural Language Processing (EMNLP)*, pages 5838–5844, Online. Association for Computational Linguistics.

Victor Sanh, Lysandre Debut, Julien Chaumond, and Thomas Wolf. 2020. Distilbert, a distilled version of bert: smaller, faster, cheaper and lighter.

Maarten Sap, Dallas Card, Saadia Gabriel, Yejin Choi, and Noah A. Smith. 2019. The risk of racial bias in hate speech detection. In *Proceedings of the 57th Annual Meeting of the Association for Computational Linguistics*, pages 1668–1678, Florence, Italy. Association for Computational Linguistics.

Anna Schmidt and Michael Wiegand. 2017. A survey on hate speech detection using natural language processing. In *Proceedings of the fifth international workshop on natural language processing for social media*, pages 1–10.

Gudbjartur Ingi Sigurbergsson and Leon Derczynski. 2020. Offensive language and hate speech detection for Danish. In *Proceedings of the 12th Language Resources and Evaluation Conference*, pages 3498–3508, Marseille, France. European Language Resources Association.

Steve Durairaj Swamy, Anupam Jamatia, and Björn Gambäck. 2019. Studying generalisability across abusive language detection datasets. In *Proceedings of the 23rd Conference on Computational Natural Language Learning (CoNLL)*, pages 940–950, Hong Kong, China. Association for Computational Linguistics.

Christina Wadsworth, Francesca Vera, and Chris Piech. 2018. Achieving fairness through adversarial learning: an application to recidivism prediction. *arXiv preprint arXiv:1807.00199*.

Zeerak Waseem. 2016. Are you a racist or am I seeing things? annotator influence on hate speech detection on Twitter. In *Proceedings of the First Workshop on NLP and Computational Social Science*, pages 138–142, Austin, Texas. Association for Computational Linguistics.

Michael Wiegand, Melanie Siegel, and Josef Ruppenhofer. 2018. Overview of the germeval 2018 shared task on the identification of offensive language.

Ellery Wulczyn, Nithum Thain, and Lucas Dixon. 2017. Ex machina: Personal attacks seen at scale. In *Proceedings of the 26th international conference on world wide web*, pages 1391–1399.

Mengzhou Xia, Anjalie Field, and Yulia Tsvetkov. 2020. Demoting racial bias in hate speech detection. In *Proceedings of the Eighth International Workshop on Natural Language Processing for Social Media*, pages 7–14, Online. Association for Computational Linguistics.

Ziqi Zhang, David Robinson, and Jonathan Tepper. 2018. Detecting hate speech on twitter using a convolution-gru based deep neural network. In *European semantic web conference*, pages 745–760. Springer.

Towards Automatic Generation of Messages Countering Online Hate Speech and Microaggressions

Mana Ashida[*] and **Mamoru Komachi**
Tokyo Metropolitan University
maashida@yahoo-corp.jp komachi@tmu.ac.jp

Abstract

Warning: *This paper discusses and contains content that may be deemed offensive or upsetting.*

With the widespread use of social media, online hate is increasing, and microaggressions, unintentional offensive remarks in everyday life (Sue et al., 2007), are receiving attention. We explore the possibility of using pre-trained language models to automatically generate messages that combat the associated offensive texts. Specifically, we focus on using *prompting* to steer model generation as it requires less data and computation than *fine-tuning* and shows the potential for using *prompting* in the proposed generation task. We also propose a human evaluation perspective; offensiveness, stance, and informativeness. After obtaining 306 counterspeech and 42 micro intervention messages generated by GPT-2, textscGPT-Neo, and textscGPT-3, we conducted a human evaluation using Amazon Mechanical Turk and found that GPT-3 produces messages of the highest quality among three systems. Also, We discuss the pros and cons of using our evaluation perspectives. We release a corpus of **c**ountering **ha**te **s**peech and **m**icroaggressions (CHASM), annotated machine-generated counternarratives along with the annotation to promote further research on automatic counternarrative generation and its evaluation.

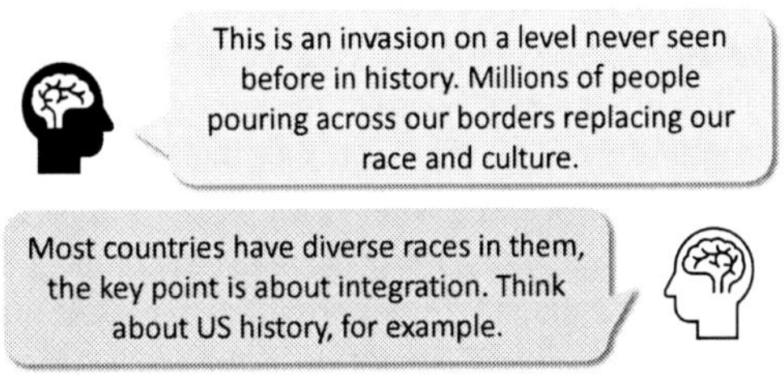

(a) A hate speech–counternarrative pair in Multitarget-CONAN (Fanton et al., 2021)

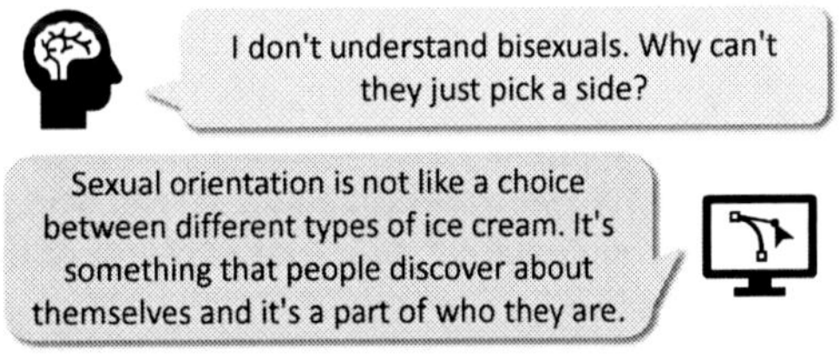

(b) An example of microaggressions in SELFMA (Breitfeller et al., 2019) and an intervention generated by GPT-3 davinci

Figure 1: Overview of the proposed message generation approach in action

1 Introduction

Concomitant with social media becoming a major means of communication, online abusive language is increasing. As abusive language can be harmful, countering it is an important way to reduce the level of danger on the Internet.

Hate speech is arguably the most well-studied form of abusive language across time and regions. It is defined by the United Nations Strategy and Plan of Action on Hate Speech[1] as "any kind of communication in speech, writing or behaviour, that attacks or uses pejorative or discriminatory language with reference to a person or a group on the basis of who they are, in other words, based on their religion, ethnicity, nationality, race, colour, descent, gender or other identity factor." Natural language processing (NLP) researchers have constructed several hate speech corpora, and some of them are publicly available (Madukwe et al., 2020).

Abusive language can be either explicitly offensive and harmful or implicitly offensive. Situations also exist where the offensiveness is executed in more subtly. One type of implicit offensive text is called "microaggression." **Microaggression** is a concept closely related to abusive language that

[*] Currently working at Yahoo Japan Corporation, Tokyo, Japan.

[1] https://www.un.org/en/genocideprevention/hate-speech-strategy.shtml

Proceedings of the Sixth Workshop on Online Abuse and Harms (WOAH), pages 11 - 23
July 14, 2022

has been receiving increased attention recently. According to Sue et al. (2007), "microaggressions are brief and commonplace daily verbal, behavioral, or environmental indignities, whether intentional or unintentional, that communicate hostile, derogatory, or negative racial slights and insults." One characteristic of microaggression is invisibility; people exhibiting microaggressions are often unaware that they engage in such communications when they interact with targeted minorities. Despite its growing interests, research on microaggression in the field of NLP is quite limited.

Identifying hate speech or microaggressions, for example, "abusive language detection," is one technique for countering hate. However, detecting abusive language has some problems; simply flagging offensive content without providing a reason may result in the infringement of free speech. A better way to combat hate speech without infringing freedom of speech is to use a counternarrative.

Counterspeech or **counternarrative** is any message countering hate speech and offensive contents. The counternarrative has been studied as a means of confronting hate speech. Many researchers report that counternarratives are effective for reducing hate online (Hangartner et al., 2021). Several NGOs, such as Dangerous Speech Project[2], are working to promote counterspeech, and social networking platforms are also encouraging the use of counterspeech. Therefore, automatically generating counternarratives and thereby reducing the labor-intensiveness involved in countering online hate speech is an important application of NLP technology for social good.

Language generation by machines is becoming a viable option with the emergence of neural generative language models (LMs). The generation quality of the pretrained generative language models has increased to such an extent that humans cannot easily differentiate machine-generated text from texts written by a human (Clark et al., 2021). As such, we explore the automatic generation of counternarratives using LMs, namely Generative Pre-trained Transformers (GPTs). Conventionally, steering the generation process of a model relies on *fine-tuning*, which requires task-specific data that are not always easily obtainable. For this reason, recent studies have employed *prompting* as an alternative to *fine-tuning*. *Prompting* requires only a small number of examples of the task, and it does not require computation for optimizing the parameters of LMs. In this paper, we investigate the possibility of using a pretrained large-scale generative language model to generate counternarratives against hate speech and microaggressions using *prompting* instead of *fine-tuning*.

Whereas the traditional counternarrative generation task is primarily focused on countering hate speech, this study extends the target to microaggressions. Identifying microaggressions and understanding why they are offensive requires an understanding of the social context and the negative stereotypes that persist in the world. Consequently, countering microaggressions is more difficult than countering hate speech. To counter microaggressions, the concept of **microinterventions** has been proposed in recent years and is being studied from the perspective of psychology and sociology (Sue et al., 2019). However, we are the first to discuss the usefulness of NLP technology for this purpose.

In this study, we generated 696 counternarratives using LMs and evaluated their quality by conducting a human evaluation exercise on a crowdsourcing platform. In addition, for qualitative evaluation, we analyze some examples from the set of counternarratives and then discuss the issue related to the counternarrative generation task as well as its evaluation.

This study makes three main contributions:

1. We propose to include **microaggressions** as a target of counternarrative generation.
2. We design a *few-shot* prompt for generating counternarratives to assess the applicability of prompting for counternarrative generation using pretrained language models.
3. We propose an annotation scheme for machine-generated counternarratives evaluation and create a corpus of **c**ountering **ha**te **s**peech and **m**icroaggressions (CHASM), annotated machine-generated counternarratives along with the offensiveness score of the abusive language post.[3]

2 Related Work

Counterspeech Generation. Considering the positive effects of counternarratives, several NLP

[2] `https://dangerousspeech.org/`

[3] The corpus is accessible from `https://github.com/tmu-nlp/CHASM`.

studies have investigated the possibility of automatically generating counterspeech or using human-in-the-loop strategies to counteract hate and harmful speech online (Qian et al., 2019; Chung et al., 2019; Tekiroğlu et al., 2020; Fanton et al., 2021; Chung et al., 2021; Zhu and Bhat, 2021; Tekiroglu et al., 2022).

Qian et al. (2019) were the first to attempt automatic counternarrative generation. They created a resource of 10,243 counternarratives against 5,257 hate speech instances in 5,020 conversations containing 22,324 comments from Reddit and 31,487 counternarratives against 14,614 hate speech instances in 11,825 conversations containing 33,776 posts from Gab. They used crowdsourcing for obtaining counternarratives and used them to train neural models. Zhu and Bhat (2021) proposed a pipeline for generating counternarrative candidates using a recurrent neural network (RNN)-based generative model trained on this dataset, pruning only grammatical candidates, and selecting the most relevant candidate.

Chung et al. (2019) created a resource of counternarratives for Islamophobia—hate or fear against Islam and Muslims—written by expert operators from three NGOs. The CONAN dataset consists of 6,645 English hate speech–counternarrative pairs, including 2,781 translated pairs from French and Italian. Chung et al. (2021) used this dataset to fine-tune GPT-2 to automatically generate counternarratives. They also adopted the same methodology of data collection on hate speech targeting other religions, races, and gender to fine-tune GPT-2 for automated generation (Fanton et al., 2021). They reported data creation via the human-in-the-loop strategy of post-editing machine-generated counternarratives by expert operators from NGOs.

These strategies require substantial amounts of data as well as human resources. Although fine-tuning pretrained models rather than training neural models requires less data, a substantial amount of data is still necessary. Herein, we explore a method that requires only a few examples for generating counternarratives. This method is called *prompting*. *Prompting* has been receiving significant amounts of attention in recent years because of its effectiveness with only a few examples. Furthermore, it does not require the training of parameters for downstream tasks. This contrasts with fine-tuning of LMs, which requires the training of newly introduced parameters with different datasets, and thus more computation. *Prompting* has also reportedly achieved performance comparable with *fine-tuning*. Further details of prompting are presented in Sec. 4.2.

Microintervention Generation. Microaggression is a less well-known concept than hate speech, little research has been conducted regarding fighting against microaggressions. In the social sciences field, Sue et al. (2019) proposed the concept of "microinterventions" as a way to deal with everyday microaggressions. They state the following goals for microinterventions: (a) make the invisible visible, (b) disarm the microaggression, (c) educate the perpetrator, and (d) seek external reinforcement or support. Some of the core differences between the countering of hate speech and the countering of microaggression are (1) lack of recognition that a microaggression has occurred, and (2) harmful impact caused by good intent. However, no studies have been conducted in the NLP field on this subject.

Studies on the generation of microinterventions in NLP are rare. One of the closest is the work on anti-stereotype generation by Fraser et al. (2021). They investigated strategies to combat negative stereotypes using anti-stereotypes that help to deconstruct harmful beliefs, and proposed the anti-stereotype generation task. Further, they analyzed the kinds of stereotypes and showed that stereotypes are multidimensional and often ambivalent. Therefore, the anti-stereotypes can also be multidimensional, not just the antonym (e.g., the anti-stereotype for "caring nurse" is not "uncaring nurse" but "rude nurse"). They provided a few examples of anti-stereotypes that seem useful for countering stereotypes (e.g., "caring and mature mother" against "caring but childish mother") while mentioning the possibility that anti-stereotypes help us to look at others as individuals instead of stereotypical group representatives.

To the best of our knowledge, this is the first work that tackles the automatic generation of counternarratives against microaggressions and the evaluation of the machine-generated microintervention quality.

Counternarrative Evaluation. Evaluation of generated text is a bottleneck in the promotion of natural language generation tasks, especially for dialogue generation. The difficulty is that there are many acceptable responses when generating output, and it is difficult to define what constitutes a good response. Therefore, the design of the evaluation scheme itself is also difficult. Whereas some relatively constrained generation tasks have established evaluation perspectives, such as "adequacy" and "fluency" for machine translation, evaluation perspectives for many other generation tasks have no common standard.

Similarly, evaluation methods for machine-generated counternarratives have not been established. Previous studies proposed various evaluation perspectives for human evaluation—such as suitableness, informativeness, intra-coherence (Chung et al., 2021), diversity, relevance, language quality (Zhu and Bhat, 2021), offensiveness, and stance (Baheti et al., 2021).

Diversity or **language quality** is designed to measure the generation ability of proposed models, and thus is not specifically designed for counternarrative generation. Because large pretrained models are known to generate fluent texts, we did not consider measuring general generation quality.

Alternatively, we adapt **offensiveness** and **stance** considering the characteristics of pretrained language models that previously found that they tend to agree with the previous comment during conversation (Baheti et al., 2021) and may generate abusive contents (Chung et al., 2021) in the counternarrative generation task. We also assume that **offensiveness** and **stance** can assess aspects that are measured by **relevance** or **suitableness** in previous studies (Chung et al., 2021; Zhu and Bhat, 2021).

Furthermore, we adapt **informativeness** from Chung et al. (2021) to reflect that counternarratives that are too generic are not considered effective. We can also presume that a system that often generates generic outputs cannot produce diverse contents. As such, we expected that **informativeness** could cover qualities that have been captured via **effectiveness** or **diversity** (Qian et al., 2019; Zhu and Bhat, 2021).

Most of the previous evaluation studies focused on comparing the generation quality of each model, and machine-generated counternarratives along with the evaluation have not been published. Baheti et al. (2021) provide the only available resource of human-written or machine-generated responses with annotations, but the original task does not involve assessing counternarrative quality but rather classifying the contextual toxicity of dialogue responses. In this study, we created a corpus of annotated machine-generated counternarratives along with the offensiveness score of the abusive language post. This allowed us to analyze counternarratives from multiple aspects. The details of the evaluation perspectives used in the experiments are presented in Sec. 4.4.

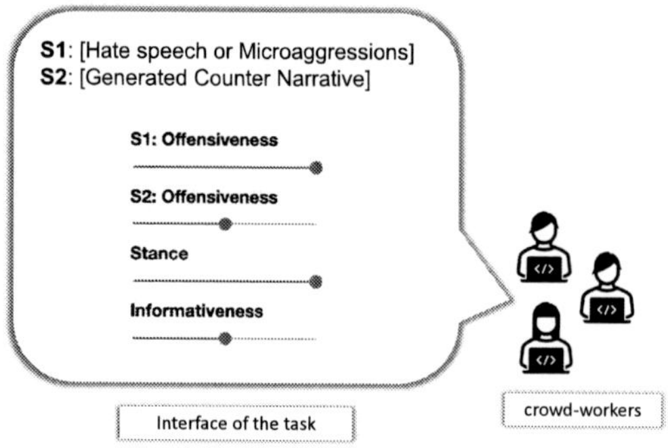

Figure 2: Interface of the annotation task

3 Counterspeech and Microintervention Generation

3.1 Task Formalization

Counternarrative generation can be viewed as a type of conditional or constrained text generation, in which the output is expected to oppose the input text. As the output is a response to the input, this task can also be considered dialogue generation with a single turn of conversation.

We formalize the counternarrative generation task following Zhu and Bhat (2021). Specifically, we assume access to a corpus of labeled pairs of conversations $D = (x_1, y_1), (x_2, y_2), ..., (x_n, y_n)$, where x_i is a hate speech or microaggression and y_i is the appropriate counternarrative as decided by experts or by crowdsourcing. The aim is to learn a model that takes as input a hate speech or a microaggression x and outputs a counternarrative y.

As output y, our goal is to produce a counternarrative that 1) is not offensive, 2) opposes the input hate speech, and 3) contains specific information on the corresponding offensive content. We propose the evaluation criteria along with the three features.

3.2 Evaluation

We conducted a human evaluation exercise to ascertain how effective and informative the counternarratives are and to obtain a fine-grained quality assessment.

For the evaluation, we considered three dimensions: **offensiveness**, **stance**, and **informativeness**. These dimensions have been proposed in the literature regarding the counternarrative generation and dialogue generation, as explained in Sec. 2. Each perspective was measured on a five-point Likert scale for counternarratives. **Offensiveness** of input was also annotated to examine how humans' perception of the offensive input differs.

Offensiveness deals with whether the sentence is offensive to anyone, such as people of a certain race, including the individuals who wrote the offensive post. Certainly, counternarratives should not include text offending other people. Also, attacking the authors themselves rather than their behavior is undesirable. Attacking the person is called *ad-hominem* (Habernal et al., 2018; Sheng et al., 2021), and is a fallacy that often occurs during conversation on the Internet. Although attacking the author of the post can be considered a countermeasure of hate speech, it cannot be regarded as a good counternarrative. The labels are presented as 0 (not sure), 1 (not offensive), 2 (maybe safe), 3 (maybe offensive), and 4 (completely offensive).

Stance (of a post) is classified into three types: agreeing, neutral, and disagreeing. A counternarrative is required to oppose the original statement; therefore, we assume that outputs that are neutral or agree with the offensive statement are not good counternarratives. Prepared labels are as follows: 0 (irrelevant), 1 (clearly agreeing), 2 (weakly agreeing), 3 (fighting but partially agreeing), and 4 (clearly fighting).

Informativeness assesses how informative and specific the counternarrative is, while not being generic. This perspective was designed as a counternarrative evaluation perspective by Chung et al. (2021). Their annotation guideline presented examples against Islamophobic hate speech: "Do you really believe that they are a problem?" received the lowest score, and "Muslims should not be forced to assimilate, since it is not right and no one wants that. And polygamy is illegal and forbidden in UK and Muslims actually respect this ban." received the highest score. We set five labels, ranging from 0 to 4, with 0 (irrelevant), 1 (not informative), 2 (generic statement and little information), 3 (relatively specific but little information), and 4 (specific and informative).

It is important to note that **informativeness** does not ask if the information is true or not. We do not explicitly ask for consulting external sources to verify if the information generated by systems is true. We discuss the issue related to this setting in Section 5.3.

Further details about the experimental settings of human evaluation will be described in Sec. 4.4.

4 Experimental Settings

4.1 Models

As for the models, we used Generative Pre-trained Transformers (**GPT**), which is an auto-regressive language model. For a given corpus $U = \{u_1, u_2, \ldots, u_n\}$ of size n, GPT is trained to maximize objective (1) where k is the size of the context window.

$$L_1(U) = \sum_i \log P(u_i | u_{i-k}, \ldots, u_{i-1}; \Theta) \quad (1)$$

The conditional probability P that the token u_i appears in the context given the tokens $u_{i-k}, \ldots, u_{i-1}$ is modeled using a neural network with parameter θ.

In this study, we examined the GPT-Neo (Black et al., 2021) model and the GPT-2 model released from Huggingface (Radford et al., 2019) as well as the GPT-3 model released from OpenAI (Brown et al., 2020). We opted for using the biggest parameter size models for each GPT, for it is reported that the bigger parameters yield the better model performance as for neural models, which is called "scaling laws for language models (Kaplan et al., 2020)"; we used GPT-2 of 1.5 B parameters trained on WebText (Radford et al., 2019), GPT-Neo of 2.5 B parameters trained on the Pile (Gao et al., 2020), and GPT-3 text-davinci-001[4] trained on CommonCrawl[5].

4.2 Methods

Sampling Parameters. We tested several sampling parameters for GPT-Neo and GPT-2 using the parameters documented in Huggingface Transformers' generation function with a fixed seed. We applied either greedy search or nucleus sampling (Holtzman et al., 2020) (with a top-*p* in {0.5,

[4]https://beta.openai.com/docs/engines/gpt-3

[5]https://commoncrawl.org/

0.95, 1.0}). We compared the four outputs to 50 randomly sampled inputs of GPT-Neo and GPT-2, respectively in terms of overall suitableness as a counterspeech, and chose the best parameter setting as greedy search. The results showed that applying nucleus sampling increases fluency and output length, but the generations contain more hallucinations and often agree to the offensive post than when no sampling was applied. One of those examples is shown in Table 4 in the Appendix. The result of annotation is also included in our dataset.

See Appendix B for further details of parameter settings.

Prompt Design. Prompts are mostly designed according to the target downstream tasks, and the design of the prompts is largely divided into three methods: *zero-shot*, *one-shot*, and *few-shot*. In a *few-shot* learning setting, the number of examples is more than one. When using zero example (only description of the task) and one example for prompts, they are called *zero-shot* and *one-shot*, respectively.

We considered *one-shot* prompt in the form of a chat-bot prompt and *few-shot* using multiple examples. The *one-shot* chat-bot prompt was obtained from presets available in OpenAI.[6] The *few-shot* prompt was created using the counterspeech in the CONAN-KN dataset (Chung et al., 2021) because they are the latest counterspeech dataset generated by experts.

Among all the pairs, an offensive post–counterspeech pair was randomly selected from each of the following five categories: Antisemitism, Homophobia, Islamophobia, Misogyny, and Racism. The actual prompt used in our experiment is shown in Table 5 in the Appendix.

As we observed that GPT-Neo and GPT-2 did not generate messages of high quality with *one-shot* prompt, we focused on using *few-shot*. However, note that GPT-3 produced some meaningful outputs, as shown in Table 6 in the Appendix; future work could analyze the differences between the use of two prompts.

4.3 Source Datasets

We used the CONAN (Chung et al., 2019), Multitarget-CONAN (Fanton et al., 2021), and Knowledge-grounded hate countering (Chung et al., 2021) datasets for hate speech inputs. For microaggression inputs, we used the Social Bias Inference Corpus (SBIC). The SBIC contains various degrees of offensive content collected from different websites. Because our interest is in microaggressions rather than directly offensive hate speech, we chose the category of "microaggression" from the dev set, which is based on the SELFMA dataset originally curated by Breitfeller et al. (2019). Further details of the chosen input texts used in the experiment are presented in Appendix A.

4.4 Evaluation

The evaluation was conducted via workers recruited through Amazon Mechanical Turk. All of the three perspectives (**offensiveness**, **stance**, **informativeness**) were evaluated using a five-point Likert scale. Each pair was evaluated by three crowd workers. We informed the workers about the risks of being exposed to offensive texts and asked for discretion. The instruction and examples presented to the workers are shown in Fig. 6.

Quality Control Recruitment was limited to those with a HIT approval rate of more than 98%, the number of approved HITs (the unit of task on Amazon Mechanical Turk) was more than 5,000. All workers were residents of the United States to ensure quality.[7] We also prepared our original qualification which can be easily answered by reading instructions. Only those who passed the additional qualification participated in our HITs.

Worker Payment We paid $2.7 per 25 sentence pair estimating 15 – 20 mins for completing. This adds up to an hourly wage of $8.4 – $11.2, which is above the federal minimum wage. Labels were obtained from three people for each pair. We collected data for 1020 sentence pairs for a total of about $400.

5 Results and Analysis

5.1 Annotation Statistics

Fig. 3 shows the annotation of offensiveness of **input** offensive text, categorized by dataset. Most of the CONAN texts are labeled as 4 (i.e., most offensive), whereas the SBIC texts have lower scores. This difference is possibly due to the characteristics of microaggressions described earlier; i.e., subtle and often unconscious discriminatory remarks.

[6] `https://beta.openai.com/examples/default-chat`

[7] However, lowering threshold is recommended considering unfair *qualification labour* to get qualified (Kummerfeld, 2021).

	CONAN			SBIC		
	off.	st.	inf.	off.	st.	inf.
GPT-2	.28	.38	.36	.25	.11	.39
GPT-Neo	.38	.32	.33	.38	.20	.31
GPT-3	.72	.76	.53	.77	.57	.42

Table 1: Inter-annotator agreement (Krippendorff's α). off., st., and inf. denote offensiveness, stance, informativeness, respectively.

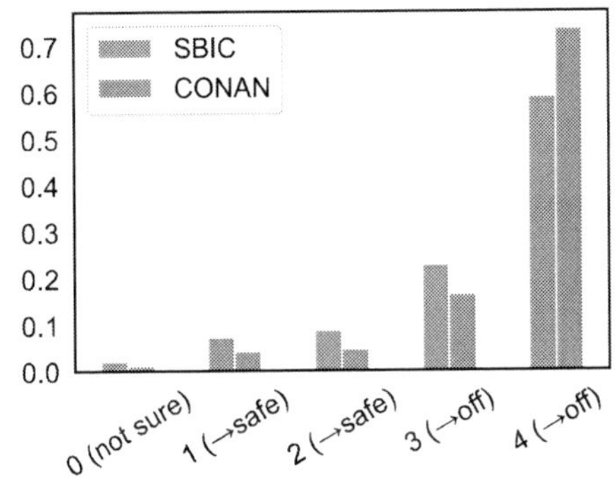

Figure 3: Offensive label distribution of input text per dataset.

However, CONAN also receives low scores for some sentences. In these cases, the annotator's belief (Sap et al., 2021) may have influenced their judgment. For example, if one believes that migrants are a threat, it is likely for them to consider discriminatory texts about migrants as not offensive. Additionally, lack of context such as whom the author is addressing affects the certainty as to whether the texts are offensive.

We report Krippendorff's α for each dataset per system in Table 1.[8] The values are comparable to previous studies dealing with relative subjectivity, such as $\alpha = 0.32$ for offensiveness and $\alpha = 0.18$ for stance of machine-generated responses reported in Baheti et al. (2021) and $\alpha = 0.51$ for offensiveness of human-written texts reported in Sap et al. (2020). Among the three systems, GPT-3 holds the higher scores for the offensive category. The higher agreement suggests that the quality of the output is more similar to the human-generated outputs, as it has been reported that machine-generated texts' agreement on offensiveness is lower than that of human-generated outputs (Baheti et al., 2021). The overall agreement reduction of SBIC compared to CONAN reflects that the generation quality is worse, and the task is more challenging. The label distribution of each perspective for CONAN is shown in Fig. 7 and for SBIC in Fig. 8 in the Appendix.

[8]To calculate α, we converted the labels of each perspective as follows: 1 and 2 of **offensiveness** into **safe**, and 3 and 4 into **offensive**; 1 and 2 of **stance** into **agree** and 3 and 4 into **disagree**; 1 and 2 of **informativeness** into **informative** and 3 and 4 into **uninformative**.

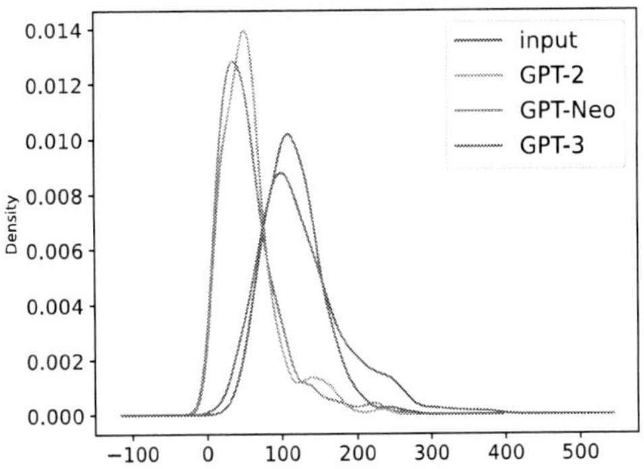

Figure 4: Kernel density estimation of the probability distribution of number of words per text for input and generated text by GPT-{2, Neo, 3}.

	DIST-1	DIST-2
GPT-2	.438	.737
GPT-Neo	.405	.681
GPT-3	**.495**	**.910**

Table 2: DIST-1 and DIST-2 of a set of generated texts by GPT-{2, Neo, 3}.

5.2 Quantitative Analysis

Generation Length. Fig. 4 shows the density distribution of the number of words for machine-generated texts. The distribution of GPT-3 corresponds to that of input texts written by a human, whereas that of GPT-2 and GPT-Neo shows that the output text lengths are much shorter. This suggests the performance of GPT-3 is the most similar to human among the three GPTs. Also, the GPT-3's output length is independent of the input length as the correlation between the number of words of each input and GPT-3 output is weak (Pearson's r of 0.29).

Generation Diversity. We report DIST (Li et al., 2016) over the outputs of three systems (Table 2). DIST calculates the percentage of different n-grams among the n-grams in all the raw sentences. DIST-1 and DIST-2 measure the proportion of different unigrams and different bigrams, respectively.

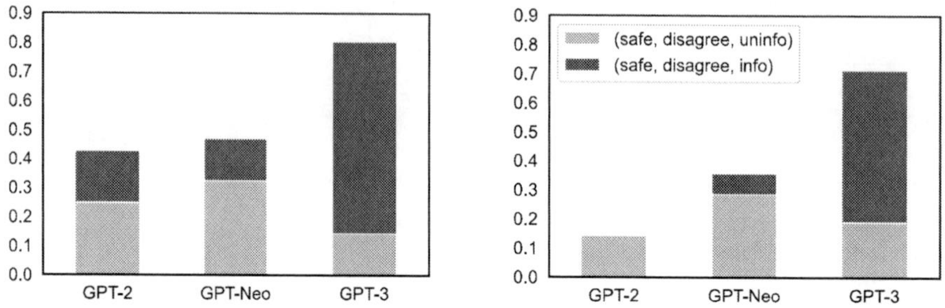

(a) CONAN

(b) SBIC

Figure 5: Ratio of {safe, disagree, uninformative} to {safe, disagree, informative}

They are automatic measures of the diversity of the generated sentences. This results suggests that GPT-3's generation is the most diverse among the three systems.

Most outputs presents facts to counter hate-speech or microaggressions. According to (Benesch et al., 2016), the types of counternarratives are multiple, such as *warning of offline or online consequences* or using *humor*. Generating different types of counternarratives as well as how to evaluate the effectiveness of different types of counternarratives are left for future work.

Generation Quality. We hereafter proceed with the analysis based on the counternarratives annotated (safe, disagree, informative) and (safe, disagree, uninformative), as we consider the former to be valid counternarratives, and the latter to be acceptable counternarratives. The result will focus on how many (safe, disagree) counternarratives are generated by each system.

Fig. 5 shows the ratio of countering messages received (safe, disagree, uninfo) to (safe, disagree, info) against CONAN's hate speech and SBIC's microaggressions. For both cases, GPT-3 performs better, followed by GPT-Neo. This can be attributed to model size: GPT-3 is the largest, and GPT-Neo is the second-largest system among the three. In CONAN, more than 14.7% (for GPT-Neo) of the generated responses receive (safe, disagree, informative). This result suggests that all the systems hold the potential to generate valid counternarratives. In SBIC, the overall score falls compared to that of CONAN, and more than half of the responses of GPT-2 and GPT-Neo are invalid as counternarratives. This can be explained by the offensiveness annotation of the input sentences that vary by individual, as illustrated in Fig. 3. This result implies that subjective offensiveness is more difficult for language models to recognize and counter.

5.3 Qualitative Analysis

The examples in Table 3a show the generated messages that counter hate speech effectively. This confirms that it is possible to generate counternarratives via *prompting*.

However, the examples in Table 3b show that some of the generated counternarratives need to be post-edited even when judged as (safe, disagree, info.). As for GPT-3, the output uses the phrases "no evidence" and "in fact." Actually, the repeated use of these phrases is found in generated texts in the corpus. However, claiming "no evidence" and "In fact" can easily lead to misinformation or hallucination as it is almost impossible to guarantee that there is no evidence on some topics. Because it is difficult for non-expert annotators to distinguish fact from misinformation, and harmless hallucination from problematic hallucination, additional fact-checking procedures would be desirable to solve this problem. Moreover, both of the generated texts argue the legitimacy of education in the isolation of children with disabilities, instead of stating the importance of diversity and inclusion in society. This is also a point that needs to be improved.

Furthermore, the issue is not only limited to the quality of generation, but also the human evaluation of the generated text. For example, in Table 3c, the majority of annotators assigned "safe." In contrast, in SBIC, it is judged to be offensive, and the annotated harmful implications include "women are responsible for their assaults," and "women shouldn't go out after dark alone." The reason the annotators assigned "agree" may be because the first half of

Post	Muslim invasion is the new plague of London. They must be repatriated to their home countries!	(offensive)
Neo:	No, they are not. They are here to work and to live in peace.	(safe, disagree, info.)
GPT-3:	So you want people to feel like second class citizens, they're only invited here to work for us and must stay silent when discriminated.	(safe, disagree, info.)

(a) Example of generated counterspeech

Post	Children with Down Syndrome should be isolated, they cannot cope with education in normal schools.	(offensive)
GPT-2:	Down syndrome is a genetic condition, not a disability.	(safe, disagree, info.)
GPT-3:	There is no evidence that children with Down Syndrome cannot cope with education in normal schools. In fact, many of them excel in these settings.	(safe, disagree, info.)

(b) Example of generated counterspeech including hallucinated contents

Post	It's terrible! And it's not like she was doing something wrong, like walking around late at night.	(56% safe, 33% offensive), offensive in SBIC
GPT-3:	It's terrible that someone was attacked and it's not right that people are blaming the victim.	(safe, agree, informative)

(c) Example of generated microintervention

Table 3: Examples of generated messages against hate speech and microaggressions

the text is identical to the input, although the latter part of GPT-3's message shows the understanding of harmful implications and countering to it. This example highlights the difficulty of the task even for humans to reach a consensus and the need for additional quality control.

6 Conclusion

This paper explored the possibility of using pretrained language models on the counternarrative generation task against hate speech and harmful social implications. We used three LMs to generate counternarratives via prompting and conducted a human evaluation exercise to ascertain the quality of the generated counternarratives using "offensiveness," "stance," and "informativeness" as our evaluation criteria. Furthermore, we analyzed the models' performance based on how many generated counternarratives are safe, informative, and opposing to abusive language input.

The overall results show the potential of language models to generate controlled content using prompting, which requires only some examples of inputs and desired outputs, compared to fine-tuning, which is computation intensive. Among the three LMs we tested, GPT-3 performed the best in terms of generating safe, informative counternarratives that oppose abusive language input. However, some of the counternarratives considered informative contained misinformation or hallucinated contents. Applying a fact-checking process to the generated contents is a possible future task.

Ethical Considerations

Our study was conducted with the approval of the Internal Review Board. We informed workers about the risk of being exposed to the hate content through the HIT title visible to workers before accepting the HIT on Amazon Mechanical Turk. The paper's theme is important as online hate speech and microaggressions continue to increase; therefore, there is a need for combating hate automatically. We hope that our corpus encourages further studies on this topic. We acknowledge the limitations that the corpus is only in English and that the hate speech contents are not fully up-to-date, such as dealing with the increasing amounts of hate speech against Asians due to the COVID pandemic.

Acknowledgements

We gratefully acknowledge the support of LINE Corporation to conduct this research. This work was partially supported by JSPS KAKENHI Grant Number 22H03651. We would like to thank anonymous reviewers and those who gave feedback on earlier versions of this paper.

References

Ashutosh Baheti, Maarten Sap, Alan Ritter, and Mark Riedl. 2021. Just say no: Analyzing the stance of neural dialogue generation in offensive contexts. In *Proceedings of the 2021 Conference on Empirical Methods in Natural Language Processing*, pages 4846–4862, Online and Punta Cana, Dominican Republic. Association for Computational Linguistics.

Susan Benesch, Derek Ruths, Kelly P Dillon, Haji Mohammad Saleem, and Lucas Wright. 2016. Counterspeech on twitter: A field study. *A report for Public Safety Canada under the Kanishka Project.*

Sid Black, Gao Leo, Phil Wang, Connor Leahy, and Stella Biderman. 2021. GPT-Neo: Large Scale Autoregressive Language Modeling with Mesh-Tensorflow. Zenodo.

Luke Breitfeller, Emily Ahn, David Jurgens, and Yulia Tsvetkov. 2019. Finding microaggressions in the wild: A case for locating elusive phenomena in social media posts. In *Proceedings of the 2019 Conference on Empirical Methods in Natural Language Processing and the 9th International Joint Conference on Natural Language Processing (EMNLP-IJCNLP)*, pages 1664–1674, Hong Kong, China. Association for Computational Linguistics.

Tom Brown, Benjamin Mann, Nick Ryder, Melanie Subbiah, Jared D Kaplan, Prafulla Dhariwal, Arvind Neelakantan, Pranav Shyam, Girish Sastry, Amanda Askell, et al. 2020. Language models are few-shot learners. In *Advances in Neural Information Processing Systems*, volume 33, pages 1877–1901. Curran Associates, Inc.

Yi-Ling Chung, Elizaveta Kuzmenko, Serra Sinem Tekiroglu, and Marco Guerini. 2019. CONAN - COunter NArratives through nichesourcing: a multilingual dataset of responses to fight online hate speech. In *Proceedings of the 57th Annual Meeting of the Association for Computational Linguistics*, pages 2819–2829, Florence, Italy. Association for Computational Linguistics.

Yi-Ling Chung, Serra Sinem Tekiroğlu, and Marco Guerini. 2021. Towards knowledge-grounded counter narrative generation for hate speech. In *Findings of the Association for Computational Linguistics: ACL-IJCNLP 2021*, pages 899–914, Online. Association for Computational Linguistics.

Elizabeth Clark, Tal August, Sofia Serrano, Nikita Haduong, Suchin Gururangan, and Noah A. Smith. 2021. All that's 'human' is not gold: Evaluating human evaluation of generated text. In *Proceedings of the 59th Annual Meeting of the Association for Computational Linguistics and the 11th International Joint Conference on Natural Language Processing (Volume 1: Long Papers)*, pages 7282–7296, Online. Association for Computational Linguistics.

Margherita Fanton, Helena Bonaldi, Serra Sinem Tekiroğlu, and Marco Guerini. 2021. Human-in-the-loop for data collection: a multi-target counter narrative dataset to fight online hate speech. In *Proceedings of the 59th Annual Meeting of the Association for Computational Linguistics and the 11th International Joint Conference on Natural Language Processing (Volume 1: Long Papers)*, pages 3226–3240, Online. Association for Computational Linguistics.

Kathleen C. Fraser, Isar Nejadgholi, and Svetlana Kiritchenko. 2021. Understanding and countering stereotypes: A computational approach to the stereotype content model. In *Proceedings of the 59th Annual Meeting of the Association for Computational Linguistics and the 11th International Joint Conference on Natural Language Processing (Volume 1: Long Papers)*, pages 600–616, Online. Association for Computational Linguistics.

Leo Gao, Stella Biderman, Sid Black, Laurence Golding, Travis Hoppe, Charles Foster, Jason Phang, Horace He, Anish Thite, Noa Nabeshima, Shawn Presser, and Connor Leahy. 2020. The Pile: An 800gb dataset of diverse text for language modeling. *arXiv preprint arXiv:2101.00027.*

Ivan Habernal, Henning Wachsmuth, Iryna Gurevych, and Benno Stein. 2018. Before name-calling: Dynamics and triggers of ad hominem fallacies in web argumentation. In *Proceedings of the 2018 Conference of the North American Chapter of the Association for Computational Linguistics: Human Language Technologies, Volume 1 (Long Papers)*, pages 386–396, New Orleans, Louisiana. Association for Computational Linguistics.

Dominik Hangartner, Gloria Gennaro, Sary Alasiri, Nicholas Bahrich, Alexandra Bornhoft, Joseph Boucher, Buket Buse Demirci, Laurenz Derksen, Aldo Hall, Matthias Jochum, et al. 2021. Empathy-based counterspeech can reduce racist hate speech in a social media field experiment. *Proceedings of the National Academy of Sciences*, 118(50).

Ari Holtzman, Jan Buys, Li Du, Maxwell Forbes, and Yejin Choi. 2020. The curious case of neural text degeneration. In *International Conference on Learning Representations.*

Jared Kaplan, Sam McCandlish, T. J. Henighan, Tom B. Brown, Benjamin Chess, Rewon Child, Scott Gray, Alec Radford, Jeff Wu, and Dario Amodei. 2020. Scaling laws for neural language models. *ArXiv*, abs/2001.08361.

Jonathan K. Kummerfeld. 2021. Quantifying and avoiding unfair qualification labour in crowdsourcing. In *Proceedings of the 59th Annual Meeting of the Association for Computational Linguistics and the 11th International Joint Conference on Natural Language Processing (Volume 2: Short Papers)*, pages 343–349, Online. Association for Computational Linguistics.

Jiwei Li, Michel Galley, Chris Brockett, Jianfeng Gao, and Bill Dolan. 2016. A diversity-promoting objective function for neural conversation models. In *Proceedings of the 2016 Conference of the North American Chapter of the Association for Computational Linguistics: Human Language Technologies*, pages 110–119, San Diego, California. Association for Computational Linguistics.

Kosisochukwu Madukwe, Xiaoying Gao, and Bing Xue. 2020. In data we trust: A critical analysis of hate speech detection datasets. In *Proceedings of the Fourth Workshop on Online Abuse and Harms*, pages 150–161, Online. Association for Computational Linguistics.

Jing Qian, Anna Bethke, Yinyin Liu, Elizabeth Belding, and William Yang Wang. 2019. A benchmark dataset for learning to intervene in online hate speech. In *Proceedings of the 2019 Conference on Empirical Methods in Natural Language Processing and the 9th International Joint Conference on Natural Language Processing (EMNLP-IJCNLP)*, pages 4755–4764, Hong Kong, China. Association for Computational Linguistics.

Alec Radford, Jeff Wu, Rewon Child, David Luan, Dario Amodei, and Ilya Sutskever. 2019. Language models are unsupervised multitask learners.

Maarten Sap, Saadia Gabriel, Lianhui Qin, Dan Jurafsky, Noah A. Smith, and Yejin Choi. 2020. Social bias frames: Reasoning about social and power implications of language. In *Proceedings of the 58th Annual Meeting of the Association for Computational Linguistics*, pages 5477–5490, Online. Association for Computational Linguistics.

Maarten Sap, Swabha Swayamdipta, Laura Vianna, Xuhui Zhou, Yejin Choi, and Noah A. Smith. 2021. Annotators with attitudes: How annotator beliefs and identities bias toxic language detection. *ArXiv*, abs/2111.07997.

Emily Sheng, Kai-Wei Chang, Prem Natarajan, and Nanyun Peng. 2021. "nice try, kiddo": Investigating ad hominems in dialogue responses. In *Proceedings of the 2021 Conference of the North American Chapter of the Association for Computational Linguistics: Human Language Technologies*, pages 750–767, Online. Association for Computational Linguistics.

Derald Wing Sue, Sarah Alsaidi, Michael N. Awad, Elizabeth Glaeser, Cassandra Z Calle, and Narolyn Mendez. 2019. Disarming racial microaggressions: Microintervention strategies for targets, white allies, and bystanders. *The American psychologist*, 74 1:128–142.

Derald Wing Sue, Christina M. Capodilupo, Gina C. Torino, Jennifer M Bucceri, Aisha M. B. Holder, Kevin L. Nadal, and Marta Elena Esquilin. 2007. Racial microaggressions in everyday life: implications for clinical practice. *The American psychologist*, 62 4:271–86.

Serra Sinem Tekiroglu, Helena Bonaldi, Margherita Fanton, and Marco Guerini. 2022. Using pre-trained language models for producing counter narratives against hate speech: a comparative study.

Serra Sinem Tekiroğlu, Yi-Ling Chung, and Marco Guerini. 2020. Generating counter narratives against online hate speech: Data and strategies. In *Proceedings of the 58th Annual Meeting of the Association for Computational Linguistics*, pages 1177–1190, Online. Association for Computational Linguistics.

Wanzheng Zhu and Suma Bhat. 2021. Generate, prune, select: A pipeline for counterspeech generation against online hate speech. In *Findings of the Association for Computational Linguistics: ACL-IJCNLP 2021*, pages 134–149, Online. Association for Computational Linguistics.

A Data Preprocessing

Hatespeech. We gather all the English hate speech in CONAN, the seed dataset in Multitarget-CONAN, and the Knowledge-grounded hate countering dataset, then select those consist of more than 10 words and less than 100 words. After excluding overlapped sentences and the texts containing #, and , we obtain 306 hate speech.

Microaggressions. We select the post consisting of more than 10 words and less than 100 words and retained all the posts which have free-text implications. We exclude the texts containing #, and ::. In this way, we select a total of 42 microaggression statements.

B Reproducibility

For GPT-3 text-davinci-001 model, we use temperature of 0.7, max tokens of 50, top_p of 1, frequency penalty of 0, and presence penalty of 0. For GPT-{2, Neo}, we use temperature of 1.0, max tokens length of 1024, top_k of 50.

Task description

Thank you for your participation!
You will be presented with a pair of sentences; offensive post (S1) and the a counter narrative (counter-speech) (S2) to the post generated by a bot.
Your task: evaluate the quality of the counter narrative from the three persepectives; **Offensiveness, Stance** and **Informativeness**

CAUTION:
The sentences presented in the task exibit overt Sexism, Racism, Xenophobia, Transphobia, Homophobia etc. Worker discretion is advised.

Offensiveness (applied to S1, S2)
Are the sentences 1 and 2 offensive to anyone, such as people of a certain race, gender or religion? "Anyone" also includes individuals such as the person who wrote S1.
So if S2 looks like it is attacking the person who wrote the S1, rate them as offensive. When you don't understand the meaning of the sentence, rank it as 0 (not sure).

Stance (applied to S2 only)
Is the counter narrative successfully disagreeing against the given offensive post or, conforming to the post.
ATTENTION: some responses use sarcasm and rhetoric to express disagreement indirectly; in that case, you are supposed to label them as either 3 or 4.

Informativeness (applied to S2 only)
How informative and specific is the counter narrative? If the counter narratives contain completely irrelevant information, mark them as 0.
If they are somewhat related, whether they agree or disagree to S1, rank them according to how much information they hold and how specific they are.

Figure 6: The instructions given to crowd-workers on Amazon Mechanical Turk

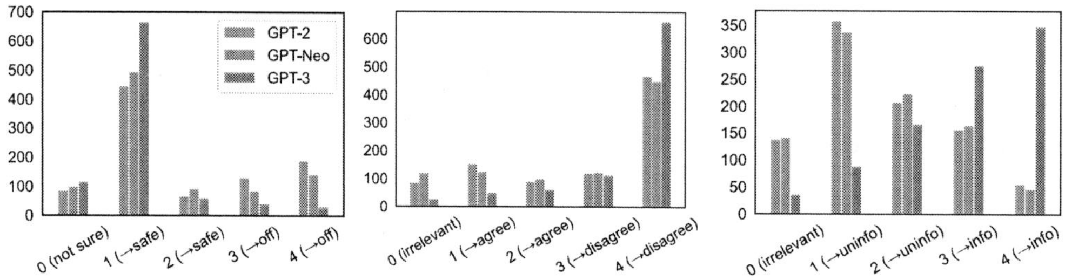

(a) offensiveness ↓ (b) stance ↑ (c) informativeness ↑

Figure 7: label distribution of CONAN

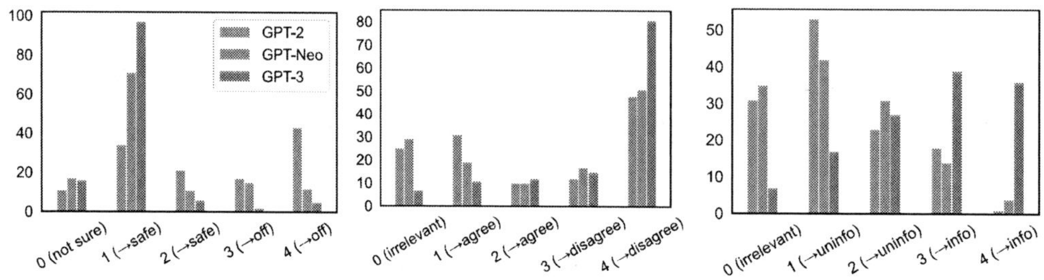

(a) offensiveness ↓ (b) stance ↑ (c) informativeness ↑

Figure 8: label distribution of SBIC

input	The overcrowd at migrant detention centers for illegals is also caused by the liberal left. Illegal immigrants have no right to be in your country and they should be taken back.
top-p=1.0	The law should be used, which has always been implemented by the American government to deport illegal immigrants who broke the law.
top-p=0.95	The liberals are also responsible for the illegal immigrants problem in the first place by not controlling the flow of illegal aliens.
top-p=0.50	Illegal immigrants are only here because of the liberal left. They should be deported and not allowed to live in your country.
greedy	You are a racist.

Table 4: Example of GPT-2's generation with different sampling parameters

Generate counterspeech to the given offensive post.
Post: Jews are born greedy. Counterspeech: Like any ethno-racial or religious group, the population of Jews is internally diverse, so it is impossible to generalize.
Post: Why gays do not try to heal? Counterspeech: Contrary to some insinuations, sexual orientation is not like a disease.
Post: We need to Burn the Koran and all the Mosques down - this will solve all problems in this country. Counterspeech: NO, we need to close Radical mosques and to expel radical Muslims. That's all. Peaceful Muslims have the right to live in peace in our country.
Post: I'm tired of woman taking part to political debate. Feminism is a divisive force in society. Counterspeech: How many women are represented in political conversations on television?
Post: This is an invasion: we must stop immigrants because they are not accepted by our people. Counterspeech: So you want people to feel like second class citizens, they're only invited here to work for us and must stay silent when discriminated.

Table 5: *Few-shot* prompt used in the experiment

Prompt	The following is a conversation with an AI assistant. The assistant is helpful, creative, clever, and very friendly. Human: Hello, who are you? AI: I am an AI. How can I help you today? Human: Hey, I don't understand bisexuals. Why can't they just pick a side?
GPT-2	AI: ____
GPT-Neo	AI:????
GPT-3	AI: Bisexuality is a term used to describe someone who is attracted to people of both genders. Some people believe that bisexuals can't just pick a side, because they are attracted to both genders. Others believe that bisexuality is simply a phase, and that people will eventually settle down with one gender. Ultimately, it is up to the individual to decide what they believe.

Table 6: Example of chat-bot prompt and generated texts

6 Appendix

6.1 GreaseTerminator

In response to the continued widespread presence of interface-based harms in digital systems, Datta et al. (Datta et al., 2021) developed *GreaseTerminator*, a visual overlay modification method. This approach enables researchers to develop, deploy and study interventions against interface-based harms in apps. This is based on the observation that it used to be difficult in the past for researchers to study the efficacy of different intervention designs against harms within mobile apps (most previous approaches focused on desktop browsers). *GreaseTerminator* provides a set of 'hooks' that serve as templates for researchers to develop interventions, which are then deployed and tested with study participants. *GreaseTerminator* interventions usually come in the form of machine learning models that build on the provided hooks, automatically detect harms within the smartphone user interface at run-time, and choose appropriate interventions (e.g. a visual overlay to hide harmful content, or content warnings). The *GreaseTerminator* architecture is shown in Figure 6(a) in contrast to the *GreaseVision* architecture.

Technical improvements w.r.t. *GreaseTerminator* The improvements of *GreaseVision* with respect to *GreaseTerminator* are two-fold: (i) improvements to the framework enabling end-user development and harms mitigation (discussed in detail in Sections 4.2, 4.3, 5 and 6), and (ii) improvements to the technical architecture (which we discuss in this section). Our distinctive and non-trivial technical improvements to the *GreaseTerminator* architecture fall under namely latency, device support, and interface-agnosticity. *GreaseTerminator* requires the end-user device to be the host device, and overlays graphics on top. A downside of this is the non-uniformity of network latency between users (e.g. depending on the internet speed in their location) resulting in a potential mismatch in rendered overlays and underlying interface. With *GreaseVision*, we send a post-processed/re-rendered image once to the end-user device's browser (stream buffering) and do not need to send any screen image from the host user device to a server, thus there is no risk of overlay-underlay mismatch and we even reduce network latency by half. Images are relayed through an HTTPS connection, with a download/upload speed $\sim$ 250Mbps, and each image sent by the server amounting to $\sim$ 1Mb). The theoretical latency per one-way transmission should be $\frac{1\times1024\times8\text{bits}}{250\times10^6\text{bits/s}}$ = 0.033ms. With each user at most requiring server usage of one NVIDIA GeForce RTX 2080, with reference to existing online benchmarks (Ignatov, 2021) the latency for 1 image (CNN) and text (LSTM) model would be 5.1ms and 4.8ms respectively. While the total theoretical latency for *GreaseTerminator* is $(2 \times 0.033 + 5)$, that of *GreaseVision* is $(0.033 + 5)$ = 5.03ms. Another downside of *GreaseTerminator* is that it requires client-side software for each target platform. There would be pre-requisite OS requirements for the end-user device, where only versions of *GreaseTerminator* developed for each OS can be offered support (currently only for Android). *GreaseVision* streams screen images directly to a login-verified browser, allowing users to access desktop/mobile on any browser-supported device. Despite variations in the streaming architecture between *GreaseVision* and *GreaseTerminator*, the interface modification framework (hooks and overlays) are retained, hence interventions (even those developed by end-users) from *GreaseVision* are compatible in *GreaseTerminator*. In addition to improvements to the streaming architecture to fulfil interface-agnosticity, adapting the visual overlay modification framework into a collaborative HITL implementation further improves the ease-of-use for all stakeholders in the ecosystem. End-users do not need to root their devices, find intervention tools or even self-develop their own customized tools. We eliminate the need for researchers to craft interventions (as users self-develop autonomously) or develop their own custom experience sampling tools (as end-users/researchers can analyze digital experiences from stored screenomes). We also eliminate the need for intervention developers to learn a new technical framework or learn how to fine-tune models. Running emulators on docker containers and virtual machines on a (single) host server is feasible, and thus allows for the browser stream to be accessible cross-device without restriction, e.g. access iOS emulator on Android device, or macOS virtual machine on Windows device. Certain limitations are imposed on the current implementation, such as a lack of access to the device camera, audio, and haptics; however, these are not permanent issues, and engineered implementations exist where a virtual/emulated device can route and access the host device's input/output sources (VrtualApp, 2016).

Proceedings of the Sixth Workshop on Online Abuse and Harms (WOAH), pages 24 - 28
July 14, 2022 ©2022 Association for Computational Linguistics

Figure 6: Architecture of *GreaseTerminator* (left) and *GreaseVision* (right).

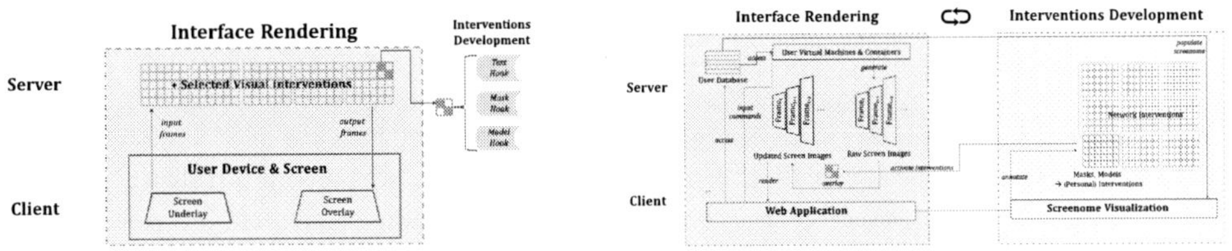

(a) The high-level architecture of *GreaseTerminator*. Details are explained in Section 2.3 and 4.2.

(b) The high-level architecture of *GreaseVision*, both as a summary of our technical infrastructure as well as one of the collaborative HITL interventions development approach.

Hooks The *text hook* enables modifying the text that is displayed on the user's device. It is implemented through character-level optical character recognition (OCR) that takes the screen image as an input and returns a set of characters and their corresponding coordinates. The EAST text detection (Zhou et al., 2017) model detects text in images and returns a set of regions with text, then uses Tesseract (Google, 2007) to extract characters within each region containing text. The *mask hook* matches the screen image against a target template of multiple images. It is implemented with *multi-scale multi-template* matching by resizing an image multiple times and sampling different subimages to compare against each instance of mask in a masks directory (where each mask is a cropped screenshot of an interface element). We retain the default majority-pixel inpainting method for mask hooks (inpainting with the most common colour value in a screen image or target masked region). As many mobile interfaces are standardized or uniform from a design perspective compared to images from the natural world, this may work in many instances. The mask hook could be connected to rendering functions such as highlighting the interface element with warning labels, or image inpainting (fill in the removed element pixels with newly generated pixels from the background), or adding content/information (from other apps) into the inpainted region. Developers can also tweak how the mask hook is applied, for example using the multi-scale multi-template matching algorithm with contourized images (shapes, colour-independent) or coloured images depending on whether the mask contains (dynamic) sub-elements, or using few-shot deep learning models if similar interface elements are non-uniform. A *model hook* loads any machine learning model to take any input and generate any output. This allows for model embedding (i.e. model weights and architectures) to inform further overlay rendering. We can connect models trained on specific tasks (e.g. person pose detection, emotion/sentiment analysis) to return output given the screen image (e.g. bounding box coordinates to filter), and this output can then be passed to a pre-defined rendering function (e.g. draw filtering box).

6.2 Related Works (extended)

6.2.1 Motivation: Pervasiveness and Individuality of Digital Harms

It is well-known that digital harms are widespread in our day-to-day technologies. Despite this, the academic literature around these harms is still developing, and it remains difficult to state exactly what the harms are that need to be addressed. Famously, Gray et al. (Gray et al., 2018) put forward a 5-class taxonomy to classify dark patterns within apps: *interface interference* (elements that manipulate the user interface to induce certain actions over other actions), *nagging* (elements that interrupt the user's current task with out-of-focus tasks) *forced action* (elements that introduce sub-tasks forcefully before permitting a user to complete their desired task), *obstruction* (elements that introduce subtasks with the intention of dissuading a user from performing an operation in the desired mode), and *sneaking* (elements that conceal or delay information relevant to the user in performing a task).

A challenge with such framework and taxonomies is to capture and understand the material impacts of harms on individuals. Harms tend to be highly individual and vary in terms of how they manifest within users of digital systems. The harms landscape is also quickly changing with ever-changing digital systems. Defining the spectrum of harms is still an open problem, the range varying from heavily-biased content (e.g. disinformation, hate speech), self-harm (e.g. eating disorders, self-cutting, suicide), cyber crime (e.g. cyber-bullying, harassment, promotion of and recruitment for extreme causes (e.g. terrorist organizations), to demographic-specific exploitation (e.g. child-inappropriate content, social engineering attacks) (HM, 2019; Pater and Mynatt, 2017; Wang et al., 2017; Honary et al., 2020; Pater et al., 2019), for which we recommend the aforementioned cited literature. The last line of defense against many digital harms is the user interface. This is why we are interested in interface-emergent harms in this paper, and how to support individuals in developing their own strategies to cope with and overcome such harms.

6.2.2 Developments in Interface Modification & Re-rendering

Digital harms have long been acknowledged as a general problem, and a range of technical interventions against digital harms are developed. Interventions, also similarly called modifications or patches, are changes to the software, which result in a change in (perceived) functionality and end-user usage. We review and categorize key *technical* intervention methods for interface modification by end-users, with cited examples specifically for digital harms mitigation. While there also exist non-technical interventions, in particular legal remedies, it is beyond this work to give a full account of these different interventions against harms; a useful framework for such an analysis is provided by Lawrence Lessig (Lessig) who characterised the different regulatory forces in the digital ecosystem.

Interface-code modifications (Kollnig et al., 2021; Higi, 2020; Jeon et al., 2012; Rasthofer et al., 2014; Davis and Chen, 2013; Backes et al., 2014; Xu et al., 2012; LuckyPatcher, 2020; Davis et al., 2012; Lyngs et al., 2020b; Freeman, 2020; rovo89, 2020; Agarwal and Hall, 2013; Enck et al., 2010; MaaarZ, 2019; VrtualApp, 2016) make changes to source code, either installation code (to modify software before installation), or run-time code (to modify software during usage). On desktop, this is done through *browser extensions* and has given rise to a large ecosystem of such extensions. Some of the most well-known interventions are ad blockers, and tools that improve productivity online (e.g. by removing the Facebook newsfeed (Lyngs et al., 2020b)). On mobile, a prominent example is *AppGuard* (Backes et al., 2014), a research project by Backes et al. that allowed users to improve the privacy properties of apps on their phone by making small, targeted modification to apps' source code. Another popular mobile solution in the community is the app *Lucky Patcher* (LuckyPatcher, 2020) that allows to get paid apps for free, by removing the code relating to payment functionality directly from the app code.

Some of these methods may require the highest level of privilege escalation to make modifications to the operating system and other programs/apps as a root user. On iOS, *Cydia Substrate* (Freeman, 2020) is the foundation for jailbreaking and further device modification. A similar system, called *Xposed Framework* (rovo89, 2020), exists for Android. To alleviate the risks and challenges afflicted with privilege escalation, *VirtualXposed* (VrtualApp, 2016) create a virtual environment on the user's Android device with simulated privilege escalation. Users can install apps into this virtual environment and apply tools of other modification approaches that may require root access. *ProtectMyPrivacy* (Agarwal and Hall, 2013) for iOS and *TaintDroid* (Enck et al., 2010) for Android both extend the functionality of the smartphone operating system with new functionality for the analysis of apps' privacy features. On desktops, code modifications tend not to be centred around a common framework, but are more commonplace in general due to the traditionally more permissive security model compared to mobile. Antivirus tools, copyright protections of games and the modding of UI components are all often implemented through interface-code modifications.

Interface-external modifications (Geza, 2019; Bodyguard, 2019; Lee et al., 2014; Ko et al., 2015; Andone et al., 2016; Hiniker et al., 2016; Löchtefeld et al., 2013; Labs, 2019; Okeke et al., 2018) are the arguably most common way to change default interface behaviour. An end-user would install a program so as to affect other programs/apps. No change to the operating system or the targeted programs/apps is made, so an uninstall of the program providing the modification would revert the device to the original state. This approach is widely used to track duration of device usage, send notifications to the user during usage (e.g. timers, warnings), block certain actions on the user device, and other aspects. The *HabitLab* (Geza, 2019) is a prominent example developed by Kovacs et al. at Stanford.

This modification framework is open-source and maintained by a community of developers, and provides interventions for both desktop and mobile.

Visual overlay modifications render graphics on an overlay layer over any active interface instance, including browsers, apps/programs, videos, or any other interface in the operating system. The modifications are visual, and do not change the functionality of the target interface. It may render sub-interfaces, labels, or other graphics on top of the foreground app. Prominent examples are *DetoxDroid* (flxapps, 2021), *Gray-Switch* (GmbH, 2021), *Google Accessibility Suite* (Google, 2021), and *GreaseTerminator* (Datta et al., 2021).

We would like to establish early on that we pursue a *visual overlay modifications* approach. Interventions should be rendered in the form of overlay graphics based on detected elements, rather than implementing program code changes natively, hence focused on changing the interface rather than the functionality of the software. Interventions should be generalizable; they are not solely website- or app-oriented, but *interface-oriented*. Interventions do not target specific apps, but general interface elements and patterns that could appear across different interface environments. To support the systemic requirements in Section 2.4, we require an interface modification approach that is (i) interface-agnostic and (ii) easy-to-use. To this extent, we build upon the work of ***GreaseTerminator*** (Datta et al., 2021), a framework optimized for these two requirements.

In response to the continued widespread presence of interface-based harms in digital systems, Datta et al. (Datta et al., 2021) developed *GreaseTerminator*, a visual overlay modification method. This approach enables researchers to develop, deploy and study interventions against interface-based harms in apps. This is based on the observation that it used to be difficult in the past for researchers to study the efficacy of different intervention designs against harms within mobile apps (most previous approaches focused on desktop browsers). *GreaseTerminator* provides a set of 'hooks' that serve as templates for researchers to develop interventions, which are then deployed and tested with study participants. *GreaseTerminator* interventions usually come in the form of machine learning models that build on the provided hooks, automatically detect harms within the smartphone user interface at run-time, and choose appropriate interventions (e.g. a visual overlay to hide harmful content, or content warnings). A visualisation of the *GreaseTerminator* approach is shown in Figure 6(a).

6.2.3 Opportunities for Low-code Development in Interface Modification

Low-code development platforms have been defined, according to practitioners, to be (i) low-code (negligible programming skill required to reach endgoal, potentially drag-and-drop), (ii) visual programming (a visual approach to development, mostly reliant on a GUI, and "what-you-see-is-what-you-get"), and (iii) automated (unattended operations exist to minimize human involvement) (Luo et al., 2021). Low-code development platforms exist for varying stages of software creation, from frontend (e.g. App maker, Bubble.io, Webflow), to workflow (Airtable, Amazon Honeycode, Google Tables, UiPath, Zapier), to backend (e.g. Firevase, WordPress, flutterflow); none exist for software modification of existing applications across interfaces. According to a review of StackOverflow and Reddit posts analysed by Luo et al. (Luo et al., 2021), low-code development platforms are cited by practitioners to be tools that enable faster development, lower the barrier to usage by non-technical people, improves IT governance compared to traditional programming, and even suits team development; one of the main limitations cited is that the complexity of the software created is constrained by the options offered by the platform.

User studies have shown that users can self-identify malevolent harms and habits upon self-reflection and develop desires to intervene against them (Cho et al., 2021; Lyngs et al., 2020a). Not only do end-users have a desire or interest in self-reflection, but there is indication that end-users have a willingness to act. Statistics for content violation reporting from Meta show that in the Jan-Jun 2021 period, $\sim$ 42,200 and $\sim$ 5,300 in-app content violations were reported on Facebook and Instagram respectively (Meta, 2022) (in this report, the numbers are specific to violations in local law, so the actual number with respect to community standard violatons would be much higher; the numbers also include reporting by governments/courts and non-government entities in addition to members of the public). Despite a willingness to act, there are limited digital visualization or reflection tools that enable flexible intervention development by end-users. There are visualization or reflection tools on browser and mobile that allow for reflection (e.g. device use time (Andone et al., 2016)), and there are separate and disconnected tools for intervention (Section 2.2), but there are limited offerings of flexible intervention development by end-users, where end-users can observe and analyze their problems while generating corresponding fixes, which thus prematurely ends the loop for action upon regret/reflection. There is a disconnect between the harms analysis ecosystem and interventions ecosystem. A barrier to binding these two ecosystems is the existence of low-code development platforms for end-users. While such tooling may exist for specific use cases on specific interfaces (e.g. web/app/game development) for mostly creationary purposes, there are limited options available for modification purposes of existing software, the closest alternative being extension ecosystems (Kollnig et al., 2021; Google, 2010a). Low-code development platforms are in essence "developer-less", removing developers from the software modification pipeline by reducing the barrier to modification through the use of GUI-based features and negligible coding, such that end-users can self-develop without expert knowledge.

Human-in-the-Loop (HITL) learning is the procedure of integrating human knowledge and experience in the augmentation of machine learning models. It is commonly used to generate new data from humans or annotate existing data by humans. Wallace et al. (Wallace et al., 2019) constructed a HITL system of an interactive interface where a human talks with a machine to generate more Q&A language and train/fine-tune Q&A models. Zhang et al. (Zhang et al., 2019) proposed a HITL system for humans to provide data for entity extraction, including requiring humans to formulate regular expressions and highlight text documents, and annotate and label data. For an extended literature review, we refer the reader to Wu et al. (Wu et al., 2021). Beyond lab settings, HITL has proven itself in wide deployment, where a wide distribution of users have indicated a willingness and ability to perform tasks on a HITL annotation tool, *reCAPTCHA*, to access utility and services. In 2010, Google reported over 100 million reCAPTCHA instances are displayed every day (Google, 2010b) to annotate different types of data, such as deciphering text for OCR of books or street signs, or labelling objects in images such as traffic lights or vehicles.

While HITL formulates the structure for human-AI collaborative model development, **model fine-tuning** and **few-shot learning** formulate the algorithmic methods of adapting models to changing inputs, environments, and contexts. Both adaptation approaches require the model to update its parameters with respect to the new input distribution. For model fine-tuning, the developer re-trains a pre-trained model on a new dataset. This is in contrast to training a model from a random initialization. Model fine-tuning techniques for pre-trained foundation models, that already contain many of the pre-requisite subnetworks required for feature reuse and warm-started training on a smaller target dataset, have indicated robustness on downstream tasks (Galanti et al., 2022; Abnar et al., 2022; Neyshabur et al., 2020). If there is an extremely large number of input distributions and few samples per distribution (small datasets), few-shot learning is an approach where the developer has separately trained a meta-model that learns how to change model parameters with respect to only a few samples. Few-shot learning has demonstrated successful test-time adaptation in updating model parameters with respect to limited test-time samples in both image and text domains (Raghu et al., 2020; Koch et al., 2015; Finn et al., 2017; Datta, 2021). Some overlapping techniques even exist between few-shot learning and fine-tuning, such as constructing subspaces and optimizing with respect to intrinsic dimensions (Aghajanyan et al., 2021; Datta and Shadbolt, 2022; Simon et al., 2020).

The raw data for harms and required interface changes reside in the history of interactions between the user and the interface. In the Screenome project (Reeves et al., 2020, 2021), the investigators proposed the study and analysis of the moment-by-moment changes on a person's screen, by capturing screenshots automatically and unobtrusively every $t = 5$ seconds while a device is on. This record of a user's digital experiences represented as a sequence of screens that they view and interact with over time is denoted as a user's **screenome**. Though not mobilized widely amongst users for their self-reflection or personalized analysis, integrating screenomes into an interface modification framework can play the dual roles of visualizing raw (harms) data to users while manifesting as parseable input for visual overlay modification frameworks.

Improving Generalization of Hate Speech Detection Systems to Novel Target Groups via Domain Adaptation

Florian Ludwig
ZITiS
Zamdorfer Str. 88
81677 München

Dr. Klara Dolos
ZITiS
Zamdorfer Str. 88
81677 München

Prof. Dr. Torsten Zesch
FernUniversität in Hagen
Universitätsstraße 47
58097 Hagen

Dr. Eleanor Hobley
ZITiS
Zamdorfer Str. 88
81677 München

Abstract

Despite recent advances in machine learning based hate speech detection, classifiers still struggle with generalizing knowledge to out-of-domain data samples. In this paper, we investigate the generalization capabilities of deep learning models to different target groups of hate speech under clean experimental settings. Furthermore, we assess the efficacy of three different strategies of unsupervised domain adaptation to improve these capabilities. Given the diversity of hate and its rapid dynamics in the online world (e.g. the evolution of new target groups like virologists during the COVID-19 pandemic), robustly detecting hate aimed at newly identified target groups is a highly relevant research question. We show that naively trained models suffer from a target group specific bias, which can be reduced via domain adaptation. We were able to achieve a relative improvement of the F1-score between 5.8% and 10.7% for out-of-domain target groups of hate speech compared to baseline approaches by utilizing domain adaptation.

Author contacts are given in the footnotes. [1]

1 Introduction

Current state-of-the-art machine learning approaches for hate speech detection reach F1-scores above 93% (Arango et al., 2019). Despite this progress, in some settings these scores drop to 50% when tested on out-of-domain data (Arango et al., 2019). The lack of generalization capabilities of hate speech detection systems hinders their suitability in real world applications.

Several challenges are faced when trying to generalize knowledge in hate speech detection tasks. Firstly, most benchmark hate speech datasets are focused on certain topics, such as hate speech directed at journalists (Charitidis et al., 2020), refugees and Muslims (Zhang et al., 2018), women only (Basile et al., 2019) or blacks, other races and women (Waseem, 2016). These datasets reflect biases towards different targets of hate, which will usually influence model training and predictive performance. Different target groups are also addressed by different perpetrators in the real world. For example, left-wing hate is frequently aimed against the 'system', with police or politicians being targeted, whereas right-wing hate is frequently aimed against Jews or foreigners. Moreover, new target groups can arise due to new phenomena such as the Corona pandemic (Fan et al., 2020). Therefore, being able to adapt models to unknown target groups of hate speech without the need of time consuming labeling of new datasets is crucial. Another challenge for generalizing knowledge across different hate speech datasets is the disagreement over the definition of hate speech (Ross et al., 2017), which is especially problematic for benchmark datasets. These disagreements lead to incompatible annotation of different datasets (MacAvaney et al., 2019; Fortuna et al., 2020), which hinders a proper assessment of the generalization capabilities of the models.

In this work we investigate the generalization and adaptation capabilities of hate speech classifiers to different domains of hate speech while eliminating errors due to incompatible datasets. This is done by conducting our experiments on a single dataset, namely the HateXplain dataset (Mathew et al., 2020), which was annotated following consistent annotation rules. There are many possibilities to categorize hate speech into different domains. For example, hate speech with common topics, hate speech that addresses common target groups, hate speech from common time periods or hate speech from common datasets can be considered as separate domains. In this work, we regard the adaptation capabilities of the

[1] torsten.zesch@fernuni-hagen.de
florian.ludwig@zitis.bund.de
eleanor.hobley@zitis.bund.de
klara.dolos@zitis.bund.de

Proceedings of the Sixth Workshop on Online Abuse and Harms (WOAH), pages 29 - 39

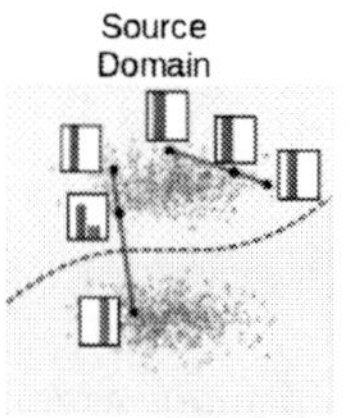

(a) **MixUp Regularization.** In manifold MixUp, virtual samples and virtual labels are computed by interpolating between the feature representations and corresponding labels (pseudo-labels for unlabeled samples) of data points.

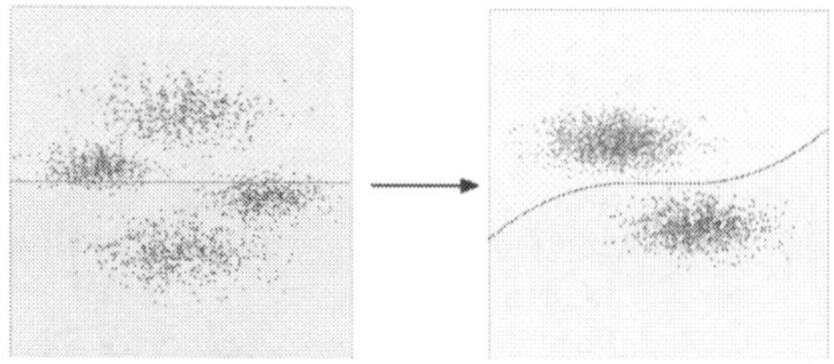

(b) **Adversarial Domain Adaptation.** The goal of adversarial domain adaptation is to align the feature distributions of source domain samples with feature distributions of target domain data samples.

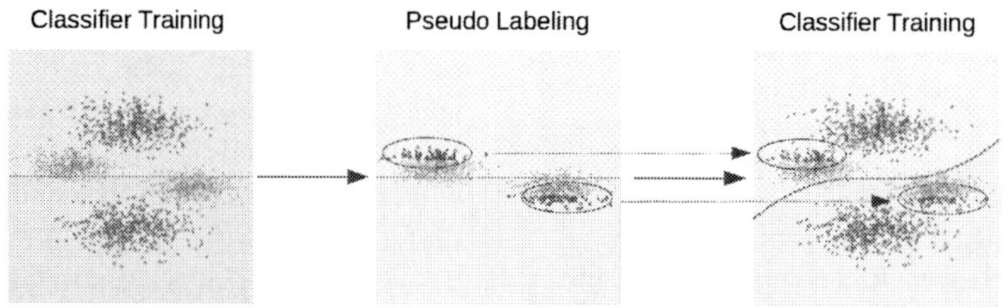

(c) **Curriculum Labeling.** After training a model on labeled samples (left), the model predicts pseudo labels (middle) for unlabeled samples from the target domain. Samples which belong to the most confident model predictions are included in the training set, together with their predicted class labels. Finally, the model is retrained from scratch on the augmented dataset (right).

Figure 1: Three different strategies for improving the generalization capabilities of models to different target groups are investigated. These approaches utilize labeled source data samples (colored data points) and unlabeled target domain data samples (grey data points).

models with respect to different target groups of hate speech due to the relevance of the topic for real world applications and the suitability of the HateXplain dataset for this research. An advantage of utilizing the HateXplain dataset for this research is, that target groups were annotated for all samples, not only the hateful ones, which allows us to appropriately select samples that correspond to different domains and therefore to properly investigate the generalization capabilities of our approaches. Adaptation of models to different target groups of hate speech is here investigated by unsupervised domain adaptation methods, namely via manifold MixUp regularization (Fig. 1a), adversarial domain adaptation (Fig. 1b) and curriculum labeling (Fig. 1c).

In summary, we make the following contributions:

- We analyze the influence of data and target group specific bias on hate speech classifiers;
- We investigate the suitability of unsupervised domain adaptation for improving model performances for out-of-domain target groups;
- Our experiments are conducted under clean conditions with properly separated domains and without data incompatibilities during model evaluation.

2 Related Work

Several approaches for machine learning based hate speech detection were investigated in recent years (Badjatiya et al., 2017; Djuric et al., 2015; Mozafari et al., 2019). An active line of research aims at improving generalization capabilities of hate speech detection systems, with most studies focusing on cross-dataset generalization capabilities of models (Bashar et al., 2021; Waseem et al., 2018).

Karan and Šnajder (2018) show the the difficulties of hate speech classifier to deal with out-domain datasets. The authors emphasize the importance of in-domain data for their generalization results. They integrated target domain data in their learning procedure using frustratingly easy domain adaptation Daumé III (2007). In contrast to our work, the authors investigated the cross-corpus generalization and adaptation capabilities of linear support vector machines. In this work, we focus on target group specific domain adaptation of deep learning based hate speech classifiers.

The generalization capabilities of deep learning models from topic generic to topic specific hate speech corpora were investigated by Chiril et al. (2021). The authors showed that models failed to generalize to domain specific corpora, but that the integration of domain specific knowledge improves the classification results in new domains. In contrast to our work, the authors focus on cross dataset generalization, which makes a clean evaluation of target group specific generalization difficult. Faal et al. (2021) suggested exploitation of multi-task learning and domain adaptation for improving the generalization capabilities of hate speech classifiers. After domain adaptive pre-training of a BERT based feature extractor (Devlin et al., 2019), the whole model was trained on multiple tasks by utilizing shared parameters as well as task specific parameters. The authors showed that the reduction of unintended target group specific model bias via multi-task learning successfully boosted generalization. In contrast to our work, they focus on general robustness with respect of target groups rather than a target group specific optimization.

In Bashar et al. (2021), the authors propose to train a language model to learn domain invariant and disentangled feature representation for different hate speech domains. After that, they trained a classifier on top of these feature representations and used it for robustly classifying hate speech from different domains. The authors demonstrated the success of the model in detecting hate speech related to the COVID-19 pandemic. On the other side, Bose et al. (2021) showed that the application of widely used unsupervised domain adaptation approaches can be problematic in the field of hate speech detection. The authors applied various pivot-based and adversarial-based approaches to generalize knowledge across different hate speech corpora. Unlike our work, which focuses on target group specific domain adaptation, these works focus on generalizing on knowledge on the level of hate speech corpora, which introduced previously discussed difficulties in model evaluation and which might be the main reason for bad adaptation results.

3 Methods and Experiments

In this section we describe the dataset, model architecture as well as the training and evaluation strategies used in our experiments.

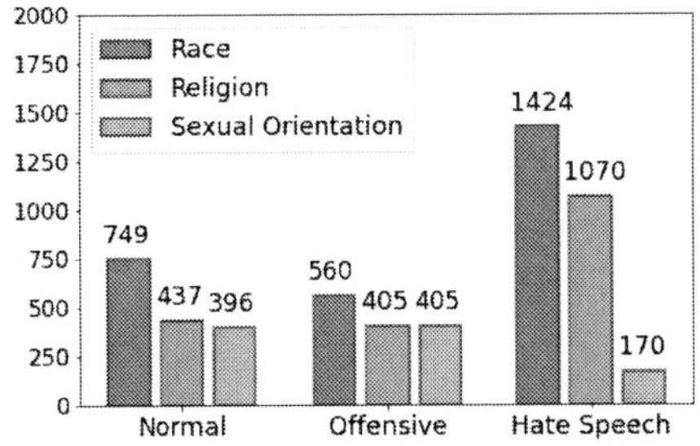

Figure 2: Number of experimental data samples by target group and and class label.

3.1 Dataset

The HateXplain dataset (Mathew et al., 2020), consisting of around $20K$ annotated posts, was used as the basis for all our experiments. The dataset was primarily annotated with the class labels $normal$, $offensive$ and $hateful$, with additional labeling of the target groups of hate ('Race', 'Religion', 'Sexual orientation', 'Gender', 'Origin', 'Other') undertaken. Unlike other datasets, such as (Del Vigna12 et al., 2017; Ousidhoum et al., 2019), each target group was annotated for all data points, including those belonging to the "normal" and "offensive" classes. This allows us to examine the generalization capabilities of different approaches with strictly separated target groups across all labels. To the best of our knowledge, the HateXplain dataset (Mathew et al., 2020) is the only dataset that explicitly annotates target groups for the classes "normal" and "offensive" as well, which is why this dataset is the only one that was used to conduct our experiments with strictly separated domains. To ensure that the trained models generalize from a single source domain to a single target domain, we select only those data points for training and validation purposes which have solely been annotated as belonging to either a source domain (e.g. "Race") or a target domain (e.g. "Religion"). We discard data points which have been annotated with multiple target groups (e.g. "Race" and "Gender"). We focus on the domains "Race," "Religion," and "Sexual Orientation" because the other target groups each contain fewer than 60 instances annotated as "Hate Speech," which risks inconsistent experimental results due to insufficient coverage of all class labels. Therefore, "Gender," "Origin," and "Other" are discarded, resulting in a final dataset that yields 170 to 1424 instances per class label (see Fig. 2). We also experiment with data augmentation. Recently, various techniques for text data augmentation have been proposed (Shorten et al., 2021), such as rule based techniques (Wei and Zou, 2019; Spasic et al., 2020; Karimi et al., 2021), feature space augmentations (Cheung and Yeung, 2020; Khosla et al., 2020) or neural augmentation (Wu et al., 2019). Due to the success of back translation based data augmentation (Xie et al., 2020; Yaseen and Langer, 2021; Corbeil and Abdi Ghadivel, 2020; Sugiyama and Yoshinaga, 2019), we decided to use this approach with pre-trained neural translation models (provided by HuggingFace [2]) in order to created an augmented version of the original HateXplain dataset. Back translation is done with the language pairs English - German, English - French and English - Spanish, resulting in nearly three times the number of instances per class.

3.2 Model Architecture and Training

In our experiments, we use the Structured Self-Attentive Sentence Embedding model (Lin et al., 2017), which provides a good trade-of between model performance and computational costs. The model is visualized in figure 3. The encoder of the model consists of a two layer bidirectional LSTM, followed by an attention module, as proposed by (Lin et al., 2017). The predictor of the model is a linear classifier, consisting of a single linear layer followed by a Softmax activation function. We use WordPiece tokenization (Devlin et al., 2018; Schuster and Nakajima, 2012). The embedding size and the hidden sizes of the LSTMs are 128, the dimension of the attention module 350, and the number of attention heads 30. A domain discriminator is applied in those experiments in which we perform adversarial domain alignment. The input of the domain discriminator is the output of the encoder of the Structured Self-Attentive Sentence Embedding model. The applied discriminator model consists of a gradient reversal layer (Ganin and Lempitsky, 2015), followed by a two layer feed forward neural network with a leaky ReLU activation function at the hidden position and a Sigmoid activation function at the output position.

We use the Adam optimizer (Kingma et al., 2015) with a learning rate of $5e^{-4}$ and beta values of $(0.9, 0.99)$ during our experiments. We apply dropout regularization (Srivastava et al., 2014) with a dropout probability of 0.6 to the LSTM modules

[2] https://huggingface.co/

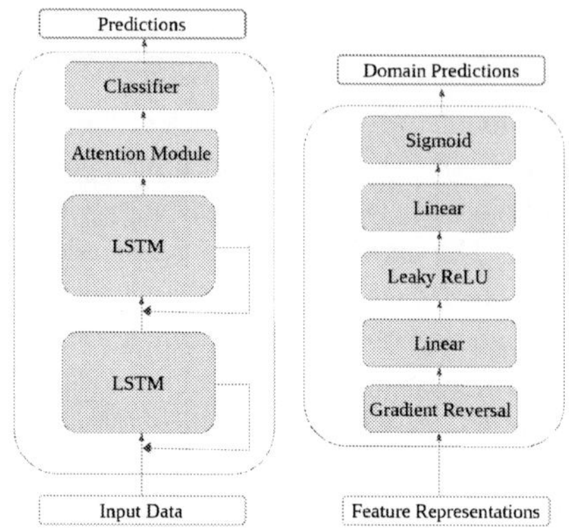

Figure 3: Structured Self-Attentive Sentence Embedding model (left) and domain discriminator (right), used in our experiments.

to prevent overfitting. All models are trained for a total of 50.000 training iterations with a batch size of 32. Our experiments are implemented using the deep learning framework Pytorch.[3]

3.3 Model Assessment

All models are evaluated using the macro-average F1-score with five-fold cross-validation. During training, we store those model states for which the models achieved the best results on the out-of-fold validation data of the training domains. For these model states, we report the results achieved on the validation data of the other domains, too. We believe that this is a realistic scenario, since we assume that only unlabeled data samples of other domains are available and we therefore need to select our models based on their performances on the source domains, for which labeled data samples are available.

3.4 Zero-Shot Approaches

In the first set of experiments, we investigate the generalization capabilities of models that use only labeled data from one domain and no data from other domains. As we examine the generalization capabilities of the models to target domains that were not present in the training data, we refer to these experiments as zero-shot approaches. In the first, naive zero-shot approach (*Zero*), models are trained with labeled data from the original HateXplain dataset (Mathew et al., 2020) that belong to a specific target group (e.g. "Race"). The training batches provided to the model in each training itera-

[3] https://pytorch.org/

tion are randomly sampled. In the second zero-shot approach (*Zero +*), models are trained with target group specific data from the augmented dataset (see Section 3.1). Similar to the first zero-shot learning approach, training batches are sampled randomly. In the last zero-shot learning approach (*Zero B+*), the training batches are sampled in a balanced manner from the augmented dataset with equal probability per class in each iteration. In all zero-shot approaches, models are evaluated with validation data from the original HateXplain dataset (Mathew et al., 2020), as described in Section 3.3.

3.5 Unsupervised Domain Adaptation

Unsupervised single source domain adaptation uses data from two different domains during the training: source data $X_S = \{(x_i, y_i)\}_{i=1}^{N}$, which consist of N labeled samples from a source domain $D_S = \{\mathcal{X}_S, P_S(X_S)\}$, and target data $X_T = \{x_j\}_{j=1}^{M}$, which consist of M unlabeled samples from a target domain $D_T = \{\mathcal{X}_T, P_T(X_T)\}$. $\mathcal{X} = \mathcal{X}_S = \mathcal{X}_T$ is a shared feature space, $P_S(X_S) \neq P_T(X_T)$ are marginal probability distributions over the feature space, which are similar, but differ. The goal of the learning algorithm is to train a model which achieves a strong performance for a task T on the target domain although no labeled data points from the target domain are available during the training. For the domain adaptation approaches, we use the same data and sampling strategy as for the last zero-shot learning approach (Zero B+).

The goal in our paper is to cover different research directions in the field of domain adaptation for hate speech detection purposes. The approaches investigated in this paper are typical candidates for their line of research, which consider the problem of domain adaptation from a regularization-based view 3.5.1, a data-based view 3.5.2 and a feature-based view 3.5.3.

3.5.1 MixUp Regularization

We adapt the approach of manifold MixUp regularization proposed by Verma et al. (2019) (Fig. 1a). Given is a deep neural network with an encoder e, which maps an input $x \in \mathcal{X}$ into hidden representation $h \in \mathbb{R}^m$, and a predictor p, which computes predictions $z \in \mathbb{R}^K$ based on the hidden representation $h \in \mathbb{R}^m$. Manifold MixUp regularization introduces an additional regularization loss based on MixUp feature representations $\tilde{h} \in \mathbb{R}^m$ and MixUp labels $\tilde{y} \in \mathbb{R}^K$, which are computed based on hidden representations $h_1, h_2 \in \mathbb{R}^m$ and corresponding labels $y_1, y_2 \in \mathbb{R}^K$ of two samples:

$$\tilde{h} = \alpha \cdot h_1 + (1 - \alpha) \cdot h_2 \tag{1}$$

$$\tilde{y} = \alpha \cdot y_1 + (1 - \alpha) \cdot y_2 \tag{2}$$

Here, $\alpha \in [0, 1]$ is sampled from a Beta distribution: $\alpha \sim Beta(2, 2)$. y_1 and y_2 are represented as one-hot encoded class labels for source domain samples and as soft pseudo-labels, which are iteratively computed by the neural network, for target domain samples.

The MixUp features are used for computing the MixUp predictions $\tilde{z} = p(\tilde{h})$ based on the predictor of the neural network. The loss between MixUp predictions and MixUp labels is computed as Cross-Entropy loss for source domain samples ($\tilde{l}_m^s$) and L1 loss for target domain samples ($\tilde{l}_m^t$). The complete MixUp loss l_m is computed as follows:

$$l_m = \lambda^s \cdot \tilde{l}_m^s + \lambda^t \cdot \tilde{l}_m^t \tag{3}$$

We set $\lambda^s = \lambda^t = 0.1$ in our experiments.

3.5.2 Curriculum Labeling

In addition to MixUp regularization, we adapt the approach of Cascante-Bonilla et al. (2020), which combines pseudo-labeling with curriculum learning, for domain adaptation purposes (Fig. 1c). Curriculum labeling is done by selecting data points from an unlabeled data pool based on the network's prediction confidences. The selected data points with corresponding pseudo-labels are iteratively included to the training procedure during the learning epochs. Following Cascante-Bonilla et al. (2020), we select data points based on percentile scores of the prediction confidences. During the training, the percentile threshold for selecting samples corresponding to the most confident predictions is increased from 0% to 100% in increments of 20%. In contrast to Cascante-Bonilla et al. (2020), we select the pseudo-labeled samples based on the model's prediction confidences independently for each predicted class. This is done to prevent a bias towards the selection of data points from majority classes, which is crucial for hate speech detection tasks. During each iteration ('curriculum epoch'), the network is re-trained from scratch with both the labeled samples and the pseudo-labeled samples selected by the model trained in the previous curriculum epoch.

Source Domain	Eval. Domain				Target Domain								
					Race			Rel.			Sex.		
		Zero	Zero +	Zero B+	Mix.	Adv.	Cur.	Mix.	Adv.	Cur.	Mix.	Adv.	Cur.
Race	Race	.56	.57	.58				**.58**	.57	.57	**.58**	.57	**.58**
	Rel.	.52	.52	.52		-		.54	.54	.51	.52	.53	.53
	Sex.	.50	.50	.51				.53	.53	.50	.51	.52	.53
Rel.	Race	.46	.46	.48	.48	.52	.52				.48	.49	.50
	Rel.	.47	.48	.50	.50	.52	.52		-		.49	.50	.50
	Sex.	.47	.48	.49	.50	.52	.51				.48	.49	.51
Sex.	Race	.36	.37	.42	.42	.48	.47	.42	.39	.42			
	Rel.	.39	.39	.43	.44	.46	.47	.43	.43	.45		-	
	Sex.	.42	.42	.46	.46	.49	.50	.45	.45	.48			

Table 1: Macro average F1 scores achieved by the approaches, averaged over five validation folds and split into target groups, approaches and domains. Improvements over the results, achieved by the best zero-shot approach are marked in green. Violet indicates negative transfer, in which the models achieved worse results than the naive zero-shot learning approach.

Approach	Source	Target	Other
Zero	0.483	0.450	
Zero +	0.490 *+1.4%*	0.455 *+1.1%*	
Zero B+	0.513 *+6.2%*	0.475 *+5.6%*	
MixUp	0.510 *+5.6%*	0.476 *+5.8%*	0.481 *+6.9%*
Adv.	0.517 *+7.0%*	0.496 *+10.2%*	0.487 *+8.2%*
Cur.	**0.525** ***+8.7%***	**0.498** ***+10.7%***	**0.488** ***+8.4%***

Table 2: Average F1-Scores of the investigated approaches and relative improvements compared to the naive zero-shot learning approach with respect to the domains.

Approach	Normal	Offensive	Hate Speech
Zero	0.479	0.287	0.618
Zero +	0.476 *-0.6%*	0.286 *-0.3%*	0.637 *+3.1%*
Zero B+	0.494 *+3.1%*	0.288 *+0.35%*	0.683 *+10.5%*
MixUp	0.490 *+2.1%*	0.281 *-2.1%*	0.690 *+11.7%*
Adv.	0.500 *+4.4%*	**0.312** ***+8.7%***	0.689 *+11.7%*
Cur.	**0.505** ***+6.5%***	0.311 *+8.4%*	**0.692** ***+12.0%***

Table 3: Average F1-Scores and its relative improvements over naive zero-shot learning, divided into approaches and classes labels.

3.5.3 Adversarial Domain Alignment

In order to learn domain invariant feature representations, Ganin et al. (2016) introduced Domain Adversarial Neural Networks (Fig. 1b). Beside the main model, a domain discriminator $D : \mathbb{R}^m \mapsto \mathbb{R}$ is trained to distinguish between feature representations $h^s \in \mathbb{R}^m$ and $h^t \in \mathbb{R}^m$ for source domain samples x^s and target domain samples x^t, computed by encoder e. At the same time, the encoder e is trained to confuse the domain discriminator D, such that the discriminator is not able to distinguish between these feature representations. To achieve this, an adversarial loss is introduced:

$$\mathcal{L}_{adv} = \mathop{\mathbb{E}}_{x^s \sim X^s}[log(D(e(x^s)))] + \mathop{\mathbb{E}}_{x^t \sim X^t}[log(1 - D(e(x^t)))] \quad (4)$$

The domain discriminator D is trained to maximize the adversarial loss $\mathcal{L}_{adv}$, while at the same time the encoder e is trained to fool the discriminator and therefore minimize $\mathcal{L}_{adv}$. The theoretical equilibrium is reached when the encoder e produces features which cannot be reliably classified as belonging either to the source or to the target domain by an optimal discriminator.

4 Results and Discussion

In this section, we present and discuss the results of our experiments. In table 1, we present macro average F1-scores, achieved by the investigated approaches. The scores are divided into source domain (first column), the domain on which the models were evaluated (second column) and the approaches used. Since the investigated domain adaptation approaches, unlike zero-shot approaches, used unlabeled target domain data in addition to labeled source domain data, their results are further subdivided into the target domain that was involved in model training. In table 2 we present the average F1-scores of the investigated approaches, split by source, target and uninvolved domain. In addition to the average values, relative improvements compared to the naive zero-shot learning approach are also given. Table 3 shows the achieved performances with respect to the class labels "normal", "offensive" and "hate speech". Again, we report the relative improvements of the approaches compared to the naive zero-shot approach. In table 4, we provide feature visualizations of our models for hate related samples based on lime (Ribeiro et al., 2016). The visualizations are provided for different approaches and combinations of source target and evaluation domains.

OFFENSIVE CONTENT WARNING: The following sections contain examples of hateful content. This is strictly for the purpose of enabling this research. Please be aware that this content could be offensive and cause you distress.

4.1 Model Bias

Although there are cases, in which models show poor generalization abilities to some out-of-domain target groups, all of our models were able to generalize knowledge to other domains to some extent. Best or equal best model performance was achieved when evaluating models against the domain on which they were trained (i.e. source domain) for both the zero-shot approaches (Table 1) as well as after averaging across domain adaptation approaches (Table 2). Data augmentation generally helped to improve the model performances, which shows that the models suffer from a bias due to the low amount of available training data. On average, the class "Hate Speech" benefits most from data augmentation (Table 3), while the performance on the classes "Normal" and "Offensive" is slightly worse compared to the naive zero-shot approach. Models additionally benefit from class balanced data sampling (Zero B+), which on average outperformed the other zero-shot learning approaches on all domains and across all class labels. Despite the improvements due to data augmentation and class balanced sampling, a gap between the performances on source domain and the other domains is still preserved. Moreover, both techniques slightly increased the performance gap between source and other domains (Table 2). We conclude that the models suffer from a target group specific bias, which occurs due to the lack of domain specific knowledge of domains other than the source domain and which cannot be reduced via typical data sampling strategies or data augmentation techniques such as back-translation. Therefore, the integration of domain specific knowledge of the target domain is crucial for reducing the performance gap between source domain and target domain.

Domain adaptation enabled models to learn domain specific features and to produce better model predictions in some instances (see samples a and b, e - h, i and l, Table 4). These results concur with the findings of (Karan and Šnajder (2018)), who highlighted the importance of in-domain knowledge for the generalization capabilities of hate speech classifiers and showed that models trained on domain general hate speech corpora failed to generalize to domain specific hate speech data Chiril et al. (2021). In contrast to our work, the authors investigated the generalization capabilities of models across different datasets, which hinders a clean evaluation due to possible dataset incompatibilities. Our results indicate that the integration of domain specific knowledge via adversarial domain adaptation and curriculum labeling is able to reduce the performance gap and achieve the largest improvements on the target domains, thereby reducing model bias (Table 2).

4.2 Effects of Domain Adaption Approaches on Model Performance

Domain adaptation was able to improve the performance over all zero-shot learning approaches for each combination of source and target domain (Table 1). Additionally, all domain adaptation approaches achieved better results on average than the zero-shot learning approaches for not only the target domain but also for the third, uninvolved domain (Table 2) and was observable for all three classes (Table 3). Moreover, the adversarial domain adaptation approach and the curriculum labeling approach on average outperformed the zero-shot learning approaches on the source domain. However, in our experiments the choice of the data included in the training procedure had greater impact to the model performances than the chosen domain adaptation approaches themselves. Furthermore, none of our investigated domain adaptation

MixUp Regularization

	Text	Source	Target	Evaluation	Prediction
a)	this little k**e is a good little donkey american	Race	Rel.	Rel.	Hate Speech
b)	luserl good job scamming you fu***ng fa**ot	Race	Rel.	Sex.	Hate Speech
c)	y' all n***as is hoes	Sex.	Race	Race	Offensive
d)	are yall n***as retarded	Sex.	Race	Race	Offensive

Adversarial Domain Adaptation

	Text	Source	Target	Eval	Prediction
e)	enjoy being a childless n****r fu**er	Rel.	Race	Race	Hate Speech
f)	deport that be**er sp**k to mexico	Sex.	Race	Race	Hate Speech
g)	like pick a struggle fa**ot	Rel.	Race	Sex.	Hate Speech
h)	kill yourself fa**ot	Rel.	Race	Sex.	Hate Speech

Curriculum Labeling

	Text	Source	Target	Eval	Prediction
i)	started as trash ending as worthless n****r trash	Rel.	Race	Race	Hate Speech
j)	those fa**ots off queer eye hate jews	Rel.	Race	Sex.	Hate Speech
k)	i fu***ng hate jews	Race	Rel.	Rel.	Offensive
l)	kill yourself fa**ot	Rel.	Race	Sex.	Hate Speech

Table 4: **Feature visualization for hate related samples.** Words highlighted in red strengthen the model to predict the class "Hate Speech", while words which are highlighted in blue, decrease this prediction confidence.

approaches outperformed the other methods in each experiment (Table 1), which makes the choice of the appropriate approach in practical settings difficult, especially when no labeled data of the target domain is available to asses the model performance on that domain.

While the two approaches curriculum labeling and adversarial domain adaptation both performed similarly, they outperform MixUp regularization in most cases. Adversarial domain adaptation improved the performances in 4 out of 6 domain combinations on the target domain, and in 5 out of 6 combinations on the uninvolved domain. Curriculum labeling resulted in better performances on the target domain in 5 out of 6 training domain pairs, and in 4 out of 6 cases on the uninvolved domain. In contrast, MixUp regularization improved performances on the target domain in only 1 out of 6 source-target domain combinations, namely "Race"-"Religion", and yielded the smallest improvements in average model performance of all three domain adaptation approaches (Table 2). Moreover, MixUp regularization was not able to correctly learn domain specific features, such as the domain specific word "n***as" for its predictions (see samples c) and d), Table 4). Thus, MixUp regularization is inferior to the other approaches for the investigated task.

Remarkably, the curriculum labeling approach resulted in worse outcomes than the zero-shot approaches in one instance (Table 1), although the risk of predicting incorrect pseudo-labels is mitigated by implementing the curriculum steps proposed in (Cascante-Bonilla et al., 2020). This performance loss or negative transfer is indicated by the phrase "hate jews" leading to a decrease in the prediction confidences of the models for the hate speech class and, in case of sample k), an incorrect prediction (samples j & k, Table 4). This negative transfer is attributable to a negative confirmation bias, which can occur in pseudo-labeling based approaches (Rizve et al., 2021) and can lead to a large number of incorrect pseudo-labels that interfere with the training procedure and thus affect the model performance. Nevertheless, the curriculum labeling approach proved to be best suitable to adapt hate speech classifiers in our study, achieving the best averaged results on the source, target and other domains.

4.3 Data Dependency of the Performance

In our experiments, the choice of the training data had the greatest impact on the model performances. Models trained on the source domain "Race" yielded the best results in general with F1 scores ranging from .50 and .58. Models, trained on the source domain "Sexual Orientation" performed worst overall and achieved F1 scores between .36 and .50. Models, trained on the source domain "Religion" achieved F1 scores between .46 and .52. A similar pattern was observed for unlabeled data from the target domain. The largest improvements via domain adaptation were achieved by utilizing unlabeled data from the target domain "Race", whereas utilizing unlabeled data from the target domain "Sexual Orientation" yielded the lowest improvements. We attribute these observations to the number of training samples available in each class. The best performances were achieved with the largest amount of labeled training data (source domain "Race"), the worst performances were achieved with the lowest amount of labeled training data (source domain "Sexual Orientation"). Additionally, the largest improvements were achieved by incorporating the largest amount of unlabeled data (target domain "Race"), the smallest improvements were achieved with the lowest amount of unlabeled data (target domain "Sexual Orientation"). Since the domain adaptation performance on the target domain depends on the performance achieved on the source domain (Zhang and Harada, 2019), this observation also holds true for the investigated domain adaptation approaches.

5 Conclusion

The goal of this work was to analyze the generalization capabilities of hate speech classifiers to different target groups of hate under clean experimental conditions. Furthermore, we aimed to investigate the suitability of unsupervised domain adaptation to improve these generalization capabilities. Our results indicate that naively trained hate speech classifiers suffer from a target group specific bias and that unsupervised domain adaptation is able to improve the generalization capabilities of models across different target groups of hate. In contrast to previous works, which mainly focus on the generalization capabilities of hate speech classifiers in cross dataset settings, we investigated the generalization capabilities of hate speech classifiers to new hate targets on a single dataset, the HateXplain dataset. This enabled us to strictly separate target groups across all class labels and therefore allowed a clean analysis of the abilities of models to generalize to different target groups of hate, while avoiding the risk of inconsistencies over the definition of hate speech between datasets. We observed a gap of the model performances on the source domains and the model performances on the target domains. While data augmentation and balanced data sampling was able to generally improve the model performances, these methods tend to preserve these gaps. The integration of domain specific knowledge via domain adaptation was able to improve the generalization capabilities of models to other target groups, whereby the number of the involved labeled and unlabeled training samples strongly influenced the results of the approaches. However, our study does not allow a clear conclusion about which domain adaptation approach is best in which constellation of available data, which makes the choice of the appropriate approach difficult in real world situations. In total, there is still potential to improve the prediction quality of the models, especially when it comes to real world applications. Failures to detect hate speech, which contain threats, may lead to life-threatening situations for people, for example. In such scenarios, the achieved model performances are not good enough to reliably support law enforcement agencies. Improvements could be made with more advanced model architectures and a larger amount of available training data, which is a limitation of our work. We also analyzed generalization capabilities for only three target groups of hate, namely "race," "religion," and "sexual orientation." These limitations should be addressed in future works, for which we suggest investigating the generalization capabilities to new targets of hate in settings with a greater amount of data, higher diversity of target groups and with more advanced models like transformer based models. Moreover, the limitations of each of the domain adaptation methods can be further investigated in order gain insight into when and why some methods might fail.

Acknowledgements

This work was funded by the German ministry of education and research (BMBF) within the framework program Research for Civil Security of the German Federal Government (KISTRA, 13N15337).

References

Aymé Arango, Jorge Pérez, and Barbara Poblete. 2019. Hate speech detection is not as easy as you may think: A closer look at model validation. In *Proceedings of the 42nd international acm sigir conference on research and development in information retrieval*, pages 45–54.

Pinkesh Badjatiya, Shashank Gupta, Manish Gupta, and Vasudeva Varma. 2017. Deep learning for hate speech detection in tweets. In *Proceedings of the 26th international conference on World Wide Web companion*, pages 759–760.

Md Abul Bashar, Richi Nayak, Khanh Luong, and Thirunavukarasu Balasubramaniam. 2021. Progressive domain adaptation for detecting hate speech on social media with small training set and its application to covid-19 concerned posts. *Social Network Analysis and Mining*, 11(1):1–18.

Valerio Basile, Cristina Bosco, Elisabetta Fersini, Nozza Debora, Viviana Patti, Francisco Manuel Rangel Pardo, Paolo Rosso, Manuela Sanguinetti, et al. 2019. Semeval-2019 task 5: Multilingual detection of hate speech against immigrants and women in twitter. In *13th International Workshop on Semantic Evaluation*, pages 54–63. Association for Computational Linguistics.

Tulika Bose, Irina Illina, and Dominique Fohr. 2021. Unsupervised domain adaptation in cross-corpora abusive language detection. In *SocialNLP 2021-The 9th International Workshop on Natural Language Processing for Social Media*.

Paola Cascante-Bonilla, Fuwen Tan, Yanjun Qi, and Vicente Ordonez. 2020. Curriculum labeling: Self-paced pseudo-labeling for semi-supervised learning. *arXiv e-prints*, pages arXiv–2001.

Polychronis Charitidis, Stavros Doropoulos, Stavros Vologiannidis, Ioannis Papastergiou, and Sophia Karakeva. 2020. Towards countering hate speech against journalists on social media. *Online Social Networks and Media*, 17:100071.

Tsz-Him Cheung and Dit-Yan Yeung. 2020. Modals: Modality-agnostic automated data augmentation in the latent space. In *International Conference on Learning Representations*.

Patricia Chiril, Endang Wahyu Pamungkas, Farah Benamara, Véronique Moriceau, and Viviana Patti. 2021. Emotionally informed hate speech detection: a multi-target perspective. *Cognitive Computation*, pages 1–31.

Jean-Philippe Corbeil and Hadi Abdi Ghadivel. 2020. Bet: A backtranslation approach for easy data augmentation in transformer-based paraphrase identification context. *arXiv e-prints*, pages arXiv–2009.

Hal Daumé III. 2007. Frustratingly easy domain adaptation. In *Proceedings of the 45th Annual Meeting of the Association of Computational Linguistics*, pages 256–263.

Fabio Del Vigna12, Andrea Cimino23, Felice Dell'Orletta, Marinella Petrocchi, and Maurizio Tesconi. 2017. Hate me, hate me not: Hate speech detection on facebook. In *Proceedings of the First Italian Conference on Cybersecurity (ITASEC17)*, pages 86–95.

Jacob Devlin, Ming-Wei Chang, Kenton Lee, and Kristina Toutanova. 2018. Bert: Pre-training of deep bidirectional transformers for language understanding. *arXiv preprint arXiv:1810.04805*.

Jacob Devlin, Ming-Wei Chang, Kenton Lee, and Kristina Toutanova. 2019. Bert: Pre-training of deep bidirectional transformers for language understanding. In *Proceedings of the 2019 Conference of the North American Chapter of the Association for Computational Linguistics: Human Language Technologies, Volume 1 (Long and Short Papers)*, pages 4171–4186.

Nemanja Djuric, Jing Zhou, Robin Morris, Mihajlo Grbovic, Vladan Radosavljevic, and Narayan Bhamidipati. 2015. Hate speech detection with comment embeddings. In *Proceedings of the 24th international conference on world wide web*, pages 29–30.

Farshid Faal, Jia Yuan Yu, and Ketra Schmitt. 2021. Domain adaptation multi-task deep neural network for mitigating unintended bias in toxic language detection. In *ICAART (2)*, pages 932–940.

Lizhou Fan, Huizi Yu, and Zhanyuan Yin. 2020. Stigmatization in social media: Documenting and analyzing hate speech for covid-19 on twitter. *Proceedings of the Association for Information Science and Technology*, 57(1):e313.

Paula Fortuna, Juan Soler, and Leo Wanner. 2020. Toxic, hateful, offensive or abusive? what are we really classifying? an empirical analysis of hate speech datasets. In *Proceedings of the 12th Language Resources and Evaluation Conference*, pages 6786–6794.

Yaroslav Ganin and Victor Lempitsky. 2015. Unsupervised domain adaptation by backpropagation. In *International conference on machine learning*, pages 1180–1189. PMLR.

Yaroslav Ganin, Evgeniya Ustinova, Hana Ajakan, Pascal Germain, Hugo Larochelle, François Laviolette, Mario Marchand, and Victor Lempitsky. 2016. Domain-adversarial training of neural networks. *The journal of machine learning research*, 17(1):2096–2030.

Mladen Karan and Jan Šnajder. 2018. Cross-domain detection of abusive language online. In *Proceedings of the 2nd workshop on abusive language online (ALW2)*, pages 132–137.

Akbar Karimi, Leonardo Rossi, and Andrea Prati. 2021. Aeda: An easier data augmentation technique for text classification. In *Findings of the Association for Computational Linguistics: EMNLP 2021*, pages 2748–2754.

Prannay Khosla, Piotr Teterwak, Chen Wang, Aaron Sarna, Yonglong Tian, Phillip Isola, Aaron Maschinot, Ce Liu, and Dilip Krishnan. 2020. Supervised contrastive learning. *Advances in Neural Information Processing Systems*, 33:18661–18673.

DP Kingma, LJ Ba, et al. 2015. Adam: A method for stochastic optimization.

Zhouhan Lin, Minwei Feng, Cicero Nogueira dos Santos, Mo Yu, Bing Xiang, Bowen Zhou, and Yoshua Bengio. 2017. A structured self-attentive sentence embedding. *arXiv preprint arXiv:1703.03130*.

Sean MacAvaney, Hao-Ren Yao, Eugene Yang, Katina Russell, Nazli Goharian, and Ophir Frieder. 2019. Hate speech detection: Challenges and solutions. *PloS one*, 14(8):e0221152.

Binny Mathew, Punyajoy Saha, Seid Muhie Yimam, Chris Biemann, Pawan Goyal, and Animesh Mukherjee. 2020. Hatexplain: A benchmark dataset for explainable hate speech detection. *arXiv preprint arXiv:2012.10289*.

Marzieh Mozafari, Reza Farahbakhsh, and Noel Crespi. 2019. A bert-based transfer learning approach for hate speech detection in online social media. In *International Conference on Complex Networks and Their Applications*, pages 928–940. Springer.

Nedjma Ousidhoum, Zizheng Lin, Hongming Zhang, Yangqiu Song, and Dit-Yan Yeung. 2019. Multilingual and multi-aspect hate speech analysis. In *Proceedings of the 2019 Conference on Empirical Methods in Natural Language Processing and the 9th International Joint Conference on Natural Language Processing (EMNLP-IJCNLP)*, pages 4675–4684.

Marco Tulio Ribeiro, Sameer Singh, and Carlos Guestrin. 2016. " why should i trust you?" explaining the predictions of any classifier. In *Proceedings of the 22nd ACM SIGKDD international conference on knowledge discovery and data mining*, pages 1135–1144.

Mamshad Nayeem Rizve, Kevin Duarte, Yogesh S Rawat, and Mubarak Shah. 2021. In defense of pseudo-labeling: An uncertainty-aware pseudo-label selection framework for semi-supervised learning. *arXiv preprint arXiv:2101.06329*.

Björn Ross, Michael Rist, Guillermo Carbonell, Benjamin Cabrera, Nils Kurowsky, and Michael Wojatzki. 2017. Measuring the reliability of hate speech annotations: The case of the european refugee crisis. *arXiv preprint arXiv:1701.08118*.

Mike Schuster and Kaisuke Nakajima. 2012. Japanese and korean voice search. In *2012 IEEE international conference on acoustics, speech and signal processing (ICASSP)*, pages 5149–5152. IEEE.

Connor Shorten, Taghi M Khoshgoftaar, and Borko Furht. 2021. Text data augmentation for deep learning. *Journal of big Data*, 8(1):1–34.

Irena Spasic, Goran Nenadic, et al. 2020. Clinical text data in machine learning: systematic review. *JMIR medical informatics*, 8(3):e17984.

Nitish Srivastava, Geoffrey Hinton, Alex Krizhevsky, Ilya Sutskever, and Ruslan Salakhutdinov. 2014. Dropout: a simple way to prevent neural networks from overfitting. *The journal of machine learning research*, 15(1):1929–1958.

Amane Sugiyama and Naoki Yoshinaga. 2019. Data augmentation using back-translation for context-aware neural machine translation. In *Proceedings of the Fourth Workshop on Discourse in Machine Translation (DiscoMT 2019)*, pages 35–44.

Vikas Verma, Alex Lamb, Christopher Beckham, Amir Najafi, Ioannis Mitliagkas, David Lopez-Paz, and Yoshua Bengio. 2019. Manifold mixup: Better representations by interpolating hidden states. In *International Conference on Machine Learning*, pages 6438–6447. PMLR.

Zeerak Waseem. 2016. Are you a racist or am i seeing things? annotator influence on hate speech detection on twitter. In *Proceedings of the first workshop on NLP and computational social science*, pages 138–142.

Zeerak Waseem, James Thorne, and Joachim Bingel. 2018. Bridging the gaps: Multi task learning for domain transfer of hate speech detection. In *Online harassment*, pages 29–55. Springer.

Jason Wei and Kai Zou. 2019. Eda: Easy data augmentation techniques for boosting performance on text classification tasks. In *Proceedings of the 2019 Conference on Empirical Methods in Natural Language Processing and the 9th International Joint Conference on Natural Language Processing (EMNLP-IJCNLP)*, pages 6382–6388.

Xing Wu, Shangwen Lv, Liangjun Zang, Jizhong Han, and Songlin Hu. 2019. Conditional bert contextual augmentation. In *International Conference on Computational Science*, pages 84–95. Springer.

Qizhe Xie, Zihang Dai, Eduard Hovy, Thang Luong, and Quoc Le. 2020. Unsupervised data augmentation for consistency training. *Advances in Neural Information Processing Systems*, 33:6256–6268.

Usama Yaseen and Stefan Langer. 2021. Data augmentation for low-resource named entity recognition using backtranslation. *arXiv e-prints*, pages arXiv–2108.

Dexuan Zhang and Tatsuya Harada. 2019. A general upper bound for unsupervised domain adaptation. *arXiv preprint arXiv:1910.01409*.

Ziqi Zhang, David Robinson, and Jonathan Tepper. 2018. Detecting hate speech on twitter using a convolution-gru based deep neural network. In *European semantic web conference*, pages 745–760. Springer.

"*Zo Grof!*": A Comprehensive Corpus for Offensive and Abusive Language in Dutch

Ward Ruitenbeek, Victor Zwart, Robin van der Noord,
Zhenja Gnezdilov, Tommaso Caselli
CLCG, University of Groningen, The Netherlands
t.caselli@rug.nl

Abstract

This paper presents a comprehensive corpus for the study of socially unacceptable language in Dutch. The corpus extends and revise an existing resource with more data and introduces a new annotation dimension for offensive language, making it a unique resource in the Dutch language panorama. Each language phenomenon (abusive and offensive language) in the corpus has been annotated with a multilayer annotation scheme modelling the explicitness and the target(s) of the abuse/offence in the message. We have conducted a new set of experiments with different classification algorithms on all annotation dimensions. Monolingual Pre-Trained Language Models prove as the best systems, obtaining a macro-average F1 of 0.828 for binary classification of offensive language, and 0.579 for the targets of offensive messages. Furthermore, the best system obtains a macro-average F1 of 0.637 for distinguishing between abusive and offensive messages.

1 Introduction

Social Media platforms have become an intrinsic part of the lives of lots of people. A phenomenon that accompanies Social Media platforms, with serious impacts on society, is the presence of socially unacceptable language. Socially unacceptable language is to be regarded as a generic umbrella term comprehending many different user-generated language phenomena such as toxic language (Karan and Šnajder, 2019; Bhat et al., 2021), offensive language (Zampieri et al., 2019c; Ranasinghe and Zampieri, 2020; Zampieri et al., 2020), abusive language (Karan and Šnajder, 2018; Caselli et al., 2020; Wiegand et al., 2021), hate speech (Waseem and Hovy, 2016a; Davidson et al., 2019; Basile et al., 2019), among others. While manually monitoring and flagging these phenomena is impossible, there has been a growing interest in the Computational Linguistics (CL) and Natural Language Processing (NLP) communities to develop automatic systems to flag messages containing these phenomena.

Besides the limitations of this type of reactive interventions, previous work (Nozza, 2021) has shown the necessity of language specific resources for these phenomena to properly train systems. This work contributes in this direction by presenting a comprehensive dataset to identify socially unacceptable language in Twitter messages in Dutch. We integrate and extend DALC v1.0 (Caselli et al., 2021) by introducing a new annotation layer for offensive language and expanding the size of the dataset from 8,156 messages to 11,292. The main contribution of this paper can be summarised as follows:

- a new release of DALC, DALC v2.0, with a) more than 3k newly annotated messages and b) annotations for the offensive language dimension;
- an extensive set of experiments to model the different annotation dimensions involved;
- an error analysis showing the limits of current models.

The annotation guidelines, the data, and the code for the reported experiments, and a data statement (Bender and Friedman, 2018) are publicly available.[1] Examples of offensive messages have been redacted to preserve privacy and explicit offensive lexical items have been obfuscated.

2 Offensive Language: Why and How

Offensive language is a broader language phenomenon when compared to other phenomena and behaviours (e.g., abusive language, hate speech or cyberbullying) and, most importantly, more subjective (Vidgen et al., 2019; Poletto et al., 2021). In

[1] https://github.com/tommasoc80/DALC

Proceedings of the Sixth Workshop on Online Abuse and Harms (WOAH), pages 40 - 56
July 14, 2022 ©2022 Association for Computational Linguistics

Offensive Language (Zampieri et al., 2019a)	Abusive Language (Caselli et al., 2021)
Posts containing any form of non-acceptable language (profanity) or a targeted offence, which can be veiled or direct. This includes insults, threats, and posts containing profane language or swear words.	Impolite, harsh, or hurtful language (that may contain profanities or vulgar language) that result in a debasement, harassment, threat, or aggression of an individual or a (social) group, but not necessarily of an entity, an institution, an organisations, or a concept.

Table 1: Definitions of offensive and abusive language adopted in this work.

general, the use of offensive language is intrinsically connected to freedom of speech. However, in the context of social media interactions, the presence and use of offensive language towards other users should raise concerns because it may escalate the exchange in deeper verbal hostility (e.g., hate speech) and give rise to highly toxic, and unsafe environments (Chowdhury et al., 2020).

While we can identify and list parameters and details that help us to narrow down whether a message is abusive or not, the offensiveness of a message is only partially dependent on its content. Other variables such as the context of occurrence, the background and experience of the reader/annotator play a relevant role. Despite these difficulties, offensive language datasets have been developed in different languages (Sigurbergsson and Derczynski, 2020; Pitenis et al., 2020; Çöltekin, 2020; Chowdhury et al., 2020) and used in recent shared tasks (Zampieri et al., 2019c, 2020).

To maximise resource interoperability and foster the study of offensive language from a multilingual perspective, we adopt the definition of offensive language from Zampieri et al. (2019c). In Table 1 the full definition is reported and compared with the definition of abusive language adopted in the Dutch Abusive Language Corpus (DALC) v1.0. A key element distinguishing these two language phenomena is the level of detail used to describe them, the different emphasis on the intentions of the producers, the presence/absence of a target, and the effects on the receivers. In particular, target is an essential and compulsory element of abusive language, while it is not the case for offensive messages. On the other hand, given its more generic nature, offensive language can be identified in messages that do not contain any target. This is particularly evident in the use of profanities to express strong (positive or negative) emotions. To better clarify the difference between the two phenomena consider the following examples from DALC v2.0:

1. ER IS EEN F***** MUG EVEN GROOT ALS MIJN DUIM
   [There is a f****** as big as my thumb]

2. Elke [identity_term] is een potentiëele terrorist
   [Every [identity_term] is a potential terrorist]

Example 1 instantiate an offensive message, due to the presence of a profanity. Its perception of being offensive can vary according to the context of use and the receivers of the message. At the same time, the message does not fully comply with the definition of abusive language for multiple reasons: there is not a (human) target and there is no intention to debase or harass an individual/group. Example 2, on the contrary, it is a clear case of abusive language. Here the abusive is express via a stereotype and a debasing act, and with an explicit target realised via a specific identity term. The message is abusive and also offensive.

In this work, we have maintained the multi-layer annotation approach of DALC v1.0, distinguishing between the explicitness of the message and its target. The explicitness and the target layers for the offensive dimension have been refined with subclasses along the existing annotation of abusive language. The explicitness layer distinguishes three subclasses: (i.) EXPLICIT; (ii.) IMPLICIT; and (iii.) NOT. While NOT is used to annotate not offensive messages, the difference between the EXPLICIT and IMPLICIT subclasses mainly rely on the surface forms of the message. Explicit offensive content refers to the presence of profanities or combination of words that unambiguously make the message offensive. Implicit messages are more subtle, lacking any surface markers, thus making the offence hidden (Waseem et al., 2017).

The target layer, on the other hand, extends the classes used for abusive language allowing for the absence of a target. In particular, we have four subclasses defined as follows: (i.) INDIVIDUAL, for messages that are addressed or target a specific

Id	Text	Explicitness	Target
1.	Dat gebeurt in het park en veel jongeren bij elkaar [That happens in a park and many young people together]	NOT	NOT
2.	En daar trap jij in. Echt slim [And you fall for that. really smart]	IMP.	IND.
3.	S*** worden ze niet gemaakt [They don't get any d****]	EXP.	GRP.
4.	j*** dat was wel schrikken geweest [J**** that was scary]	EXP.	NOT
5.	ons geld vervangen door die sh** euro [replace our money by that sh** euro]	EXP.	OTH.

Table 2: Examples of the annotation of the explicitness and the target layers. EXP. = EXPLICIT, IMP. = IMPLICIT; IND. = INDIVIDUAL, GRP. = GROUP, OTH. = OTHER. English translations in brackets.

person or individual (who could be named or not); (ii.) GROUP, for messages that target a group of people considered as a unity because of ethnicity, gender, political affiliation, religion, disabilities, or other common properties; (iii.) OTHER, for messages that target concepts, institutions and organisations, or non-living entities; and (iv.) NOT, for offensive messages without a target. In Table 2, we report some redacted examples from the dataset to illustrate the combination of the two layers in the annotation process.

Data Collection and Annotation DALC v1.0 is a corpus of 8,156 messages from Twitter in Dutch obtained by applying three different collection methods: keywords extraction, message geolocation, and seed users. We have extracted a total of 10k messages using only the keywords and seed users data from DALC v1.0, since these two sources proved to be denser and more suitable for the language phenomenon of interest. Following the settings of DALC v1.0, there is no overlap of messages concerning topic and authors between train and test distributions. Consequently, the 10k messages are equally and independently extracted from the train and test candidates - resulting in 5k messages per distribution. We divided the messages of each distribution in batches of 1k each for the annotation.

Given the highly subjective nature of offensive language, all annotations for both layers have been conducted in parallel by four annotators. [2] Annotators were asked to apply the definition of offensive language as reported in Table 1. Each offensive message was then annotated for the explicitness and the target layers.

The annotation has been conducted in two steps. In the first step, the annotators focused on all 6,267 messages that were marked as not abusive in DALC v1.0. This is a necessary curation phase in order to be compliant with the distinction between offensive and abusive language. In the second steps, we have annotated 5 additional batches for train and 1 batch for test. The final amount of annotated data is 12,251.[3]

Table 3 reports the pairwise Cohen's Kappa score for all the four annotators for the explicitness and the target layers. The agreement scores have been computed on all the annotated data. The agreement for explicitness layer ranges between a minimum of 0.330 to a maximum of 0.541, indicating a slight/substantial agreement, with a global Fleiss' Kappa of 0.430. It is worth noting that there is a variation in agreement across the annotators, with A.1 and A.3 being the strongest pair. Kappa scores slightly increase when aggregating the explicitness subclasses into a generic offensive (OFF) label. In this case, the values range between 0.358 (A.2–A.4) and 0.593 (A.1–A.3), with a Fleiss' Kappa of 0.473. The results for the annotation of the target layer are slightly worse, with the minimum agreement being a Cohen's Kappa of 0.250 (A.2–A.3) and a maximum of 0.474 (A.1–A.3). Overall Fleiss's Kappa for the target layer is 0.402.

To better understand these results, we have anal-

[2]The annotators are also authors of this paper.

[3]15 messages from the last training batch were not annotated.

Explicitness	A.1	A.2	A.3	A.4
A.1	–	0.457	0.541	0.412
A.2	–	–	0.373	0.330
A.3	–	–	–	0.471

Target	A.1	A.2	A.3	A.4
A.1	–	0.391	0.474	0.379
A.2	–	–	0.304	0.250
A.3	–	–	–	0.457

Table 3: Inter-Annotator Agreement for the Explicitness and the Target layers - pairwise Cohen's Kappa.

ysed the pairwise confusion matrices of all the annotators.[4] For the explicitness layer, it clearly appears that the biggest source of disagreement is the offensive status of the message rather than the distinction between explicit or implicit, further supporting the claim that offensiveness is subjective. This has also an impact on the target layer: if a message is not annotated as offensive, the target annotation is ignore.

Handling of disagreements We adopt a majority voting for handling the disagreements and assigning final labels. In all cases where a tie is reached, the examples have been discussed collectively to reach a consensus. However, when subjectivity is an essential property of a language phenomenon, disagreements are more informative than detrimental (Aroyo et al., 2019; Basile, 2020; Leonardelli et al., 2021). In line with this vision, the final distribution contains the disaggregated annotations to promote further research on the relationship of subjectivity and annotation of natural language phenomena.

3 Data Overview

The annotated corpus contains 11,292 Twitter messages in Dutch, covering a time period between November 2015 and August 2020. For completeness, all messages marked as offensive and containing a target have also been further annotated for abusiveness. For abusive language, we applied the same annotation procedure used in DALC v1.0. Table 4 illustrates the distribution of the data for the abusive and offensive dimensions, and the target layers across the Train/Dev and Test distributions.

The unbalanced distribution between the negative and the positive examples for both the abusive and the offensive dimensions is part of the design strategy. While the actual distribution of these classes in social media is unknown, a distribution of 2/3 *vs.* 1/3 between negative and positive examples appears to be more realistic than a perfectly balanced dataset and in line with previous work (Basile et al., 2019; Davidson et al., 2017; Zampieri et al., 2019c, 2020).

[4]See Appendix B for details.

Annotated Dimension	Subclass	Train	Dev	Test	Total
Abusive	EXP	855	127	328	1,310
	IMP	536	116	135	787
	NOT	5,426	962	2,807	9,195
Offensive	EXP	1,407	230	584	2,221
	IMP	1,070	209	283	1,562
	NOT	4,340	766	2,403	7,509
Target - Abusive	IND	777	127	254	1,158
	GRP	470	87	158	715
	OTH	144	29	51	224
Target - Offensive	IND	1,147	191	361	1,699
	GRP	705	133	244	1,082
	OTH	489	93	157	739
	NOT	136	22	105	263

Table 4: DALC v2.0: Distribution of subclasses in Train, Dev, and Test splits for abusive, offensive dimensions and target layers. Target is split between target of abusive messages and target of offensive messages.

Overall, 2,097 messages have been annotated as abusive, with an increase of 208 messages when compared to DALC v1.0. On the other hand, 3,783 messages have been marked as offensive. In both dimensions, the explicit subclass represents the majority, with 62.47% of cases for the abusive dimension and 58.71% for the offensive one. The difference in the distribution of the implicit subclass is striking, with implicit offensive messages being almost the double of the abusive counterpart. A possible explanation can be found in the definitions of the two phenomena and their annotations: offensive messages have been labelled as such either because they contained a profanity, or because the annotators *subjectively perceived* them as offensive.

As for the targets, we observe that only a minority of offensive messages does not have a target (6.95%). When compared to other datasets for offensive language, the amount of messages associated with this class varies - for instance, being the majority class in Sigurbergsson and Derczynski (2020) but not the minority in Zampieri et al. (2019b) - suggesting that there may be a dependency of this subclass on the method(s) used for collecting the data. On the other hand, differences in the realisation of the targets are more evident when focusing on the IND and GRP subclasses. Offensive messages have a balanced distribution between these two subclasses corresponding to 28.25% and 28.60% of all the targets, respectively. On the contrary, abusive messages see a majority of cases (55.22%) for the IND subclass, and relatively fewer cases for GRP (34.09%). Lastly, the OTH subclass has been selected more often (19.53%) with offensive messages than with the abusive ones (only 10.68%). This difference can be again explained in the light of the definitions of the two phenomena.

No significant difference in length has been found between abusive and offensive messages (average length abusive 28.79 words; average length offensive 28.44),[5] while this is not the case for offensive and not offensive messages (average length not offensive 21.93 words; average length offensive 28.44). [6] Similarly to DALC v1.0, significant differences in length between implicit and explicit messages appear only in the Test distribution, where implicit offensive messages have an average of 30.04 words compared to the 23.55 words of the explicit messages.

To gain better insights into the data and the differences between the two dimensions, we have extracted and compared the top-50 keywords between the Train and Test distributions by collapsing the subclass in the explicitness layer, resulting in OFFENSIVE, ABUSIVE, NOT (Table 11 in Appendix B illustrates the top-10 keywords). While we observe a lack of overlapping lexical items between Train and Test distributions, and the absence of any topic-specific lexical items, the differences between offensive and abusive language are not as neat as one would imagine. Besides the presence of some profanities or slurs, most of the keywords do not present any specific denotative or connotative markings for offensive and/or abusive language.

4 Experiments

We ran a set of experiments to validate the newly annotated corpus. We first focused on the identification of the offensiveness dimension (§ 4.1), and then on the target layer (§ 4.2). We also investigate the ability of systems to distinguish between offensive and abusive dimensions (§ 4.3). We tested four different architectures: a Linear SVM combining character and word n-gram TF-IDF vectors, a Bi-LSTM model initialised Coosto pre-trained word embeddings,[7] and two monolingual Transformer-based pre-trained Language Models (PTLMs), namely BERTje (de Vries et al., 2019) and RobBERT (Delobelle et al., 2020). The two PTLMs differ with respect to their architectures (BERT *vs.* RoBERTa), the size (12GB *vs.* 39GB) and origin of the data used to generate the models (manually selected data *vs.* the Dutch section of the automatically derived OSCAR corpus (Suárez et al., 2019)). All models are trained on the Train split and evaluated against the held-out, non-overlapping Test split. The Dev split is used for tuning of the systems' (hyper)parameters. Models are compared using the macro-average F1. However, given the imbalance among the subclasses in the different layers, for each subclass, we also report Precision and Recall. For the offensiveness and the offensive target dimensions, systems are compared against a dummy classifier based on the majority class. In all experiments, a common preprocessing approach is applied. All preprocessing steps and (hyper)parameters are detailed in Appendix A for replicability.

4.1 Detecting Offensive Language

We have first modeled the offensiveness dimension both as a binary classification task, by collapsing the EXPLICIT and IMPLICIT subclasses into a single value, namely OFF(ENSIVE). Given the distribution of the annotated data, the task is already challenging. The second experiment setting follows the fine-grained, tripartite distinction between EXPLICIT, IMPLICIT and NOT.

Table 5 presents the results for the binary setting. All models outperform the dummy baseline, with RobBERT achieving the best results (macro-average F1 of 0.828). Interestingly, the second best system is the Bi-LSTM rather than the other PTLM, BERTje, with a macro-average F1 of 0.823. When comparing the results of these two latter models, we observe that BERTje underpeforms on the OFF label, especially for Recall. A possible ex-

[5]Statistical test: Mann-Whitney Test; $p > 0.05$

[6]Statistical test: Mann-Whitney Test; $p < 0.05$

[7]https://github.com/coosto/dutch-word-embeddings

System	Class	Precision	Recall	Macro-F1
Dummy	OFF NOT	0.0 0.734	0.0 1.0	0.423
SVM	OFF NOT	0.644 0.836	0.513 0.898	0.718
Bi-LSTM	OFF NOT	$0.733_{0.015}$ $0.908_{0.004}$	$0.749_{0.015}$ $0.901_{0.009}$	$0.823_{0.004}$
BERTje	OFF NOT	$0.721_{0.010}$ $0.891_{0.006}$	$0.693_{0.022}$ $0.903_{0.008}$	$0.802_{0.002}$
RobBERT	OFF NOT	$0.756_{0.005}$ $0.906_{0.004}$	$0.737_{0.013}$ $0.914_{0.001}$	$\mathbf{0.828}_{0.006}$

Table 5: DALC v2.0: Offensive language, binary classification. Lower script numbers show standard deviations over 3 different runs. Best scores in bold.

planation can be found by taking into account the properties of the embedding representations of the models. The Coosto word embeddings used to initialise the Bi-LSTM have been obtained by using a large amount of messages from social media (624 million messages out of a total of 660 million texts), making them more suitable and inline with the text variety of the dataset. This may also be one of the reasons why RobBERT performs best: the data used to generate its embeddings are also from the Web, although not specifically from social media posts. To further validate the behaviour of the Bi-LSTM model, we ran a further set of experiments using random pre-trained embeddings obtained from the Dutch CoNLL17 corpus[8] (Fares et al., 2017). The embeddings are smaller than the Coosto ones (100 dimensions *vs.* 300 dimensions for Coosto), and obtained from a different data distribution. While the results[9] are lower (macro-F1 $0.799_{0.004}$), they are still competitive, with the macro-F1 falling within the standard deviation of BERTje.

All systems achieve very good results on the negative class but suffer on the positive one. This is mainly due to the lack of overlapping elements between the Train/Dev and the Test split, besides the impact of the unbalanced distribution of the data in the training data. This is particularly evident for the Recall of the OFF class of the SVM which is barely above 0.5. Finally, in absolute terms, the results of the top systems are in line with those reported for comparable datasets in other languages (Zampieri et al., 2020).

[8] http://vectors.nlpl.eu/repository/

[9] OFF Precision: $0.737_{0.058}$, OFF Recall: $0.680_{0.064}$; NOT Precision: $0.888_{0.016}$, NOT Recall: $0.908_{0.034}$

The outcome of the fine-grained experiments are detailed in Table 6. Rather than focusing only on the best systems, we have experimented with all of them to see whether the patterns observed in the binary classification remain valid.

System	Class	Precision	Recall	Macro-F1
SVM	EXP IMP NOT	0.710 0.297 0.820	0.395 0.212 0.936	0.543
Bi-LSTM	EXP IMP NOT	$0.766_{0.044}$ $0.423_{0.039}$ $0.889_{0.009}$	$0.709_{0.058}$ $0.268_{0.025}$ $0.942_{0.014}$	$0.658_{0.004}$
BERTje	EXP IMP NOT	$0.762_{0.015}$ $0.374_{0.033}$ $0.887_{0.007}$	$0.639_{0.054}$ $0.434_{0.032}$ $0.904_{0.032}$	$0.663_{0.018}$
RobBERT	EXP IMP NOT	$0.735_{0.007}$ $0.370_{0.007}$ $0.904_{0.005}$	$0.724_{0.012}$ $0.358_{0.042}$ $0.911_{0.02}$	$\mathbf{0.667}_{0.005}$

Table 6: DALC v2.0: Explicitness layer classification. Lower script numbers show standard deviations over 3 different runs. Best scores in bold.

The picture that emerges is slightly different. The performances on the EXP and the NOT subclasses are almost unchanged for the neural-based systems, while they dramatically drop for the EXP subclass for the SVM model. All systems struggle to distinguish the IMP subclass, with the Bi-LSTM achieving the best Precision. When compared to the binary classification, the results of the two PTLMs are closer and marginally better than the Bi-LSTM, confirming RobBERT as the best system (macro-average F1 0.667). Interestingly, BERTje has the highest Recall score for the IMP subclass.

4.2 Detecting the Targets

Target identification has an important role within the more general task of offensive language identification, especially because it can help to better assess the seriousness of the offence and contribute to the study of more specific phenomena such as hate speech (Waseem et al., 2017; Zampieri et al., 2019b). In particular, messages containing a target can be further annotated by distinguishing whether they express an insult or stronger forms of degradation (e.g., abusive language, or hate speech), and by refining the types of target (e.g., gender, race/ethnicity, political orientation, disabilities, among others).

In these experiments, we have assumed a perfect labelling of the messages for offensiveness.

This results in a reduced number of messages that we can use for training and testing our systems. Similarly to the offensiveness dimension, we have compared our results against a dummy classifier that always predicts the most frequent label, i.e., IND. The results are reported in Table 7.

System	Class	Precision	Recall	Macro-F1
Dummy	IND	0.416	1.0	0.147
	GRP	0.0	0.0	
	OTH	0.0	0.0	
	NOT	0.0	0.0	
SVM	IND	0.587	0.892	0.467
	GRP	0.631	0.561	
	OTH	0.535	0.286	
	NOT	0.666	0.114	
Bi-LSTM	IND	$0.605_{0.023}$	$0.844_{0.054}$	$0.471_{0.009}$
	GRP	$0.673_{0.049}$	$0.551_{0.065}$	
	OTH	$0.466_{0.075}$	$0.346_{0.047}$	
	NOT	$0.359_{0.068}$	$0.130_{0.033}$	
BERTje	IND	$0.692_{0.005}$	$0.863_{0.009}$	**$0.579_{0.002}$**
	GRP	$0.685_{0.016}$	$0.677_{0.020}$	
	OTH	$0.600_{0.034}$	$0.438_{0.025}$	
	NOT	$0.501_{0.068}$	$0.285_{0.041}$	
RobBERT	IND	$0.681_{0.009}$	$0.862_{0.011}$	$0.567_{0.006}$
	GRP	$0.701_{0.005}$	$0.666_{0.004}$	
	OTH	$0.590_{0.033}$	$0.448_{0.022}$	
	NOT	$0.441_{0.013}$	$0.244_{0.021}$	

Table 7: DALC v2.0: Target layer classification. Lower script numbers show standard deviations over 3 different runs. Best scores in bold.

Given the higher number of subclasses and the reduced number of messages useful for training the systems, target identification is more challenging. All systems outperform the dummy baseline, with varying degrees of performance. The first striking result is the (relatively) close performance of the SVM and the Bi-LSTM models, with a macro F1 delta of 0.004. While the Bi-LSTM has a better performance for the IND and GRP subclasses, the SVM obtains better results on the OTH and the NOT. The PTLMs confirm as the best systems and for this task BERTje outperforms RobBERT, with a macro-average F1 of 0.579.

Similarly to the offensive dimension, the distribution of the labels in the Train split clearly has an impact on the results of the trained systems (see Table 4). Thus, it is not surprising that all systems tend to overgeneralise the IND subclass since it is the most frequent one. When analysing the confusion matrices across all systems, it appears that the most confounded class is OTH. The class tends to be wrongly assigned to the IND and the GRP subclasses.

4.3 Distinguishing between Offensive and Abusive Language

System	Class	Precision	Recall	Macro-F1
SVM	OFF	0.383	0.170	0.530
	ABU	0.570	0.410	
	NOT	0.820	0.941	
Bi-LSTM	OFF	$0.451_{0.014}$	$0.231_{0.096}$	$0.607_{0.021}$
	ABU	$0.596_{0.027}$	$0.637_{0.042}$	
	NOT	$0.883_{0.014}$	$0.941_{0.022}$	
BERTje	OFF	$0.339_{0.021}$	$0.383_{0.020}$	$0.599_{0.009}$
	ABU	$0.600_{0.024}$	$0.495_{0.009}$	
	NOT	$0.891_{0.005}$	$0.901_{0.013}$	
RobBERT	OFF	$0.384_{0.015}$	$0.359_{0.036}$	**$0.637_{0.009}$**
	ABU	$0.625_{0.012}$	$0.644_{0.018}$	
	NOT	$0.903_{0.005}$	$0.907_{0.011}$	

Table 8: DALC v2.0: Abusive *vs.* Offensive classification. Lower script numbers show standard deviations over 3 different runs. Best scores in bold.

In this section, we present a set of experiments that challenges systems to distinguish between three categories: whether a message is offensive but not abusive (OFF; see example 1), whether a message is abusive (ABU; see example 2), and whether a message is neither (NOT). The task is framed as a multi-class classification problem rather than as a multi-label classification one. This results in a slightly different distribution of the labels, namely in Train we have 1,391 (20.51%) messages marked as ABU, 1,086 (16.01%) messages marked as OFF, and 4,304 (63.47%) messages for NOT. The test split has 463 (14.15%) ABU messages, 404 (12.35%) OFF messages, and 2,403 (73.48%) messages marked as NOT. The distribution between the ABU and OFF classes is unbalanced in favour of the ABU class.

Results for these experiments are illustrated in Table 8. As the figures show, the imbalance of the classes in the Train split affects the performance of all systems, with the results for the ABU messages being better than those labelled as OFF, but worse than those labelled as NOT. RobBERT qualifies again as the best system followed by the Bi-LSTM, and with the SVM being the worst. The results for BERTje are comparable to those obtained for the offensive experiments in the binary setting (see Table 5). Across all systems, we observe a tendency to wrongly classify OFF as NOT, and ABU as OFF. Connecting this with our analysis of the top- keywords per class indicates that the systems trained in this way heavily rely on superficial linguistic cues rather than grasping deeper and more heavily discriminating cues. In addition to this, when focusing on the combination of the explicitness layers and the ABU and OFF classes, we observe that in the Train split the majority of ABU messages (i.e, 62.25%) are marked as EXPLICIT, while this holds only for 49.81% of the OFF messages. It thus appears that with varying degrees all systems have identified a clear shortcut in these experiments whereby messages that are marked as EXPLICIT are then more often associated with the ABU class.

5 Error Analysis

We have conducted an error analysis for the offensive dimension and the offensive target layer since they represents the new annotations in the dataset. The error analysis has been conducted on the Dev set using the best performing system for each dimension.

Offensive Language For the offensive language dimension, we have used the predictions by RobBERT in the binary settings. The system wrongly classifies 179 messages, with the majority (101 messages) being OFF messages wrongly labelled as NOT. To gain better insights, we have classified all the errors into six categories:

- **criticism**: 13.40% of the errors are due to messages expressing some form of criticism; 75% of them are OFF wrongly labelled as NOT;
- **obfuscation**: only 3.35% of OFF messages wrongly labelled are due to obfuscation or abbreviation of profanities or slurs;
- **sarcasm/irony**: 8.93% of the errors are due to presence of irony or sarcasm; the majority (62.5%) concerns errors for the OFF subclass wrongly considered as NOT;
- **world knowledge**: 13.4% of the errors could have been correctly classified by means of some form of world knowledge;
- **gold errors**: 7.82% of the errors are due to potential annotation mistakes in the gold standard data;
- **bias**: this category comprises the largest amount of errors, 48.6% of the messages. 60.91% of the errors are False Positives for the OFF subclass containing identity terms (e.g. "gay"), names of political parties or politicians, or religious terms; the remainder of the messages are False Negatives for the OFF subclass containing stereotypes or being implicitly offensive.

Target For targets, 127 messages are wrongly classified. When analysing the confusion matrices across all systems, it appears that the most confounded class is OTH. The class tends to be wrongly assigned to the IND and the GRP subclasses. On the contrary, the errors for the NOT subclass are limited and they seem to be due to lack of training data.

The large part of the errors (31.49%) are due to different elements such as mixture of pronouns in the message (e.g., "jij" and "ze"), presence of collective nouns, or presence of a user's placeholder (i.e., MENTION) but no direct address in the text, and even mentions of concepts. The second largest block of errors, 23.62%, is due to the presence of multiple placeholders in the message, often happening in Twitter when replying to a long conversation but not necessarily addressing all the users involved. 18.11% of the errors could have been avoided by correctly processing the verb form. Given the larger amount of classes, 15.74% of the messages present some errors in the gold data - note, however, that these messages also include the errors in the gold standard for the offensive language dimension. Finally, 11.02% of the targets could have been correctly assigned if some form of commonsense knowledge was available to the system.

6 Related Work

The interest for the development of datasets and systems for the detection of abusive and offensive language phenomena has seen a steep growth in recent years. Different phenomena have been investigated including racism (Waseem and Hovy, 2016b; Davidson et al., 2017, 2019), hate speech (Alfina et al., 2017; Founta et al., 2018; Mishra et al., 2018; Basile et al., 2019), toxicity[10], verbal aggression (Kumar et al., 2018), and misogyny (Frenda et al., 2018; Pamungkas et al., 2020; Guest et al., 2021).

Offensive language, as we have detailed in § 2, is a more general and subjective phenomenon than abusive language. Founta et al. (2018) provides an

[10]The Toxic Comment Classification Challenge `https://bit.ly/2QuHKD6`

extensive analysis of the correlations between different phenomena and decide to collapse messages labelled as abusive, offensive and aggressive into a single category, namely abusive. Early attempts to annotate offensive language have been conducted in German as part of broader evaluation on hate speech (Wiegand et al., 2018). The SemEval 2019 Task 6: OffensEval (Zampieri et al., 2019c) has set up a common reference framework for the definition and the annotation of offensive language. The follow-up edition of the task (Zampieri et al., 2020) applied the original definition and annotation approach to four additional languages other than English, namely Turkish, Danish, Arabic, Greek. This corpus complements these annotation efforts with a further compatible dataset to fill a gap in the Dutch language resource panorama and to promote the advancement of multilingual approaches.

A different direction to the development of multilingual offensive language datasets has been presented with XHATE-99 (Glavaš et al., 2020). In this case, the authors have semi-automatically translated selected messages from three English datasets into five target languages (Albanian, Croatian, German, Russian, and Turkish). By working with translations, the authors have managed to better disentangle the impact of language versus domain shift in a transfer learning setting. As a matter of fact, the language alignments have ensured that losses observed in the cross-lingual setting are solely due to language shift rather than domain.

7 Conclusion and Future Work

This paper has presented DALC v2.0, a corpus for detecting offensive and abusive language in social media for Dutch. The corpus is composed of 11,292 messages manually annotated and it currently represents the largest available resource for these language phenomena in Dutch. Offensive language captures a more subjective dimension when compared to abusive language. For this reason, the data have been annotated in parallel by all annotators. We have applied a multi-layered annotation scheme targeting two key dimensions: the explicitness of the message and the presence of a potential target. For both annotation layers, the final labels have been assigned by means of majority voting. However, in the release of the corpus, we also distribute the disaggregated labels for both layers.

We have conducted a series of experiments by applying different algorithms. We have obtained the best results by using two monolingual PTLMs, namely RobBERT for the offensive dimension, and BERTje for the targets. For the offensive dimension, we have found that a Bi-LSTM architecture is very competitive when compared to the PTLMs also when using non-domain specific embeddings. We have also experimented on the ability of the models to distinguish between abusive and offensive language, obtaining promising results, showing that the distinction between offensive and abusive language is a more complex task than targeting each phenomenon individually.

Our error analysis has indicated limits of the systems and of the dataset. In particular, it seems that systems heavily rely on surface cues to assign a label to the message, showing a lack of "comprehension" of the content of the message and a high sensitivity to the distribution of the data in the training split.

Future work will focus on further testing the abilities of the dataset to train robust system by applying trained models to dynamic benchmark on the line of the HateCheck approach (Röttger et al., 2021). Furthermore, given the presence of multiple compatible corpora in different languages, we plan to explore the application of multilingual systems to address this task.

Ethical Statement

Dual use DALC v2.0 and all the accompanying models are exposed to risks of dual use from malevolent agents. However, by making publicly available the resource and documenting the process behind its creation and the training of the models (including their limitations and errors), we may mitigate such risks.

Misrepresentation As the error analysis has shown (§ 5), even the best system is far from being perfect, with a relatively high number of False Positive for the OFF subclass. We thus recommend caution before deploying such a model without any additional human supervision.

Privacy Collection of data from Twitter's users has been conducted in compliance with Twitter's Terms of Service. Given the large amount of users that may be involved, we could not collect informed consent from each of them. To comply with this limitations, we have made publicly available only the tweet IDs. This will protect the users' rights to delete their messages or accounts. However, releasing only IDs exposes DALC to fluctuations in terms of potentially available messages, thus making replicability of experiments and comparison with future work impossible. To obviate to this limitation, we make available another version of the corpus, Full Text. This version of the corpus allows users to access to the full text message of all 11,292 tweets. The Full Text dataset is released with a dedicated licence. In this case, we make available only the text, removing any information related to the time periods or seed users. We have also anonymised all users' mentions and external URLs. The licence explicitly prevents users to actively search for the text of the messages in any form. We deem these sufficient steps to protect users' privacy and rights to do research using internet material.

References

Ika Alfina, Rio Mulia, Mohamad Ivan Fanany, and Yudo Ekanata. 2017. Hate speech detection in the indonesian language: A dataset and preliminary study. In *2017 International Conference on Advanced Computer Science and Information Systems (ICACSIS)*, pages 233–238. IEEE.

Lora Aroyo, Lucas Dixon, Nithum Thain, Olivia Redfield, and Rachel Rosen. 2019. Crowdsourcing subjective tasks: The case study of understanding toxicity in online discussions. In *Companion Proceedings of The 2019 World Wide Web Conference*, WWW '19, page 1100–1105, New York, NY, USA. Association for Computing Machinery.

Valerio Basile. 2020. It's the end of the gold standard as we know it. on the impact of pre-aggregation on the evaluation of highly subjective tasks. In *DP@AI*IA*.

Valerio Basile, Cristina Bosco, Elisabetta Fersini, Debora Nozza, Viviana Patti, Francisco Manuel Rangel Pardo, Paolo Rosso, and Manuela Sanguinetti. 2019. SemEval-2019 task 5: Multilingual detection of hate speech against immigrants and women in twitter. In *Proceedings of the 13th International Workshop on Semantic Evaluation*, pages 54–63, Minneapolis, Minnesota, USA. Association for Computational Linguistics.

Emily M Bender and Batya Friedman. 2018. Data statements for natural language processing: Toward mitigating system bias and enabling better science. *Transactions of the Association for Computational Linguistics*, 6:587–604.

Meghana Moorthy Bhat, Saghar Hosseini, Ahmed Hassan Awadallah, Paul Bennett, and Weisheng Li. 2021. Say 'YES' to positivity: Detecting toxic language in workplace communications. In *Findings of the Association for Computational Linguistics: EMNLP 2021*, pages 2017–2029, Punta Cana, Dominican Republic. Association for Computational Linguistics.

Tommaso Caselli, Valerio Basile, Jelena Mitrović, Inga Kartoziya, and Michael Granitzer. 2020. I feel offended, don't be abusive! implicit/explicit messages in offensive and abusive language. In *Proceedings of the 12th Language Resources and Evaluation Conference*, pages 6193–6202, Marseille, France. European Language Resources Association.

Tommaso Caselli, Arjan Schelhaas, Marieke Weultjes, Folkert Leistra, Hylke van der Veen, Gerben Timmerman, and Malvina Nissim. 2021. DALC: the Dutch abusive language corpus. In *Proceedings of the 5th Workshop on Online Abuse and Harms (WOAH 2021)*, pages 54–66, Online. Association for Computational Linguistics.

Shammur Absar Chowdhury, Hamdy Mubarak, Ahmed Abdelali, Soon-gyo Jung, Bernard J. Jansen, and Joni Salminen. 2020. A multi-platform Arabic news comment dataset for offensive language detection. In *Proceedings of the 12th Language Resources and Evaluation Conference*, pages 6203–6212, Marseille, France. European Language Resources Association.

Çağrı Çöltekin. 2020. A corpus of Turkish offensive language on social media. In *Proceedings of the 12th Language Resources and Evaluation Conference*, pages 6174–6184, Marseille, France. European Language Resources Association.

Thomas Davidson, Debasmita Bhattacharya, and Ingmar Weber. 2019. Racial bias in hate speech and abusive language detection datasets. In *Proceedings of the Third Workshop on Abusive Language Online*, pages 25–35, Florence, Italy. Association for Computational Linguistics.

Thomas Davidson, Dana Warmsley, Michael Macy, and Ingmar Weber. 2017. Automated hate speech detection and the problem of offensive language. In *Proceedings of the International AAAI Conference on Web and Social Media*.

Wietse de Vries, Andreas van Cranenburgh, Arianna Bisazza, Tommaso Caselli, Gertjan van Noord, and Malvina Nissim. 2019. Bertje: A dutch bert model. *arXiv preprint arXiv:1912.09582*.

Pieter Delobelle, Thomas Winters, and Bettina Berendt. 2020. RobBERT: a Dutch RoBERTa-based Language Model. In *Findings of the Association for Computational Linguistics: EMNLP 2020*, pages 3255–3265, Online. Association for Computational Linguistics.

Murhaf Fares, Andrey Kutuzov, Stephan Oepen, and Erik Velldal. 2017. Word vectors, reuse, and replicability: Towards a community repository of large-text resources. In *Proceedings of the 21st Nordic Conference on Computational Linguistics*, pages 271–276, Gothenburg, Sweden. Association for Computational Linguistics.

Antigoni Maria Founta, Constantinos Djouvas, Despoina Chatzakou, Ilias Leontiadis, Jeremy Blackburn, Gianluca Stringhini, Athena Vakali, Michael Sirivianos, and Nicolas Kourtellis. 2018. Large scale crowdsourcing and characterization of twitter abusive behavior. In *Twelfth International AAAI Conference on Web and Social Media*.

Simona Frenda, Ghanem Bilal, et al. 2018. Exploration of misogyny in spanish and english tweets. In *Third Workshop on Evaluation of Human Language Technologies for Iberian Languages (IberEval 2018)*, volume 2150, pages 260–267. Ceur Workshop Proceedings.

Goran Glavaš, Mladen Karan, and Ivan Vulić. 2020. XHate-999: Analyzing and detecting abusive language across domains and languages. In *Proceedings of the 28th International Conference on Computational Linguistics*, pages 6350–6365, Barcelona, Spain (Online). International Committee on Computational Linguistics.

Ella Guest, Bertie Vidgen, Alexandros Mittos, Nishanth Sastry, Gareth Tyson, and Helen Margetts. 2021. An expert annotated dataset for the detection of online misogyny. In *Proceedings of the 16th Conference of the European Chapter of the Association for Computational Linguistics: Main Volume*, pages 1336–1350.

Mladen Karan and Jan Šnajder. 2018. Cross-domain detection of abusive language online. In *Proceedings of the 2nd Workshop on Abusive Language Online (ALW2)*, pages 132–137, Brussels, Belgium. Association for Computational Linguistics.

Mladen Karan and Jan Šnajder. 2019. Preemptive toxic language detection in Wikipedia comments using thread-level context. In *Proceedings of the Third Workshop on Abusive Language Online*, pages 129–134, Florence, Italy. Association for Computational Linguistics.

Ritesh Kumar, Atul Kr. Ojha, Shervin Malmasi, and Marcos Zampieri. 2018. Benchmarking aggression identification in social media. In *Proceedings of the First Workshop on Trolling, Aggression and Cyberbullying (TRAC-2018)*, pages 1–11, Santa Fe, New Mexico, USA. Association for Computational Linguistics.

Elisa Leonardelli, Stefano Menini, Alessio Palmero Aprosio, Marco Guerini, and Sara Tonelli. 2021. Agreeing to disagree: Annotating offensive language datasets with annotators' disagreement. In *Proceedings of the 2021 Conference on Empirical Methods in Natural Language Processing*, pages 10528–10539, Online and Punta Cana, Dominican Republic. Association for Computational Linguistics.

Pushkar Mishra, Marco Del Tredici, Helen Yannakoudakis, and Ekaterina Shutova. 2018. Author profiling for abuse detection. In *Proceedings of the 27th International Conference on Computational Linguistics*, pages 1088–1098.

Debora Nozza. 2021. Exposing the limits of zero-shot cross-lingual hate speech detection. In *Proceedings of the 59th Annual Meeting of the Association for Computational Linguistics and the 11th International Joint Conference on Natural Language Processing (Volume 2: Short Papers)*, pages 907–914, Online. Association for Computational Linguistics.

Endang Wahyu Pamungkas, Valerio Basile, and Viviana Patti. 2020. Misogyny detection in twitter: a multilingual and cross-domain study. *Information Processing & Management*, 57(6):102360.

Zesis Pitenis, Marcos Zampieri, and Tharindu Ranasinghe. 2020. Offensive language identification in Greek. In *Proceedings of the 12th Language Resources and Evaluation Conference*, pages 5113–5119, Marseille, France. European Language Resources Association.

Fabio Poletto, Valerio Basile, Manuela Sanguinetti, Cristina Bosco, and Viviana Patti. 2021. Resources and benchmark corpora for hate speech detection: a systematic review. *Lang. Resour. Evaluation*, 55(2):477–523.

Tharindu Ranasinghe and Marcos Zampieri. 2020. Multilingual offensive language identification with cross-lingual embeddings. In *Proceedings of the 2020 Conference on Empirical Methods in Natural Language Processing (EMNLP)*, pages 5838–5844, Online. Association for Computational Linguistics.

Paul Röttger, Bertie Vidgen, Dong Nguyen, Zeerak Waseem, Helen Margetts, and Janet Pierrehumbert. 2021. HateCheck: Functional tests for hate speech detection models. In *Proceedings of the 59th Annual Meeting of the Association for Computational Linguistics and the 11th International Joint Conference on Natural Language Processing (Volume 1: Long Papers)*, pages 41–58, Online. Association for Computational Linguistics.

Gudbjartur Ingi Sigurbergsson and Leon Derczynski. 2020. Offensive language and hate speech detection for Danish. In *Proceedings of the 12th Language Resources and Evaluation Conference*, pages 3498–3508, Marseille, France. European Language Resources Association.

Pedro Javier Ortiz Suárez, Benoît Sagot, and Laurent Romary. 2019. Asynchronous pipeline for processing huge corpora on medium to low resource infrastructures. In *7th Workshop on the Challenges in the Management of Large Corpora (CMLC-7)*. Leibniz-Institut für Deutsche Sprache.

Bertie Vidgen, Alex Harris, Dong Nguyen, Rebekah Tromble, Scott Hale, and Helen Margetts. 2019. Challenges and frontiers in abusive content detection. In *Proceedings of the Third Workshop on Abusive Language Online*, pages 80–93, Florence, Italy. Association for Computational Linguistics.

Zeerak Waseem, Thomas Davidson, Dana Warmsley, and Ingmar Weber. 2017. Understanding abuse: A typology of abusive language detection subtasks. In *Proceedings of the First Workshop on Abusive Language Online*, pages 78–84.

Zeerak Waseem and Dirk Hovy. 2016a. Hateful symbols or hateful people? predictive features for hate speech detection on Twitter. In *Proceedings of the NAACL Student Research Workshop*, pages 88–93, San Diego, California. Association for Computational Linguistics.

Zeerak Waseem and Dirk Hovy. 2016b. Hateful symbols or hateful people? predictive features for hate speech detection on twitter. In *Proceedings of the NAACL Student Research Workshop*, pages 88–93, San Diego, California. Association for Computational Linguistics.

Michael Wiegand, Josef Ruppenhofer, and Elisabeth Eder. 2021. Implicitly abusive language – what does it actually look like and why are we not getting there? In *Proceedings of the 2021 Conference of the North American Chapter of the Association for Computational Linguistics: Human Language Technologies*, pages 576–587, Online. Association for Computational Linguistics.

Michael Wiegand, Josef Ruppenhofer, Anna Schmidt, and Clayton Greenberg. 2018. Inducing a lexicon of abusive words–a feature-based approach. In *Proceedings of the 2018 Conference of the North American Chapter of the Association for Computational Linguistics: Human Language Technologies, Volume 1 (Long Papers)*, pages 1046–1056.

Marcos Zampieri, Shervin Malmasi, Preslav Nakov, Sara Rosenthal, Noura Farra, and Ritesh Kumar. 2019a. Predicting the type and target of offensive posts in social media. In *Proceedings of the 2019 Conference of the North American Chapter of the Association for Computational Linguistics: Human Language Technologies, Volume 1 (Long and Short Papers)*, pages 1415–1420, Minneapolis, Minnesota. Association for Computational Linguistics.

Marcos Zampieri, Shervin Malmasi, Preslav Nakov, Sara Rosenthal, Noura Farra, and Ritesh Kumar. 2019b. Predicting the Type and Target of Offensive Posts in Social Media. In *Proceedings of NAACL*.

Marcos Zampieri, Shervin Malmasi, Preslav Nakov, Sara Rosenthal, Noura Farra, and Ritesh Kumar. 2019c. SemEval-2019 task 6: Identifying and categorizing offensive language in social media (OffensEval). In *Proceedings of the 13th International Workshop on Semantic Evaluation*, pages 75–86, Minneapolis, Minnesota, USA. Association for Computational Linguistics.

Marcos Zampieri, Preslav Nakov, Sara Rosenthal, Pepa Atanasova, Georgi Karadzhov, Hamdy Mubarak, Leon Derczynski, Zeses Pitenis, and Çağrı Çöltekin. 2020. SemEval-2020 task 12: Multilingual offensive language identification in social media (OffensEval 2020). In *Proceedings of the Fourteenth Workshop on Semantic Evaluation*, pages 1425–1447, Barcelona (online). International Committee for Computational Linguistics.

Appendix A: Replicability

Preprocessing All experiments have been conducted with common pre-processing steps, namely:

- lowercasing of all words
- all users' mentions have been substituted with a placeholder (MENTION);
- all URLs have been substituted with a with a placeholder (URL);
- all ordinal numbers have been replaced with a placeholder (NUMBER);
- emojis have been replaced with text (e.g. 🥺 → `:pleading_face:`) using Python `emoji` package;
- hashtag symbol has been removed from hashtags (e.g. #kadiricinadalet → kadiricinadalet);
- extra blank spaces have been replaced with a single space;
- extra blank new lines have been removed.

Models' hyperparameters All hyperparamters used for the experiments are reported in Table 9.

Model	Task	Hyperparm.	Value
SVM	Offensive Off. Target	n-gram range	1–2
		character n-gram range	3–5
		C	1.0
Bi-LSTM	Offensive	LSTM nodes	32
		Hidden Layers	0
		Embeddings	Coosto Word2Vec
		Embedding dim.	300
		Recurrent dropout	0.1
		Batch size	32
		Loss	categorical crossentropy
		Layer activation	ReLu
		Output layer activation	SoftMax
		Fully connected layer size	16
		Optimizer	Adam
		Max. training epochs	100
		Early stopping patience	3
Bi-LSTM	Off. Target	LSTM nodes	50
		Hidden Layers	0
		Embeddings	Coosto Word2Vec
		Embedding dim.	300
		Recurrent dropout	0.1
		Batch size	32
		Loss	categorical crossentropy
		Layer activation	ReLu
		Output layer activation	SoftMax
		Fully connected layer size	64
		Optimizer	Adam
		Max. training epochs	100
		Early stopping patience	3
BERTje RobBERT	Offensive	Learning rate	4e-5
		Training Epochs	5
		Optimzer	AdamW
		Max sequence length	123
		Batch size	16
		Num. warmup steps	2
BERTje	Off. Target	Learning rate	6e-5
		Training Epochs	5
		Max seq. length	123
		Batch size	16
		Num. warmup steps	2
RobBERT	Off. Target	Learning rate	5e-5
		Training Epochs	5
		Max seq. length	123
		Batch size	16
		Num. warmup steps	2

Table 9: Hyperparameters for each of the models used in the experiments.

Appendix B: Supplementary Analyses

B.1. Data Distribution

Table 10 illustrates the distribution of the data per topic/source across the Train, Dev, and Test split, respectively.

Split	Data Source	Messages Included
Train	Paris Attack	511
	Dutch Parliament Election	464
	Protests/BLM	1,255
	Seed users	2,539
	June 2018	1,044
	May 2019	1,004
Dev	Paris Attack	98
	Dutch Parliament Election	84
	Protests/BLM	237
	Seed users	436
	June 2018	182
	May 2019	168
Test	*Intoch* Sinterklass	240
	April 2017	1,275
	September 2019	1,100
	Seed users	655

Table 10: DALC v2.0: distribution of the sources across Train, Dev, and Test.

B.2. Pairwise Inter-Annotator Agreement

Figures 1 to 12 illustrate the pairwise confusion matrix for each pair of annotators for the offensive explicitness layer and the offensive target layer. Note: for completeness, the target layer contains an extra subclass (NOT OFF) indicating cases where one annotator has marked the message as OFFENSIVE and, consequently, he has annotated also the target while the other has consider the message as not containing any offence.

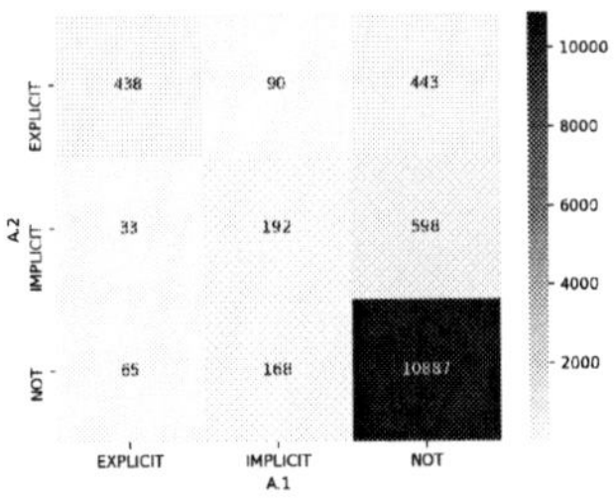

Figure 1: Explicitness Layer: A.1-A.2.

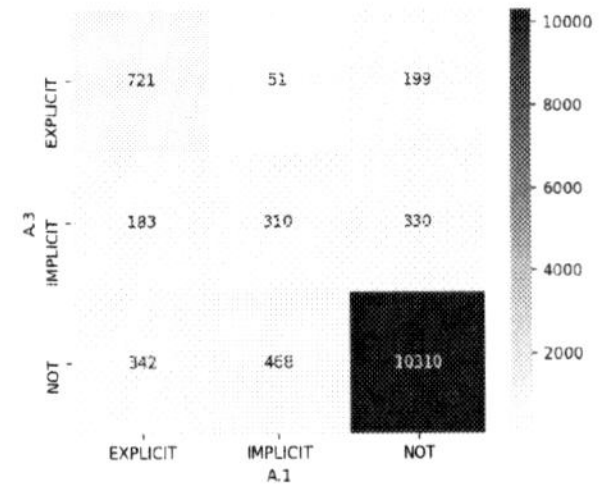

Figure 2: Explicitness Layer: A.1-A.3.

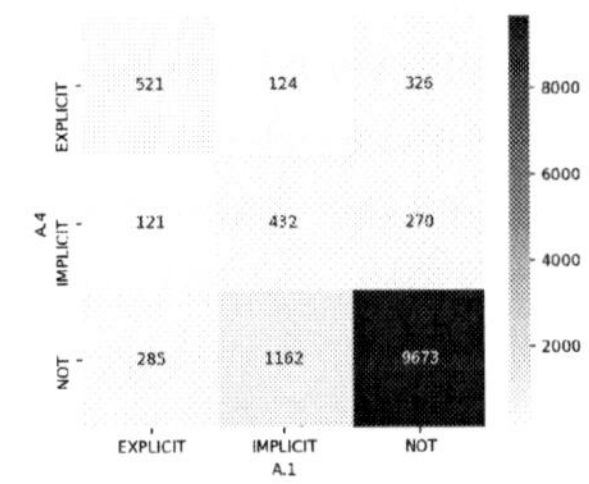

Figure 3: Explicitness Layer: A.1-A.4.

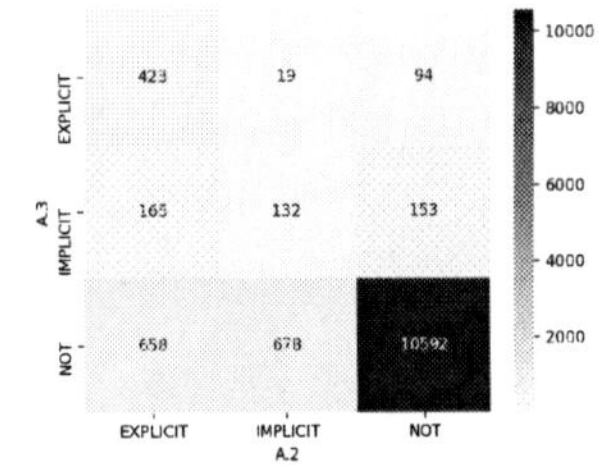

Figure 4: Explicitness Layer: A.2-A.3.

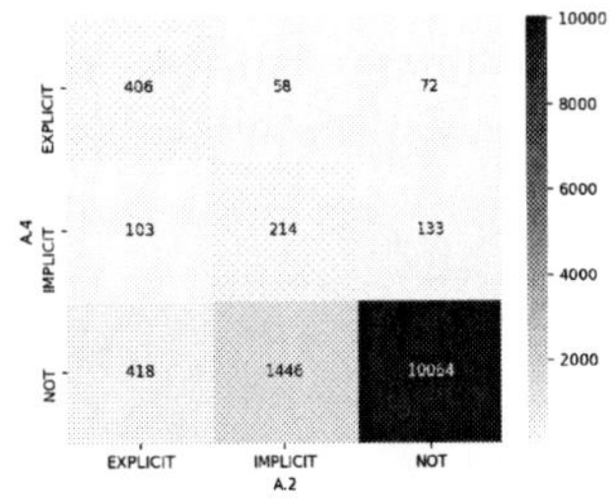

Figure 5: Explicitness Layer: A.2-A.4.

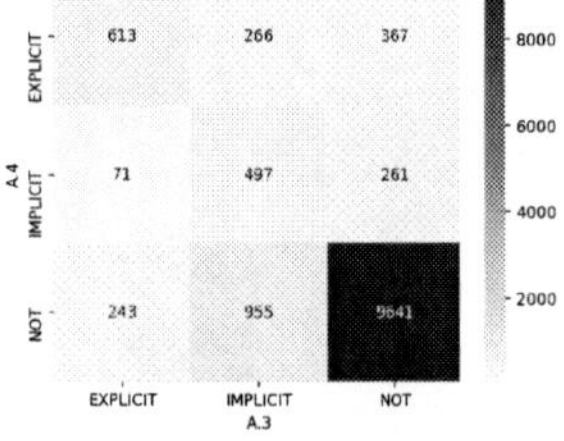

Figure 6: Explicitness Layer: A.3-A.4.

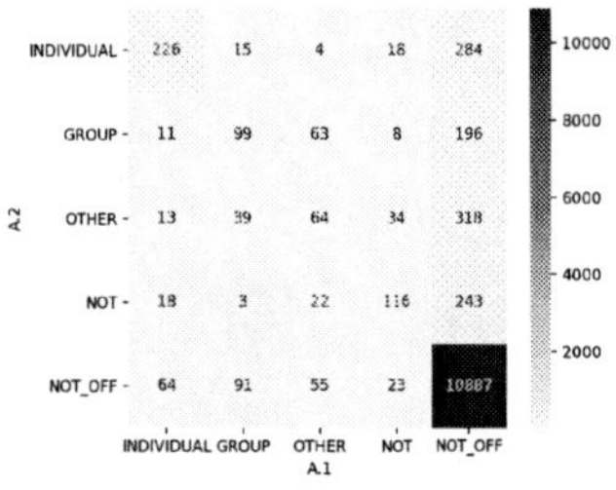

Figure 7: Target Layer: A.1-A.2.

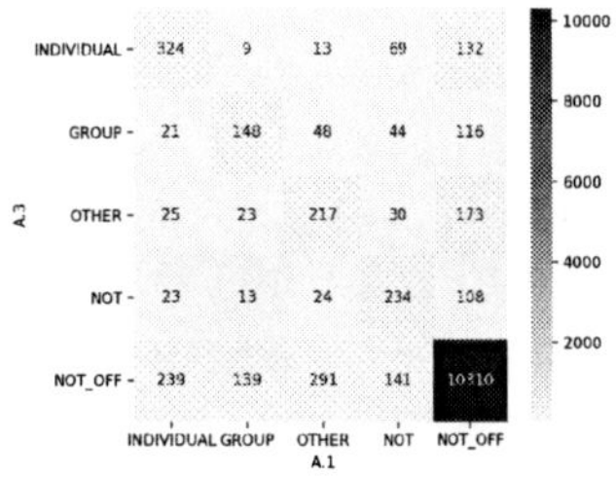

Figure 8: Target Layer: A.1-A.3.

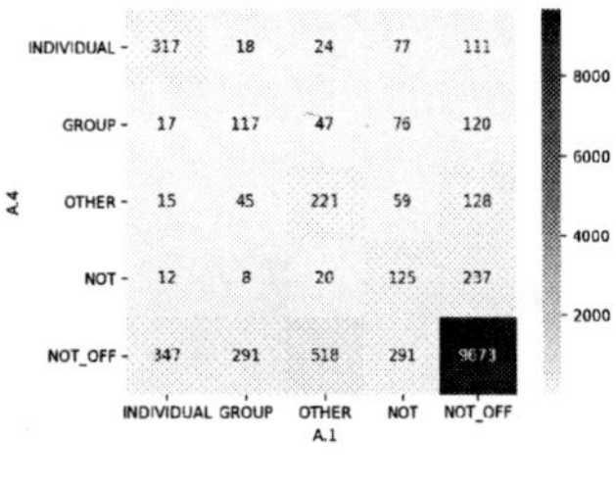

Figure 9: Target Layer: A.1-A.4.

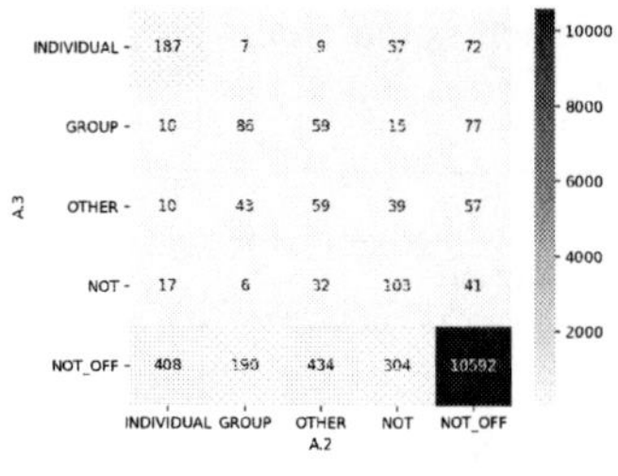

Figure 10: Target Layer: A.2-A.3.

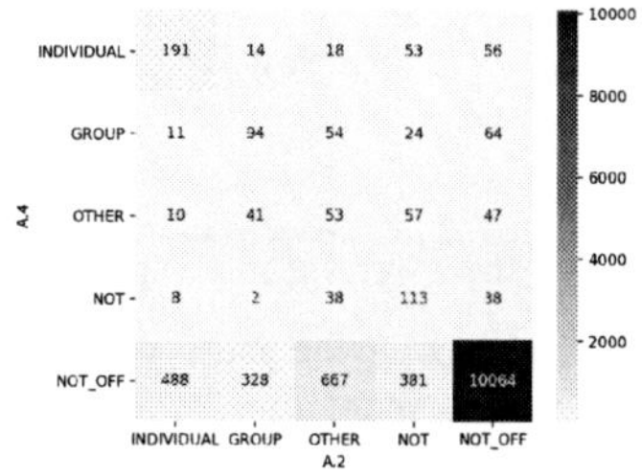

Figure 11: Target Layer: A.2-A.4.

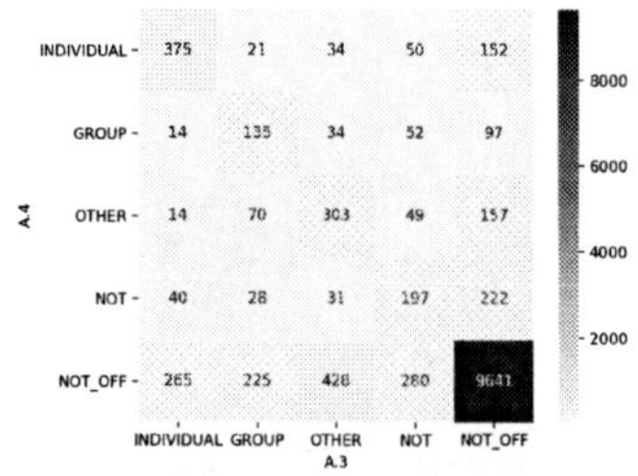

Figure 12: Target Layer: A.3-A.4.

B.3 Keywords

Table 11 illustrates the keywords for the messages labeled as OFFENSIVE, ABUSIVE, and NOT OFFENSIVE. The keywords have been extracted using TF-IDF per language phenomenon rather than per subclass by collapsing the explicitness layers (i.e., offensive *vs.* abusive rather than abusive explicit *vs.* offensive explicit, and so forth).

B.4 Error Analysis

Figure 13 illustrates the confusion matrix for the offensive language dimension (binary classification), while Figure 14 illustrates the confusion matrix for the target classification (offensive messages only)

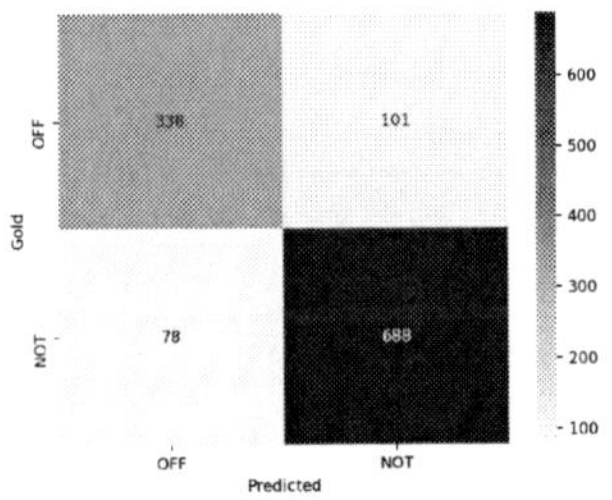

Figure 13: Confusion Matrix: Offensive Binary.

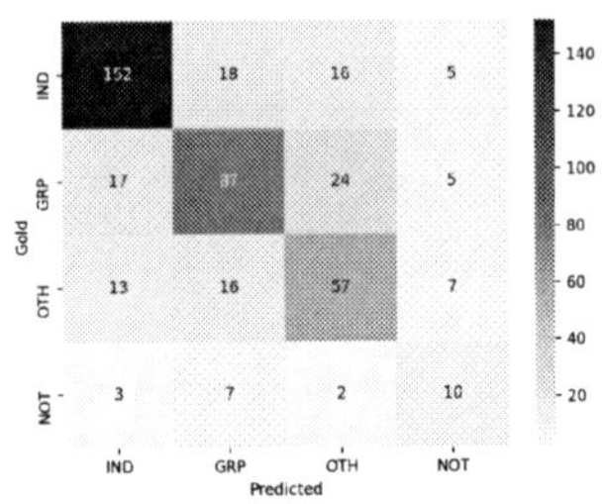

Figure 14: Confusion Matrix: Offensive Target.

Train				Test			
OFF.	**ABU.**	**NOT OFF.**	**NOT ABU.**	**OFF.**	**ABU.**	**NOT OFF.**	**NOT ABU.**
sod*****er	sod*****er	schaambeek	zand	onderbuikonzin	lelijk	peuzelen	amaai
klimaatwappie	lelijkerd	prop	klimaatwappie	😜	😃	jonko	🎈
j**d	ontslaan	geboorteplaats	fokken	ha	arrogante	😹	ha
fari***r	kansloze	fokken	fari***r	och	😂	sad	🥺
lelijkerd	veenendaal	bong	bong	beesten	ma****ten	haarpijn	💪
zeur	lijpo	opstandig	opstandig	😃	laffe	amaai	meter
veenendaal	huile	tier	tier	k*****stad	stap	uhhh	boekenweek geschenk
kansloze	flathead	webshops	vrolijk	ma****ten	k*****stad	hierzo	beesten
ontslaan	oogeruimd	datacenters	busje	catsuit	iek	zeldzame	mannelijkheid
huilie	sowieso	busje	wishlist	iek	k*****	leukkkk	geverfd

Table 11: DALC v2.0: Top 10 keywords per target phenomenon in Train and Test. Explicitly offensive/abusive content have been masked with $*$

Counter-TWIT: An Italian Corpus for Online Counterspeech in Ecological Contexts

Pierpaolo Goffredo[◇] **Valerio Basile**[♡] **Bianca Cepollaro**[♠] **Viviana Patti**[♡]
[◇] Université Côte d'Azur, France / Inria, CNRS, I3S, France
[♠] Università Vita-Salute San Raffaele, Italy
[♡] Dipartimento di Informatica, Università degli Studi di Torino, Italy
[◇]pierpaolo.goffredo@inria.fr, [♡]{name.surname}@unito.it,
[♠]cepollaro.biancamaria@hsr.it

Abstract

This work describes the process of creating a corpus of Twitter conversations annotated for the presence of *counterspeech* in response to toxic speech related to axes of discrimination linked to sexism, racism and homophobia. The main novelty is an annotated dataset comprising relevant tweets in their context of occurrence. The corpus is made up of tweets and responses captured by different profiles replying to discriminatory content or objectionably couched news. An annotation scheme was created to illustrate the relevant dimensions of toxic speech and counterspeech. An analysis of the collected and annotated data and of the Inter-Annotator Agreement (IAA) that emerged during the annotation process is included. Moreover, we report about preliminary experiments on automatic *counterspeech* detection, based on supervised automatic learning models trained on the new dataset. The results highlight the fundamental role played by the context in this detection task, confirming our intuitions about the importance to collect tweets in their context of occurrence.

1 Introduction

Billions of users are active every day on the main social media platforms and they are regularly exposed to toxic discourse, i.e. speech that inflicts psychological or emotional harm and/or incites people to participate in bigoted practices ranging from sexism to homophobia, to racism. To protect users from online toxicity, social media providers have been increasingly implementing censorship-based measures. Such measures are highly controversial and only targeted to the most extreme and explicit forms of toxic speech. Implicit toxic contents are particularly dangerous because they can go under the radar, they are hard to question, and may end up being accepted without conversation participants fully realizing it.

The question arises: how can we counter online toxic speech? Recent studies in social philosophy of language investigated the strategy that consists in engaging in interventions aimed at avoiding that toxic contents get (wittingly or unwittingly) accepted by the conversation participants. Such strategy is often dubbed *counterspeech* and has been mostly analyzed by taking into account face-to-face exchanges. Philosophers of language (Lepoutre, 2017; Langton, 2018) have focused on how counterspeech could work in idealized conversational models. In particular, they have focused on speech that counters implicit toxic contents by (i) spelling out, unpacking, articulating the objectionable contents implicitly conveyed by a given utterance and then (ii) challenging, questioning, rejecting, disputing, confronting it. This counterspeech strategy seems very costly. The first move is cognitively costly: it's hard to unpack implicit content on the spot. The second move is about social cost: it may be tough to go and take a confrontational attitude.

Interestingly, certain features of how communication works on social networks make social media particularly interesting venues to easily observe real instances of counterspeech in ecological contexts. For counterspeech to succeed in face-to-face interactions, the counterspeaker needs to be ready to intervene saying the right thing, in the right place, at the right moment. On social networks, on the other hand, counterspeech can well be asynchronous: this may lighten its cognitive load. As for the social cost of counterspeech, note that social network users enjoy a bit of anonymity in their online intervention and online interactions follow a different etiquette than face-to-face exchanges in terms of interruption of the "conversation". This may possibly lighten the social cost associated with counterspeech. A further interesting aspect is that online counterspeech can reach many more people than offline interventions. In fact, users often challenge offline contents (newspapers articles, pieces of public speeches, reported conversations, passages of textbooks, and so on) on social networks,

Proceedings of the Sixth Workshop on Online Abuse and Harms (WOAH), pages 57 - 66
July 14, 2022

in order to give their conversational moves more attention.

Studying counterspeech online comes with the added benefit of enabling the researcher to build computational models of language interactions involving toxic speech and counterspeech. By leveraging the most recent Natural Language Processing techniques, a corpus of counterspeech represents the first step towards automated systems to detect, support or even generate effective responses to toxic speech online.

The exploratory theoretical investigation conducted in philosophy raises many empirical questions. In our work, we address a few ones. For instance: do people on social networks ever employ such an idealized model where in order to reject implicit toxic content one has to first make explicit what was wrong with it? Or do users prefer less sophisticated strategy, like insulting and attacking bigoted contributions? Does the use of irony make the counterspeaker sound more or less aggressive? Do users support counterspeakers with reactions and comments or is it a solitary enterprise? Many more questions are still left unanswered, but this work paves the way for illuminating further the nature and working of online counterspeech.

The contributions of this article can be summarized as follows:

- A novel corpus of toxic speech and counterspeech in a conversational context from Italian social media, covering different target groups.
- A novel annotation schema encoding a fine-grained classification of toxic speech and argumentative relations between utterances.
- A pilot experiment on automatic counterspeech detection, showing the importance of taking the conversational context into account rather than modeling single utterances in isolation.

2 Related Work

There is a growing concern among the ICT (Information and Communication Technologies) companies leading the development of Social Networks about toxic speech: as it can undermine the image of such social environments as "safe" place, they must implement methods to cut off this phenomenon (Mathew et al., 2019). Some countries started to considered hate speech as a crime and sentencing it as such[1]. In other cases, institutions invited the ICT companies to subscribe codes of conduct concerning hate speech moderation and censorship on their platforms. This is the case of the Code of Conduct issued by the EU Commission in 2016 (EU Commission, 2016). Moreover, Social Networks regulated *hateful conduct*, publishing guidelines to avoid harmful behaviors subscribed by users as part of their terms of service[2]. However, such measures don't seem to suffice to effectively combat the phenomenon (Gagliardone, 2015).

Approaches to counterspeech have been investigated by the Computational Linguistics community, suggesting that counterspeech can reduce or limit the hateful content on the Web, especially in Social Networks (Mathew et al., 2018). However, especially from a computational point of view, the development of corpora and models for the automatic detection and generation of counterspeech is still underdeveloped, while most of the efforts have been devoted to the detection of various forms of toxic speech, hate speech included (Poletto et al., 2021; Jurgens et al., 2019).

Most literature focuses on English language and considers toxic speech data collected from specific templates, which limits the coverage of explicit toxic speech and leaves out implicit toxic speech altogether. Chung et al. (2019) recently created a large multilingual corpus of short texts in English, French and Italian, called CONAN, consisting of <hate speech (HS) - counterspeech (CS)> pairs created ad hoc in the context of the HateMeter project[3], with the effort of more than 100 operators from NGOs and with a special focus on Anti-Muslim hatred online in different European countries. Annotated corpora like CONAN enable a systematic study of Counter-Narratives (CNs), a study which is still in its beginnings, but differs from the one we presented here. In particular, counterspeech in CONAN is not observed in an ecological setting, which is the perspective we hold in the current study.

A similar work to Chung et al. (2019) is realized by Chung et al. (2020), where off-the-shelf

[1] https://en.wikipedia.org/wiki/Hate_speech_laws_by_country

[2] Twitter's measures: https://help.twitter.com/it/rules-and-policies/hateful-conduct-policy and Facebook's measure: https://www.facebook.com/communitystandards/hate_speech

[3] http://hatemeter.eu/

NMT models are used to synthesize silver data from other languages using the CONAN dataset as kick-start for generation to overcome the scarcity of gold standard data for training and the lack of huge datasets made of counter narratives in Italian language. The accomplishment is done under different resource conditions, testing the effect of using (i) silver data, (ii) gold standard data, and (iii) their combination. Tekiroğlu et al. (2020) investigate methods to obtain high quality Counter-Narratives while reducing efforts from experts trained by some Non-Governmental Organizations (NGOs) to intervene in online hateful conversations.

Orbach et al. (2020) created benchmark data for training and evaluating the performance of an automatic detection system of counterspeech debates in order to introduce a novel NLU task. Mathew et al. (2019) propose a study to understand how the counterspeech phenomenon is related to statistics of comments collected from YouTube. Menini et al. (2021) present experimental results obtained considering different methods with and without context referring to abusive vs. not abusive tweets.

Unlike the related works presented in this section, the contribution of this work in Automatic Counterspeech Detection is the development of a multi-layer corpus of Italian Twitter data in the context of their conversation thread.

3 The Counter-TWIT corpus

We developed a novel corpus, called **Counter-TWIT**, to study counterspeech online in an ecological setting, based on Twitter conversation threads in the Italian language.

3.1 Collecting Conterspeech Twitter Data

We collected a new dataset of tweets. Counter speech is rare across all of social media, and we considered several strategies for ensuring there were sufficient instances in our dataset.

We chose Twitter as the source platform, in particular collecting tweets and their replies, because of the accessibility of its API.

Collecting counterspeech in an ecological setting is a very challenging task, since there are not obvious keyword-based strategies to filter out the relevant tweets from the ones that are posted everyday and that can be collected by relying on the Twitter API. Let us recall that the creation of the novel corpus was a stage, necessary to the following preliminary experimental phase, where the corpus will be exploited for training a machine learning model able to recognize automatically counterspeech discourse on misogyny, homophobia and racism. We initially selected the profiles of activists, organizations, or pages especially devoted to calling out common instances of bigotry. Users interacting in such contexts are likely to comment on hate speech and thus engage in counterspeech. Such profiles are not as popular as those of public figures such as actresses and politicians. In some cases, however, a few comments are enough to start an interesting conversation thread. In such pages users often highlight how certain news are presented in troublesome ways implicitly conveying discriminatory contents. In addition, these profiles allow their followers to reply in order to share their personal opinion giving rise to counterspeech as a *collective enterprise*, which is an interesting trait.

For collecting data different tools for Python language have been used in favor of rebuilding the conversation tree.

3.2 Data annotation

To annotate the tweets we developed a custom annotation platform. Expert annotators were selected among bachelor's, master's and PhD students and university researchers, within disciplines related to Humanities and Social Sciences such as philosophy and psychology, with some specific background in the study of hate speech and counterspeech.

The annotators were trained in various areas of language sciences, ranging from philosophy of language to computational linguistics. Therefore, they were trained to be sensitive to the relevant distinctions at play in the annotation, e.g., between explicit and implicit communication, irony, and so on. The annotation scheme was applied by seven annotators to a collection of 624 messages, including 344 root tweets and their replies (280 posts). The annotators were provided clear and detailed guidelines[4].

At first, the annotators tested a preliminary version of the platform on a small sample of tweets and replies, sharing comments and discussing doubts and controversial issues that needed explanation or modification. This process led to settling on the final version of the annotation scheme and guidelines.

[4]Guidelines are available at `https://github.com/pierpaologoffredo/Counter-TWIT/blob/main/Readme.md` (in Italian).

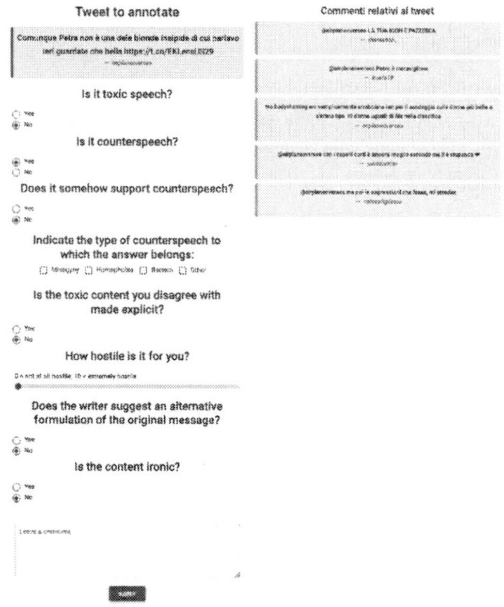

Figure 1: Screenshot of the annotation interface of Counter-TWIT.

The annotation process was based on two layers: firstly, annotators were called to judge whether a tweet or reply could be considered as (Yes/No): TOXIC SPEECH, COUNTERSPEECH, SUPPORT TO COUNTERSPEECH. All of these are binary questions and not mutually exclusive. Figure 1 shows a screenshot of the annotation interface.

In case a tweet or reply is marked as "counterspeech", the annotator is asked to annotate the type of counterspeech and the target group considered (Misogyny, Homophobia, Racism and Other [5]), as a second annotation layer.

Counterspeech often denounces the nature of the discriminatory content it aims to counter. There are several possible labels that can be used for marking different classes of counterspeech, also based on previous studies (Mathew et al., 2019). After a careful discussion and inspired by the reflections in (Cepollaro, 2021), we decided to select four labels associated to the different type of counterspeech: EXPLICITATION, HOSTILITY, IRONY/HUMOR, ALTERNATIVE. In the second-level each label is binary and they are not mutually exclusive, except for hostility that is rated on a scale from 1 to 10. In the following all the layers included in our annotation scheme are described.

Toxic Speech Toxic speech promotes discrimination or deprives people of important powers of self-determination and social and civic participation. Racist, sexist and homophobic slurs count as systemic toxic discourse that generally worsens its targets' well being. Furthermore, note that toxic speech is not about impolite language or vulgar expressions: speech can be toxic and damage people's dignity without employing "bad" words.

Therefore, we call toxic speech the discourse that explicitly or implicitly expresses or promotes unjust discrimination on the basis of gender, ethnicity, geographical origin, sexual orientation, the presence of disabilities, and so on. The **toxic speech** label applies both to explicit and obvious cases, and to implicit and more difficult to grasp cases. What distinguishes toxic speech is that it implicitly or explicitly conveys content that contributes to extant social injustice, e.g., those due to sexism, homophobia, and racism. This could be in principle performed via aggressive as well as non-aggressive speech. Take for instance a scenario where one attacks their interlocutor with a racial insult: this is aggressive toxic speech. Then take a scenario where one claims that the members of a given group should not benefit from certain rights: this is toxic speech too because of its content, but it is not aggressive in the sense of the former. In other words, the feature of aggressiveness or hostility does not primarily concern the content but the form of a contribution. This said, it appears clear how a counterspeech intervention can also display a different degree of aggressiveness or hostility in its form. Counterspeech in general (at least of the kind we considered in this study) is confrontational in character, for it challenges a piece of discriminatory content. But confrontation can be carried out in more or less aggressive ways. What's the difference between toxic speech and counterspeech hostility? Possibly none, but this does not blur the divide between the two notions: while the former conveys discriminatory content, the latter challenges it.

Counterspeech Counterspeech is a second-round speech expressing disagreement with a content or attitude. The type of counterspeech we are

[5] We did not constrain the definition of the main axes of discrimination in place, because we wanted annotators to be aligned with the folk understanding of such notions. We introduced the category "Other" to collect any other targets, with the idea of qualitatively analyzing any choices on this item. The small number of such selections (only 33 within the entire corpus) seems to confirm that the choice of targets was reasonable.

interested in is the one that tries to combat discriminatory or stereotyped contents (e.g., sexist, homophobic, racist, etc.) occurring in another post, comment, newspaper article, song, film, etc. expressed using a toxic language. In our framework, counterspeech is meant to be used to address toxic speech, rather than merely false speech. It is particularly interesting when it is exploited to address *implicit* rather then explicit toxic speech (speech conveying toxic contents via implications, presupposition, and the like): "implicit toxic contents are particularly dangerous: they can go under radar, they are hard to question, and may end up being accepted in the common ground without conversation participants fully realizing it. They may be immune to censorship, slipping through it" (Cepollaro, 2021).

Support to counterspeech Support consists in giving resonance and visibility to a certain counterspeech intervention (inside or outside the Twitter thread), in expressing approval and support for another user's intervention. For example, in this exchange[6]:

> -**"Miley Cyrus video reveals all the sexualization of lesbians."**
> -*"Quite right!"*

The answer expresses approval and support for the counterspeech intervention, therefore it counts as support for the counterspeech.

Explicitation The explicitation of the implicit meaning unpacks, articulates and brings out what was implicit in a message (Sbisà, 1999). This typology is particularly interesting because discriminatory contents are often conveyed. Social media users sometimes employ explicitation to point out how certain apparently harmless interventions actually communicated discriminatory contents. Explicitation, by articulating what is implicit, opens up the possibility that implicit content will be criticized or questioned.

The practice of explicitation highlights implicitly transmitted information monitors and filters the influence that the implicit meaning can have on. Here is an example of what the practice of explicitation looks like:

> -**"Emma Watson is beautiful but smart"**
> -*"What does 'but' mean, that a beautiful woman is not smart?!"*

In this case the second speaker challenges the first's assumption that there would be a contrast for a woman between being beautiful and being smart.

Hostility In engaging in counterspeech, users can express various degrees of hostility and antagonism. This is often carried out through (but is not limited to) the use of aggressive and insulting language. For instance:

> *"Good giant? What a bunch of morons"*

The speaker in the example gets angry at the newspaper that called "good giant" a man who murdered a lesbian woman for rejecting him.
To conceptualize and then measure the efficacy of counterspeech is still an open question. Among the most promising candidates, we find its capabilities to change people's minds and raise awareness about discrimination in the toxic speaker and in the audience. It is also an open question what modulates counterspeech efficacy. It may well be that hostility backfires, and that less confrontational counterspeech styles obtain better effects, but it is not said. This could easily depend on the context and the kind of content that counterspeech aims to reject. For this reason, our study is not yet concerned with counterspeech efficacy, but rather on the ways in which it is performed and perceived. A further step in this research is then to conceptualize and measure its efficacy, relying on a classification of its most salient features.

Alternative In engaging in counterspeech, users can propose an alternative to the main topic being discussed: they may for instance object to the way a newspaper title an article and come up with an alternative that in their view would avoid the troublesome contents conveyed by the actual one.

This kind of correcting interventions typically targets the wording of the text or some aspects of its content, suggesting a more "fair" point of view or providing a more detailed description of the facts.

> *The news to report is not that there are baby prostitutes in Parioli, but that there are pedophile customers in Parioli. Stop blaming the victims!*

The speaker in the example suggests that newspaper shouldn't talk about "baby prostitutes" but "pedophile clients" since their way of couching the news implicitly blames victims.

[6]The main tweet is in **bold**, while the reply is in *italic*, the tweets are translated into English by the authors.

Irony/Humor Irony detection consists in reporting if a text contains traces of irony. In this context we call "irony" a plethora of phenomena, such as humor, something witty, black humor, sarcasm, etc.

Irony can be expressed in many ways and there is no single definition of what is ironic and what is not. In this task users are asked, expanding as much as possible the definition of irony, to note as ironic any humorous, sarcastic, ironic intent, be it positive or negative.

> *"And thank goodness he's a good giant. If he was bad that he did, would he eat it?"*

This tweet ironically remarks how ridiculous it is to call "good" someone who murdered a woman for rejecting it. Note that the labels on this layer are not mutually exclusive: more then one typology label could be selected during the annotation.

3.3 Annotation Results

For each tweet, the gold label was obtained by aggregating the results of the individual judgments, by applying simple mathematical operations: majority vote for binary labels and arithmetic mean for labels with numeric values (only *Hostility* in our scheme). Figure 2 shows the distribution of the gold standard labels. 3.04% of tweets were labeled as both Counterspeech and Support, while no overlap was found between Toxic and the other labels.

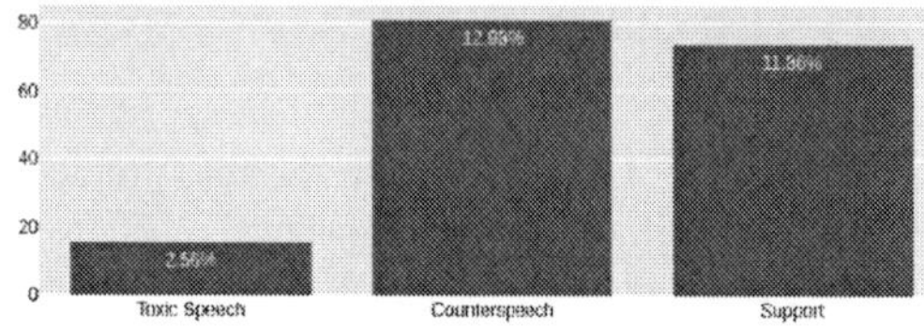

Figure 2: Distribution of the Layer 1 labels over the Counter-TWIT corpus.

The labels are not evenly distributed between tweets and replies. It is possible to observe in Figure 3 that TOXIC SPEECH is more present in replies (3.5%) than in tweets (1.7%), as well as SUPPORT (17.5% in replies and 7.2% in tweets). The opposite is true for the COUNTERSPEECH label, present in 16.2% of the tweets and 8.9% of the replies.

Interestingly, the presence of counterspeech at the root tweet level is significant. This indicates that tweets classified as counterspeech have led users to comment to support counterspeech. These

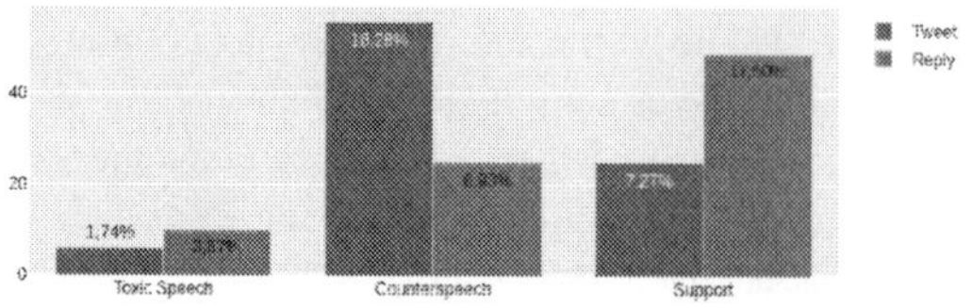

Figure 3: Distribution of Layer 1 labels (root tweets and replies).

first analysis results confirm that collecting data from target profiles is effective for the purpose of filtering samples of counterspeech in the wild, given that the phenomenon is very sparse and a simple keyword-based or hashtag approach is harder to be applied. We can also see that in the debate generated around these profiles there is often an attempt of countering toxic speech generated elsewhere (news, TV, etc). This is interesting because it allows us to analyze the phenomenon of toxic speech in social media (and its reactions) in more comprehensive way such as by investigating cross-references between various media, and framing the overall debate in the context of a media ecosystem. This latter includes social media but also others toxic information sources to be countered. As a consequence, the support label among annotated replies is also significant.

Figure 4 shows the distribution of the gold standard labels for the second level of annotation considering the whole corpus made of 642 tweets.

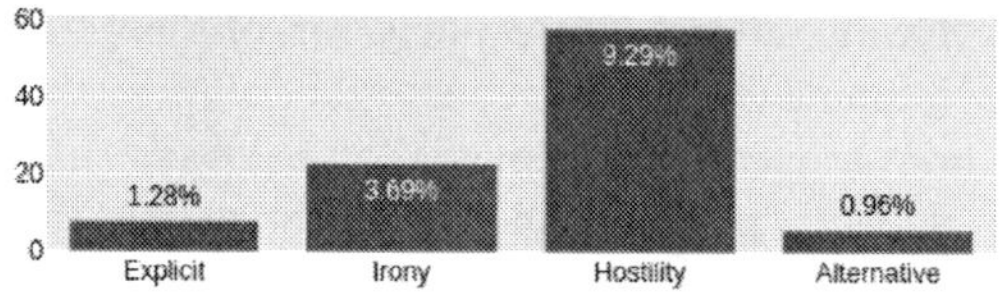

Figure 4: Distribution of the counterspeech typology labels over the Counter-TWIT corpus

Also in this case it is possible to notice that a tweet or a reply can be considered belonging to different type of counterspeech rather than a single one as illustrated in the Figure 5.

Regarding the neutral class, this is represented by all those tweets and replies that are not classified as toxic, counterspeech and support to counterspeech. It includes 472 tweets and replies. This imbalance in the data highlights once again how difficult it can be to collect these types of tweets and replies and subsequently categorize them.

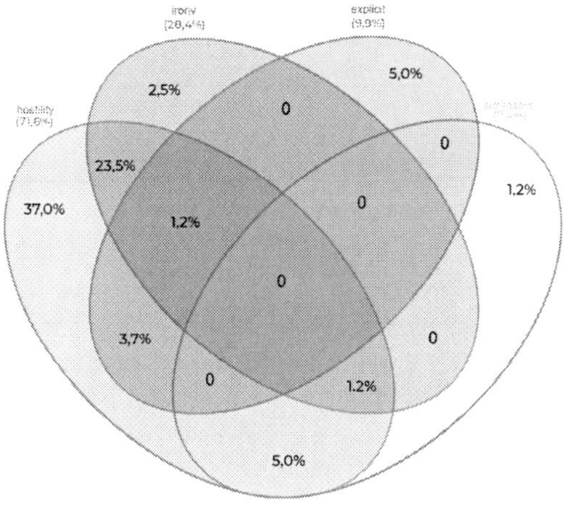

Figure 5: Intersection of counterspeech typology labels over the Counter-TWIT corpus (% refers to the total of tweets annotated as counterspeech).

3.4 Inter-Annotator Agreement

The quality of the gold standard is evaluated in terms of inter-annotator agreement using Krippendorff's α , a generalization of Cohen's Kappa to an arbitrary number of annotators applicable to incomplete question-answer matrices, which was suitable to our case (Artstein and Poesio, 2008). The analysis is limited to the binary labels.

Table 1: Krippendorff's α values for each label on tweets and replies.

Label	α (tweets)	α (replies)
TOXIC SPEECH	0.25	0.15
COUNTERSPEECH	0.46	0.03
SUPPORT	0.36	0.37
EXPLICITATION	0.38	0.02
IRONY	0.40	0.05
ALTERNATIVE	0.25	0.02

Table 1 shows that the annotation of the replies in particular is controversial and the issue deserves a deeper investigations. One possible reason could be that different annotators interpret the main tweet differently, and then, with a cascade effect, diverge more in assigning the label to the reply tweets. The agreement on the root tweets is, instead, generally higher, in particular on the core label COUNTERSPEECH.

In addition, the label which created disagreement the most has been EXPLICITATION. The annotators reported that during the annotation task it was very difficult to understand when a tweet or a reply could be marked with this tag, which highlighted a difficulty in reaching a common understanding of the meaning of the label. Recent literature postulates how disagreement stems from different sources. We hypothesize that in the case of this work, the disagreement on the main level of annotation (toxic/counterspeech) is dependent on the highly subjective nature of the annotation task. However, the disagreement on the finer-grained level may be due to the more difficult, ambiguous nature of the task, which needs greater knowledge of linguistic phenomena under observation.

Furthermore, a deeper analysis on that tweets (25) and replies (4) which have been considered as counterspeech by all three annotators reveals confusion in agreeing on EXPLICITATION as showed in Table 2.

Table 2: Krippendorff's α values for data considered counterspeech by all three annotators.

explicitation	irony	alternative
0.09790	0.41364	0.46749

Thus, the label which created a visible disagreement has been the **explicitation**. The annotators reported that during the annotation task it was very difficult to understand when a tweet or a reply could be marked with this tag, which highlighted a difficulty in reaching a common understanding of the meaning of the label.

However, the disagreement on the finer-grained level may be due to the more difficult, ambiguous nature of the task, which needs greater knowledge of linguistic phenomena under observation. The IAA results reflect the problems described.

4 Evaluation

We carried our a battery of experiments in order to perform three independent binary classifications: toxic vs. non-toxic speech, counterspeech vs. not counterspeech, and support to counterspeech vs. not support to counterspeech. We employ a supervised classifier based on BERT (Devlin et al., 2019) pre-trained on a large corpus of Italian tweets named AlBERTo (Polignano et al., 2019).

The metrics used to evaluate AlBERTo's performance are Precision, Recall, and F1-Score for the individual labels, and their macro-average.

The three experiments are 5-fold cross-validation experiments with 9 fine-tuning epochs and a learning rate of 10^{-5}. The results are shown

Table 3: Model performance over three binary classification using reply text as dataset for training. (0), (1), and (avg) refer respectively to positive class, negative class, and their macro-average.

Label	Prec.(0)	Rec.(0)	F1 (0)	Prec.(1)	Rec.(1)	F1 (1)	Prec. (avg)	Rec.(avg)	F1 (avg)
COUNTERSPEECH	.914	.884	.898	.441	.408	.402	.661	.663	.650
TOXIC	.978	.985	.981	.295	.183	.186	.637	.584	.584
SUPPORT	.932	.929	.930	.550	.500	.501	.741	.714	.716

in Table 3. Despite the small size of the corpus and the representative items for each class, the classifiers for COUNTERSPEECH and SUPPORT perform reasonably well, while the classification of TOXIC SPEECH turned out to be a challenge, in particular for detecting the positive class.

The results are obtained with the model fine-tuned only with the tweet or reply text in isolation. We performed an additional experiment taking into account the root of the conversations where the replies belong. We do so by concatenating the text of the reply to the text of the original tweet it replies to, with the goal of observing how the performance of the model changes when considering the context of the reply. The results of this second experiment are shown in Table 4. The experiment is performed with the same hyperparameters of the previous experiment, in order to provide a consistent comparison.

Including context in the training improves the classification of counterspeech. This is due mainly to a higher recall on the positive class. This is true for all labels, and particularly for COUNTERSPEECH, which is about 65% higher. However, the extra training data seem to confuse the classifiers for the other two labels.

5 Error Analysis

In order to get some deeper insight about the difficulties in classifying a **counterspeech** content, we selected False Positives (FP), i.e., counterspeech tweets hat have not been classified as such by the model, and exploited the information included in the finer-grained annotation layer regarding counterspeech categories, namely EXPLICITATION, HOSTILITY, IRONY/HUMOR, ALTERNATIVE.

We considered all the FPs for the first annotation layer, counting all the data (tweets or reply) that were labeled as belonging to the counterspeech category from humans but not from the model. Thus, for those tweets we checked the values attached to the counterspeech typology labels in order to find a meaning among the classification errors and the counterspeech typologies' relation.

The proportion of False Positives over all the predictions obtained from the language model is the following: false positives represent about 7% of the total. Of these, the vast majority are *Ironic* (~34%) and *Hostile* (~76%), also considering that the labels are not mutually exclusive.

This qualitative analysis can lead to affirm that the model tends to confuse **hostile** and **ironic** content more than explicit and suggestion of alternative ones probably due to a higher cost from a cognitive and social point of view.

There are two layers of complexity that give rise to disagreement in classifying correctly the tweets. Detecting toxic speech depends on how each subject is sensitive to detecting each axis of discrimination (which often varies along demographic and psychological factors). A further source of disagreement stems from the relative unconstrained character of the notions deployed (toxic speech and counterspeech) (Basile et al., 2021).

Finally, we analyzed the False Positive Rate by counterspeech category. **Irony** and **Hostility** are by far the most difficult categories to predict, with a FP ratio of about 60% and 70% respectively, while next to no FPs are predicted for *Explicit* and *Alternative*.

6 Discussion and Conclusions

In this work we studied hate speech in online environments. To address the dangers of toxic speech, Social Networks defined policies that regulate speech inciting hatred, while some countries started to introduce norms to treat this phenomenon as a crime and sentenced as such. This way to address the problem showed some limitations as the main approaches consist in blocking or suspending the problematic content or the user account itself. Therefore several involved parties, such as institutions and organizations, started to consider counterspeech as an alternative to blocking (Gagliardone, 2015). Thus, adding "more speech" has been considered as a valid alternative to counter hate speech.

We collected and annotated data from Twitter in

Table 4: Model performance over three binary classification using reply text and root tweet for training. (0), (1), and (avg) refer respectively to positive class, negative class, and their macro-average.

Label	Prec.(0)	Rec.(0)	F1 (0)	Prec.(1)	Rec.(1)	F1 (1)	Prec. (avg)	Rec.(avg)	F1 (avg)
COUNTERSPEECH	.960	.883	.920	.466	.730	.564	.713	.807	.742
TOXIC	.979	.840	.903	.037	.283	.065	.508	.561	.484
SUPPORT	.922	.816	.865	.317	.544	.396	.620	.680	.630

order to create the Counter-TWIT Italian corpus to study counterspeech in an ecological setting. The corpus includes content that is considered to unleash hate speech and to receive replies in the form of counterspeech.

Specifically, data were collected with the aim of observing counterspeech within the context of occurrence, i.e. collecting not only tweets in isolation, but conversation threads including a root tweet and the corresponding replies. Finally, we validated the corpus with cross-validation experiments.

We developed the **Counter-TWIT** corpus made of tweets and replies collected from accounts that has been selected after a deep research based on shared contents. All the data collected have been annotated, by exploiting a web-based annotation platform developed roughly from the scratch and published online[7], where a group of expert annotators were applying a novel multi-layer annotation scheme devoted to mark whether the tweets or replies were counterspeech, toxic speech or in support of counterspeech (layer 1). In case counterspeech was marked as present, users were asked to label the text as belonging to some typology of counterspeech for the sake of a deeper understanding of the phenomenon (Layer 2).

Thus, the annotated corpus has been used for training the **AlBERTo** neural language model for performing a battery of binary classification task related to the detection of toxic, counterspeech, and support to counterspeech. We used this language model since it has been trained and developed using an Italian vocabulary instead of using other multilingual model that presented limitations to the type of language learned and the size of vocabulary (Polignano et al., 2019).

We executed two type of experiments: one using only the replies of conversation tree and the second with also the "main" tweet. This approach has been designed in order to go deep into the intuition that this classification task needs the context. Results show that performance, Recall in particular, improves when conversation context data are provided, and this supports the original hypothesis that counterspeech must be studied in a context, which is intuitive given the definition of counterspeech as second-turn intervention aimed to contrast a previous contribution (Cepollaro, 2021), taken as reference definition in this work.

Finally, we performed a statistical and qualitative evaluation of the results obtained from the neural language model evaluating the number of data classified as not belonging to counterspeech class rather than being considered as such (False Positives data). We discovered that the model tends to confuse most with Irony and Hostility labels rather than Explicitation and suggestion to Alternative ones.

Given the promising preliminary results, we plan to expand the corpus in our future research. Furthermore, other qualitative analysis could be run by considering the correlation of types of counterspeech and the predictions made with a language model in order to understand in greater detail how the model behaves towards a specific counterspeech category. Indeed, annotating content as counterspeech is not an easy task, due to different shapes of the textual meaning based on the context and the language used. There is not a unique pattern to individuate and mark the tweet as belonging to a specific categories. A large annotated corpus will provide a more solid base for training the model in detecting counterspeech and, in possible future developments, for generating automatically counterspeech content in order to fight hate speech, which is another very interesting direction (Tekiroğlu et al., 2020).

Counter-TWIT[8] is made available online to further study the phenomenon described and other issue related to counterspeech classification in Italian Twitter.

[7] `http://thesiscounterspeech.altervista.org/`

[8] `https://github.com/pierpaologoffredo/Counter-TWIT`

References

Ron Artstein and Massimo Poesio. 2008. Survey article: Inter-coder agreement for computational linguistics. *Computational Linguistics*, 34(4):555–596.

Valerio Basile, Michael Fell, Tommaso Fornaciari, Dirk Hovy, Silviu Paun, Barbara Plank, Massimo Poesio, and Alexandra Uma. 2021. We need to consider disagreement in evaluation. In *Proceedings of the 1st Workshop on Benchmarking: Past, Present and Future*, pages 15–21, Online. Association for Computational Linguistics.

Bianca Cepollaro. 2021. Remedies to discriminatory contents: On and offline counterspeech. Talk at HaLO Workshop.

Yi-Ling Chung, Elizaveta Kuzmenko, Serra Sinem Tekiroglu, and Marco Guerini. 2019. CONAN - COunter NArratives through nichesourcing: a multilingual dataset of responses to fight online hate speech. In *Proceedings of the 57th Annual Meeting of the Association for Computational Linguistics*, pages 2819–2829, Florence, Italy. Association for Computational Linguistics.

Yi-Ling Chung, Serra Sinem Tekiroglu, and Marco Guerini. 2020. Italian counter narrative generation to fight online hate speech. In *Proceedings of the Seventh Italian Conference on Computational Linguistics, CLiC-it 2020, Bologna, Italy, March 1-3, 2021*, volume 2769 of *CEUR Workshop Proceedings*. CEUR-WS.org.

Jacob Devlin, Ming-Wei Chang, Kenton Lee, and Kristina Toutanova. 2019. BERT: Pre-training of deep bidirectional transformers for language understanding. In *Proceedings of the 2019 Conference of the North American Chapter of the Association for Computational Linguistics: Human Language Technologies, Volume 1 (Long and Short Papers)*, pages 4171–4186, Minneapolis, Minnesota. Association for Computational Linguistics.

EU Commission. 2016. Code of conduct on countering illegal hate speech online.

Iginio Gagliardone. 2015. *Countering Online Hate Speech - UNESCO*. UNESCO Publishing.

David Jurgens, Libby Hemphill, and Eshwar Chandrasekharan. 2019. A just and comprehensive strategy for using NLP to address online abuse. In *Proceedings of the 57th Annual Meeting of the Association for Computational Linguistics*, pages 3658–3666, Florence, Italy. Association for Computational Linguistics.

R. Langton. 2018. *Blocking as counter-speech*, pages 144–164. Oxford Scholarship Online.

Maxime Lepoutre. 2017. Hate speech in public discourse: A pessimistic defense of counterspeech. *Social Theory and Practice*, 43(4):851–883.

Binny Mathew, Navish Kumar, Ravina, Pawan Goyal, and Animesh Mukherjee. 2018. Analyzing the hate and counter speech accounts on twitter. *CoRR*, abs/1812.02712.

Binny Mathew, Punyajoy Saha, Hardik Tharad, Subham Rajgaria, Prajwal Singhania, Suman Kalyan Maity, Pawan Goyal, and Animesh Mukherjee. 2019. Thou shalt not hate: Countering online hate speech. *Proceedings of the International AAAI Conference on Web and Social Media*, 13(01):369–380.

Stefano Menini, Alessio Palmero Aprosio, and Sara Tonelli. 2021. Abuse is contextual, what about nlp? the role of context in abusive language annotation and detection. *CoRR*, abs/2103.14916.

Matan Orbach, Yonatan Bilu, Assaf Toledo, Dan Lahav, Michal Jacovi, Ranit Aharonov, and Noam Slonim. 2020. Out of the echo chamber: Detecting countering debate speeches. In *Proceedings of the 58th Annual Meeting of the Association for Computational Linguistics*, pages 7073–7086, Online. Association for Computational Linguistics.

Fabio Poletto, Valerio Basile, Manuela Sanguinetti, Cristina Bosco, and Viviana Patti. 2021. Resources and benchmark corpora for hate speech detection: a systematic review. *Language Resources and Evaluation*, 55(2):477–523.

Marco Polignano, Pierpaolo Basile, Marco de Gemmis, Giovanni Semeraro, and Valerio Basile. 2019. AlBERTo: Italian BERT Language Understanding Model for NLP Challenging Tasks Based on Tweets. In *Proceedings of the Sixth Italian Conference on Computational Linguistics (CLiC-it 2019)*, volume 2481. CEUR.

Marina Sbisà. 1999. Ideology and the persuasive use of presupposition. *Language and ideology. Selected papers from the 6th International Pragmatics Conference*, 1:492–509.

Serra Sinem Tekiroğlu, Yi-Ling Chung, and Marco Guerini. 2020. Generating counter narratives against online hate speech: Data and strategies. In *Proceedings of the 58th Annual Meeting of the Association for Computational Linguistics*, pages 1177–1190, Online. Association for Computational Linguistics.

StereoKG: Data-Driven Knowledge Graph Construction for Cultural Knowledge and Stereotypes

Awantee Deshpande, Dana Ruiter, Marius Mosbach, Dietrich Klakow
Spoken Language Systems Group, Saarland University, Germany
{adeshpande,druiter,mmosbach,dietrich}@lsv.uni-saarland.de

Abstract

Analyzing ethnic or religious bias is important for improving fairness, accountability, and transparency of natural language processing models. However, many techniques rely on human-compiled lists of bias terms, which are expensive to create and are limited in coverage. In this study, we present a fully data-driven pipeline for generating a knowledge graph (KG) of cultural knowledge and stereotypes. Our resulting KG covers 5 religious groups and 5 nationalities and can easily be extended to include more entities. Our human evaluation shows that the majority (59.2%) of non-singleton entries are coherent and complete stereotypes. We further show that performing intermediate masked language model training on the verbalized KG leads to a higher level of cultural awareness in the model and has the potential to increase classification performance on knowledge-crucial samples on a related task, i.e., hate speech detection.

1 Introduction

Fairness, accountability, and transparency to fight model-inherent bias and discrimination have become a major branch of machine learning research in recent years. This includes studying cultural bias and stereotypes in datasets and language models. Stereotypes are cognitive schemas that aid in categorizing and perceiving other social groups (Hilton and von Hippel, 1996), and becoming conscious of this stereotyping can increase cultural knowledge and sensitivity (Buchtel, 2014). However, without mindfulness, stereotypes lead to inferring traits of individuals from their (e.g., socio-economic) status or social group (Hoffman and Hurst, 1990), which then leads to systemic discrimination. Stereotypes as inherent cognitive functions are equally present in human-generated content, e.g., text resources used to train machine learning algorithms, which then further propagate and lead to discrimination (Hovy and Spruit, 2016). Within the natural language processing community, bias reduction includes work in reducing gender (Bolukbasi et al., 2016), ethnic or religious bias (Manzini et al., 2019) in word embeddings or classification tasks (Dixon et al., 2018; Badjatiya et al., 2020; Mozafari et al., 2020). Nevertheless, these techniques often rely on predefined lexicons, which are mostly human-written and thus expensive in their creation. Instead, we present an entirely data-driven pipeline for the creation of a scalable knowledge graph (KG) of cultural knowledge and stereotypes. Our resulting knowledge graph, called StereoKG, consists of 4,722 entries about 10 different social groups, i.e., 5 religious groups and 5 nationalities. This knowledge graph has several use cases, ranging from analyzing existing stereotypical and cultural knowledge online, to removing ethnic and religious bias or increasing the cultural awareness of classifiers. In our experiments, we focus on the latter: integration of cultural knowledge to improve classification performance. Overall, our contributions are threefold:

- Development of a fully **data-driven** knowledge graph construction approach on Twitter and Reddit data.
- **Manual evaluation** and analysis of the resulting knowledge graph of cultural knowledge and stereotypes, highlighting the importance of multiple-mention entries in representing cultural stereotypes, which achieve higher quality than single-mention entries.
- Classification experiments showing that performing intermediate masked language model training on linearized stereotype knowledge can improve the **classification performance** on knowledge-crucial samples on a hate speech task.

The rest of the paper is structured as follows:

Proceedings of the Sixth Workshop on Online Abuse and Harms (WOAH), pages 67 - 78
July 14, 2022

After describing the related work (Section 2), we present our knowledge graph creation technique (Section 3) which is then evaluated in a quantitative and qualitative fashion (Section 4). Section 5 describes the knowledge integration experiments, which constitute downstream task performance on hate speech detection and masked language modelling predictions of cultural content. We then discuss (Section 6) and conclude (Section 7) our findings. Ethical concerns are addressed in Appendix A.

2 Related Work

Cultural knowledge about different social groups and entities plays an important role in responding to contextual situations. In this work, we target cultural knowledge as a form of commonsense (LoBue and Yates, 2011). Incorporating cultural commonsense in reasoning tasks is an understudied practice in NLP. Anacleto et al. (2006) study the variation of cultural commonsense and how it affects computer applications. While there exist knowledge base resources for general commonsense (Lenat, 1995; Speer et al., 2017; Tandon et al., 2014), to the best of our knowledge, Acharya et al. (2020) have provided the only work targeting the construction of a cultural knowledge graph, which comprises various rituals and customs for two cultures. However, since it relies on crowdsourcing, it is limited in its coverage and is not easily extendable.

Cultural knowledge is largely correlated to **stereotypes**. Contrary to exhaustive research avenues analyzing gender and ethnic stereotypes, our work focuses on the lesser-studied nationality and religious stereotypes. Snefjella.B et al. (2018) have shown that national stereotypes could be grounded in the collective linguistic behavior of nations, while the Harvard Pluralism Project[1] stresses the importance of considering religion as a factor for prejudice. Because of the diversity of social groups and their behavioral traits, stereotypes and cultural attributes have unclear boundaries, making it difficult to distinguish between the two. Keeping this in mind, we treat cultural knowledge and stereotypes as interchangeable terms.

Stereotypes have been used to estimate **bias** in language models using curated datasets (Nadeem et al., 2021; Nangia et al., 2020). Stereotypical data has also been extracted from search engine autocomplete predictions using query prompts (Baker and Potts, 2013) and then used for analyzing how language models learn these concepts (Choenni et al., 2021). Bolukbasi et al. (2016) use minimal pairs of male-female terms to debias word embeddings.

In our work, we create a unified resource of cultural knowledge and stereotypes. Knowledge graphs serve as sources of representing knowledge in a structured format. Factual knowledge bases such as DBPedia (Auer et al., 2007), Freebase (Bollacker et al., 2008) and Wikidata (Vrandečić and Krötzsch, 2014) contain grounded knowledge about individual entities. **Knowledge graph construction** for commonsense reasoning has also been a common object of research (Lenat, 1995; Speer et al., 2017; Tandon et al., 2014). While some KGs comprise an if-then reasoning scheme (Sap et al., 2019; Forbes and Choi, 2017), some contain knowledge in the form of triples (Vrandečić and Krötzsch, 2014) or as simple natural language sentences (Bhakthavatsalam et al., 2020; Thorne et al., 2021). Crowdsourced KGs, e.g., Wikidata, result in good quality knowledge, but require large-scale manual annotation and resources. In contrast, KGs constructed in an automated manner have a lower cost in construction, are easily extendable, and have been shown to be useful in several downstream applications (Suchanek et al., 2007; Bhakthavatsalam et al., 2020). For example, Romero et al. (2019) use questions as prompts for learning commonsense cues from search engine query logs and question-answering forums and construct a commonsense knowledge base.

Explicit **knowledge integration** of knowledge resources into language models can be roughly categorized into fusion based approaches and language modeling based approaches. Fusion based approaches (Peters et al., 2019; Wang et al., 2021; Yan et al., 2021) typically perform knowledge integration by combining language model representations with representations extracted from knowledge bases. Compared to language modeling based approaches, as explored by us, they rely on aligned data and are typically applied during the pre-training stage. Language modeling based approaches commonly start from a pre-trained language model and perform knowledge integration via intermediate pre-training. For example, Bosselut et al. (2019) integrate commonsense knowledge by performing language modeling on triples ob-

[1] https://pluralism.org/stereotypes-and-prejudice

tained from ATOMIC and ConceptNet. Recently, Da et al. (2021) analyzed this approach in the few-shot training setting. In contrast to our study, both works consider autoregressive language models and use the resulting models for knowledge base construction, while we study the impact of knowledge integration on downstream task performance. Similar to our work, Lauscher et al. (2020) integrate commonsense knowledge via masked language modeling. They obtain sentences for intermediate pre-training by randomly traversing the ConceptNet knowledge graph. Unlike our work, they do not update the weights of the pre-trained model and train adapter layers instead. Moreover, while we focus on hate-speech classification as our downstream task, they evaluate on GLUE.

Query Templates
Why is <*SUB*>
Why isn't <*SUB*>
Why are <*SUB*>
Why aren't <*SUB*>
Why can <*SUB*>
Why can't <*SUB*>
Why do <*SUB*>
Why don't <*SUB*>
Why doesn't <*SUB*>
How is <*SUB*>
How do <*SUB*>
What makes <*SUB*>
Why does <*SUB*> culture
<*SUB*> are so
<*SUB*> is such a

Table 1: Question-based (top) and statement-based (bottom) query templates.

3 Knowledge Graph Construction

We focus our cultural KG on 5 religious (*Atheism*[2], *Christianity, Hinduism, Islam, Judaism*) and 5 national (*American, Chinese, French, German, Indian*) entities. Previous work on automatic KG creation depended on external algorithms, i.e., autocompletion of search engine queries (Romero et al., 2019; Choenni et al., 2021; Baker and Potts, 2013). This dependency is limiting, as external providers may filter[3] outputs of their autocomplete algorithm, especially on sensitive topics such as *culture* and *identity*. Instead, we keep control over the whole KG creation process. The entire KG construction pipeline is illustrated in Figure 1.

Using statement and **question mining**, cultural knowledge and stereotypes regarding our entities of interest are collected from two social media platforms, Reddit and Twitter. For Reddit, we limit our search to subreddits relevant for the respective subjects (e.g. *r/germany* for Germans) together with common question-answering subreddits (e.g., *r/AskReddit*) using the PRAW[4] library. The complete list of queried subreddits is given in Appendix B. Similar to the commonsense mining approach by Romero et al. (2019) and Choenni et al. (2021), we use fixed question and statement templates (Table 1) to identify potential sentences containing cultural knowledge with the assumption that questions posted about various national and religious entities act as cues for underlying stereotypical notions about them. This results in 11,259 mined questions and statements. The questions are then **converted into statements** using `Quasimodo`[5] (Romero et al., 2019), as OpenIE does not process interrogative sentences.

To reduce redundancies in the KG triples, we **cluster** the mined sentences with similar content together using the fast clustering method for community detection implemented in the `SentenceTransformers`[6] (Reimers and Gurevych, 2019) library. This step results in 6,993 singletons and 610 clusters with more than one instance. We hypothesize that non-singleton clusters are better representatives of cultural knowledge and stereotypes, as these are based on questions that have been asked by several users, while singletons may be based on unique thoughts which do not represent a popular stereotype or cultural reality. The qualitative difference between singletons and clusters is evaluated in Section 4.2.

All assertions are then **converted into triples** using `OpenIE` (Mausam, 2016). As OpenIE outputs multiple triples which may be noisy or irrelevant, they are filtered using the following heuristics:

- Eliminate triples containing personal pronouns, e.g., *I, he*.
- Eliminate triples not containing the original subject entity.
- Remove colloquialisms (e.g, *lol*) and modalities (e.g., *really*) from triples.

[2]Although atheism is not a religion, we still include it under the list of religious dispositions as a religious belief.

[3]In its battle against biased or hateful content, Google has imposed filters on its autocomplete predictions for targeted questions.

[4]`https://github.com/praw-dev/praw`

[5]`https://github.com/Aunsiels/CSK`

[6]`https://www.sbert.net/examples/applications/clustering/README.html`

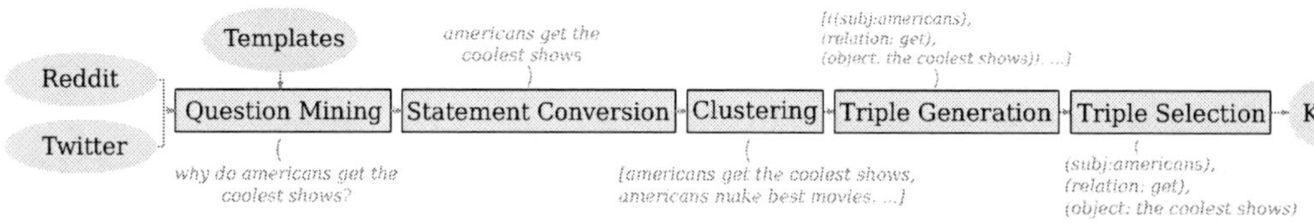

Figure 1: From noisy social media content to structured knowledge graph: the creation pipeline of StereoKG.

While most triples are singletons, many are part of a cluster. In order to **select the triple** to represent a cluster in the final KG, triples within a cluster are converted into sentences via concatenation of their subject-predicate-object terms. These are ranked on their grammaticality using a binary classification model[7] trained on the corpus of linguistic acceptability (CoLA) (Warstadt et al., 2019). Concretely, the rank of a sentence is the score assigned to the *grammatical* class by the classification model, and the triple with the highest rank is chosen as the representative for the entire cluster. Since CoLA and the resulting classifier are restricted to English, our triple selection currently only works for English data. However, our method provides an advantage over standard cluster representative selection methods such as centroid identification, since we ensure that the chosen representative triple is the most fluent choice in its cluster. This is important, since (grammatical) completeness is an important quality feature for a KG, which we also assess as part of our human evaluation.

4 Knowledge Graph Evaluation

The resulting KG consists of 4,722 entries, with Americans being the largest represented group (1,071 entries) and Jews (43) the smallest. The proposed pipeline can also be utilised to extend the KG with additional entities. In the following section, we describe the qualitative and quantitative evaluation of the generated KG.

4.1 KG Statistics

To gain insights into the sentiments and overall distribution of descriptive predicates, we evaluate the KG on two criteria.

Sentiment Analysis We perform a ternary (*positive, neutral, negative*) sentiment analysis over the KG triples by verbalizing them into sentences. We use a pre-trained sentiment classification model[8] (Barbieri et al., 2020) for this task. We observe that for certain subjects, e.g. *atheists*, the triples have a higher tendency to be negatively evaluated by the simple presence of the entity term. In order to mitigate this bias in the sentiment analysis classifier, we mask[9] the subject entities with their type, e.g. *"islam seems to be conservative"* → *"religion seems to be conservative"* and *"french culture is pure"* → *"nation culture is pure"*, and then perform classification.

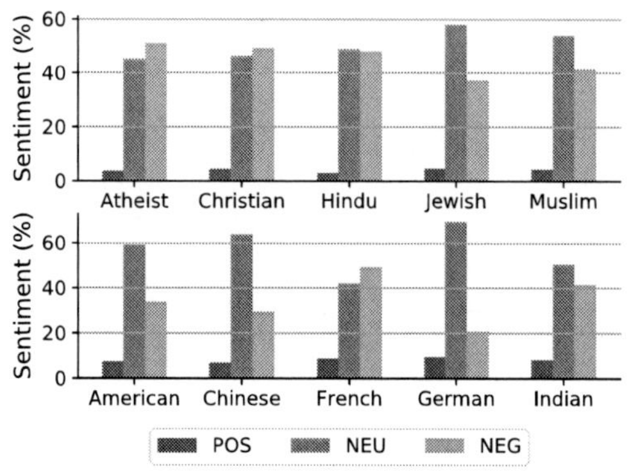

Figure 2: Percentage of POSitive, NEUtral and NEGatively evaluated triples per religious (top) and nationality (bottom) entity.

Pointwise Mutual Information (PMI) PMI $\pi(x, y)$ measures the association of two events. We calculate π between entities $E = e_1, ..., e_n$ and their co-occurring predicate and object tokens w as:

$$\pi(e, w) = \log \frac{p(e, w)}{p(e)p(w)} \tag{1}$$

[7] https://huggingface.co/textattack/distilbert-base-uncased-CoLA

[8] https://huggingface.co/cardiffnlp/twitter-roberta-base-sentiment

[9] Note that the more generic term used to mask the specific religion or nationality terms may also have a biased representation in the pre-trained classifier. However, when applying masking via generic terms, we observe a large decrease in the negative classification of otherwise neutral/positive samples for certain subjects, indicating a decreased level of model bias.

Infrequent tokens co-occurring with a single entity will have higher PMI scores with the said entity. To focus our analysis on common tokens co-occurring with one entity while maintaining low co-occurrence with other entities, we use the following PMI-based **association metric** α:

$$\alpha(e, w) = (\pi(e, w) - \overline{\pi}(e, w)) \cdot f(e, w) \quad (2)$$

Where $f(e, w)$ is the frequency of w amongst all tokens co-occurring with e and

$$\overline{\pi} = \sum_{e_i \in E \setminus \{e\}} \pi(e_i, w) \quad (3)$$

Intuitively, Equation 2 mitigates the effect of infrequent tokens in the PMI calculation and gives a relative score across all the entities. We calculate α between entities and their co-occurring predicates and objects to identify trends in the contents of the triples.

Results Figure 2 shows the results of the sentiment classification. Overall, positively evaluated instances are rare across all entities, with most being neutral or negatively evaluated. The results of the association analysis are highlighted in Table 2. The most positively (4.7%) and least negatively (37.2%) evaluated religious group are *Jews*, where positive stereotypes include *strong* for Jewish women (α = 5.19). Most (58.1%) instances about Judaism are neutral reports of cultural practices, e.g., about *circumcision* (α = 6.78). Hindus have the smallest proportion of positive stereotypes (2.9%) and Atheists have the largest amount of negative evaluations (51.0%) which often include strong negative actions and emotions such as *attack* (α = 2.04), *angry* (α = 1.37) and *obnoxious* (α = 2.69). Nationalities tend to be more frequently positively evaluated than religious groups, with Germans being the most positively evaluated (9.5%) and the least negatively evaluated (21.0%) with most instances being neutral mentions of the countries role during *ww2* (α = 3.76). Chinese (6.7%) have the lowest proportion of positive stereotypes, however neutral sentiments are most common (63.9%) and are often about topics such as Chinese *food* (α = 2.77). The nationality with the largest proportion of negative stereotypes are the French (49.3%), which are mostly described with negative traits such as *elitist* (α = 5.09) or *vulgar* (α = 5.09), while neutral and positive mentions are often related to food, e.g., *croissants* (α = 5.09).

Since most stereotypical questions asked online have more negative connotations than positive, it confirms the premise that stereotypes can represent prejudicial opinions of different cultural groups.

4.2 Human Evaluation

We perform a **human evaluation** to gain insights into the quality of StereoKG. We focus on three quality metrics, namely *coherence* (COH), *completeness* (COM), and *domain* (DOM) evaluated on a nominal 3-point scale for negation (0), ambiguity (1), and affirmation (2) respectively. COH measures the semantic logicality of a triple, while COM measures if the grammatical valency of the predicate is fulfilled. DOM measures whether the triple belongs to our domain of interest, i.e., whether it can be considered a stereotype or cultural knowledge. We also measure two subjective *credibility* measures CR1 and CR2, where CR1 is a binary measure asking whether the annotator has heard of this stereotype/knowledge before, and CR2 asks whether they believe the information to be true on a scale of 0-4. To evaluate the overall quality of triples, we calculate the success rate (SUC), where a triple is considered successful if it achieves an above average (> 1) rating across all three quality metrics COH, COM, and DOM. The evaluation is performed on a total of 100 unique triples from the KG, where 50 triples each were randomly sampled from the subset of triples stemming from singleton and non-singleton clusters respectively. Each sample was annotated by 3 annotators, all of whom are students with different cultural backgrounds (*German (irreligious), Indian (Hindu), and Iranian (Muslim)*).

We assess **inter-annotator agreement** using the average observed agreement (OA) as calculated using the `NLTK agreement`[10] function, which does not penalize repeated entries of a single value[11] unlike other common metrics (e.g. Krippendorff-α). We observe high levels of agreement for both quality measures COH (0.82) and COM (0.74), while OA for DOM is lower (0.59) due to the subjective nature of what constitutes a *stereotype* (Table

[10] `https://www.nltk.org/_modules/nltk/metrics/agreement.html`

[11] Repeated entries of a single value are quite common in our annotations, since for most quality measures we use a 3-point or even 2-point scale.

Entity	#Instances	Top Tokens (α)
Atheist	731	*god, christians, annoying, believe, theists, obsessed, attack, vocal, angry, argue, troll, hate*
Christian	823	*obsessed, follow, bible, weird, hate, jesus, abortion, afraid, jewish, covid, non-christians*
Hindu	102	*men, india, hindustan, uc, muslim, caste, tolerant, babas, shameless, fool, jihads,marrying*
Jewish	43	*jew,wear, israel, circumcisions, conversion, discourage, evangelize, progressive, shiksas, leftist*
Muslim	842	*hate, countries, allowed, ex-muslims, obsessed, quran, eat, laws, allah, islamophobia, sharia*
American	1071	*culture, call, obsessed, pronounce, different, countries, afraid, healthcare, hate, british, soccer*
Chinese	277	*restaurants, companies, citizens, food, workers, students, tourists, menus, consumers*
French	138	*eat, speak, obsession, call, egg, pretty, croissants, depicted, proud, culture, exaggerate, elitist*
German	262	*obsessed, pronounce, words, ww2, water, war, nazi, prepare, berlin, love, disciplined, manual*
Indian	431	*culture, obsessed, hate, pakistanis, pictures, marriages, heads, defensive, afraid, stare, army*
Total	4722	

Table 2: Number of instances per entity and predicate/object tokens with highest association score α to entity.

	COH (0-2)	COM (0-2)	DOM (0-2)	CR1 (0-1)	CR2 (0-4)	SUC (%)
SD	1.55	1.11	0.97	0.13	1.17	44.0
CD	1.70	1.42	1.18	0.29	1.56	59.2
All	1.63	1.26	1.07	0.21	1.36	51.5
OA	0.82	0.74	0.59	0.81	0.39	

Table 3: Human annotated COHerence, COMpleteness, DOMain and CRedibility metrics and SUCcess rate over the complete KG test sample (All) as well as its singleton-derived (SD) and cluster-derived (CD) subsamples. Average observed agreement (OA) given for each metric.

3). Similarly, OA for subjective measures CR{1,2} is mixed, as can be expected. To measure intra-annotator agreement, we duplicated 10 random samples. Intra-annotator agreement is high across all annotators (0.79, 0.95, 1.00).

The COH **quality metric** of the KG is high for both singleton (1.55) and non-singleton-derived entries (1.70), and COM is slightly lower (average COM=1.26). That indicates that the vast majority of entities are meaningful (COH), with some missing relevant information (COM). Overall, DOM is close to 1, suggesting that it was often not clear to annotators whether an entity can be considered a stereotype, which is also reflected in the overall lower inter-annotator agreement on this metric. Entities stemming from non-singleton clusters have a high success rate of 59.2, meaning that the majority of non-singleton-derived entities lean positively across all three quality metrics COH, COM, and DOM. Overall, non-singleton entities are of higher quality than singleton-derived entities (SUC $+15.2$), underlining the initial hypothesis that multiple occurrences of questions online are better indicators of a stereotype than unique

Corpus	Train	Dev	Test
OLID	3504/7088	894/1752	242/620
WSF	830/6662	105/965	261/1880

Table 4: Number of *hate/neutral* instances in the train, dev and test set of downstream tasks.

questions. Moreover, stereotypical knowledge in non-singleton entities is more likely to be known (CR1 $+0.16$) and believed to be true (CR2 $+0.39$) by annotators.

5 Knowledge Integration

To explore how StereoKG can be used to integrate knowledge into an existing language model, we perform intermediate masked language modeling (MLM) on it in its structured (verbalized triple) and unstructured (sentence) form. The unstructured knowledge is more expressive and verbose, while the structured knowledge from triples is concise and less noisy as compared to the unstructured data. We then fine-tune and evaluate the language model performance on hate speech detection, a task for which we esteem stereotype knowledge to be of use.

5.1 Experimental Setup

Data We experiment with the effect of intermediate pre-training focusing on two kinds of downstream datasets for fine-tuning: one of the same domain as the pre-training corpus (Twitter), and another which is outside the domain data. We use the Twitter-based OLID (Zampieri et al., 2019) dataset as our in-domain dataset and the White Supremacy Forum (WSF) dataset (de Gibert et al., 2018) as our out-of-domain dataset. Both tasks are binary *hate/neutral* classification tasks. As OLID does not have an official validation set, we split off 20% of samples from the training data for validation. Similarly, WSF is randomly split into 70-10-20% splits for training, validation, and testing respectively.

We manually identify 9 and 33 samples containing a stereotype or cultural knowledge about the subject entities of interest in the dev and test splits of OLID and WSF respectively. To analyze the effect of cultural knowledge integration on these samples exclusively, we use these to create dedicated stereotype test sets. To avoid breaking the exclusivity between validation and testing, we remove the samples found in the validation sets from the original validation splits. During our testing phase, we test the models on the complete test sets as well as the dedicated stereotype test sets. We give the final dataset statistics in Table 4.

Our unstructured knowledge (UK) comprises the original sentences from the clusters from which the triples are formed. Since pre-training requires a sentence format, we create our structured knowledge (SK) by verbalizing the triples from the KG with a T5-based (Raffel et al., 2020) triple-to-text conversion model (details in Appendix C).

Models For the **knowledge integration** experiments, we use the sequence classification pipeline in the `simpletransformers`[12] library. As baselines, we fine-tune two models: general-domain (BASE) RoBERTa[13](Liu et al., 2019) and domain-trained (DT) Twitter RoBERTa[14](Barbieri et al., 2020). Additionally, we continue MLM training of the baseline models before fine-tuning using i) unstructured (+UK) KG knowledge and ii) structured (+SK) verbalized triples to investigate the impact of stereotypical knowledge. All models are fine-tuned with early stopping (δ=0.01, patience=3) using the validation F1 score as the stopping criterion. We fine-tune 10 models for each configuration, each having a different random seed and report their averaged Macro-F1 with standard errors.

5.2 Knowledge vs. Domain

We fine-tune the BASE(+UK/SK) and DT(+UK/SK) RoBERTa models on the in-domain (OLID) and out-of-domain (WSF) training data and report Macro-F1 on the entire test set. To quantify the impact of injecting stereotypes, we also report results on the dedicated stereotype test set. Results on the complete test set and stereotype test set are shown in Table 5 (top) respectively.

Model	**OLID** (F1)		**WSF** (F1)	
	Complete	Stereotype	Complete	Stereotype
BASE	69.7±.7	65.1±2.3	60.5±.6	73.3±1.7
BASE+UK	70.6±.4	67.9±2.6	60.7±.5	72.7±1.3
BASE+SK	70.4±.6	66.9±2.0	59.5±1.2	67.5±3.2
DT	70.5±.4	72.5±1.7	60.8±.6	**77.7**±1.6
DT+UK	70.6±.4	73.4±3.4	**61.4**±.4	77.0±2.9
DT+SK	**71.2**±.2	**73.8**±1.8	60.6±.5	75.6±1.8
Our best	71.2	–	91.3*	–
Benchmark	80.0	–	78.0*	–

Table 5: Averaged Macro-F1 and standard errors of BASE and domain trained (DT) models with intermediate MLM training on unstructured (UK) and structured (SK) knowledge tested on OLID and WSF. Top results in **bold**. We compare our best model per test set against its corresponding OLID/WSF benchmark implementation. Values with * are accuracies.

For the **complete test set**, knowledge integration does not seem to have a significant effect, with most model variations being within the error bounds of each other. Only domain training positively affects the classification performance, with all DT models outperforming their BASE counterparts on the OLID dataset with gains of up to F1 +1.5. As expected, domain training does not have an effect on the performance for the out-of-domain WSF data.

While the effect of cultural knowledge integration is not significant on the full test sets, its effect becomes clearer when focusing only on the subset of instances that contain **stereotypes**. Firstly, domain training has a larger effect on these samples, with the DT model showing an increase of F1 +7.4 over BASE on OLID. When the DT model has additionally undergone intermediate MLM training on cultural knowledge, we observe further improvements in F1 for +UK and +SK respectively. While these improvements are within each other's error bounds, this suggests that the training on cultural knowledge can increase downstream task performance on knowledge-crucial samples, i.e., in our case, those that require cultural or stereotypical knowledge. A larger stereotype-containing test set is required to further verify this hypothesis by reducing error bounds. On the out-of-domain WSF data, we do not observe these trends, similar to the BASE model on OLID. This suggests that domain training is a prerequisite for effective knowledge integration.

To set our model results into perspective, we

[12]`https://simpletransformers.ai/docs/classification-models/`

[13]`https://huggingface.co/roberta-base`

[14]`https://huggingface.co/cardiffnlp/twitter-roberta-base`

compare our best models against the **benchmarks** provided by Zampieri et al. (2019) and de Gibert et al. (2018) for OLID and WSF, respectively (Table 5, bottom). On OLID, the benchmark model outperforms our best model by a large margin (F1 +8.8). However, their reported models are single runs without reported standard errors, thus it is unclear whether this specific run is representative for the underlying average model performance. For WSF, our best model outperforms the benchmark by a large margin (Acc +13.3), which is due to the simpler long short-term memory approach that constitutes this benchmark.

5.3 Cultural Knowledge Prediction

To further quantify the degree to which cultural and stereotype knowledge is encoded in the models, we compare their MLM predictions on **masked stereotypes**. We manually collected 100 sentences from the verbalized KG and masked tokens which require either cultural or stereotype knowledge to be completed. By taking into account the top 5 predictions and comparing them to the masked gold standard, we calculate the prediction accuracy at 5 (ACC@5)[15] and analyze common trends.

Our results in Table 6 show that both, the generic BASE and Twitter-based DT models have the same low level of **cultural awareness** (ACC@5=37%), with most predictions being vague e.g, *he, this, that*. However, adding 4,895 unstructured knowledge instances as intermediate MLM training data drastically improves results to 48% (BASE+UK) and 49% (DT+UK). Both +UK models show higher sensitivity to cultural correlations e.g., *Americans* and their struggle with *healthcare*, or *Muslims* and reading the *Quran*, which was not displayed by the baseline models. Further, adjective predictions about minorities tend to be more positive, e.g. *Jewish women are [strong] →beautiful*. The structured knowledge also improves cultural sensitivity to a large margin, i.e., +7% points (BASE+SK) and +4% points (DT+SK). However, their predictions are often more generic and less culture-specific than the +UK models, which may be due to the lack of variable context in which these stereotypes are seen due to the denoising factor of using SK.

[15]If the gold standard is present in the top 5 predictions, it is considered accurate.

6 Discussion

We create an automated pipeline to extract cultural and stereotypical knowledge from the internet in the form of queries. While this overcomes the limitations and expenses of crowdsourcing and is easily extendable to a large number of entities, several shortcomings still need to be addressed. Automated extraction results in irrelevant and noisy data, which is augmented by erroneous outputs during triple creation. This is also evidenced in the human evaluation that corroborates the existence of many incomplete triples in the resultant KG, which could also be due to the noisy OpenIE outputs. Other stages in the analysis, such as statement conversion, fast clustering, and triple verbalization give sufficiently good approximations.

Our knowledge integration experiments suggest that performing intermediate MLM training on (verbalized) cultural knowledge can improve the classification performance on knowledge-crucial samples. However, the sample of stereotypical examples in the test/dev sets of both hate speech corpora is low (9 for OLID and 33 for WSF), indicating that a more extensive dedicated hate speech test set focusing on stereotype entities is required to reduce error margins and verify results. Our experiments are limited to intermediate MLM training and we leave the exploration of other knowledge integration techniques for future work.

Our work serves as a preliminary research for studying stereotypes and cultural knowledge across different entities. Extending the KG for other entities than the one proposed in our work is easily done by plugging in new entities into our query templates (Table 1) and the pre-existing pipeline can be used to scrape data, create clusters and finally extract triples without the need of manual intervention. Nevertheless, the current version of StereoKG does not differentiate between (true) cultural knowledge and (untrue or stigmatizing) stereotypes. In reality, making this distinction is a challenge for human experts too, due to the fuzzy boundary between false "stereotypes" and perfectly true cultural "facts" because of the subjective nature of cultural knowledge.

The content used for the construction of StereoKG stems from English-speaking Twitter and Reddit. This comprises a specific demographic which is only a subset of our global society. The stereotypes and cultural knowledge included in StereoKG therefore also underlie this sampling

Model	ACC@5 (%)	Example	Pred (top 3)
BASE	37	*Muslims are turning away [science].*	*too, now, again*
BASE+UK	48	*Americans don't have free [healthcare].*	*healthcare, lunch, tuition*
BASE+SK	45	*Americans are voting for [Trump].*	*freedom, democracy, them*
DT	37	*Atheists unilaterally support [abortion].*	*fascism, abortion, terrorism*
DT+UK	49	*Muslims compare apostasy to [treason]*	*treason, sin, genocide*
DT+SK	41	*Chinese toilets are [dirty].*	*disgusting, awful, shit*

Table 6: Cultural MLM prediction accuracy at 5 (ACC@5) of different models together with example instances with masked [gold standard] token and the top 3 predictions of the model.

bias. Extending the KG to other languages as well as data sources could yield a more global view on stereotypes regarding a specific entity.

7 Conclusion

This study presents StereoKG, a scalable data-driven knowledge graph of 4,722 cultural knowledge and stereotype entries spanning 5 religions and 5 nationalities. We describe our automated KG creation pipeline and evaluate the resulting KG quality through human annotation, showing that the majority of cluster-derived entries in the KG are of high quality (success rate 59.2%) and more common and credible than their singleton counterparts. The KG can easily be extended to include other nationalities as well as genders, sexual orientations, professions, etc., as the underlying subjects. Further, performing intermediate MLM training on verbalized instances of StereoKG greatly improves the models' capabilities to predict culture-related content. This improvement of cultural awareness has a positive effect on knowledge-crucial samples, where we observe a slight improvement in classification performance on a related downstream task, i.e., hate speech detection. Future work should focus on differentiating between cultural facts that should be represented in language models and stigmatizing stereotypes that should not be present in language models.

We make StereoKG and the code of our KG creation pipeline available under `https://github.com/uds-lsv/StereoKG`.

Acknowledgements

We thank our annotators for their keen work as well as the reviewers for their valuable feedback. This study has been partially funded by the DFG (WI 4204/3-1), EU Horizon 2020 project ROXANNE (833635) and the Deutsche Forschungsgemeinschaft (DFG, German Research Foundation) – Project-ID 232722074 – SFB 1102.

References

Anurag Acharya, Kartik Talamadupula, and Mark A. Finlayson. 2020. An atlas of cultural commonsense for machine reasoning. *CoRR*, abs/2009.05664.

Oshin Agarwal, Heming Ge, Siamak Shakeri, and Rami Al-Rfou. 2021. Knowledge graph based synthetic corpus generation for knowledge-enhanced language model pre-training. In *Proceedings of the 2021 Conference of the North American Chapter of the Association for Computational Linguistics: Human Language Technologies*, pages 3554–3565, Online. Association for Computational Linguistics.

Junia Anacleto, Henry Lieberman, Marie Tsutsumi, Vânia Neris, Aparecido Carvalho, Jose Espinosa, Muriel Godoi, and Silvia Zem-Mascarenhas. 2006. Can common sense uncover cultural differences in computer applications? In *Artificial Intelligence in Theory and Practice*, pages 1–10, Boston, MA. Springer US.

Sören Auer, Christian Bizer, Georgi Kobilarov, Jens Lehmann, Richard Cyganiak, and Zachary Ives. 2007. Dbpedia: A nucleus for a web of open data. In *Proceedings of the 6th International The Semantic Web and 2nd Asian Conference on Asian Semantic Web Conference*, ISWC'07/ASWC'07, page 722–735, Berlin, Heidelberg. Springer-Verlag.

Pinkesh Badjatiya, Manish Gupta, and Vasudeva Varma. 2020. Stereotypical bias removal for hate speech detection task using knowledge-based generalizations. *CoRR*, abs/2001.05495.

Paul Baker and Amanda Potts. 2013. Why do white people have thin lips? Google and the perpetuation of stereotypes via auto-complete search forms. *Critical Discourse Studies*, 10(2):187–204.

Francesco Barbieri, Jose Camacho-Collados, Luis Espinosa Anke, and Leonardo Neves. 2020. TweetEval: Unified benchmark and comparative evaluation for tweet classification. In *Findings of the Association for Computational Linguistics: EMNLP 2020*, pages 1644–1650, Online. Association for Computational Linguistics.

Sumithra Bhakthavatsalam, Chloe Anastasiades, and Peter Clark. 2020. Genericskb: A knowledge base of generic statements.

Kurt D. Bollacker, Colin Evans, Praveen K. Paritosh, Tim Sturge, and Jamie Taylor. 2008. Freebase: a collaboratively created graph database for structuring human knowledge. In *SIGMOD Conference*.

Tolga Bolukbasi, Kai-Wei Chang, James Zou, Venkatesh Saligrama, and Adam Kalai. 2016. Man is to computer programmer as woman is to homemaker? debiasing word embeddings. In *Proceedings of the 30th International Conference on Neural Information Processing Systems*, NIPS'16, page 4356–4364, Red Hook, NY, USA. Curran Associates Inc.

Antoine Bosselut, Hannah Rashkin, Maarten Sap, Chaitanya Malaviya, Asli Celikyilmaz, and Yejin Choi. 2019. COMET: Commonsense transformers for automatic knowledge graph construction. In *Proceedings of the 57th Annual Meeting of the Association for Computational Linguistics*, pages 4762–4779, Florence, Italy. Association for Computational Linguistics.

Emma E. Buchtel. 2014. Cultural sensitivity or cultural stereotyping? positive and negative effects of a cultural psychology class. *International Journal of Intercultural Relations*, 39:40–52.

Rochelle Choenni, Ekaterina Shutova, and Robert van Rooij. 2021. Stepmothers are mean and academics are pretentious: What do pretrained language models learn about you? In *Proceedings of the 2021 Conference on Empirical Methods in Natural Language Processing*, pages 1477–1491, Online and Punta Cana, Dominican Republic. Association for Computational Linguistics.

Emilie Colin, Claire Gardent, Yassine M'rabet, Shashi Narayan, and Laura Perez-Beltrachini. 2016. The WebNLG challenge: Generating text from DBPedia data. In *Proceedings of the 9th International Natural Language Generation conference*, pages 163–167, Edinburgh, UK. Association for Computational Linguistics.

Jeff Da, Ronan Le Bras, Ximing Lu, Yejin Choi, and Antoine Bosselut. 2021. Analyzing commonsense emergence in few-shot knowledge models. In *3rd Conference on Automated Knowledge Base Construction*.

Ona de Gibert, Naiara Perez, Aitor García-Pablos, and Montse Cuadros. 2018. Hate Speech Dataset from a White Supremacy Forum. In *Proceedings of the 2nd Workshop on Abusive Language Online (ALW2)*, pages 11–20, Brussels, Belgium. Association for Computational Linguistics.

Lucas Dixon, John Li, Jeffrey Sorensen, Nithum Thain, and Lucy Vasserman. 2018. Measuring and mitigating unintended bias in text classification. In *Proceedings of the 2018 AAAI/ACM Conference on AI, Ethics, and Society*. ACM.

John F. Dovidio, Miles Hewstone, Peter Glick, and Victoria M. Esses. 2010. Prejudice, stereotyping and discrimination: Theoretical and empirical overview. In *The SAGE handbook of prejudice, stereotyping and discrimination*, pages 3–28. SAGE Publications Ltd.

Maxwell Forbes and Yejin Choi. 2017. Verb physics: Relative physical knowledge of actions and objects. In *Proceedings of the 55th Annual Meeting of the Association for Computational Linguistics (Volume 1: Long Papers)*, pages 266–276, Vancouver, Canada. Association for Computational Linguistics.

James L. Hilton and William von Hippel. 1996. Stereotypes. *Annual Review of Psychology*, 47(1):237–271. PMID: 15012482.

Curt Hoffman and Nancy Hurst. 1990. Gender stereotypes: Perception or rationalization? *Journal of Personality and Social Psychology*, 58(2):197–208.

Dirk Hovy and Shannon L. Spruit. 2016. The social impact of natural language processing. In *Proceedings of the 54th Annual Meeting of the Association for Computational Linguistics (Volume 2: Short Papers)*, pages 591–598, Berlin, Germany. Association for Computational Linguistics.

Anne Lauscher, Olga Majewska, Leonardo F. R. Ribeiro, Iryna Gurevych, Nikolai Rozanov, and Goran Glavaš. 2020. Common sense or world knowledge? investigating adapter-based knowledge injection into pretrained transformers. In *Proceedings of Deep Learning Inside Out (DeeLIO): The First Workshop on Knowledge Extraction and Integration for Deep Learning Architectures*, pages 43–49, Online. Association for Computational Linguistics.

Douglas B. Lenat. 1995. Cyc: A large-scale investment in knowledge infrastructure. *Commun. ACM*, 38(11):33–38.

Yinhan Liu, Myle Ott, Naman Goyal, Jingfei Du, Mandar Joshi, Danqi Chen, Omer Levy, Mike Lewis, Luke Zettlemoyer, and Veselin Stoyanov. 2019. Roberta: A robustly optimized bert pretraining approach.

Peter LoBue and Alexander Yates. 2011. Types of common-sense knowledge needed for recognizing textual entailment. In *Proceedings of the 49th Annual Meeting of the Association for Computational Linguistics: Human Language Technologies*, pages 329–334, Portland, Oregon, USA. Association for Computational Linguistics.

Thomas Manzini, Lim Yao Chong, Alan W Black, and Yulia Tsvetkov. 2019. Black is to criminal as caucasian is to police: Detecting and removing multiclass bias in word embeddings. In *Proceedings of the 2019 Conference of the North American Chapter of the Association for Computational Linguistics: Human Language Technologies, Volume 1 (Long and Short Papers)*, pages 615–621, Minneapolis, Minnesota. Association for Computational Linguistics.

Mausam. 2016. Open information extraction systems and downstream applications. In *Proceedings of the Twenty-Fifth International Joint Conference on Artificial Intelligence*, IJCAI'16, page 4074–4077. AAAI Press.

Marzieh Mozafari, Reza Farahbakhsh, and Noël Crespi. 2020. Hate speech detection and racial bias mitigation in social media based on BERT model. *PLOS ONE*, 15(8):e0237861.

Moin Nadeem, Anna Bethke, and Siva Reddy. 2021. StereoSet: Measuring stereotypical bias in pretrained language models. In *Proceedings of the 59th Annual Meeting of the Association for Computational Linguistics and the 11th International Joint Conference on Natural Language Processing (Volume 1: Long Papers)*, pages 5356–5371, Online. Association for Computational Linguistics.

Nikita Nangia, Clara Vania, Rasika Bhalerao, and Samuel R. Bowman. 2020. CrowS-pairs: A challenge dataset for measuring social biases in masked language models. In *Proceedings of the 2020 Conference on Empirical Methods in Natural Language Processing (EMNLP)*, pages 1953–1967, Online. Association for Computational Linguistics.

Matthew E. Peters, Mark Neumann, Robert Logan, Roy Schwartz, Vidur Joshi, Sameer Singh, and Noah A. Smith. 2019. Knowledge enhanced contextual word representations. In *Proceedings of the 2019 Conference on Empirical Methods in Natural Language Processing and the 9th International Joint Conference on Natural Language Processing (EMNLP-IJCNLP)*, pages 43–54, Hong Kong, China. Association for Computational Linguistics.

Colin Raffel, Noam Shazeer, Adam Roberts, Katherine Lee, Sharan Narang, Michael Matena, Yanqi Zhou, Wei Li, and Peter J. Liu. 2020. Exploring the limits of transfer learning with a unified text-to-text transformer. *Journal of Machine Learning Research*, 21(140):1–67.

Nils Reimers and Iryna Gurevych. 2019. Sentence-BERT: Sentence embeddings using Siamese BERT-networks. In *Proceedings of the 2019 Conference on Empirical Methods in Natural Language Processing and the 9th International Joint Conference on Natural Language Processing (EMNLP-IJCNLP)*, pages 3982–3992, Hong Kong, China. Association for Computational Linguistics.

Julien Romero, Simon Razniewski, Koninika Pal, Jeff Z. Pan, Archit Sakhadeo, and Gerhard Weikum. 2019. Commonsense properties from query logs and question answering forums. In *Proceedings of the 28th ACM International Conference on Information and Knowledge Management*, CIKM '19, page 1411–1420, New York, NY, USA. Association for Computing Machinery.

Maarten Sap, Ronan Le Bras, Emily Allaway, Chandra Bhagavatula, Nicholas Lourie, Hannah Rashkin, Brendan Roof, Noah A. Smith, and Yejin Choi. 2019. Atomic: An atlas of machine commonsense for if-then reasoning. *Proceedings of the AAAI Conference on Artificial Intelligence*, 33(01):3027–3035.

Snefjella.B, Schmidtke.D, and Kuperman.V. 2018. National character stereotypes mirror language use: A study of canadian and american tweets. *PLoS One*.

Robyn Speer, Joshua Chin, and Catherine Havasi. 2017. Conceptnet 5.5: An open multilingual graph of general knowledge. In *Proceedings of the Thirty-First AAAI Conference on Artificial Intelligence*, AAAI'17, page 4444–4451. AAAI Press.

Fabian M. Suchanek, Gjergji Kasneci, and Gerhard Weikum. 2007. Yago: A core of semantic knowledge. In *Proceedings of the 16th International Conference on World Wide Web*, WWW '07, page 697–706, New York, NY, USA. Association for Computing Machinery.

Niket Tandon, Gerard de Melo, Fabian Suchanek, and Gerhard Weikum. 2014. Webchild: Harvesting and organizing commonsense knowledge from the web. In *Proceedings of the 7th ACM International Conference on Web Search and Data Mining*, WSDM '14, page 523–532, New York, NY, USA. Association for Computing Machinery.

James Thorne, Majid Yazdani, Marzieh Saeidi, Fabrizio Silvestri, Sebastian Riedel, and Alon Halevy. 2021. From natural language processing to neural databases. *Proc. VLDB Endow.*, 14(6):1033–1039.

Denny Vrandečić and Markus Krötzsch. 2014. Wikidata: A free collaborative knowledgebase. *Commun. ACM*, 57(10):78–85.

Ruize Wang, Duyu Tang, Nan Duan, Zhongyu Wei, Xuanjing Huang, Jianshu Ji, Guihong Cao, Daxin Jiang, and Ming Zhou. 2021. K-Adapter: Infusing Knowledge into Pre-Trained Models with Adapters. In *Findings of the Association for Computational Linguistics: ACL-IJCNLP 2021*, pages 1405–1418, Online. Association for Computational Linguistics.

Alex Warstadt, Amanpreet Singh, and Samuel R. Bowman. 2019. Neural network acceptability judgments. *Transactions of the Association for Computational Linguistics*, 7:625–641.

Ruiqing Yan, Lanchang Sun, Fang Wang, and Xiaoming Zhang. 2021. K-xlnet: A general method for combining explicit knowledge with language model pretraining. *CoRR*, abs/2104.10649.

Marcos Zampieri, Shervin Malmasi, Preslav Nakov, Sara Rosenthal, Noura Farra, and Ritesh Kumar. 2019. Predicting the type and target of offensive posts in social media. In *Proceedings of the 2019 Conference of the North American Chapter of the Association for Computational Linguistics: Human Language Technologies, Volume 1 (Long and Short Papers)*, pages 1415–1420, Minneapolis, Minnesota. Association for Computational Linguistics.

A Ethics Statement

Human Evaluation We perform a human evaluation using human raters. After making an internal call for participation that included a task description and the amount of compensation, we selected participants based on their timely response to our call. The chosen raters were compensated fairly.

Modeling Stereotypes Stereotypes are fundamentally cognitive schemas that help the perceiver process the dynamics of different groups. They are made up of a collection of traits that are ascribed to a given social group (Dovidio et al., 2010). If made conscious, they can aid in improving cultural sensitivity (Buchtel, 2014). However, in most cases, these are unconscious beliefs and can then lead to bias and discrimination (Hoffman and Hurst, 1990). Human-written content reflects these cognitive biases, and when natural language processing (NLP) models are trained on this biased data, they can further propagate stereotypes and discrimination (Hovy and Spruit, 2016). Mitigating bias in NLP has thus become a major research direction. These works often require structured knowledge or lists about biased terms, e.g., Bolukbasi et al. (2016) rely on a list of male-female minimal pairs. Our work's contribution is to automatize this process by exploiting social media users' beliefs about social groups, i.e., we collect assertions and questions about social groups which appear often in both Reddit and Twitter data. In this sense, our approach can be described as a similar process that occurs in humans as they become aware of their own mental processes, including stereotypes (Buchtel, 2014). If we are aware of stereotypes, we can use them to improve cultural sensitivity and mitigate the effects of bias and discrimination.

StereoKG could be used to generate stereotypical content (e.g., through verbalization). While verbalized stereotypes can improve the downstream task performance on knowledge crucial samples (Section 5), they could, however, also be **misused** in a hurtful manner, e.g., by using stereotypical knowledge in question-answering systems. However, this is a general issue pertaining to language models which we are trying to mitigate through our work: if trained on bias(ed) data, they could be misused to generate harmful content.

Environmental Impact Our models are trained on Titan X GPUs with 12GB RAM. In order to economize the energy use, we did not perform any extensive hyperparameter exploration.

Entity	Subject-specific	Generic
Atheist	*r/TrueAtheism, r/religion, r/DebateReligion, r/atheism*	*r/explainlikeimfive, r/AskReddit, r/TooAfraidToAsk, r/NoStupidQuestions*
Christian	*r/religion, r/DebateReligion, r/TrueChristian, r/DebateAChristian, r/AskAChristian, r/atheism, r/Christianity, r/Christian, r/Christianmarriage, r/Bible*	*r/AskReddit, r/NoStupidQuestions, r/explainlikeimfive*
Hindu	*r/India, r/hindusim, r/librandu, r/IndiaSpeaks, r/awakened, r/IAmA, r/atheismindia, r/india, r/AskHistorians*	*r/explainlikeimfive, r/AskReddit, r/TooAfraidToAsk, r/NoStupidQuestions*
Jewish	*r/Judaism, r/AskHistorians, r/religion, r/DebateReligion, r/AskSocialScience*	*r/explainlikeimfive, r/AskReddit, r/TooAfraidToAsk, r/NoStupidQuestions, r/Discussion*
Muslim	*r/religion, r/DebateReligion, r/TraditionalMuslims, r/progressive_islam, r/atheism, r/islam, r/exmuslim, r/Hijabis, r/indianmuslims, r/AskSocialScience*	*r/AskReddit, r/NoStupidQuestions, r/explainlikeimfive, r/ask*
American	*r/AskAnAmerican*	*r/explainlikeimfive, r/OutOfTheLoop, r/TooAfraidToAsk, r/offmychest, r/NoStupidQuestions, r/linguistics, r/AskReddit*
Chinese	*r/shanghai, r/China, r/asianamerican, r/HongKong, r/Sino*	*r/explainlikeimfive, r/AskReddit, r/TooAfraidToAsk, r/NoStupidQuestions*
French	*r/French, r/france, r/AskAFrench, r/AskEurope*	*r/explainlikeimfive, r/AskReddit, r/NoStupidQuestions*
German	*r/germany, r/German, r/europe, r/AskGermany, r/AskAGerman*	*r/explainlikeimfive, r/AskReddit, r/offmychest, r/TooAfraidToAsk, r/NoStupidQuestions*
Indian	*r/India, r/india, r/indiadiscussion, r/IndianFood, r/indianpeoplefacebook, r/ABCDesis*	*r/explainlikeimfive, r/retailhell,r/AskReddit, r/TooAfraidToAsk, r/NoStupidQuestions*

Table 7: Section 3 - Subreddits for Reddit extraction

B List of Subreddits

We gather data from several subject-specific and generic subreddits as listed in Table 7.

C Triple Verbalization

The triple verbalization technique takes inspiration from KELM (Agarwal et al., 2021). We use the WebNLG 2020 (Colin et al., 2016) corpus to fine-tune a T5-base[16] model for 5 epochs and then apply it to triples in StereoKG. It results in a corpus of verbalized triples in sentence form:

> *<jewish men, get, circumcisions>* → *"Jewish men get circumcisions."*
> *<american culture, obsessed with, novelty>* → *"The American culture is obsessed with novelty."*

These sentences constitute the structured knowledge (SK) and are used for intermediate MLM pre-training of the baseline models.

[16] https://huggingface.co/t5-base

The subtle language of exclusion: Identifying the Toxic Speech of Trans-exclusionary Radical Feminists

Christina Lu
Dartmouth College*
christinalu@deepmind.com

David Jurgens
University of Michigan
jurgens@umich.edu

Abstract

Toxic language can take many forms, from explicit hate speech to more subtle microaggressions. Within this space, models identifying transphobic language have largely focused on overt forms. However, a more pernicious and subtle source of transphobic comments comes in the form of statements made by Trans-exclusionary Radical Feminists (TERFs); these statements often appear seemingly-positive and promote women's causes and issues, while simultaneously denying the inclusion of transgender women as women. Here, we introduce two models to mitigate this antisocial behavior. The first model identifies TERF users in social media, recognizing that these users are a main source of transphobic material that enters mainstream discussion and whom other users may not desire to engage with in good faith. The second model tackles the harder task of recognizing the masked rhetoric of TERF messages and introduces a new dataset to support this task. Finally, we discuss the ethics of deploying these models to mitigate the harm of this language, arguing for a balanced approach that allows for restorative interactions.

1 Introduction

Transgender individuals are frequent targets of toxic language in online spaces (Craig et al., 2020; Haimson et al., 2020). Multiple approaches to recognizing such abusive language have focused on identifying explicit forms of abuse, such as using trans-specific slurs (Waseem et al., 2017; Schmidt and Wiegand, 2017; Fortuna and Nunes, 2018). However, not all verbal abuse directed towards the transgender community is so explicit. Within those transphobic groups, trans-exclusionary radical feminists (TERFs) are a community who is critical of the notion of gender, and position the existence of trans women as antithetical to "womanhood."[1]

I find it increasingly harder to believe that the people saying this nonsense actually believe it. A man is a woman because he wears some lipstick and says he's a woman, but a woman isn't a woman because of biology??
Some would say that LGB have already been "thrown under the bus" to accommodate an ideology that relies heavily upon gender stereotypes and "being in the wrong body." I hear there're a lot of lesbians who feel like this.
Guarantee they'll expect more rigorous research to debate the ethics of fancy shoes than they did for men in women's sports

Figure 1: Examples of harmful rhetoric by TERFs which reference notions of biological essentialism in defining gender and exclusion of transgender women from sports. While offensive, we include the examples here to highlight the subtlety in their exclusionary messages. Throughout the paper, all messages are lightly paraphrased for privacy.

As such, the language of their attacks is frequently couched in arguments promoting women's safety and rights—nominally positive language. TERF groups maintain an active presence across public social media and are often a source of transphobia online (Pearce et al., 2020). However, their masked rhetoric is unrecognized by current models for hate speech detection, and indeed, identifying TERFs in general can be difficult if one is not familiar with their lines of argumentation, as seen in the examples in Figure 1. Interacting with individuals propagating these beliefs can be materially harmful and as a result, multiple transgender communities and allies have established lists of known TERF accounts to help individuals block or avoid abuse. However, the recruitment of new individuals with TERF beliefs as well as sockpuppet accounts make

* Work performed in part at the University of Michigan

[1] We acknowledge that the use of the term TERF is potentially contentious, as some individuals who identify these views consider it derogatory. Nonetheless, our use follows current academic practice in naming (e.g., Williams, 2020).

Proceedings of the Sixth Workshop on Online Abuse and Harms (WOAH), pages 79 - 91
July 14, 2022

manually keeping these lists up-to-date a challenge for mitigating their impact. In this paper, we widen the scope of abusive detection online by demonstrating a model for detecting both TERFs and nuanced TERF rhetoric on Twitter by analyzing their tweets and community features.

Work in abusive language detection for social media has become more widespread (Fortuna et al., 2020; Zampieri et al., 2020), but more subtle forms of hate speech such as dog whistles are notoriously difficult to capture (Caselli et al., 2020). TERF rhetoric directly falls into this category, as it consists of a particular brand of transphobia that employs dog whistles and bad faith argumentation. Prior work has only begun to address these subtle form of offensive such as microaggressions (Breitfeller et al., 2019; Han and Tsvetkov, 2020), condescension (Wang and Potts, 2019; Perez Almendros et al., 2020), and other social biases (Sap et al., 2020). Our work identifying TERFs and their rhetoric extends this recent line of research by filling the gap into an under-researched but important area of transphobic hate speech.

We introduce the first computational method for detecting TERF accounts on Twitter, which combines information from user messages and network representations. Using community-sourced data of over 22K users, we show that social and content information can accurately identify TERF accounts, attaining a F1 of 0.93. To support identifying TERF messages directly, we introduce a new dataset of gender and trans-identity related messages annotated for TERF-specific rhetoric, showing that despite the challenging nature of the task, we can obtain 0.68 F1. Together, these methods allow individuals to recognize and screen out the uniquely transphobic rhetoric of TERFs.

This paper provides the following contributions. First, little computational attention has been paid to TERFs and transphobic speech in previous work within the realm of abusive content detection. Our model is the first to tackle the challenge of capturing nuanced, transphobic rhetoric from TERFs, and leveraging it to identify TERFs on Twitter. Second, we introduce a new dataset for recognizing TERF-specific rhetoric, allowing the community to expand current efforts at combating abusive language. Finally, acknowledging the dual use of NLP (Hovy and Spruit, 2016), we consider the ethics of deploying these technologies in the risks and benefits of censuring versus allowing engagement with TERFs, arguing for a balanced approach that facilitates restorative justice.

2 TERFs in Online Spaces

Feminist ideals aim to promote women's rights and mainstream feminism is considered inclusive of transgender women (Williams, 2016). However, a small number of individuals claiming to be feminists have taken an opposite stance, arguing for transphobic views that push for biological essentialism and criticizing the notion of gender (Williams, 2020). This group was given the name "trans-exclusionary radical feminists" or TERFs as a way of separating their views. Drawing in part upon feminist arguments in Raymond (1979), TERFs argue that gender derives fully from the biological sex, which is dependent on a person's chromosomes and thus is binary and immutable (Riddell, 2006; Serano, 2016); it follows in their biological reductivist reasoning that a transgender woman is a man. As a result, TERFs frequently make claims seeded with anxiety about the encroachment of transgender women into women's spaces and rights (e.g., participation in sports or use of restrooms), as well as the need for biological tests of gender (Earles, 2019).[2]

For many TERFs, their rationale is embedded with real but misdirected fear of violence against and subjugation of women. Regardless, such harmful rhetoric directly marginalizes and excludes transgender women (Hines, 2019; Vajjala, 2020), often invalidating their very existence. These arguments frequently follow the subtle language of microaggressions (Sue, 2010, Ch.2). TERFs themselves are also not a monolithic bloc; individuals may vary in their stances towards transgender people, from claiming to openly support them as a separate group to radically opposing them and arguing such identities themselves are flawed. While all such attitudes are harmful, this range suggests that some viewpoints could be changed.

Less prevalent in the United States and Canada, TERFs within the United Kingdom hold an unfortunately mainstream position within feminism (Lewis, 2019), with a notable proponent being J.K. Rowling (Kelleher, 2020), author of the Harry Potter series. TERFs are present on multiple platforms; TERFs maintained an active community of over

[2]We note that recent proponents of this ideology have adopted the name "gender critical" but espouse the same offensive beliefs of biological essentialism (Tadvick, 2018).

64K users on the r/gendercritical subreddit, until June of 2020, after which it was banned by Reddit for the promotion of hate speech.

The presence of TERFs in online communities represents a significant risk to transgender individuals, as they perpetuate targeted harassment and doxxing. Online spaces are particularly critical for transgender individuals due to their role in facilitating the transition experience (Fink and Miller, 2014) and seeking social support during the coming out process (Haimson and Veinot, 2020; Pinter et al., 2021). As some individuals may not have publicly come out to family and coworkers (but do so online, potentially anonymously), targeted harassment poses risks for some individuals (Kade, 2021). Potential interactions between TERFs and transgender individuals can further marginalize individuals and reduce the perceived support.

3 A Dataset for Recognizing TERFs

As frequent targets of abusive language, transgender individuals and their allies have curated lists of known TERF users on Twitter in attempts to mitigate the harm they cause. These user lists form the basis for our dataset, described next.

3.1 User Lists

Our ultimate goal is to identify TERF users and their rhetoric. Prior work has shown that user-created lists on Twitter are reliable signals of identity that can be used for classification tasks (Kim et al., 2010; Faralli et al., 2015). Accordingly, we collect curated lists from two communities, along with a random sample of users as a control set.

First, TERFblocklist is a manually-curated list of TERF accounts by trans women and activists. The block list uses a third-party Twitter API web app, Block Together,[3] which enables users to screen out content and interaction from users on shareable, custom block lists. Potential additions to this list are sent to the maintainer who verifies the accusations of transphobia before they are added. Through manual submissions, users identified 13,399 TERF accounts, which forms the basis for our list of Twitter users who are TERFs.[4]

[3]As of June 2020, Block Together shut down but other alternatives such as Block Party and Moderate have the same functionality.

[4]We recognize that block lists are themselves products of exclusion that can potentially include users who do not have a particular view or identity. However, we still use such lists here, as they have been curated by members of the trans community we trust their judgments in who poses risks.

Category	No. users	No. tweets	Description
TERF	8,631	13,508,673	TERFs
Trans-friendly	14,827	1,291,908†	Explicitly trans-friendly
Control	11,510	33,573,308	Random English speakers

Table 1: Summary of the sizes of the datasets used in these studies, reflecting only English-language tweets per category. †Only up to 100 recent tweets were collected for each user in the Trans-friendly category.

Second, as a direct response to TERFblocklist, TERF users created a separate block list of their own on Block Together, which contained 17,091 "transactivists and transcultists," as a way of identifying users whom they could actively target or selectively ignore. While initially designed for unethical reasons (targeting users), this data forms the basis for our list of trans-friendly users. Because both TERF and trans-friendly users share high-level themes in their discussion around transgender issues, having representation of both groups is essential for ensuring that trans-friendly accounts are not being mistakenly labeled as TERFs.

Third, as not all users discuss transgender issues, we randomly sample 13,152 "control" English-speaking users from the Twitter decahose in May 2020 and retain all users who are not on either of the two blocklists. As some users had private Twitter accounts, the final number of users in our corpus is a subset of these original lists.

3.2 Linguistic and Social Data

For each user, we collect two types of data that we hypothesize will capture whether they are a TERF or not: tweet text and the user's friends (i.e., the Twitter users they follow). While the text of a tweet carries the most information about the stance of the user, the people they follow are also strong signals for both the community they are a member of and what content they willingly engage with. This task is particularly context-sensitive due to the dog whistles employed by TERFs, and necessitates both types of data.

Through Tweepy and the Twitter API, we collect all recent (2019 onward) tweets from each user in the TERF (13,508,673 tweets), trans-friendly (1,291,908 tweets), and control (33,573,308 tweets) groups and discard non-English tweets using the language classifier of Blodgett et al. (2016) for labeling social media English. Due to API limitations when retrieving tweets, we keep only up-to-100 recent tweets for each user in the Trans-friendly category to maximize the diversity in that sample, without overrepresenting any one user. We also collect the list of user IDs belonging to each user's friends using the Twitter API. At the time of collection, some users had taken their accounts private, which prevented collecting all data. Table 1 shows the statistics for our final dataset.

4 Building a TERF classifier

To recognize TERF users, we use a multi-stage approach that combines information from individual messages on topics discussed by TERFs with social features representing who they follow. Following, we describe the three stages: how we (1) recognize topics closely related to TERF rhetoric, (2) identify individual messages likely to come from TERFs, and (3) combine textual and social features to detect TERF users themselves.

4.1 Identifying TERF Topics

Despite espousing harmful rhetoric, individuals with TERF beliefs routinely engage in conversations about commonplace topics. As a result, training any TERF-specific classifier is likely to mistakenly pick up on idiosyncratic content not related to TERF rhetoric. Therefore, in the first stage, we build a topic model to identify content themes that are related to TERF rhetoric and focus our later analysis primarily on this content.

To identify potentially TERF content, we fit a STTM topic model (Qiang et al., 2019), which suits the brevity of character-limited tweets. Prior to fitting the model, tweets are preprocessed to remove links and tokens under three characters and to filter out tokens appearing in fewer than 10 tweets or more than half of all, as these words are either unlikely to be content words related to our target construct or too rare to aid in topic inference. All remaining tweets with four or more tokens are used to fit the topic model. The number of topics is determined using topical coherence and we vary the number from 5 to 80 in 5-topic increments. Coherence was maximized at 15 topics; following best practice from Hoyle et al. (2021), a separate human evaluation was also done by the authors who also found 15 topics resulted in the most-coherent, least-redundant themes. As a robustness test, this procedure was replicated three times in each configuration to manually ensure that topical themes

Topic	Top words
0	people like police country know trump illegal think right state want border time iran years world government going need america
2	labour brexit vote party people like think corbyn deal leave want know voted election time tory right boris tories remain
5	jesus like love people church life christ know lord good world time think catholic bible christian great right said family
8	like movie good think time people love know watch great character best star film thing going better movies shit story
9	**women trans people male female gender woman rights like think males know right want girls spaces need biological lesbians females**
14	twitter people like tweet know read think account news time media video tweets good said youtube right women article going

Figure 2: The most probable words for a sample of topics learned from TERF tweets. Topic 9 (bolded) reflects the content most likely to pertain to transgender issues and contain transphobic messages.

were roughly consistent across runs.

All runs demonstrated a manually-identified topic that contained content about trans women, gender, and other common transphobic TERF talking points. The most-probable words for a sample of topics are shown in Figure 2, where Topic 9 was identified by experts as most related to TERF-related rhetoric. Across all content, approximately 7.4% of tweets from TERFs are from this topic, compared to 4.3% for transgender individuals and 0.2% for individuals from the randomly-sampled control group. The use of this topic by non-TERF users underscores that the topic itself is broad and not necessarily solely TERF rhetoric, but rather a more general topic that includes material related to gender and trans issues (both appropriate and abusive). We refer to this topic as the *trans topic* in later sections. Finally, we note that the topic models consistently identified topics relating to British-specific content (e.g., Brexit), shown in Topic 2 in Figure 2, underscoring the association of TERFs with the UK (Hines, 2019; Lewis, 2019).

4.2 Classifying TERF-signaling Tweets

Using the topic model, the subsequently-identified trans topic act as an initial feature for helping distinguish TERF users. To identify whether messages with this topic are offensive, we fine-tune a language model to identify trans topic tweets from TERF users, using the topic as a weak label on whether the content is offensive—i.e., that content from TERF users in this topic is likely to be offensive, while content from others would not be. We train a BERT model (Devlin et al., 2019) to recognize whether a tweet with this topic came from a known-TERF user versus a user in our control set, which includes transgender individuals, their allies, and a sample of English-speaking users. Because of the heuristic labeling of data, this classifier's decisions are intended to act as features for the downstream task of recognizing users, rather than being designed for recognizing TERF rhetoric (which is addressed later in §5).

Tweets were selected for the training set as follows. To avoid potential confounds from multiple tweets from a single user, we partition users 90:10 into training and test sets.[5] We added all TERF-topic tweets across the three groups of training users into the training set, so the model could learn to distinguish when TERF-topic tweets came specifically from TERFs. We also supplemented the corpus with a sample of other tweets from non-TERFs, in order to make the model more robust against unrelated tweets. In total, this yielded 491,998 TERF-topic tweets from TERFs and 275,189 and 315,202 mixed topic tweets from the transgender and control user sets, respectively, which reflect inoffensive content in this topic. The BERT model is fine-tuned for four epochs using AdamW (η=2e-5, ϵ=1e-8) on a batch size of 32.

Results The classifier ultimately had high performance on the test set, attaining an F1 of 0.98 on identifying control tweets from non-TERFs and an F1 of 0.96 on recognizing that a TERF-topic tweet came from a TERF.[6] Such tweets were labeled as TERF 92% of the time, while signal tweets from non-TERFs (which are supposed to be the most difficult to distinguish) were labeled as TERF approximately 45% of the time. This result points to strong linguistic differences in the language of the two groups and that the BERT classifier can potentially be useful for distinguishing the two user types. However, the high false-positive rate for signal tweets from non-TERFs (i.e., those not espousing such rhetoric) underscores the risks in using single-tweet classifications alone to label a user as a TERF; great care is needed to reduce the rate of false positives at the user label. We refer to this classifier as the TERF-*signal* classifier in later analyses.

4.3 Identifying TERF users

In the final phase, we aim to identify TERF users themselves through their linguistic and social features. While linguistic features such as those of our BERT and STTM models identify TERF-related content, extra-linguistic features of accounts can also be powerful signals of the account type (Al Zamal et al., 2012; Lynn et al., 2019) and can even help identify accounts known to engage in abusive behavior (Abozinadah and Jones Jr, 2017). In particular, the social network aspect of Twitter allows us to use particular frequently-followed accounts as features—e.g., accounts by high-profile users that promote TERF ideology. Following, we build a classifier to identify these users using linguistic and network features. Our ultimate goal is to help supplement existing TERF user lists to mitigate the users' effect on the transgender community.

Experimental Setup Information on who a person follows on Twitter is potentially informative of their world view and what information they are regularly exposed to. We encode a user's social network as a set of binary features corresponding to whether the user follows specific accounts on Twitter. We include features for (i) each of the thousand most-followed users overall in our training data and (ii) each of the thousand most-followed accounts by users in our TERF list.

Our linguistic features combine different aspects of the STTM and BERT models, computed over the 100 most-recent tweets from each user. Six features are used: (1, 2) the mean posterior probability of a tweet being from the trans topic and the max across all tweets, (3) the percentage of tweets that are from the transgender topic, (4) the mean probability of a transgender-topic tweet being a signal tweet, (5) the mean probability of a tweet in any other topic tweet being a signal tweet, and (6) the maximum probability of any tweet being a signal tweet.

A logistic regression model is trained on these network and linguistic features using the same train and test partitions in previous experiments to avoid data leakage. To test the contribution of each feature type, we evaluate ablation models that reflect using (i) only features from the STTM topic model, (ii) only features from the signal classifier, (iii) all the text-based features from the STTM and signal

[5] No hyperparameter optimization was performed, so no development set was used.

[6] Throughout the paper, we use Binary F1 with the TERF-related category as the positive class.

Model	AUC	Prec.	Rec.	F1
Random	0.50	0.18	0.53	0.27
LR Baseline	0.92	0.64	0.68	0.66
Topic Feats.	0.70	0.55	0.29	0.38
BERT Feats.	0.89	0.89	0.68	0.77
Topic & BERT Feats.	0.91	0.94	0.78	0.85
Network Feats.	0.95	0.92	0.80	0.86
All Features	**0.98**	**0.96**	**0.90**	**0.93**

Table 2: Performance at recognizing TERF accounts from different feature types. The Logistic Regression (LR) baseline was trained solely on unigram and bigram features of the text; The All Features model does not include the baseline's lexical features, only those of the non-baseline models.

models, and (iv) only the network features (no text-related features). Finally, as a test for whether this high-level aggregation is needed to improve performance, we include a Logistic Regression baseline trained on unigrams and bigrams from the concatenated messages of a user.[7] Models are compared with a random baseline.

Results The combined model was highly accurate at identifying TERF accounts, attaining an F1 of 0.93 as shown in Table 2. Models trained on individual feature categories outperformed the random baseline, indicating they each contained meaningful signals. Only the signal features and network features were able to outperform the Logistic Regression text-based baseline ($p<0.01$ using McNemar's test). However, the transgender topic features still capture complementary information as the signal features, where combining them still improves performance ($p<0.01$) over models trained on each feature individually.

The social network features and combined-linguistic features provided similar performance, with network features outperforming slightly ($p=0.04$). This network result suggests that many TERF users actively engage in strategic social networking to the point that the users they follow are reliable indicators of their underlying attitudes on transgender issues. This high performance of network features mirrors similar types of inferences for social attitudes like political affiliation (Barberá et al., 2015) and topical stance (Lynn et al., 2019).

Ultimately, the combination of all features was essential for high performance and significantly improved ($p<0.01$) over any individual feature type. Performance gains over both feature types came from increased Recall, which indicates that not all TERF users engage in following prominent TERF accounts or frequently share TERF rhetoric.

The act of classifying users as TERFs potentially carries a risk of harm. While the model's performance is notably high, misclassifications can potentially disenfranchise users who are mistakenly labeled as TERFs—e.g., labeling an individual from the transgender community as a TERF themself—or lead to ostracizing. The best model's performance indicates that most errors are of omission, not labeling a TERF as such, which we view as the appropriate type of error to avoid the risk of harm.[8] While the model is highly accurate, we explicitly call for avoiding its use in fully automated settings, e.g., automatically banning or censuring users; instead, this classification tool is only meant to help humans identify accounts among the huge search space and then manually review such accounts.

Compared to users in the random sample portion of our dataset, both TERFs and transgender individuals likely have overlap in their topical content. As a result, errors that are introduced through the topic model and signal tweets could potentially bias the model so that most false positive errors are made for transgender users. However, examining the false positive error rates shows that between these groups, individuals from the random sample are more likely to be labeled as TERFs (1.9%) versus those in the trans-friendly group (1.3%), suggesting the features are not biased due to shared topicality.

5 Recognizing TERF Rhetoric

When making transphobic statements, TERFs employ regular arguments that delegitimize the status and inclusion of transgender women in the definition of woman. While recent work has aimed to identify explicit slurs used against transgender individuals (Kurrek et al., 2020), the TERF rhetoric is more subtle. However, the high performance of our signal classifier (§4.2) indicates TERF users can be accurately identified when discussing transgender topics. Now, we test whether we can explicitly recognize which statements contain harmful TERF rhetoric. We first create a topically-focused dataset of transgender-related content and label messages

[7] Minimum ngram frequency was set to 50, with limited hyperparameter tuning on the development set showing lower performance for including higher-order ngrams or when using a lower (25) or higher (100) minimum frequency threshold.

[8] We also note that because these labels are derived through public lists, we speculate that some noise may exist due to misunderstanding or even users changing beliefs over time.

by whether they contain a TERF rhetoric, and then use this corpus to train classifiers.

Data and Annotation Data was sampled from the transgender topic (§4.1) from a balanced number of TERF-identified, transgender, and control users. Content labeled with the topic represents an ideal dataset for recognizing TERF language, as it focuses primarily on trans and gender-related discussion (not necessarily TERF-related) and likely contains both TERF arguments and rebuttals to TERF arguments.

The two authors first reviewed hundreds of messages as an open coding exercise to identify salient themes used in TERF arguments. Salient categories included (a) bad-faith arguments, (b) concerns about transgender women competing in women's sports, (c) and biological essentialist exclusion of transgender women; these three themes were sufficient to cover all TERF arguments seen in the reviewed data. Following the construction of the categories, the authors completed two rounds of training annotation where each independently labeled 50 tweets and then discussed all labels. Comments were labeled as either (i) not TERF-related or (ii) having any of the three different categories of TERF rhetoric.

Annotators completed 580 items and attained a Krippendorff's α of 0.53, reflecting moderate agreement. Disagreements often stemmed from the difficulty of interpreting the intention of the message. For example, the tweet "Gender is a form of oppression, which only serves the patriarchy" could be viewed through the lens of TERF rhetoric that defines gender fully as a biological construct; alternatively, such a message could be promoting gender fluidity and the rejection of hegemonic norms of gender, which is not a TERF argument. Other disagreements were due to ambiguity around sarcasm or whether the perceived attack on women was related to transgender issues. Disagreements were adjudicated and ultimately 34.4% of the instances were labeled as transphobic arguments in the final dataset.

Experimental Setup Our task mirrors analogous work on stance detection, which aims to identify a user's latent beliefs towards some entity, which may or may not be present in the message. Recent work has shown that pretrained language models are state of the art for stance detection (Samih and Darwish, 2021), so we test one such model here.

Model	AUC	Prec.	Rec.	F1
Random	0.50	0.23	0.54	0.32
Perspective API	0.52	0.45	0.43	0.44
Logistic Regression	0.63	0.17	0.08	0.11
RoBERTa	**0.76**	**0.67**	**0.70**	**0.68**

Table 3: Performance on recognizing TERF rhetoric.

Data was split into train, development, and test sets using an 80:10:10 percent random partitioning. We test two models: a RoBERTa model (Liu et al., 2019) initialized with the `roberta-base` parameters and a Logistic Regression model. The RoBERTa model was fine-tuned using AdamW with ϵ=1e-8 and η=4e-5 and a batch size of 32; the model was fine-tuned over 10 epochs, selecting the epoch that performed highest on the development data (#6). The logistic regression model used unigram and bigrams with no minimum token frequency due to the dataset size. We compare these against a uniform random baseline and a competitive baseline of a commercial model for recognizing toxic language, Perspective API using 0.5 as a cut-off for determining toxicity.

Results The RoBERTa model was effective at recognizing the rhetoric of tweets, attaining an F1 of 0.68 (Table 3), which is slightly above inter-annotator agreement. This performance suggests that the model is near the upper bound for performance in the current data (due to IAA) and that TERF rhetoric can be easily recognized by deep neural models. In contrast, the simple lexical baseline performed poorly and, surprisingly, below chance. When viewed in contrast to a similar baseline for recognizing TERF users in §4.3, this low performance suggests that simple lexical features alone are insufficient for recognizing TERF rhetoric specifically due to their nuance, even if they may be useful for identifying TERF users themselves or identifying other kinds of more explicit hate speech (e.g., Waseem and Hovy, 2016). The competitive baseline of Perspective API was not able to recognize the subtle offensive language of TERF rhetoric, though it does surpass chance; as Perspective API is widely deployed, this result suggests TERF rhetoric is unlikely to be flagged for review.

The RoBERTa model was robust to hard cases such as paraphrased TERF arguments by non-TERF as a rebuttal to strong rhetoric, which included the language of the rhetoric itself. Examining the error shows that the model struggled with cases where

Label	Pred.	Tweet
TERF	NOT	Definitive signs of an unbearable human: using queer as an umbrella category. That's it.
TERF	NOT	The ease with which women's rights can be sidelined by the government underscores the vulnerability of those rights: we can't take anything for granted
NOT	TERF	Talking about gender "incongruence" as well as dysphoria is never limited to the body of the trans-identified person. They describe misery within their gender roles. Men are tired of demands for invulnerability while women want to be looked in the eye and spoken to like adults.
NOT	TERF	How do you know for sure Yaniv isn't trans? How does anyone tell whether someone is a "genuine" trans identifying male and a predator?

Table 4: Examples of misclassifications by the model for recognizing TERF rhetoric show false negatives from subtle arguments (top two) and false positives likely-innocuous questions (bottom two).

the interpretation of the message could be ambiguous. Table 4 shows a sample of four misclassifications; the first two false negatives highlight subtle arguments that the model misses, while the last two suggest the model is overweighting arguments that could appear to be made in bad faith. Overall, the moderately-high performance suggests that TERF rhetoric can be recognized but represents a challenging NLP task if deployed solely in a manner designed to censure such content.

6 Values and Design Considerations

The computational tools developed in this paper in §4 and §5 facilitate the detection of TERFs and their rhetoric. To what end should these tools be used? The majority of antisocial or toxic language detectors are used punitively for censure or removal—uses of toxic speech are removed from public visibility and the transgressing individuals are potentially subject to temporary suspensions or even account removals. Given that at their core, many TERFs are feminists who are primarily concerned with women's rights and safety (albeit mistakenly latching onto a biological essentialist definition of "women"), we view the application and deployment of our tools as an ideal ethical case study for alternatives to the traditional punitive uses of abusive language detection. As NLP moves from focusing on the language of bad actors to examining nuanced discourse in a gray area, we must rethink how our methods are deployed and what the ultimate goals of such tools are: reconciliation and rehabilitation, or potential radicalization through alienation.

Due to the political nature of a TERF detector, it is worth critically examining such work through contemporary lenses of "cancel culture" (Bouvier, 2020) and restorative justice (Braithwaite, 2002). This work intends to provide a useful tool allowing marginalized people in the trans community to curate their online experiences and avoid doxxing and harassment at the hands of TERFs. However, examining its impact could raise concerns of censorship or evoke the echo chambers of algorithmically-constructed Facebook feeds—which we explicitly acknowledge and seek to avoid.

"Cancel culture" is a contemporary form of ostracism that straddles online and real-world spheres and often leads to material loss for the "cancelled" (Bouvier, 2020). The phenomenon is largely punitive and, combined with other forms of online censorship such as deplatforming, generates further polarization; it pushes people away to be radicalized in remote spaces. Online moderation tools have typically relied on these types of actions to remove content (Srinivasan et al., 2019). While community-level bans have been effective at reducing harm without creating spill-over into other communities (Chandrasekharan et al., 2017), such actions still run the risk of removing the possibility of further engagement that leads to a change in underlying views. Thus, we do not label people as TERFs in order to silence or "cancel" them. Rather, we consider it a tool to better engage, understand, and ultimately find a path to reconciliation.

We reiterate that the methods outlined in this paper should *not* supersede human judgment, but rather be used in tandem to best inform the user. It is worth being cautious of the fact that people take AI models to be objective arbiters when in reality, they can and do embed bias in many facets (e.g., Sap et al., 2019; Ghosh et al., 2021). Such a system should not be viewed as the end-all-be-all in decision-making.

The ideal use-case of TERF detection should be grounded within a framework of restorative justice (Schoenebeck and Blackwell, 2021); instead of punitive retribution, we seek rehabilitation through mutual engagement, dialogue, and consensus. Users should be able to decide how to engage upon encountering a TERF guided by an assessment of TERFs stance (e.g., transphobic severity) and whether they are equipped and able to put in the labor of understanding and addressing their fears.

As potential next steps for deploying our models in a manner to minimize risk, Kwon et al. (2018) and Im et al. (2020) have proposed visual mechanisms for displaying "social signals" of other individuals on social media to create an informed decision about potential interactions; our tool could easily lend itself to such mechanisms by identifying users by their likelihood of being a TERF and also, if the user is willing, to show content our model has identified as being TERF rhetoric to assess their stance. While promoting interactions between the transgender community and TERFs poses risks, we retain some optimism for establishing shared common ground to facilitate dialogue. Indeed, as our topic model showed, the bulk of TERF users' message is *not* about transgender issues and much of this content overlaps with that written by transgender women; for those willing to engage, new NLP methods could be used to (i) identify particular non-confrontational topics to foster an initial dialogue, (ii) suggest potential counterspeech, building upon recent work on counterspeech for hate speech (Garland et al., 2020; Mathew et al., 2019; Chung et al., 2019; He et al., 2021), and (iii) analyze their statements to identify those TERFs whose stances signal they could be open to change (Mensah et al., 2019).

7 Conclusion

Online communities serve essential roles as places of support and information. For transgender individuals, these spaces are especially critical as they provide access to accepting and supportive communities, which may not be available locally. However, the public forums of social media can also harbor less than welcoming users. Trans-exclusionary radical feminists (TERFs) promote a harmful rhetoric that rejects transgender women as women, pushes an agenda that reduces gender to biology, and seeks to invalidate transgender women in policy and practice. As a result, transgender individuals and their allies have adopted technological solutions to limit interactions with TERFs by manually curating block lists, which require frequent updating and currently rely only on self-reporting to recognize those users who pose harm.

This paper introduces new datasets and models for supporting the trans community through automatically identifying TERF users and their rhetoric. We present a new multi-stage model that identifies salient themes in TERF users' content and show that these signals, when combined with social network features, result in a highly accurate classifier (0.93 F1) that reliably identifies TERF users with minimal risk of mistakenly labeling trans-friendly users as TERFs, despite sharing similar content themes. Further, we introduce a new dataset for directly identifying the often-subtle rhetoric of TERFs and show that despite the challenging task, our model can attain moderately high performance (0.68 F1). Together, these two tools can aid the trans community in mitigating harm through preemptive identification of TERFs. All data, code, models, and annotation guidelines will be available at `https://github.com/lu-christina/terfspot`.

Acknowledgments

We thank the members of the Blablablab for their helpful thoughts and comments as well as the WOAH reviewers for their thoughtful critiques—with a special shout out to R3 for an exceptionally helpful and detailed review. Finally, we also thank the work of the trans women and activists who have curated the initial TERFblocklist and their work in helping keep the community safe.

8 Ethics

Data Privacy Our data includes lists of Twitter users who belong to marginalized categories, notably transgender individuals. This data is obtained from entirely public sources of Twitter lists and is not directly maintained by the research team. While we are not able to minimize the privacy implications of this public data, the research team took additional steps to maintain the privacy of the data on our servers. Further, this data will only be shared further to researchers who agree to ensure future privacy and use the data in ethical ways.

Using TERF as a term The TERF acronym has been considered by some to be a derogatory term directed at a group of people and some have called for the term not to be used (e.g., Flaherty, 2018). While recognizing these views, we opt to follow common scholarly practice and use the term. However, we took additional precautions when writing to ensure that the framing of such users was from a neutral point of view.

Do we *need* to predict TERF users? Labeling a user as a TERF is a potentially risky act. Misclassifications could lead to being socially ostracised by peers and increased mistrust. However, this risk is offset, in part, by the risk of *not* developing such technology. Transgender individuals actively and manually identify TERF users to minimize their interactions with such toxic content. However this identification is labor intensive and (i) exposes users to TERF content, increasing harm and (ii) is likely to miss some users due to the scale of finding TERF users on social media. As a result, inaction increases the harm to transgender users. Recognizing this trade-off, we have performed additional analyses to minimize the risk of false positive classifications of users as a TERF, showing that our model has a low false positive rate (§4.3).

Who should be on a block list? Our models are trained on community-curated block lists, with a goal of helping individuals identify others who might be engaged in harmful TERF rhetoric. Yet, it is worth considering whether such actions potentially perpetuate harm by minimizing discourse, increasing polarization, or even serving as a "marker of success" for antagonistic users to aim for. We explicitly do not advocate automatically including any user on a block list and, instead, as outlined in §6, argue for more nuance and consideration in how users apply this technology. We view an ideal application of our model as one that allows each person to define their own comfort level in exposure and engagement in an informed manner. Our tool can serve as a social signal to help others guide their decision but should not be taken as ground truth for blocking anyone.

Dual-use Risks Many NLP methods, including those presented here, have dual-use for good and bad purposes. Our models could be used to deployed to identify and "cancel" TERF users, cutting them off from the larger social media community. Further, TERF users could use our models adversarially to test how their own accounts are classified and systematically change their behavior to avoid future detection. Yet, in our setting, the technology offers substantial benefits for a marginalized group, transgender individuals, who have been overlooked by NLP methods for identifying transgender-targeted content. Our models augment their ability to identify TERF users and use this knowledge as they see fit. Given the harm faced by transgender individuals, we view the benefits as substantially outweighing risks.

References

Ehab A Abozinadah and James H Jones Jr. 2017. A statistical learning approach to detect abusive twitter accounts. In *Proceedings of the International Conference on Compute and Data Analysis*, pages 6–13.

Faiyaz Al Zamal, Wendy Liu, and Derek Ruths. 2012. Homophily and latent attribute inference: Inferring latent attributes of Twitter users from neighbors. In *Proceedings of the International Conference on Web and Social Media (ICWSM)*.

Pablo Barberá, John T. Jost, Jonathan Nagler, Joshua A. Tucker, and Richard Bonneau. 2015. Tweeting From Left to Right: Is Online Political Communication More Than an Echo Chamber? *Psychological Science*, 26(10):1531–1542.

Su Lin Blodgett, Lisa Green, and Brendan O'Connor. 2016. Demographic dialectal variation in social media: A case study of African-American English. In *Proceedings of the 2016 Conference on Empirical Methods in Natural Language Processing*, pages 1119–1130, Austin, Texas. Association for Computational Linguistics.

Gwen Bouvier. 2020. Racist call-outs and cancel culture on twitter: The limitations of the platform's ability to define issues of social justice. *Discourse, Context & Media*, 38:100431.

John Braithwaite. 2002. *Restorative justice & responsive regulation*. Oxford University press on demand.

Luke Breitfeller, Emily Ahn, David Jurgens, and Yulia Tsvetkov. 2019. Finding microaggressions in the wild: A case for locating elusive phenomena in social media posts. In *Proceedings of the 2019 Conference on Empirical Methods in Natural Language Processing and the 9th International Joint Conference on Natural Language Processing (EMNLP-IJCNLP)*, pages 1664–1674, Hong Kong, China. Association for Computational Linguistics.

Tommaso Caselli, Valerio Basile, Jelena Mitrović, Inga Kartoziya, and Michael Granitzer. 2020. I feel offended, don't be abusive! implicit/explicit messages in offensive and abusive language. In *Proceedings of the 12th Language Resources and Evaluation Conference*, pages 6193–6202, Marseille, France. European Language Resources Association.

Eshwar Chandrasekharan, Umashanthi Pavalanathan, Anirudh Srinivasan, Adam Glynn, Jacob Eisenstein, and Eric Gilbert. 2017. You can't stay here: The efficacy of reddit's 2015 ban examined through hate speech. *Proceedings of the ACM on Human-Computer Interaction*, 1(CSCW):1–22.

Yi-Ling Chung, Elizaveta Kuzmenko, Serra Sinem Tekiroglu, and Marco Guerini. 2019. CONAN - COunter NArratives through nichesourcing: a multilingual dataset of responses to fight online hate speech. In *Proceedings of the 57th Annual Meeting of the Association for Computational Linguistics*, pages 2819–2829, Florence, Italy. Association for Computational Linguistics.

Shelley L Craig, Andrew D Eaton, Lauren B McInroy, Sandra A D'Souza, Sreedevi Krishnan, Gordon A Wells, Lloyd Twum-Siaw, and Vivian WY Leung. 2020. Navigating negativity: a grounded theory and integrative mixed methods investigation of how sexual and gender minority youth cope with negative comments online. *Psychology & Sexuality*, 11(3):161–179.

Jacob Devlin, Ming-Wei Chang, Kenton Lee, and Kristina Toutanova. 2019. BERT: Pre-training of deep bidirectional transformers for language understanding. In *Proceedings of the 2019 Conference of the North American Chapter of the Association for Computational Linguistics: Human Language Technologies, Volume 1 (Long and Short Papers)*, pages 4171–4186, Minneapolis, Minnesota. Association for Computational Linguistics.

Jennifer Earles. 2019. The "penis police": Lesbian and feminist spaces, trans women, and the maintenance of the sex/gender/sexuality system. *Journal of lesbian studies*, 23(2):243–256.

Stefano Faralli, Giovanni Stilo, and Paola Velardi. 2015. Large scale homophily analysis in twitter using a twixonomy. In *Proceedings of the Twenty-Fourth International Joint Conference on Artificial Intelligence, IJCAI 2015, Buenos Aires, Argentina, July 25-31, 2015*, pages 2334–2340. AAAI Press.

Marty Fink and Quinn Miller. 2014. Trans media moments: Tumblr, 2011–2013. *Television & New Media*, 15(7):611–626.

Colleen Flaherty. 2018. "TERF" War. *Inside Higher Ed*.

Paula Fortuna and Sérgio Nunes. 2018. A survey on automatic detection of hate speech in text. *ACM Computing Surveys (CSUR)*, 51(4):85.

Paula Fortuna, Juan Soler, and Leo Wanner. 2020. Toxic, hateful, offensive or abusive? what are we really classifying? an empirical analysis of hate speech datasets. In *Proceedings of the 12th Language Resources and Evaluation Conference*, pages 6786–6794, Marseille, France. European Language Resources Association.

Joshua Garland, Keyan Ghazi-Zahedi, Jean-Gabriel Young, Laurent Hébert-Dufresne, and Mirta Galesic. 2020. Countering hate on social media: Large scale classification of hate and counter speech. In *Proceedings of the Fourth Workshop on Online Abuse and Harms*, pages 102–112, Online. Association for Computational Linguistics.

Sayan Ghosh, Dylan Baker, David Jurgens, and Vinodkumar Prabhakaran. 2021. Detecting cross-geographic biases in toxicity modeling on social media. In *Proceedings of the Seventh Workshop on Noisy User-generated Text (W-NUT 2021)*, pages 313–328, Online. Association for Computational Linguistics.

Oliver L Haimson, Justin Buss, Zu Weinger, Denny L Starks, Dykee Gorrell, and Briar Sweetbriar Baron. 2020. Trans time: Safety, privacy, and content warnings on a transgender-specific social media site. *Proceedings of the ACM on Human-Computer Interaction*, 4(CSCW2):1–27.

Oliver L Haimson and Tiffany C Veinot. 2020. Coming out to doctors, coming out to "everyone": Understanding the average sequence of transgender identity disclosures using social media data. *Transgender health*, 5(3):158–165.

Xiaochuang Han and Yulia Tsvetkov. 2020. Fortifying toxic speech detectors against disguised toxicity. In *Proceedings of the 2020 Conference on Empirical Methods in Natural Language Processing (EMNLP)*, pages 7732–7739.

Bing He, Caleb Ziems, Sandeep Soni, Naren Ramakrishnan, Diyi Yang, and Srijan Kumar. 2021. Racism is a virus: anti-asian hate and counterspeech in social media during the covid-19 crisis. In *Proceedings of the 2021 IEEE/ACM International Conference on Advances in Social Networks Analysis and Mining*, pages 90–94.

Sally Hines. 2019. The feminist frontier: On trans and feminism. *Journal of Gender Studies*, 28(2):145–157.

Dirk Hovy and Shannon L. Spruit. 2016. The social impact of natural language processing. In *Proceedings of the 54th Annual Meeting of the Association for Computational Linguistics (Volume 2: Short Papers)*, pages 591–598, Berlin, Germany. Association for Computational Linguistics.

Alexander Hoyle, Pranav Goel, Andrew Hian-Cheong, Denis Peskov, Jordan Boyd-Graber, and Philip Resnik. 2021. Is automated topic model evaluation broken? the incoherence of coherence. *Advances in Neural Information Processing Systems*, 34.

Jane Im, Sonali Tandon, Eshwar Chandrasekharan, Taylor Denby, and Eric Gilbert. 2020. Synthesized social signals: Computationally-derived social signals from account histories. In *CHI '20: CHI Conference on Human Factors in Computing Systems, Honolulu, HI, USA, April 25-30, 2020*, pages 1–12. ACM.

Tristen Kade. 2021. "hey, by the way, i'm transgender": Transgender disclosures as coming out stories in social contexts among trans men. *Socius*, 7:23780231211039389.

Terri M Kelleher. 2020. Jk rowling: Guilty, of crime of stating that sex is determined by biology. *News Weekly*, (3072):10.

Dongwoo Kim, Yohan Jo, Il-Chul Moon, and Alice Oh. 2010. Analysis of twitter lists as a potential source for discovering latent characteristics of users. In *ACM CHI workshop on microblogging*, volume 6. Citeseer.

Jana Kurrek, Haji Mohammad Saleem, and Derek Ruths. 2020. Towards a comprehensive taxonomy and large-scale annotated corpus for online slur usage. In *Proceedings of the Fourth Workshop on Online Abuse and Harms*, pages 138–149, Online. Association for Computational Linguistics.

Saebom Kwon, Puhe Liang, Sonali Tandon, Jacob Berman, Pai-ju Chang, and Eric Gilbert. 2018. Tweety holmes: A browser extension for abusive twitter profile detection. In *Companion of the 2018 ACM Conference on Computer Supported Cooperative Work and Social Computing*, pages 17–20.

Sophie Lewis. 2019. How british feminism became anti-trans. *The New York Times*.

Yinhan Liu, Myle Ott, Naman Goyal, Jingfei Du, Mandar Joshi, Danqi Chen, Omer Levy, Mike Lewis, Luke Zettlemoyer, and Veselin Stoyanov. 2019. Roberta: A robustly optimized bert pretraining approach. *ArXiv preprint*, abs/1907.11692.

Veronica Lynn, Salvatore Giorgi, Niranjan Balasubramanian, and H. Andrew Schwartz. 2019. Tweet classification without the tweet: An empirical examination of user versus document attributes. In *Proceedings of the Third Workshop on Natural Language Processing and Computational Social Science*, pages 18–28, Minneapolis, Minnesota. Association for Computational Linguistics.

Binny Mathew, Punyajoy Saha, Hardik Tharad, Subham Rajgaria, Prajwal Singhania, Suman Kalyan Maity, Pawan Goyal, and Animesh Mukherjee. 2019. Thou shalt not hate: Countering online hate speech. In *Proceedings of the International AAAI Conference on Web and Social Media*, volume 13, pages 369–380.

Humphrey Mensah, Lu Xiao, and Sucheta Soundarajan. 2019. Characterizing susceptible users on reddit's changemyview. In *Proceedings of the 10th International Conference on Social Media and Society*, pages 102–107.

Ruth Pearce, Sonja Erikainen, and Ben Vincent. 2020. Terf wars: An introduction. *The Sociological Review*, 68(4):677–698.

Carla Perez Almendros, Luis Espinosa Anke, and Steven Schockaert. 2020. Don't patronize me! an annotated dataset with patronizing and condescending language towards vulnerable communities. In *Proceedings of the 28th International Conference on Computational Linguistics*, pages 5891–5902, Barcelona, Spain (Online). International Committee on Computational Linguistics.

Anthony T Pinter, Morgan Klaus Scheuerman, and Jed R Brubaker. 2021. Entering doors, evading traps: Benefits and risks of visibility during transgender coming outs. *Proceedings of the ACM on Human-Computer Interaction*, 4(CSCW3):1–27.

Jipeng Qiang, Qian Zhenyu, Yun Li, Yunhao Yuan, and Xindong Wu. 2019. Short text topic modeling techniques, applications, and performance: A survey. *ArXiv preprint*, abs/1904.07695.

Janice G Raymond. 1979. *The Transsexual Empire the Making of the She-Male*. Beacon Press (Ma).

Carol Riddell. 2006. *Divided sisterhood: a critical review of Janice Raymond's*. Routledge London and New York.

Younes Samih and Kareem Darwish. 2021. A few topical tweets are enough for effective user stance detection. In *Proceedings of the 16th Conference of the European Chapter of the Association for Computational Linguistics: Main Volume*, pages 2637–2646, Online. Association for Computational Linguistics.

Maarten Sap, Dallas Card, Saadia Gabriel, Yejin Choi, and Noah A. Smith. 2019. The risk of racial bias in hate speech detection. In *Proceedings of the 57th Annual Meeting of the Association for Computational Linguistics*, pages 1668–1678, Florence, Italy. Association for Computational Linguistics.

Maarten Sap, Saadia Gabriel, Lianhui Qin, Dan Jurafsky, Noah A. Smith, and Yejin Choi. 2020. Social bias frames: Reasoning about social and power implications of language. In *Proceedings of the 58th Annual Meeting of the Association for Computational Linguistics*, pages 5477–5490, Online. Association for Computational Linguistics.

Anna Schmidt and Michael Wiegand. 2017. A survey on hate speech detection using natural language processing. In *Proceedings of the Fifth International Workshop on Natural Language Processing for Social Media*, pages 1–10, Valencia, Spain. Association for Computational Linguistics.

Sarita Schoenebeck and Lindsay Blackwell. 2021. Reimagining social media governance: Harm, accountability, and repair. *Yale Journal of Law and Technology*, 23(1). Justice Collaboratory Special Issue.

Julia Serano. 2016. *Whipping girl: A transsexual woman on sexism and the scapegoating of femininity*. Hachette UK.

Kumar Bhargav Srinivasan, Cristian Danescu-Niculescu-Mizil, Lillian Lee, and Chenhao Tan. 2019. Content removal as a moderation strategy: Compliance and other outcomes in the changemyview community. *Proceedings of the ACM on Human-Computer Interaction*, 3(CSCW):1–21.

Derald Wing Sue. 2010. *Microaggressions in everyday life: Race, gender, and sexual orientation*. John Wiley & Sons.

Teresa Tadvick. 2018. Practicing gender in online spaces. Bachelor's thesis, University of Colorado, Boulder.

Emily Vajjala. 2020. *Gender-critical/Genderless? A Critical Discourse Analysis of Trans-Exclusionary Radical Feminism (TERF) in Feminist Current*. Ph.D. thesis, Southern Illinois University, Carbondale.

Zijian Wang and Christopher Potts. 2019. TalkDown: A corpus for condescension detection in context. In *Proceedings of the 2019 Conference on Empirical Methods in Natural Language Processing and the 9th International Joint Conference on Natural Language Processing (EMNLP-IJCNLP)*, pages 3711–3719, Hong Kong, China. Association for Computational Linguistics.

Zeerak Waseem, Thomas Davidson, Dana Warmsley, and Ingmar Weber. 2017. Understanding abuse: A typology of abusive language detection subtasks. In *Proceedings of the First Workshop on Abusive Language Online*, pages 78–84, Vancouver, BC, Canada. Association for Computational Linguistics.

Zeerak Waseem and Dirk Hovy. 2016. Hateful symbols or hateful people? predictive features for hate speech detection on Twitter. In *Proceedings of the NAACL Student Research Workshop*, pages 88–93, San Diego, California. Association for Computational Linguistics.

Cristan Williams. 2016. Radical inclusion: Recounting the trans inclusive history of radical feminism. *Transgender Studies Quarterly*, 3(1-2):254–258.

Cristan Williams. 2020. The ontological woman: A history of deauthentication, dehumanization, and violence. *The Sociological Review*, 68(4):718–734.

Marcos Zampieri, Preslav Nakov, Sara Rosenthal, Pepa Atanasova, Georgi Karadzhov, Hamdy Mubarak, Leon Derczynski, Zeses Pitenis, and Çağrı Çöltekin. 2020. SemEval-2020 task 12: Multilingual offensive language identification in social media (OffensEval 2020). In *Proceedings of the Fourteenth Workshop on Semantic Evaluation*, pages 1425–1447, Barcelona (online). International Committee for Computational Linguistics.

Lost in Distillation: A Case Study in Toxicity Modeling

Alyssa Chvasta and **Alyssa Lees** and **Jeffrey Sorensen** and
Lucy Vasserman and **Nitesh Goyal**
Google Jigsaw, New York
achvasta,alyssalees,sorenj,lucyvasserman,teshg@google.com

Abstract

In an era of increasingly large pre-trained language models, knowledge distillation is a powerful tool for transferring information from a large model to a smaller one. In particular, distillation is of tremendous benefit when it comes to real-world constraints such as serving latency or serving at scale. However, a loss of robustness in language understanding may be hidden in the process and not immediately revealed when looking at high-level evaluation metrics. We investigate the hidden costs: what is "lost in distillation", especially in regards to identity-based model bias using the case study of toxicity modeling. With reproducible models using open source training sets, we investigate models distilled from a BERT teacher baseline. Using both open source and proprietary big data models, we investigate these hidden performance costs.

1 Introduction

The revolution in natural language processing brought on by transformers, which have now been employed in virtually all major text processing applications, also brought substantially higher computational costs. The typical BERT model (Devlin et al., 2019) has over 100M parameters and 12 layers. The prospect of using these models in production settings without special purpose hardware quickly led practitioners to seek techniques to reduce the computational costs.

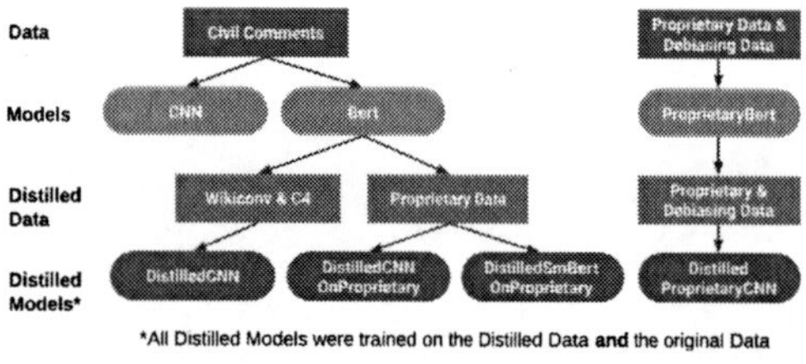

Figure 1: Map of data and results presented

An approach widely advocated is to employ the technique of *knowledge distillation* to improve the performance of a simpler *student model* by training on additional unsupervised data that has been labeled by the larger *teacher model* (Hinton et al., 2015).

The ability to draw upon the wellspring of nearly unlimited unsupervised data and to leverage the higher performance of a much larger model, while maintaining the lower serving costs of a smaller model, has led to rapid adoption of this practice. However, closer analysis of the performance of distilled models reveals that while they may be able to erect a facade of high accuracy, they fail to capture important aspects of the knowledge represented in the teacher models.

We present a particular method of using distillation that we used to improve the performance of our models through pseudo-labeling of unsupervised data, while retaining the model architecture and number of parameters. While, for some metrics we saw nearly asymptotic performance to the teacher model, using other metrics we discovered important differences. While we do not know if this problem will manifest across all differences in architecture and parameterization - we want to caution researchers who are exploring distillation as a potential quick fix.

2 Related Work

BERT models and transformer models in general have structures that are layered with computation units that limit the degrees that parallelism can be used. Focusing on task performance alone, as is often the case for benchmark tasks, has been criticized for failing to account for resource costs (Ethayarajh and Jurafsky, 2020). Knowledge distillation is one of many techniques authors have proposed schemes to reduce the size and complexity.

Proceedings of the Sixth Workshop on Online Abuse and Harms (WOAH), pages 92 - 101
July 14, 2022 ©2022 Association for Computational Linguistics

Models with unintended biases has received considerable attention with multiple survey papers both generally (Pessach and Shmueli, 2022) and for natural language in particular (Kurita et al., 2019; Czarnowska et al., 2021).

Two popular implementations of the distillation paradigm of creating a vast training set using large models to label unsupervised data are presented in Jiao et al. (2020) and Sanh et al. (2020). The primary goal of this work is producing a model with similar performance characteristics on the target task, but with lower a resource footprint. Turc et al. (2019) suggests pre-training and fine-tuning compact models as an alternative to traditional distillation. However, the effects on model bias were not reported in these studies.

Several other works explore this idea in modes similar to the work we present here, although often with a different array of model architectures. Wasserblat et al. (2020) and Mangalwedhekar (2021) both include CNNs as one of the target models. Tang et al. (2019); Chia et al. (2019); Adhikari et al. (2020) all present additional studies regarding distillation and the performance of the models in terms of fidelity to the teacher model.

Specifically regarding bias in the distillation or model compression setting, Xu and Hu (2022) report reduction in bias in contrast to our findings, although in a generation application. However, Gupta et al. (2022) makes clear that biases from the training data can also be preserved or exacerbated in a similar distillation setting.

Bender et al. (2021) raises several risks of large language models overall, including identity-based bias. We show that these risks can be magnified with the use of distillation, and that high-level accuracy metrics can hide nuances in performance, especially when large models are built to address a wide range of use cases.

3 Toxicity Modeling

We have chosen to use the problem of "toxic" comment classification to illustrate the difficulty that we observed in distillation. This is due to the ready availability of training resources for this task, the practical real-world need to address this problem, and the clear risks (Xu et al., 2021) of identity term bias and other modeling pitfalls.

Several diagnostic frameworks that were proposed to highlight the limitations of classification systems *in general* can also be used to highlight the problems with distillation in particular. Our primary framework is the method of measuring classifier unintended bias associated with neutral or ambiguous identity terms. This framework was introduced in Dixon et al. (2018) and expanded in Borkan et al. (2019) along with the Civil Comments dataset that is our primary source of supervised training data. In addition we use the diagnostic HateCheck test set (Röttger et al., 2021). Recently works that study implicitly abusive language (Wiegand et al., 2021; Lees et al., 2021), where careful attention to the context and implication of the comments is required. We include these evaluation challenges for our models.

4 Models

We found the bias effects of distillation to be remarkably persistent from a small to a very large scale. We created smaller, reproducible models entirely from publicly available resources, and duplicated the same findings on a very large model to show the generality of these findings. Table 1 provides a list of data sources and models described in the next sections. [1]

4.1 Teacher Models

We trained state of the art text classification models using both publicly available resources, and a larger model trained on resources that we are not authorized to release. Here, our intent is to show that the effects persist into the big data domain.

4.1.1 Civil Comments based Models

All of the models described in this section are based upon publicly available resources and data. The Civil Comments dataset introduced in Borkan et al. (2019) is a public domain corpus of 1.8M user comments labeled for toxicity by crowd raters. These comments originated from a distributed commenting platform that ceased operation in 2017. A subset of the data, ~400K comments were additionally rated for specific identity subgroup associations such as gender, religion, or sexual orientation. The identity labels in the test set are used for bias evaluation.

Our Civil Comments based models were constructed both for the purposes of reproducibility and for experiments in distillation size. All of these

[1] A Python notebook demonstrating the ideas presented in this paper can be found at `http://github.com/conversationai/Lost_in_Distillation`.

Model	Data Sources	Training Instances
CNN	Civil Comments	1.8M
Bert	Civil Comments	1.8M
ProprietaryBERT	Civil Comments + Human Labeled Proprietary (3M) + Bias Mitigation (2M)	6.8M
DistilledCNN	Civil Comments + WikiConv (400K) + C4 (640k)	2.8M
DistilledCNNOnProprietary	Civil Comments + BERT-labeled proprietary (20M)	21.8M
DistilledSmBERTOnProprietary	Civil Comments + BERT-labeled proprietary (20M)	21.8M
DistilledProprietaryCNN	proprietaryBERT data + ProprietaryBERT-labeled proprietary (28M) + Bias Mitigation (1.7M)	36.5M

Table 1: Model Training Data Size

were fine-tuned or trained only using the public domain Civil Comments training corpus. Also for the sake of reproducibility, all BERT model versions used open-source checkpoints. It should be noted that in addition to models listed below, we also experimented with distilling via alternate compact architectures. The results were worse in terms of performance and as such we omitted the results.

All CNN models are trained until convergence. For these models, no bias mitigation or data enhancement was employed. Some discrepancies between the big data models and the Civil Comments models, both in overall results metrics and bias, are due to these differences in data.

CNN A baseline CNN trained exclusively on Civil Comments data with a BERT-base checkpoint as initial embedding. With 5 layers (2-gram, 3-gram, 4-gram, 5-gram and 6-gram layers of 300) and a max pooling layer. The model hyperparameters were tuned on a held-out evaluation set. The final model employed batch size of 64, max token sequence length of 1536 and learning rate of $1e-5$. The hyper-tuned parameters were used for all of the distilled CNN student models below. The best model on the Civil Comments test set (.965 AUC-ROC) was selected for evaluation. This baseline CNN model is used as a control to ascertain whether a distilled CNN has demonstrable improvements over a model without the benefits of teacher pre-training.

BERT A task-specific teacher model built from a BERT-base public checkpoint with 768 dimensions, 12 layers, 12 heads that was fine-tuned exclusively on the Civil Comments training data. The model used a batch size of 64, a learning rate of $1e-5$, max token length of 512 and Adam optimizer. The model was trained for 1M steps and the best performing checkpoint in terms of AUC-ROC was selected.

4.1.2 Big Data Models

Using a combination of publicly available datasets and our much larger proprietary datasets, we show the distillation bias effects in the toxicity space scale to big data. We start with a competitive teacher BERT model that is distilled using a compact CNN architecture. Both teacher and student incorporate the open-source Civil Comments training corpus as well as proprietary human-labeled data and bias mitigation data. We follow the best practices of data augmentation described in (Dixon et al., 2018) by including bias mitigation data to help mitigate discrepancies in identity subgroup metrics.

PROPRIETARYBERT A state-of-the-art BERT toxicity model that has been pre-trained on more than 1.5B user comments in English. This baseline was additionally fine-tuned on rater labeled comments. The model uses a custom sentence-piece vocabulary of size 200K. The teacher model is constructed with 768 dimensions, 12 layers, 12 heads, consistent with BERT-base (Devlin et al., 2019). The pre-training consists of MLM loss with uniform masking at 15%. Pretraining was conducted with batch size of 32 for over 100K steps. The model was fine-tuned on 3M user generated comments scored by raters for toxicity, bias mitigation data, and the Civil Comments training set with batch size of 512 until convergence.

4.2 Distilled Models

Several models are used to examine distillation. For reference, knowledge distillation is defined as training a smaller neural network on a dataset called the *transfer set*. Using cross entropy as the loss function between the output of the smaller distilled model $y(x|t)$ and the output of the teacher model $\hat{y}(x|t)$, where t is the temperature and for a standard softmax

$$E(x|t) = -\sum_i \hat{y}_i(x|t) \log y_i(\mathbf{x}|t)$$

is normally set to 1.

DISTILLEDCNN The transfer data, scored by the above BERT model, is drawn from WikiConv (Hua et al., 2018), a corpus encompassing the history of conversations on Wikipedia Talk pages, and

C4 (Raffel et al., 2019), a cleaned version of Common Crawl's web crawl corpus. For both sources a large quantity of data was scored with BERT and then examples were dropped to ensure a 50/50 distribution of toxic and nontoxic examples using a 0.5 threshold. Since both sources are extremely non-toxic (0.004% and 0.00005% respectively), this process produced only 400k examples from WikiConv and 640k from C4.

DISTILLEDCNNONPROPRIETARY CNN model distilled on a much larger volume of unsupervised user comments as the transfer set labeled by BERT. As with DISTILLEDCNN, the architecture and training parameters replicate those used by CNN. The model was trained on the Civil Comments golden data and 20M teacher-labeled comments, including proprietary comments.

DISTILLEDSMBERTONPROPRIETARY Small BERT model distilled on the same larger volume of unsupervised corpus of user-domain comments as DISTILLEDCNNONPROPRIETARY by using BERT as teacher. As with DISTILLEDCNNONPROPRIETARY the model uses Civil Comments golden data and 20M teacher-labeled comments from a proprietary dataset. The model is included to ascertain whether Small BERT for distillation yields improvements in bias over a CNN.

DISTILLEDPROPRIETARYCNN A CNN student model distilled on 28M user comments scored with PROPRIETARYBERT. The model is also trained on the the same golden data as the teacher model. In addition, the model training data also includes 1.7M bias mitigation examples added to the golden data to mitigate identity term bias. The model uses the same tokenizer as the teacher model and is initialized from the teacher word embeddings. The CNN is 5 layers: one layer of 300 bi-grams, one layer of 300 tri-grams, one layer of 300 quad-grams, one layer of 300 5-grams, one layer of 300 6-grams and a max pool of the entire sequence. The model is trained with an Adam optimizer (Kingma and Ba, 2017), learning rate of .1, a batch size of 128 and a maximum token sequence length of 1536 until convergence.

The distilled student model DISTILLEDPROPRIETARYCNN achieves equivalent (if slightly better performance) to the teacher model PROPRIETARYBERT on the Civil Comments test set, as shown in Table 3. The *Short Synthetic* test set is used to measure bias, as shown in Table 3, and further illustrates the similar performance of the two models.

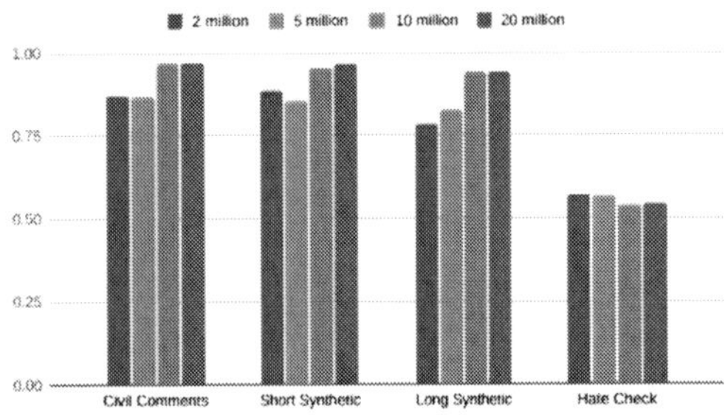

Figure 2: AUC-ROC performance of the BERT model distilled on proprietary data and evaluated on various test sets, broken down by distilled train set size.

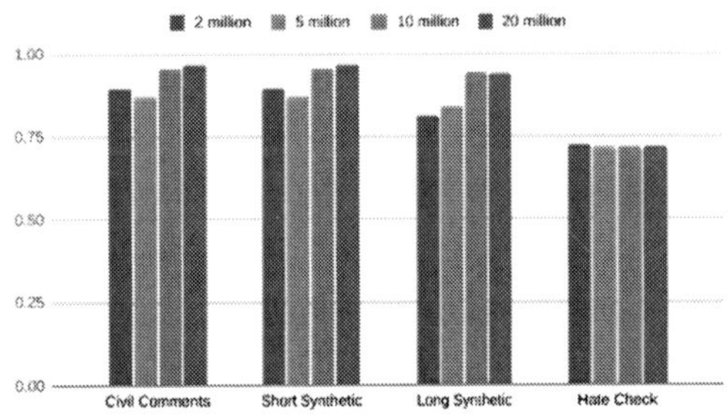

Figure 3: AUC-PR performance of the BERT model distilled on proprietary data and evaluated on various test sets, broken down by distilled train set size.

5 Evaluating Performance and Bias

Experiments are run on a variety of evaluation sets to assess the classification performance of the teacher, baseline and distilled models. In assessing both the Civil Comments based models and the big data models, we compare the distilled student and baseline models performance against the teacher models. Results are shown in Table 2 (Civil Comments based models) and Table 3 (big data models). The final column in each of these tables shows the difference in AUC-ROC between the student model and the teacher.

Civil Comments The test set from Civil Comments, drawn from the same distribution of comments as the training data, and is similar to the data distribution contained in the big data datasets.

Given the matched distribution between training and test, we expect this to be a best case result. All of the Civil Comments-based distilled and baseline models are within $\sim 1\%$ of BERT AUC-ROC).

In the big data case, in fact DISTILLEDPROPRIETARYCNN yields better performance than PROPRIETARYBERT in Table 3. These results show the strong promise of distillation, which leverages unsupervised data and produces an improvement without additional model complexity.

Short Synthetic A synthetic test set created by substituting identity terms into toxic and non-toxic sentence templates (Dixon et al., 2018; Borkan et al., 2019).

The performance of DISTILLEDCNN and DISTILLEDCNNONPROPRIETARY along with CNN begins to degrade (-3.5%) with respect to the teacher model BERT on this dataset. This yields some evidence that the distillation process, when used with CNN architectures, may increase identity term bias.

On the other hand, minimal degradation in performance occurred for DISTILLEDPROPRIETARYCNN where carefully selected bias mitigation data was included as part of the teacher model training and distillation process.

Long Synthetic A dataset similar to Short Synthetic but with the addition of *random filler text* meant to be more confusing.

This more challenging dataset begins to show degradation for the DISTILLEDPROPRIETARYCNN model, despite the addition of bias mitigation data. Table 3 shows almost a -5% fall in AUC-ROC performance with respect to the teacher PROPRIETARYBERT.

Likewise, larger drops in performance can be seen for the Civil Comments-based models in table 2. Interestingly, DISTILLEDCNNONPROPRIETARY starts to slightly outperform the baseline CNN and DISTILLEDCNN with only a -4% drop in AUC versus $-6\%+$.

Hate Check A targeted diagnostic test for hate detection models from Röttger et al. (2021). This dataset explicitly attempts to probe the generalisability of a model, measuring systemic gaps and biases in other datasets using a suite of synthetically generated tests.

While the big data teacher model PROPRIETARYBERT begins to show slightly more robust performance than the smaller BERT model (.831 AUC vs .701), all distilled and baseline CNN models suffer significant falls in performance. DISTILLEDPROPRIETARYCNN has nearly a -17% fall in AUC to .664. Both DISTILLEDCNN and DISTILLEDCNNONPROPRIETARY models have $\sim 10\%$ or greater falls in AUC to (.575 and .595 respectively).

Examining the Hate Check functionalities, the categories with the largest differences where the teacher model outperforms the student model are in the non-hate comments that contain a negative term with negation (F14), followed by the comments that have a character swap (F25), and implicit derogation (F4). The teacher model, however, did not perform as well on abuse targeted against a non-protected object or individual (F22, F23). In 22 of the 29 categories, the student model performed worse than the teacher.

We continue our testing with a suite of more robust tests that demonstrate the limitations and weak-points in the distilled model versions.

False Positives A dataset inspired and derived from the work of Welbl et al. (2021), where authors trained a generative LM specifically to not produce toxic content. This dataset includes the sentences generated that had a large discrepancy in score between the publicly available toxicity model, Perspective API (Jigsaw, 2017), and human raters. Human annotations marked far fewer examples as toxic than the automated models, and the authors note a strong bias towards false positives in this set.

The False Positives dataset includes 50% auto-generated texts that had Perspective API scores $>$ .75 but were marked by human raters as non-toxic and the rest as randomly selected auto-generated comments with corresponding human annotations.

Notably all models perform poorly on the challenging dataset with PROPRIETARYBERT and BERT yielding only .635 and .651 AUC-ROC respectively. However all distilled CNN models faired even worse when compared to the teacher models, varying between -11% and -15%.

Identity Swaps Inspired by the work in Prabhakaran et al. (2019), where Perturbation Sensitivity Analysis is used to detect unintended model bias related to named entities, we repeat a similar experiment in relation to curated swapped identity terms. A small subset of curated phrases with explicit identity terms meant to detect *hard* toxic and non-toxic instances. The phrases each have 23 identity terms which are swapped with correct associated grammar specifications. Examples from this data set appear in Table 8. The identity swaps sets shows similar drops in performance for all distilled model instances as compared to the teacher.

Covert Toxicity Detecting implicit abuse or covert toxicity, where clearly hateful or abusive words are not used in the comment, presents an especially hard challenge. Given the documented difficulty of toxicity models and hate models to identify such text, we included a representative set as a further baseline. Using a published test dataset (Lees et al., 2021) we select an output label that is defined as the max of the covert and overt toxic scores. Notably all models performed extremely poorly on this set with $< .6$ AUC. The effects of distillation were more mixed, suggesting that identifying covert toxicity or implicit abuse is a more nuanced and unsolved task and perhaps more reliant on training data.

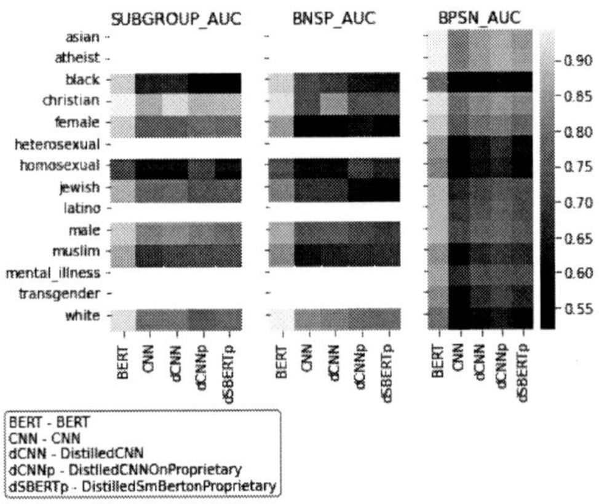

Figure 4: Civil Comments Bias Metric Breakdowns for Identity Subtypes on Civil Comments-based Models

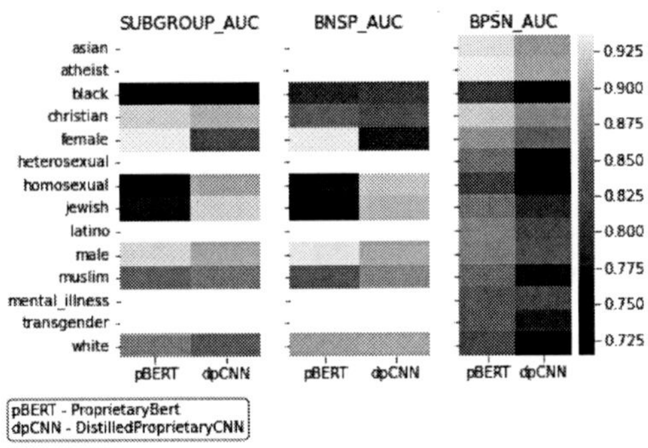

Figure 5: Civil Comments Eval Set Bias Metric Breakdowns for Identity Subtypes on Proprietary Big Data Models with bias mitigation implemented

6 Bias in Distilled Models

For evaluation of model bias, we employ a subset of the suite of metrics introduced in Borkan et al. (2019). In particular, we utilize the following metrics for identifying unintended bias along with averaging the differences in these metrics across a subsection of identity categories:

Subgroup AUC The AUC computed only for the data labeled as including a mention of a particular identity

Background Positive, Subgroup Negative AUC BPSN AUC is computed for a split dataset of positive background data and negative examples for a particular subgroup. Lower metrics for this particular category suggest that a particular identity is linked to a high false positive rate, which could imply that specific identities are associated with toxicity, independent of context.

Background Negative, Subgroup Positive AUC BNSP AUC is computed for a split dataset of negative background data and positive subgroup examples.

6.1 Civil Comments Identities Bias

Civil Comments Identities subset includes rater labeled categories for subgroup identities. The overall bias metrics for the Civil Comments-based models in Figure 6 show a notable discrepancy between the teacher BERT style model BERT and baseline and distilled versions of the models. Also, a drop in overall performance for BPSN, suggesting strong links between the presence of any identity subtype and a false positive value.

Figure 4 shows subgroup bias metric breakdowns for individual subgroups. The missing subgroup metrics are due to insufficient data to accurately assess the subgroup positive performance. Outside of the wide discrepancy between the teacher BERT model and the distilled CNNs, certain identity categories perform far worse than others such as *black* and *homosexual*.

On the other hand, DISTILLEDPROPRIETARYCNN, which contains explicit bias mitigating data, does not show the same overall average bias metric degradation for subgroup AUC and BNSP AUC. However, there is a fall in performance for average BPSN, suggesting, despite the existence of bias mitigation data, some identity groups are linked with false positives (see Figure 7). Figure 4 better illustrates the identity subgroup breakdowns. The distilled student model DISTILLEDPROPRIETARYCNN shows a uniform drop in performance for BPSN

Dataset	Model Type	Model	Params	AUC-PR	AUC-ROC	Teacher AUC-ROC Diff
Civil Comments	BERT Teacher	BERT	110M	**.815**	**.981**	0
	Distilled Student	DISTILLEDCNN	8M	.755	.970	-.011
		DISTILLEDCNNONPROPRIETARY	8M	.757	.971	-.010
		DISTILLEDSMBERTONPROPRIETARY	NA	.702	.958	-.023
	Baseline	CNN	8M	.738	.965	-.016
Short Synthetic	BERT Teacher	BERT	110M	**.997**	**.997**	0
	Distilled Student	DISTILLEDCNN	8M	.952	.955	-.042
		DISTILLEDCNNONPROPRIETARY	8M	.961	.961	-.036
		DISTILLEDSMBERTONPROPRIETARY	NA	.936	.936	-.061
	Baseline	CNN	8M	.956	.961	-.036
Long Synthetic	BERT Teacher	BERT	110M	**.984**	**.983**	0
	Distilled Student	DISTILLEDCNN	8M	.911	.916	-.067
		DISTILLEDCNNONPROPRIETARY	8M	.938	.943	-.040
		DISTILLEDSMBERTONPROPRIETARY	NA	.915	.913	-.070
	Baseline	CNN	8M	.915	.923	-.060
Hate Check	BERT Teacher	BERT	110M	**.813**	**.701**	0
	Distilled Student	DISTILLEDCNN	8M	.712	.575	-.126
		DISTILLEDCNNONPROPRIETARY	8M	.715	.595	-.106
		DISTILLEDSMBERTONPROPRIETARY	NA	.706	.531	-.170
	Baseline	CNN	8M	.731	.560	-.141
False Positives	BERT Teacher	BERT	110M	**.103**	**.651**	0
	Distilled Student	DISTILLEDCNN	8M	.061	.500	-.151
		DISTILLEDCNNONPROPRIETARY	8M	.074	.547	-.104
		DISTILLEDSMBERTONPROPRIETARY	NA	.065	.532	-.119
	Baseline	CNN	8M	.07	.538	-.113
Identity Swaps	BERT Teacher	BERT	110M	**.321**	**.892**	0
	Distilled Student	DISTILLEDCNN	8M	.360	.754	-.138
		DISTILLEDCNNONPROPRIETARY	8M	.346	.791	-.101
		DISTILLEDSMBERTONPROPRIETARY	NA	.356	.760	-.132
	Baseline	CNN	8M	.354	.774	-.118
Covert Toxicity	BERT Teacher	BERT	110M	**.130**	**.586**	0
	Distilled Student	DISTILLEDCNN	8M	.128	.585	-.001
		DISTILLEDCNNONPROPRIETARY	8M	.127	.562	-.024
		DISTILLEDSMBERTONPROPRIETARY	NA	.117	.564	-.022
	Baseline	CNN	8M	.126	.568	-.018

Table 2: Evaluation Results for Civil Comments based models: **BERT** - BERT model trained on Civil Comments, **CNN** - CNN trained on Civil Comments, **DISTILLEDCNN** - CNN distilled from BERT on 2M comments(reproducible) **DISTILLEDCNNONPROPRIETARY** - CNN distilled from BERT on 20M proprietary comments, **DISTILLEDSMBERTONPROPRIETARY** - Small Bert model distilled from BERT on 20M proprietary comments

AUC metrics (false positives for identity terms) when compared to PROPRIETARYBERT. However, certain subgroups such as *jewish* and *homosexual* have worse subgroup and BNSP AUC performance for the teacher model, where the abundance of bias mitigation data may be compromising the model's toxicity sensitivity

7 Effect of Distilled Data Size

Another variable to consider is the size of the distilled transfer data used for training. For these experiments we use variable-sized subsets of the data used by DISTILLEDCNNONPROPRIETARY above. This data matches the distribution of toxic comments found in Civil Comments, but is not publicly available.

In this experiment we consider the effect of increasing the ratio of the size of the transfer dataset to the size of the golden human-labeled data. We find in Figure 2 and Figure 3 that more distilled transfer data increases performance but only to a certain point. Increasing the distilled data size beyond 10M comments had little effect.

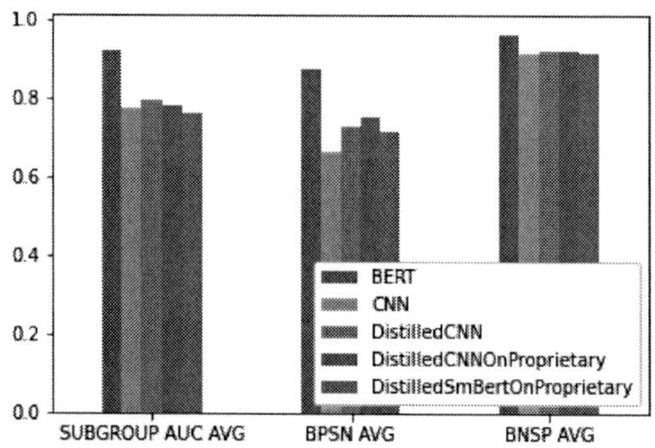

Figure 6: Civil Comments Eval Set Average Bias Metrics for Reproducible Models

8 Conclusion

The experimental section illustrates for both our more robust big data toxicity models and smaller reproducible versions that we are able to distill large transformer teacher models into smaller student models with very similar metrics on the evaluation datasets drawn from the same distribution. However, upon closer inspection, the distilled models consistently under-perform and even demon-

Dataset	Model Type	Model	Params	AUC-PR	AUC-ROC	Teacher AUC-ROC Diff
Civil Comments	BERT Teacher	PROPRIETARYBERT	235M	.734	.969	0
	Distilled Student	DISTILLEDPROPRIETARYCNN	23M	.771	.974	+.005
Short Synthetic	BERT Teacher	PROPRIETARYBERT	235M	.993	.994	0
	Distilled Student	DISTILLEDPROPRIETARYCNN	23M	.992	.993	-.001
Long Synthetic	BERT Teacher	PROPRIETARYBERT	235M	.997	.996	0
	Distilled Student	DISTILLEDPROPRIETARYCNN	23M	.958	.949	-.047
Hate Check	BERT Teacher	PROPRIETARYBERT	235M	.898	.831	0
	Distilled Student	DISTILLEDPROPRIETARYCNN	23M	.791	.664	-.167
False Positives	BERT Teacher	PROPRIETARYBERT	235M	.113	.635	0
	Distilled Student	DISTILLEDPROPRIETARYCNN	23M	.061	.520	-.115
Identity Swaps	BERT Teacher	PROPRIETARYBERT	235M	.311	.954	0
	Distilled Student	DISTILLEDPROPRIETARYCNN	23M	.329	.854	-.100
Covert Toxicity	BERT Teacher	PROPRIETARYBERT	235M	.117	.538	0
	Distilled Student	DISTILLEDPROPRIETARYCNN	23M	.131	.583	+.045

Table 3: Big Data Model Evaluation Results

id	text	label	PROPRIETARYBERT	DISTILLEDPROPRIETARYCNN	Diff
1	Never trust a single word said by a gay	true	.847 (TP)	.574 (TP)	-.273
2	Never trust a single word said by a married man	true	.321 (FN)	.139 (FN)	-.182
3	Never trust a single word said by a black	true	.794 (TP)	.347 (FN)	-.447
4	I do not know many blacks	false	.162 (TN)	.610 (FP)	+.448
5	I do not know many immigrants	false	.017 (TN)	.250 (TN)	+.233
6	I wish I could date a gay	false	.158 (TN)	.563 (FP)	+.334
7	I wish I could date a married man	false	.019 (TN)	.040 (TN)	+.021
8	asexuals being in charge are a danger to our country	true	.718 (TP)	.313 (FN)	-.405
9	lesbians being in charge are a danger to our country	true	.818 (TP)	.640 (TP)	-.178
10	Three unmarried men were elected to parliament today.	false	.032 (TN)	.031 (TN)	-.001

Table 4: Identity Swaps Toxicity Evaluation Results (TP, FP, TN, FN assuming a .5 threshold for toxicity label)

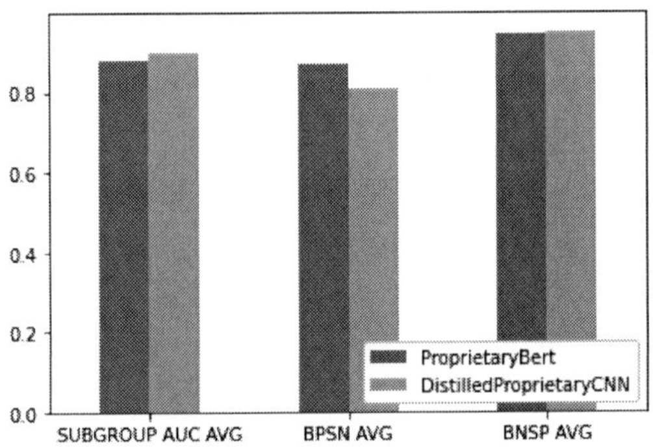

Figure 7: Civil Comments Eval Set Average Bias Metrics for Proprietary Models with bias mitigation

strate serious weakness when examined on larger and more difficult suites of test sets. In particular, identity-based bias for the toxicity models is noticeably worse in the distilled model versions, even with the addition of significant quantities bias-mitigating data. Table 4 shows specific examples with high discrepancy of score between the teacher and student models for both True/False toxicity labels from the curated Identity Swaps set. Even distilled models are complex, so we do not have a systemic way to characterize what's different between the teacher and the student models. But our analysis suggests that the student models are emphasizing lexical features.

Balancing costs versus performance is an unavoidable part of building machine learning systems. Much of the work within the academic community presents techniques that bring marginal improvements often at much higher costs. The popularity of ensemble models in machine learning competitions is but one example of such a technique that is usually impractical in production settings.

In our own work, we became interested in distillation because it allowed us to maintain our existing architecture and serving costs, but allowed us to improve our models to what seemed like performance parity with the promising new BERT models.

We quickly noticed that distilled models performed worse, consistently, in our bias metrics. While the technique of data augmentation has helped us mitigate these biases, that technique has proven to be less effective in distillation settings.

In trying to tackle biases, whether caused by sampling methods, the annotators, or the models themselves, there are always other potential biases that we are not yet measuring. For these reasons we have concluded that there may be subtle and intangible benefits to using large models. Importantly for us, data augmentation techniques for bias mitigation perform better with transformer models, at least to the limits of our ability to measure. While distillation seemingly lifts student model performance to new heights of accuracy, it may be a pale imitation of the often profound context sensitive classifications that are produced by the teacher models. We hope that this caution and advice with help other practitioners who face similar choices.

References

Ashutosh Adhikari, Achyudh Ram, Raphael Tang, William L. Hamilton, and Jimmy Lin. 2020. Exploring the limits of simple learners in knowledge distillation for document classification with DocBERT. In *Proceedings of the 5th Workshop on Representation Learning for NLP*, pages 72–77, Online. Association for Computational Linguistics.

Emily M. Bender, Timnit Gebru, Angelina McMillan-Major, and Shmargaret Shmitchell. 2021. On the dangers of stochastic parrots: Can language models be too big? 🦜. In *Proceedings of the 2021 ACM Conference on Fairness, Accountability, and Transparency*, FAccT '21, page 610–623, New York, NY, USA. Association for Computing Machinery.

Daniel Borkan, Lucas Dixon, Jeffrey Sorensen, Nithum Thain, and Lucy Vasserman. 2019. Nuanced metrics for measuring unintended bias with real data for text classification. In *Companion Proceedings of The 2019 World Wide Web Conference*, WWW '19, page 491–500, New York, NY, USA. Association for Computing Machinery.

Yew Ken Chia, Sam Witteveen, and Martin Andrews. 2019. Transformer to cnn: Label-scarce distillation for efficient text classification.

Paula Czarnowska, Yogarshi Vyas, and Kashif Shah. 2021. Quantifying social biases in NLP: A generalization and empirical comparison of extrinsic fairness metrics. *Transactions of the Association for Computational Linguistics*, 9:1249–1267.

Jacob Devlin, Ming-Wei Chang, Kenton Lee, and Kristina Toutanova. 2019. BERT: Pre-training of deep bidirectional transformers for language understanding. In *Proceedings of the 2019 Conference of the North American Chapter of the Association for Computational Linguistics: Human Language Technologies, Volume 1 (Long and Short Papers)*, pages 4171–4186, Minneapolis, Minnesota. Association for Computational Linguistics.

Lucas Dixon, John Li, Jeffrey Sorensen, Nithum Thain, and Lucy Vasserman. 2018. Measuring and mitigating unintended bias in text classification. In *Proceedings of the 2018 AAAI/ACM Conference on AI, Ethics, and Society*, AIES '18, page 67–73, New York, NY, USA. Association for Computing Machinery.

Kawin Ethayarajh and Dan Jurafsky. 2020. Utility is in the eye of the user: A critique of NLP leaderboards. In *Proceedings of the 2020 Conference on Empirical Methods in Natural Language Processing (EMNLP)*, pages 4846–4853, Online. Association for Computational Linguistics.

Umang Gupta, Jwala Dhamala, Varun Kumar, Apurv Verma, Yada Pruksachatkun, Satyapriya Krishna, Rahul Gupta, Kai-Wei Chang, Greg Ver Steeg, and Aram Galstyan. 2022. Mitigating gender bias in distilled language models via counterfactual role reversal. In *Findings of the Association for Computational Linguistics: ACL 2022*, pages 658–678, Dublin, Ireland. Association for Computational Linguistics.

Geoffrey Hinton, Oriol Vinyals, and Jeff Dean. 2015. Distilling the knowledge in a neural network.

Yiqing Hua, Cristian Danescu-Niculescu-Mizil, Dario Taraborelli, Nithum Thain, Jeffrey Sorensen, and Lucas Dixon. 2018. WikiConv: A corpus of the complete conversational history of a large online collaborative community. In *Proceedings of the 2018 Conference on Empirical Methods in Natural Language Processing*, pages 2818–2823, Brussels, Belgium. Association for Computational Linguistics.

Xiaoqi Jiao, Yichun Yin, Lifeng Shang, Xin Jiang, Xiao Chen, Linlin Li, Fang Wang, and Qun Liu. 2020. TinyBERT: Distilling BERT for natural language understanding. In *Findings of the Association for Computational Linguistics: EMNLP 2020*, pages 4163–4174, Online. Association for Computational Linguistics.

Google Jigsaw. 2017. Perspective api. `https://www.perspectiveapi.com/`. Accessed: 2021-02-02.

Diederik P. Kingma and Jimmy Ba. 2017. Adam: A method for stochastic optimization.

Keita Kurita, Nidhi Vyas, Ayush Pareek, Alan W Black, and Yulia Tsvetkov. 2019. Measuring bias in contextualized word representations. In *Proceedings of the First Workshop on Gender Bias in Natural Language Processing*, pages 166–172, Florence, Italy. Association for Computational Linguistics.

Alyssa Lees, Daniel Borkan, Ian Kivlichan, Jorge Nario, and Tesh Goyal. 2021. Capturing covertly toxic speech via crowdsourcing. In *Proceedings of the First Workshop on Bridging Human–Computer Interaction and Natural Language Processing*, pages 14–20, Online. Association for Computational Linguistics.

Bansidhar Mangalwedhekar. 2021. Distilling bert for low complexity network training.

Dana Pessach and Erez Shmueli. 2022. A review on fairness in machine learning. *ACM Comput. Surv.*, 55(3).

Vinodkumar Prabhakaran, Ben Hutchinson, and Margaret Mitchell. 2019. Perturbation sensitivity analysis to detect unintended model biases. *CoRR*, abs/1910.04210.

Colin Raffel, Noam Shazeer, Adam Roberts, Katherine Lee, Sharan Narang, Michael Matena, Yanqi Zhou, Wei Li, and Peter J. Liu. 2019. Exploring the limits of transfer learning with a unified text-to-text transformer. *arXiv e-prints*.

Paul Röttger, Bertie Vidgen, Dong Nguyen, Zeerak Waseem, Helen Margetts, and Janet Pierrehumbert. 2021. HateCheck: Functional tests for hate speech detection models. In *Proceedings of the 59th Annual Meeting of the Association for Computational Linguistics and the 11th International Joint Conference on Natural Language Processing (Volume 1: Long Papers)*, pages 41–58, Online. Association for Computational Linguistics.

Victor Sanh, Lysandre Debut, Julien Chaumond, and Thomas Wolf. 2020. Distilbert, a distilled version of bert: smaller, faster, cheaper and lighter.

Raphael Tang, Yao Lu, Linqing Liu, Lili Mou, Olga Vechtomova, and Jimmy Lin. 2019. Distilling task-specific knowledge from bert into simple neural networks.

Iulia Turc, Ming-Wei Chang, Kenton Lee, and Kristina Toutanova. 2019. Well-read students learn better: The impact of student initialization on knowledge distillation. *CoRR*, abs/1908.08962.

Moshe Wasserblat, Oren Pereg, and Peter Izsak. 2020. Exploring the boundaries of low-resource BERT distillation. In *Proceedings of SustaiNLP: Workshop on Simple and Efficient Natural Language Processing*, pages 35–40, Online. Association for Computational Linguistics.

Johannes Welbl, Amelia Glaese, Jonathan Uesato, Sumanth Dathathri, John Mellor, Lisa Anne Hendricks, Kirsty Anderson, Pushmeet Kohli, Ben Coppin, and Po-Sen Huang. 2021. Challenges in detoxifying language models.

Michael Wiegand, Maja Geulig, and Josef Ruppenhofer. 2021. Implicitly abusive comparisons – a new dataset and linguistic analysis. In *Proceedings of the 16th Conference of the European Chapter of the Association for Computational Linguistics: Main Volume*, pages 358–368, Online. Association for Computational Linguistics.

Albert Xu, Eshaan Pathak, Eric Wallace, Suchin Gururangan, Maarten Sap, and Dan Klein. 2021. Detoxifying language models risks marginalizing minority voices. In *Proceedings of the 2021 Conference of the North American Chapter of the Association for Computational Linguistics: Human Language Technologies*, pages 2390–2397, Online. Association for Computational Linguistics.

Guangxuan Xu and Qingyuan Hu. 2022. Can model compression improve nlp fairness.

Cleansing and expanding the HURTLEX(EL) with a multidimensional categorization of offensive words

Vivian Stamou* **Iakovi Alexiou†** **Antigone Klimi†** **Eleftheria Molou†**
Alexandra Saivanidou† **Stella Markantonatou***

*Institute for Language and Speech Processing, Athena R.C.
†Faculty of Philology, University of Athens
{vivianstamou, iakovi.alexiou, antyklimi, moloueleftheria,
alexansaivan, stiliani.markantonatou}@gmail.com

Abstract

We present a cleansed version of the Modern Greek branch of the multilingual lexicon HURTLEX.[1] The new version contains 737 offensive words. We worked bottom-up in two annotation rounds and developed detailed diagnostics of "offensiveness" by cross-classifying words on three dimensions: context, reference, and thematic domain. Our work reveals a wider spectrum of thematic domains concerning the study of offensive language than those identified in the Greek lexicographic literature as well as social and cultural aspects that are not included in the original HURTLEX categories.

1 Introduction

The term *offensive language* (OL) is used to describe “hurtful, derogatory or obscene comments made by one person to another person” and the term *hate speech* (HS) to describe speech that is possibly harmful to disadvantaged social groups.[2] Although both legal and ethical aspects have been considered in an effort to differentiate between HS and OL, the line between the two terms is difficult to be drawn (Davidson et al. 2017; Waseem et al. 2017) and they are often used interchangeably (Jacobs and Potter, 1998). In this work, terms in the domains of OL and HS are considered together.

Many of the studies referring to OL detection use vocabularies (Chen et al. 2012; Colla et al. 2020; Njagi et al. 2015; Pedersen 2019; Razavi et al. 2010) or patterns as a starting point and depend heavily on the selection of “seed words”. Keyword-based approaches might be more effective in the case of explicit abuse according to the typology provided in Waseem et al. (2017). Also, there are strong indications that key-word and lexicon-based approaches score better when there is a shortage of annotated corpora (Sazzed, 2021); Modern Greek (MG) is an underresourced language in terms of corpora annotated for OL.

Resource development for OL detection is an issue in itself. Firstly, "offense" is a subjective notion and as a result, the social (in general) and personal characteristics of the annotators as well as the annotation method may put bias on the resources for OL detection (lists of offensive words, corpora). The so-called "descriptive" approaches to resource development try to represent various stances in the same resource while the so-called "prescriptive" approaches try to represent few or even only one stance. High interranotator scores seem to correlate with the prescriptive approach (Röttger et al., 2022). Furthermore, Schmidt and Wiegand (2017) point out that little is known about the creation process and the theoretical concepts underlying collections of offensive words. The context in which words occur also affects their offensive nature; for instance, Pelosi et al. (2017) observe that words collected in vulgar lexicons, sometimes may be considered neutral or even positive.

Our group represents female native speakers of MG with middle to high education aged 20-60; none belongs to marginal social groups. Our work is of the prescriptive persuasion. We did not make use of a pre-existing list of guidelines for recognising offensive words; instead we developed our own list of diagnostics with an iterative bottom-up procedure. We offer a cleansed version of the HURTLEX-(EL) lexicon containing 737 words after removing the wrong words and the words that were not considered offensive by all the annotators. Explanations whether the OL value of the words is context-dependent or not are offered as well as descriptions of certain contexts that trigger the offensive meanings.

[1] The lexicon is available here: `https://osf.io/t5jey/?view_only=e910e28ea21e4895905aff2d0c0ac162` (archived under: DOI 10.17605/OSF.IO/T5JEY).

[2] https://thelawdictionary.org/offensive-language/.

Proceedings of the Sixth Workshop on Online Abuse and Harms (WOAH), pages 102 - 108
July 14, 2022

2 OL identification studies and resources for Modern Greek

Pitenis et al. (2020) presented the first annotated MG dataset, the Offensive Greek Tweet Dataset (OGTD) that was extracted with a yet unpublished list of profane or obscene keywords (e.g., μαλάκας 'asshole', πουτάνα 'whore'). Tweets were marked as "offensive", "not offensive" or "spam". As "offensive" were labelled tweets that contained profane or obscene language or when they could be considered offensive on the basis of the context (Pitenis 2019:32-33). These general annotation guidelines were meant for texts. Lekea and Karampelas (2018) has investigated HS in the context of terrorist argument drawing on an also unpublished list of 1265 words. Perifanos and Goutsos (2021) have combined visual and textual cues in a multimodal approach for HS detection on Twitter. 4004 tweets with the hashtag #απέλαση 'deportation' and the term λάθρο 'illegal' were annotated manually as hateful, xenophobic and racist by 3 annotators with the majority vote.

Overall, the literature on Modern Greek OL detection does not provide annotated corpora representing a wide range of registers, sizeable OL lexica or annotation guidelines. In this context, and given that lexical resources are crucial for OL identification when few or no labelled corpora exist (Sazzed 2021), the Greek (EL) branch of HURTLEX (Bassignana et al., 2018) seemed a promising starting point.

HURTLEX is a domain-independent lexicon of 53 languages with offensive, aggressive and hateful words. Its kernel consists of ~1000 manually selected words corresponding to 17 fine-grained thematic categories that were enriched in a semi-automatic manner by drawing on the MultiWodrnet synsets and Babelnet.[3,4] In HURTLEX each lemma-sense pair is classified as "non-offensive" or "neutral" or "offensive". The neutral cases were further divided into "not literally pejorative" and "negative connotation" (not a directly derogatory use). An agreement of 61% between two annotators was reported. The senses judged as non offensive were removed and two versions of the lexicon were received: one containing the translations of offensive senses and one with the additional distinction concerning the neutral cases. Notably, HURTLEX aims to support the development of resources for underrepresented languages (Bassignana et al. 2018:5).

OL has been discussed in the context of MG lexicography. Efthymiou et al. (2014) show that the classification of the negative terms as derogatory, offensive, slang and taboo words in two celebrated dictionaries of MG, the LNEG2 (Babiniotis, 2002) and the LKN (Triantafyllidis, 2007) do not converge. In Table 1 a tick in the sixth column denotes an overlap between the categories of OL words identified by Efthymiou et al. (2014) and our classification. Christopoulou (2012) and Xydopoulos (2012) discuss extensively experiments on the measuring of word offensiveness but do not expand on how native speakers offer the relevant evaluation.

3 Working with HURTLEX-(EL)

Although filtering has been applied to prevent noise propagation in the semi-automatically enriched HURTLEX, its EL branch still includes synsets with no offensive meaning and incorrect terms. First, we manually removed clearly incorrect terms. Two linguists agreed that these included: (i) foreign words (384 words; either in English or French), (ii) combinations of Greek and foreign words (33 words), i.e., ευρασίας griffon, Lit. eurasia's griffon, (iii) about 194 meaningless phrases, i.e., πουτίγκα κεφάλι, Lit. pudding head, (iv) terms with morphological errors (23 words) i.e., φυσιογνωμονική 'physiognomic' instead of φυσιογνωμική 'physiognomic' (v) agreement errors (46 words), i.e., σεξουαλικά επίθεση, instead of σεξουαλική επίθεση 'sexual assault' (vi) different inflectional forms of the same lemma (298 words); MG makes heavy use of inflectional morphology and HURTLEX seemed unable to filter out types in the same inflectional paradigm, and (vii) archaic words (37 words), i.e., αιχμαλωτίζων 'capturer' which is an active present participle of a verb still used in MG but these particular participles belong to older forms of the language. At this stage, annotators also removed words that they all considered "unoffensive" in MG, i.e., μοτσαρέλα 'mozzarella'. 2143 words (about 69% of the original HURTLEX-(EL) contents) were retained out of the 3114 original entries of HURTLEX -(EL).

Given the growing body of literature (Chakrabarty et al. 2019; Naseem et al. 2019; Ashraf et al. 2021) emphasizing the role of context in characterising a word as offensive, we adopted

[3] https://multiwordnet.fbk.eu/english/home.php.

[4] https://babelnet.org/.

an annotation schema with three categories, namely *offensive (context-independent), context (context-dependent)*, following the distinction introduced in Vargas et al. (2021), and *non-offensive* entries. Representative examples were provided for terms assigned the label "context-dependent".

Next, four independent annotators, all undergraduate linguists who offered volunteer work, assigned one of the three labels: context-independent, context-dependent, non-offensive. General diagnostics of offensiveness mainly about profane and obscene language were offered as suggestions at this stage. The interannotator agreement score in this first step was 0.77 (Fleiss kappa), which indicates an already substantial agreement.

In the final step, a somewhat different annotation procedure was adopted (see Poletto et al. 2017 for a similar approach). The four annotators were provided with a set of more detailed diagnostics of offensiveness, e.g.: "Names of animals that are stereotypically related with negative properties in the Greek culture, such as ugliness, e.g., φώκια 'seal' or dirt, e.g., γουρούνι 'pig', are offensively used when they target individuals." These diagnostics were not developed on the basis of the classification of offensive words in the original HURTLEX or in the MG lexica (Section 2); instead, we preferred to work bottom-up and develop our own diagnostics. The motivation for this decision was that the rich material in HURTLEX-(EL) would present more classification challenges than the material in Greek printed lexica and that a Greek group's idea of offensiveness might not be identical to that of HURTLEX, a possibility that is recognised by the HURTLEX developers (Bassignana et al. 2018:5). The annotators were asked to consult these diagnostics when classifying the terms as un/offensive but (i) they might propose changes such as deletions, additions and redefinitions of categories (ii) a term might fit to more than one category. The annotators would meet with the group leaders to discuss the diagnostics. There were three rounds of this procedure and eventually the system of thematic categories was developed as a set of diagnostics for recognising offensive words in Modern Greek; this system is presented in Section 4.

Lastly, the labels context-independent, context-dependent and non-offensive were reassigned independently by the annotators and an interannotator agreement Fleiss kappa score of 0.96 was received. We did not resort to majority vote so only 737 terms that were shared by all the four annotators were included in the final lexicon; of them, as "context independent" were marked 448 words and as "context dependent" 289 words.

4 Annotation Diagnostics

Prose in this Section should be read with constant reference to Table 1. The final annotation diagnostics scheme comprises:

1. 17 thematic categories of offensive words

2. Tripartite distinction: offensive context-dependent, offensive context-independent and non-offensive words (Section 3). The role of the context is illustrated with the following examples: (i) the word φυτό 'plant' acquires derogatory meaning when it is attributed to a person ('nerd'), (ii) the word μαλάκας 'asshole' loses its offensive connotation when it is used to address someone in a friendly social context (Christopoulou, 2012; Xydopoulos, 2012).

3. A subtler specification of context where words are classified by the entities that are the targets of the offensive meaning: individuals (indv.), groups, non-humans and events / properties / states (ESP). This is helpful, for instance, when individuals are assigned stereotypically negative characteristics of animals.

Below are given indicative terms and clarifications regarding the identified 17 thematic categories listed in Table 1:

1. **Social class and hierarchy**: Words implying stereotypical negative characteristics of the members of the respective social communities, e.g., χωριάτης 'peasant', νεόπλουτος 'nouveau riche', φτωχός 'poor', βαρώνος 'baron'.

2. **Historical and social context**: Historical events, movements or acts are assigned a negative characterization that is absent in the their historical context but it may have occurred because of the their contemporary obsolete nature (Hamilton et al., 2016), e.g., σχολαστικισμός 'scholasticism', ηθικολόγος 'moralist', ακαδημαϊσμός 'academicism', μεσαιωνικός 'medieval'.

3. **Crime and immoral behavior & respective agents**, e.g., δολοφονία 'murder' and δολοφόνος 'murderer', τρομοκρατία 'terrorism' and τρομοκράτης 'terrorist', ληστεία 'robbery', συκοφαντία 'slander' and σούφρωμα 'puckering'.

4. **Religion** is viewed as a behavior not congruent with the beliefs of the Greek population and its duly constituted religion (Moon, 2018), e.g., ειδωλολατρία 'idololatry', μασόνος 'mason'.
5. **Nationality/ethnicity**: Negative stereotypical ethnic characteristics are assigned to individuals of other nationalities and minorities, e.g., Εβραίος 'Jew', γύφτος 'gypsy' (Razavi et al. 2010; Warner and Hirschberg 2012). These words might be acceptable in a casual conversation if the speaker and the recipient belong to the same cultural group (Warner and Hirschberg, 2012).
6. **Politics**: In the context of democratic and liberal societies especially (Razavi et al., 2010), extreme political regimes or acts receive negative political evaluation, e.g., φασισμός 'fascism', χούντα 'junta', αποστάτης 'renegade'.
7. **Professions of low prestige and sexual occupations**, e.g., σκαφτιάς 'digger', παπαράτσι 'paparazzi', ιερόδουλη 'prostitute', ζιγκολό 'gigolo'.
8. **Animals**: Transfer of animal characteristics to humans, e.g., γουρούνι 'pig', γάιδαρος 'donkey', πρόβατα 'cattle', φίδι 'snake', τσιμπούρι 'tick' (Efthymiou et al., 2014).
9. **Plants**: Stereotypical negative attributes are assigned to humans regarding their cognitive skills and physical appearance, e.g., αγγούρι 'cucumber', πατάτες 'potatoes', φάβα 'fava bean', φυτό 'nerd'.
10. **Characteristics of inannimates** are transferred to humans e.g., σκουπίδι 'trash', βαρίδι 'sinker'.
11. **Sentiments/psychological states**: e.g., τρελός 'crazy', δυστυχισμένος 'miserable', θυμωμένος 'mad', μανιασμένος 'raging'.
12. **Behavior**: People tend to criticize other people's manner based on social norms and their own way of perceiving reality, e.g., κακότροπος 'snappy', λεχρίτης 'asswipe', εξυπνάκιας 'smartass', κλόουν 'clown'.
13. **Physical and cognitive disabilities / appearance**: Assignment of specific physical or cognitive disabilities to humans (καμπούρης 'hunchback', τυφλός 'blind', χωλός 'lame', βλάκας 'idiot', κουτορνίθι 'dumb'.
14. **Sexuality / gender identity**: Some are official terms, e.g., ομοφυλόφιλος 'homosexual', λεσβία 'lesbian', τραβεστί 'tranny' (Narváez et al., 2009).
15. **Taboo body parts** are context-independent offensive, e.g., αρχίδια 'balls', κώλος 'ass', παπάρι 'whatchamacallit', ψωλή 'dick'. Scientific terms, e.g., χολή 'spleen', οπίσθια 'buttock' may be used offensively or as formal / scientific terminology (Crespo-Fernández, 2018).
16. **Scientific or medical terms**, e.g., ναρκισσισμός 'narcissism', μικρόβιο 'germ'.
17. **Places** related to offensive occupations, e.g., μπουρδέλο 'brothel'.

Figure 1 presents the distribution of words per diagnostic. Behavior is the most populated diagnostic followed by Crime & immoral behavior and Animals.

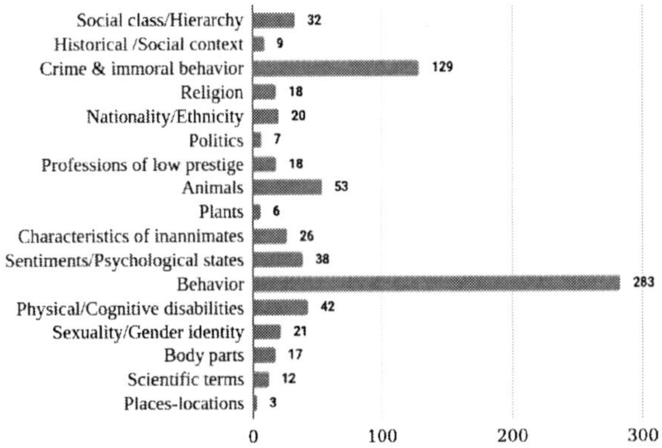

Figure 1: Word distribution per diagnostic.

5 Comparison to HURTLEX-(EL)

HURTLEX relies on a classification of OL words in 17 categories (Bassignana et al., 2018). We have defined our own diagnostics in a bottom-up iterative fashion (Section 3). The comparison of these diagnostics against the OL categories in the MG literature (sixth column of Table 1) justifies our expectations that HURTLEX would provide access to more thematic categories of offensive/derogatory words (note that all the OL categories defined in the MG literature feature among our diagnostics).

Our 17 diagnostics are equal in number with the original HURTLEX categories, but they present, probably expected, similarities and differences.

Similarities were expected because we worked on the expansion of the original 17 HURTLEX categories. However, this similarity of our independently derived diagnostics -also with the lexicographic OL categories of Greek- indicates a certain stability of OL diagnostics across different social settings, namely those of HURTLEX, of Greek lexicography which refers to the Greek society of at

	Classes	OL Target	Cont. Ind.	Cont. Dep.	Efthymiou (2014)
1.	Social class/ hierarchy	indv., groups		+	
2.	Historical/ social context	indv., groups, ESP		+	
3.	Crime immoral behavior	indv., groups, ESP	+	+	
4.	Religion	indv., groups, ESP		+	✓
5.	Nationality ethnicity	indv., groups	+	+	✓
6.	Politics	indv., groups, ESP	+	+	✓
7.	Professions of low prestige/ sexual occup.	indv., groups, ESP	+	+	
8.	Animals	indv., groups, non-human		+	
9.	Plants	indv., groups, non human		+	
10.	Characteristics of inannimates	indv., groups, non-human		+	
11.	Sentiments, psychological states	indv., ESP	+	+	
12.	Behavior	indv., groups, ESP	+	+	✓
13.	Physical/ cognitive disabilities, appearance	indv., groups, non humans	+	+	✓
14.	Sexuality gender identity	indv., groups, ESP	+	+	✓
15.	Body parts	indv., groups, ESP, non-human	+	+	✓
16.	Scientific terms	indv., groups, ESP, non-human		+	
17.	Places-locations	indv., groups, ESP, non human	+		

Table 1: Presentation of the OL diagnostics & comparison to the study by Efthymiou et al. (2014).

least 20 years ago and the contemporary Greek social settings that our group represents.

The deviation was expected because OL phenomena are influenced by regional and cultural patterns (Bassignana et al. 2018). As a fact, mainly historically and culturally marked diagnostics deviate from the HURTLEX categories. The differences between HURTLEX's categories and our diagnostics are: (i) HURTLEX's category "SVP—words related to the seven deadly sins of the Christian tradition": Our diagnostic 4 reflects tendencies of Greek society and contains words referring to different religions or religious states (ii) HURTLEX's "IS—social class/ hierarchy": Our diagnostic 1 also comprises terms denoting social and economic (dis)advantages, e.g., νεόπλουτος 'nouveau riche' and βαρώνος 'baron' (iii) We included the new diagnostic 2 "Historical / social context", which contains contemporary terms particular to Greek history, e.g., κλέφτες 'armatole / militiamen' (Greek armed groups of the Ottoman occupation era); HURTLEX distributes these words in the categories "Potential negative connotations (QAS)", "Derogatory words (CDS)" and, "Felonies and words related to crime and immoral behavior (RE)" (iv) We added the new diagnostic 5 containing terms about nationalities/minorities within the Greek ethnicity and words reflecting social and cultural differentiation, e.g., 'Jew', 'gypsy' (vi) We included the words related to sexual orientation (HURTLEX's OM) in the single diagnostic 16 "Sexuality / gender identity".

6 Conclusions and future work

We have discussed our experience regarding the development of an openly available, cleansed version of the Greek branch of HURTLEX; in doing so, we have defined diagnostics of offensiveness that will be useful in future offensive word and text categorisation tasks.

This was the first step in a longer-term effort that aims to offer reasonable MG lexica and corpora for the task of OL detection. On the lexicon development front we plan to study the effect of evaluative morphology on OL (Christopoulou, 2012; Stavrianaki, 2009), enlarge the lexicon semi-automatically drawing on corpora (Wiegand et al., 2018) and test its coverage and contribution to OL identification tasks using texts from a variety of registers. On the corpora development front, we intend to use the lexicon in order to leverage corpora for OL detection and for a variety of registers.

References

Noman Ashraf, Arkaitz Zubiaga, and Alexander Gelbukh. 2021. Abusive language detection in youtube comments leveraging replies as conversational context. *PeerJ Computer Science*, 7:e742.

George Babiniotis. 2002. *Dictionary of Modern Greek Language*. Center Lexicology.

Elisa Bassignana, Valerio Basile, and Viviana Patti. 2018. Hurtlex: A multilingual lexicon of words to hurt. In *Proceedings of the Fifth Italian Conference on Computational Linguistics (CLiC-it)*.

Tuhin Chakrabarty, Kilol Gupta, and Smaranda Muresan. 2019. Pay "attention" to your context when classifying abusive language. In *Proceedings of the Third Workshop on Abusive Language Online*, pages 70–79, Florence, Italy. Association for Computational Linguistics.

Ying Chen, Yilu Zhou, Sencun Zhu, and Heng Xu. 2012. Detecting offensive language in social media to protect adolescent online safety. *2012 International Conference on Privacy, Security, Risk and Trust and 2012 International Confernece on Social Computing*, pages 71–80.

Aikaterini Christopoulou. 2012. *A lexicological analysis of slang vocabulary of Modern Greek*. PhD dissertation, University of Patras.

Davide Colla, Tommaso Caselli, Valerio Basile, Jelena Mitrović, and Michael Granitzer. 2020. GruPaTo at SemEval-2020 task 12: Retraining mBERT on social media and fine-tuned offensive language models. In *Proceedings of the Fourteenth Workshop on Semantic Evaluation*, pages 1546–1554, Barcelona (online). International Committee for Computational Linguistics.

Eliecer Crespo-Fernández. 2018. Taboos in speaking of sex and sexuality. *The Oxford Handbook of Taboo Words and Language*, pages 41–60.

Thomas Davidson, Dana Warmsley, Michael Macy, and Ingmar Weber. 2017. Automated hate speech detection and the problem of offensive language. In *Proceedings of the 11th International AAAI Conference on Web and Social Media*, ICWSM '17, pages 512–515.

Angeliki Efthymiou, Zoe Gavriilidou, and Eleni Papadopoulou. 2014. *Labeling of Derogatory Words in Modern Greek Dictionaries*, pages 27–40. De Gruyter Open Poland.

William L. Hamilton, Kevin Clark, Jure Leskovec, and Dan Jurafsky. 2016. Inducing domain-specific sentiment lexicons from unlabeled corpora. In *Proceedings of the 2016 Conference on Empirical Methods in Natural Language Processing*, pages 595–605, Austin, Texas. Association for Computational Linguistics.

James B. Jacobs and Kimberly Potter. 1998. *Hate Crimes: Criminal Law and Identity Politics*. Oxford University Press USA.

Ioanna K. Lekea and Panagiotis Karampelas. 2018. Detecting hate speech within the terrorist argument: A greek case. In *Proceedings of the 2018 IEEE/ACM International Conference on Advances in Social Networks Analysis and Mining*, ASONAM '18, page 1084–1091. IEEE Press.

Richard Moon. 2018. *Putting Faith in Hate: When Religion Is the Source or Target of Hate Speech*. Cambridge University Press.

Dr. Rafael F. Narváez, Ilan H. Meyer, Robert M. Kertzner, Suzanne C. Ouellette, and Allegra R. Gordon. 2009. A qualitative approach to the intersection of sexual, ethnic, and gender identities. *Identity*, 9(1):63–86. PMID: 27683200.

Usman Naseem, Imran Razzak, and Ibrahim A. Hameed. 2019. Deep context-aware embedding for abusive and hate speech detection on twitter. *Aust. J. Intell. Inf. Process. Syst.*, 15:69–76.

Dennis Njagi, Z. Zuping, Damien Hanyurwimfura, and Jun Long. 2015. A lexicon-based approach for hate speech detection. *International Journal of Multimedia and Ubiquitous Engineering*, 10:215–230.

Ted Pedersen. 2019. Duluth at SemEval-2019 task 6: Lexical approaches to identify and categorize offensive tweets. In *Proceedings of the 13th International Workshop on Semantic Evaluation*, pages 593–599, Minneapolis, Minnesota, USA. Association for Computational Linguistics.

Serena Pelosi, Alessandro Maisto, Pierluigi Vitale, and Simonetta Vietri. 2017. Mining offensive language on social media. In *CLiC-it*.

Konstantinos Perifanos and Dionysis Goutsos. 2021. Multimodal hate speech detection in greek social media. *Multimodal Technologies and Interaction*, 5(7).

Zeses Pitenis. 2019. *Detecting Offensive Posts in Greek Social Media*. Master thesis, University Of Wolverhampton, School Of Humanities.

Zesis Pitenis, Marcos Zampieri, and Tharindu Ranasinghe. 2020. Offensive language identification in Greek. In *Proceedings of the 12th Language Resources and Evaluation Conference*, pages 5113–5119, Marseille, France. European Language Resources Association.

Fabio Poletto, Marco Antonio Stranisci, Manuela Sanguinetti, Viviana Patti, and Cristina Bosco. 2017. Hate speech annotation: Analysis of an italian twitter corpus. In *CLiC-it*.

Amir H. Razavi, Diana Inkpen, Sasha Uritsky, and Stan Matwin. 2010. Offensive language detection using multi-level classification. In *Advances in Artificial Intelligence*, pages 16–27, Berlin, Heidelberg. Springer Berlin Heidelberg.

Paul Röttger, Bertie Vidgen, Dirk Hovy, and Janet B. Pierrehumbert. 2022. Two contrasting data annotation paradigms for subjective nlp tasks. ArXiv 2112.07475.

Salim Sazzed. 2021. A lexicon for profane and obscene text identification in Bengali. In *Proceedings of the International Conference on Recent Advances in Natural Language Processing (RANLP 2021)*, pages 1289–1296, Held Online. INCOMA Ltd.

Anna Schmidt and Michael Wiegand. 2017. A survey on hate speech detection using natural language processing. In *Proceedings of the Fifth International Workshop on Natural Language Processing for Social Media*, pages 1–10, Valencia, Spain. Association for Computational Linguistics.

Aikaterini Stavrianaki. 2009. –άκι και –ette: diminutive suffixes of Modern Greek and French. A comparative analysis and extensions regarding language learning and teaching. In *Proceedings of International Conference 2008, European year of intercultural dialogue: Talking with languages-cultures. Thessaloniki: Department of French Language, AUTH*, pages 759–769.

Manolis Triantafyllidis. 2007. *Dictionary of Standard Modern Greek.* Institute of Modern Greek Studies.[Manolis Triandaphyllidis Foundation].

Francielle Alves Vargas, Isabelle Carvalho, and Fabiana Rodrigues de Goes. 2021. Identifying offensive expressions of opinion in context. *ArXiv*, abs/2104.12227.

William Warner and Julia Hirschberg. 2012. Detecting hate speech on the world wide web. In *Proceedings of the Second Workshop on Language in Social Media*, pages 19–26, Montréal, Canada. Association for Computational Linguistics.

Zeerak Waseem, Thomas Davidson, Dana Warmsley, and Ingmar Weber. 2017. Understanding abuse: A typology of abusive language detection subtasks. In *Proceedings of the First Workshop on Abusive Language Online*, pages 78–84, Vancouver, BC, Canada. Association for Computational Linguistics.

Michael Wiegand, Josef Ruppenhofer, Anna Schmidt, and Clayton Greenberg. 2018. Inducing a lexicon of abusive words – a feature-based approach. In *Proceedings of the 2018 Conference of the North American Chapter of the Association for Computational Linguistics: Human Language Technologies, Volume 1 (Long Papers)*, pages 1046–1056, New Orleans, Louisiana. Association for Computational Linguistics.

George Xydopoulos. 2012. *Lexicology: An Introduction to the Analysis of Words and Dictionaries.* Patakis Publishers, Athens.

Free speech or Free Hate Speech? Analyzing the Proliferation of Hate Speech in Parler

Abraham Israeli isabrah@post.bgu.ac.il
Oren Tsur orentsur@bgu.ac.il
Department of Software and Information System Engineering
Ben-Gurion University of the Negev
Beer-Sheva, Israel

Abstract

Social platforms such as Gab and Parler, branded as 'free-speech' networks, have seen a significant growth of their user base in recent years. This popularity is mainly attributed to the stricter moderation enforced by mainstream platforms such as Twitter, Facebook, and Reddit. In this work we provide the first large scale analysis of hate-speech on Parler. We experiment with an array of algorithms for hate-speech detection, demonstrating the limitations of transfer learning in that domain, given the illusive and ever changing nature of the ways hate-speech is delivered. In order to improve classification accuracy we annotated 10K Parler posts, which we use to fine-tune a BERT classifier. Classification of individual posts is then leveraged for the classification of millions of users via label propagation over the social network. Classifying users by their propensity to disseminate hate, we find that hate mongers make about 16% of Parler active users, and that they have distinct characteristics comparing to other user groups. We find that hate mongers are more active, more central, express distinct levels of sentiment, and convey a distinct array of emotions like anger and sadness. We further complement our analysis by comparing the trends observed in Parler to those found in Gab. To the best of our knowledge, this is among the first works to analyze hate speech in Parler in a quantitative manner and on the user level.

1 Introduction

Social platforms like Twitter, Facebook, and Reddit have become a central communication channel for billions of users.[1] The immense popularity of social platforms resulted in a significant rise in the toxicity of the discourse, ranging from cyberbullying to explicit hate speech and calls for violence against individuals and groups (Waseem and Hovy, 2016; Mondal et al., 2017; Laub, 2019; Ziems et al., 2020). Women, people of color, the LGBT community, Muslims, immigrants, and Jews are among the most targeted groups. Recent studies report on a surge in Islamophobia (Akbarzadeh, 2016; Sunar, 2017; Osman, 2017; Chandra et al., 2021), antisemitism (ADL, 2020; Zannettou et al., 2020), xenophobia (Iwama, 2018; Entorf and Lange, 2019), hate of Asians (An et al., 2021; Vidgen et al., 2020a) and hate crimes (Dodd and Marsh, 2017; Levin and Reitzel, 2018; Edwards and Rushin, 2018; Perry et al., 2020).

Facing an increased public and legislature scrutiny, mainstream social platforms (e.g., Facebook, Twitter, Reddit) committed to a stricter enforcement of community standards, curbing levels of hate on the platform.[2]

The stricter moderation of content drove many users into joining alternative social platforms such as Parler and Gab. Touting their commitment to 'free speech' and 'no moderation' policy, these platforms attract users that were suspended from mainstream platforms, conspiracy theorists, extremists, unhinged users, free-speech advocates, political activists as well as others.

User migration to Parler and Gab was not only grass-root. The platforms were promoted by prominent news anchors and political figures. For example, U.S. Senator Ted Cruz (R-TX) tweeted *"I'm proud to join @parler_app – a platform gets what free speech is all about – and I'm excited to be a part of it. Let's speak. Let's speak freely. And let's end the Silicon Valley censorship"* (6/25/2020). Sean Hannity, a popular host and commentator on Fox news, informed the viewers of his daily show that *"I saw that the president had joined it. At least there is a place, it's like Twitter, it's called Parler, I have an account there... good for you because the president joined, because they are censoring him and Dan Scavino and everybody else"* (1/8/2021).

[1] E.g., Facebook 2021 Q2 report (Meta, 2021a).

[2] e.g., Facebook 2021 report on hate-speech (Meta, 2021b), and the Time magazine cover of hate-speech in Twitter: (Time, 2021).

Proceedings of the Sixth Workshop on Online Abuse and Harms (WOAH), pages 109 - 121
July 14, 2022

Hate, brewing online, often spills to the streets (Hankes and Amend, 2019; Munn, 2019; Malevich and Robertso, 2019; Thomas, 2019). Thus, defending 'hate speech' under the right for 'free speech' may result in very concrete actions in real life. The perpetrator of the Pittsburgh synagogue shooting[3] was active on Gab, referring to "kike infestation" and "the children of satan". His final post, minutes before opening fire in the synagogue, was *"I can't sit by and watch my people get slaughtered. Screw your optics, I'm going in."*. Similarly, the storming of the U.S. Capitol on January 6, 2021 was found by the U.S. Senate Investigation Committee to be encouraged and coordinated on Parler (Peters et al., 2021).

In this work we focus on Parler, investigating the proliferation of hate speech on the platform, both on the post level and on the user level. We identify three distinct groups of users, denoted as hate mongers, standard users and hate flirts. We show significant differences between the groups in terms of language, emotion, activity level and role in the network. We further compare our results to the hateful dynamics reported for Gab.

2 Related Work

A growing body of work studies the magnitude and the different manifestations of hate speech in social media (Chandrasekharan et al., 2017; Zannettou et al., 2018; Zampieri et al., 2020; Ranasinghe and Zampieri, 2020), among others. Here, we present an overview of the current literature in three different perspectives: (i) The detection of hate speech on the *post* level, (ii) The detection of hate-promoting *users*, and (iii) The characterization of hate speech on the *platform* level.

Post-level classification Most previous works adress the detection of hate in textual form. Keywords and sentence structure in Twitter and Whisper were used in (Mondal et al., 2017; Saleem et al., 2017), demonstrating the limitations of a lexical approach. The use of code words, ambiguity and dog-whistling, and the challenges they introduce to text-based models were studied by (Davidson et al., 2017; Ribeiro et al., 2017; Arviv et al., 2021). The detection of implicit forms of hate speech is addressed by Magu et al. (2017) which detects the use of hate code words (e.g., google, skype, bing and skittle to refer to Black people, Jews, Chinese, and Muslims, respectively) using an SVM classifier based on bag-of-words. ElSherief et al. (2021) introduced a benchmark corpus of 22.5K tweets to study implicit hate speech. The authors presented baseline results over this dataset using Jigsaw Perspective,[4] SVM, and different variants of BERT (Devlin et al., 2018).

The use of demographic features such as gender and location in the detection of hate speech is explored by Waseem and Hovy (2016). User meta features, e.g., account age, posts per day, number of followers/friends, are used by Ribeiro et al. (2017).

Computational methods for the detection of hate speech and abusive language range from SVM and logistic regression (Davidson et al., 2017; Waseem and Hovy, 2016; Nobata et al., 2016; Magu et al., 2017), to neural architectures. Recently, Transformer-based architectures (Mozafari et al., 2019; Aluru et al., 2020; Samghabadi et al., 2020; Salminen et al., 2020; Qian et al., 2021; Kennedy et al., 2020; Arviv et al., 2021) achieved significant improvements over RNN and CNN models (Zhang et al., 2016; Gambäck and Sikdar, 2017; Del Vigna12 et al., 2017; Park and Fung, 2017). In an effort to mitigate the need for extensive annotation some works use transformers to generate more samples, e.g., (Vidgen et al., 2020b; Wullach et al., 2020, 2021). Zhou et al. (2021) integrate features from external resources to support the model performance.

In order to account for the often elusive and coded language and for the unfortunate variety of targeted groups (Schmidt and Wiegand, 2017; Ross et al., 2017), a set of functional test was suggested by Röttger et al. (2020), allowing an quick evaluation of hate-detection models.

Classification of hate *users* Characterizing *accounts* that are instrumental in the propagation of hate is gaining interest from the research community and industry alike, whether in order to better understand the social phenomena or in order to suspend major perpetrators instead of removing sporadic content. Detection and characterization of hateful Twitter and Gab users was tackled by Ribeiro et al. (2018); Mathew et al. (2018, 2019) and Arviv et al. (2021), among others. An annotated dataset of a few hundreds Twitter users was released as part of a shared task in CLEF 2021, see (Bevendorff et al., 2021) for an overview of the data and the submissions. Das et al. (2021) intro-

[3]ADL report on the attack: `https://tinyurl.com/yz87jn69` (accessed: 4/17/22)

[4]`https://www.perspectiveapi.com`

duced a user-level annotated dataset of 798 Gab users which we use for evaluation and comparison.

Hate speech on Parler and Gab While most prior work focus on the manifestations of hate in mainstream platforms, a number of works do address alternative platforms such as Gab and Parler. Two annotated Gab datasets were introduced by Kennedy et al. (2018) and by Qian et al. (2019). We use these datasets in this work as we compare Parler to Gab.

Focusing on users, rather than posts, Das et al. (2021) experiment with an array of models for hate users classification. Lima et al. (2018) aims to understand what users join Gab and what kind of content they share, while Jasser et al. (2021) conduct a qualitative analysis studying Gab's platform norms, given the lack of moderation. Gallacher and Bright (2021) explore whether users seek out Gab in order to express hate, or that the toxic attitude is adopted after joining the platform. The diffusion dynamics of the content posted by hateful and non-hateful Gab users is modeled by Mathew et al. (2019) and by Mathew et al. (2020).

Parler, launched in August 2018 and experiencing its impressive expansion of user base from late 2020, is only beginning to draw the attention of the research community. Early works analysed the language in Parler in several aspects such as QAnon content (Sipka et al., 2021), COVID-19 vaccines (Baines et al., 2021), and the 2021 Capitol riots (Esser, 2021). The first dataset of Parler messages was introduced by Aliapoulios et al. (2021), along with a basic statistical analysis of the data, e.g., the number of posts and the number of registered users per month, along with the most popular tokens, bigrams, and hashtags. We use this dataset in the current work to analyze hate speech on Parler. Ward (2021) used a list of predefined keywords (hate terms), assessing the level of hate-speech on the platform.

Our work differs from these works in a number of fundamental aspects. First, we combine textual and social (network) signals in order to detect both hateful posts and hate-promoting accounts. Second, we suggest models that rely on state-of-the-art neural architectures and computational methods, while previous work detects hate speech by matching a fixed set of keywords from a predefined list of hate terms. Furthermore, we provide a thorough analysis of the applicability of different algorithms, trained and fine-tuned on various datasets and tasks. Third, we provide a broader context to our analysis of the proliferation of hate in Parler, as we compare and contrast it to trends observed on Gab.

3 Data

In this section we describe the datasets used for this work – starting with a general overview of the platforms, then providing a detailed description of the datasets and the annotation procedure.

3.1 Parler and Gab Social Platforms

Parler Alluding to the french verb 'to speak', Parler was launched on August 2018. The platform brands itself as "The World's Town Square" a place in which users can *"Speak freely and express yourself openly, without fear of being "deplatformed" for your views"*.[5]

Parler users post texts (called *parlays*) of up to 1000 characters. Users can reply to parlays and to previous replies. Parler supports a reposting mechanism similar to Twitters retweets (called 'echos'). Throughout this paper we refer to echo posts as *reposts*, not to confuse with the ((())) (echo) hate symbol (Arviv et al., 2021).

Parler's official guidelines[6] explicitly allow "trolling" and "not-safe-for-work" (NSFW) content, include only two "principles" prohibiting "unlawful acts", citing "Obvious examples include: child sexual abuse material, content posted by or on behalf of terrorist organizations, intellectual property theft".

By January 2021, 13.25M users have joined Parler and its application was the most downloaded app in Apple's App Store. This growth is attributed to celebrities and political figures promoting the platform (see Section 1) and the stricter moderation enforced by Facebook and Twitter, culminating with the suspension of Donald Trump (`@realDonaldTrump`), the 45th President of the United States, from Twitter and Facebook.

Gab Gab, launched on August 2016, was created as an alternative to Twitter, positioning itself as putting "people and free speech first", welcoming users suspended from other social networks (Zannettou et al., 2018). Gab posts (called *gabs*) are limited to 300-characters, and users can repost, quote or reply to previously created gabs. Gab permits

[5]Parler branding on its landing page (accessed: 3/10/2022)

[6]https://parler.com/documents/guidelines.pdf (accessed: 4/17/2022)

	Parler	Gab
Users	4.08M	144.3K
Posts	20.59M	7.95M
Replies	84.55M	5.92M
Reposts	77.93M	8.24M
Time-Span	08/2018 – 01/2021	08/2016 – 01/2018

Table 1: Datasets Statistics. Replies are responses to main posts. Reposts are equivalent to Twitter retweets.

pornographic and obscene content, as long as it is labeled *NSFW*. Previous work finds the majority of Gab users to be Caucasians-conservatives-males (Lima et al., 2018). For more details about Gab usage, users and manifestations of hate see references at Section 2.

3.2 Parler and Gab Corpora

We use the Parler and Gab datasets published by Aliapoulios et al. (2021) and Zannettou et al. (2018), respectively. The Parler dataset is unlabeled, therefore annotation is required. We describe the annotation procedure and label statistics in Section 3.3.

Both datasets include posts and users' meta data, though the Parler dataset is richer, containing more attributes such as registration time. Each of the datasets is composed of millions of posts and replies, see Table 1. The Parler dataset is bigger, containing more posts and more users, however, on average, Gab users post more content per user. We note that there is no temporal overlap between the two datasets. In Section 7 we discuss this point and its possible impacts on our analysis.

We use three Gab *annotated* datasets which are all sampled from the unlabeled Gab corpus we use: (i) The Gab Hate Corpus – 27.5K Gab posts published by Kennedy et al. (2018), (ii) 9.5K Gab posts published by Qian et al. (2019), and (iii) 5K posts published by Arviv et al. (2021).[7]. In total, we collect a corpus of 42.1K annotated Gab posts. 7.7K (18.4%) of the posts are tagged as hateful.

3.3 Annotation of Parler Data

Hate speech takes different forms in different social platforms (Wiegand et al., 2019) and across time (Florio et al., 2020). It is often implicit (ElSherief et al., 2021), targeting a variety of groups. Consequently, transfer learning remains a challenge for hate-speech detection, and an annotated Parler dataset is needed in order to achieve accurate classification. These challenges and the significant improvements in performance achieved by proper fine-tuning are demonstrated through extensive experimentation in Section 4.1. In the remainder of this section we describe the annotation procedure.

The annotation task was designed as follows: 10K posts were sampled from the Parler corpus. All posts are: (i) in English; (ii) at least 10 characters long; (iii) neither a repost nor a comment; and (iv) do not contain a URL.

The 10K annotated posts *were not* randomly selected from the Parler corpus. A random selection of posts would have led to an extremely imbalanced dataset as most of the posts are not expected to express hate. Hence, we opt to stratified sampling. This sampling process relies on an approximation of the likelihood of each post to include hateful content. We used a pretrained hate speech prediction model to approximate this likelihood.

Annotation was done by 112 student (more than half of them are graduate students), who were provided detailed guidelines and training involving the various types of hate speech, the elusiveness of hate expressions using coded language, how to detect it, and a number of examples of different types. Each of the annotators was prompted with a list of 300 posts and had to assign each with a Lickert score ranging from 1 (not hate) to 5 (extreme or explicit hate). We provided annotators only with the textual content of the post. Each of the 10K posts was annotated by three annotators. Annotators presented a satisfying agreement level of 72% and a Cohen's Kappa of 0.44. Labels of posts with a low agreement level[8] were ignored (~7% of the annotated posts). We define a post as hateful (non-hateful) if its average score is higher (lower) than three. We omit posts with an average score of exactly three. Accordingly, 3224 of the 10K posts (32.8%) were labeled as hateful and 6053 (59.8%) as non-hateful.

We make this annotated corpus available under our public GitHub repository[9] – the first public annotated corpus of Parler.

4 Methods

In this work we are interested in the detection of hate, both on the post level and the account

[7]This work models Twitter data but also published an annotated dataset of Gab

[8]Low agreement is defined as either an annotation with at least three different Likert values, or a difference greater than 2 between the Likert values.

[9]https://github.com/NasLabBgu/parler-hate-speech

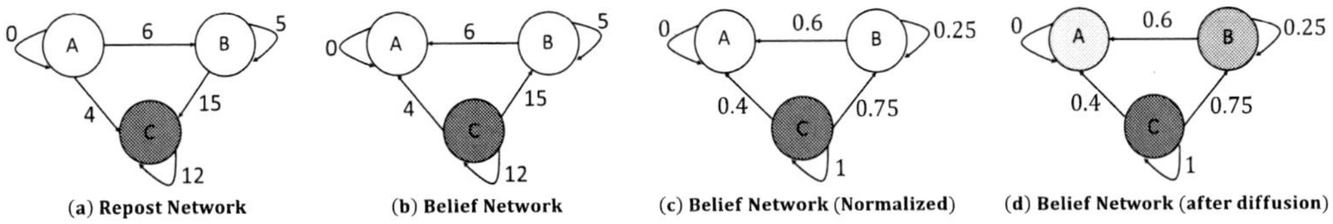

Figure 1: An illustration of the diffusion model over three nodes. Self loops represent the total number of posts per node. In step (a) The repost network is built and nodes are assigned an initial belief – seed hate mongers with a value of 1 (orange) and others with a value of 0 (white). In steps (b) and (c) The network is converted to a belief network – reversing edges direction and normalizing weights. In step (d) The diffusion process is simulated. Belief updates are indicated by darker shades.

level. Our interest in the post level classification is twofold. Given an accurate classifier, we can: (a) Approximate the hate degree in different aggregation levels – e.g., over the full network or and per user, and (b) Use the post-level predictions to support training a user level classifier. A review of the various post level classifiers is provided in Section 4.1 and our modifications to a diffusion-based model for user classification are presented in Section 4.2. Ethical considerations related to user classification are discussed at the end of Section 7.

4.1 Post Level Classification Models

We fine-tune the DistilBERT (Sanh et al., 2019) transformer on each of the datasets, obtaining two fine-tuned models (referred to as Our-FT BERT). We compare the models performance on the respective datasets against four competitive models:

1. **Jigsaw Perspective**: A widely used commercial model geared toward detection of hateful and toxic content, developed by Google. Jigsaw was found to perform well in an array of tasks related to hate-speech detection (Röttger et al., 2020). Jigsaw implementation is not public and the service is provided as a black-box through an online API.[10]

2. **deHateBERT** (Aluru et al., 2020): An adaptation of the BERT Transformer for hate-speech detection – the pretrained transformer was fine-tuned on a corpus of 96.3K text snippets from Twitter and from the white supremacist forum Stormfront.org. The authors indicate that 15.01K (15.6%) training samples were labeled as hate-speech.

3. **Twitter-roBERTa** (Barbieri et al., 2020): This model uses the RoBERTa (Liu et al., 2019) architecture, specifically fine-tuned on the task of hate-speech detection of micro-messages. The authors used a corpus of 13K tweets, 5.2K (40%) of them are labeled as hate speech.

4. **HateBase** (Tuckwood, 2017): HateBase is a multilanguage vocabulary of hate terms that is maintained in order to assist in content moderation and research. We use 68 explicit hate terms that were used in prior works (Mathew et al., 2018, 2019). These terms were manually selected from HateBase's English lexicon. All the terms in the list are *explicit*, e.g., 'kike' (slur targeting Jews), 'paki' (slur against Muslims, especially with Pakistani roots), and 'cunt'. Text is labeled as hate if it contains at least a single hate term.

4.2 User Level Classification

In order to leverage the network structure, we view each platform as a social network with users as nodes and *reposts* as directed edges. Edges are weighted to reflect levels of engagement, as illustrated in Figure 1(a): a directed edge (A, B) with a weight of 6 indicates that user A reposted 6 posts originally posted by user B.

We modify the diffusion-based approach for the detection of hate mongers proposed by Ribeiro et al. (2018) in order to achieve a more accurate classification. The basic diffusion-based classification is performed in two stages: (a) Identifying a *seed* group of hate mongers; and (b) Applying a diffusion model over the social network. We use the DeGroot's hate diffusion model (Golub and Jackson, 2010) which outputs an estimated belief value (i.e., "hate") per user, over the [0,1] range. A toy example of the diffusion process is illustrated in Figure 1. In our experiments we set the number of diffusion iterations to three. One clear advantage of this approach over fully supervised methods is that it does not require a large dataset annotated on the user level.

[10]https://www.perspectiveapi.com

Modified Diffusion Model We introduced two modifications to the diffusion model used by Ribeiro et al. (2018) and Mathew et al. (2019): (i) *Seed definition*: Instead of taking a lexical approach in order to identify users posting more than *k* hateful posts, we use our fine-tuned Transformers. We argue that fine-tuning the classifiers for each social network significantly improves the classification on the post level (as demonstrated in Section 5.1), and ultimately, improves the performance of the diffusion model; and (ii) *Hateful users definition*: In the original diffusion process, hate (as well as "not-hate") labels are diffused through the network. This way, seed hate mongers may end with a low hate score, which in turn propagates to their neighbours. However, seed users were chosen due to the fact that they post a significant number of undoubtedly hateful posts. Fixing the hate score of seed users results in a more accurate labeling of the accounts in the network.

5 Classification Results

5.1 Post Level Results

We use the annotated corpora (see Sections 3.2 and 3.3) to fine-tune the pretrained Transformer on each social platform, splitting the labeled data to train (60%), validation (20%), and test (20%) sets.

The precision-recall curves of the Parler and Gab models are presented in Figure 2. Our fine-tuned models significantly outperforms the other models in both datasets. We wish to point out that while the popular keywords base approach (HateBase) achieves a high precision and a moderate recall on the Gab data, outperforming all Transformer models except the platform fine-tuned ones, it collapses in both measures on the Parler dataset. These results revalidate the limitations of lexical approaches, and of neural methods that are not fine-tuned for the specific dataset.

5.2 User Level Results

As described in Section 4.2, in order to classify accounts we use a diffusion model. The diffusion process is seeded with a set of hateful accounts. The choice of seed accounts involves the following steps: (i) After establishing the accuracy of the fine-tuned models (Section 5.1) we use these models to label *all* the posts in the respective datasets; (ii) Opting for a conservative assignment of seed users, we consider only posts with hate score (likelihood) over 0.95 (0.9) in the Parler (Gab) dataset to be hateful. This threshold setting yields a precision of 0.801 (0.902) and a recall of 0.811 (0.903) over the Parler (Gab) dataset.[11]; Finally, (iii) Users posting 10 or more hateful posts are labeled as seed accounts. We take the conservative approach in steps (ii) and (iii) in order to control the often noisy diffusion process.

Simulating the modified diffusion process described in Section 4.2 we obtain a hate score per *user*. For analysis purposes we divide users to three distinct groups – hate mongers (denoted HM), composed of the users making the top quartile of hate scores; Standard users (denoted S) making the bottom quartile; the rest of the users (denoted $\widetilde{HM}$) suspected as "flirting" with hate mongers and hate dissemination. Users with a low level of activity (less than five posts or users who joined the network less than 60 days prior to data collection) were not considered.[12] The distribution of *active* users by type in Parler is 16.1%/42.4%/41.5% per $HM/\widetilde{HM}/S$ populations, and 10%/41.7%/48.3% in Gab.

Evaluation of the diffusion model A user-level annotated dataset of 798 Gab users was shared by Das et al. (2021). We use this dataset to validate the performance of the diffusion models – both the standard model and our modified model (see Section 4.2). We find our modified model to outperform the standard model, achieving precision/recall/F1-scores of 0.9/0.54/0.678, comparing to 0.95/0.34/0.5. Therefore, results and analysis in the remainder of the paper are based on the modified diffusion model.

6 Analysis: The Propensity of Hate

6.1 Hate on the Post Level

Taking our conservative approach, we find that the frequency of hate posting is higher in Parler (3.29%), compared in Gab (2.13%). However, we find that 13.95% of Parler users share at least one hateful post – a significantly lower number compared to Gab (18.58%). We find that 65.5% of the hate content in Parler is posted as a reply to other parlays. This reflects a significant over-representation of replies compared with full corpus distribution (46.2% of posts are replies, see Table 1). Similarly, 38.9% of the hate content on Gab are replies.

[11]These measures are the weighted average precision/recall over both hate/non-hate classes.

[12]87.1% (63.4%) of the users in Parler (Gab)

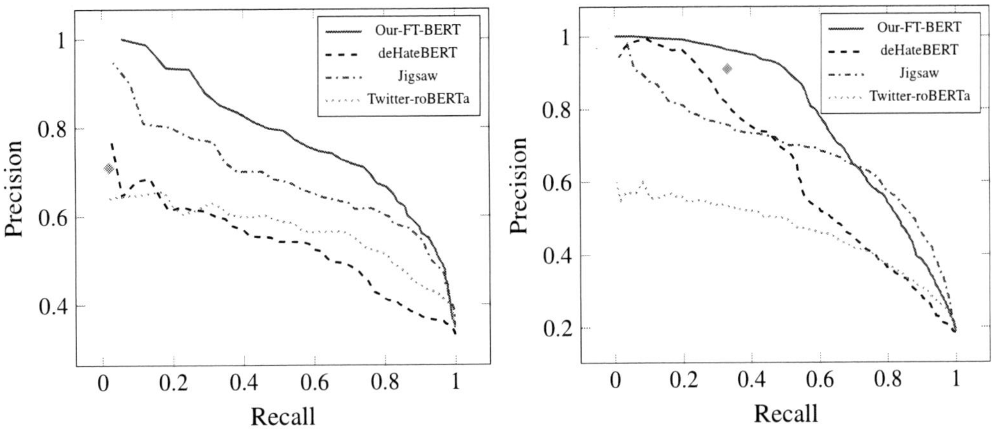

Parler Classifiers

Gab Classifiers

Figure 2: Post level Precision-Recall (PR) curves. FT-BERT: Fine Tuned BERT; Orange diamond (◈) marks the PR performance of the lexical-based approach (HateBase). Unlike the other four methods, this approach cannot be controlled by a threshold parameter, hence only a single PR value is available.

6.2 Hate on the User Level

We provide an analysis of the characteristics of the HM, $\widetilde{HM}$ and S accounts on an array of attributes, ranging from activity levels to centrality, sentiment and the emotions they convey.

Activity Level Activity levels are compared via four features – number of posts, replies, reposts, and users' age (measured in days).

HM are the most active user group in both platforms across all activity types (see Figure 3). We find that the $\widetilde{HM}$ users have similar characteristics in both platforms – overall, they post less content than the HM users, repost more content than the S group, and their tendency to reply is lower compared to the S users.

Interestingly, although the HM make only 16.1% (10%) of the active users in Parler (Gab) – they generate a disproportional number of posts: 30.6% (59.45%) of the posts in Parler (Gab). The same holds for replies – the HM users post 36.68% (75.57%) of the replies in Parler (Gab). When aggregating all activity types (post/reply/repost) – the HM users generate 41.23% (71.38%) of the content in Parler (Gab).

User *Age* (days from account creation to the most recent post in the data), is an exceptional feature. We observe only insignificant differences between the three user groups. This observation holds for both platforms. However, collapsing the groups – we do find a significant difference between the two platforms. Gab users are "older" with an average age of 323.9 compared to 189.6 of the Parler users. We hypothesize that the difference is a result of the way both platform evolve over time, given the unfolding of events driving users to these platforms (see Sections 1 and 3.1).

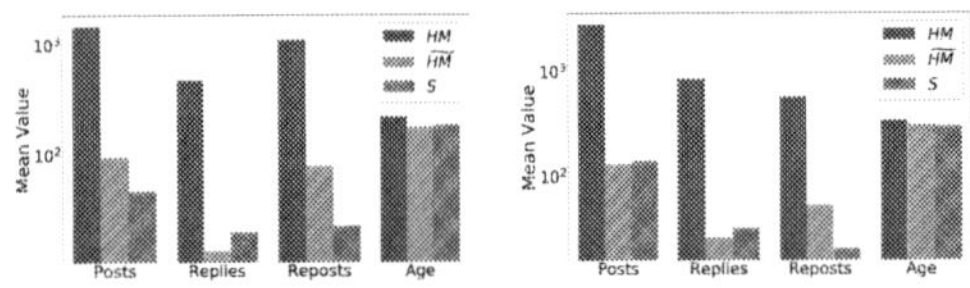

(a) Parler (b) Gab

Figure 3: Activity measures per user group. Numbers are averaged per measure and group. We use a log-scale over the y-axis.

Popularity and Engagement We quantify the popularity level of users based on the number of *followers* they have. Figure 4 presents numbers for both platforms. On both platforms hate mongers (HM) are significantly more popular compared to users in other user groups. In Parler, the median number of followers is 121 compared to 15 and 12 of $\widetilde{HM}$ and S, respectively. The same holds for Gab – a median value of 160 for HM users compared to 43 and 41 of the other two user groups. Interestingly, although Parler is a much larger social platform (mainly in terms of registered users, see Section 3 and Table 1) we do not see a significantly higher number of followers in Parler. Moreover, when calculating the number of followers over the

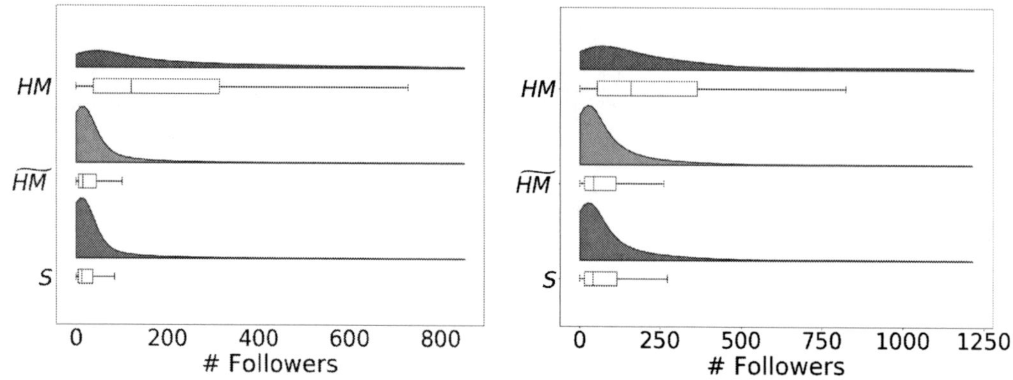

(a) Parler Followers

(b) Gab Followers

Figure 4: Followers distributions. The extreme percentiles (2.5%) of the data are omitted for visualization purposes. Rectangles indicate the ± standard division around the average; The median is indicated by a vertical line.

whole population, the median in Gab is three times higher – 48 vs. 16.

Engagement level is measured by the number of *followees* each account has (the number of accounts a user follows). We find that HM are highly engaged in both platforms, compared to other user groups. In Parler, the median number of followees of HM users is 106 – significantly higher than 46 and 36 median values of the $\widetilde{HM}$ and S users, respectively.

Account's Self Description Analogous to the account's description in Twitter, Parler users can provide a short descriptive/biographical text to appear next to the user's avatar. For example, the biography that is associated with a specific Parler user is: *"Conservative banned by mainstream social media outlets for calling the leftists out for what they really are! Been awake for YEARS! #trump2020"*.

We use this content to further assess users' commitment to the Parler platform,[13] assuming more engaged users are, the more likely they add the description to their profile. We find that while only 35.8% of the S users use the biography field, 59.6% of the HM users provide the description in their profile. We also find that the average (median) biographical text length of HM users is 128.6 (134). This is considerably longer, compared to $\widetilde{HM}$ and S users who included the description in their profile, with an average (median) of 99.4 (90) and 94.6 (84) text length, respectively.

[13]In this part, we do not compare Parler to Gab since account's self description is not available for the Gab corpus.

Social Structure Analysing the degree distribution of users provides an interesting difference between the platforms. As observed in Figure 5, HM users have the most distinctive distribution in both Parler and Gab. However, while the $\widetilde{HM}$ and the S group distributions are inseparable in Gab, the Parler user groups have distinct distributions. These distributions highlight the distinctiveness of the position of HM users in the network, as well the role of the $\widetilde{HM}$ compared to S users.

Emotional Features We compare the sentiment expressed and the emotions conveyed by different user groups. We use pretrained BERT models for both the sentiment[14] and emotion[15] predictions. Results are presented in Table 2. Looking at the Parler users, we find a small though significant (p-value $< 10^{-3}$) tendency of HM to express a more negative sentiment. The same holds for Gab, although the sentiment expressed by $\widetilde{HM}$ is closer to the sentiment of the HM users, rather to that of the S users. Aggregating the emotion predictions, we find that HM users tend to convey more *Anger* and *Sadness* than the other groups. This observation holds for both Parler and Gab, although *Anger* is more prominent.

7 Discussion

Time span Given that we provide a comparison between trends in Parler and Gab, it is im-

[14]https://huggingface.co/nlptown/bert-base-multilingual-uncased-sentiment

[15]https://huggingface.co/bhadresh-savani/distilbert-base-uncased-emotion

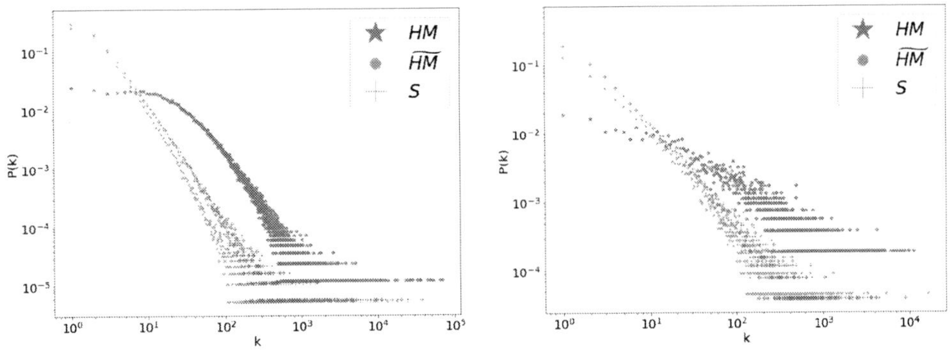

(a) Parler (b) Gab

Figure 5: Social networks degree distribution. We present the in-degree distributions. Network is based on reposts. p(k) (y-axis) is the probability value per a each node's degree (x-axis). We use a log-scale over both axis.

		Anger	Joy	Sad	Fear	Sentiment
Parler	*HM*	48%	37.9%	7.4%	5.1%	2.63
	$\widetilde{HM}$	41.9%	44.3%	6.7%	5.3%	2.84
	S	33.6%	55.7%	5%	4.3%	2.84
Gab	*HM*	40.0%	44.5%	7.2%	6.3%	2.55
	$\widetilde{HM}$	35.9%	49.7%	5.9%	7.1%	2.56
	S	35.5%	51.1%	6.0%	5.7%	2.67

Table 2: Emotions and sentiment analysis. The four leftmost columns are the distribution of emotions per user group while the rightmost column is the median sentiment score. The sentiment spans over [1,5] (i.e., 5 is the highest score).

portant to note the datasets span different and non-overlapping time-frames (see Table 1). Therefore, the comparison we provide should be read cautiously. We do note, however, that each of the datasets was crawled from the early days of the social platform and spans over a similar time range (17 months). Moreover, the temporal disparity between the dataset could be considered as an advantage – allowing us to examine the generalization performance of hate speech models, as we report in Section 5.1.

Ethical Considerations Analysing and modeling hate speech in a new social platform such as Parler is of great importance. However, classifying *users* as hate mongers, based on the output of an algorithm, may result in marking users falsely (which may result in suspension or other measures taken against them). While we always opted for a conservative approach, as well as focusing on aggregated measures characterizing the trends of a *platform*, we note that user labeling should be carefully used, ideally involving a 'man-in-the-loop'.

Considering the annotation task – the annotation process did not include any information about the identity of the users. In addition, we warned our human annotators about the possible inappropriate and triggering content of the posts. We also make sure to remove users' information from the annotated dataset that we publish.

8 Conclusion and Future Work

To the best of our knowledge, we present the first large-scale computational analysis of hate speech on Parler, and provide a comparison to trends observed in the Gab platform.

We tag and share the first annotated Parler dataset, containing 10K posts labeled by the level of hate they convey. We used this dataset to fine-tune a transformer model to be used to mark a seed set of users in a diffusion model, resulting in user-level classification. We find significant differences between hate mongers (*HM*) and other user groups: *HM* represent only 16.1% and 10% of the active users in Parler and Gab respectively. However, they generate *41.23%* of the content in Parler and *71.38%* of the content in Gab. We find that *HM* show higher engagement levels and they have significantly more followers and followees. Other differences are manifested through the sentiment level expressed and the emotions conveyed.

Future work takes two trajectories: (i) Comparison of the current results with a more traditional social platform (e.g., Twitter); and (ii) An early detection of hate mongers – building a classifier to detect hate mongers based on their very first steps in the social platform.

References

ADL. 2020. Antisemitic incidents hit all-time high in 2019.

Shahram Akbarzadeh. 2016. The muslim question in australia: Islamophobia and muslim alienation. *Journal of Muslim Minority Affairs*, 36(3):323–333.

Max Aliapoulios, Emmi Bevensee, Jeremy Blackburn, Barry Bradlyn, Emiliano De Cristofaro, Gianluca Stringhini, and Savvas Zannettou. 2021. An early look at the parler online social network. *arXiv preprint arXiv:2101.03820*.

Sai Saketh Aluru, Binny Mathew, Punyajoy Saha, and Animesh Mukherjee. 2020. Deep learning models for multilingual hate speech detection. *arXiv preprint arXiv:2004.06465*.

Jisun An, Haewoon Kwak, Claire Seungeun Lee, Bogang Jun, and Yong-Yeol Ahn. 2021. Predicting anti-asian hateful users on twitter during covid-19. *arXiv preprint arXiv:2109.07296*.

Eyal Arviv, Simo Hanouna, and Oren Tsur. 2021. It'sa thin line between love and hate: Using the echo in modeling dynamics of racist online communities. In *Proceedings of the International AAAI Conference on Web and Social Media*, volume 15, pages 61–70.

Annalise Baines, Muhammad Ittefaq, and Mauryne Abwao. 2021. # scamdemic,# plandemic, or# scaredemic: What parler social media platform tells us about covid-19 vaccine. *Vaccines*, 9(5):421.

Francesco Barbieri, Jose Camacho-Collados, Leonardo Neves, and Luis Espinosa-Anke. 2020. Tweeteval: Unified benchmark and comparative evaluation for tweet classification. *arXiv preprint arXiv:2010.12421*.

Janek Bevendorff, Berta Chulvi, Gretel Liz De La Peña Sarracén, Mike Kestemont, Enrique Manjavacas, Ilia Markov, Maximilian Mayerl, Martin Potthast, Rangel Francisco, Paolo Rosso, Efstathios Stamatatos, Benno Stein, Wiegmann Matti, Magdalena Wolska, and Eva Zangerle. 2021. Overview of PAN 2021: Authorship Verification,Profiling Hate Speech Spreaders on Twitter,and Style Change Detection. In *12th International Conference of the CLEF Association (CLEF 2021)*. Springer.

Mohit Chandra, Manvith Reddy, Shradha Sehgal, Saurabh Gupta, Arun Balaji Buduru, and Ponnurangam Kumaraguru. 2021. " a virus has no religion": Analyzing islamophobia on twitter during the covid-19 outbreak. In *Proceedings of the 32nd ACM Conference on Hypertext and Social Media*, pages 67–77.

Eshwar Chandrasekharan, Umashanthi Pavalanathan, Anirudh Srinivasan, Adam Glynn, Jacob Eisenstein, and Eric Gilbert. 2017. You can't stay here: The efficacy of reddit's 2015 ban examined through hate speech. *Proceedings of the ACM on Human-Computer Interaction*, 1(CSCW):31.

Mithun Das, Punyajoy Saha, Ritam Dutt, Pawan Goyal, Animesh Mukherjee, and Binny Mathew. 2021. You too brutus! trapping hateful users in social media: Challenges, solutions & insights. In *Proceedings of the 32nd ACM Conference on Hypertext and Social Media*, pages 79–89.

Thomas Davidson, Dana Warmsley, Michael Macy, and Ingmar Weber. 2017. Automated hate speech detection and the problem of offensive language. In *Eleventh international aaai conference on web and social media*.

Fabio Del Vigna12, Andrea Cimino23, Felice Dell'Orletta, Marinella Petrocchi, and Maurizio Tesconi. 2017. Hate me, hate me not: Hate speech detection on facebook. In *Proceedings of the First Italian Conference on Cybersecurity (ITASEC17)*, pages 86–95.

Jacob Devlin, Ming-Wei Chang, Kenton Lee, and Kristina Toutanova. 2018. Bert: Pre-training of deep bidirectional transformers for language understanding. *arXiv preprint arXiv:1810.04805*.

Vikram Dodd and Sarah Marsh. 2017. Anti-muslim hate crimes increase fivefold since london bridge attacks. *The Guardian*, 7.

Griffin Sims Edwards and Stephen Rushin. 2018. The effect of president trump's election on hate crimes. *Available at SSRN 3102652*.

Mai ElSherief, Caleb Ziems, David Muchlinski, Vaishnavi Anupindi, Jordyn Seybolt, Munmun De Choudhury, and Diyi Yang. 2021. Latent hatred: A benchmark for understanding implicit hate speech. *arXiv preprint arXiv:2109.05322*.

Horst Entorf and Martin Lange. 2019. Refugees welcome? understanding the regional heterogeneity of anti-foreigner hate crimes in germany. *Understanding the Regional Heterogeneity of Anti-Foreigner Hate Crimes in Germany (January 30, 2019). ZEW-Centre for European Economic Research Discussion Paper*, (19-005).

Arne C Esser. 2021. How does the language of corpora from radicalized communities discovered on parler compare to online conversations on twitter regarding the 2021 capitol riots and election fraud? Master's thesis.

Komal Florio, Valerio Basile, Marco Polignano, Pierpaolo Basile, and Viviana Patti. 2020. Time of your hate: The challenge of time in hate speech detection on social media. *Applied Sciences*, 10(12):4180.

John Gallacher and Jonathan Bright. 2021. Hate contagion: Measuring the spread and trajectory of hate on social media.

Björn Gambäck and Utpal Kumar Sikdar. 2017. Using convolutional neural networks to classify hate-speech. In *Proceedings of the first workshop on abusive language online*, pages 85–90.

Benjamin Golub and Matthew O Jackson. 2010. Naive learning in social networks and the wisdom of crowds. *American Economic Journal: Microeconomics*, 2(1):112–49.

Keegan Hankes and Alex Amend. 2019. Aspi explains: 8chan.

Janice A Iwama. 2018. Understanding hate crimes against immigrants: C onsiderations for future research. *Sociology compass*, 12(3):e12565.

Greta Jasser, Jordan McSwiney, Ed Pertwee, and Savvas Zannettou. 2021. 'welcome to# gabfam': Far-right virtual community on gab. *New Media & Society*, page 14614448211024546.

Brendan Kennedy, Mohammad Atari, Aida Mostafazadeh Davani, Leigh Yeh, Ali Omrani, Yehsong Kim, Kris Coombs, Shreya Havaldar, Gwenyth Portillo-Wightman, Elaine Gonzalez, et al. 2018. The gab hate corpus: A collection of 27k posts annotated for hate speech.

Brendan Kennedy, Xisen Jin, Aida Mostafazadeh Davani, Morteza Dehghani, and Xiang Ren. 2020. Contextualizing hate speech classifiers with post-hoc explanation. *arXiv preprint arXiv:2005.02439*.

Zachary Laub. 2019. Hate speech on social media: Global comparisons.

Brian Levin and John David Reitzel. 2018. Report to the nation: hate crimes rise in us cities and counties in time of division and foreign interference.

Lucas Lima, Julio CS Reis, Philipe Melo, Fabricio Murai, Leandro Araujo, Pantelis Vikatos, and Fabricio Benevenuto. 2018. Inside the right-leaning echo chambers: Characterizing gab, an unmoderated social system. In *2018 IEEE/ACM International Conference on Advances in Social Networks Analysis and Mining (ASONAM)*, pages 515–522. IEEE.

Yinhan Liu, Myle Ott, Naman Goyal, Jingfei Du, Mandar Joshi, Danqi Chen, Omer Levy, Mike Lewis, Luke Zettlemoyer, and Veselin Stoyanov. 2019. Roberta: A robustly optimized bert pretraining approach. *arXiv preprint arXiv:1907.11692*.

Rijul Magu, Kshitij Joshi, and Jiebo Luo. 2017. Detecting the hate code on social media. In *Eleventh International AAAI Conference on Web and Social Media*.

Simon Malevich and Tom Robertso. 2019. Violence begetting violence: An examination of extremist content on deep web social networks.

Binny Mathew, Ritam Dutt, Pawan Goyal, and Animesh Mukherjee. 2019. Spread of hate speech in online social media. In *Proceedings of the 10th ACM conference on web science*, pages 173–182.

Binny Mathew, Anurag Illendula, Punyajoy Saha, Soumya Sarkar, Pawan Goyal, and Animesh Mukherjee. 2020. Hate begets hate: A temporal study of hate speech. *Proceedings of the ACM on Human-Computer Interaction*, 4(CSCW2):1–24.

Binny Mathew, Navish Kumar, Pawan Goyal, Animesh Mukherjee, et al. 2018. Analyzing the hate and counter speech accounts on twitter. *arXiv preprint arXiv:1812.02712*.

Meta. 2021a. Facebook reports second quarter 2021 results. `https://tinyurl.com/2p8r4wd6`. Accessed: 2022-04-17.

Meta. 2021b. Update on our progress on ai and hate speech detection. `https://tinyurl.com/muvn4hma`. Accessed: 2022-04-17.

Mainack Mondal, Leandro Araújo Silva, and Fabrício Benevenuto. 2017. A measurement study of hate speech in social media. In *Proceedings of the 28th acm conference on hypertext and social media*, pages 85–94.

Marzieh Mozafari, Reza Farahbakhsh, and Noël Crespi. 2019. A bert-based transfer learning approach for hate speech detection in online social media. In *International Conference on Complex Networks and Their Applications*, pages 928–940. Springer.

Luke Munn. 2019. Alt-right pipeline: Individual journeys to extremism online.

Chikashi Nobata, Joel Tetreault, Achint Thomas, Yashar Mehdad, and Yi Chang. 2016. Abusive language detection in online user content. In *Proceedings of the 25th international conference on world wide web*, pages 145–153.

Mohamed Nawab Bin Mohamed Osman. 2017. Retraction: Understanding islamophobia in asia: The cases of myanmar and malaysia. *Islamophobia Studies Journal*, 4(1):17–36.

Ji Ho Park and Pascale Fung. 2017. One-step and two-step classification for abusive language detection on twitter. *arXiv preprint arXiv:1706.01206*.

Barbara Perry, Davut Akca, Fatih Karakus, Mehmet Fatih Bastug, et al. 2020. Planting hate speech to harvest hatred: How does political hate speech fuel hate crimes in turkey? *International Journal for Crime, Justice and Social Democracy*, 9(2).

Gary Peters, Rob Portman, Amy Klobuchar, and Roy Blunt. 2021. Examining the u.s. capitol attack: a review of the security planning and response failures.

Jing Qian, Anna Bethke, Yinyin Liu, Elizabeth Belding, and William Yang Wang. 2019. A benchmark dataset for learning to intervene in online hate speech. *arXiv preprint arXiv:1909.04251*.

Jing Qian, Hong Wang, Mai ElSherief, and Xifeng Yan. 2021. Lifelong learning of hate speech classification on social media. *arXiv preprint arXiv:2106.02821*.

Tharindu Ranasinghe and Marcos Zampieri. 2020. Multilingual offensive language identification with cross-lingual embeddings. *arXiv preprint arXiv:2010.05324*.

Manoel Ribeiro, Pedro Calais, Yuri Santos, Virgílio Almeida, and Wagner Meira Jr. 2018. Characterizing and detecting hateful users on twitter. In *Proceedings of the International AAAI Conference on Web and Social Media*, volume 12.

Manoel Horta Ribeiro, Pedro H Calais, Yuri A Santos, Virgílio AF Almeida, and Wagner Meira Jr. 2017. "like sheep among wolves": Characterizing hateful users on twitter. *arXiv preprint arXiv:1801.00317*.

Björn Ross, Michael Rist, Guillermo Carbonell, Benjamin Cabrera, Nils Kurowsky, and Michael Wojatzki. 2017. Measuring the reliability of hate speech annotations: The case of the european refugee crisis. *arXiv preprint arXiv:1701.08118*.

Paul Röttger, Bertram Vidgen, Dong Nguyen, Zeerak Waseem, Helen Margetts, and Janet Pierrehumbert. 2020. Hatecheck: Functional tests for hate speech detection models. *arXiv preprint arXiv:2012.15606*.

Haji Mohammad Saleem, Kelly P Dillon, Susan Benesch, and Derek Ruths. 2017. A web of hate: Tackling hateful speech in online social spaces. *arXiv preprint arXiv:1709.10159*.

Joni Salminen, Maximilian Hopf, Shammur A Chowdhury, Soon-gyo Jung, Hind Almerekhi, and Bernard J Jansen. 2020. Developing an online hate classifier for multiple social media platforms. *Human-centric Computing and Information Sciences*, 10(1):1.

Niloofar Safi Samghabadi, Parth Patwa, PYKL Srinivas, Prerana Mukherjee, Amitava Das, and Thamar Solorio. 2020. Aggression and misogyny detection using bert: A multi-task approach. In *Proceedings of the Second Workshop on Trolling, Aggression and Cyberbullying*, pages 126–131.

Victor Sanh, Lysandre Debut, Julien Chaumond, and Thomas Wolf. 2019. Distilbert, a distilled version of bert: smaller, faster, cheaper and lighter. *ArXiv*, abs/1910.01108.

Anna Schmidt and Michael Wiegand. 2017. A survey on hate speech detection using natural language processing. In *Proceedings of the fifth international workshop on natural language processing for social media*, pages 1–10.

Andrea Sipka, Aniko Hannak, and Aleksandra Urman. 2021. Comparing the language of qanon-related content on parler, gab, and twitter. *arXiv preprint arXiv:2111.11118*.

Lütfi Sunar. 2017. The long history of islam as a collective "other" of the west and the rise of islamophobia in the us after trump. *Insight Turkey*, 19(3):35–52.

Elise Thomas. 2019. Aspi explains: 8chan.

Time. 2021. Twitter penalizes record number of accounts for posting hate speech. `https://time.com/6080324/twitter-hate-speech-penalties/`. Accessed: 2022-04-17.

Christopher Tuckwood. 2017. Hatebase: Online database of hate speech. *The Sentinal Project. Available at: https://www. hatebase. org*.

Bertie Vidgen, Austin Botelho, David Broniatowski, Ella Guest, Matthew Hall, Helen Margetts, Rebekah Tromble, Zeerak Waseem, and Scott Hale. 2020a. Detecting east asian prejudice on social media. *arXiv preprint arXiv:2005.03909*.

Bertie Vidgen, Tristan Thrush, Zeerak Waseem, and Douwe Kiela. 2020b. Learning from the worst: Dynamically generated datasets to improve online hate detection. *arXiv preprint arXiv:2012.15761*.

Ethan Ward. 2021. Parlez-vous le hate?: Examining topics and hate speech in the alternative social network parler. Master's thesis, University of Waterloo.

Zeerak Waseem and Dirk Hovy. 2016. Hateful symbols or hateful people? predictive features for hate speech detection on twitter. In *Proceedings of the NAACL student research workshop*, pages 88–93.

Michael Wiegand, Josef Ruppenhofer, and Thomas Kleinbauer. 2019. Detection of abusive language: the problem of biased datasets. In *Proceedings of the 2019 conference of the North American Chapter of the Association for Computational Linguistics: human language technologies, volume 1 (long and short papers)*, pages 602–608.

Tomer Wullach, Amir Adler, and Einat Minkov. 2020. Towards hate speech detection at large via deep generative modeling. *IEEE Internet Computing*, 25(2):48–57.

Tomer Wullach, Amir Adler, and Einat Minkov. 2021. Fight fire with fire: Fine-tuning hate detectors using large samples of generated hate speech. *arXiv preprint arXiv:2109.00591*.

Marcos Zampieri, Preslav Nakov, Sara Rosenthal, Pepa Atanasova, Georgi Karadzhov, Hamdy Mubarak, Leon Derczynski, Zeses Pitenis, and Çağrı Çöltekin. 2020. Semeval-2020 task 12: Multilingual offensive language identification in social media (offenseval 2020). *arXiv preprint arXiv:2006.07235*.

Savvas Zannettou, Barry Bradlyn, Emiliano De Cristofaro, Haewoon Kwak, Michael Sirivianos, Gianluca Stringini, and Jeremy Blackburn. 2018. What is gab: A bastion of free speech or an alt-right echo chamber.

In *Companion Proceedings of the The Web Conference 2018*, pages 1007–1014. International World Wide Web Conferences Steering Committee.

Savvas Zannettou, Joel Finkelstein, Barry Bradlyn, and Jeremy Blackburn. 2020. A quantitative approach to understanding online antisemitism. In *Proceedings of the International AAAI Conference on Web and Social Media*, volume 14, pages 786–797.

Ziqi Zhang, David Robinson, and Jonathan Tepper. 2016. Hate speech detection using a convolution-lstm based deep neural network.

Xianbing Zhou, Yang Yong, Xiaochao Fan, Ge Ren, Yunfeng Song, Yufeng Diao, Liang Yang, and Hongfei Lin. 2021. Hate speech detection based on sentiment knowledge sharing. In *Proceedings of the 59th Annual Meeting of the Association for Computational Linguistics and the 11th International Joint Conference on Natural Language Processing (Volume 1: Long Papers)*, pages 7158–7166.

Caleb Ziems, Bing He, Sandeep Soni, and Srijan Kumar. 2020. Racism is a virus: Anti-asian hate and counter-hate in social media during the covid-19 crisis. *arXiv preprint:2005.12423*.

Multilingual Resources for Offensive Language Detection

Aymé Arango[1,3] Jorge Pérez[1,3] Bárbara Poblete[1,3] Valentina Proust[2,3] Magdalena Saldaña[2,3]

[1]Departament of Computer Science, University of Chile
[2]Communication Faculty, Pontifical Catholic University of Chile
[3]Millennium Institute of Data Foundation, Santiago, Chile

Abstract

Most of the published approaches and resources for offensive language and hate speech detection are tailored for the English language. In consequence, cross-lingual and cross-cultural perspectives lack some essential resources. The lack of diversity of the datasets in Spanish is notable. Variations throughout Spanish-speaking countries make existing datasets not enough to encompass the task in the different Spanish variants. We manually annotated 9834 tweets from Chile to enrich the existing Spanish resources with different words and new targets of hate that have not been considered in previous studies. We conducted several cross-dataset evaluation experiments of the models published in the literature using our Chilean dataset and two others in English and Spanish. We propose a comparative framework for quickly conducting comparative experiments using different previously published models. In addition, we set up a Codalab competition for further comparison of new models in a standard scenario, that is, data partitions and evaluation metrics. All resources can be accessed through a centralized repository for researchers to get a complete picture of the progress on the multilingual hate speech and offensive language detection task.

1 Introduction

Offensive language frequently appears on social network interactions [1]. According to Sigurbergsson and Derczynski (2020) *offensive language* encompass a range of expressions from profanities to much more severe types of language among which is *hate speech*. Hate speech is usually defined as communications of animosity or disparagement of an individual or a group on account of a group characteristic[2]. Offensive language and hate speech bring along the risk of encouraging real hate crimes. Due to the large amount of content generated in social media, automatic moderation is necessary to perform offensive content detection.

Machine learning models are used in most of the published approach for this purpose. The necessary resources are available almost exclusively for the English language (Anzovino et al., 2018; Hosseinmardi et al., 2015; Davidson et al., 2017). On the other hand, the cross-lingual and cross-cultural perspectives have been under addressed in the related literature. The lack of adequately annotated datasets is one of the limiting factors for developing these subtasks (Yin and Zubiaga, 2021; Fortuna and Nunes, 2018). In addition, the publicly available resources are accessible through the correspondent description papers. These resources have insufficient lack of centralized repositories for datasets and classification models. This situation makes it difficult for researchers to get a complete picture of the progress on the task.

Most of these existing datasets contain English examples, though we have gathered some datasets in Portuguese (Fortuna et al., 2019), Arabic (Mulki et al., 2019), Italian (Sanguinetti et al., 2018) and Spanish (Pereira-Kohatsu et al., 2019). In the particular case of the Spanish language, only a few datasets can be found. The geographical origin of them is limited to Spain (Pereira-Kohatsu et al., 2019), México (Álvarez-Carmona et al., 2018), or unknown (Basile et al., 2019). Since the hate speech phenomenon depends on the socio-cultural context (Sap et al., 2019), the targets of hate could change depending on the origin of the messages. The Spanish language specific features spoken in different countries, makes models poorly generalizable when training with these existing resources. We propose a manually annotated dataset for offensive language detection. The dataset is composed of 9834 tweets from Chile and is meant to enrich the existing Spanish resources with different words

[1] https://www.channel4.com/news/george-floyd-death-has-led-to-increasing-online-hate-speech-report-claims

[2] https://www.encyclopedia.com/international/encyclopedias-almanacs-transcripts-and-maps/hate-speech

Proceedings of the Sixth Workshop on Online Abuse and Harms (WOAH), pages 122 - 130
July 14, 2022

and new targets of hate that have not been considered in previous studies.

We conducted several evaluation experiments of the models published in the literature using our Chilean dataset and two others in English and Spanish. We propose a comparative framework for quickly conducting comparative experiments. This framework facilitates the application of existing models by including each original implementation as sub-models. In addition, we set up a Codalab competition for further comparison of new models in a standard scenario, that is, data partitions and evaluation metrics.

In summary, we developed the following resources for multilingual hate speech detection:

1. Chilean dataset for offensive language detection: We annotated a Spanish Twitter dataset in several categories related to the phenomenon of offensive language, including a hate speech category. This dataset is composed of 9834 Spanish tweets and is, as far as we know, the first one where the data was originated in South America.

2. Comparative framework: We constructed a library of models using published cross-lingual offensiveness detectors. The library facilitates the use of models by providing a common interface. Moreover, we set up a Codalab competition for further comparison of emergent models.

3. Resource repository: We organized the existing datasets into a structured repository to facilitate authors finding existing resources in several languages. The repository contains annotations of the main characteristics of the existing datasets and direct links for downloading them. In addition to datasets, it contains tools for using existing multilingual hate speech detection models.

In Section 2, we describe the existing datasets for offensive language detection as well as we comment on the diversity of existing Spanish resources. Next, in Section 3, we describe the Chilean dataset we constructed for offensive language detection, including a hate speech category. Finally, in Section 4, we describe the tools we created for helping the authors to replicate and compare new approaches with the existing ones in a cross-lingual environment. All resources described in the paper will be integrated in our centralized code repository[3].

Ethical Considerations: The annotators inferred only female and male genders of the authors and targets of tweets. The genders were inferred from names and pronouns. Due to the non-binary nature of gender, this label should be used carefully to avoid unfair models.

OFFENSIVE CONTENT WARNING. Because of the topic of our research, certain examples are potentially offensive. We minimized as much as possible the number of examples and obfuscated offensive words.

2 Related Work

One of the essential steps for the research in *offensive language* detection using machine learning is dataset acquisition. Even when several social media platforms exist to get data from them, constructing a balanced labeled dataset is a costly task in time and effort. There is not a dataset considered as standard for this task. Therefore researchers have to search in the related literature for the adequate one for their experiment.

Most of the existing datasets have been annotated for the English language (Dinakar et al., 2011; Hosseinmardi et al., 2015; Waseem and Hovy, 2016; Founta et al., 2018) though there exist a few in other languages such as Spanish (Basile et al., 2019), Italian (Sanguinetti et al., 2018) and Arabic (Mubarak et al., 2017). It is important to mention that even for English, the task is far from being solved (Arango et al., 2020).

In most cases, the datasets only contain texts messages and not other information regarding authors, localication, or the conversation to which the tweet belongs. The lack of information makes the datasets out of context and limits the use of different features. Regarding the data sources, most of the datasets have been recovered from the Twitter platform, though a few are composed of Facebook messages (Bosco et al., 2018) or Youtube comments (Dinakar et al., 2011). As far as we know, there exists one data repository[4] for organizing offensive language datasets.

[3]https://github.com/aymeam/Datasets-for-Hate-Speech-Detection

[4]https://hatespeechdata.com/

2.1 Spanish Datasets and the Multicultural Problem:

To the best of our knowledge, there are four different datasets (Basile et al., 2019; Pereira-Kohatsu et al., 2019; Álvarez-Carmona et al., 2018; Fersini et al., 2018) in the Spanish language, related to the task of offensive language detection, with a total of 26 000 messages labeled for hate speech or aggressive content. One of these datasets contained messages that originated in Spain (Pereira-Kohatsu et al., 2019) (6000 tweets). Two of them from unknown origin: IberEval 2018 (Fersini et al., 2018) (4138 tweets) and SemEval 2019 (Basile et al., 2019) (5365 tweets). The remaining dataset was constructed with messages from Mexico: MEX-A3T (11 000 tweets) being the only resource related to the hate speech phenomenon built for Latin-American Spanish.

Being the hate speech phenomenon a cultural problem, we consider that a model trained on these datasets would not be able to generalize over different Spanish data from different cultures.

3 Chilean Dataset for Offensive Language Detection

The research in the Spanish language has been limited, in part, due to the lack of resources. As we described in Section 2, the few Spanish available datasets are composed of examples of the variant of Spanish spoken in specific regions of the world with the cultural background associated with it.

We consider it necessary to leverage the first dataset representative of the Spanish spoken in South America, particularly Chile. The examples in this dataset would enrich the understanding of pffensive language and hate speech by introducing terms mainly used in this region and targets of hate unconsidered in previous studies. Next, we describe the process of annotation and general features of our datasets.

3.1 Data Recovering

For recovering an initial corpus, we followed a strategy commonly used in the related literature (Basile et al., 2019; Waseem and Hovy, 2016) which is identifying words that serve as seeds for querying online platforms. The use of seeds would guarantee a higher probability for hateful content to appear in the crawled data.

Seeds The seeds were gathered by surveying a group of seven Chilean students. The list includes terms (or phrases) used in Chile. Some of these terms are offensive, but others are neutral terms related to polemic subjects such as sexual nature, immigration, and others (e.g. *haitianos, indígenas, lesbianas*). We recovered a total of 132 seeds that can be read in our code repository.

Search Parameters Using the pre-defined seeds and with the help of the Twitter API[5], we downloaded approximately 61 000 tweets. The tweets' language was restricted to Spanish, and the geolocation was prefixed for the Chile area. Along with each tweet, we recovered the conversation (sequence of tweets) that originated them in case of existing. These conversations serve as context for each tweet (Qian et al., 2019).

Sample for Annotation From the 61 000 tweets recovered, we selected 10 000 (one-sixth), taking a proportional amount of tweets originating from each seed. In this way, we maintained a representative sample of all sources.

3.2 Annotation

Three external annotators under contract conducted the process of labeling the dataset, all three were native Chileans. First, they went through a training process, where the three of them labeled the same set of tweets to make sure they annotated the content as similarly as possible. They repeated this process with different sets of tweets until achieving an inter-annotator agreement higher than 90% agreement and a Krippendorff's alpha higher than 0.7 in all the pre-defined labels (Neuendorf, 2002). After the training process, they proceeded to label the final dataset, a portion each. Table 1 contains a summary of this measure obtained during the training process.

3.3 Chilean Dataset Description

The final dataset contains 9834 tweets annotated with several labels, some of them related to offensive content based on Chen's categorization of uncivil speech (Chen, 2017). In addition, it includes annotations that contextualize the messages, such as the target of offensive speech and the use of irony. As described above, the dataset also contains the conversation that originated each of them. These conversations serve as context for the annotated tweets. Next, we explore the main characteristics of the resulting dataset.

[5]https://developer.twitter.com/en/docs/twitter-api

3.3.1 Offensive Content Labels

Some of the labels in the final dataset encompass different types of offensive content. These labels are *hate speech*, *unintended profanity/vulgarity*, *insult/appellation*, *intentional profanity/vulgarity*. The other labels are not directly related to the offensive phenomenon, but help contextualize the messages and generalize the dataset.

hate speech The tweet contains hate speech if it includes stereotypical language to offend minority groups such as women, immigrants, sexual or racial minorities.

For example, the tweet: *"La mapuche es un asqueroso trapo y los mapuches; cero aporte, son gasto, daño y destrucción, tampoco originarios."* (*"The Mapuche woman is a disgusting rag and the Mapuche people; zero contribution, they are a waste of money, damage, and destruction, not natives either."*) is labeled as hateful because the author is attributing detrimental characteristics to the *mapuche* people which are a minority group of indigenous people in Chile and Argentina.

Hate against this particular minority is also an example of the dependence of the hate speech phenomenon on socio-cultural factors.

insult/appellation A tweet is labeled as positive for insults or name calling if the tweet includes nicknames, phrases, or words that are not profane but are offensive (such as "s***id" or "j**k").

For example: " *está "mujer" me da vergüenza ajena."* (" *This "woman" embarrases me"*), is labeled as containing insulting language because the intention is to offend a person (this woman) without using profane words. On the other hand, the tweet: *"Ma***to flaite hediondo a marihuana."* (*"D**n marijuana-smelly chav."*) also belongs to this class because of the use of *"flaite"* a pejorative word used in Chile for referring to marginal or uneducated people (Rojas, 2015).

unintended profanity/vulgar language Some tweets may contain profane words without the intention of offending anyone, like in: *"Que manera de echar de menos ese estadio por la grandísima co***a de su madre* (*"I really miss that mother f*** stadium"*). This kind of tweet is labeled as containing unintended profanity. In this case, *mother f**** is an expression used for making emphasis on how much the author misses the stadium.

Label	Positives (%)	K
intentional profanity/vulgarity grosería c/intención	2668 (27,13)	0,72
unintended profanity/vulgarity grosería s/intención	1358 (13,80)	0,75
insult/appellation insulto/sobrenombre	4036 (41,04)	0,86
hate speech discurso de odio	633 (6,43)	0,74
migration migración	405 (4,11)	0,84
Venezuela Venezuela	199 (20.2)	0,73
domestic politics política nacional	3438 (34,96)	0,81
marginalized gropus grupos marginalizados	886 (9,0)	0,74
"others" "otros"	5220 (53,08)	0,73
sarcasm/irony/mockery sarcasmo/ironía/burla	2125 (21,60)	0,7
legitimate question pregunta legítima	89 (0,9)	1
evidence evidencia	427 (4,34)	0,71
female figure figura femenina	1436 (14,60)	0,72
male figure figura masculina	2872 (29,20)	0,75
anonymous author autor anonimo	6391 (6498)	0,92
female author author femenino	2102 (21,37)	
male author author masculino	4695 (47,74)	0,81
unk-gender author género desconocido	3037 (30,88)	

Table 1: The column "Label" shows each label of the dataset in both, English and in Spanish languages. The column "Positives (%)" shows the number and percent of tweets labeled as positive for each label. Finally, the column "K" shows the Krippendorff's measure obtained during the training stage for each of the labels.

intentional profanity/vulgar language: A different type of profanity can be found in the tweet: *"Les dije que el árbitro era un CO***A DE SU MADRE* " (*"I told you the referee was a MOTHER F**** "). Even when we have the same words as in previous example, in this case, the annotators marked this tweet as containing *intentional profanity*, as the author has the intention to insult a person using profane words (*the referee*).

3.3.2 Tweets Content

Other labels are meant to enrich the dataset by spotting linguistic and semantic information of the tweets. In this sense, we can find annotations regarding the content of the tweet.

male figure: The tweet labels containing male or female figures are the ones, offensive or not, directed to a particular person identified by annotators as male, for example: *"Tremendo hijo de p**a eres Marcos."* (*"You are a tremendous son of a b***, Marcos."*) is labeled as *male or female figure* since the message is directed to *Antonio*, a male.

female figure: Similar to the *male figure* label, the tweet: *"Y q dice la autodenominada candidata feminista al respecto"* (*"And what does the self-appointed feminist candidate have to say about it?"*) is labeled as *female figure* since the author poses a question to a female (*feminist candidate*).

mention to [topic] There are five labels used to mark when a tweet makes reference to different topics such as *immigration, domestic politics, marginalized groups* and *others*. As an example of *domestic politics* is the tweet "*Vamos a botar a la feminazi,* 👍 *#VOTACIONES2021*" ("*We are going to kick out the feminazi,* 👍 *# ELECTIONS2021*")".

sarcasm/irony/mockery The use of humor or sarcasm was also identified in this label. This label could be helpful to disambiguate the message's intention, that is, the intention of hurting. (e.g. *"Aquí llenando la piscina con las lágrimas de los fachos"* (*"Here filling the pool with fascists' tears"*).

evidence This category is based on Chen's (Chen, 2017) definition of deliberative speech, a condition set to foster healthy conversations on social media. The tweets are labeled positive for evidence if they provide statistical evidence, citations, or links with extra information instead of a mere opinion. For example: *"Expulsión de migrantes efectuada este domingo en la RM https://t.co/*** vía @***"* (*"Expulsion of migrants carried out this Sunday in the Metropolitan Region https://t.co/*** via @***"*) is labeled as *evidence* because it includes a link to a news source.

legitimate question Also based on Chen's work (2017), a tweet contains a *legitimate question* if it poses a non-rhetorical question, for example asking for more information about a particular event, like in the tweet: *"¿A los venezolanos le están solicitando visa para entrar a Peru?"* (*"Are Venezuelans requested to have a visa to enter Peru?"*).

		insult	prof/vulg	hate	off
dummy	F1	48.7	45.9	49.3	48.6
seed	F1	58.8	51.8	47.9	51.6
EMB +RF	F1	66.3	69.8	55.5	66.0
	ROC	77.3	76.0	79.8	71.8

Table 2: The Table shows the F-score obtained using different baselines in different classification tasks over our dataset. Baselines: dummy = random predictions; seed = all messages containing one of the offensive seeds used for recovering the dataset is predicted as positive; EMB+RF = Spanish Glove Embeddings and Radom Forest Classifier; Tasks: insult, profanity/vulgarity (prof/vulg); hate and offensive (off) detection.

3.3.3 Tweets' Author Information

All the tweets contain a label of the authors' gender: 2102 tweets were sent by a *female author*, 4694 by a *male author*. The rest of the authors were identified as *undetermined-gender* since the user name does not suggest either a male or female gender (e.g., "DVM"; "Patria y Libertad"). The annotators also labeled information about the anonymity of the authors. The tweet is labeled as anonymous if the username is a nickname (e.g. "DVM") or a name without last name (e.g. "patricia"). There are 5371 unique Twitter users in the dataset.

The 50,67% of the tweets in any offensive categories were sent by users labeled as males, 20,22% by females and the rest from undetermined-gender users.

Table 1 contains a summary of the dataset columns. A sample of the dataset can be found in our repository [6] and will be completly published soon.

3.4 Offensive Content Detection Baselines

We implemented some baselines for offensive language detection over our dataset. We defined different classification tasks: *insult, profanity/vulgarity* (intentional or not) and *hate speech* detection. In addition, we tested baselines to identify if a tweet belongs to any of the offensive classes. Therefore, we set the target *offensive* if the tweet is labeled as any of the offensive labels (*insult* or *profanity/vulgarity* or *hate speech*. The results were obtained with a 5-Fold cross validation .

[6] https://anonymous.4open.science/r/Datasets-for-Hate-Speech-Detection-0D50/Chilean%20dataset/Dataset_sample_500.csv

dummy classifier We predict the values of the classes randomly, making use of the Sklearn[7] dummy classifier.

seed classifier: To verify that there is no seed bias, we conducted a baseline classification method consisting of labeling as positive those tweets containing one of the offensive seeds previously used to recover the dataset (See Section 3.1). Our results show the best performance on the *insult* detection task showing a higher bias in this category. The list of offensive seeds can be found in our code repository. This result was expected since this category is positive depending on the existence of certain words. On the other hand, the rest of the tasks showed nearly random results.

EMB + RF We tested a third baseline using Spanish FastText embeddings[8] and Random Forest classifier. The word embeddings of 100 dimensions were first averaged into one single vector and used as input for a Random Forest Classifier with default parameters. We show the results for 5-fold cross-validation. The results with this approach, compare to dummy and seed classifiers, showed the best results.

The F-Score obtained with the different methods in the four tasks can be shown in Table 2.

		ACL19	EMNLP20	ECML20
$EN \rightarrow ES$	F1	48.42	53.26	64.56
	ROC	50.83	63.42	73.14
$ES \rightarrow EN$	F1	45.54	60.22	60.09
	ROC	49.20	69.53	63.91
$EN \rightarrow CL$	F1	49.17	38.19	48.83
	ROC	50.12	48.16	60.85
$CL \rightarrow EN$	F1	44.58	47.33	51.6
	ROC	51.25	47.83	54.33

Table 3: Cross-lingual experiments using there different datasets: English (Basile et al., 2019) (EN), Spanish (Basile et al., 2019) (ES), and our Spanish dataset recovered from Chile (CL). Models: ACL19 (Pamungkas and Patti, 2019); EMNLP20 (Ranasinghe and Zampieri, 2020); ECML20 (Aluru et al., 2020); WEBSCi21 (Vitiugin et al., 2021).

4 Comparative Framework

In the related literature of offensive language detection, there is a lack of comparative studies. This situation is more noticeable in cross-lingual approaches as a relatively new sub-area. There is no consensus about the best approaches for solving the cross-lingual detection task.

With the purpose of alleviating this situation, we propose two tools for cross-lingual approaches comparison:

1. A python library that contains published cross-lingual hate speech detection models as methods: The library has five published models. Each model consists of the original implementation code as a sub-module, plus a class interface that standardizes all models' input to simplify their use. In addition, the library contains the main class whose attributes are the previously mentioned models and auxiliary tools for evaluation and data management. A brief description of the models can be found in Section 4.1

2. An open competition in Codalab[9] for further comparison. We set up an open competition in Codalab to promote fair comparison among cross-lingual approaches. Different leaderboards can be found for the different configurations.

4.1 Cross-lingual Models

We found a few papers describing cross-lingual approaches. We included them in our library using the original companion code.

ACL19 As a preparation stage for the model proposed by Pamungkas et al. (2021), it is necessary to translate the data into the target language. The model consists of training two different LSTM architectures. The first one is trained with the original training data, and the other is trained using the data translated into the testing language. Finally, the two outputs are concatenated and used as input for a final linear output layer.

ECML20 In this paper, Aluru et al. (2020) described different approaches for cross-lingual hate speech detection with different architectures. Those are the multilingual Bert model, the GRU model, and a combination of LASER embeddings and Logistic Regression (LR) classifier. The model

[7]https://scikit-learn.org/stable/

[8]https://github.com/dccuchile/spanish-word-embeddings

[9]https://codalab.lisn.upsaclay.fr/competitions/1221?secret_key=c1de3893-de48-4ca1-8071-89e82f189039

that combines LASER embeddings and LR classifier turned to be the best approach. Our library includes three types of models, though in Table 3 we only report the best results.

EMNLP20 Ranasinghe and Zampieri (2020) proposed a transfer learning strategy. First, an XLM-R classification model is trained using data from one language, and the weights are saved. Then, these weights are used to initialize the model and predict labels in a different language.

We used our library for reproducing the previously mentioned models in a cross-lingual way using three different languages English, Spanish (Basile et al., 2019), and our Chilean dataset. In Table 3, we show the results we obtained in different cross-lingual experiments.

4.2 Evaluation Datasets

For evaluation, we used the Spanish (*ES*) and English (*EN*) datasets constructed for the SemEval 2019 competition (Basile et al., 2019). As we mentioned in Section 2, the authors of these datasets did not specify any location for recovering the data. Examining the tweets objects of the Spanish dataset, we noticed only a few with geo-location information, some belonging to Spain, México, though most of them were unknown. We compare the cross-datasets performance with the performance across different variants of Spanish: general Spanish (ES) and the variant of Spanish spoken in Chile (CL). To this end, we add experiments using our previously described Chilean (*CL*) dataset. We show precision, recall, and F-score metrics, the commonly used metrics, and the ROC metric.

4.2.1 Cross-lingual Results

In general, the cross-lingual setup, including the Spanish (ES) dataset, performed better than Chilean (CL). One of the reasons for this could be the data used for pre-trained models; for example, *ECML20* model is based on LASER representations. These are multilingual sentence embeddings constructed from parallel data. The data used may not encompass some of the words used in South America, though a more profound analysis is needed. Despite presenting a simple structure (LASER + LR), *ECML20* model showed the overall best results.

4.2.2 Cross-cultural Results

We tested the models in monolingual Spanish setups but using datasets from different socio-cultural contexts.

		ACL19	EMNLP20	ECML20
$CL \rightarrow ES$	F1	50.0	53.1	56.7
	ROC	51.2	57.0	64.2
$ES \rightarrow CL$	F1	46.1	41.3	46.7
	ROC	49.9	46.6	53.0

Table 4: Cross-cultural experiments using two different datasets: Spanish (Basile et al., 2019) (ES) and our Spanish dataset recovered from Chile (CL). Models: ACL19 (Pamungkas and Patti, 2019); EMNLP20 (Ranasinghe and Zampieri, 2020); ECML20 (Aluru et al., 2020); WEBSCi21 (Vitiugin et al., 2021).

One of the datasets is the SemEval Spanish dataset (Basile et al., 2019) with examples originated in Spain. The other is our dataset, also in Spanish, but originated in Chile. The results in terms of F1 and ROC are shown in Table 4.

The best overall results were obtained using the *ECML20* model in the $CL \rightarrow ES$ configuration. Despite being datasets from the same language, the knowledge transfer was, in general, poor. All the results were lower than the ones obtained in an inside-dataset experiment shown in Table 2. These results evidence of the differences between the two Spanish variants, the different hate targets of the two geographical regions, though much more inside in this regard is needed.

4.3 Repository Description

To facilitate finding an appropriate dataset, we organized them in a centralized repository. So far, we have listed 39 datasets, 20 of which are in the English language and 19 others in different languages such as Arabic (5), Spanish (4), Italian (3), Portuguese (1), among others.

In our repository the datasets are separated by languages and have the following structure:

- Datasets (Link to paper): Abbreviated name of the dataset with a link for downloading the paper description.
- Objects: Which are the type of objects (e.g. *tweets, images, sentences*).
- Size: The number of objects in the dataset.
- Available: A direct link for downloading the dataset is provided if the dataset is publicly available.

- Labels: The labels in which the objects are categorized (e.g. *(hateful, non-hateful), (racist, sexist, either))*

Approximately, 64% are composed of tweets, but other objects can be found, such as Facebook comments or Twitter users. Although some of the below-listed datasets are not explicitly available, they could be obtained from the authors if requested. ee Our comparative framework (Section 4) facilitates the use of previously published models for cross lingual hate speech detection.

5 Conclusions

We described three resources for the multilingual offensive language detection task. These resources would be helpful in the development of the multilingual sub-area, which have been under-addressed.

We constructed the first Chilean dataset for hate speech and offensive language to alleviate this situation. The dataset contains 9834 tweets in the Spanish language that originated in Chile. The tweets are labeled in several categories related to offensive content. Furthermore, it includes annotations associated with the content of the tweets.

Finally, we created a comparative framework (library + competition) to facilitate researchers to compare new models with the existing ones. The library is implemented in python and contains, as submodels, previously published cross-lingual approaches for hate speech detection. The competition is hosted in Codalab and offers a scenario for comparing new models with the existing ones.

The resource repository would facilitate researchers to find, in one place, the datasets that better meet their needs as well as tools for easily comparing their work with previously existing models. From our repository, it is noticeable the lack of available Spanish examples. Moreover, there is a low representation of different types of Spanish spoken worldwide.

6 References

References

Sai Saketh Aluru, Binny Mathew, Punyajoy Saha, and Animesh Mukherjee. 2020. Deep learning models for multilingual hate speech detection. *CoRR*, abs/2004.06465.

Miguel Á Álvarez-Carmona, Estefanıa Guzmán-Falcón, Manuel Montes-y Gómez, Hugo Jair Escalante, Luis Villasenor-Pineda, Verónica Reyes-Meza, and Antonio Rico-Sulayes. 2018. Overview of mex-a3t at ibereval 2018: Authorship and aggressiveness analysis in mexican spanish tweets. In *Notebook papers of 3rd sepln workshop on evaluation of human language technologies for iberian languages (ibereval), seville, spain*, volume 6.

Maria Anzovino, Elisabetta Fersini, and Paolo Rosso. 2018. Automatic identification and classification of misogynistic language on twitter. In *International Conference on Applications of Natural Language to Information Systems*, pages 57–64. Springer.

Aymé Arango, Jorge Pérez, and Barbara Poblete. 2020. Hate speech detection is not as easy as you may think: A closer look at model validation (extended version). *IS*, page 101584.

Valerio Basile, Cristina Bosco, Viviana Patti, Manuela Sanguinetti, Elisabetta Fersini, Debora Nozza, Francisco Rangel, and Paolo Rosso. 2019. Shared task on multilingual detection of hate. SemEval 2019, Task 5.

Cristina Bosco, Dell'Orletta Felice, Fabio Poletto, Manuela Sanguinetti, and Tesconi Maurizio. 2018. Overview of the evalita 2018 hate speech detection task. In *EVALITA 2018-Sixth Evaluation Campaign of Natural Language Processing and Speech Tools for Italian*, volume 2263, pages 1–9. CEUR.

Gina Masullo Chen. 2017. *Online incivility and public debate: Nasty talk*. Springer.

Thomas Davidson, Dana Warmsley, Michael W. Macy, and Ingmar Weber. 2017. Automated hate speech detection and the problem of offensive language. pages 512–515.

Karthik Dinakar, Roi Reichart, and Henry Lieberman. 2011. Modeling the detection of textual cyberbullying. In *The Social Mobile Web, Papers from the 2011 Workshop (ICWSM)*.

Elisabetta Fersini, Paolo Rosso, and Maria Anzovino. 2018. Overview of the task on automatic misogyny identification at ibereval 2018. *IberEval@ SEPLN*, 2150:214–228.

Paula Fortuna, Joao Rocha da Silva, Leo Wanner, Sérgio Nunes, et al. 2019. A hierarchically-labeled portuguese hate speech dataset. In *Proceedings of the Third Workshop on Abusive Language Online*, pages 94–104.

Paula Fortuna and Sérgio Nunes. 2018. A survey on automatic detection of hate speech in text. *ACM Computing Surveys (CSUR)*, 51(4):1–30.

Antigoni-Maria Founta, Constantinos Djouvas, Despoina Chatzakou, Ilias Leontiadis, Jeremy Blackburn, Gianluca Stringhini, Athena Vakali, Michael Sirivianos, and Nicolas Kourtellis. 2018. Large scale crowdsourcing and characterization of twitter abusive behavior. In *Proceedings of the Twelfth International Conference on Web and Social Media, ICWSM 2018, Stanford, California, USA, June 25-28, 2018*, pages 491–500. AAAI Press.

Homa Hosseinmardi, Sabrina Arredondo Mattson, Rahat Ibn Rafiq, Richard Han, Qin Lv, and Shivakant Mishra. 2015. Analyzing labeled cyberbullying incidents on the instagram social network. In *International Conference on Social Informatics*, pages 49–66. Springer.

Hamdy Mubarak, Kareem Darwish, and Walid Magdy. 2017. Abusive language detection on arabic social media. In *Proceedings of the First Workshop on Abusive Language Online*, pages 52–56.

Hala Mulki, Hatem Haddad, Chedi Bechikh Ali, and Halima Alshabani. 2019. L-HSAB: A Levantine Twitter dataset for hate speech and abusive language. In *Proceedings of the Third Workshop on Abusive Language Online*, pages 111–118, Florence, Italy. Association for Computational Linguistics.

Kimberly A Neuendorf. 2002. Defining content analysis. *Content analysis guidebook. Thousand Oaks, CA: Sage*.

Endang Wahyu Pamungkas, Valerio Basile, and Viviana Patti. 2021. A joint learning approach with knowledge injection for zero-shot cross-lingual hate speech detection. *Information Processing & Management*, 58(4):102544.

Endang Wahyu Pamungkas and Viviana Patti. 2019. Cross-domain and cross-lingual abusive language detection: A hybrid approach with deep learning and a multilingual lexicon. In *Proc. 57th ACL*, pages 363–370.

Juan Carlos Pereira-Kohatsu, Lara Quijano Sánchez, Federico Liberatore, and Miguel Camacho-Collados. 2019. Detecting and monitoring hate speech in twitter. *Sensors*, 19(21):4654.

Jing Qian, Anna Bethke, Yinyin Liu, Elizabeth Belding, and William Yang Wang. 2019. A benchmark dataset for learning to intervene in online hate speech. *arXiv preprint arXiv:1909.04251*.

Tharindu Ranasinghe and Marcos Zampieri. 2020. Multilingual offensive language identification with cross-lingual embeddings. *arXiv preprint arXiv:2010.05324*.

Darío Rojas. 2015. Flaite: algunos apuntes etimológicos. *Alpha (Osorno)*, (40):193–200.

Manuela Sanguinetti, Fabio Poletto, Cristina Bosco, Viviana Patti, and Marco Stranisci. 2018. An italian twitter corpus of hate speech against immigrants. pages 2798–2895.

Maarten Sap, Dallas Card, Saadia Gabriel, Yejin Choi, and Noah A. Smith. 2019. The risk of racial bias in hate speech detection. In *Proceedings of the 57th Conference of the Association for Computational Linguistics, ACL 2019, Florence, Italy, July 28- August 2, 2019, Volume 1: Long Papers*, pages 1668–1678.

Gudbjartur Ingi Sigurbergsson and Leon Derczynski. 2020. Offensive language and hate speech detection for danish. In *Proceedings of the 12th Language Resources and Evaluation Conference*, pages 3498–3508.

Fedor Vitiugin, Yasas Senarath, and Hemant Purohit. 2021. Efficient detection of multilingual hate speech by using interactive attention network with minimal human feedback. In *13th ACM Web Science Conference 2021*.

Zeerak Waseem and Dirk Hovy. 2016. Hateful symbols or hateful people? predictive features for hate speech detection on twitter. In *Proc. SRW@HLT-NAACL*, pages 88–93.

Wenjie Yin and Arkaitz Zubiaga. 2021. Towards generalisable hate speech detection: a review on obstacles and solutions. *PeerJ Computer Science*, 7:e598.

Enriching Abusive Language Detection with Community Context

Jana Kurrek †
McGill University
School of Computer Science
jana.kurrek@mail.mcgill.ca

Haji Mohammad Saleem †
McGill University
School of Computer Science
haji.saleem@mail.mcgill.ca

Derek Ruths
McGill University
School of Computer Science
derek.ruths@mcgill.ca

Abstract

Uses of pejorative expressions can be benign or actively empowering. When models for abuse detection misclassify these expressions as derogatory, they inadvertently censor productive conversations held by marginalized groups. One way to engage with non-dominant perspectives is to add context around conversations. Previous research has leveraged user- and thread-level features, but it often neglects the spaces within which productive conversations take place. Our paper highlights how community context can improve classification outcomes in abusive language detection. We make two main contributions to this end. First, we demonstrate that online communities cluster by the nature of their support towards victims of abuse. Second, we establish how community context improves accuracy and reduces the false positive rates of state-of-the-art abusive language classifiers. These findings suggest a promising direction for context-aware models in abusive language research.

1 Introduction

Existing models for abuse detection struggle to grasp subtle knowledge about the social environments that they operate within. They do not perform natural language understanding and consequently cannot generalize when tested out-of-distribution (Bender et al., 2021). This problem is often the result of training data imbalance, which encourages language models to overestimate the significance of certain lexical cues. For instance, Wiegand et al. (2019) observe that "commentator", "football", and "announcer" end up strongly correlated with hateful tweets in the Waseem and Hovy (2016) corpus. This trend is caused by focused sampling, and it does not reflect an underlying property of abusive expressions.

When models rely on pejorative or demographic words, they can encode systemic bias through *false positives* (Kennedy et al., 2020). For example, research has established that detection algorithms are more likely to classify comments written in African-American Vernacular English (AAVE) as offensive (Davidson et al., 2019; Xia et al., 2020). Benign tweets like "*Wussup, n*gga*!" and "*I saw his ass yesterday*" both score above 90% for toxicity (Sap et al., 2019). Similarly, Zhang et al. (2020) analyze the Wikipedia Talk Pages Corpus (Dixon et al., 2018) and find that 58% of comments that contain the term "gay" are labelled as toxic, while only 10% of all comments are toxic. This enables the misclassification of positive phrases like "*she makes me happy to be gay*". Even Twitter accounts belonging to drag queens have been rated higher in terms of average toxicity than the accounts associated with white nationalists (Oliva et al., 2021). These findings underline how language models with faulty correlations can facilitate the censorship of productive conversations held by marginalized communities.

Productive conversations containing slurs are common, and they take many forms (Hom, 2008). Research inspired by the #MeToo movement has focused on the detection of sexual harassment disclosures by victims (Deal et al., 2020), but this research has not been sufficiently integrated into the literature on abusive language detection. The distinction between actual sexist messages and messages calling out sexism is rarely addressed in the field (Chiril et al., 2020). A similar trend is seen with sarcasm. Humor and self-irony can be employed as coping mechanisms by victims of abuse (Garrick, 2006), yet they constitute frequent sources of error for state-of-the-art classifiers (Vidgen et al., 2019). For example, the median toxicity score for language on `transgendercirclejerk`, a "parody [subreddit] for trans people", is as high as 90% (Kurrek et al., 2020). More broadly, transgender users are "excluded, harmed, and misrepresented in existing

† These authors made equal contributions.

Proceedings of the Sixth Workshop on Online Abuse and Harms (WOAH), pages 131 - 142
July 14, 2022 ©2022 Association for Computational Linguistics

platforms, algorithms, and research methods" related to network analysis (Stewart and Spiro, 2021).

Meaningful improvements in abusive language detection require a thoughtful engagement with the perspectives of marginalized communities and their allies. One way to ensure that machine learning frameworks are socially conscientious is to add context around conversations. Past research has explored the contextual information within conversation threads (Pavlopoulos et al., 2020; Ziems et al., 2020), user demographics (Unsvåg and Gambäck, 2018; Founta et al., 2019), user history (Saveski et al., 2021; Qian et al., 2018; Dadvar et al., 2013), user profiles (Unsvåg and Gambäck, 2018; Founta et al., 2019), and user networks (Ziems et al., 2020; Mishra et al., 2018) with varying degrees of success in improving performance. However, most modelling efforts for abusive language detection neglect one major aspect of online conversations: the community environment they take place within.

Online communities adhere to a variety of sociologistic norms that reinforce their identities. This phenomenon is easily observed on Reddit, where community structure is an explicit component of platform design. For example, the majority of comments on the pro-Trump subreddit `The_Donald` delegitimize liberal ideas (McLamore and Uluğ, 2020; Soliman et al., 2019). Similarly, a collection of "manosphere" subreddits espouse misogynistic ideologies (Stewart and Spiro, 2021; Ging, 2019). More broadly, communities can reinforce "toxic technocultures" (Massanari, 2017), and those technocultures are not limited to Reddit. Community structure is present across 4chan, Facebook, Voat, etc., and it exists in a less explicit manner on platforms like Twitter (Silva et al., 2017).

In this paper, we study community context on Reddit, and we focus specifically on language that is collected using slurs. We demonstrate that subreddits cluster by the nature of their support towards marginalized groups, and we use subreddit embeddings to improve the accuracy and false positive rates of state-of-the-art abusive language classifiers. While our analysis is platform-specific, it suggests a promising new direction for context-aware models.

2 Related Work

2.1 Methods in Abusive Language Detection

Abusive language detection is a relatively new field of research, with "very limited" work from as recently as 2016 (Waseem and Hovy, 2016). Early methods featured Naive Bayes (Liu and Forss, 2014), SVMs (Tulkens et al., 2016), Random Forests (Warner and Hirschberg, 2012), Decision Trees (Del Vigna et al., 2017), and Logistic Regression (Burnap and Williams, 2014; Greevy, 2004).

However, recent developments in NLP have directed the field towards neural and Transformer-based approaches. CNNs, LSTMs (+ Attention), and GRUs have been widely used in the literature (Mathur et al., 2018; Meyer and Gambäck, 2019; Chakrabarty et al., 2019; Zhang et al., 2018; Modha et al., 2018). As of 2019, researchers have begun adopting pre-trained language models. Contemporary work leverages BERT, DistilBERT, ALBERT, RoBERTA, and mBERT (Alonso et al., 2020; Davidson et al., 2020). In fact, Bodapati et al. (2019) note that seven of the top ten performing models for offensive language identification at SEMEVAL-2019 were BERT-based. A similar trend was seen at SEMEVAL-2020, where "most teams used some kind of pre-trained Transformers" (Zampieri et al., 2020). Regardless of architecture, methods in abusive language detection can be divided into content- and context- based approaches.

Content-based approaches rely on comment text for feature engineering. Researchers have used TF-IDF weighted n-gram counts as well as distributional embeddings for text representation (Davidson et al., 2017; Nobata et al., 2016; Van Hee et al., 2018), POS tags or dependency relations for encoding syntactic information (Narang and Brew, 2020), and the frequencies of hashtags, URLs, user mentions, emojis, etc. for detecting platform-specific tokens. Lexicons are also popular for capturing sentiment, politeness, emotion, and hate words (Cao et al., 2020; Nobata et al., 2016; Markov and Daelemans, 2021; Koufakou et al., 2020). The central assumption behind content-based abusive language detection is that comments can be exclusively assessed using textual features. However, this assumption neither holds in theory nor in practice because linguistic structures are discourse-determined, and that discourse is shaped by social, historical, and political context (Bridges, 2017). Semantics cannot be completely interpreted using content cues alone. Even human annotators struggle to classify comments that involve satire or homonymy in the absence of broader context (Kurrek et al., 2020). In light of these concerns, researchers are increasingly identifying the impor-

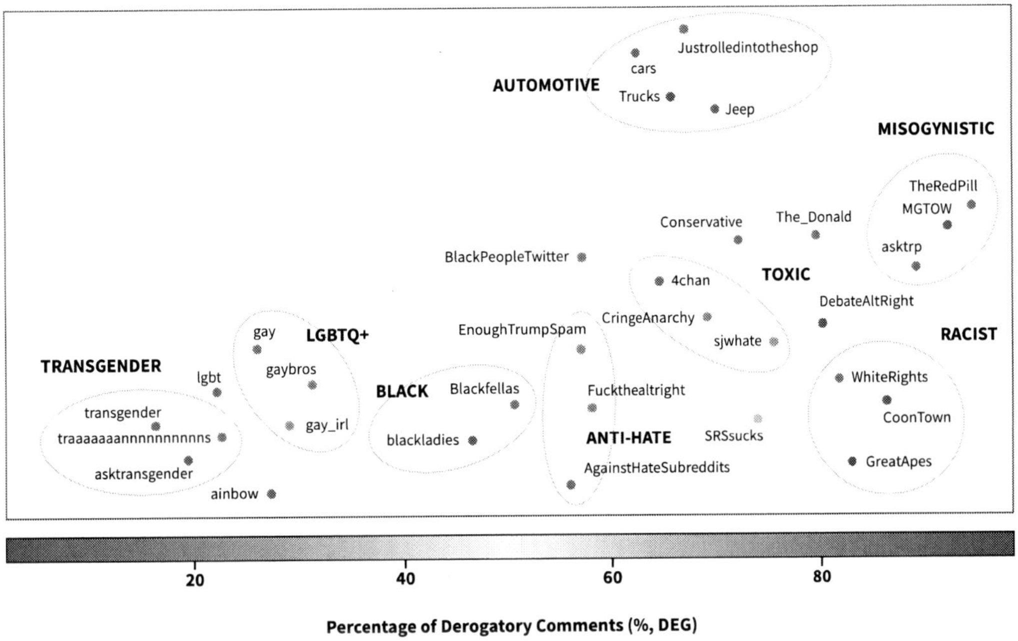

Figure 1: A subset of our subreddit embeddings plotted in two-dimensions using UMAP. Community clusters emerge based on the nature of users' support towards marginalized groups.

tance of user and conversational features to their detection frameworks. We summarize five main trends in the literature below.

Conversational Context. Attempts have been made to situate abusive comments within conversation threads. Threads have been studied using preceding comments (Pavlopoulos et al., 2020; Karan and Šnajder, 2019), discussion titles (Gao and Huang, 2017), and counts for aggressive comments (Ziems et al., 2020). The position of a comment in a thread - start or end - has also been considered (Joksimovic et al., 2019). Finally, researchers have analyzed conversation graphs for topological indicators of abuse (Papegnies et al., 2017).

User Demographics. Researchers have attempted to incorporate user-level context through demographic signals for age, location, and gender. Age has been extracted from user disclosures, but these disclosures can be unreliable when users have an incentive to view adult-rated content (Dadvar et al., 2013). Previous work has inferred gender from user names (Waseem and Hovy, 2016; Unsvåg and Gambäck, 2018), expressions in user biographies (Waseem and Hovy, 2016; Unsvåg and Gambäck, 2018), and in-game avatar choices (Balci and Salah, 2015), but these methods can fail when names are gender-neutral. Location information obtained through geo-coding has also been used to analyze hateful tweets (Fan et al., 2020).

User History. Patterns in user behaviour, including daily logins (Balci and Salah, 2015), favourites (Unsvåg and Gambäck, 2018), and posting history (Saveski et al., 2021; Ziems et al., 2020), can be used as features in abusive language detection models. Some work focuses directly on the content of past comments. For example, Dadvar et al. (2013) look for the prevalence of profanity in text. Conversely, Qian et al. (2018) encode all historical posts by a user. Similarly, Ziems et al. (2020) create TF-IDF vectors derived from a user's timeline.

User Profiles. Several elements of profile metadata have been studied as a proxy for digital identity. These elements include usernames (Gao and Huang, 2017), user anonymity, the presence of updated profile pictures (Unsvåg and Gambäck, 2018), biographies (Miró-Llinares et al., 2018), verified account status (Ziems et al., 2020), counts for followers (Founta et al., 2019), and friends (Balci and Salah, 2015). Some other profile features include profile language (Galán-García et al., 2016) and account age (Founta et al., 2019).

User Networks. Homophily in social networks induces user clusters based on shared identities. These clusters have been shown to represent collective ideologies and moralities (Dehghani et al., 2016), motivating researchers to examine local user networks for markers of abusive behaviour. Interaction and connection-based social graphs are analyzed using Jaccard's similarity and eigenvalue or closeness centrality (Ziems et al., 2020; Chatzakou et al., 2017; Founta et al., 2019; Unsvåg and Gambäck, 2018; Papegnies et al., 2017), which are also relevant for creating user embeddings.

2.2 Methods in Community Profiling

Network data may capture localized trends about individual users, but it often overlooks how groups of users behave as a whole. There are connection- and content-based solutions for explicit community profiling which, to the best of our knowledge, exist outside of contemporary abusive language research. Connection-based solutions evolved out of the idea that similar communities house similar users. In contrast, content-based solutions claim that similar communities contain similar content.

Connection-based Representations. Vector representations of online communities are known to encode semantics (Martin, 2017). Popular techniques for obtaining these representations require the construction of a community graph. Kumar et al. (2018) construct a bipartite multigraph between Reddit users and subreddits. An edge $u_i \rightarrow s_j$ is added for each post by a user u_i in a subreddit s_j. The graph is then used to learn subreddit embeddings by a "node2vec-style" approach.

Martin (2017) creates a symmetric matrix of subreddit-subreddit user co-occurrences, where $\mathbf{X}_{ij}$ is the number of unique users who have commented at least ten times in the subreddits i and j. Skip-grams with negative sampling or `GloVe` can then be used to obtain subreddit embeddings. Here, subreddits and user co-occurrences inherit the role of words and word co-occurrences respectively. Waller and Anderson (2019) also treat communities as "words" and users who comment in them as "contexts" and adapt word2vec for community representations. The subreddit graph proposed in Janchevski and Gievska (2019) contains edges weighted by the number of shared users between the two subreddits. They only consider users who participate in at least ten subreddits and use node2vec to generate node embeddings.

Content-based Representations. Content-based solutions for community profiling rely on methods for document similarity. Janchevski and Gievska (2019) average the word2vec representations for the top 30 words in each subreddit, ranked by TF-IDF score. This research is currently limited, relative to other techniques.

3 Methodology

3.1 Corpus

We select the `Slur-Corpus` by Kurrek et al. (2020). It consists of 40k human-annotated Reddit comments. Every comment contains a slur and is labelled as either derogatory (`DEG`), appropriative (`APR`), non-derogatory non-appropriative (`NDNA`), or homonym (`HOM`). The corpus is nearly evenly split between derogatory and non-derogatory (`APR, NDNA, HOM`) slur usages, with 51% of comments labelled `DEG` (see Table 1).

The `Slur-Corpus` is one of few community-aware resources for abusive language detection. The data is sampled over the course of a decade (October 2007 to September 2019), reflecting a variety of users and language conventions. Every comment is published with the subreddit from which it was sourced, and the authors curate content across a number of antagonistic, supportive, and general discussion communities. As opposed to random sampling, this method guarantees the representation of targeted and minority voices. We see this as crucial for investigating the role of social context within abusive language conventions.

3.2 Definitions

Subreddits are niche communities dedicated to the discussion of a particular topic, with users participating in subreddits that engage their personal interests. As a result, subreddits often exhibit language specificity that can be leveraged for making inferences about slur usages.

Consider the slur *tr*nny*. The comment, "*I am genuinly surpised at a suicidal tr*nny*" from `CringeAnarchy` is derogatory. In contrast, "*So do I. Just that the tr*nny is dying on me lol.*" from `Honda` is non-derogatory because *tr*nny* is being used as a homonym. Both of these subreddits adhere to different linguistic norms and appeal to different user bases. Quantifying these differences is important. Niche or small automotive subreddits are likely to be related to `Honda`, and their users may also use *tr*nny* to mean *transmission*.

Label	Count	%	Stats	Count
DEG	20531	51%	Users	36962
NDNA	16729		Posts	34610
HOM	1998	49%	Subreddits	2691
APR	553			
Total	39811			

Table 1: Characteristics of the Slur-Corpus. The split between DEG and NDG comments is nearly equal.

3.3 Constructing Subreddit Embeddings

We construct subreddit embeddings based on user comment co-occurrence. This method aligns with prior work on the subject (Martin, 2017; Kumar et al., 2018; Waller and Anderson, 2019), but extends it by considering data collected at a much larger scale. We use all publicly available Reddit comments prior to September 2019 in order to generate lists of users that comment in each found subreddit (Baumgartner et al., 2020). We then store frequency counts for each list and, in total, identify 998K unique subreddits and 42.7M unique authors over the course of 12 years. There is a long tail because many subreddits have low participation.

Next, we identify active users, defined as being any users with at least ten comments in a subreddit. We exclude bot accounts and focus on top subreddits by activity. This leaves 10.4K subreddits and 12.2M unique users. With this data, we build a subreddit adjacency matrix $\mathbf{A}$, where $\mathbf{A}_{ij}$ is the number of co-occurring users in subreddits i and j. We use GloVe to generate dense embeddings from $\mathbf{A}$, and we run it over 100 epochs with a learning rate of 0.05 and a representation size of 150.

3.4 Evaluating Subreddit Embeddings

Our tests for subreddit similarity seek to capture two conditions: (1) compositionality: similar subreddits have similar constituent subreddits; and (2) analogy: subreddit similarity is preserved under analogical argument. We rely on vector algebra to model each of these two conditions.

3.4.1 Similarity

The similarity between subreddits S_i and S_j is simply the cosine similarity of their representations:

$$sim(S_i, S_j) = \frac{\vec{S_i} \cdot \vec{S_j}}{|\vec{S_i}||\vec{S_j}|}$$

3.4.2 Composition Tests

We find a subreddit S_k that represents the sum of S_i and S_j. We create $\vec{V} = \vec{S_i} + \vec{S_j}$, and then compute $S_k := max_x(\{sim(\vec{V}, \vec{S_x})\})$. We run the composition test to identify local sports team subreddits from combinations of sport and city subreddits ($\overrightarrow{sport} + \overrightarrow{city} = \overrightarrow{team}$). We base these tests on the evaluations of Martin (2017).

3.4.3 Analogy Tests

We find a subreddit S_n such that $\vec{S_i} : \vec{S_j} :: \vec{S_m} : \vec{S_n}$ for a triad of subreddits S_i, S_j and S_m. We create $\vec{V} = \vec{S_i} - \vec{S_j} + \vec{S_m}$ and then compute $S_n = max_x(\{sim(\vec{V}, \vec{S_x})\})$. The analogy tests, based on Waller and Anderson (2019), identify:

1. A local team given a city and sport:
   $\overrightarrow{city} : \overrightarrow{team} :: \overrightarrow{city'} : \overrightarrow{team'}$
2. A sport given a team and its city:
   $\overrightarrow{team} : \overrightarrow{sport} :: \overrightarrow{team'} : \overrightarrow{sport'}$
3. A city given a university
   $\overrightarrow{university} : \overrightarrow{city} :: \overrightarrow{university'} : \overrightarrow{city'}$

In total, we ran 157 composition tests and 6349 analogy tests. In 81% of cases, the correct answer to a composition test was in the top five most similar subreddits. Similarly, in 84% of cases, the correct answer to an analogy test was in the top five most similar subreddits. Examples are highlighted in Table 2, and we note that they are in line with the results reported in the original paper.

3.5 Context Insensitive Classifiers

To assess the importance of community context, we run a series of context sensitive and context insensitive experiments. We run all experiments using a 5-fold cross validation in order to label the entire corpus. Moreover, we use stratified sampling to ensure a uniform distribution of slurs, subreddits, and labels across all folds. Below, we describe the models used for our context insensitive experiments.

(LOG-REG) Our first classifier is a Logistic Regression with L2 regularization. We preprocess the corpus by lowercasing and stemming the text, removing stop words, and masking user mentions and URLs prior to tokenization. Each token is then weighed using TF-IDF to create unigram, bigram, and trigram features. We use scikit-learn to create our classification pipeline.

city	+	sport	=	team	city	:	team	::	city	:	team
toronto	+	baseball	=	Torontobluejays	boston	:	BostonBruins	::	toronto	:	leafs
chicago	+	baseball	=	CHICubs	boston	:	Patriots	::	chicago	:	CHIBears
chicago	+	hockey	=	hawks	**team**	:	**sport**	::	**team**	:	**sport**
chicago	+	nba	=	chicagobulls	redsox	:	baseball	::	BostonBruins	:	hockey
boston	+	baseball	=	redsox	redsox	:	baseball	::	Patriots	:	nfl
boston	+	hockey	=	BostonBruins	**university**	:	**city**	::	**university**	:	**city**
boston	+	nba	=	bostonceltics	mcgill	:	montreal	::	UBC	:	vancouver
boston	+	nfl	=	Patriots	mcgill	:	montreal	::	UofT	:	toronto

Table 2: Examples of subreddit embedding evaluation, based on our composition and analogy tests.

gaybros	**Blackfellas**	**trans**	**AgainstHateSubreddits**
askgaybros	blackladies	transpositive	Fuckthealtright
gay	BlackHair	ask_transgender	TopMindsOfReddit
gaymers	racism	MtF	beholdthemasterrace
4chan	**CoonTown**	**GenderCritical**	**MGTOW**
ImGoingToHellForThis	GreatApes	itsafetish	WhereAreAllTheGoodMen
classic4chan	WhiteRights	GCdebatesQT	TheRedPill
CringeAnarchy	AntiPOZi	Gender_Critical	asktrp
changemyview	**hiphop**	**cars**	**relationships**
PoliticalDiscussion	90sHipHop	Autos	AskWomen
bestof	rap	BMW	relationship_advice
TrueAskReddit	hiphop101	carporn	offmychest

Table 3: Top three subreddits by cosine similarity to each subreddit in bold (experiments run on top five).

(BERT) Our second classifier is BERT. We use BERT-BASE pre-trained on uncased data with the AdamW optimizer, which has a final linear layer. It takes the top-level embedding of the [CLS] token as input. We do fine-tuning over four epochs with a batch size of 32, and we choose a learning rate of 2e-05 and epsilon 1e-8[1].

$$\text{[CLS]}\ c\ \text{[SEP]}$$

(PERSPECTIVE) We use a publicly available commercial tool for toxicity detection[2]. It is a CNN-based model that is trained on a high volume of user-generated comments across social media platforms. While the tool is updated by PERSPECTIVE, the API cannot be retrained, fine-tuned, or modified. We use 0.8 as our threshold for DEG.

3.6 Context Sensitive Classifiers

Below, we describe the models used for our context sensitive experiments.

(LOG-REG-COMM) We use the same setup as in LOG-REG, but we include an additional feature for the name of each subreddit that comments are sourced from. This is done with the purpose of incorporating a social prior with which the algorithm can contextualize the comment text.

(BERT-COMM) We concatenate the name of each source subreddit to the beginning of each text before passing the comment to BERT.

$$\text{[CLS]}\ s + c\ \text{[SEP]}$$

(BERT-COMM-SEP) In our second variant for context sensitivity, we use the sentence entailment format for BERT. This model concatenates the comment with the source subreddit, separated by BERT's [SEP] token. The model is fine-tuned in the same way as our other BERT models.

$$\text{[CLS]}\ c\ \text{[SEP]}\ s\ \text{[SEP]}$$

(BERT-COMM-NGH) We use our trained GloVe embeddings (see Section 3.3) to obtain the five most similar subreddits to each source subreddits. This allows us to build a direct community neighborhood that we concatenate to the source subreddit. We train this variant of BERT using the same sentence entailment format as was described above.

$$\text{[CLS]}\ c\ \text{[SEP]}\ s_1\ s_2\ ...\ s_6\ \text{[SEP]}$$

4 Results

4.1 Subreddits Cluster around Social Polarity

Prior work has established that communities cluster around topics like music, movies, and sports (Martin, 2017). We want to examine how subreddit neighbourhoods behave based on the nature of their support towards marginalized groups. We identify

[1] All BERT experiments were performed on Google Colab with Tesla V100-SXM2-16GB GPU, and we use BERTForSequenceClassification from huggingface for our implementation.

[2] www.perspectiveapi.com

	Performance				% Classified DEG			
	Accuracy	Precision	Recall	F1	DEG	NDNA	APR	HOM
PERSPECTIVE	0.6132	0.6147	0.6102	0.6079	70.75%	53.10%	53.16%	10.71%
LOG-REG	0.8003	0.8009	0.7994	0.7997	82.85%	22.46%	61.30%	16.67%
LOG-REG-COMM	0.8002	0.8001	0.7999	0.8000	81.10%	20.53%	58.95%	15.67%
BERT	0.8856	0.8854	0.8857	0.8855	88.06%	10.26%	47.20%	6.31%
BERT-COMM	0.8905	0.8904	0.8908	0.8905	88.08%	9.38%	42.31%	5.36%
BERT-COMM-SEP	**0.8930**	**0.8930**	**0.8934**	**0.8930**	**88.12%**	8.95%	**39.60%**	5.11%
BERT-COMM-NGH	0.8923	0.8924	0.8928	0.8923	87.82%	**8.80%**	39.78%	**4.75%**

Table 4: Results from our classification task. We report the percentage of each gold label that is classified as DEG. This indicates the percentage of true positives for DEG and the percentage of false positives for the other three labels.

eight supportive and antagonistic subreddits and use our GloVe embeddings to extract the three most similar communities to each of them (see: Table 3). We make two main observations.

First, we observe that supportive subreddits are most similar to other supportive subreddits that cater towards the same marginalized community. For instance, the neighbourhood of gaybros, a subreddit built for the LGBTQ+ community, contains other subreddits based on pride and support: askgaybros, gay, and gaymers. A similar trend is observed with the neighbours of Blackfellas and trans.

Second, we see that antagonistic subreddits are most similar to other antagonistic subreddits. GenderCritical is contained in a cluster of anti-trans subreddits, MGTOW is near misogynistic subreddits, and CoonTown is surrounded by racist subreddits. This highlights how polarizing communities tend to cluster around other communities with the same, or similar, polarities.

Figure 1 shows the embeddings of a sample of subreddits from Slur-Corpus plotted in two-dimensions using UMAP. There are independent groups for misogynistic, racist, toxic, anti-hate, black, gay, and trans subreddits.

4.2 Subreddit Context Reduces False Positives

We present the results from our classification experiments in Table 4[3]. The results will be discussed through two lenses: (1) overall performance; and (2) performance by label.

BERT-based models outperformed classifiers based on Logistic Regression. This is unsurprising, given that Transformers are the current state-of-the-art in NLP. However, LOG-REG achieves nearly 20% higher accuracy than PERSPECTIVE. While this performance gap is likely the result of the data used to train both models, it is concerning given that the Perspective API is widely used as a tool for toxicity detection with both commercial[4] and academic applications (Cuthbertson et al., 2019).

		BERT	∩	BERT-COMM-SEP	
FP		765	1339	480	
TP	1067{	587	17492	599	}1364
TN		480	16696	765	
FN		599	1853	587	
	2.68%	6.11%	93.89%	6.11%	3.43%

Table 5: The effect of community context on BERT classification outcomes. The column ∩ counts the number of comments with identical labels from BERT and BERT-COMM-SEP, while the columns relating to each classifier only describe comments with different labels. The percentages 2.68% and 3.43% represent the share of true positives and negatives for BERT and BERT-COMM-SEP, respectively.

For both BERT and LOG-REG, the addition of subreddit context reduced the number of false positives across all three non-derogatory labels. Performance on DEG comments remained relatively unchanged. The highest increase in performance was seen with BERT-COMM-SEP, which had each source subreddit concatenated to the comment with a middle [SEP] token. Adding subreddit context led to a significant improvement for appropriative text, across which the false positive rate decreased by almost 8%. For example, "*Tr*nny* here, some of us are actually really cool." was originally misclassified without community context.

Surprisingly, BERT-COMM-NGH, our model with expanded neighbourhood context, showed little improvement over BERT-COMM-SEP. While the identification of NDNA and HOM improved marginally, the false positive rate for appropriative language increased. One possible explanation is that smaller communities did not have a significant presence in the Slur-Corpus (8% of all subreddits accounted for 80% of all comments), and consequently the performance gains associated

[3]We report Macro F1.

[4]Trusted partners include Reddit, The New York Times, The Financial Times, and the Wall Street Journal.

with comments belonging to these subreddits was marginal. We still believe that neighbourhood context is important for determining the nature of niche communities based on their proximity to larger, established supportive or antagonistic communities. Further analysis of this model is required to understand its full potential.

4.3 Understanding Context Sensitivity

We call a comment "context sensitive" if the addition of context changed its classification label. BERT and BERT-COMM-SEP have comparable performance on the majority of the corpus: 94% of comments are context insensitive (see Table 5). However, 1364 of the total classification errors made by BERT were rectified with the inclusion of social context. These classifications represented $> 3\%$ of the actual corpus, but 56% of context-sensitive comments within it. In Table 6, we present examples of top subreddits for both *true positive* and *true negative* context sensitive comments, along with comments for each. The *true positive* comments largely belonged to antagonistic subreddits, while the *true negative* ones belonged to supportive subreddits. Community context helped BERT-COMM-SEP identify community polarity.

True Positives
CringeAnarchy I am genuinly surpised at a suicidal *tr*nny*
4chan This is basically everyday in Atlanta. It's *n*gger/sp*c* central. Give a useful warning next time.
True Negatives
BlackPeopleTwitter Shit Britney rides for us too, idk if you seen when she was about to let the hands fly on some dude for calling her security a *n*gger*
askgaybros Masc bear here. Twinks are my favorite and *f*ggot* is a pretty funny word :b

Table 6: Top subreddits across comments whose labels were correctly classified with the addition of context.

5 Discussion

Our analysis points to two key resources that would benefit future abusive language research.

Subreddit embeddings for community sampling. Systems for abuse detection should reliably identify different variations of abuse (e.g. sexism, racism, etc.), while still exhibiting sensitivity towards non-derogatory comments (e.g. appropriation, reclamation, etc.). One way to achieve this is to ensure content diversity in training data. Kurrek et al. (2020) specifically use community sampling to achieve this kind of diversity. The authors collect comments from various Reddit communities, but their work is limited by the absence of resources that identify and consolidate supportive or antagonistic subreddits. Instead, they rely on manual data exploration. There are several issues with this approach. First, knowing which communities to look for (and how to find them) requires a high degree of domain knowledge. Second, manual comment analysis is an expensive task, which makes it difficult to scale or reuse as new communities form. Third, this method is prone to overlooking smaller, niche subreddits that would otherwise have been found using a neighborhood exploration of community clusters. We propose the use of subreddit embeddings in future research to further extend efforts on diverse and representative content collection.

Community context for protecting productive conversations. One of our primary research objectives was to ensure that detection frameworks do not mistakenly classify productive conversations as abusive. Community contextualized models, based on Logistic Regression and BERT, better identified non-derogatory comments than their context-insensitive counterparts. Context was found to be particularly helpful for identifying appropriative language, resulting in an 8% increase in accuracy with the addition of a subreddit name. Appropriation is a tool used by marginalized populations to counteract oppression. When abuse detection frameworks misclassify reclamation, they censor the empowerment tools of the very communities that they are installed to protect. Our analysis of the Slur-Corpus suggests that productive conversations tend to happen in safe and supportive social spaces. It is therefore crucial that these spaces be considered for nuanced classification of abuse.

6 Conclusion and Future Work

The subjectivity of abuse makes it challenging to annotate and detect reliably. One method for making the problem tractable is to position online conversations within a larger context. This paper was an exploration of one type of contextual information: community identity. We found that the context derived from community identity can help in the collection and classification of abusive language. We therefore believe that community context is integral to all stages of abusive language research. We leave as future work the inclusion of community information in existing, platform-agnostic, ensemble detection frameworks.

References

Pedro Alonso, Rajkumar Saini, and György Kovács. 2020. Hate speech detection using transformer ensembles on the hasoc dataset. In *International Conference on Speech and Computer*, pages 13–21. Springer.

Koray Balci and Albert Ali Salah. 2015. Automatic analysis and identification of verbal aggression and abusive behaviors for online social games. *Computers in Human Behavior*, 53:517–526.

Jason Baumgartner, Savvas Zannettou, Brian Keegan, Megan Squire, and Jeremy Blackburn. 2020. The pushshift reddit dataset. In *Proceedings of the International AAAI Conference on Web and Social Media*, volume 14, pages 830–839.

Emily M Bender, Timnit Gebru, Angelina McMillan-Major, and Shmargaret Shmitchell. 2021. On the dangers of stochastic parrots: Can language models be too big? In *Proceedings of the 2021 ACM Conference on Fairness, Accountability, and Transparency*, pages 610–623.

Sravan Bodapati, Spandana Gella, Kasturi Bhattacharjee, and Yaser Al-Onaizan. 2019. Neural word decomposition models for abusive language detection. In *Proceedings of the Third Workshop on Abusive Language Online*, pages 135–145.

Judith Bridges. 2017. Gendering metapragmatics in online discourse:"mansplaining man gonna mansplain...". *Discourse, Context & Media*, 20:94–102.

Peter Burnap and Matthew Leighton Williams. 2014. Hate speech, machine classification and statistical modelling of information flows on twitter: Interpretation and communication for policy decision making. *Internet, Policy & Politics*.

Rui Cao, Roy Ka-Wei Lee, and Tuan-Anh Hoang. 2020. Deephate: Hate speech detection via multi-faceted text representations. In *12th ACM Conference on Web Science*, pages 11–20.

Tuhin Chakrabarty, Kilol Gupta, and Smaranda Muresan. 2019. Pay "attention" to your context when classifying abusive language. In *Proceedings of the Third Workshop on Abusive Language Online*, pages 70–79.

Despoina Chatzakou, Nicolas Kourtellis, Jeremy Blackburn, Emiliano De Cristofaro, Gianluca Stringhini, and Athena Vakali. 2017. Mean birds: Detecting aggression and bullying on twitter. In *Proceedings of the 2017 ACM on web science conference*, pages 13–22.

Patricia Chiril, Véronique Moriceau, Farah Benamara, Alda Mari, Gloria Origgi, and Marlène Coulomb-Gully. 2020. He said "who's gonna take care of your children when you are at acl?": Reported sexist acts are not sexist. In *Proceedings of the 58th Annual Meeting of the Association for Computational Linguistics*, pages 4055–4066.

Lana Cuthbertson, Alex Kearney, Riley Dawson, Ashia Zawaduk, Eve Cuthbertson, Ann Gordon-Tighe, and Kory Wallace Mathewson. 2019. Women, politics and twitter: Using machine learning to change the discourse. In *Proceedings AI for Social Good workshop at NeurIPS*.

Maral Dadvar, Dolf Trieschnigg, Roeland Ordelman, and Franciska de Jong. 2013. Improving cyberbullying detection with user context. In *Proceedings of the 35th European conference on Advances in Information Retrieval*, pages 693–696.

Sam Davidson, Qiusi Sun, and Magdalena Wojcieszak. 2020. Developing a new classifier for automated identification of incivility in social media. In *Proceedings of the Fourth Workshop on Online Abuse and Harms*, pages 95–101.

Thomas Davidson, Debasmita Bhattacharya, and Ingmar Weber. 2019. Racial bias in hate speech and abusive language detection datasets. In *Proceedings of the Third Workshop on Abusive Language Online*, pages 25–35. Association for Computational Linguistics.

Thomas Davidson, Dana Warmsley, Michael Macy, and Ingmar Weber. 2017. Automated hate speech detection and the problem of offensive language. In *Proceedings of the International AAAI Conference on Web and Social Media*, volume 11.

Bonnie-Elene Deal, Lourdes S Martinez, Brian H Spitzberg, and Ming-Hsiang Tsou. 2020. "i definitely did not report it when i was raped...# webelievechristine# metoo": A content analysis of disclosures of sexual assault on twitter. *Social Media+ Society*, 6.

Morteza Dehghani, Kate Johnson, Joe Hoover, Eyal Sagi, Justin Garten, Niki Jitendra Parmar, Stephen Vaisey, Rumen Iliev, and Jesse Graham. 2016. Purity homophily in social networks. *Journal of Experimental Psychology: General*, 145.

Fabio Del Vigna, Andrea Cimino, Felice Dell'Orletta, Marinella Petrocchi, and Maurizio Tesconi. 2017. Hate me, hate me not: Hate speech detection on facebook. In *Proceedings of the First Italian Conference on Cybersecurity (ITASEC)*, pages 86–95.

Lucas Dixon, John Li, Jeffrey Sorensen, Nithum Thain, and Lucy Vasserman. 2018. Measuring and mitigating unintended bias in text classification. In *Proceedings of the 2018 AAAI/ACM Conference on AI, Ethics, and Society*, pages 67–73.

Lizhou Fan, Huizi Yu, and Zhanyuan Yin. 2020. Stigmatization in social media: Documenting and analyzing hate speech for covid-19 on twitter. *Proceedings of the Association for Information Science and Technology*, 57(1):e313.

Antigoni Maria Founta, Despoina Chatzakou, Nicolas Kourtellis, Jeremy Blackburn, Athena Vakali, and Ilias Leontiadis. 2019. A unified deep learning architecture for abuse detection. In *Proceedings of the 10th ACM conference on web science*, pages 105–114.

Patxi Galán-García, José Gaviria de la Puerta, Carlos Laorden Gómez, Igor Santos, and Pablo García Bringas. 2016. Supervised machine learning for the detection of troll profiles in twitter social network: application to a real case of cyberbullying. *Logic Journal of the IGPL*, 24(1):42–53.

Lei Gao and Ruihong Huang. 2017. Detecting online hate speech using context aware models. In *Proceedings of the International Conference Recent Advances in Natural Language Processing, RANLP 2017*, pages 260–266. INCOMA Ltd.

Jacqueline Garrick. 2006. The humor of trauma survivors: Its application in a therapeutic milieu. *Journal of aggression, maltreatment & trauma*, 12(1-2):169–182.

Debbie Ging. 2019. Alphas, betas, and incels: Theorizing the masculinities of the manosphere. *Men and Masculinities*, 22(4):638–657.

Edel Greevy. 2004. *Automatic text categorisation of racist webpages*. Ph.D. thesis, Dublin City University.

Christopher Hom. 2008. The semantics of racial epithets. *The Journal of Philosophy*, 105(8):416–440.

Andrej Janchevski and Sonja Gievska. 2019. A study of different models for subreddit recommendation based on user-community interaction. In *International Conference on ICT Innovations*, pages 96–108. Springer.

Srecko Joksimovic, Ryan S Baker, Jaclyn Ocumpaugh, Juan Miguel L Andres, Ivan Tot, Elle Yuan Wang, and Shane Dawson. 2019. Automated identification of verbally abusive behaviors in online discussions. In *Proceedings of the Third Workshop on Abusive Language Online*, pages 36–45.

Mladen Karan and Jan Šnajder. 2019. Preemptive toxic language detection in wikipedia comments using thread-level context. In *Proceedings of the Third Workshop on Abusive Language Online*, pages 129–134.

Brendan Kennedy, Xisen Jin, Aida Mostafazadeh Davani, Morteza Dehghani, and Xiang Ren. 2020. Contextualizing hate speech classifiers with post-hoc explanation. In *Proceedings of the Annual Meeting of the Association for Computational Linguistics*.

Anna Koufakou, Endang Wahyu Pamungkas, Valerio Basile, and Viviana Patti. 2020. HurtBERT: Incorporating lexical features with BERT for the detection of abusive language. In *Proceedings of the Fourth Workshop on Online Abuse and Harms*, pages 34–43. Association for Computational Linguistics.

Srijan Kumar, William L Hamilton, Jure Leskovec, and Dan Jurafsky. 2018. Community interaction and conflict on the web. In *Proceedings of the 2018 world wide web conference*, pages 933–943.

Jana Kurrek, Haji Mohammad Saleem, and Derek Ruths. 2020. Towards a comprehensive taxonomy and large-scale annotated corpus for online slur usage. In *Proceedings of the Fourth Workshop on Online Abuse and Harms*, pages 138–149.

Shuhua Liu and Thomas Forss. 2014. Combining n-gram based similarity analysis with sentiment analysis in web content classification. In *Proceedings of the International Joint Conference on Knowledge Discovery, Knowledge Engineering and Knowledge Management-Volume 1*, pages 530–537.

Ilia Markov and Walter Daelemans. 2021. Improving cross-domain hate speech detection by reducing the false positive rate. In *Proceedings of the Fourth Workshop on NLP for Internet Freedom: Censorship, Disinformation, and Propaganda*.

Trevor Martin. 2017. community2vec: Vector representations of online communities encode semantic relationships. In *Proceedings of the Second Workshop on NLP and Computational Social Science*, pages 27–31.

Adrienne Massanari. 2017. # gamergate and the fappening: How reddit's algorithm, governance, and culture support toxic technocultures. *New media & society*, 19(3):329–346.

Puneet Mathur, Rajiv Shah, Ramit Sawhney, and Debanjan Mahata. 2018. Detecting offensive tweets in hindi-english code-switched language. In *Proceedings of the Sixth International Workshop on Natural Language Processing for Social Media*, pages 18–26.

Quinnehtukqut McLamore and Özden Melis Uluğ. 2020. Social representations of sociopolitical groups on r/the_donald and emergent conflict narratives: A qualitative content analysis. *Analyses of Social Issues and Public Policy*.

Johannes Skjeggestad Meyer and Björn Gambäck. 2019. A platform agnostic dual-strand hate speech detector. In *ACL 2019 The Third Workshop on Abusive Language Online Proceedings of the Workshop*. Association for Computational Linguistics.

Fernando Miró-Llinares, Asier Moneva, and Miriam Esteve. 2018. Hate is in the air! but where? introducing an algorithm to detect hate speech in digital microenvironments. *Crime Science*, 7(1):1–12.

Pushkar Mishra, Marco Del Tredici, Helen Yannakoudakis, and Ekaterina Shutova. 2018. Author profiling for abuse detection. In *Proceedings of the 27th international conference on computational linguistics*, pages 1088–1098.

Sandip Modha, Prasenjit Majumder, and Thomas Mandl. 2018. Filtering aggression from the multilingual social media feed. In *Proceedings of the First Workshop on Trolling, Aggression and Cyberbullying (TRAC-2018)*, pages 199–207.

Kanika Narang and Chris Brew. 2020. Abusive language detection using syntactic dependency graphs. In *Proceedings of the Fourth Workshop on Online Abuse and Harms*, pages 44–53.

Chikashi Nobata, Joel Tetreault, Achint Thomas, Yashar Mehdad, and Yi Chang. 2016. Abusive language detection in online user content. In *Proceedings of the 25th international conference on world wide web*, pages 145–153.

Thiago Dias Oliva, Dennys Marcelo Antonialli, and Alessandra Gomes. 2021. Fighting hate speech, silencing drag queens? artificial intelligence in content moderation and risks to lgbtq voices online. *Sexuality & Culture*, 25(2):700–732.

Etienne Papegnies, Vincent Labatut, Richard Dufour, and Georges Linares. 2017. Graph-based features for automatic online abuse detection. In *International conference on statistical language and speech processing*, pages 70–81. Springer.

John Pavlopoulos, Jeffrey Sorensen, Lucas Dixon, Nithum Thain, and Ion Androutsopoulos. 2020. Toxicity detection: Does context really matter? In *Proceedings of the 58th Annual Meeting of the Association for Computational Linguistics*.

Jing Qian, Mai ElSherief, Elizabeth Belding, and William Yang Wang. 2018. Leveraging intra-user and inter-user representation learning for automated hate speech detection. In *Proceedings of the 2018 Conference of the North American Chapter of the Association for Computational Linguistics: Human Language Technologies*, volume 2, pages 118–123.

Maarten Sap, Dallas Card, Saadia Gabriel, Yejin Choi, and Noah A Smith. 2019. The risk of racial bias in hate speech detection. In *Proceedings of the 57th Annual Meeting of the Association for Computational Linguistics*, pages 1668–1678.

Martin Saveski, Brandon Roy, and Deb Roy. 2021. The structure of toxic conversations on twitter. In *Proceedings of the Web Conference 2021*, pages 1086–1097.

Wendel Silva, Ádamo Santana, Fábio Lobato, and Márcia Pinheiro. 2017. A methodology for community detection in twitter. In *Proceedings of the International Conference on Web Intelligence*, pages 1006–1009.

Ahmed Soliman, Jan Hafer, and Florian Lemmerich. 2019. A characterization of political communities on reddit. In *Proceedings of the 30th ACM conference on hypertext and Social Media*, pages 259–263.

Leo G. Stewart and Emma S. Spiro. 2021. Nobody puts redditor in a binary: Digital demography, collective identities, and gender in a subreddit network. In *Proceedings of the 24th ACM Conference on Computer-Supported Cooperative Work and Social Computing*. Association for Computing Machinery.

Stéphan Tulkens, Lisa Hilte, Elise Lodewyckx, Ben Verhoeven, and Walter Daelemans. 2016. A dictionary-based approach to racism detection in dutch social media. In *Proceedings of the First Workshop on Text Analytics for Cybersecurity and Online Safety*, page 11. LREC.

Elise Fehn Unsvåg and Björn Gambäck. 2018. The effects of user features on twitter hate speech detection. In *Proceedings of the 2nd workshop on abusive language online (ALW2)*, pages 75–85.

Cynthia Van Hee, Gilles Jacobs, Chris Emmery, Bart Desmet, Els Lefever, Ben Verhoeven, Guy De Pauw, Walter Daelemans, and Véronique Hoste. 2018. Automatic detection of cyberbullying in social media text. *PloS one*, 13.

Bertie Vidgen, Alex Harris, Dong Nguyen, Rebekah Tromble, Scott Hale, and Helen Margetts. 2019. Challenges and frontiers in abusive content detection. In *Proceedings of the Third Workshop on Abusive Language Online*, pages 80–93.

Isaac Waller and Ashton Anderson. 2019. Generalists and specialists: Using community embeddings to quantify activity diversity in online platforms. In *The World Wide Web Conference*, pages 1954–1964.

William Warner and Julia Hirschberg. 2012. Detecting hate speech on the world wide web. In *Proceedings of the second workshop on language in social media*, pages 19–26.

Zeerak Waseem and Dirk Hovy. 2016. Hateful symbols or hateful people? predictive features for hate speech detection on twitter. In *Proceedings of the NAACL student research workshop*, pages 88–93.

Michael Wiegand, Josef Ruppenhofer, and Thomas Kleinbauer. 2019. Detection of abusive language: the problem of biased datasets. In *Proceedings of the 2019 Conference of the North American Chapter of the Association for Computational Linguistics: Human Language Technologies*, pages 602–608.

Mengzhou Xia, Anjalie Field, and Yulia Tsvetkov. 2020. Demoting racial bias in hate speech detection. In *Proceedings of the Eighth International Workshop on Natural Language Processing for Social Media*, pages 7–14. ACL.

Marcos Zampieri, Preslav Nakov, Sara Rosenthal, Pepa Atanasova, Georgi Karadzhov, Hamdy Mubarak, Leon Derczynski, Zeses Pitenis, and Çağrı Çöltekin. 2020. SemEval-2020 task 12: Multilingual offensive language identification in social media (OffensEval 2020). In *Proceedings of the Fourteenth Workshop on Semantic Evaluation*, pages 1425–1447. International Committee for Computational Linguistics.

Guanhua Zhang, Bing Bai, Junqi Zhang, Kun Bai, Conghui Zhu, and Tiejun Zhao. 2020. Demographics should not be the reason of toxicity: Mitigating discrimination in text classifications with instance weighting. In *Proceedings of the 58th Annual Meeting of the Association for Computational Linguistics*, pages 4134–4145.

Ziqi Zhang, David Robinson, and Jonathan Tepper. 2018. Detecting hate speech on twitter using a convolution-gru based deep neural network. In *European semantic web conference*, pages 745–760. Springer.

Caleb Ziems, Ymir Vigfusson, and Fred Morstatter. 2020. Aggressive, repetitive, intentional, visible, and imbalanced: Refining representations for cyberbullying classification. In *Proceedings of the International AAAI Conference on Web and Social Media*, volume 14, pages 808–819.

DeTox: A Comprehensive Dataset for German Offensive Language and Conversation Analysis

Christoph Demus[2,3], Jonas Pitz[1], Mina Schütz[1], Nadine Probol[1], Melanie Siegel[1], Dirk Labudde[2,3]

[1] Darmstadt University of Applied Sciences
Max-Planck-Straße 2, 64807 Dieburg
{jonas.pitz, mina.schuetz, melanie.siegel}@h-da.de
{nadine.probol}stud.@h-da.de

[2] Fraunhofer Institute for Secure Information Technology
Rheinstraße 75, 64295 Darmstadt
{christoph.demus, dirk.labudde}@sit.fraunhofer.de

[3] Mittweida University of Applied Sciences
Technikumplatz 17, 09648 Mittweida
{christoph.demus, dirk.labudde}@hs-mittweida.de

Abstract

In this work, we present a publicly available offensive language dataset (DeTox-dataset) containing 10,278 annotated German social media comments collected in the first half of 2021. With twelve different annotation categories annotated by six annotators, it is far more comprehensive than other datasets, and goes beyond just hate speech detection. The labels aim in particular also at toxicity, criminal relevance and discrimination types of comments. Furthermore, about half of the comments are from coherent parts of conversations, which opens the possibility to consider the comments contexts and do conversation analyses in order to research the contagion of offensive language in conversations. The dataset is available in our GitHub repository: https://github.com/hdaSprachtechnologie/detox

1 Introduction

With the increasing popularity of social networks in the last decade, people started to communicate more and more online, organising themselves in groups and social networks in general. It became easier than ever before to interact with foreign people because geographical distance played no role any more. While this is a great opportunity for our society, it does not come without risks regarding toxic and offensive language.

Whereas many research groups focus mainly on binary hate speech classification, offensive language contains several other aspects. These include insult, threat, and discrimination based on characteristics such as age, gender, ethnicity, religion, and sexual orientation.

The two main tasks to limit the amount of toxic language are detection and classification, e.g., to identify threats at an early stage or to effectively support criminal investigators in their work. The basis to train algorithms that can support such assessments are labelled datasets of high quality as well as quantity.

Such datasets exist only for a few languages, e.g. Vidgen et al. (2021) provided the Contextual Abuse Dataset with fine grained labels for English language. For many languages, including German, this is a limiting research factor. Therefore, motivated by the concrete application to assist a fine granular classification of offensive comments in a reporting centre for hate comments[1] of the German state government, we present a new German dataset that aims among others at hate speech, toxicity, sentiment, target, but also at criminal relevance (regarding German law) and threat. It contributes in three main aspects: (1) With 10,278 annotated comments it provides a new valuable resource for the German hate speech community. (2) Having twelve different labels per comment opens broad research and application options beyond basic hate speech detection and (3) the inclusion of whole conversation threads being partly annotated allows to make use of comments contexts as well as other supervised and unsupervised conversation analyses.

[1] https://hessengegenhetze.de/

Proceedings of the Sixth Workshop on Online Abuse and Harms (WOAH), pages 143 - 153
July 14, 2022

Dataset	Source	# Comments	Tasks
Bretschneider and Peters (2017)	Facebook	5,600	binary hate speech and intensity (moderate or clearly)
Ross et al. (2017)	Twitter	470	binary hate speech and intensity (scale 1-6)
GermEval 2018 and 2019 (Wiegand et al., 2018; Struß et al., 2019)	Twitter	15,567	coarse: offense, other fine: abuse, insult, profanity
	Twitter	2,888	implicit, explicit
HASOC 2019 (Mandl et al., 2019)	Twitter, Facebook	4,669	coarse: binary offense fine: hate, offensive, profane
GermEval 2021 (Risch et al., 2021)	Facebook	4,188	toxic, non-toxic engaging comments fact-claiming comments

Table 1: **Overview of Public German Datasets with Hate Speech Related Annotations.**

2 Related Work

2.1 German Datasets

In the last years, shared tasks played a major role for research in the hate speech detection field as they were accompanied with appropriate annotated datasets for the German language (Tab. 1). The largest dataset was created by the organizers of the GermEval 2018 and 2019 shared tasks (Struß et al., 2019), with the dataset of 2019 being an extended version of the data in 2018 and containing a total of over 15,000 comments with offensive language annotations. In the following version of GermEval in 2021 (Risch et al., 2021) a new dataset with slightly different tasks was published. The dataset of the HASOC 2019 (Mandl et al., 2019) has similar annotations to those of the GermEval 2018 and 2019 datasets. Bretschneider and Peters (2017) focused on detecting hate against foreigners. All presented datasets contain data from social networks, which represent typical online conversations.

2.2 Data quality

Aside from the quantity, the quality of the data in a dataset is of major importance. The data quality can be examined from three different viewpoints: Interpretability, relevance and accuracy (Kiefer, 2016). Interpretability describes whether the data is technically interpretable by the algorithm. An example would be a NLP-Model that was designed for text inputs and therefore cannot process images. Relevance describes whether the data is appropriate for the given problem that should be solved. For hate speech detection this means that the data should contain a certain amount of hate speech but also non hate speech comments, and it should ideally be unbiased. Finally, accuracy indicates, whether the data reflects the reality. All those factors influence each other.

2.3 Data Collection Strategies

As there is no perfect strategy to create a dataset that fulfils the aforementioned factors as much as possible, research groups use different methods for data collection. One main issue for hate speech collections is that the real proportion of hateful comments in social networks is too low to train models on (Schmidt and Wiegand, 2017). Therefore, it is often necessary to enrich the corpus with additional hate speech comments. Waseem and Hovy (2016) suggest to first identify frequently used swearwords and slurs, and then search for comments containing these words. For example, Zampieri et al. (2019a) created a dataset (OLID) - for the OffensEval shared task 2019 (Zampieri et al., 2019b) - using only ten keywords. Wiegand et al. (2018) concern that this strategy could lead to a missing variety of offensive terms, which could lead to hate speech detection models just learning those keywords (Schmidt and Wiegand, 2017). Therefore, for the GermEval 2018 and 2019 datasets (Wiegand et al., 2018; Struß et al., 2019), the authors first identified Twitter accounts that regularly post hate speech by using keyword lists. Then they sampled comments that were posted by these users. On the one hand, this omits the keyword search, but on the other hand, a single user might use a certain vocabulary. To counteract this problem, they separated the users for the train and test set splits. A combination of both methods was used by Mandl et al. (2019). In 2020 the HASOC organizers (Mandl et al., 2020) used preliminary datasets to train a simple SVM model with an average performance which they then used to identify possible hate speech comments on Twitter to create a new dataset. In addition, they included a small amount of random comments.

2.4 Annotation Strategies

Three main factors that contribute to a high annotation quality are (1) the selection of annotators, (2) the annotation schema and (3) the annotation process itself, including the process of quality insurance.

There are three options for who annotates the collected data (Poletto et al., 2020). In the best case, the data is annotated by selected subject-matter experts. However, this is not always possible due to the amount of work involved. Therefore, amateurs are often used for annotation. These can also be selected individuals (e.g., students) who are familiar with the subject background. The third possibility is the use of crowdsourcing platforms, where the annotators are not known in advance.

In all cases where non-experts annotate data, they should ideally go through a training process before they start the labelling process to ensure a high quality of the annotations. In the mentioned shared tasks, the first two methods were used, i.e. the data was either annotated by the authors themselves or by selected individuals.

2.5 Inter-Annotator Agreement

The inter-annotator agreement (IAA) is an important measure to assess the quality of the annotations. Depending on the number of annotators and the data type, there are several measures that can be used to evaluate the IAA. The most popular are Kappa-measures like Cohens (Cohen, 1960) or Fleiss Kappa (Fleiss, 1971) and Krippendorff's alpha (Krippendorff, 1980). The latter is especially used for datasets containing missing data values.

Gwet (2008) introduced the AC_1 (AC - Agreement Coefficient) measure for IAA. The author shows that this measure is more resistant against the paradoxes of Kappa measures, which is described in detail in Feinstein and Cicchetti (1990) and Gwet (2015) (despite the name the paradoxes are also valid for Krippendorff's alpha). Furthermore, its weighted version AC_2 (Gwet, 2014) is able to handle different scales (e.g. ordinal scale).

3 Data Collection and Description

For this dataset we used Twitter as the data source, as it grants free access to most of its tweets for research purposes, and it is possible to (automatically) extract tweets by multiple criteria via the Twitter-API. The use of Twitter text data guarantees a high interpretability (see Sec. 2.2) and thus allows algorithms to be developed using this data.

In contrast to previous related work, we aimed not only at collecting single comments but also at collecting whole conversations or parts thereof, which means tweets or comments and their reply trees. Both require different data collection strategies, which will be explained in the following sections. All collected comments and conversations are in German language and posted in the first half of 2021. The most present topics in the media during the time we crawled the data were the Corona pandemic with all its aspects, as well as politics related to the elections of the German Bundestag in September 2021.

3.1 Comments

As we intended to cover a wide range of topics, types of discrimination, and political attitudes, we manually created keyword lists for the fields we wanted to receive comments for. As keywords, we used words that we expected to occur in offensive comments as well as offensive words. Furthermore, we determined keywords with the help of Google Trends in order to capture currently much discussed topics. For example, we used "merkelmussweg" (engl. "Merkel must go", often used as a hashtag) as one keyword for political attitude and "Querdenker" (engl. "lateral thinkers"), which is a pejorative term for Corona deniers, for Corona-related hate speech, but also words like "Jude" (engl. "jew") that are neutral by its own but often used in discriminating comments. In the end, our keyword lists contained a total of 131 words. During the comment search we did not only search the comment text for the keywords but also the hashtags. With these keyword lists, we pulled 781,991 comments from 154,151 Twitter users.

In a second step - to create a smaller dataset with a higher probability to contain offensive and relevant content - we filtered these comments with two additional lists: 1) a hate word list and 2) a list containing profane words.[2] The hate word list was set up for an earlier participation at GermEval 2018 (Siegel and Meyer, 2018). It was extended on different hate speech corpora using the tf-idf mechanism. The profane word list was extracted from a website containing around 2,000 offensive and profane words in German. For our sampling strategy each of the filtered tweets needed to con-

[2] https://www.insult.wiki/schimpfwort-liste

Comments	annotated	not annotated	Total
single Com.	4,936	0	4,936
Com. of Conv.	5,342	444,300	449,642
Total	10,278	444,300	454,578

Table 2: **General Statistics of the complete Dataset:** Numbers of annotated and additional not annotated comments in the single comments and conversation part of our dataset.

Single Comments	
# hate word filtered	3,214
# unfiltered	1,722
Conversations	
# Convs	514
Mean # Com. per Conv.	873.09
Mean # Authors per Conv.	502.14

Table 3: **Additional Dataset Statistics:** Statistics regarding the composition of the single comments and the number and size of conversations. All together the datasets contains 100 conversations with more than five annotated comments those conversations contain on average 45 annotated comments (max. 463 annotated comments per conversation).

tain at least one word from each of the two lists. Finally, we took the comments for the annotation from about two thirds from the pre-filtered stream and one third from the 781,991 comments set (Tables 2 and 3).

3.2 Conversations

For the selection of conversations, we first selected parent tweets on Twitter and then pulled the whole response tree. This can be done by searching for all tweets having the same conversation ID as the parent tweet.

We expected that by involving entire conversations, the hate speech portion on Twitter would be reflected more realistically, addressing the requirement for data accuracy. But, we also expected that this dataset would contain less hate speech overall than the dataset with individual comments, thus leading to a problem of relevancy. To counteract this problem, we selected a total of 25 Twitter pages containing content of politicians, scientists related to the Corona pandemic, conspiracy theorists and influencers. The selection was based on those figures often being a catalyst for controversial discussions in recent media. This resulted in 4,698 conversations containing 637,027 comments. For annotation, we intended to select coherent conversation parts that may contain - with a high probability - hate speech. Therefore, in a first step we selected comments from these conversations, which have 10 to 199 direct replies but, to avoid major biases, are not posts of the owners of the crawled twitter pages. This resulted in 1,665 comments that were annotated. As it is known that offensive comments trigger other users to post offensive responses (Cheng et al., 2017; Almerekhi et al., 2020) we used this knowledge to find offensive passages in the conversation trees. Therefore, in a second step, we noted 57 comments from 49 conversations that were annotated as hate speech (majority voting) or toxic (averaged toxicity annotation > 2.5). Finally, we extracted these comments' parent comments and all their successor comments (the whole conversation after each selected comment). This resulted in 5,342 annotated comments belonging to captured conversations (Tables 2 and 3). Next to the annotated comments belonging to conversations, we also included all not annotated comments of conversations where at least one comment was annotated from as these comments could be useful for unsupervised analyses.

4 Data Annotation

The annotation scheme was established to best support the specific task of building models for fine grained classification in the mentioned reporting office for hate comments but also with a view to future research. This resulted in a comprehensive annotation schema with twelve different categories at two levels. Furthermore, various metadata such as annotation time and duration were logged to leave the possibility not only to use the dataset to train models but also for future analyses like the Inter-Rater-Agreement-Learning described by Hanke et al. (2020) that uses annotation metadata to compute the reliability of annotators.

4.1 Annotation Schema

An overview over the annotation schema is given in Figure 1. Initially, comments that could not be (fully) understood, i.e. because of missing context, could be labelled as "Incomprehensible" which made further annotations to a comment voluntary. If this was not the case, the other main categories had to be annotated. "Sentiment" refers to the assumed emotional state of the comment's author when writing the comment: negative, neutral or positive. "Expression" describes whether the author expressed its message in an implicit or explicit manner. With the "Target" of a comment, we refer

Categories
- Incomprehensible .... [y / n]
- Sentiment .... [-1, 0, 1]
- Hate Speech .... [y / n]
  - Hate Speech Entities .... [free text input]
  - Type of Discrimination .... [10 types]
- Criminal Relevance .... [y / n]
  - Legal Paragraphs .... [14 paragraphs]
- Expression .... [implicit / explicit]
- Toxicity .... [1 - 5]
- Extremism .... [y / n]
- Target .... [person / group / public]
- Threat .... [y / n]

Figure 1: **Overview of the Annotation Schema:** The categories and their respective labels ("y" - yes, "n" - no). Categories in second order depend on their parent category.

to who is addressed, as this is of importance for hate speech contagion in conversations (Kwon and Gruzd, 2017). The comment can be addressed to a single or multiple separate persons, a group or groups of people, or it can have no specific target (public). With the category "Threat" we address comments that invoke or announce acts of violence and therefore pose a direct danger or threat to the public.

While "Toxicity" and "Hate Speech" are closely related, they are not interchangeable and can even occur independently of each other. To distinguish between the two categories, we used the following definitions:

Toxicity: Toxicity indicates the potential of a comment to "poison" a conversation. The more it encourages aggressive responses or triggers other participants to leave the conversation, the more toxic the comment is. We introduced a scale of 1 (not toxic) to 5 (very toxic) to be able to model the impact of toxic comments on the conversation more accurately.

Hate Speech [3] **:** Hate speech is defined as any form of expression that attacks or disparages persons or groups by characteristics attributed to the groups. Discriminatory statements can be aimed at, for example, political attitudes, religious affiliation or sexual identity of the victims.

In a free text input form, the annotators could submit words or phrases that were pivotal in their decision to label the comment as "Hate Speech". The type of discrimination could also be specified. The following types of discrimination were available for selection (zero, one or multiple selections were possible):

Types of Discrimination: Job; Political Attitude; Personal Engagement and Interests; Sexual Identity; Physical, Psychological or Mental Characteristics; Nationality; Religion; Social Status; World View; Ethnicity.

The category "Criminal Relevance" indicates whether a comment can be considered as relevant under German criminal law. If a comment was selected to be criminally relevant, annotators had to further specify the legal paragraphs that were applicable. This was one of the most difficult tasks for the annotators, as they did not have a legal background. The following paragraphs were considered to be applicable to online comments:

Legal Paragraphs (StGB[4]): § 86, § 86a, § 111, § 126, § 130, § 131, § 140, § 166, § 185, § 186, § 187, § 189, § 240, § 241.

4.2 Annotation Disagreements

Labelling hate speech data relates a lot to personal beliefs, experience and demographic properties (Sap et al., 2021). As our main goal was to train models for classification, we applied a prescriptive annotation standard, meaning we aimed at having clear decisions regarding to annotation guidelines and not surveying personal annotator beliefs (Röttger et al., 2021). Nevertheless, also the use of detailed annotation guidelines cannot reach full objectivity. As a result disagreements between the annotators will necessarily appear and can be handled in multiple ways. Common strategies are majority voting for classification on a nominal (incl. binary) scale and averaging for classification on an ordinal scale. Majority voting has the property, that underrepresented opinions get likely voted out, in particular if the number of annotators is high (Davani et al., 2022). If this is good or bad depends on the specific application. To avoid this behaviour other approaches model annotators separately and even make it possible to estimate uncertainty which could be used to make no decision if uncertainty is high (Davani et al., 2022). We used majority voting and averaging for this work but also included the single annotations of each annotator in the dataset to allow other approaches.

[3] Based on the definition of the United Nations: https://www.un.org/en/genocideprevention/documents/UN%20Strategy%20and%20Plan%20of%20Action%20on%20Hate%20Speech%2018%20June%20SYNOPSIS.pdf

[4] StGB (engl. German Criminal Code): https://www.gesetze-im-internet.de/englisch_stgb/index.html

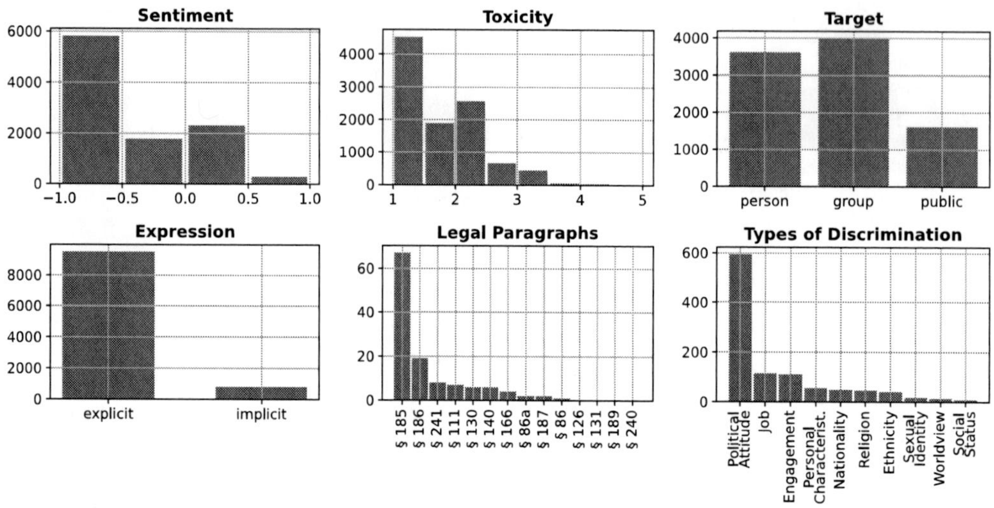

Figure 2: **Frequency Distributions for the Labels Sentiment, Toxicity, Target, Expression, Legal Paragraphs and Types of Discrimination:** Sentiment values reach from -1 (negative) to +1 (positive), Toxicity values reach from 1 (not toxic) to 5 (most toxic). The categories Legal Paragraphs and Type of Discrimination are multi label classes related to the labels Criminal Relevance and Hate Speech respectively. The paragraphs meant to be paragraphs in the German "Strafgesetzbuch (StGB)" (engl. German Criminal Code).

4.3 Annotation Process

The group of annotators consisted of six students, four of them studying Information Science and two studying General and Digital Forensics. The complete annotation process was permanently monitored. First, we introduced the annotators for the task, including an explanation of the annotation guidelines. Afterwards, we started a training phase, where each annotator annotated 200 comments split in two sets. After each set, we identified controversial annotated comments and discussed them. Then, the annotators were split in two groups of three persons each according to their annotations in the training phase. That means, annotators were divided such that the annotators are equally distributed on how offensive they labelled comments on average. The goal was to avoid that all annotators, who tend to label comments more toxic than others, are in the same group, as this would bias the annotations. In the next step, we began with the annotation phase, which run over about five months. In this phase, the data was annotated in 8 batches. To cut it short, finally every comment was annotated by three annotators and every annotator annotated 5139 comments (half of the data). In the datasets, single Twitter comments and comments from conversations were mixed and roughly equally distributed. During this phase the inter annotator agreement was permanently monitored and every one to three weeks unclear comments were extracted and discussed, also under consideration of the agreement in all categories.

For subsequent analyses on consistency (Sec. 5.2) of the annotations, each annotator had to annotate 20 randomly selected comments per annotation set twice. This results in 123 to 138 twice annotated comments per annotator (it is not $8 \cdot 20 = 160$ as we additionally had some other non-public comments in the annotation datasets).

5 Results and Discussion

In this section, we will first outline general specifications like the frequencies of the annotated labels of the dataset. In the second part the annotation quality containing measures for the IAA and the annotator consistency are presented and finally a closer look at the conversations is taken. As the dataset is very comprehensive, we can only show selected, most important statistics and results.

5.1 General

After the annotation process, the dataset contains 31,327 Annotations for 10,278 Twitter comments. The 141 comments for which the annotations differed the most (difference of > 7 annotations, with 12 being the maximum) were re-examined by the

Category	Com.	Conv.	Total
Incompre-hensible	117 2.39 %	214 4.01 %	332 3.23 %
Hate Speech	880 17.83 %	235 4.40 %	1,115 10.85 %
Criminal Relevance	99 2.01 %	32 0.60 %	131 1.27 %
Extremism	55 1.11 %	27 0.51 %	82 0.80 %
Threat	11 0.22 %	1 0.02 %	12 0.12 %

Table 4: **Frequencies of the Annotation Categories:** Absolute and percentage values for the frequencies of the binary annotation categories separated in single comments (Com.) and comments from conversations (Conv.).

Category	Group A	Group B
Incomprehensible	0.7982	0.9343
Sentiment	0.7744	0.8785
Hate speech	0.7286	0.8056
Criminal Relevance	0.9368	0.9364
Expression	0.9625	0.9515
Toxicity	0.8584	0.9159
Target	0.7281	0.7701
Extremism	0.5441	0.6086
Threat	0.9987	0.9997
Mean	**0.8144**	**0.8667**

Table 5: **Inter-Annotator Agreement:** IAA for all labels and both groups of annotators containing three annotators each. Sentiment and Toxicity values are computed with the AC_2 measure, all others with AC_1.

authors.

For the analysis, we separated the labels in binary ones (Tab. 4) and non-binary ones (Fig. 2). For the binary labels, except for the category Threat, we did a majority voting to achieve a gold standard. As the category Threat is much less represented than the other categories, we lowered the border and assumed a comment as Threat, if at least one annotator labelled it as Threat. In real applications, one would likely do the same, not to miss any comments that pose a threat. The analysis of the binary label frequencies shows that the hate speech proportion of the complete dataset is 10.85 % (1,115 comments) and 1.27 % (131 comments) are labelled as criminally relevant. The categories Extremism and Threat were only in less than 1 % of the comments labelled as true. In contrast to that, 3.23 % (329 comments) were annotated as incomprehensible by the majority of the annotators, which means the sense of the comment could not fully be understood, and therefore was not (completely) labelled. Table 4 also shows that the single comments part of the dataset contains a higher proportion of offensive comments. This is visible most clearly in the category Hate Speech, where the proportion in the single comments part is 17.83 % but in the conversations part only 4.40 %. The reason is that each comment in the single comments part was selected only by its own properties, in particular by keyword search. In contrast to that, in the conversations part not the comments were selected but whole conversations with all comments. Therefore, this is an expected observation.

Figure 2 shows the frequency distributions for the labels Sentiment, Toxicity, Target, Expression, Legal Paragraphs, and Type of Discrimination. It is noticeable that most of the comments have a toxicity of less than 2.5, although the sentiment of the majority of the comments is negative (-1 is the most negative). Nevertheless, the percentage of toxic comments is with 9.63 % just a little lower than the hate speech proportion in the dataset. Concerning the target of the comments, it shows that specific persons and groups are almost equally addressed, and it is rare that a comment addresses no specific target.

The categories Legal Paragraphs and Type of Discrimination differ from the others as they are connected to other categories (Criminal Relevance and Hate Speech respectively) and they are multi-label categories. As before also for the paragraphs and the types of discrimination a majority voting was done. The most often annotated paragraph is by far § 185 "Beleidigung" (engl. insult) followed by § 186 "Üble Nachrede" (engl. malicious gossip). Regarding the Type of Discrimination, the dominating category is "Political Attitude" which suggests, that most of the hate speech comments seem to be offensive towards the political view of people.

5.2 Inter-Annotator Agreement and Consistency

To assess the quality of the annotations, we measured the IAA and the consistency of the annotators using Gwets agreement coefficients (AC_1, AC_2), as they are resistant against the paradoxes of Kappa-measures and resulted in more realistic values here (see Sec. 2.5). AC_1 (with a nominal scale) was used for all classes except Sentiment and Toxicity. As they have an ordinal scale, we used AC_2 for them. For both, the IAA and the consistency, we did not evaluate the categories "Legal Paragraphs" and "Type of Discrimination" here, as they depend

Category	A1	A2	A3	B1	B2	B3	Mean
Incomprehensible	0.94	0.96	0.80	0.97	0.98	0.93	**0.93**
Sentiment	0.86	0.94	0.69	0.92	0.94	0.94	**0.88**
Hate speech	0.90	0.95	0.77	0.90	0.89	0.93	**0.89**
Criminal Relevance	0.95	0.99	0.83	0.95	0.95	0.91	**0.93**
Expression	0.89	0.85	0.67	0.77	0.89	0.86	**0.82**
Toxicity	0.94	0.96	0.97	0.97	0.95	0.94	**0.95**
Target	0.82	0.73	0.62	0.80	0.76	0.76	**0.75**
Extremism	0.99	1.00	0.78	0.94	0.95	0.98	**0.94**
Threat	1.00	1.00	0.80	0.96	0.98	0.97	**0.95**
Mean	**0.92**	**0.93**	**0.77**	**0.91**	**0.92**	**0.91**	**0.89**

Table 6: **Annotator Consistencies:** Every annotator labelled around 130 comments twice. From these duplicate annotations, the agreements for every annotator and every category were computed using Gwets AC_1 and AC_2 (for Sentiment and Toxicity) measures.

	Random Selection	Answers of offensive Comments
Toxic	1.97 %	5.97 %
Hate Speech	2.81 %	6.24 %

Table 7: **Proportion of Offensive Comments in Conversations:** Random Selection shows the proportion of toxic and hate speech comments in 1,673 random selected comments from conversations. The second column shows the proportion of toxic and hate speech comments in 881 answers to comments that were labelled as toxic / hate speech.

on the categories "Criminal Relevance" and "Hate Speech" respectively which would require more complex analyses to get reliable results.

The IAA (Tab. 5) was measured over all comments for each of the two groups of annotators. The table shows that the mean agreement of group A is about 0.05 lower than the agreement of group B. Still, both groups have mean values over 0.8 which indicates a very good agreement. Looking at the IAA of each label category, it is visible that the category "Extremism" has by far the lowest agreement in both groups (0.54 and 0.61) and "Threat" has with over 0.99 the highest agreement. The latter is caused by the fact that there are just 12 comments in the whole dataset that are labelled threatening at all.

In addition, we analysed the consistency of the annotators using the duplicate annotations of each annotator (see Sec. 4.3). An ideal annotator would annotate the same comment always the same (high consistency) but in reality this is not the case.

The analysis (Tab. 6) shows that five of the six annotators have - with an agreement over 0.80 in their twice annotated comments - a very good consistency, which indicates that they labelled the same comment both times almost equally. Annotator A3 has with a value of 0.77 a lower consistency but still being good (> 0.6). This could also be one reason, why Group A has a lower average IAA. In contrast to the IAA, the consistency of the category Extremism is, except of annotator A3, very good (over 0.90). This shows that there might have been different interpretations of these category as it would have lead to a better IAA otherwise.

5.3 Conversations

A main question in the conversation analysis related to hate speech is, what impact an offensive comment to the following conversation has. In our analysis, we define all comments as offensive that are labelled as hate speech (majority voting) or toxic (averaged toxicity annotation > 2.5). Then we compared the proportion of offensive comments in the random selection (from the first annotation step, see Sec. 3.2) with the proportion of offensive comments in direct answers to offensive comments (annotated in step 2). The results in Table 7 show, that the proportion of toxic comments in answers to offensive comments is with almost 6 % three times higher than in the random selection. For hate speech it is with 6.24 % even a bit higher. This observation indicates that offensive comments trigger users to answer with offensive speech.

6 Baseline Models

The categories hate speech, toxicity and sentiment were selected to train simple baseline models on. We did not make use of comments contexts so far, this will be done in later work. Even though toxicity and sentiment are regression tasks, we used classification models for them as this heavily improved the performance for the underrepresented classes (high toxicity and positive Sentiment).

We used a multi layer perceptron (MLP) with an

Category	MLP Prec	MLP Re	MLP F1	SVM Prec	SVM Re	SVM F1	GBert Prec	GBert Re	GBert F1	XLM-R Prec	XLM-R Re	XLM-R F1
Hate Speech	0.67 (0.85)	0.54 (0.89)	0.56 (0.85)	0.65 (0.90)	0.79 (0.80)	0.67 (0.83)	0.78 (0.89)	0.67 (0.91)	0.71 (0.89)	0.53 (0.79)	0.58 (0.89)	0.55 (0.83)
Toxicity	0.28 (0.53)	0.27 (0.54)	0.27 (0.53)	0.35 (0.66)	0.41 (0.61)	0.35 (0.62)	0.41 (0.67)	0.37 (0.68)	0.39 (0.67)	0.56 (0.67)	0.56 (0.66)	0.54 (0.65)
Sentiment	0.60 (0.62)	0.44 (0.63)	0.45 (0.60)	0.58 (0.71)	0.63 (0.70)	0.59 (0.70)	0.66 (0.71)	0.55 (0.71)	0.58 (0.71)	0.64 (0.72)	0.64 (0.71)	0.63 (0.71)

Table 8: **Performance measures of our baseline models on the given labels:** The values are macro averaged and in round brackets the weighted values are given.

additional embedding layer with a vocabulary size of 15,000 and softmax function, an SVM model that uses an 200 dimensional Fasttext feature vector as input as well as GBert and XLM-R Transformer models. We did a stratified train-test-split (80 % training, 20 % test) and evaluated the results (Tab. 8) using macro and weighted (values in round brackets) precision, recall and F1-score. The bigger the difference between the macro and weighted value, the bigger is the difference of the recall scores of the classes.

In most categories the SVM outperforms the MLP and the transformer models slightly outperform the SVM. In particular, the macro recall scores of the SVM, which are relevant for detection of offensive language, are higher compared to the MLP and on a same level as the transformer models. Overall the MLP tended to have a higher performance on the majority class but a much lower performance on the minority class. In the other models this gap was mostly smaller. GBert produced better results for Hate Speech detection while XLM-R had better macro average scores for Toxicity.

7 Limitations of the Dataset

Even though the data collection and annotations were done as properly as possible, the dataset has some limitations. Twitter as a data source has some disadvantages: First, it is just one of many social networks. Every network brings its own properties and influences therefore the people, their writing style and communication standards. Second, comments on Twitter are moderated and therefore offensive language might have already been removed before our data collection. A more general problem, which is partly but not exclusively caused by the method of keyword search, is the presence of selected topics limiting generalizability. Regarding the annotations, even with three annotations per comment the number is relatively small resulting to a high influence of possible biased annotations or annotators. The comprehensive annotation schema is complex to annotate, and the definitions of hate speech and toxicity naturally leave a lot of room for personal interpretations. Further, the annotations for the legal paragraphs should be treated carefully, as no annotator (and also no one of the authors) has a legal background. Finally, the annotations for legal paragraphs are specific to German legislation.

8 Conclusion

Modern machine learning methods require sufficient amounts of annotated data that are of high quality and at the same time, the annotations must be granular enough that the learned models can be used effectively in real applications.

For this dataset the data was carefully selected and biases were avoided as much as possible. The annotation schema was developed together with first-hand users from a reporting office for offensive comments in Germany. During the annotation process, the quality was systematically monitored and adjusted. Parts of the data are available together with their conversation contexts (i.e. its parent comments and replies). We have conducted initial statistical data analyses with the annotated data, which we will continue in the future and trained baseline models on selected categories.

The dataset gives the possibility to train models on high quality annotated data that go beyond binary classification tasks. Moreover, it can be used to build more complex algorithms which may take the comments' context into account and even conversation analyses and analyses regarding the spread of offensive language are possible.

9 Acknowledgements

This work is enhanced by the Darmstadt University of Applied Sciences, which supported this work with the research in Information Science (https://sis.h-da.de/), in collaboration with the Fraunhofer Institute for Secure Information Technology. Additionally, this contribution has been funded by the project "DeTox" (Cybersecurity research funding of the Hessian Ministry of the Interior and Sports) which is a collaboration with the Hessian CyberCompetenceCenter (Hessen3C).

References

Hind Almerekhi, Haewoon Kwak, Joni Salminen, and Bernard J. Jansen. 2020. Are these comments triggering? predicting triggers of toxicity in online discussions. In *Proceedings of The Web Conference 2020*. ACM.

Uwe Bretschneider and Ralf Peters. 2017. Detecting offensive statements towards foreigners in social media. In *Proceedings of the 50th Hawaii International Conference on System Sciences (2017)*. Hawaii International Conference on System Sciences.

Justin Cheng, Michael Bernstein, Cristian Danescu-Niculescu-Mizil, and Jure Leskovec. 2017. Anyone can become a troll: Causes of trolling behavior in online discussions. In *Proceedings of the 2017 ACM Conference on Computer Supported Cooperative Work and Social Computing*, CSCW '17, page 1217–1230, New York, NY, USA. Association for Computing Machinery.

Jacob Cohen. 1960. A coefficient of agreement for nominal scales. *Educational and Psychological Measurement*, 20(1):37–46.

Aida Mostafazadeh Davani, Mark Díaz, and Vinodkumar Prabhakaran. 2022. Dealing with Disagreements: Looking Beyond the Majority Vote in Subjective Annotations. *Transactions of the Association for Computational Linguistics*, 10:92–110.

Alvan R. Feinstein and Domenic V. Cicchetti. 1990. High agreement but low kappa: I. the problems of two paradoxes. *Journal of Clinical Epidemiology*, 43(6):543–549.

Joseph L. Fleiss. 1971. Measuring nominal scale agreement among many raters. *Psychological Bulletin*, 76(5):378–382.

Kilem Gwet. 2015. On krippendorff's alpha coefficient.

Kilem Li Gwet. 2008. Computing inter-rater reliability and its variance in the presence of high agreement. *British Journal of Mathematical and Statistical Psychology*, 61(1):29–48.

Kilem Li Gwet. 2014. *Handbook of Inter-Rater Reliability*, chapter Agreement Coefficients for Ordinal, Interval, and Ratio Data. Advanced Analytics, LLC.

Kai-Jannis Hanke, Andy Ludwig, Dirk Labudde, and Michael Spranger. 2020. Towards inter-rater-agreement-learning. In *The Tenth International Conference on Advances in Information Mining and Management*.

Cornelia Kiefer. 2016. Assessing the quality of unstructured data: An initial overview. In *LWDA*, pages 62–73.

Klaus Krippendorff. 1980. *Content Analysis: An Introduction to its Methodology*, chapter 12. Sage Publications, Beverly Hills.

K. Hazel Kwon and Anatoliy Gruzd. 2017. Is offensive commenting contagious online? examining public vs interpersonal swearing in response to donald trump's YouTube campaign videos. *Internet Research*, 27(4):991–1010.

Thomas Mandl, Sandip Modha, Anand Kumar M, and Bharathi Raja Chakravarthi. 2020. Overview of the hasoc track at fire 2020: Hate speech and offensive language identification in tamil, malayalam, hindi, english and german. In *Forum for Information Retrieval Evaluation*, FIRE 2020, page 29–32, New York, NY, USA. Association for Computing Machinery.

Thomas Mandl, Sandip Modha, Prasenjit Majumder, Daksh Patel, Mohana Dave, Chintak Mandlia, and Aditya Patel. 2019. Overview of the HASOC track at FIRE 2019. In *Proceedings of the 11th Forum for Information Retrieval Evaluation*. ACM.

Fabio Poletto, Valerio Basile, Manuela Sanguinetti, Cristina Bosco, and Viviana Patti. 2020. Resources and benchmark corpora for hate speech detection: a systematic review. *Language Resources and Evaluation*, pages 1–47.

Julian Risch, Anke Stoll, Lena Wilms, and Michael Wiegand. 2021. Overview of the GermEval 2021 shared task on the identification of toxic, engaging, and fact-claiming comments. In *Proceedings of the GermEval 2021 Workshop on the Identification of Toxic, Engaging, and Fact-Claiming Comments : 17th Conference on Natural Language Processing KONVENS 2021*.

Björn Ross, Michael Rist, Guillermo Carbonell, Benjamin Cabrera, Nils Kurowsky, and Michael Wojatzki. 2017. Measuring the reliability of hate speech annotations: The case of the european refugee crisis. *Proceedings of NLP4CMC III: 3rd Workshop on Natural Language Processing for Computer-Mediated Communication (Bochum), Bochumer Linguistische Arbeitsberichte, vol. 17, sep 2016, pp. 6-9*.

Paul Röttger, Bertie Vidgen, Dirk Hovy, and Janet B. Pierrehumbert. 2021. Two contrasting data annotation paradigms for subjective nlp tasks.

Maarten Sap, Swabha Swayamdipta, Laura Vianna, Xuhui Zhou, Yejin Choi, and Noah A. Smith. 2021. Annotators with attitudes: How annotator beliefs and identities bias toxic language detection.

Anna Schmidt and Michael Wiegand. 2017. A survey on hate speech detection using natural language processing. In *Proceedings of the Fifth International Workshop on Natural Language Processing for Social Media*, pages 1–10, Valencia, Spain. Association for Computational Linguistics.

Melanie Siegel and Markus Meyer. 2018. h_da submission for the GermEval shared task on the identification of offensive language. In *Proceedings of the GermEval 2018 Workshop*, Vienna, Austria. Austrian Academy of Sciences.

Julia Maria Struß, Melanie Siegel, Josef Ruppenhofer, Michael Wiegand, and Manfred Klenner. 2019. Overview of germeval task 2, 2019 shared task on the identification of offensive language. In *Proceedings of the 15th Conference on Natural Language Processing (KONVENS 2019)*, pages 354–365, Erlangen, Germany. German Society for Computational Linguistics & Language Technology.

Bertie Vidgen, Dong Nguyen, Helen Margetts, Patricia Rossini, and Rebekah Tromble. 2021. Introducing CAD: the contextual abuse dataset. In *Proceedings of the 2021 Conference of the North American Chapter of the Association for Computational Linguistics: Human Language Technologies*, pages 2289–2303, Online. Association for Computational Linguistics.

Zeerak Waseem and Dirk Hovy. 2016. Hateful symbols or hateful people? predictive features for hate speech detection on Twitter. In *Proceedings of the NAACL Student Research Workshop*, pages 88–93, San Diego, California. Association for Computational Linguistics.

Michael Wiegand, Melanie Siegel, and Josef Ruppenhofer. 2018. Overview of the GermEval 2018 shared task on the identification of offensive language. In *Proceedings of the GermEval 2018 Workshop*, Vienna, Austria. Austrian Academy of Sciences.

Marcos Zampieri, Shervin Malmasi, Preslav Nakov, Sara Rosenthal, Noura Farra, and Ritesh Kumar. 2019a. Predicting the type and target of offensive posts in social media. In *Proceedings of the 2019 Conference of the North American Chapter of the Association for Computational Linguistics: Human Language Technologies, Volume 1 (Long and Short Papers)*, pages 1415–1420, Minneapolis, Minnesota. Association for Computational Linguistics.

Marcos Zampieri, Shervin Malmasi, Preslav Nakov, Sara Rosenthal, Noura Farra, and Ritesh Kumar. 2019b. Semeval-2019 task 6: Identifying and categorizing offensive language in social media (offenseval). In *Proceedings of the 13th International Workshop on Semantic Evaluation*, pages 75–86.

MULTILINGUAL HATECHECK: Functional Tests for Multilingual Hate Speech Detection Models

Paul Röttger[1,2], **Haitham Seelawi**[1], **Debora Nozza**[1,3], **Zeerak Talat**[1,4], and **Bertie Vidgen**[1]

[1]Rewire [2]University of Oxford [3]Bocconi University [4]Simon Fraser University

Abstract

Hate speech detection models are typically evaluated on held-out test sets. However, this risks painting an incomplete and potentially misleading picture of model performance because of increasingly well-documented systematic gaps and biases in hate speech datasets. To enable more targeted diagnostic insights, recent research has thus introduced functional tests for hate speech detection models. However, these tests currently only exist for English-language content, which means that they cannot support the development of more effective models in other languages spoken by billions across the world. To help address this issue, we introduce MULTILINGUAL HATECHECK (MHC), a suite of functional tests for multilingual hate speech detection models. MHC covers 34 functionalities across ten languages, which is more languages than any other hate speech dataset. To illustrate MHC's utility, we train and test a high-performing multilingual hate speech detection model, and reveal critical model weaknesses for monolingual and cross-lingual applications.

1 Introduction

Hate speech detection models play a key role in online content moderation and also enable scientific analysis and monitoring of online hate. Traditionally, models have been evaluated by their performance on held-out test sets. However, this practice risks painting an incomplete and misleading picture of model quality. Hate speech datasets are prone to exhibit systematic gaps and biases due to how they are sampled (Wiegand et al., 2019; Vidgen and Derczynski, 2020; Poletto et al., 2021) and annotated (Talat, 2016; Davidson et al., 2019; Sap et al., 2021). Therefore, models may perform deceptively well by learning overly simplistic decision rules rather than encoding a generalisable understanding of the task (e.g. Niven and Kao, 2019; Geva et al., 2019; Shah et al., 2020). Further, aggregate and thus abstract performance metrics such as accuracy and F1 score may obscure more specific model weaknesses (Wu et al., 2019).

For these reasons, recent hate speech research has introduced novel test sets and methods that allow for a more targeted evaluation of model functionalities (Calabrese et al., 2021; Kirk et al., 2021; Mathew et al., 2021; Röttger et al., 2021b). However, these novel test sets, like most hate speech datasets so far, focus on English-language content. A lack of effective evaluation hinders the development of higher-quality hate speech detection models for other languages. As a consequence, billions of non-English speakers across the world are given less protection against online hate, and even the largest social media platforms have clear language gaps in their content moderation (Simonite, 2021; Marinescu, 2021).

As a step towards closing these language gaps, we introduce MULTILINGUAL HATECHECK (MHC), which extends the English HATECHECK functional test suite for hate speech detection models (Röttger et al., 2021b) to ten more languages. Functional testing evaluates models on sets of targeted test cases (Beizer, 1995). Ribeiro et al. (2020) first applied this idea to structured model evaluation in NLP, and Röttger et al. (2021b) used it to diagnose critical model weaknesses in English hate speech detection models. We create novel functional test suites for Arabic, Dutch, French, German, Hindi, Italian, Mandarin, Polish, Portuguese and Spanish.[1] To our knowledge, MHC covers more languages than any other hate speech dataset.

The functional tests for each language in MHC broadly match those of the original HATECHECK, which were selected based on interviews with civil society stakeholders as well as a review of hate speech research. In each language, there are be-

[1]On dialects: we use Egyptian Arabic in Arabic script, European Dutch and French, High German, Standard Italian and Polish, Standard Hindi in Latin script, Standard Mandarin in Chinese script, Brazilian Portuguese and Argentinian Spanish.

Proceedings of the Sixth Workshop on Online Abuse and Harms (WOAH), pages 154 - 169

tween 25 and 27 tests for different kinds of hate speech (e.g. dehumanisation and threatening language) as well as contrasting non-hate, which may lexically resemble hate speech but is clearly non-hateful (e.g. counter speech). These contrasts make the test suites particularly challenging to models that rely on overly simplistic decision rules and thus enable more accurate evaluation of model functionalities (Gardner et al., 2020). For each functional test, native-speaking language experts hand-crafted targeted test cases with clear gold standard labels, using the English cases as a starting point but adapting them to retain realism and cultural compatibility in the target language.

We demonstrate MHC's utility as a diagnostic tool by evaluating a multilingual XLM-T model (Barbieri et al., 2021) fine-tuned on a combination of three widely-used hate speech datasets in Spanish, Italian and Portuguese. This model achieves strong performance on the respective held-out test sets. However, testing with MHC reveals that the model is 1) overly sensitive to key words and key phrases, 2) biased in its target coverage and 3) error-prone and inconsistent in cross-lingual transfer, in both zero- and many-shot settings. If this model was used to moderate content, these critical weaknesses could cause serious harm, leaving some users unprotected from hate while others are restricted in their freedom of expression. We hope that by revealing such weaknesses, MHC can play a key role in the development of better multilingual hate speech detection models.[2]

Definition of Hate Speech Following Röttger et al. (2021b), we define hate speech as *abuse that is targeted at a protected group or at its members for being a part of that group.* Protected groups are groups based on age, disability, gender identity, race, national or ethnic origins, religion, sex or sexual orientation, which broadly reflects Western legal consensus, particularly the US 1964 Civil Rights Act, the UK's 2010 Equality Act and the EU's Charter of Fundamental Rights. Based on these definitions, we approach hate speech detection as the binary classification of content as either hateful or non-hateful.

Content Warning This article contains examples of hateful and abusive language. All examples are taken from MHC in their original language, to illustrate MHC's composition.

[2]We make MHC available on GitHub.

2 Constructing MHC

2.1 Defining Functional Tests

Functional tests in MHC test the ability of hate speech detection models to correctly classify different types of hateful and non-hateful content. The tests are fine-grained, distinct and contrastive. For example, we have separate tests for hate expressed using profanity (e.g. DE:"F*ck alle Juden"[3]) and non-hateful uses of profanity (e.g. DE:"Ich hatte noch nie so einen guten F*ck") in every language. Related functional tests are grouped into classes.

2.2 Selecting Functional Tests

We selected functional tests for each language in MHC to broadly match those from the original HATECHECK. Röttger et al. (2021b), in turn, motivated their selection of tests based on two factors: 1) a series of 21 interviews with NGO workers from the UK, US and Germany whose work directly relates to online hate, and 2) a review of previous hate speech research, particularly taxonomy work (e.g. Zampieri et al., 2019; Banko et al., 2020; Kurrek et al., 2020), error analyses (e.g. Davidson et al., 2017; van Aken et al., 2018; Vidgen et al., 2020) and survey articles (e.g. Schmidt and Wiegand, 2017; Fortuna and Nunes, 2018; Vidgen et al., 2019). All test cases are short text statements, and they are constructed to be clearly hateful or non-hateful according to our definition of hate speech.

Overall, there are 27 functional tests grouped into 11 classes for each of the ten languages in MHC, except for Mandarin, which has 25 functional tests. Compared to the 29 functional tests in HATECHECK, we 1) exclude slur homonyms and reclaimed slurs, because they have no direct equivalents in most MHC languages, and 2) adapt functional tests for spelling variations to non-Latin script in Arabic and Mandarin. For Mandarin, there are two fewer tests for spelling variations and thus two fewer tests overall compared to the other nine languages. As in HATECHECK, the tests cover **distinct expressions of hate**, as well as **contrastive non-hate**, which shares lexical features with hate but is unambiguously non-hateful. We provide example cases in different languages for each functional test in Appendix A.

Distinct Expressions of Hate MHC tests different types of derogatory hate speech (**F1-4**) and hate

[3]We use ISO 639-1 codes to denote the different languages when giving test case examples. See Table 2 for a legend.

expressed through threatening language (**F5/6**). It tests hate expressed using slurs (**F7**) and profanity (**F8**). MHC also tests hate expressed through pronoun reference (**F10/11**), negation (**F12**) and phrasing variants, specifically questions and opinions (**F14/15**). Lastly, MHC tests hate containing spelling variations such as missing characters or leet speak (**F23-34**), as well as spelling variations in non-Latin script for Arabic (**F28-31**) and Mandarin (**F32-34**). For example, there is an Arabic-specific test for spellings in Arabizi, the Arabic chat alphabet (**F30**), and a Mandarin-specific test for spellings in Pinyin, Mandarin's romanised version (**F34**).

Contrastive Non-Hate MHC tests non-hateful contrasts which use profanity (**F9**) and negation (**F13**) as well as protected group identifiers (**F16/17**). It also tests non-hateful contrasts in which hate speech is quoted or referenced, specifically *counter speech*, i.e. direct responses to hate speech which seek to act against it (**F18/19**). Lastly, MHC tests non-hateful contrasts which target out-of-scope entities such as objects (**F20-22**) rather than a protected group.

2.3 Generating Test Cases

All test cases in MHC are hand-crafted by native-speaking language experts who have prior experience researching and/or annotating hate speech.[4] Each test case is a short statement that corresponds to exactly one gold standard label. HATECHECK's English test cases provide a starting point for MHC, but experts were encouraged to creatively adapt cases rather than providing literal translations, so as to retain relevance and realism. Adapting language-specific idioms (e.g. "murder that beat"), slurs (e.g. "c*nt") and profanity (e.g. "f*ck") in particular required more creativity.

Test cases are generated at scale using templates (Dixon et al., 2018; Garg et al., 2019; Ribeiro et al., 2020), in which we replace tokens for protected group identifiers (e.g. NL:"Ik haat [IDENT].") and slurs (e.g. NL:"Voor mij ben je een [SLR]."). Compared to HATECHECK, the templates for MHC required more granular placeholders for gender- and case-inflected languages. German templates, for example, were instantiated based on gender and count of the identity group term, as well as its case: the male singular of Jew ("[male_IDENT_S]") in the German Akkusativ would be "den Juden" whereas its Nominativ would be "der Jude". The benefits of the template approach are that 1) MHC has an equal number of cases targeted at different protected groups in each language, and 2) the templates can easily be used to generate more test cases targeted at other protected groups in the future.

MHC covers seven protected groups in each language. The selection of protected groups varies by language, with the goal of maximising the relevance of MHC to the cultural context of each language. Some groups, like women, are covered in all ten languages, whereas others, like lower caste people (HI:"shudra") are only covered in one language. For cases targeted at or referencing a particular protected group, we provide a secondary label for the group that is targeted. For an overview of protected groups covered by MHC in each language, see Appendix B.

In total, we generate 36,582 test cases across the ten languages in MHC, of which 25,511 (69.7%) are hateful and 11,071 (30.2%) are non-hateful. There is some variation in the number of test cases between different languages due to different numbers of functional tests and slurs, with Polish having the most cases (3,815) and Mandarin the least (3,378). 88.6% of all test cases are generated from templates. The remaining test cases do not use template tokens (e.g. PT:"O clima hoje está f*da") and are crafted individually. The average test case length is 8.5 words (std. dev. = 3.6) or 46.0 characters (std. dev. = 21.3). This resembles the composition of the original English HATECHECK.

Validation To validate gold standard labels in MHC, all 36,582 test cases were reviewed by three native-speaking annotators. For each language we recruited at least 12 annotators, so that in total more than 120 annotators worked on MHC.[5] Annotation was prescriptive (Röttger et al., 2021a), meaning that annotators were tasked with adhering to clear annotation guidelines reflecting our definition of hate speech, rather than sharing their personal view on what is and is not hateful.[6] Compared to the original HATECHECK, where four out of five annotators confirmed the gold label for 99.4% of all test cases, there was more disagreement on MHC (see Appendix D). Upon review, language experts found that the vast majority of disagreement in MHC stemmed from annotators failing to apply the provided guidelines. For example, annotators mislabelled several instances of clearly hateful slurs

[4]See Appendix C for more detail on the language experts.

[5]See Appendix C for more detail on annotator recruitment.

[6]Annotation guidelines are available on GitHub.

(e.g. DE:"Du bist eine F*tze, mehr nicht"). Therefore, we did not exclude any cases from MHC. To enable further analysis and data filtering, we publish all annotator labels and mark up cases and templates where annotator majority labels differ from the gold labels.

3 Testing Models with MHC

3.1 Model Setup

As a suite of functional tests, MHC is broadly applicable across hate speech detection models for the ten languages that it covers. Users can test multilingual models across all ten languages or use a language-specific test suite to test monolingual models. MHC is model agnostic, and can be used to compare different architectures or different datasets in zero-, few- or many-shot settings, and even commercial models for which public information on architecture and training data is limited.

Multilingual Transformer Models We test XLM-T (Barbieri et al., 2021), an XLM-R model (Conneau et al., 2020) pre-trained on an additional 198 million Twitter posts in over 30 languages.[7] XLM-R is a widely-used architecture for multilingual language modelling, which has been shown to achieve near state-of-the-art performance on multilingual hate speech detection (Banerjee et al., 2021; Mandl et al., 2021). We chose XLM-T over XLM-R after initial experiments showed the former to outperform the latter on several hate speech detection datasets as well as MHC.

We fine-tune XLM-T on three widely-used hate speech datasets – one Spanish (Basile et al., 2019), one Italian (Sanguinetti et al., 2020) and one Portuguese (Fortuna et al., 2019). Accordingly, model performance is many-shot for Spanish, Italian and Portuguese, and zero-shot for all other languages.

All three datasets have an explicit label for hate speech that matches our definition of hate (§1), so that we can collapse all other labels into a single non-hateful label, to match MHC's binary format. The Spanish Basile et al. (2019) dataset contains 4,950 tweets, of which 41.5% are labelled as hateful. The Italian Sanguinetti et al. (2020) dataset contains 8,100 tweets, of which 41.8% are labelled as hateful. The Portuguese Fortuna et al. (2019) dataset contains 5,670 tweets, of which 31.5% are labelled as hateful.

[7]We use the XLM-T implementation hosted on HuggingFace: huggingface.co/cardiffnlp/twitter-xlm-roberta-base.

We focus our discussion on XTC, an XLM-T model fine-tuned on a combination of these three datasets, which outperforms XLM-T models fine-tuned on the three datasets individually (see Appendix F). For the Spanish and Portuguese data, we use stratified 80/10/10 train/dev/test splits. For the Italian data, we use the original 91.6/8.4 train/test split, and then split the original training set into 90/10 train/dev portions. On the held-out test sets, XTC achieves 84.7 macro F1 for Spanish, 76.3 for Italian, and 73.3 for Portuguese, which is better than results reported in the original papers.[8]

Testing Commercial Models Few commercial models for hate speech detection are available for research use, and only a small subset of them can handle non-English language content. The best candidate for testing is Perspective, a free API built by Google's Jigsaw team.[9] Given an input text, Perspective provides percentage scores for attributes such as "toxicity" and "identity attack". The "toxicity" attribute covers a wide range of languages, including the ten in MHC. However, compared to hate speech, "toxicity" is a much broader concept, which includes other forms of abuse and profanity – some of which would be considered contrastive non-hate in the context of MHC. On the other hand, Perspective's "identity attack" aims to identify "negative or hateful comments targeting someone because of their identity" and thus aligns with our definition of hate speech (§1), but it is only available for three languages in MHC – German, Italian and Portuguese. For these three languages, XTC consistently outperforms Perspective (see Appendix H).

3.2 Results

Performance Across Labels MHC reveals clear gaps in XTC's performance across all ten languages (Table 2). Overall performance in terms of macro F1 is best on Mandarin (71.5), Italian (69.6) and Spanish (69.5), and worst on Hindi (58.1), Arabic (59.4) and Polish (66.2). F1 scores are higher for hateful cases than for non-hateful cases across all languages, with Hindi and Arabic exhibiting the biggest differences between hate and non-hate (∼40pp). For hateful cases, XTC performs best in terms of F1 score on Portuguese (83.5) and worst on Polish (76.1), but performance differences are

[8]See Appendix E for details on each dataset and preprocessing, and Appendix G for details on model training.

[9]www.perspectiveapi.com/

	Functionality	Gold Label	Accuracy (%) AR	NL	FR	DE	HI	<u>IT</u>	ZH	PL	<u>PT</u>	<u>ES</u>
Derogation	**F1**: Expression of strong negative emotions (explicit)	hateful	82.9	80.0	82.1	82.9	75.0	75.0	76.4	67.9	**83.6**	80.7
	F2: Description using very negative attributes (explicit)	hateful	87.9	87.1	84.3	82.1	77.1	82.1	85.7	72.9	**91.4**	78.6
	F3: Dehumanisation (explicit)	hateful	92.9	91.4	92.1	94.3	82.9	95.0	**97.9**	87.9	91.4	84.3
	F4: Implicit derogation	hateful	75.2	72.1	74.3	63.4	**85.0**	62.1	52.1	55.7	76.1	64.3
Threat. language	**F5**: Direct threat	hateful	85.0	94.3	92.9	93.6	84.3	88.6	**97.9**	76.4	90.0	89.3
	F6: Threat as normative statement	hateful	95.0	91.4	92.1	93.6	**96.4**	91.4	92.1	84.3	90.7	91.0
Slurs	**F7**: Hate expressed using slur	hateful	76.9	55.3	73.8	67.5	64.4	52.1	70.7	51.1	**77.1**	*43.3*
Profanity usage	**F8**: Hate expressed using profanity	hateful	94.3	83.6	91.0	90.0	80.0	80.0	**97.1**	79.3	94.3	75.7
	F9: Non-hateful use of profanity	non-hate	61.0	91.0	77.0	91.0	57.0	79.0	74.0	92.0	79.0	**99.0**
Pronoun reference	**F10**: Hate expressed through reference in subsequent clauses	hateful	84.3	81.4	**94.0**	89.3	90.7	91.4	83.6	65.0	86.4	84.1
	F11: Hate expressed through reference in subsequent sentences	hateful	88.6	90.0	**91.4**	**91.4**	89.3	87.9	89.3	69.3	85.0	79.3
Negation	**F12**: Hate expressed using negated positive statement	hateful	**89.3**	67.9	72.1	70.0	87.9	72.9	72.1	65.0	82.1	67.6
	F13: Non-hate expressed using negated hateful statement	non-hate	*17.9*	*33.6*	*27.9*	*28.6*	*10.0*	*33.6*	*43.6*	*35.0*	*19.3*	*35.7*
Phrasing	**F14**: Hate phrased as a question	hateful	88.6	73.6	84.3	91.4	77.9	87.9	74.3	75.0	**93.6**	72.9
	F15: Hate phrased as an opinion	hateful	90.7	77.9	**92.9**	87.9	78.6	89.3	90.0	75.0	92.1	78.6
Non-hateful group identifier	**F16**: Neutral statements using protected group identifiers	non-hate	*44.3*	67.1	67.1	67.9	*49.3*	83.6	80.0	**88.6**	56.6	68.6
	F17: Positive statements using protected group identifiers	non-hate	*47.6*	51.0	56.0	59.0	*40.0*	**81.4**	75.7	73.8	67.1	71.4
Counter speech	**F18**: Denouncements of hate that quote it	non-hate	*10.3*	*47.6*	*22.8*	*31.6*	*17.1*	*37.9*	*43.9*	**61.4**	*22.4*	*40.9*
	F19: Denouncements of hate that make direct reference to it	non-hate	*9.6*	*32.9*	*18.6*	*34.8*	*13.7*	*31.7*	*45.1*	*44.9*	*24.8*	**64.6**
Abuse against non-protected targets	**F20**: Abuse targeted at objects	non-hate	53.8	73.8	72.3	66.2	*49.2*	73.8	70.8	87.7	70.8	**86.2**
	F21: Abuse targeted at individuals (not as member of a protected group)	non-hate	56.2	66.2	72.3	67.7	*41.5*	60.0	52.3	90.8	55.4	**92.3**
	F22: Abuse targeted at non-protected groups (e.g. professions)	non-hate	*27.7*	*47.7*	55.4	*33.8*	*26.2*	56.9	*38.5*	61.5	*44.6*	**70.8**
Spelling variations	**F23**: Swaps of adjacent characters	hateful	-	82.1	89.3	89.3	87.9	75.7	-	69.3	**94.3**	84.3
	F24: Missing characters	hateful	-	85.0	75.0	82.9	74.3	69.3	-	72.9	**85.7**	68.6
	F25: Missing word boundaries	hateful	-	81.2	91.0	80.6	87.7	90.7	-	71.6	**95.0**	76.8
	F26: Added spaces between chars	hateful	65.8	61.2	86.8	85.8	**89.7**	77.0	-	58.0	83.2	71.3
	F27: Leet speak spellings	hateful	-	94.7	**95.2**	93.5	87.7	86.3	-	71.6	95.0	81.1
	F28: AR: Latin char. replacement	hateful	**83.0**	-	-	-	-	-	-	-	-	-
	F29: AR: Repeated characters	hateful	**82.9**	-	-	-	-	-	-	-	-	-
	F30: AR: Arabizi (Arabic chat alphabet)	hateful	**60.9**	-	-	-	-	-	-	-	-	-
	F31: AR: Accepted alt. spellings	hateful	**85.6**	-	-	-	-	-	-	-	-	-
	F32: ZH: Homophone char. replacement	hateful	-	-	-	-	-	-	**89.3**	-	-	-
	F33: ZH: Character decomposition	hateful	-	-	-	-	-	-	**87.7**	-	-	-
	F34: ZH: Pinyin spelling	hateful	-	-	-	-	-	-	**76.5**	-	-	-

Table 1: MHC covers 34 functionalities in 11 classes with a total of n = 36,582 test cases. 69.74% of cases (25,511 in 25 functional tests) are labelled hateful, 30.26% (11,071 in 9 functional tests) are labelled non-hateful. The right-most columns report accuracy (%) of the the XTC model (§3.1) across functional tests for each language. Languages which XTC was directly trained on are <u>underlined</u>, to highlight many-shot vs. zero-shot settings. Best performance on each functional test is **bolded**. Below random choice performance (<50%) is in *cursive red*. Examples of test cases for each functional test are listed in Appendix A.

relatively small across languages (< 8pp). For non-hateful cases, on the other hand, performance varies considerably across languages (< 24pp), with XTC performing best on Mandarin (61.1) and worst on Hindi (39.8).

Language	F1-h	F1-nh	Mac. F1
Arabic / AR	79.1	39.8	59.4
Dutch / NL	80.1	53.3	66.7
French / FR	82.6	52.6	67.6
German / DE	82.6	55.2	68.9
Hindi / HI	78.5	37.7	58.1
Italian / IT	81.5	57.8	69.6
Mandarin / ZH	81.8	61.1	71.5
Polish / PL	76.1	56.4	66.2
Portuguese / PT	83.5	53.4	68.5
Spanish / ES	79.9	59.1	69.5

Table 2: Performance of XTC across the ten languages in MHC. Many-shot settings are underlined. All other languages are zero-shot. F1 score for **h**ateful and **n**on-**h**ateful cases, and overall macro F1 score.

Performance Across Functional Tests Evaluating XTC on each functional test across languages (Table 1) reveals specific model weaknesses.

XTC performs better than a random binary-choice baseline (50% accuracy) on all functional tests for hate, with the exception of Spanish statements with hateful slurs (**F7**, 43.3% accuracy). Explicit dehumanisation (**F3**), threatening language (**F5/6**) and hate expressed using profanity (**F8**) appear to be the least challenging for the model, with relatively high and consistent accuracy across languages. In comparison, XTC generally performs worse on implicit hate (**F4**) and spelling variations (**F23+**). For other hateful functional tests, performance differs noticeably between languages. For example, XTC is very accurate on **F10**: hate expressed through reference in subsequent clauses in Spanish (94.0%), but much less so on Polish hate of the same kind (65.0%). Performance is worst on hate expressed using slurs (**F7**), with XTC misclassifying Spanish (43.3%), Polish (51.1%) and Italian statements (52.1%) at particularly high rates.

The only non-hateful functional test where performance is better than a random choice baseline across all ten languages is for non-hateful uses of profanity (**F9**). In contrast, negated hate (**F13**) and counter speech (**F18/19**), are misclassified at very high rates in every language. For example, XTC is only 9.6% accurate on Arabic denouncements of hate that make direct reference to it (**F22**). Performance differs more noticeably across languages for non-hateful uses of protected group identity terms (**F16/17**) and abuse against non-protected targets (**F20-22**). For example, XTC is 81.4% accurate on positive statements using group identifiers in Italian, but only 40.0% accurate on the same type of statement in Hindi.

Performance Across Target Groups MHC can show whether models exhibit *unintended biases* in target coverage (Dixon et al., 2018) by testing their performance on cases generated from [IDENT] templates. These cases are exactly the same, apart from the group that is targeted (e.g. IT: "Odio i gay" and IT:"Odio gli immigrati"). To illustrate, Table 3 shows model accuracy on these cases for French, Italian and Mandarin, which all cover the same seven protected groups.

Target Group	FR	IT	ZH
Women	70.9	70.1	74.5
Trans people	65.4	67.6	71.0
Gay people	56.4	68.2	70.3
Black people	61.5	67.7	66.7
Disabled people	61.2	64.4	72.6
Muslims	66.2	69.0	68.3
Immigrants	66.8	72.4	74.0

Table 3: Macro F1 of XTC on French, Italian and Mandarin test cases in MHC generated from [IDENT] templates, split by targeted protected group.

In French, XTC performs substantially worse on cases targeting gay people (56.4 macro F1) than on equivalent cases targeting women (70.9) or immigrants (66.8). In Italian, XTC performs particularly poorly on cases targeting disabled people (64.4), and in Mandarin on cases targeting black people (66.7), compared to other target groups.

3.3 Discussion

MHC reveals clear functional weaknesses in the XTC model across all ten languages.

First, XTC is overly sensitive to key words and phrases. XTC does have some ability to distinguish between different uses of potentially hateful key words, as demonstrated by its relatively good performance on both hateful and non-hateful uses of profanity across languages (**F8/9**). However, in languages like Hindi and Arabic, even entries which refer positively to protected groups (**F17**) are misclassified as hateful at high rates. Accuracy on non-hateful contrasts to hateful phrases, like negated hate (**F13**) and counter speech (**F18/19**), is low across all languages. Thus, XTC appears to rely at least in part on overly simplistic decision rules (e.g. that the use of group identifiers is a signal for hate speech). It does not sufficiently register linguistic signals like negation, that reframe hateful phrases into clearly non-hateful statements (e.g. FR:"Je ne déteste pas les blacks.").

Second, XTC is biased in its target coverage across languages, classifying hate directed against some protected groups less accurately than equivalent cases directed at others (Table 3).

These are clear weaknesses that were not apparent from XTC's strong performance on held-out test sets. They match findings from HATECHECK for monolingual English models (Röttger et al., 2021b). If XTC was used to moderate content, these weaknesses could cause serious harm. In particular, misclassifying counter speech risks undermining positive efforts to fight hate speech, and biased target coverage may create and entrench biases in the protections afforded to different groups. However, the multilingual nature of MHC also allows for additional, novel insights.

First, we can evaluate cross-lingual performance in both zero- and many-shot settings (Table 2). XTC performs particularly well on Italian, Spanish and Portuguese – the languages it was fine-tuned on – but also on French, which is another Romance language. Performance on other European languages is also relatively high. By contrast, Hindi and Arabic clearly stand out as particularly challenging, with substantially lower performance. This suggests that cross-lingual transfer works better across more closely related languages and poses a challenge for more dissimilar languages.[10] Cultural differences across language settings may also affect transferability. We may for example expect hate in Italian and French to be more similar to each other than to hate in Hindi, along such dimensions as who the targets of hate are, which would likely affect the cross-lingual performance of hate speech detection models. Both hypotheses could be explored in future research.

Second, we can evaluate differences in language-specific model behaviour, again in zero- as well as many-shot settings. For example, XTC tends to overpredict hate in Hindi and Arabic, both zero-shot, whereas it tends to underpredict hate in many-shot Spanish and zero-shot Polish (Table 1). XTC also exhibits different target biases across languages, for zero-shot settings like in French and Mandarin as well as many-shot Italian (Table 3). This suggests that, in addition to accounting for differences in high-level performance, multilingual models may require very different calibration and adaptation across languages, even for languages they were not directly fine-tuned on.

Overall, the insights generated by MHC suggest two potential steps towards the development of more effective multilingual hate speech detection models: 1) creating training data in diverse languages to reduce language gaps, even for models with significant cross-lingual transfer abilities, and 2) evaluating and addressing language-specific model biases as well as differences in performance across languages.

4 Limitations

The limitations of the original HATECHECK also apply to MHC. First, MHC diagnoses specific model weaknesses rather than generalisable model strengths, and should be used to complement rather than substitute evaluation on held-out test sets of real-world hate speech. Second, MHC does not test functionalities related to context outside of individual documents or modalities other than text. Third, MHC only covers a limited set of protected groups and slurs across languages, but can easily be expanded using the provided case templates.

The multilingual nature of MHC creates additional considerations. First, comparisons of performance between languages are not strictly like-for-like, because cases in different languages are not literal translations of each other. This limitation is compounded for Arabic and Mandarin, which have unique functional tests for spelling variations. Second, even though MHC includes a diverse set of ten languages, these languages still only make up a fraction of languages spoken across the world. To our knowledge, MHC covers more languages than any other hate speech dataset, but hundreds of other languages remain neglected and should be considered for future expansions of MHC. Third, the selection of functional tests in MHC is based on HATECHECK, which was informed in part by

[10] The surprisingly good performance of XTC on Mandarin is a caveat, which may in part be explained by Mandarin being more prevalent than Arabic or Hindi in XLM-R's pre-training corpus (Conneau et al., 2020).

interviews in an anglo-centric setting. We worked with native-speaking language experts and created additional tests to account for non-Latin scripts in Arabic and Mandarin, but future research may consider additional interviews or other language-specific steps to inform expansions of MHC. Lastly, individual languages, like the ten included in MHC, are not monolithic but vary between speakers, especially across geographic regions and sociodemographic groups. We use widely-spoken dialects for the ten languages in MHC (see §1), but cannot cover all variations.

5 Related Work

Diagnostic Hate Speech Datasets The concept of functional testing from software engineering (Beizer, 1995) was first applied to NLP model evaluation by Ribeiro et al. (2020). The original HATECHECK (Röttger et al., 2021b) then introduced functional tests for hate speech detection models, using hand-crafted test cases to diagnose model weaknesses on different kinds of hate and non-hate. Kirk et al. (2021) applied the same framework to emoji-based hate. Manerba and Tonelli (2021) provide smaller-scale functional test for abuse detection systems. Other research has instead collected real-world examples of hate and annotated them for more fine-grained labels, such as the hate target, to enable more comprehensive error analysis (e.g. Mathew et al., 2021; Vidgen et al., 2021). Instead of creating a static dataset, Calabrese et al. (2021) devise a hate speech-specific data augmentation technique based on simple heuristics to create additional test cases based on model training data. MHC is the first non-English diagnostic dataset for hate speech detection models.

Non-English Hate Speech Data English is by far the most common language for hate speech datasets, as recent reviews by Vidgen and Derczynski (2020) and Poletto et al. (2021) confirm. Encouragingly, more and more non-English datasets are being created, particularly for shared tasks (e.g. Wiegand et al., 2018; Ptaszynski et al., 2019; Fersini et al., 2020; Zampieri et al., 2020; Mulki and Ghanem, 2021). However, very few datasets cover more than one language (Ousidhoum et al., 2019; Basile et al., 2019), and to our knowledge no dataset covers as many languages as MHC.

Multilingual Hate Speech Detection The scarcity of non-English hate speech datasets has motivated research into few- and zero-shot cross-lingual hate speech detection, i.e. detection with little or no training data in the target language. However, model performance is generally found to be lacking in such settings (Stappen et al., 2020; Leite et al., 2020; Nozza, 2021). Others have thus explored data augmentation techniques based on machine translation, which yield limited improvements (Pamungkas et al., 2021; Wang and Banko, 2021). Overall, multilingual models trained or fine-tuned directly on the target languages, i.e. in many-shot settings, are still consistently found to perform best (Aluru et al., 2020; Pelicon et al., 2021). MHC's functional tests are model-agnostic and can be used to evaluate multilingual hate speech detection models trained on any amount of data.

6 Conclusion

In this article, we introduced MULTILINGUAL HATECHECK (MHC), a suite of functional tests for multilingual hate speech detection models. MHC expands the English-language HATECHECK (Röttger et al., 2021b) to ten additional languages: Arabic, Dutch, French, German, Hindi, Italian, Mandarin, Polish, Portuguese and Spanish. To our knowledge, MHC covers more languages than any other hate speech dataset. Across the languages, native-speaking language experts created 36,582 test cases, which provide contrasts between hateful and non-hateful content. This makes MHC challenging to hate speech detection models and allows for a more effective evaluation of model quality.

We demonstrated MHC's utility as a diagnostic tool by testing a high-performing multilingual transformer model, which was fine-tuned on three widely-used hate speech datasets in three different languages. MHC revealed the model to be 1) overly sensitive to key words and key phrases, 2) biased in its target coverage and 3) error-prone and inconsistent in cross-lingual transfer, in both zero- and many-shot settings.

So far, hate speech research has primarily focused on English-language content and thus neglected billions of non-English speakers across the world. We hope that MHC can contribute to closing this language gap and that by diagnosing specific model weaknesses across languages it can support the development of better multilingual hate speech detection models in the future.

Acknowledgments

This research was commissioned from Rewire by Google's Jigsaw team. All authors worked on this project in their capacity as researchers at Rewire. We thank all annotators and language experts for their work, and all reviewers for their constructive feedback.

References

Sai Saketh Aluru, Binny Mathew, Punyajoy Saha, and Animesh Mukherjee. 2020. A deep dive into multilingual hate speech classification. In *Machine Learning and Knowledge Discovery in Databases. Applied Data Science and Demo Track: European Conference, ECML PKDD 2020, Ghent, Belgium, September 14–18, 2020, Proceedings, Part V*, page 423–439, Berlin, Heidelberg. Springer-Verlag.

Somnath Banerjee, Maulindu Sarkar, Nancy Agrawal, Punyajoy Saha, and Mithun Das. 2021. Exploring transformer based models to identify hate speech and offensive content in english and indo-aryan languages. *arXiv preprint arXiv:2111.13974*.

Michele Banko, Brendon MacKeen, and Laurie Ray. 2020. A Unified Taxonomy of Harmful Content. In *Proceedings of the Fourth Workshop on Online Abuse and Harms*, pages 125–137. Association for Computational Linguistics.

Francesco Barbieri, Luis Espinosa Anke, and Jose Camacho-Collados. 2021. XLM-T: A multilingual language model toolkit for twitter. *arXiv preprint arXiv:2104.12250*.

Valerio Basile, Cristina Bosco, Elisabetta Fersini, Nozza Debora, Viviana Patti, Francisco Manuel Rangel Pardo, Paolo Rosso, Manuela Sanguinetti, et al. 2019. Semeval-2019 task 5: Multilingual detection of hate speech against immigrants and women in twitter. In *13th International Workshop on Semantic Evaluation*, pages 54–63. Association for Computational Linguistics.

Boris Beizer. 1995. *Black-box testing: techniques for functional testing of software and systems*. John Wiley & Sons, Inc.

Emily M. Bender and Batya Friedman. 2018. Data statements for natural language processing: Toward mitigating system bias and enabling better science. *Transactions of the Association for Computational Linguistics*, 6:587–604.

Cristina Bosco, Dell'Orletta Felice, Fabio Poletto, Manuela Sanguinetti, and Tesconi Maurizio. 2018. Overview of the evalita 2018 hate speech detection task. In *EVALITA 2018-Sixth Evaluation Campaign of Natural Language Processing and Speech Tools for Italian*, volume 2263, pages 1–9. CEUR.

Agostina Calabrese, Michele Bevilacqua, Björn Ross, Rocco Tripodi, and Roberto Navigli. 2021. Aaa: Fair evaluation for abuse detection systems wanted. In *13th ACM Web Science Conference 2021*, pages 243–252.

Arthur TE Capozzi, Mirko Lai, Valerio Basile, Fabio Poletto, Manuela Sanguinetti, Cristina Bosco, Viviana Patti, Giancarlo Ruffo, Cataldo Musto, Marco Polignano, et al. 2019. Computational linguistics against hate: Hate speech detection and visualization on social media in the" contro l'odio" project. In *6th Italian Conference on Computational Linguistics, CLiC-it 2019*, volume 2481, pages 1–6. CEUR-WS.

Alexis Conneau, Kartikay Khandelwal, Naman Goyal, Vishrav Chaudhary, Guillaume Wenzek, Francisco Guzmán, Edouard Grave, Myle Ott, Luke Zettlemoyer, and Veselin Stoyanov. 2020. Unsupervised cross-lingual representation learning at scale. In *Proceedings of the 58th Annual Meeting of the Association for Computational Linguistics*, pages 8440–8451, Online. Association for Computational Linguistics.

Thomas Davidson, Debasmita Bhattacharya, and Ingmar Weber. 2019. Racial bias in hate speech and abusive language detection datasets. In *Proceedings of the Third Workshop on Abusive Language Online*, pages 25–35, Florence, Italy. Association for Computational Linguistics.

Thomas Davidson, Dana Warmsley, Michael Macy, and Ingmar Weber. 2017. Automated hate speech detection and the problem of offensive language. In *Proceedings of the 11th International AAAI Conference on Web and Social Media*, pages 512–515. Association for the Advancement of Artificial Intelligence.

Lucas Dixon, John Li, Jeffrey Sorensen, Nithum Thain, and Lucy Vasserman. 2018. Measuring and mitigating unintended bias in text classification. In *Proceedings of the 2018 AAAI/ACM Conference on AI, Ethics, and Society*, pages 67–73. Association for Computing Machinery.

Elisabetta Fersini, Debora Nozza, and Paolo Rosso. 2020. AMI @ EVALITA2020: Automatic misogyny identification. In *Proceedings of the 7th evaluation campaign of Natural Language Processing and Speech tools for Italian (EVALITA 2020)*, Online. CEUR.org.

Paula Fortuna and Sérgio Nunes. 2018. A survey on automatic detection of hate speech in text. *ACM Computing Surveys (CSUR)*, 51(4):1–30.

Paula Fortuna, João Rocha da Silva, Juan Soler-Company, Leo Wanner, and Sérgio Nunes. 2019. A hierarchically-labeled Portuguese hate speech dataset. In *Proceedings of the Third Workshop on Abusive Language Online*, pages 94–104, Florence, Italy. Association for Computational Linguistics.

Matt Gardner, Yoav Artzi, Victoria Basmov, Jonathan Berant, Ben Bogin, Sihao Chen, Pradeep Dasigi, Dheeru Dua, Yanai Elazar, Ananth Gottumukkala, Nitish Gupta, Hannaneh Hajishirzi, Gabriel Ilharco, Daniel Khashabi, Kevin Lin, Jiangming Liu, Nelson F. Liu, Phoebe Mulcaire, Qiang Ning, Sameer Singh, Noah A. Smith, Sanjay Subramanian, Reut Tsarfaty, Eric Wallace, Ally Zhang, and Ben Zhou. 2020. Evaluating models' local decision boundaries via contrast sets. In *Findings of the Association for Computational Linguistics: EMNLP 2020*, pages 1307–1323, Online. Association for Computational Linguistics.

Sahaj Garg, Vincent Perot, Nicole Limtiaco, Ankur Taly, Ed H. Chi, and Alex Beutel. 2019. Counterfactual fairness in text classification through robustness. In *Proceedings of the 2019 AAAI/ACM Conference on AI, Ethics, and Society*, AIES '19, page 219–226, New York, NY, USA. Association for Computing Machinery.

Mor Geva, Yoav Goldberg, and Jonathan Berant. 2019. Are we modeling the task or the annotator? an investigation of annotator bias in natural language understanding datasets. In *Proceedings of the 2019 Conference on Empirical Methods in Natural Language Processing and the 9th International Joint Conference on Natural Language Processing (EMNLP-IJCNLP)*, pages 1161–1166, Hong Kong, China. Association for Computational Linguistics.

Hannah Rose Kirk, Bertram Vidgen, Paul Röttger, Tristan Thrush, and Scott A Hale. 2021. Hatemoji: A test suite and adversarially-generated dataset for benchmarking and detecting emoji-based hate. *arXiv preprint arXiv:2108.05921*.

Jana Kurrek, Haji Mohammad Saleem, and Derek Ruths. 2020. Towards a comprehensive taxonomy and large-scale annotated corpus for online slur usage. In *Proceedings of the Fourth Workshop on Online Abuse and Harms*, pages 138–149, Online. Association for Computational Linguistics.

João Augusto Leite, Diego Silva, Kalina Bontcheva, and Carolina Scarton. 2020. Toxic language detection in social media for Brazilian Portuguese: New dataset and multilingual analysis. In *Proceedings of the 1st Conference of the Asia-Pacific Chapter of the Association for Computational Linguistics and the 10th International Joint Conference on Natural Language Processing*, pages 914–924, Suzhou, China. Association for Computational Linguistics.

Ilya Loshchilov and Frank Hutter. 2019. Decoupled weight decay regularization. In *Proceedings of the 7th International Conference on Learning Representations*.

Thomas Mandl, Sandip Modha, Gautam Kishore Shahi, Hiren Madhu, Shrey Satapara, Prasenjit Majumder, Johannes Schäfer, Tharindu Ranasinghe, Marcos Zampieri, Durgesh Nandini, et al. 2021. Overview of the hasoc subtrack at fire 2021: Hate speech and offensive content identification in english and indo-aryan languages. *arXiv preprint arXiv:2112.09301*.

Marta Marchiori Manerba and Sara Tonelli. 2021. Fine-grained fairness analysis of abusive language detection systems with CheckList. In *Proceedings of the 5th Workshop on Online Abuse and Harms (WOAH 2021)*, pages 81–91, Online. Association for Computational Linguistics.

Delia Marinescu. 2021. Facebook's content moderation language barrier. *New America*.

Binny Mathew, Punyajoy Saha, Seid Muhie Yimam, Chris Biemann, Pawan Goyal, and Animesh Mukherjee. 2021. Hatexplain: A benchmark dataset for explainable hate speech detection. In *Proceedings of the AAAI Conference on Artificial Intelligence*, volume 35, pages 14867–14875.

Hala Mulki and Bilal Ghanem. 2021. Working notes of the workshop arabic misogyny identification (armi-2021). In *Forum for Information Retrieval Evaluation*, FIRE 2021, page 7–8, New York, NY, USA. Association for Computing Machinery.

Timothy Niven and Hung-Yu Kao. 2019. Probing neural network comprehension of natural language arguments. In *Proceedings of the 57th Annual Meeting of the Association for Computational Linguistics*, pages 4658–4664, Florence, Italy. Association for Computational Linguistics.

Debora Nozza. 2021. Exposing the limits of zero-shot cross-lingual hate speech detection. In *Proceedings of the 59th Annual Meeting of the Association for Computational Linguistics*, Online. Association for Computational Linguistics.

Nedjma Ousidhoum, Zizheng Lin, Hongming Zhang, Yangqiu Song, and Dit-Yan Yeung. 2019. Multilingual and multi-aspect hate speech analysis. In *Proceedings of the 2019 Conference on Empirical Methods in Natural Language Processing and the 9th International Joint Conference on Natural Language Processing (EMNLP-IJCNLP)*, pages 4675–4684, Hong Kong, China. Association for Computational Linguistics.

Endang Wahyu Pamungkas, Valerio Basile, and Viviana Patti. 2021. A joint learning approach with knowledge injection for zero-shot cross-lingual hate speech detection. *Information Processing & Management*, 58(4):102544.

Andraž Pelicon, Ravi Shekhar, Blaž Škrlj, Matthew Purver, and Senja Pollak. 2021. Investigating cross-lingual training for offensive language detection. *PeerJ Computer Science*, 7:e559. Publisher: PeerJ Inc.

Fabio Poletto, Valerio Basile, Manuela Sanguinetti, Cristina Bosco, and Viviana Patti. 2021. Resources and benchmark corpora for hate speech detection: a systematic review. *Language Resources and Evaluation*, 55(2):477–523.

Michal Ptaszynski, Agata Pieciukiewicz, and Paweł Dybała. 2019. Results of the poleval 2019 shared task 6: First dataset and open shared task for automatic cyberbullying detection in polish twitter. *Proceedings of the PolEval 2019 Workshop*, page 89.

Marco Tulio Ribeiro, Tongshuang Wu, Carlos Guestrin, and Sameer Singh. 2020. Beyond accuracy: Behavioral testing of NLP models with CheckList. In *Proceedings of the 58th Annual Meeting of the Association for Computational Linguistics*, pages 4902–4912, Online. Association for Computational Linguistics.

Paul Röttger, Bertie Vidgen, Dirk Hovy, and Janet B Pierrehumbert. 2021a. Two contrasting data annotation paradigms for subjective nlp tasks. *arXiv preprint arXiv:2112.07475*.

Paul Röttger, Bertie Vidgen, Dong Nguyen, Zeerak Talat, Helen Margetts, and Janet Pierrehumbert. 2021b. HateCheck: Functional tests for hate speech detection models. In *Proceedings of the 59th Annual Meeting of the Association for Computational Linguistics and the 11th International Joint Conference on Natural Language Processing (Volume 1: Long Papers)*, pages 41–58, Online. Association for Computational Linguistics.

Manuela Sanguinetti, Gloria Comandini, Elisa Di Nuovo, Simona Frenda, Marco Antonio Stranisci, Cristina Bosco, Caselli Tommaso, Viviana Patti, Irene Russo, et al. 2020. Haspeede 2@ evalita2020: Overview of the evalita 2020 hate speech detection task. In *EVALITA 2020 Seventh Evaluation Campaign of Natural Language Processing and Speech Tools for Italian*, pages 1–9. CEUR.

Manuela Sanguinetti, Fabio Poletto, Cristina Bosco, Viviana Patti, and Marco Stranisci. 2018. An Italian Twitter corpus of hate speech against immigrants. In *Proceedings of the 11th International Conference on Language Resources and Evaluation (LREC 2018)*.

Maarten Sap, Swabha Swayamdipta, Laura Vianna, Xuhui Zhou, Yejin Choi, and Noah A. Smith. 2021. Annotators with attitudes: How annotator beliefs and identities bias toxic language detection.

Anna Schmidt and Michael Wiegand. 2017. A survey on hate speech detection using natural language processing. In *Proceedings of the Fifth International Workshop on Natural Language Processing for Social Media*, pages 1–10, Valencia, Spain. Association for Computational Linguistics.

Deven Santosh Shah, H. Andrew Schwartz, and Dirk Hovy. 2020. Predictive biases in natural language processing models: A conceptual framework and overview. In *Proceedings of the 58th Annual Meeting of the Association for Computational Linguistics*, pages 5248–5264, Online. Association for Computational Linguistics.

Tom Simonite. 2021. Facebook is everywhere; its moderation is nowhere close. *Wired*.

Lukas Stappen, Fabian Brunn, and Björn W. Schuller. 2020. Cross-lingual zero- and few-shot hate speech detection utilising frozen transformer language models and AXEL. *CoRR*, abs/2004.13850.

Zeerak Talat. 2016. Are you a racist or am I seeing things? Annotator influence on hate speech detection on Twitter. In *Proceedings of the First Workshop on NLP and Computational Social Science*, pages 138–142, Austin, Texas. Association for Computational Linguistics.

Betty van Aken, Julian Risch, Ralf Krestel, and Alexander Löser. 2018. Challenges for toxic comment classification: An in-depth error analysis. In *Proceedings of the 2nd Workshop on Abusive Language Online (ALW2)*, pages 33–42, Brussels, Belgium. Association for Computational Linguistics.

Bertie Vidgen and Leon Derczynski. 2020. Directions in abusive language training data, a systematic review: Garbage in, garbage out. *PLOS ONE*, 15(12):e0243300.

Bertie Vidgen, Scott Hale, Ella Guest, Helen Margetts, David Broniatowski, Zeerak Talat, Austin Botelho, Matthew Hall, and Rebekah Tromble. 2020. Detecting East Asian prejudice on social media. In *Proceedings of the Fourth Workshop on Online Abuse and Harms*, pages 162–172, Online. Association for Computational Linguistics.

Bertie Vidgen, Alex Harris, Dong Nguyen, Rebekah Tromble, Scott Hale, and Helen Margetts. 2019. Challenges and frontiers in abusive content detection. In *Proceedings of the Third Workshop on Abusive Language Online*, pages 80–93, Florence, Italy. Association for Computational Linguistics.

Bertie Vidgen, Tristan Thrush, Zeerak Talat, and Douwe Kiela. 2021. Learning from the worst: Dynamically generated datasets to improve online hate detection. In *Proceedings of the 59th Annual Meeting of the Association for Computational Linguistics and the 11th International Joint Conference on Natural Language Processing (Volume 1: Long Papers)*, pages 1667–1682, Online. Association for Computational Linguistics.

Cindy Wang and Michele Banko. 2021. Practical Transformer-based Multilingual Text Classification. In *Proceedings of the 2021 Conference of the North American Chapter of the Association for Computational Linguistics: Human Language Technologies: Industry Papers*, pages 121–129, Online. Association for Computational Linguistics.

Michael Wiegand, Josef Ruppenhofer, and Thomas Kleinbauer. 2019. Detection of abusive language: The problem of biased datasets. In *Proceedings of the 2019 Conference of the North American Chapter of the Association for Computational Linguistics: Human Language Technologies, Volume 1 (Long and Short Papers)*, pages 602–608, Minneapolis, Minnesota. Association for Computational Linguistics.

Michael Wiegand, Melanie Siegel, and Josef Ruppenhofer. 2018. Overview of the GermEval 2018 Shared Task on the Identification of Offensive Language. In *Proceedings of GermEval 2018, 14th Conference on Natural Language Processing (KONVENS 2018)*.

Thomas Wolf, Lysandre Debut, Victor Sanh, Julien Chaumond, Clement Delangue, Anthony Moi, Pierric Cistac, Tim Rault, Remi Louf, Morgan Funtowicz, Joe Davison, Sam Shleifer, Patrick von Platen, Clara Ma, Yacine Jernite, Julien Plu, Canwen Xu, Teven Le Scao, Sylvain Gugger, Mariama Drame, Quentin Lhoest, and Alexander Rush. 2020. Transformers: State-of-the-art natural language processing. In *Proceedings of the 2020 Conference on Empirical Methods in Natural Language Processing: System Demonstrations*, pages 38–45, Online. Association for Computational Linguistics.

Tongshuang Wu, Marco Tulio Ribeiro, Jeffrey Heer, and Daniel Weld. 2019. Errudite: Scalable, reproducible, and testable error analysis. In *Proceedings of the 57th Annual Meeting of the Association for Computational Linguistics*, pages 747–763, Florence, Italy. Association for Computational Linguistics.

Marcos Zampieri, Shervin Malmasi, Preslav Nakov, Sara Rosenthal, Noura Farra, and Ritesh Kumar. 2019. Predicting the type and target of offensive posts in social media. In *Proceedings of the 2019 Conference of the North American Chapter of the Association for Computational Linguistics: Human Language Technologies, Volume 1 (Long and Short Papers)*, pages 1415–1420, Minneapolis, Minnesota. Association for Computational Linguistics.

Marcos Zampieri, Preslav Nakov, Sara Rosenthal, Pepa Atanasova, Georgi Karadzhov, Hamdy Mubarak, Leon Derczynski, Zeses Pitenis, and Çağrı Çöltekin. 2020. SemEval-2020 Task 12: Multilingual Offensive Language Identification in Social Media (OffensEval 2020). In *Proceedings of SemEval*.

A Example MHC Test Cases

See Table 4 on the next page.

B Protected Groups in MHC

MHC covers seven protected groups per language.

Arabic: women /نساء, trans people / متحولين جنسيا, gay people / مثلين, black people / سود, Jews / يهود, disabled people / معاقيين, immigrants / لاجئين

Dutch: women / vrouwen, trans people / transgenders, gay people / homoseksuelen, black people / zwarte personen, disabled people / gehandicapten, immigrants / immigranten, Muslims / Moslims

French: women / femmes, trans people / trans, gay people / homos, black people / blacks, disabled people / handicapés, Muslims / musulmans, refugees / réfugiés

German: women / Frauen, trans people / Transmenschen, gay people / Schwule, black people / Schwarze, disabled people / Behinderte Jews / Juden, refugees / Flüchtlinge

Hindi: women / aurato, trans people / hijro, gay people / gays, North-East Indians / assamese, Muslims / musalmano, Lower Caste / shudro, Black people / negro

Italian: women / donne, trans people / trans, gay people / gay, black people / persone di colore, disabled people / disabili, Muslims / musulmani, immigrants / immigrati

Mandarin: women / 女人, trans people / 跨性别者, gay people / 同性恋, black people / 黑人, disabled people / 残疾人, Muslims / 穆斯林, foreigners / 外国人

Polish: women / kobiety, trans people / osoby transpłciowe, gay people / geje, Asian people / azjaci, disabled people / niepełnosprawni, Jews / Żydzi, immigrants / imigranci

Portuguese: women / mulheres, black people / negros, gay people / gays, trans people / pessoas trans, indigenous people / indígenas, Jews / judeus, disabled people / deficientes

Spanish: women / mujeres, black people / negros, gay people / gays, trans people / trans, indigenous people / indígenas, Jews / judíos, disabled people / discapacitados

C Data Statement

Following Bender and Friedman (2018), we provide a data statement, which documents the generation and provenance of test cases in MHC.

A. CURATION RATIONALE The goal of our research was to construct MHC, a multilingual suite of functional tests for hate speech detection models. For this purpose, our team of native-speaking language experts generated a total of 36,582 short text documents in ten different languages, by hand and by using simple templates for group identifiers and slurs (§2.3). Each document corresponds to one functional test and a binary gold standard label (hateful or non-hateful).

B. LANGUAGE VARIETY MHC covers ten languages: Arabic, Dutch, French, German, Hindi, Italian, Mandarin, Polish, Portuguese and Spanish.

C. SPEAKER DEMOGRAPHICS All test cases across the ten languages in MHC were hand-crafted by native-speaking language experts – one per language. All ten had previously worked on hate speech as researchers and/or annotators. Six out of ten experts identify as women, the rest as men. Four out of ten identify as non-White.

D. ANNOTATOR DEMOGRAPHICS More than 120 annotators provided annotations on MHC, with at least 12 annotators per language. Annotators were recruited on Appen, a crowdworking provider. Appen gave no demographic information beyond guaranteeing that annotators were native speakers of the languages in which they completed their work. In setting up the annotation task and communicating with annotators, we followed guidance for protecting and monitoring annotator well-being provided by Vidgen et al. (2019).

E. SPEECH SITUATION All test cases were created between November 2021 and January 2022.

F. TEXT CHARACTERISTICS The composition of the dataset is described in detail in §2.2 and §2.3 of the article.

D Annotator Disagreement on MHC

Annotator disagreement on MHC (Table 5) is higher than on the original HATECHECK (Röttger et al., 2021b), where four out of five annotators agreed on the gold label in 99.4% of cases. There is a lot of variation in disagreement across languages, with most having less than 5% disagreement, and only Mandarin and French more than 10%. Upon review, our language experts found that the vast majority of disagreements stemmed from annotator error, where annotators failed to apply the explicit, prescriptive annotation guidelines they received.

	Functionality	Gold Label	Language	Example
Derogation	**F1**: Expression of strong negative emotions (explicit)	hateful	FR	Il n'y a rien de plus horrible qu'une femme.
	F2: Description using very negative attributes (explicit)	hateful	HI	duniya mai sabse zyada murkh bas gays hi hote hain.
	F3: Dehumanisation (explicit)	hateful	NL	Gehandicapten zijn een plaag.
	F4: Implicit derogation	hateful	PL	Życie każdego owada jest cenniejsze niż życie kobiety.
Threat. language	**F5**: Direct threat	hateful	ZH	只能给女人死刑才能解决问题。
	F6: Threat as normative statement	hateful	ES	En un mundo justo, los negros como ustedes estarían todos muertos.
Slurs	**F7**: Hate expressed using slur	hateful	PT	Anormais simplesmente não conseguem ajudar a si mesmos.
Profanity usage	**F8**: Hate expressed using profanity	hateful	IT	Tipico di un trans essere un pezzo di merda.
	F9: Non-hateful use of profanity	non-hate	AR	لازم احاول قد مقدر ما بقاش حمار.
Pronoun reference	**F10**: Hate expressed through reference in subsequent clauses	hateful	HI	wo shudra insaan dikhte hai par hai wo parijeevi hi.
	F11: Hate expressed through reference in subsequent sentences	hateful	PT	É obvio que eles são estúpidios, afiinal são gays
Negation	**F12**: Hate expressed using negated positive statement	hateful	DE	Behinderte sind uns grundsätzlich nicht ebenbürtig.
	F13: Non-hate expressed using negated hateful statement	non-hate	PL	Nie stójmy bezczynnie, gdy niepełnosprawni są mordowani.
Phrasing	**F14**: Hate phrased as a question	hateful	IT	Sbaglio a pensare che questi disabili debbano essere condannati a morte?
	F15: Hate phrased as an opinion	hateful	ES	Si me preguntas, los negros como tú no son mejores que las ratas.
Non-hateful group identifier	**F16**: Neutral statements using protected group identifiers	non-hate	ZH	我和两个跨性别者住在一起。
	F17: Positive statements using protected group identifiers	non-hate	NL	Homoseksuelen horen thuis in de regering.
Counter speech	**F18**: Denouncements of hate that quote it	non-hate	AR	ايه اللي خلاك تقول انك بتتقرف من النساء.
	F19: Denouncements of hate that make direct reference to it	non-hate	HI	logo ko kinnar bulana bilkul theek nahi hai.
Abuse against non-protected targets	**F20**: Abuse targeted at objects	non-hate	IT	Questa serie di esercizi è così nauseante.
	F21: Abuse targeted at individuals (not as member of a protected group)	non-hate	PL	Nienawidzę cię.
	F22: Abuse targeted at non-protected groups (e.g. professions)	non-hate	DE	Ich kann Politiker wie dich wirklich nicht ausstehen.
Spelling variations	**F23**: Swaps of adjacent characters	hateful	NL	Zulke transgenders moeten worden geëxecueterd.
	F24: Missing characters	hateful	FR	Typique d'un homo d'être à ce point stupde.
	F25: Missing word boundaries	hateful	PT	Essas mulheresme dão tanto nojo.
	F26: Added spaces between chars	hateful	ES	Quiero m a t a r a todos los indígenas.
	F27: Leet speak spellings	hateful	HI	keval aurat hi 1tni badi murkh ho sakta hai.
	F28: AR: Latin char. replacement	hateful	AR	انا بكرهكم 5الص يا يهود.
	F29: AR: Repeated characters	hateful	AR	ما حد فيكو ينزل ضررررررب بالمثلين دول بالطوة.
	F30: AR: Arabizi (Arabic chat alphabet)	hateful	AR	Alanwa3 dee mal el yahood lazm ytnafth feha el23dam.
	F31: AR: Accepted alt. spellings	hateful	AR	النساء لازمهم حبس في الاآقاص.
	F32: ZH: Homophone char. replacement	hateful	ZH	我想沙死所有黑人。
	F33: ZH: Character decomposition	hateful	ZH	这些外国人就该闭上他们的犭句嘴。
	F34: ZH: Pinyin spelling	hateful	ZH	所有女人都去si。

Table 4: Example test cases for each of the 34 functional tests in MHC. Examples were selected at random.

For example, hate and more general abuse were often confused, and abuse against non-protected targets was often labelled as hateful. Therefore, we did not exclude any cases from MHC. To enable further analysis and data filtering, we provide annotator labels with the test suite and mark up cases and templates where there is disagreement between the annotator majority labels and the gold labels from our language experts.

Language	% Disagreement	n Disagreement
Arabic / AR	7.05	252
Dutch / NL	9.61	362
French / FR	21.22	789
German / DE	4.20	153
Hindi / HI	4.88	174
Italian / IT	0.73	27
Mandarin / ZH	11.48	388
Polish / PL	2.04	78
Portuguese / PT	4.12	152
Spanish / ES	2.40	90

Table 5: Proportion of entries and absolute number of entries where at least 2/3 annotators disagreed with the expert gold label, for each language in MHC.

E Datasets for Model Fine-Tuning

E.1 Sanguinetti et al. (2020) Italian Data

Sampling The authors compiled 8,100 tweets sampled using keywords. 4,000 tweets come from HaSpeeDe 2018 (Bosco et al., 2018), which in turn originates in the Sanguinetti et al. (2018) dataset. The other 4,100 tweets were collected as part of the Italian hate speech monitoring project "Contro l'Odio" (Capozzi et al., 2019).

Annotation The Sanguinetti et al. (2018) tweets were annotated in two phases, first by expert annotators, then by crowdworkers from CrowdFlower. Each tweet was annotated by two to three annotators for six attributes: *hate speech*, *aggressiveness*, *offensiveness*, *irony*, *stereotype*, and *intensity*. For inter-annotator agreement, the authors report a Krippendorff's Alpha of 38% for CrowdFlower, and a Cohen's Kappa of 45% for the expert annotators. The "Contro l'Odio" tweets were annotated by crowdworkers, but inter-annotator agreement was not reported. (Sanguinetti et al., 2020).

Data We use all 8,100 tweets (41.8% hate).

Definition of Hate Speech "Language that spreads, incites, promotes or justifies hatred or violence towards the given target, or a message that aims at dehumanizing, delegitimizing, hurting or intimidating the target. The targets are Immigrants, Muslims, and Roma groups, or individual members of such groups."

E.2 Fortuna et al. (2019) Portuguese Data

Sampling Fortuna et al. (2019) initially collected 42,930 tweets based on a search of 29 user profiles, 19 keywords and ten hashtags. They then filtered the tweets, keeping only Portuguese-language tweets, and removing duplicates and retweets, resulting in 33,890 tweets. Finally, they set a cap of a maximum of 200 tweets per search method, to create the final dataset of 5,668 tweets.

Annotation All tweets in the dataset were annotated as either hateful or non-hateful by 18 non-expert Portuguese native speakers were hired. Each tweet was annotated by three annotators, and inter-annotator agreement was low, with a Cohen's Kappa of 0.17.

Data We use all 5,668 tweets (31.5% hate).

Definition of Hate Speech "Hate speech is language that attacks or diminishes, that incites violence or hate against groups, based on specific characteristics such as physical appearance, religion, descent, national or ethnic origin, sexual orientation, gender identity or other, and it can occur with different linguistic styles, even in subtle forms or when humour is used."

E.3 Basile et al. (2019) Spanish Data

Sampling Tweets were sampled using three methods: 1) monitoring potential victims of hate accounts, 2) retrieving tweets from the history of identified haters, and 3) retrieving tweets using neutral and derogatory keywords, polarising hashtags, and stems. This yielded 19,600 tweets, of which 6,600 are in Spanish and the rest in English.

Annotation The dataset was annotated for three attributes: *hate speech*, *target range* (individuals or groups), and *aggressiveness*. First, all data was annotated by at least three Figure Eight crowdworkers. Inter-annotator agreement on Spanish *hate speech* was high, with a Cohen's Kappa of 0.89. Second, two experts annotated each tweet. The final label was assigned based on majority vote across the crowd and expert annotators.

Data We use all 6,600 Spanish tweets, of which 41.5% are labelled as hateful.

Definition of Hate Speech "Any communication that disparages a person or a group on the basis of some characteristic such as race, color, ethnicity, gender, sexual orientation, nationality, religion, or other characteristics."

E.4 Pre-Processing

Before using the datasets for fine-tuning, we remove newline and tab characters. We replace URLs and user mentions with [URL] and [USER] tokens.

F XLM-T Model Comparison

We denote the three XLM-T models trained on Italian Sanguinetti et al. (2020), Portuguese Fortuna et al. (2019) and Spanish Basile et al. (2019) as XLM-IT, XLM-PT and XLM-ES respectively. XTC denotes the XLM-T model trained on the combination of all three datasets, for which we report results in the main body of this article. XTC generally outperforms the monolingual models when compared on the respective held-out test sets (Table 6) as well as MHC (Table 7).

Dataset	XLM-IT	XLM-PT	XLM-ES	XTC
IT	73.2	-	-	**76.3**
PT	-	**75.3**	-	73.3
ES	-	-	84.0	**84.7**

Table 6: Macro F1 for each fine-tuned model on its respective test set and for XTC on all test sets.

Lang.	XLM-IT	XLM-PT	XLM-ES	XTC
AR	51.3	45.8	51.4	**59.4**
NL	59.9	49.5	59.6	**66.7**
FR	57.5	50.5	62.2	**67.6**
DE	62.1	46.9	59.5	**68.9**
HI	48.2	44.4	47.4	**58.1**
IT	53.6	47.0	54.6	**69.6**
ZH	61.8	42.7	53.2	**71.5**
PL	57.5	49.2	58.2	**66.2**
PT	58.6	64.2	56.0	**68.5**
ES	60.0	50.1	64.4	**69.5**

Table 7: Macro F1 across languages on MHC for each of our fine-tuned models.

G XLM-T Model Details

Model Architecture We implemented XLM-T model (Barbieri et al., 2021) using the `transformers` Python library (Wolf et al., 2020). XLM-T is an XLM-R (Conneau et al., 2020) model pre-trained on an additional 198 million Twitter posts in over 30 languages. It has 12 layers, a hidden layer size of 768, 12 attention heads and a total of 278 million parameters. For sequence classification, we added a linear layer with softmax output.

Fine-Tuning All models use unweighted cross-entropy loss and the AdamW optimiser (Loshchilov and Hutter, 2019) with a 5e-5 learning rate and a 0.01 weight decay. For regularisation, we set a 10% dropout probability, and for batch size we use 32. For each model, we train for 50 epochs, with an early stopping strategy with a patience of 5 epochs, with respect to improvements in the binary F1-score on the validation split. We store the checkpoint with the highest binary F1-score and use it as our final model.

Computation We ran all computations on an AWS "g4dn.2xlarge" server equipped with one NVIDIA T4 GPU card. The average wall time for each each training step was around 3 seconds.

Model Access We make the XTC model available for download on HuggingFace.

H Google Perspective Results

We test Perspective's "identity attack" attribute and convert the percentage score to a binary label using a 50% cutoff. Testing was done in February 2022.

On the held-out test sets for Italian (Sanguinetti et al., 2020) and Portuguese (Fortuna et al., 2019), Perspective scored 70.7 and 64.1 macro F1. Perspective is outperformed on both languages by XTC, which scored 76.3 and 84.7 (Table 6).

On MHC, for the three languages it supports, Perspective (Table 8) performs worse than XTC (Table 2) in terms of macro F1 for Italian and Portuguese, and around equally well for German.

Language	F1-h	F1-nh	Macro F1
German / DE	84.1	54.9	69.5
Italian / IT	69.6	61.2	65.4
Portuguese / PT	84.2	47.6	65.9

Table 8: Performance of the Perspective API across the three languages it supports in MHC. F1 score for **h**ateful and **n**on-**h**ateful cases, and overall macro F1 score.

Distributional properties of political dogwhistle representations in Swedish BERT

Niclas Hertzberg* and **Asad Sayeed*** and **Ellen Breitholtz*** and **Robin Cooper***
and **Elina Lindgren**† and **Gregor Rettenegger**† and **Björn Rönnerstrand**†‡
*Dept. of Philosophy, Linguistics, and Theory of Science
†Dept. of Journalism, Media, and Communication
‡SOM Institute
University of Gothenburg, Sweden
asad.sayeed@gu.se

Abstract

"Dogwhistles" are expressions intended by the speaker to have two messages: a socially-unacceptable "in-group" message understood by a subset of listeners and a benign message intended for the out-group. We take the result of a word-replacement survey of the Swedish population intended to reveal how dogwhistles are understood, and we show that the difficulty of annotating dogwhistles is reflected in the separability of the space of a sentence-transformer Swedish BERT trained on general data.[1]

1 Introduction

We explore whether contemporary vector-space sentence representation techniques also provide a structured representation of the different messages in "dogwhistle" political communication. A dogwhistle refers to a word or phrase used in manipulative communication, usually in a political context. Dogwhistles carry at least two messages: one message intended for the broader community, and another "payload" message intended to communicate a specific, less acceptable message to a receptive "in-group". Dogwhistles depend on the "out-group" members not picking up on the payload message (Albertson, 2014; Bhat and Klein, 2020).

We take several Swedish-language dogwhistles and survey data from the Swedish population about the interpretation of these dogwhistles, and we apply clustering techniques based on the transformer-derived representation of the responses. We ask the question: are the responses clearly partitioned in the semantic space, and does the "sharpness" of this partitioning reflect the ease of dogwhistle identification by expert annotators?

While there has been work exploring dogwhistles through the lens of linguistics (Henderson and McCready, 2019; Bhat and Klein, 2020; Saul, 2018), automated approaches to exploring dogwhistles using NLP techniques are generally lacking (Xu et al., 2021). Considering the volume of social media data and the extent to which dogwhistles have been employed on these channels, it is important to create new computational techniques to detect and analyze dogwhistles that might succeed at higher data volumes. The first step in accomplishing this is to show that automatic techniques can be used to reliably extend and enhance manual analysis.

Dogwhistles can be strategically used, e.g. politically to send a veiled message to one group of voters while avoiding alienating another group (Bhat and Klein, 2020). This could pose a problem in a representative democracy since the out-group portion of the voter-base are deceived into voting for a certain candidate that might not represent their political views (Goodin and Saward, 2005).

Therefore, we contribute the following:

- We present a preliminary dataset of a word replacement task by members of the Swedish population as part of a survey of political attitudes, including a manual annotation for dogwhistle identification with inter-annotator agreement (IAA; Krippendorff's α) scores.
- We use a transformer-based model to represent the responses in a semantic space and apply classification (SVM) and clustering techniques (K-means) to the vectors.
- We evaluate the clusterings in terms of cluster purity metrics, and we show that the lower the IAA, the lower the linear separability of the responses in the vector space.

We then conclude that a Swedish BERT variant already represents important aspects of the underlying semantics of dogwhistles.

[1] Authors other than Niclas Hertzberg and Asad Sayeed are listed in ascending alphabetical order.

Proceedings of the Sixth Workshop on Online Abuse and Harms (WOAH), pages 170 - 175
July 14, 2022 ©2022 Association for Computational Linguistics

2 Dataset

Dogwhistle politics has become increasingly salient in the current mass and social media environment. This is also the case in Swedish society. Recent studies have shown that certain issues, in particular immigration, have produced examples of emergent dogwhistles gaining in public use (Åkerlund, 2021; Filimon et al., 2020).

Using a professional polling firm, we anonymously sampled 1000 members of the Swedish public using a word replacement task. We constructed 5 sentences containing words or phrases we suspected were being used as dogwhistles and asked survey participants to replace the words with what they thought it "really" meant. Then we manually annotated these responses for whether they identified a dogwhistle use or not. The survey was conducted under institutional ethical review in a process that involved survey administration and anonymized data compilation at a remove from the authors.

Each item therefore contains the substitution of participant-provided words or phrases for the original dogwhistle in the full context of the corresponding stimulus sentence. An illustrative stimulus example would be the following: "The Swedish unions are controlled by **globalists**". Each person taking the survey would replace "globalists" with a word or phrase they believe to convey the same information. The replacements can vary widely: someone might replace "globalists" with "communists" or an anti-Semitic slur, which might be considered an "in-group" response. Others would replace "globalists" with, e.g., "people concerned with international affairs" thus not showing an understanding of the dogwhistle as having any associations with the aforementioned groups. The actual Swedish dogwhistles we use and their English translations are listed in table 1.

Each replacement thus gave rise to a slightly altered sentence that, according to the person taking the survey, would convey the same information as the original sentence. The replacements for each dogwhistle was manually labeled depending on a person picking up on the dogwhistle meaning or not. An inter-annotator score was then calculated for the labeling of each dogwhistle.

IAA was calculated in two rounds, an initial round and a confirmatory round partway through the annotation. We report both scores in table 2.

Role of inter-annotator agreement[2] The goal of the annotation and the computation of IAA is to determine whether or not the annotation task can be designed with the following criterion in mind: that a panel of trained annotators with access to the guidelines can reliably distinguish between participant responses that *did* pick up on the "in-group" dogwhistle meaning from those that *did not*.

The identification and interpretation of a dogwhistle is an inherently subjective task which stems directly from one of the reasons to use a dogwhistle in the first place: to take advantage of the ambiguity of interpretation based on the standpoint of the individual recipients of the message. There are good reasons to critique the widespread use of IAA statistics to represent reader or listener reaction in subjective tasks like these (Sayeed, 2013). However, in this case, the annotation guidelines were developed in an iterative process to be presented in future publications that ensured that Swedish-speaking annotators informed about Swedish politics could consistently identify the dogwhistle interpretations of survey participants. The focus of this work is to explore the extent to which the intuitions behind the annotation guidelines are reflected in a Swedish BERT model trained on a multi-genre corpus.

3 Method

3.1 Sentence transformers

Sentence transformers (Reimers and Gurevych, 2019) are based on BERT (Devlin et al., 2018) and produce state of the art semantic representations of entire sentences and paragraphs. A high performing sentence model returns semantic representations of sentences, with a cosine distance that correlates with their semantic similarity. Different sentences can thus be compared computationally. The specific sentence model we used was Swedish sentence-Bert (Rekathati, 2021).

Resources for training machine learning models on Swedish text are somewhat limited. The lack of resources prevents training a sentence transformer in Swedish using the same procedure as training sentence transformers in English. However, the training of a sentence transformer in the target language can be obtained by fine-turning a Swedish model (Malmsten et al., 2020)[3] on the output of an

[2] We thank Reviewer 3 for raising this point.

[3] Pre-trained on books, newspapers official government reports, a small amount of social media, and Swedish Wikipedia.

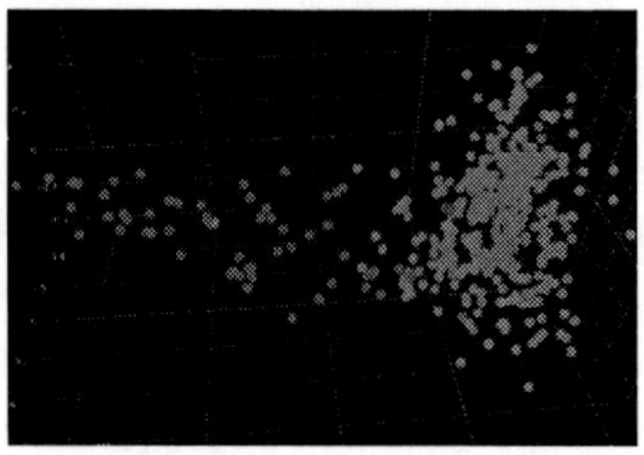

Figure 1: Responses for dogwhistle "enrich" represented in the semantic space. Coded in-group responses colored green.

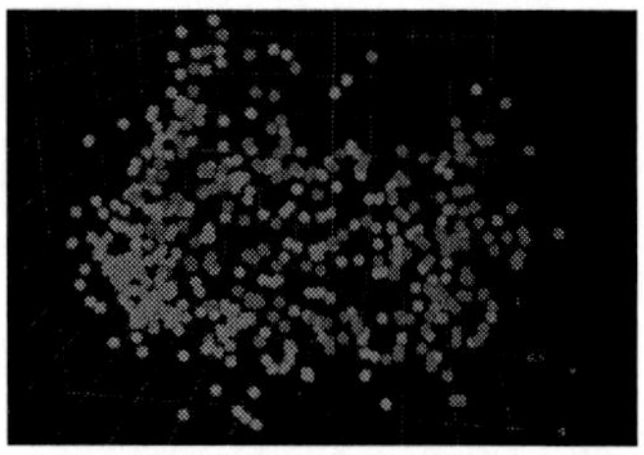

Figure 2: Dogwhistle "remigration" represented in the semantic space. Coded in-group responses colored green. Additional plots are in supplementary material.

already trained English sentence transformer and a parallel corpora of the source and target language. (Reimers and Gurevych, 2020). This procedure is an accessible way to train sentence transformers in a variety of languages faced with the same data limitations as Swedish.

3.2 Procedure

As we were interested in the semantic representations given by the sentence replacements for each dogwhistle response, we did the following: we input each of the sentences containing the replaced dogwhistle from the dataset into a sentence transformer in order to get dense 768-dimensional vector representations.

Then in order to visualize the semantic clustering of these sentence representations we used Principal Component Analysis (PCA; Abdi and Williams, 2010) to reduce the vectors to 3 dimensions.

3.3 Evaluation metrics

The general purpose of the clustering validations is to measure the compactness, i.e., how similar objects within a cluster are, and separation, which measures how far apart the clusters are. We evaluated the clustering created in the semantic space using two different evaluation metrics:

Davies-Bouldin (DB; Davies and Bouldin, 1979) score measures the average of the intra-cluster dispersion within each individual cluster divided by the distance between the centroid of one cluster to the centroid of the other cluster. A more compact cluster further apart from the other cluster will result in a lower score, with 0 indicating two very distinct clusters.

Calinski-Harabasz (CH; Caliński and Harabasz, 1974), measures intra-cluster dispersion and each cluster center's distance from the global centroid.

3.3.1 Unsupervised approach

We then used K-means with two cluster centroids to label each point in the space based on that point's distance from the nearest cluster centroid.

We did this with both the dimensionality-reduced sentence representations and the original 768-dimensional vectors. The sentence representations and the K-means labels were then evaluated using the aforementioned evaluation metrics.

3.3.2 Supervised approach

We evaluated the same sentence representations using the previous metrics, but with the annotated labels rather than the K-means labels. In addition, we trained a linear-kernel support vector machine (SVM). When training the SVM, we randomly sampled the sentence representations and labels, and split the data into training and testing (70%-30%). A higher F_1 score corresponds to a better division of the clusters.

4 Experiment and analysis

Our main question: is there an easily detected separation between the in-group responses and the out-group responses in the representation space?

If this was the case, it would mean that the model has picked up on some distinction between the responses that corresponds to the distinction made by the annotators. Given the distance in the semantic space between the two groups, it should be possible to separate the space with a linear SVM trained on a subset of the data.

A further question is whether there is a correlation between the clusterings and the IAA scores? Being able to linearly separate the two groups is a necessary but not sufficient condition for good clustering scores. The dogwhistle replacements might vary widely enough to not cluster well while still being separatable using a hyperplane to a high de-

The overwhelming bulk of the training data is news media.

Swedish	English
Flyktingpolitik	refugee policy
Berikar	enrich
Återvandring	remigration
Förortsgäng	suburban gang
Hjälpa på plats	help on location

Table 1: Swedish dogwhistles discussed in the present work and their English translations.

Dogwhistle	IAA	Responses/DWs
Flyktingpolitik	0.73/0.87	801/216
Berikar	0.79/0.91	813/102
Återvandring	0.74/0.55	776/268
Förortsgäng	1/1	816/172
Hjälpa på plats	1/0.82	788/108

Table 2: IAA for two annotation development phases and the total number of unique responses along with the subset that are in-group dogwhistle (DW) responses.

gree of accuracy. Ideally, two differentiable dense clusters would correspond to the IAA.

4.1 Results

The results in Table 3 show that a high separability among clusters does indeed correspond with the IAA agreement, which indicates the annotators ease of categorizing a response as "in-group" or "out-group". For example, the dogwhistle "remigration" had the lowest F1 score for both the dimensionality reduced sentence representations (0.72) and the original sentence representations (0.85), as well as the lowest IAA overall (0.74/0.55), as can be seen in table 2. Similarly, "suburban gang" had the highest IAA (1/1) and very high F1 scores as well (0.98/0.97).

However, the evaluation of the K-means labeled clusters did not correspond well to the IAA. The evaluation metrics for "refugee policy" is higher than "help on location" (1/0.82) despite having a much lower IAA score (0.74/0.55).

An explanation for this might be that some dogwhistle clusterings are spread over a wider semantic space, while still being linearly separatable (with an SVM) from other clusterings. This type of data distribution will still obtain good clustering results. For example, "enrich" in table 4 reports the best defined clusters overall (measured by a low DB score and high CH score), while only having a marginally greater F1 score (0.98/0.98) on the SVM task than "suburban gang" (0.98/0.97).

	3-dim	768-dim
Dogwhistle	F_1	F_1
Flyktingpolitik	0.77	0.91
Berikar	0.98	0.98
Återvandring	0.72	0.85
Förortsgäng	0.98	0.97
Hjälpa på plats	0.94	0.96

Table 3: SVM F_1 metrics for each dogwhistle.

Dogwhistle	3-dim		768-dim	
Clustering	CH	DB	CH	DB
Flyktingpolitik				
K-means	568.86	0.99	159.79	2.06
Human	65.29	2.90	40.41	3.85
Berikar				
K-means	1111.32	0.49	327.34	0.96
Human	978.04	0.61	303.33	1.12
Återvandring				
K-means	580.85	1.07	175.32	1.95
Human	148.15	2.05	64.39	3.16
Förortsgäng				
K-means	607.61	0.94	243.29	1.59
Human	241.03	1.39	115.59	2.06
Hjälpa på plats				
K-means	398.04	0.92	119.72	1.93
Human	300.58	1.02	97.16	2.02

Table 4: Cluster separability metrics for each dogwhistle for K-means and human clustering.

4.1.1 Support Vector Machine

The SVM was generally able to separate the two clusters well, even given fairly small amounts of training data. The general correlation with IAA scores were higher with PCA dimensionality-reduced vector representations. Possible reasons for the performance of the SVM might be that the SVM does not take into account the separation of the data from its cluster centroid in the opposite direction of the other cluster or the dispersion of the datapoints along an axis orthogonal to the separating plane. The SVM measurement only takes into account the overlapping of the semantic meanings of the sentences, represented in the space.

4.1.2 Internal clustering evaluation

The evaluation metrics for the K-means labeled points in the space does not seem to correspond to the IAA values. The lowest scoring dogwhistles, "refugee policy" and "remigration", cluster fairly well compared to the other dogwhistles with higher IAA values.

4.1.3 External clustering evaluation

The results for the evaluation metrics on the human labeled points indicate that there is an overall correspondence between the IAA and those measurements: the lowest rated IAA dogwhistles always have the lowest clustering score. This indicates that there is a semantic distinction between in-group responses and out-group responses that is captured fairly well by sentence transformers.

5 Conclusions and future work

Our work contributes a computationally straightforward method to extend the manual analysis of dogwhistles that is available for many languages at a resource level similar to Swedish. Our evaluations show that easily identified dogwhistle interpretations are partitioned well enough in the vector space given by SOTA sentence models that they are linearly separable using a simple SVM.

The representation of sentences given by the model is largely derived from the corpora that the model is trained on. The corpora thus has a large impact on the semantic space. Given this, models trained on different corpora would give rise to different semantic spaces where the clustering of the sentences would be different. Since K-means does not seem to be able to differentiate between in-group sentence replacements and out-group sentence replacements, future work might include an investigation into modeling the semantic space by training a sentence transformer on different sources of text. This would also allow us to investigate the role of specific lexical choices in the detection and representation of dogwhistles. In theory, it should be possible to train a model that creates a semantic space that clusters the points in a way that that the labels can be retrieved by an algorithm like K-means using only the data itself.

Acknowledgements

Funding for this work was provided by the Gothenburg Research Initiative for Politically Emergent Systems (GRIPES) supported by the Marianne and Marcus Wallenberg Foundation grant 2019.0214. Christoffer Olsson assisted with some of the annotations used in the work.

References

Hervé Abdi and Lynne J Williams. 2010. Principal component analysis. *Wiley interdisciplinary reviews: computational statistics*, 2(4):433–459.

Mathilda Åkerlund. 2021. Dog whistling far-right code words: the case of 'culture enricher'on the swedish web. *Information, Communication & Society*, pages 1–18.

Bethany Albertson. 2014. Dog-whistle politics: Multivocal communication and religious appeals. *Political Behavior*, 37.

P. Ishwara Bhat and Ofra Klein. 2020. Covert hate speech: White nationalists and dog whistle communication on twitter.

Tadeusz Caliński and Jerzy Harabasz. 1974. A dendrite method for cluster analysis. *Communications in Statistics-theory and Methods*, 3(1):1–27.

David L Davies and Donald W Bouldin. 1979. A cluster separation measure. *IEEE transactions on pattern analysis and machine intelligence*, (2):224–227.

Jacob Devlin, Ming-Wei Chang, Kenton Lee, and Kristina Toutanova. 2018. BERT: pre-training of deep bidirectional transformers for language understanding. *CoRR*, abs/1810.04805.

Luiza Maria Filimon et al. 2020. Nordic dog whistles. analyzing discriminatory discourses in the parlance of the scandinavian radical right parties. *Revista Română de Studii Baltice şi Nordice*, 12(1):7–40.

Robert E Goodin and Michael Saward. 2005. Dog whistles and democratic mandates. *The Political Quarterly*, 76(4):471–476.

Robert Henderson and Elin McCready. 2019. Dogwhistles and the at-issue/non-at-issue distinction. *Secondary Content*.

Martin Malmsten, Love Börjeson, and Chris Haffenden. 2020. Playing with words at the national library of sweden - making a swedish BERT. *CoRR*, abs/2007.01658.

Nils Reimers and Iryna Gurevych. 2019. Sentence-bert: Sentence embeddings using siamese bert-networks. *ArXiv*, abs/1908.10084.

Nils Reimers and Iryna Gurevych. 2020. Making monolingual sentence embeddings multilingual using knowledge distillation. In *Proceedings of the 2020 Conference on Empirical Methods in Natural Language Processing*. Association for Computational Linguistics.

Faton Rekathati. 2021. The kblab blog: Introducing a swedish sentence transformer.

Jennifer Saul. 2018. Dogwhistles, political manipulation, and philosophy of language. *New work on speech acts*, 360:84.

Asad Sayeed. 2013. An opinion about opinions about opinions: subjectivity and the aggregate reader. In *Proceedings of the 2013 Conference of the North American Chapter of the Association for Computational Linguistics: Human Language Technologies*, pages 691–696, Atlanta, Georgia. Association for Computational Linguistics.

Canwen Xu, Wangchunshu Zhou, Tao Ge, Ke Xu, Julian McAuley, and Furu Wei. 2021. Blow the dog whistle: A Chinese dataset for cant understanding with common sense and world knowledge. In *Proceedings of the 2021 Conference of the North American Chapter of the Association for Computational Linguistics: Human Language Technologies*, pages 2139–2145, Online. Association for Computational Linguistics.

Hate Speech Criteria: A Modular Approach to Task-Specific Hate Speech Definitions

Urja Khurana[1*] and **Ivar Vermeulen**[2] and **Eric Nalisnick**[3]
and **Marloes van Noorloos**[4] and **Antske Fokkens**[1,5*]
[1]Computational Linguistics and Text Mining Lab, Vrije Universiteit Amsterdam
[2]Department of Communication Science, Vrije Universiteit Amsterdam
[3]Informatics Institute, University of Amsterdam
[4]Department of Criminal Law, Tilburg University
[5]Dept. of Mathematics and Computerscience, Eindhoven University of Technology

Abstract

Offensive Content Warning: This paper contains offensive language only for providing examples that clarify this research and do not reflect the authors' opinions. Please be aware that these examples are offensive and may cause you distress.

The subjectivity of recognizing *hate speech* makes it a complex task. This is also reflected by different and incomplete definitions in NLP. We present *hate speech* criteria, developed with perspectives from law and social science, with the aim of helping researchers create more precise definitions and annotation guidelines on five aspects: (1) target groups, (2) dominance, (3) perpetrator characteristics, (4) type of negative group reference, and the (5) type of potential consequences/effects. Definitions can be structured so that they cover a more broad or more narrow phenomenon. As such, conscious choices can be made on specifying criteria or leaving them open. We argue that the goal and exact task developers have in mind should determine how the scope of *hate speech* is defined. We provide an overview of the properties of English datasets from `hatespeechdata.com` that may help select the most suitable dataset for a specific scenario.

1 Introduction

The surge in online *hate speech* has resulted in an increased need for its automatic detection. Its presence can be highly consequential as it creates an unsafe environment and threatens the freedom of speech (Kiritchenko et al., 2021). Effects of hate speech range from a personal level (e.g. anxiety or stress (Cervone et al., 2021)) to societal level (e.g. discrimination or violence (Waldron, 2012)) and such speech can disrupt social debate severely (Vidgen and Derczynski, 2020). Due to the large volumes of data on social media, automatizing the task is essential as hate speech can violate the law, depending on the country, in addition to its negative consequences in society. This makes automatic hate speech detection a very important task that needs to be carried out responsibly.

What is considered *hate speech* is subjective (Fortuna et al., 2020), there are a variety of valid viewpoints on what does (not) fall under this concept. Current hate speech datasets in NLP reflect this, having similar yet (subtly) different or incomplete definitions. For instance, similar terms are used interchangeably across publications and datasets, e.g. abusive, offensive, or toxic (Madukwe et al., 2020; Fortuna et al., 2020). We posit that a clear relation to (membership of) a target group of the victim sets *hate speech* apart from other forms of toxic or abusive language. Underspecified definitions and guidelines increase the level of subjectivity in annotations. This subjectivity propagates into the model, which can lead to biased models (Sap et al., 2019; Davidson et al., 2019). Even if annotations are systematic, it may remain unclear which phenomena (e.g. target groups or types of abusive) are covered and thus captured by models.

It depends on the task for which a dataset is created whether subjectivity is desired or not. We will argue that, even for scenarios where the goal is to collect multiple viewpoints, it is important to clearly define on what aspects of the phenomenon this subjectivity is sought. At the same time, we must keep in mind that it is impossible to fully remove subjectivity when determining whether something is *hate speech* or not. Even in law, where *hate speech* is aimed to be defined as objectively as possible, it is inevitable that courts have difficulties interpreting such a context-dependent and sensitive topic in consistent and predictable ways (Van Noorloos, 2014b). Nevertheless, a clear definition can help reduce subjectivity to borderline cases.

What would then be a good definition of *hate*

*Main correspondence: `u.khurana@vu.nl` and `antske.fokkens@vu.nl`

Proceedings of the Sixth Workshop on Online Abuse and Harms (WOAH), pages 176 - 191
July 14, 2022

speech? We advocate that a good definition of *hate speech* starts with a good understanding of the intention that it serves. For instance, a social media platform may want a *broader* consideration of *hate speech*, as it needs to keep its platform safe, in comparison to a law-enforcing model, which has to take legal action only when there is a clear punishable presence. One may decide to focus on hate speech towards one specific group or to keep this completely open to investigate which groups are considered potential targets by (crowd) annotators.

Rather than specifying what "the" definition should be, we provide a meta-prescriptive setup to construct definitions and guidelines through a modular approach, where modifications can be made according to the task at hand. Concretely, we propose five criteria which should be taken into account when defining *hate speech*[1] and creating annotation guidelines: (1) target groups, (2) social status of target groups, (3) perpetrator, (4) type of negative reference, (5) type of potential effect/consequence. These criteria were developed with insights from law and social science. We provide an overview of all English datasets from *www.hatespeechdata.com* according to these criteria, so that people working with a specific definition in mind can easily identify which existing English datasets[2] may be of direct use or provide a good starting point.

2 Background and Motivation

In this section, we describe related work that provided the motivation and insights for the operationalization we propose in this paper.

2.1 Annotations for Hate Speech Tasks

The quality of annotations directly influences the quality of hate speech detection models trained on the annotated data. The subjective nature of the task makes obtaining high inter-annotator agreement, often used as a quality metric for annotations, difficult (Talat et al., 2017). Awal et al. (2020) analyze and find evidence for inconsistency in the annotation for different widely-used hate speech datasets. They discover that some of the retweets in the dataset of Founta et al. (2018) have different labels while the tweet is the same, as also found by Isaksen and Gambäck (2020).

Demographic factors such as language, age, and educational background have an impact on how annotation is done (Al Kuwatly et al., 2020; Schmidt and Wiegand, 2017) as well as expertise (Talat, 2016). This subjectivity of the annotator also brings in possible biases of their own, as illustrated in Sap et al. (2019), Davidson et al. (2019), and Talat (2016). Sap et al. (2019) show that priming annotators and making them aware of their racial bias can decrease such inclinations which could stem from misunderstanding the intent of the text.

Vidgen and Derczynski (2020) point out that annotators need more appropriate guidelines with clear examples to get better annotations. They also argue that it is good practice to create training sets in such a way that they address the task. We follow this point of view and start from the assumption that any annotation task (whether it is intended for training, evaluation or exploration) starts with establishing the purpose of the annotations: How will the system trained on them be used? What is investigated in case of exploratory research?

2.2 Task Specific Annotations

One factor in settling how annotations can support the purpose of the task is how much subjectivity is desired. Röttger et al. (2021a) distinguish two types of approaches to annotation: descriptive and prescriptive. Descriptive annotations encourage subjectivity of annotators (where inconsistency is not an issue), while prescription instructs annotators to strictly follow carefully defined criteria (the less subjectivity, the better). Accordingly, they require definitions that are either more open to interpretation or that are more specific as to what falls under the phenomenon under investigation (in our case *hate speech*).

Most datasets we explored are built to serve as training data for discrete classification identifying if a message contains hate speech (or another form of abusive language). This requires consistently annotated data.[3] As such, most existing datasets should ideally follow a prescriptive paradigm. However, many use definitions that can introduce unintended forms of subjectivity leading to problematic forms of inconsistency.

[1] We emphasize that the focus of this definition is on textual *hate speech*. Introducing other modalities (e.g. images or sound) adds other layers of complexity.

[2] We limit our overview to English for reasons of space, but plan to apply the criteria to all sets mentioned on the site in the future.

[3] We found a notable exception in Ousidhoum et al. (2019) following a *descriptive* approach, who aim to assess how people view and react to *hate speech*. Röttger et al. (2021a) give an overview of abusive language datasets and how they correspond to the annotation paradigm of prescriptive vs. descriptive based on the definition.

As mentioned in Section 1, even in the most prescriptive scenario of all, criminal law, experts may differ in their judgment. A certain level of disagreement is thus inevitable due to the nature of the task. This should nevertheless be limited to borderline cases and the definition should make explicit where this borderline is situated, e.g. should it include all potentially harmful messages to create a pleasant online environment for users or focus on the most extreme cases that potentially break the law?

While borderline cases are inevitable, there are also clear cases where there is wide agreement on a message being an example of hate speech, or contrarily benign without any signal that could possibly be problematic. In general, the fact that there is disagreement on a specific example can be valuable information (Aroyo and Welty, 2015). A system trained on data that captures disagreement could for instance reflect the perception of various annotators (e.g. providing scores that reflect how many annotators would consider an utterance to constitute hate speech). Subjectivity is a strength in this scenario, but the racial bias reported by Sap et al. (2019) would still be problematic. It therefore remains desirable to raise the annotators' awareness of their biases. This would not be the case if the goal of annotating would be to investigate annotator bias rather than creating data for training or evaluating a system. Here, influence on annotators should be kept to a minimum. These examples illustrate that it is important to make conscious decisions as to where subjectivity is desired in annotations and to clearly specify which criteria annotators should not deviate from.

2.3 Defining Hate Speech

There is large variation in current NLP definitions and datasets. This begins with the inconsistent usage of terms. *Abusive* and *offensive language* are examples of terms that have been used to express the same or similar concepts (Schmidt and Wiegand, 2017; Talat et al., 2017; Fortuna et al., 2020; Madukwe et al., 2020). Talat et al. (2017) introduce a typology that aims to further specify types of abusive language by distinguishing between (1) explicit and implicit and (2) directed or generalized forms. We limit ourselves to *hate speech*. We pose that the relation of the negativity of an abusive utterance to a target's (membership of a) specific group is a defining characteristic of *hate speech*.

Even while working on the same phenomenon, there are several (subtle) differences in work addressing *hate speech*. Some datasets have a broader understanding of *hate speech*, e.g. Davidson et al. (2017) take a(n unintended) descriptive approach by not defining potential targets. Fortuna et al. (2020) contrast the more vague definition of Davidson et al. (2017) to the explicit list in Talat et al. (2017), who intentionally focus on a more narrow phenomenon covering only racism and sexism. Fortuna et al. (2020) confirm that different datasets "provide their own flavor of hate speech" (Fortuna et al., 2020, p. 6782).

Varying and vague definitions can lead to inconsistencies that can (unknowingly) be problematic (Madukwe et al., 2020). For instance, users may have a different expectation from a dataset than what its annotations actually cover. Ensuring that datasets are used and created appropriately starts with awareness. Therefore, we introduce *hate speech criteria* (detailed in Section 3) that can be used to construct (prescriptive or descriptive) definitions with annotational guidelines. Individual steps can be adapted depending on the task. Definitions can support a broader or more narrow focus. They can try to leave subjectivity to a minimum or explicitly keep specific aspects underspecified to collect multiple perspectives. Clear definitions can address some challenges around *hate speech* identification, but not all. We elaborate on remaining open issues, such as influence of individual annotators in Section 5.

Our proposal resembles prior work by Kennedy et al. (2022). They translate their definition into a hierarchical coding typology that is used to annotate their *hate speech* dataset. They also use insights from legal (Germany, Australia, The Netherlands, and other countries), sociology, and psychology disciplines. Like us, they point out that *hate speech* is treated differently per country and recognize the importance of having a negative reference relating to (membership of) a group in the utterance. Fortuna and Nunes (2018) discuss differences of hate speech definitions between different sources[4] and recognize different dimensions that are mostly present: having a target, inciting hate or violence, to attack or diminish, and humor having a special status. Zufall et al. (2020) introduce a schema to assess if utterances are hate speech according to the EU law. In contrast to these works, we take a broader approach and present criteria to construct

[4]Platforms, code of conducts, and one scientific paper.

definitions that fit a diverse set of operationalizations according to the desired research. Our criteria can thus support the same definitions Zufall et al. (2020) cover, but is also wide enough to support other types of definitions. In addition, we introduce new aspects that are essential to *hate speech*, such as the dominance of a group and perpetrator characteristics to our criteria.

We furthermore go beyond these prior studies in that we provide an overview of existing English NLP datasets that address *hate speech*. This overview is powered by the dimensions provided in our criteria, which are complementary to the aspects introduced in the typology by Talat et al. (2017), who cover abusive language in general. Their typology does not focus on definitional *hate speech* dimensions but captures the (dis)similarities between different types of abusive language. As mentioned above, they distinguish between abuse directed at an individual or generally addressing a target group and between implicit or explicit abuse. Our approach relates to that typology as follows. Their examples of generalized abusive language would typically fall under *hate speech*. Speech directed at individuals also falls under *hate speech* if there is direct evidence for the abuse being related to group membership. We add specifications on potential targets, group dominance, perpetrator information and the effect of the message which can encapsulate both implicit and explicit *hate speech*.

3 Proposed Hate Speech Criteria

This section provides our proposed procedure to define *hate speech*. As outlined above, we follow the view that hate speech is characterized by problematic statements that are related to a target's (presumed) membership of a specific group. Starting from this assumption, we propose the following criteria, represented in Figure 1, to define the scope of *hate speech*:

1. Identify the target group(s).
2. Specify the social status of the target group
3. Consider properties of the perpetrator
4. Identify the type of negative reference (in relation to the target) present.
5. Identify the potential effects/consequences of the utterance.

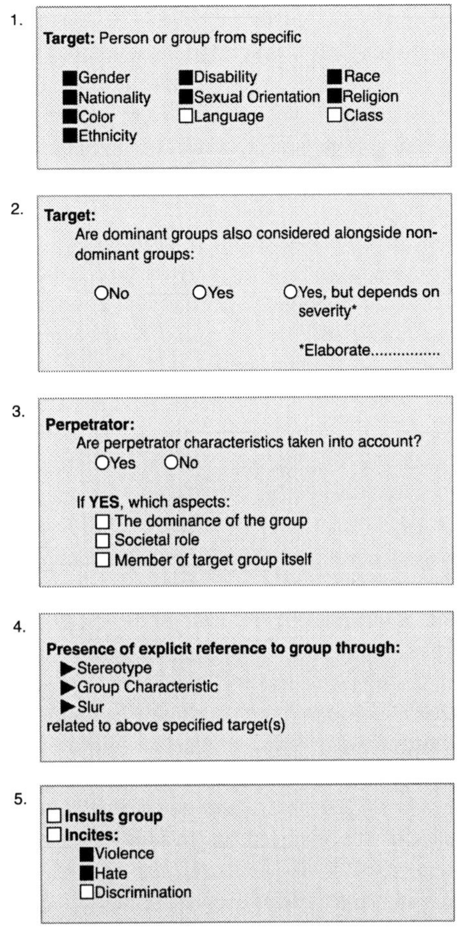

Figure 1: Our proposed *Hate Speech Criteria* to support modular task-specific definition and annotation guidelines construction.

Per step, we indicate the considerations that should be taken into account. These can differ depending on the task, but certain elements are standard across many definitions found in NLP and are also generally supported by law. We call these cases *standard* cases and indicate them in our figure with a filled checkbox. Other facets which are known to be considered in existing definitions (but not all) are *optional* cases and these are left unfilled. This corresponds to how European countries have defined *hate speech*, with some target groups being more common and/or obliged by EU law and other target groups differing among member states (Commission et al., 2021). The options can be adjusted in any way the use case requires: one can extend the definition, narrow it down to investigate a specific form of hate speech or purposely leave a component underspecified. It is specifically possible to work with multiple definitions that apply in different legal or social contexts (e.g. being more lenient to what is allowed in artistic context or being more protective towards users on a social platform). Note that the criteria do not intend to distinguish different forms of *hate speech*, but allow researchers to define or distinguish a specific form themselves when necessary for a task. An example of applying the criteria to a task is given in Appendix B.

3.1 Considered Targets

The inclusion of specific target groups depends heavily on the task (e.g. women- and immigrants-focused (Basile et al., 2019) or racism- and sexism-focused (Talat and Hovy, 2016)). For instance, a law-supporting detection system in Belgium would also consider *language*[5] a basis of a group, while that would not be the case in the Netherlands.[6] Thus, the first step in defining the scope under consideration is to specify which target groups are being considered for your task. In Figure 1, the most common target groups are indicated as the **standard** groups. The list of possible characteristics is not exhaustive and others that historically have been disparaged can be added. Vice-versa, a study may focus on a subset of these groups. Which specific target groups people consider potential victims of hate speech can furthermore be the topic of descriptive research. In this case, it should be defined that this is intentionally left unspecified.

3.2 Target Group Dominance

An important distinction that can be made in the target group is the dominance of a group in society, depending on where the model will be deployed. We define a dominant (cultural) group as a group whose members are (possibly without them being aware) positively privileged (Razzante and Orbe, 2018), unstigmatized (Rosenblum and Toni-Michelle, 2000), and generally favored by societal institutions (Marger, 1997). Hateful sentences against non-dominant groups can be far more consequential than those addressing groups that are in power and can control the narrative. As such, objectionable speech against (an individual from) a dominant group does not necessarily have to be considered *hate speech*. While for some tasks this distinction would be sensible to make, the law does not always make it, e.g. in The Netherlands (Van Noorloos, 2014b).

We ask the question if the task at hand also takes the dominant group into account as a potential target of *hate speech*. There are three different options: The option *no* excludes all forms of negative speech addressed at the dominant group from consideration. The option *yes* does not distinguish between targets from the dominant group and other targets. The third option assumes that utterances targeting the dominant group can be *hate speech*, but under stricter conditions. For instance, a definition may exclude the possibility of discriminating against the dominant group, but would consider calls for violence against them *hate speech*.

3.3 Speaker/Perpetrator

The third distinction we propose is considering perpetrator characteristics (Geldenhuys and Kelly-Louw, 2020). It should be made explicit whether, for a particular task, it matters who the perpetrator is. Because it is a common scenario in NLP that only text is available and the background of a speaker cannot be determined, there are **no standard** aspects to consider here. We describe how speaker characteristics may be taken into account for those scenarios where they can be retrieved. For instance, a person uttering possible *hate speech* against their own group may be "exempted". It is also important to consider what such a speaker is doing with their utterance. If they are "re-appropriating"[7] speech to reject the negative statement (Galinsky et al., 2013), that would not be considered *hate speech* while if the intention is justification, it would be. Additionally, the societal role of the perpetrator may play a role: a person in a powerful position saying something derogating can be much more harmful than an average person saying the same thing, e.g. a CEO of a tech company making derogatory remarks about female engineers. In contrast, e.g. artists can be given more freedom due to artistic expression. Some

[5]Belgian Criminal Code: Articles 377bis, 405quater, 422quater, 438bis, 442ter, 453bis, 514bis, 525bis, 532bis, and 534quater https://www.ejustice.just.fgov.be/cgi_loi/change_lg.pl?language=nl&la=N&cn=1867060801&table_name=wet

[6]Dutch Criminal Code: Articles 137d and 137e https://wetten.overheid.nl/BWBR0001854/2022-03-01

[7]*Reappropriate:* "to take possession for oneself that which was once possessed by another, and we use it to refer to the phenomenon whereby a stigmatized group revalues an externally imposed negative label by self-consciously referring to itself in terms of that label." - Galinsky et al. (2003)

countries, e.g. The Netherlands also allow more space for politicians:[8] Statements that contribute to the political debate are given more protection in lieu of freedom of expression, but remarks may not infringe other rights.[9]

3.4 Types of References to Target Groups

Hate speech is a specific kind of abuse that is characterized by a negative reference that is either aimed at a target group or *explicitly* related to membership of a target group. We thus differentiate between negative behavior toward someone from a potential target group from negative behavior *because of* someone's membership of a target group. For illustration, *"They should lock you up!"* clearly is a problematic message due to its threatening nature. It would nevertheless not be considered hate speech as there is no explicit reference to the individual being a part of a targeted group, even if they are in fact a member of such a group. Now, if we change it to *"They should lock you up, SLUR!"* where the slur specifically targets a group, this *would* be considered hate speech, as the slur clearly signals a relation between the threat and the group the target belongs to.

We explicitly state that the text should contain one (or more) of the following: (i) a stereotype (ii) a group characteristic (this can be the group itself as well) or (iii) a slur that is connected to the target groups specified in the first block. This is the only step where all the references provided are **standard** and cannot be optional. Only if the addressed task enables using more contextual clues while annotating then the reference may be found in a larger context (e.g. another tweet in the thread), but some evidence for the direct link between group membership and the abuse must be present. If there is no larger context, then reliance should be only on the present text.

3.5 Potential Consequence of Utterance

The last step in setting up the scope of *hate speech* is evaluating its strength and potential effects. The actual effects need not be proved, also not in criminal law. However, the words need to be liable to incite to hatred, violence, discrimination or to insult (Van Noorloos, 2014a). Most definitions consider inciting violence and hate as *hate speech*, as these consequences make *hate speech* stand out from other offensive expressions. These two incitements are **standard** cases. Additional broader potential consequences can also be considered, such as inciting discrimination, or a general insult toward a group. The latter is specifically recognized by Dutch law. Which possible consequences should be taken into account depends on the severity of *hate speech* the task should address. It furthermore depends on the context wherein the narrative exists. Is there a relation to a threatening historical situation? Does the uttering call for exclusion of particular target groups? Furthermore, a threat can be implicitly present, i.e. "What should we do with your *stereotypical object*?". While there is not an explicit *call* for it, violence *is* implied: destruction. The threat lies in its potential consequences. It is important to understand the implications and where the possible violence or hate stems from in a statement. Once this is understood, one may decide if different consequences, depending on severity, should apply to different targets or not.

4 Overview of Definitions and Datasets

To highlight the differences between existing datasets and to comprehend what kind of tasks they would fit, we present an overview of widely-used datasets based on their definitions. Our scope is restricted to all English datasets found on `hatespeechdata.com` that tackle *hate speech*, since it has the most datasets and a variety of definitions.[10] The overview can be found in Table 1, where we indeed observe this variation.

For each step in our criteria, we indicate if it is explicitly specified in the definition or not. There is a difference between defining *hate speech* and specifying a particular focus. We follow the descriptions of the annotations in the dataset for our classification. In cases where *only* a definition is given, we assume that that is the focus of the dataset as well, unless stated otherwise (e.g. in Talat and Hovy (2016); Basile et al. (2019)). An ✗ signals that the aspect is unspecified in the definition, therefore it is still possible that the specifics are present in the dataset but this cannot be guaranteed. E.g.

[8] `https://mensenrechten.nl/nl/vrijheid-van-meningsuiting`

[9] An example of a politician violating this freedom: `https://uitspraken.rechtspraak.nl/inziendocument?id=ECLI:NL:RBAMS:2021:7392`, `https://www.politico.eu/article/dutch-mep-guilty-anti-semitism-holocaust/`

[10] We leave out Sarkar and KhudaBukhsh (2020) as it presents a challenge for hate speech detection models but does not address the task itself. We include Zufall et al. (2020) to illustrate that our criteria also fits a legal perspective of *hate speech*.

	T	ND	P	Explicit Ref	Effects/Consequences
Talat and Hovy (2016)	✓	✓	✗	Stereotype & Slur	Insult, Violence, Hate, *Other*
ElSherief et al. (2021)	✓	✗	✗	Slur & Group Characteristics	Insult, Violence, Hate, Discrimination, *Other*
Kennedy et al. (2022)	✓	✗	✗	Slur, Group Characteristics, & Stereotypes	Violence or Hate
Basile et al. (2019)	✓	✓	✗	✗	*Other*
Kirk et al. (2021)	✓	✗	✗	✗	Discrimination, *Other*
Founta et al. (2018)	✓	✗	✗	✗	Insult, Hate, *Other*
Mandl et al. (2019)	✓	✗	✗	Stereotypes & Group Characteristics	✗
Mollas et al. (2020)	✓	✗	✗	✗	Insult, Violence
Zufall et al. (2020)	✓	✗	✗	✗	Violence, Hate
ElSherief et al. (2018)	✓	✗	✗	✗	*Other*
Gao and Huang (2017)	✓	✗	✗	✗	*Other*
Qian et al. (2019)	✓	✗	✗	✗	*Other*
Ribeiro et al. (2018)	✓	✗	✗	✗	Violence, *Other*
Röttger et al. (2021b)	✓	✗	✗	*Other*	✗
Chung et al. (2019)	✓	✓	✗	✗	✗
Fanton et al. (2021)	✓	✓	✗	✗	✗
Mathew et al. (2021)	✓	-	✗	✗	✗
Davidson et al. (2017)	✗	✗	✗	✗	Insult, Violence, Hate, *Other*
de Gibert et al. (2018)	✗	✗	✗	*Other*	✗
Ousidhoum et al. (2019)	✓	✗	✗	✗	✗

Table 1: Overview of existing datasets according to the hate speech criteria that we propose. **T:** target groups specified, **ND:** considering only non-dominant groups specified, **Explicit Ref**: explicit reference specified, if yes; which ones, **Effects/Consequences:** effects/consequences specified, if yes; which ones. Per paper we indicate for each aspect if they are present in the definition or focus.

several datasets might only consider non-dominant groups but do not explicitly state so, or when left unspecified it is unclear which explicit references to the group are always present.

Under column **T** we see if there are specific target groups in the definition. There are very few datasets that do not explicitly mention their target groups (Davidson et al., 2017; de Gibert et al., 2018). Although there is some overlap in groups between different datasets, there are also (subtle) differences. Due to this variety, we provide an overview of different target groups covered per dataset in Appendix A.

For the second step, most definitions do not mention anything about dominance. Mathew et al. (2021) are the only ones to mention *Caucasian* as a target group, which we mark with a '-' to signal that this paper is explicit about not restricting itself to non-dominant groups. Most papers with a ✓for **ND** specifically define their targets to apply to non-dominant groups only (Chung et al., 2019; Basile et al., 2019; Fanton et al., 2021), with the exception of Talat and Hovy (2016), who mention *minorities*.

None of the datasets mention taking perpetrator characteristics into account (column **P**). Similarly, the explicit references are left unspecified in most datasets' definitions (column **Explicit Ref**). This means that for such datasets it cannot be guaranteed whether explicit references are present, nor whether they include specifications as to which ones. Looking at **Effects/Consequences**, *violence* and *hate* occur the most. Other terminology for negative relations and effects/consequences widely differs and the interpretation with respect to our criteria can be subjective (e.g. is 'humiliate' a form of discrimination, an insult or something else?), we mark such terminology as *Other*.

The idea behind the overview is that it can illustrate the need for future datasets that specify their aspects more explicitly and aids in deciding which dataset is suitable for a specific task. For instance, if a task requires a dataset that guarantees a focus on non-dominant groups, then column **ND** can easily point to the datasets that fit this prerequisite explicitly. If the dominance being specified is not very important but the presence of an explicit reference of a negative relation like a slur is, then Mandl et al. (2019) could be fitting for the task. If, in addition, incitement of hate and violence is essential, then Kennedy et al. (2022) should be considered. If dominance is important as well, one might consider to further annotate samples from these sets that are labeled as *hate speech*, saving the time to separate 'clean' messages. In combination with the overview of which datasets cover which target groups, we believe these outlines to be helpful for identifying useful datasets.

5 Discussion

The presented *hate speech* criteria aim to include those aspects of *hate speech* needed to arrive at clearer definitions and to provide better annotation guidelines, while supporting a wide range of use cases. We are aware, however, that they do not provide a magic solution to all challenges around this complex phenomenon. In this section we briefly discuss (1) possible extensions, (2) possible further specifications and (3) challenges that a clear definition cannot (fully) address on its own.

We tried to create an extensive overview of relevant aspects, but are well aware that we may have missed things. Moreover, *hate speech* is strongly connected to culture and what is perceived as *hate speech* may change. The criteria can thus be **extended** to cover new target groups, more perpetrator characteristics, or additional potential consequences. This particularly holds for the fourth step: *Types of References to Target Groups*. We maintain that *evidence* of the abuse being related to (assumed) group membership is a requirement, but researchers may decide that other clues can also serve as possible evidence for an utterance being *hate speech*. These clues may include the history of a certain perpetrator, who in the past has uttered instances of *hate speech* multiple times. As mentioned, the evidence may also come from e.g. what the utterance is responding to.

The typology of Talat et al. (2017) is not included in our criteria. We explained in Section 2 how our criteria relate to this typology. It is however straightforward to add **further specifications** to a *hate speech* definition created through our criteria. Note that, even though our criteria relies on the clear presence of group characteristics, stereotypes, and/or slurs, they do not exclude implicit forms of abuse, especially since we also evaluate the potential consequences e.g.: *"Everything was quite ominous with the train accident. Would like to know whether the train drivers were called StereotypicalName1, StereotypicalName2 or StereotypicalName3 #RefugeeCrisis"* (Benikova et al., 2017). Here, the stereotypical names indicate that this falls under *hate speech*. Utterances like *"white revolution is the only solution"*(ElSherief et al., 2021) may seem problematic due to the lack of an explicit slur, stereotype or target group characteristic. It nevertheless provides direct evidence, since "white" implies that the revolution would be against non-white and the violent nature of the threat.

A clear definition can help avoid inconsistencies and unwanted forms of subjectivity in the data, but it cannot address all challenges involved in determining whether an instance exhibits *hate speech*. First, we mentioned multiple times that some form of **subjectivity** remains inevitable when dealing with *hate speech*. Though people will always differ as to where they draw the line, instructions on the level of severity that should be included with illustrating discussions can be helpful. Even for the seemingly clear case of inciting violence, which is a core aspect, there is a vast difference between uttering *"Throw tomatoes at them!"* and an actual life-threatening *"Gun them down!"*. The class of group insult in particular can include a large variety, from merely unkind statements *"Women really have a horrible sense of fashion with their white sneakers!"* to insults that question people's capabilities or attack someone's morals. Questioning a groups capabilities can lead to discrimination, especially when uttered by people with authority or in power. The remark *"I'm not sexist but female comedians just are not funny!"* (Shvets et al., 2021) may seem relatively harmless when coming from a tweeter with few followers, but when coming from an influential critic or the president of a comedians' union, it can actively harm women's careers. Attacks on a group's morals can also have an impact beyond merely insulting. For instance, saying that a non-dominant group are leeches can incite hate or lead to violent ramifications.

Explanations that illustrate the potential affect on different targets can help annotators to determine the severity of a specific statement and may help them to make more systematic decisions on where to draw the line. This leads to the second challenge that a definition by itself cannot solve: **annotator bias**. Explanations and training may help annotators to tackle their bias and may make them more sensitive to more subtle attacks to groups they are not part of, but the affect of an annotator's background will not be completely eliminated. Our criteria are meant to support creating a definition and guidelines. They do not mention gathering annotator information, because we believe that the definition crafted for a specific task does not change based on annotator information. However, we want to emphasize that it is essential that annotator demographics are taken into account and that the goal of the task should be kept in mind when establishing annotators' background. E.g. if the target group considered for the task is *Gender*, it is of utmost importance to have annotators that can capture experiences of all genders. In general, it is vital to include members of potential target groups, since they are more likely to pick up on subtleties.

A third issue that can only partially be addressed by means of a clear definition lies in the relation between *hate speech* and **freedom of speech**. As mentioned, *hate speech* can create unsafe environments that hamper freedom of speech. At the same time, opinions can differ regarding whether specific remarks are harmful or should be allowed because they are part of an important debate (and where marking them as *hate speech* would hamper freedom of speech). Law has to clearly define what is punishable *hate speech* and what on the other hand should be protected by freedom of speech. In Dutch law, a distinction is made for e.g. public debates where politicians are given more (but not unlimited) space for *controversial* statements. Another example is that Dutch law protects members of a religion from problematic utterances (which is prohibited in all EU countries), but leaves ample space for negative statements about specific religions (decriminalized in many Western countries) (Van Noorloos, 2014a). In the context of creating a safe environment for discussion, this distinction between attacking a religion or people can be hard to make sometimes and there are cases where it does not seem to make sense. The example *#BanIslam* from Talat and Hovy (2016), for instance, might be aimed at religion and not at people, but it can clearly be harmful to Muslims and it is hard to see how such a hashtag would contribute to a useful public debate or discussion. In this context, both the potential harm and added value of statements to a debate should be taken into account. Though the example of *#BanIslam* seems clear, it is easy to imagine that it is not always straightforward to make this call.

The challenges mentioned above show that a clear definition may be a good starting point, but cannot solve everything. We provided examples that illustrate the complexity, but full discussions would merit individual papers on each of these topics. A final limitation we want to point out is that our overviews are currently limited to English datasets. Our framework leaves variables related to linguistic properties or cultural aspects open and can thus be easily applied to datasets covering other languages.

6 Conclusion

We presented modular criteria to construct definitions and annotator guidelines to address *hate speech*. These steps include aspects that have, to our knowledge, not been prominent before. We propose five components for defining hate speech: (1) identifying the target group(s), (2) specifying the consideration of dominant groups, (3) considering perpetrator characteristics, (4) finding explicit negative reference(s) of the target(s), and (5) identifying the potential consequences/effects. Based on the task at hand, the definition can be modified as, depending on the application for which *hate speech* is addressed, a different description may be needed. This ties into how strictly each specific aspect needs to be defined as well: do we need annotations that are as consistent as possible (prescriptive) or do we want to investigate diversity in perspectives on this particular aspect (descriptive)?

We provided an overview of a large variety of English *hate speech* datasets based on the dimensions that are present in our criteria. We hope that the criteria and discussions in this paper will motivate NLP researchers working on *hate speech* to critically think about the tasks they are addressing and evaluate how fitting current definitions and datasets are for their task. The overview can then help select the most suitable datasets that can either be directly used or used as starting points that serve the task after adding further specifications. We particularly hope that the discussion in this work will help those working on new datasets to take these aspects into account from the start.

Acknowledgements

This research was (partially) funded by the Hybrid Intelligence Center, a 10-year programme funded by the Dutch Ministry of Education, Culture and Science through the Netherlands Organisation for Scientific Research. We would additionally like to thank the reviewers for providing us with valuable feedback that has helped improving this paper.

References

Hala Al Kuwatly, Maximilian Wich, and Georg Groh. 2020. Identifying and measuring annotator bias based on annotators' demographic characteristics. In *Proceedings of the Fourth Workshop on Online Abuse and Harms*, pages 184–190, Online. Association for Computational Linguistics.

Lora Aroyo and Chris Welty. 2015. Truth is a lie: Crowd truth and the seven myths of human annotation. *AI Magazine*, 36(1):15–24.

Md Rabiul Awal, Rui Cao, Roy Ka-Wei Lee, and Sandra Mitrović. 2020. On analyzing annotation consistency in online abusive behavior datasets. *arXiv preprint arXiv:2006.13507*.

Valerio Basile, Cristina Bosco, Elisabetta Fersini, Debora Nozza, Viviana Patti, Francisco Manuel Rangel Pardo, Paolo Rosso, and Manuela Sanguinetti. 2019. SemEval-2019 task 5: Multilingual detection of hate speech against immigrants and women in Twitter. In *Proceedings of the 13th International Workshop on Semantic Evaluation*, pages 54–63, Minneapolis, Minnesota, USA. Association for Computational Linguistics.

Darina Benikova, Michael Wojatzki, and Torsten Zesch. 2017. What does this imply? examining the impact of implicitness on the perception of hate speech. In *International Conference of the German Society for Computational Linguistics and Language Technology*, pages 171–179. Springer.

Carmen Cervone, Martha Augoustinos, and Anne Maass. 2021. The language of derogation and hate: Functions, consequences, and reappropriation. *Journal of language and social psychology*, 40(1):80–101.

Yi-Ling Chung, Elizaveta Kuzmenko, Serra Sinem Tekiroglu, and Marco Guerini. 2019. CONAN - COunter NArratives through nichesourcing: a multilingual dataset of responses to fight online hate speech. In *Proceedings of the 57th Annual Meeting of the Association for Computational Linguistics*, pages 2819–2829, Florence, Italy. Association for Computational Linguistics.

European Commission, Directorate-General for Justice, Consumers, P Ypma, C Drevon, C Fulcher, O Gascon, K Brown, A Marsavelski, and S Giraudon. 2021. *Study to support the preparation of the European Commission's initiative to extend the list of EU crimes in Article 83 of the Treaty on the Functioning of the EU to hate speech and hate crime : final report.* Publications Office.

Thomas Davidson, Debasmita Bhattacharya, and Ingmar Weber. 2019. Racial bias in hate speech and abusive language detection datasets. In *Proceedings of the Third Workshop on Abusive Language Online*, pages 25–35, Florence, Italy. Association for Computational Linguistics.

Thomas Davidson, Dana Warmsley, Michael Macy, and Ingmar Weber. 2017. Automated hate speech detection and the problem of offensive language. In *Proceedings of the International AAAI Conference on Web and Social Media*, volume 11.

Ona de Gibert, Naiara Perez, Aitor García-Pablos, and Montse Cuadros. 2018. Hate speech dataset from a white supremacy forum. In *Proceedings of the 2nd Workshop on Abusive Language Online (ALW2)*, pages 11–20, Brussels, Belgium. Association for Computational Linguistics.

Mai ElSherief, Shirin Nilizadeh, Dana Nguyen, Giovanni Vigna, and Elizabeth Belding. 2018. Peer to peer hate: Hate speech instigators and their targets. In *Proceedings of the International AAAI Conference on Web and Social Media*, volume 12.

Mai ElSherief, Caleb Ziems, David Muchlinski, Vaishnavi Anupindi, Jordyn Seybolt, Munmun De Choudhury, and Diyi Yang. 2021. Latent hatred: A benchmark for understanding implicit hate speech. In *Proceedings of the 2021 Conference on Empirical Methods in Natural Language Processing*, pages 345–363, Online and Punta Cana, Dominican Republic. Association for Computational Linguistics.

Margherita Fanton, Helena Bonaldi, Serra Sinem Tekiroğlu, and Marco Guerini. 2021. Human-in-the-loop for data collection: a multi-target counter narrative dataset to fight online hate speech. In *Proceedings of the 59th Annual Meeting of the Association for Computational Linguistics and the 11th International Joint Conference on Natural Language Processing (Volume 1: Long Papers)*, pages 3226–3240, Online. Association for Computational Linguistics.

Paula Fortuna and Sérgio Nunes. 2018. A survey on automatic detection of hate speech in text. *ACM Computing Surveys (CSUR)*, 51:1 – 30.

Paula Fortuna, Juan Soler, and Leo Wanner. 2020. Toxic, hateful, offensive or abusive? what are we really classifying? an empirical analysis of hate speech datasets. In *Proceedings of the 12th Language Resources and Evaluation Conference*, pages 6786–6794, Marseille, France. European Language Resources Association.

Antigoni Founta, Constantinos Djouvas, Despoina Chatzakou, Ilias Leontiadis, Jeremy Blackburn, Gianluca Stringhini, Athena Vakali, Michael Sirivianos, and Nicolas Kourtellis. 2018. Large scale crowdsourcing and characterization of twitter abusive behavior. In *Proceedings of the International AAAI Conference on Web and Social Media*, volume 12.

Adam D Galinsky, Kurt Hugenberg, Carla Groom, and Galen V Bodenhausen. 2003. The reappropriation of stigmatizing labels: Implications for social identity. In *Identity issues in groups*, volume 5, pages 221–256. Emerald Group Publishing Limited.

Adam D Galinsky, Cynthia S Wang, Jennifer A Whitson, Eric M Anicich, Kurt Hugenberg, and Galen V Bodenhausen. 2013. The reappropriation of stigmatizing labels: The reciprocal relationship between power and self-labeling. *Psychological science*, 24(10):2020–2029.

Lei Gao and Ruihong Huang. 2017. Detecting online hate speech using context aware models. In *Proceedings of the International Conference Recent Advances in Natural Language Processing, RANLP 2017*, pages 260–266, Varna, Bulgaria. INCOMA Ltd.

Judith Geldenhuys and Michelle Kelly-Louw. 2020. Demystifying hate speech under the pepuda. *Geldenhuys J and Kelly-Louw M" Demystifying Hate Speech underthe PEPUDA" PER/PELJ*.

Vebjørn Isaksen and Björn Gambäck. 2020. Using transfer-based language models to detect hateful and offensive language online. In *Proceedings of the Fourth Workshop on Online Abuse and Harms*, pages 16–27, Online. Association for Computational Linguistics.

Brendan Kennedy, Mohammad Atari, Aida Mostafazadeh Davani, Leigh Yeh, Ali Omrani, Yehsong Kim, Kris Coombs, Shreya Havaldar, Gwenyth Portillo-Wightman, Elaine Gonzalez, et al. 2022. Introducing the gab hate corpus: defining and applying hate-based rhetoric to social media posts at scale. *Language Resources and Evaluation*, pages 1–30.

Svetlana Kiritchenko, Isar Nejadgholi, and Kathleen C Fraser. 2021. Confronting abusive language online: A survey from the ethical and human rights perspective. *Journal of Artificial Intelligence Research*, 71:431–478.

Hannah Rose Kirk, Bertram Vidgen, Paul Röttger, Tristan Thrush, and Scott A Hale. 2021. Hatemoji: A test suite and adversarially-generated dataset for benchmarking and detecting emoji-based hate. *arXiv preprint arXiv:2108.05921*.

Kosisochukwu Madukwe, Xiaoying Gao, and Bing Xue. 2020. In data we trust: A critical analysis of hate speech detection datasets. In *Proceedings of the Fourth Workshop on Online Abuse and Harms*, pages 150–161, Online. Association for Computational Linguistics.

Thomas Mandl, Sandip Modha, Prasenjit Majumder, Daksh Patel, Mohana Dave, Chintak Mandlia, and Aditya Patel. 2019. Overview of the hasoc track at fire 2019: Hate speech and offensive content identification in indo-european languages. In *Proceedings of the 11th forum for information retrieval evaluation*, pages 14–17.

Martin Marger. 1997. *Chapter 5: Foundations of the American Ethnic Hierarchy: Anglo-Americans and Native Americans*, 4th edition, page 146–169. Wadsworth, Belmont.

Binny Mathew, Punyajoy Saha, Seid Muhie Yimam, Chris Biemann, Pawan Goyal, and Animesh Mukherjee. 2021. Hatexplain: A benchmark dataset for explainable hate speech detection. In *Proceedings of the AAAI Conference on Artificial Intelligence*, volume 35, pages 14867–14875.

Ioannis Mollas, Zoe Chrysopoulou, Stamatis Karlos, and Grigorios Tsoumakas. 2020. Ethos: an online hate speech detection dataset. *arXiv preprint arXiv:2006.08328*.

Nedjma Ousidhoum, Zizheng Lin, Hongming Zhang, Yangqiu Song, and Dit-Yan Yeung. 2019. Multilingual and multi-aspect hate speech analysis. In *Proceedings of the 2019 Conference on Empirical Methods in Natural Language Processing and the 9th International Joint Conference on Natural Language Processing (EMNLP-IJCNLP)*, pages 4675–4684, Hong Kong, China. Association for Computational Linguistics.

Jing Qian, Anna Bethke, Yinyin Liu, Elizabeth Belding, and William Yang Wang. 2019. A benchmark dataset for learning to intervene in online hate speech. In *Proceedings of the 2019 Conference on Empirical Methods in Natural Language Processing and the 9th International Joint Conference on Natural Language Processing (EMNLP-IJCNLP)*, pages 4755–4764, Hong Kong, China. Association for Computational Linguistics.

Robert J Razzante and Mark P Orbe. 2018. Two sides of the same coin: Conceptualizing dominant group theory in the context of co-cultural theory. volume 28, pages 354–375. Oxford University Press.

Manoel Ribeiro, Pedro Calais, Yuri Santos, Virgílio Almeida, and Wagner Meira Jr. 2018. Characterizing and detecting hateful users on twitter. In *Proceedings of the International AAAI Conference on Web and Social Media*, volume 12.

Karen E Rosenblum and C. Travis Toni-Michelle. 2000. *The Meaning of Difference: American Constructions of Race Sex and Gender Social Class and Sexual Orientation*, 2nd edition. McGraw-Hill, Boston.

Paul Röttger, Bertie Vidgen, Dirk Hovy, and Janet B Pierrehumbert. 2021a. Two contrasting data annotation paradigms for subjective nlp tasks. *arXiv preprint arXiv:2112.07475*.

Paul Röttger, Bertie Vidgen, Dong Nguyen, Zeerak Waseem, Helen Margetts, and Janet Pierrehumbert. 2021b. HateCheck: Functional tests for hate speech detection models. In *Proceedings of the 59th Annual Meeting of the Association for Computational Linguistics and the 11th International Joint Conference on Natural Language Processing (Volume 1: Long Papers)*, pages 41–58, Online. Association for Computational Linguistics.

Maarten Sap, Dallas Card, Saadia Gabriel, Yejin Choi, and Noah A. Smith. 2019. The risk of racial bias in hate speech detection. In *Proceedings of the 57th Annual Meeting of the Association for Computational Linguistics*, pages 1668–1678, Florence, Italy. Association for Computational Linguistics.

Rupak Sarkar and Ashiqur R KhudaBukhsh. 2020. Are chess discussions racist? an adversarial hate speech data set. *arXiv preprint arXiv:2011.10280*.

Anna Schmidt and Michael Wiegand. 2017. A survey on hate speech detection using natural language processing. In *Proceedings of the Fifth International Workshop on Natural Language Processing for Social Media*, pages 1–10, Valencia, Spain. Association for Computational Linguistics.

Alexander Shvets, Paula Fortuna, Juan Soler, and Leo Wanner. 2021. Targets and aspects in social media hate speech. In *Proceedings of the 5th Workshop on Online Abuse and Harms (WOAH 2021)*, pages 179–190, Online. Association for Computational Linguistics.

Zeerak Talat. 2016. Are you a racist or am I seeing things? annotator influence on hate speech detection on Twitter. In *Proceedings of the First Workshop on NLP and Computational Social Science*, pages 138–142, Austin, Texas. Association for Computational Linguistics.

Zeerak Talat, Thomas Davidson, Dana Warmsley, and Ingmar Weber. 2017. Understanding abuse: A typology of abusive language detection subtasks. In *Proceedings of the First Workshop on Abusive Language Online*, pages 78–84, Vancouver, BC, Canada. Association for Computational Linguistics.

Zeerak Talat and Dirk Hovy. 2016. Hateful symbols or hateful people? predictive features for hate speech detection on Twitter. In *Proceedings of the NAACL Student Research Workshop*, pages 88–93, San Diego, California. Association for Computational Linguistics.

Marloes Van Noorloos. 2014a. Criminalising defamation of religion and belief. *European Journal of Crime, Criminal Law and Criminal Justice*, 22(4):351–375.

Marloes Van Noorloos. 2014b. The politicisation of hate speech bans in the twenty-first-century netherlands: Law in a changing context. *Journal of Ethnic and Migration Studies*, 40(2):249–265.

Bertie Vidgen and Leon Derczynski. 2020. Directions in abusive language training data, a systematic review: Garbage in, garbage out. *Plos one*, 15(12):e0243300.

Jeremy Waldron. 2012. The harm in hate speech. In *The Harm in Hate Speech*. Harvard University Press.

Frederike Zufall, Marius Hamacher, Katharina Kloppenborg, and Torsten Zesch. 2020. A legal approach to hate speech: Operationalizing the eu's legal framework against the expression of hatred as an nlp task. *arXiv preprint arXiv:2004.03422*.

A Overview of Target Groups in Datasets

Since many of the datasets have varied target groups that are taken into consideration, we present an overview of the target groups that are mentioned in their definitions, or are explicitly stated to be their focus, in Table 2. Due to different terminology used for related concepts, we use umbrella terms for the distinct categories and indicate the precise terms if those categories are present in the dataset (e.g. health concerns, disease, and disability grouped under health). Under **Other** we illustrate target groups that do not fit the other categories and do not occur enough to be specified by themselves. Furthermore, we also indicate if definitions keep the target groups open to unspecified ones by using wordings like "groups such as ..." (e.g. Kirk et al. (2021); Mandl et al. (2019)).

Datasets that do not have any target groups indicated, as can be seen in Table 1, are left out from this overview.

When a specific focus is mentioned (e.g. Chung et al. (2019); Basile et al. (2019)), instead of using the umbrella terms, we use the exact targets as mentioned by the paper. Moreover, when both *Gender* and *Gender Identity* are considered by a dataset, this is indicated as *Gender (Identity)*.

	Gender	Origin	Religion	Sexual Orientation	Health	Other
Talat and Hovy (2016)	Gender	Race				
ElSherief et al. (2021)	Gender (Identity), Sex	Race, Ethnicity, Nationality	Religion	Sexual Orientation	Disability, Disease	Age
Kennedy et al. (2022)	Gender	Race, Ethnicity, Nationality, Regionalism	Religion, Spiritual Identity		Mental, Physical Health	Ideology, Political Identification
Basile et al. (2019)	Women	Immigrants				
Kirk et al. (2021)	Gender	Race, Ethnicity, Nationality, Color, Descent	Religion			"Other identity factor"
Founta et al. (2018)	Gender	Ethnicity, Race	Religion	Sexuality	Disability	"Attributes such as"
Mandl et al. (2019)	Gender	Race		Sexual Orientation	Health Condition	Political Opinion, Social Status, "or similar"
Mollas et al. (2020)	Gender	Race, National Origin	Religion	Sexual Orientation	Disability	
Zufall et al. (2020)		Race, Colour, Descent, National or Ethnic Origin	Religion			
ElSherief et al. (2018)	Gender, Sex	Race, Ethnicity, National Origin	Religion	Sexual Orientation	Disability, Disease	
Gao and Huang (2017)	Gender	Ethnicity		Sexual Orientation		"Facet of identity"
Qian et al. (2019)	Gender (Identity), Sex	Race, Ethnicity, National Origin, Caste	Religion	Sexual Orientation	Disease, Disability	
Ribeiro et al. (2018)	Gender (Identity)	Race, Ethnicity, National Origin	Religion	Sexual Orientation	Disability, Disease	Age
Röttger et al. (2021b)	Women, Trans people	Black people, Immigrants	Muslims	Gay people	Disabled people	
Chung et al. (2019)			Islamophobia			
Fanton et al. (2021)	Women	People of Color, Romani, Migrants	Jews, Muslims	LGBT+	Disabled people	Overweight people
Mathew et al. (2021)	Gender	Race, Indigenous, Refugee, Immigrant	Religion	Sexual Orientation		
Ousidhoum et al. (2019)	Gender	Origin	Religion	Sexual Orientation	Special Needs	

Table 2: Overview of target groups. Each column represents a type of target, under which we indicate the specific targeted group per dataset. An empty cell indicates that the target group type was not mentioned in the definition/focus.

B Example of Applying the Criteria to a Task

To showcase the utility of the proposed criteria to create a definition and associated annotation guidelines, we will apply the criteria to a prescriptive and descriptive scenario. For reasons of simplicity, we assume the questions are applied to texts that contain some form of abuse (where we use *abuse* as an overarching term which includes any form of *hate speech* as well as other forms potentially harmful content).

B.1 Prescriptive scenario

Consider the following scenario where we want to create a definition for a task that takes down *hate speech* on a social media platform that goes against the Dutch law for *hate speech.*[11] We initially want annotations in a prescriptive setting: as the addressed task concerns the law, we strive to reduce subjectivity to a minimum.

For each step, we fill in what is specified according to the Dutch law. Correspondingly, the target groups considered are: race, religion or philosophy of life, gender, hetero- or homo-sexuality, and physical and mental disability. As the law does not make a distinction between dominant and non-dominant groups, the task will not either. The step around perpetrator is more complex: the law does not define a distinction for the kind of perpetrator, but does allow for more lenience in a political or artistic context. We require the presence of all the explicit references mentioned in the criteria as all of them are standard cases: stereotype, group characteristic, and slur. Furthermore, the incitement of violence, hate or discrimination is considered. In addition, group insult is also seen as a consequence for all target groups except for gender.

This brings us to the following definition for the task: *For this task, hate speech is defined as language targeted at a person or group based on their race, religion or philosophy of life, gender, hetero- or homo-sexuality, and physical and mental disability and incites violence, hate or discrimination or insults a group on the basis of aforementioned targets, barring gender.*

Then, we transfer this definition using the criteria to annotation guidelines. For each step, we ask the question if the specification is present or not. If any step is not considered, we keep the lack of consideration as a note to prevent personal judgments in such cases as much as possible. If the answer to a question is *yes*, the annotator can proceed to the next question. If an answer is no, the instance is not covered by the task definition of *hate speech* and the annotator can directly label the instance as *not hate speech*.

For this specific task, we ask the following questions to be answered for texts that contain a form of abuse:

1. Does the target (group) belong to one of the following groups: *race, religion or philosophy of life, gender, hetero- or homo-sexuality, and physical and mental disability*?

2. **NOTE:** The target (group) can belong to both non-dominant and dominant groups.

3. Does the text contain an explicit reference to the group (related to above specified target(s)) through a stereotype, group characteristic or slur?

4. Does the text incite violence, hate, or discrimination or group insult? If the text incites violence, hate or discrimination, it should be labeled as *hate speech.* If the text only contains a group insult proceed to the next question.

5. Is the group insult directed at a group based on the following characteristics: *race, religion or philosophy of life, hetero- or homo-sexuality, and physical and mental disability*? If yes, it should be labeled as *hate speech.*

6. If the text contains *hate speech*: Is the speaker an artist or politician making the utterance in a context of their work? Please indicate "political or artistic context" (it can still be hate speech).

Please note that the instructions above literally follow Dutch law and we are aware that these targets does not cover all groups (notably this is a rather limited view on LGBTQ+) and that the exclusion of gender from group insult is debatable. It should also be noted that aspects such as group dominance or who the speaker is can have an influence on a verdict, but applying those subtleties would, in this scenario, be up to judges making a final verdict rather than annotators marking potential violations of the law. For similar reasons, we

[11] Dutch Criminal Code: Articles 137d and 137e `https://wetten.overheid.nl/BWBR0001854/2022-03-01`.

choose to mark the artistic or political context as a relevant aspect rather than specifying what this would mean for the ultimate decision.

B.2 Descriptive Scenario

Suppose that we want to study what groups various annotators consider potential victims of *hate speech*, including whether they distinguish between dominant or non-dominant groups. We focus on forms of hate speech that incite violence hate or discrimination, leaving the more vague category of group insults out. The questions they should then answer about texts containing some form of abuse are:

1. Is the abuse aimed at a specific target group or a member of such a group?
2. Does the text contain an explicit reference to the group (related to above specified target(s)) through a stereotype, group characteristic or slur?
3. Does the text incite violence, hate, or discrimination?

By making it clear for which aspects the subjectivity from annotators is desired, it is easier to ensure that annotators will deviate from the given instructions for that facet and that other researchers are aware of the variation. We know, for instance, that they did check whether there is an explicit reference to the group. The awareness can help in making an informed decision if the dataset is useful for their task or not. Naturally, the outcome will remain somewhat cluttered by subjective interpretations whether a specific remark could incite, e.g., discrimination. We can however distinguish between these motivations by making annotators answer the question rather than making them label the data. As such, we learn whether their reason for 'no' was related to the specific group being a potential target or to the severity or nature of the abuse.

For reasons of simplicity, we left the criterion of perpetrator information out of this example. Investigating this aspect would probably require a different setup. For instance, first defining *hate speech* as something that incites violence, hate or discrimination, and then asking the following questions:

1. Is the abuse aimed at a specific target group or a member of such a group?
2. Does the text contain an explicit reference to the group (related to above specified target(s)) through a stereotype, group characteristic or slur?
3. Is the speaker a member of the target group?
4. Do you consider this utterance to be *hate speech* based on the definition provided above?

Note that the examples in this appendix are included for purposes of illustration as how definitions may help specifying annotation tasks. We are well aware that providing a good annotation setup, especially for descriptive scenarios, is complex. As many aspects mentioned in this paper, the next step of actually setting up such tasks can merit a paper on its own.

Accounting for Offensive Speech as a Practice of Resistance

Mark Díaz*
Google Research
markdiaz@google.com

Razvan Amironesei*
Google Research
amironesei@gmail.com

Laura Weidinger
DeepMind
lweidinger@deepmind.com

Iason Gabriel
DeepMind
iason@deepmind.com

Abstract

Tasks such as toxicity detection, hate speech detection, and online harassment detection have been developed for identifying interactions involving offensive speech. In this work we articulate the need for a relational understanding of offensiveness to help distinguish denotative offensive speech from offensive speech serving as a mechanism through which marginalized communities resist oppressive social norms. Using examples from the queer community, we argue that evaluations of offensive speech must focus on the impacts of language use. We motivate this use of language in Cynic philosophy and use it to frame a use of offensive speech as a practice of resistance. We also explore the degree to which NLP systems may encounter limits to modeling relational context.

1 Introduction

Tasks such as the detection of toxicity, hate speech, and online harassment have been developed to identify and intervene in situations that have the potential to cause significant social harm. These tasks for identifying and classifying offensive or undesirable language have gone by different names (see: (Waseem et al., 2017; Balayn et al., 2021)) and have employed varying task definitions, but they are united by a goal of reducing harm and breakdowns in civil discourse. Because language use varies contextually, it is difficult to model the nuanced social context that informs whether language produces harm. Offensive language classification and related tasks capture different forms of undesirable language, such as language that is rude, incites hate, causes offense, or causes people to disengage from online interaction.

In this paper, we discuss a form of offensive language that has not previously received much research attention in the machine learning (ML) community, namely offensive language that is beneficial in its use and whose prosocial effects are sociologically and historically documented. In other words, language that uses terminology which is often noted as offensive, but which is not perceived as offensive in particular contexts of use. We distinguish this language with contextually-specific beneficial impacts as *reappropriated*. Understanding how to characterize and model this kind of language is important not only because of its widespread use, but also because of the critical sociological role it can play, particularly within marginalized communities.

We contribute: 1) a framing of offensiveness that accounts for socially productive uses of denotatively offensive language; 2) a general understanding of offensive language that builds from definitions of hate speech and toxicity to show the difficulty of operationalizing relational context; 3) specific challenges and directions for improving how we operationalize relational aspects of offensiveness.

We also call on researchers developing offensive speech classification tasks to engage with offensiveness as a social relation that arises not just between individuals in communication but also between communities of discourse. In other words, offensiveness and its impacts are best understood from the perspectives of those already embedded in relationships that structure who produces, receives, perceives and who is targeted (i.e., who is implicitly or explicitly named) by offensive speech. We separately name reception and perception to distinguish between the recipient(s) of a message, such as an alias tagged in a Tweet, and those who may not be the intended audience but to whom the content is visible. However, practical challenges in data collection and annotation task design can cause offensiveness to be implicitly operationalized as a semantic property of language.

Our discussion begins with the foundations of

*Authors contributed equally

Proceedings of the Sixth Workshop on Online Abuse and Harms (WOAH), pages 192 - 202
July 14, 2022

offensiveness, adding to challenges that have been highlighted by others. We also provide considerations and steps forward for improving automated offensiveness classification. We argue that accounting for the social and historical constitution of offensive language is important for the responsible development of automated and semi-automated tools to identify offensive language. To do so, in turn, deepens our understanding of offensive speech and recognizes the disparate impacts or ends of offensive language (e.g., as a means to silence others; as a means to challenge existing social structures).

2 A Working Definition of Offensiveness

Natural language processing (NLP) systems have historically faced challenges identifying and classifying denotatively offensive language used with inoffensive connotation (Ashwitha et al., 2021; Weitzel et al., 2016; Sun et al., 2021). A challenge inherent to defining different forms of hateful, toxic, or offensive language is that the characterization of these terms is necessarily socially, culturally, and politically specific. For this reason, Hovy and Yang (2021) identify the robust inclusion of social context in understanding language as a key missing component for the success of modeling approaches. Building from definitions of hate speech and toxicity, we establish a working definition of offensiveness that can better account for missing social context.

Hate speech is typically defined to link the use of derogatory language to a person or people based on group membership, such as "some characteristic such as race, color, ethnicity, gender, sexual orientation, nationality, religion, or other characteristics" (Basile et al., 2019). One of the key characteristics of this definition is that it focuses on the injury applied to a specific subject of offense. Broadly, definitions of hate speech underscore a need to identify who the target is in order to assess offense or harm. We argue that the target of offensive language is best understood with respect to differential relations and power dynamics between them and the producers, receivers, and perceivers of offensive speech.

In contrast to hate speech and other definitions of offensive language, toxicity is specifically oriented around the measurable outcome of language use. Defined as, "a rude, disrespectful, or unreasonable comment that is likely to make people leave a discussion,"[1] it does not engage explicitly with injury or harm, but links it to measurable behavior. Toxicity helps bring attention to the ends of reappropriated offensive language, and what characteristics can help distinguish it from denotative uses of offensive language. On its own, however, it is not clear that it suffices to protect the user's best interest, as it does not engage explicitly with the subject of verbal injury. The definition serves those with an interest to maximize user engagement, i.e. to minimize the chances of the user "leaving a discussion". It is conceivable that users who experience offense may not leave a discussion, for example in cases where users are habitually exposed to the relevant offense, such as microaggressions.

Hate speech and toxicity help us to construct a relational view for grounding a more robust definition of offensiveness– that is, a view that considers the social relations among targets of offensive language, and the producers, receivers, and perceivers (each of whom can also be a target) of denotatively offensive speech. This view is focused on identifying the network of social relations rather than some essential attribute of words or phrases.

3 Drag Queens and the Cynic Perspective

In this section, we analyze language use within the queer community to show how social relations and the ends of targeted language can help us to understand how denotatively offensive language 1) can have expressly beneficial ends and 2) can work as a social practice of collective resistance which fulfills a function of "self-innoculation" against out-group antagonism. We specifically analyze mock impoliteness used by drag queens that implicitly offers a critique of exclusionary sexual mores and social attitudes that hinder the self-expression of queer communities. These social attitudes include the demonization of queer sexuality, gender expression and visibility. We foreground our example with the case of Cynic offensive speech, which we present as a historical practice of resistance to unreflective social conventions. We show that denotatively offensive language as vehiculated by drag queens is not an isolated sociological phenomenon but instead should be inscribed in a history of practices of resistance.

[1] https://developers.perspectiveapi.com/s/about-the-api-attributes-and-languages: :text=%EF%BB%BFAttributestext= Perspective's%20main%20attribute%20is%20TOXICITY,make %20you%20leave%20a%20discussion%E2%80%9D

Culpeper (2011) defines mock impoliteness as language which "consists of impolite forms whose effects are (at least theoretically for the most part) canceled by the context." The author continues "[...] mock impoliteness in theoretical terms [is understood] as involving the canceling of impoliteness' perlocutionary effects flowing from a conventionalised impoliteness formula when an obvious mismatch emerges with the context it is used in." One key aspect that we want to emphasize here is how mock impoliteness works to both reduce the harmful effects of targeted insult while supporting social bonding and relationship building.

3.1 Mock Impoliteness in the Queer Community

The use of mock impoliteness is not exclusive to the queer community. However, compared with other uses of mock impoliteness, its use in the queer community acts as a form of social resistance (McKinnon, 2017). Although, building in-group solidarity and social bonding are significant effects of mock impoliteness, we focus on what it means for queer individuals to "self-innoculate" against offensive language by practicing employing it themselves. McKinnon (2017) uses mock impoliteness to show that "utterances, which could potentially be evaluated as genuine impoliteness outside of the appropriate context, are positively evaluated by in-group members who recognize the importance of "building a thick skin" to face a hostile environment both explicitly via the deployment of offensive language which targets marginalized communities (e.g., slurs) and implicitly via the structures of civil language, which may inhibit certain forms of expression by marginalized communities (e.g., comments highlighting nontraditional gender expression). One complexity in interpreting language that relies heavily on context, is the "context collapse" that takes place on platforms such as Twitter (Marwick and Boyd, 2011). A drag queen may target the drag community in a Tweet, relying on shared contextual markers with their targeted audience - for example, assuming shared norms of mock impoliteness, and a mutual understanding that slurs are not intended literally. However on platforms such as Twitter, where the wider public can see these messages, perceivers may lack this context and thus interpret such utterances as offensive. This "context collapse" must be accounted for to assess the content of a given Tweet.

(b)

Figure 1: Examples of mock impoliteness from prominent drag queens featured on RuPaul's Drag Race.

Oliva et al. (2021) describe erroneously high toxicity probabilities (provided by the Perspective API) for language from drag queens on Twitter[2]. Although toxicity is distinct from offensiveness, their analysis shows how the difficulty of implementing a relational approach and detecting relational context in practice can cause the concept to be misapplied. This difficulty applies not only to classifying toxicity, but also classifying hate speech, offensiveness, and other language rooted in relational context. The authors compare tweets that contain queer vernacular produced by drag queens to racist tweets written by white supremacists that are predicted to have low toxicity. As the authors point out, many of the swear words and slurs used among drag queens that might otherwise be considered insulting or rude, are used playfully. To characterize the constructive nature of language in this example, it is not only important to understand the individual relation and the type of humor between two drag queens engaging with each other, but also to understand their marginalized social positions relative to broader society. This example brings to light the difficulty of not only developing a relational framing but also practical challenges in identifying this relational context in data.

[2]Oliva et al. (2021) offer an example tweet of mock impoliteness: tweet by drag queen Darienne Lake, "So proud of this bitch. Love seeing you on @AmericanIdol."

Contrary to Oliva et al., we are not focused here on toxicity. Rather, we assess the above example in terms of offensiveness and disambiguate between hate speech, toxicity and offensive speech not only at the definitional level but also at a conceptual level. For example, applying Perspective API's definition of toxicity is complicated by the fact that, presented without context to a perceiver or data annotator, this language may be indistinguishable from rude, uncivil, indecent and impolite exchange. In addition, with context but without knowledge of sociological norms within the community, it may still be assumed by a perceiver that the exchange also leads to disengagement, thus qualifying the interaction as toxic. This challenge for outside perceivers highlights a need to identify which context is required in instances where members of a community of discourse - in this case drag queens - may break normative rules of civility (such as by using widely acknowledged hateful terms like "fag", "tranny", or "dyke") and consensually use language deemed uncivil by mainstream standards.

3.2 Mutual Recognition and Consent

It is important to emphasize that social positionality, (that is, the roles one can fulfill in a given social context) is crucial for disambiguating offensive content. Take the example of the Cynics to whom offense fulfills an ascetic role as part of a larger project of living one's life by practicing spiritual exercises. Cynic philosophy is defined by a denunciation of normative social conventions and by a demand to "return to a simple life in conformity with nature" (Hadot, 2002). Cynic philosophy, as set out by the philosopher Diogenes, established ethical practices that its proponents put forward to support a virtuous way of life, which was achieved through severe self-discipline and the strategic use of offensive language. Similar to mock impoliteness, cynic insult was used as a way to critique unreflective social norms from a position of subjugation. In this respect they both play a sociological role as practices of resistance. However, whereas the outcome of offensive language for Cynics was to further the way of life of an ancient school of thought, for drag queens, the outcome is solidaristic bonding, identity formation, and queer survival in the face of marginalization.

Thus, we must ask if consenting to being both the producer and recipient of offensive language is a sufficient condition for an observer to identify the language as inoffensive or for a platform to tolerate it. In this case, the drag queens directing tweets at each other recognize a shared queer identity referenced in a specific type of offensive language and can be reasonably confident that their messages will be considered a practice of mock impoliteness based on queer vernacular and social dynamics. Critically, mock impoliteness as used by drag queens and members of the queer community features slurs and insults that have precisely been used in targeted harassment against them. Among members of the queer community, interactions such as these are predicated upon a dynamic of group exchanges, recognition of group membership, and awareness of such language as used by outgroup members (e.g., the use of slurs such as 'faggot' or 'tranny' and insults focused on sexual behavior and femininity).

Recognition of the sociological norms of mock impoliteness is reflected in reciprocal, consensual engagement. In this way, mock impoliteness is a mutually socially constructed phenomenon. However, it is critical to note that language use within groups may not be consistently used or recognized by all. For example, someone new to the drag community might be initially unfamiliar with mock impoliteness, mistaking it for malice, and others within the community may simply not engage in mock impoliteness. In these cases, reciprocal, consensual engagement is not achieved. This shows that recognition of offensive discourse is still an insufficient condition to identify mock impoliteness and that it may need to be followed by explicit consent to offensive language.

Although we name the combination of recognition and mutual consent to offensive language as reasons for potentially tolerating its use on a platform, we do not argue in favor of protecting hateful exchanges among producers and receivers who target individuals or groups outside of their own. This would include, for example, two homophobic individuals bonding over and consenting to uses of queer slurs among themselves. Any community of discourse that promotes racist, homophobic, xenophobic, or similar ideas should be submitted to scrutiny. Out of context, drag queen's reappropriated offensive speech may appear to do just this, showing that recognition and consent between producer and recipient to offensive language are not sufficient conditions for identifying mock impoliteness. To build from linguistic recognition and consent, we ask why and, in particular, to what ends do drag queens invoke offensive language on the platform?

As Oliva et al. describe, much of the language used in the tweets they analyzed is reflective of mock impoliteness among members of the queer community, which is a critically important act of socializing– or training– ingroup members to inure and defend themselves from derogatory remarks lobbed by outgroup members. While mock impoliteness features swear words and often employs homophobic slurs, this language can be distinguished from offensive language invoked by outgroup harassers in at least two important ways.

First, mock impoliteness serves to inure queer individuals to homophobic attacks from outgroup members, as well as to hostility from other community members (McKinnon, 2017; Murray, 1979). In this way, offensiveness is used as a rhetorical means to prosocial ends that effectively resist to exclusionary social norms that seek to define queer existence. Taking automated action on offensiveness as an end in itself to be identified stands to ignore its prosocial impacts and ignores the web of social relations that support queer survival. In order to develop content moderation and related processes that predict and mitigate harm, offensiveness must also be conceptualized in such a way that accounts for the beneficial impacts, or ends, of language rather than treating offensiveness as a fixed, negative property of language itself. While mock impoliteness might be read as targeted harassment by a random or non-queer audience, a relational lens makes clear that offensiveness can operate within a dynamic relation of in-group recognition that consolidates the formation of a social identity.

In this respect, the queer practice of mock impoliteness parallels a Cynic practice of training for adversity. The Cynic analogy of the adaptive mouse describes the actions of a mouse adapting itself to harsh living environments. The analogy describes how Diogenes, the preeminent Cynic, rolled himself "over hot sand, while in winter he used to embrace statues covered with snow, using every means of inuring himself to hardship." The practice of inuring oneself to hardship is consistent with the description of the drag queens practice of "building a thick skin." The Cynics and drag queens have distinct motivations and engage in distinct behavior, however queer practices of self-inoculation parallel a lineage of "building a thick skin", figuratively and literally within a history of practices of training for adversity.

Second, as the case of mock impoliteness illustrates, characterizing the ends (or potential ends) of offensiveness is central. The goal of this work is not to propose a universal taxonomy of offensiveness. Instead, we turn attention to understanding how offensiveness functions as a social practice and the ends it produces in order for us to account for the various ways of operationalizing it. Focusing on the complex intentions of offensiveness allows us to describe its relational nature.

We characterize two types of ends – those that are individual and those that are plural or collective and related to belonging to a recognized social identity. Individual ends refer to the impacts local to a specific interaction and the people directly engaged. This includes the interlocutors as well as individual entities named explicitly or implicitly in an utterance. Plural ends refer to those that impact individuals who are not specifically named or involved but who may bear witness to an interaction describing their social group, such as through a curated social media feed. This includes utterances that name groups or communities. Though they don't specifically discuss the ends of offensiveness or abusive language (Waseem et al., 2017) importantly highlight that many classification tasks can be understood in relation to whether they focus on language that is directed toward a specific individual or entity or whether they focus on language directed toward a generalized group. In discussing ends we posit that intergroup linguistic based recognition between parties are necessary but insufficient conditions for identifying offensive language with beneficial outcomes. A sufficient condition for allowing the presence of offensive language is the verifiable absence of harm.

But our argument with respect to the articulation of ends goes further. As a way to illustrate the sociological relevance of mock impoliteness in the context of drag queen discourse as a practice of "building a thick skin," we placed the concept in a history of ethical and spiritual practice of offensive language in the Cynic philosophy.

In both the case of mock impoliteness and the case of the Cynics there are distinct yet connected practices of engaging with adversarial conditions and social norms. The Cynic use of offensive speech is focused on creating a space for the practice of a virtuous way of life actualized via systematic practices of training and endurance. Offense as a public act of provocation instantiates the ethical substance of a "life of battle and struggle against and for others (Foucault and Foucault, 2012)." queer practices of building thick skin via offensive speech is similarly defined by the preservation and self-expression of a social identity. In this way, queer mock impoliteness also stands as an example of reclaiming offensive language, which has been studied and documented in relation to social justice targets, such as misogyny (Gaucher et al., 2015) and ableism (Smith, 2012).

4 Rethinking Offensiveness for Machine Learning Practice

In our assessment of mock impoliteness, we motivate a relational frame with an example of marginal discourse to bring attention to social relations reflective of power dynamics in society. However this does not emerge from a void. Rather, it is grounded in a broad range of conceptual precedents that articulate the social, ethical and epistemological role of relationality. For example, Foucault's analyzes power (pouvoir) as a techno-social relation of subjection (Foucault, 2012) and of freedom (Foucault, 1982), Arendt theorizes power as a capacity to act in concert with others (Arendt, 2013), Weber understands power (Macht) as the exercise of a will on another will (Weber, 2019), and Patricia Hill Collins' analysis of lived experience within the domain of Black feminist epistemologies are key to our argument (Collins, 2002). In particular, Hill Collins analyzes the "connections between knowledge and power relations" and the particular forms of knowledge operative in Black women's lived experience.

In all of these cases, relationality unveils and constitutes new forms of knowledge, new forms of ethical action, and new forms of individual and collective experience. More specifically, in the space of AI ethics, Birhane (2021) discusses relational ethics as a "framework" that re-examines "hierarchical power asymmetries," how the "contingent and interconnected background that algorithmic systems emerge from (and are deployed to) in the process of protecting the welfare of the most vulnerable." Cooper et al. (2022) put forward a framework for relational accountability, Viljoen (2021) proposes a relational theory of data governance which shows how "data relations result in supra-individual legal interests" that in turn "materialize unjust social relations" via data flows which order in particular ways social existence.

At the conceptual level a relational frame shows that particular social and historical context is crucial to account for how offensive speech emerges and is constituted in a network of social relations by introducing discursive markers of style (as our example of mock impoliteness in drag queen shows) rather than relying on the perceived essential attribute of words or phrases. It also lays the foundation for practical experimentation and highlights avenues for designing classification tasks and identifying what context must be accounted for in data annotation, dataset construction, and modeling techniques.

4.1 Providing Context to Annotators

Drawing from a relational frame, there are opportunities to improve annotation task design and data collection by leveraging intuitive human understandings of social context. For example, annotation task instructions can invoke relational context that humans implicitly use to judge the offensive nature of language. Sap et al. (2019) introduced dialect priming to annotators as a contextual cue to the origins of an utterance. They primed annotators with a measure of an utterances' alignment with AAE, which significantly reduced the degree to which they rated AAE utterances as toxic. In addition, when asked to consider the tweet author's likely race, annotators were also less likely to identify AAE tweets as toxic.

Identifying an utterance as in alignment with AAE implicitly introduces sociologically informed norms about language use, the contexts in which it is likely to be used and consented to, and broader social context about how language produced by the likely author may be perceived. However, other work has found limited success in providing annotators with more context (Pavlopoulos et al., 2020). More work is needed to explore how exactly annotators use additional context, and in which instances additional context is most influential it is not clear exactly how annotators used contextual information to make sense of the tweet prompts.

Moreover, research is needed to explore the role of context in data annotation, for example, to explore avenues of capturing why a rater may annotate utterances the way that they do. Annotators' sense making practices– how they rely on different contextual clues when making judgments– remain generally unclear in text labeling. Significant correlations have been shown between annotators' political views and their ratings of antiblack speech, suggesting that political viewpoints may also be worth considering or documenting when selecting annotators or evaluating interrater agreement (Sap et al., 2021). Similarly, Prabhakaran et al. (2021) found differences between black and non-black annotator's labels of sentiment on age-related text prompts. Conversely, little work has explored how raters fill in contextual gaps when details are not provided, for example what kinds of assumptions might be made about the producer of an utterance, which, in terms of race, critical race scholars would suggest Whiteness is assumed (Sue, 2006). Given the use of the globally distributed crowd workforce, the ways in which these assumptions may differ across regions also stands to be explored.

A parallel direction to highlighting additional social context is to select data annotators with the ability to recognize the sociological norms embedded in context. The recognition of the norms surrounding language use is predicated on knowledge of, experience with, or proximity to specific forms of language use. In this vein, machine learning researchers have highlighted a need for considering annotator social identity in both dataset documentation (Prabhakaran et al., 2021; Díaz et al., 2022) as well as in modeling techniques (Davani et al., 2021). In Sap et al. (2019)'s work it is not clear whether and how individual annotators may have taken race and dialect information into account when making judgments.

However, prior work on data annotation by Patton et al. (2019) shows that annotators' social identity and lived experiences can shape the cues they draw from when making annotation judgments. Moreover, they demonstrate that lived experience can inform different judgments in comparison with annotators who have been formally educated and trained on the concepts being annotated. This has particularly important implications for the annotation of linguistic phenomena such as mock impoliteness by drag queens and others in the queer community, which may not be familiar or legible to annotators who do not share a queer social identity.

Mock impoliteness and the Cynic thought are key to unveiling historical and sociological reasons for offensiveness language use. We rely on the intuition that annotators with knowledge and/or shared group membership are more likely to be exposed to sociological norms used within their own social groups than to norms in other groups. For members of marginalized groups, recognizing these sociological norms is also an implicit recognition of the social and ethical modes of resistance that they represent and embody. At the same time, it is critical to acknowledge that no social group is monolithic, so there are inherent limits to both the degree to which members are representative of other members as well as the degree to which they can be expected to recognize mock impoliteness from other in-group members.

4.2 Ends and Outcomes of Offensiveness

Another avenue for improving offensiveness classification is to bring its measurable outcomes into focus. Treating offensive language as a means to an end underscores decisions about which of its different ends we seek to identify, whether beneficial in the case of queer resistance or more negative in cases of insult. Identifying which impacts to focus on can shift design and implementation practices.

By bringing focus to the likelihood of offensive language to cause a person to disengage from interaction, toxicity as defined by Jigsaw provides an example of incorporating measurable ends into the definition of the classification task. As such, the definition inspires specific behaviors or outcomes to be measured. Acknowledging the ways in which members of marginalized communities stand to be disproportionately harmed, it is also prudent to consider how people with marginalized identities may respond to negative or harmful language differently from others. For example, because they are more likely to endure disrespectful or harassing language, people with marginalized identities may endure offensive language in interactions longer than others. This means that a behavioral measure, such as exiting a conversation, may be differently predictive of offensiveness depending on the social identities of targets involved.

Nonetheless, capturing offensive language under the label 'toxicity' is an interesting departure from other labels used to describe offensiveness, such as 'misogynous' or 'aggressive', because of its focus on using observable behavior as a metric. Mishra et al. (2019) also take into account observable behavior by modeling sexist and racist tweets using author profiles. Doing so captured repeated behaviors and hateful discourses represented in certain profiles and improved model performance. Modeling user profile discourse stands as a way to combine language modeling with measurable behavior for identifying offensive language. As Cheng et al. (2017) show, trolling behavior can be predicted, in part, from user mood as measured through recent user history, which offers a signal of unwanted speech. . Of course, not all offensive language is produced by online trolls and not all online trolls produce offensive language. However, as Mishra et al. show, capturing histories of behavior and interactions, including their associated norms and patterns of speech can be an avenue for using behavioral measures to improve language modeling.

Bringing focus to platform and account-level behavior also affords the ability to infer additional social context, such as user political alignment, which scholars have predicted based on interactions and follower lists on Twitter (Colleoni et al., 2014). In addition, Hovy (2015) found that training gender- and age-"aware" classifiers using embeddings created from user reviews filtered by author age and gender provided modest, consistent improvements in topic classification and sentiment analysis tasks. Using similar techniques, information about content producers might be used to prevent their content from over-moderation, which Oliva et al. suggest impacts drag queens on Twitter. As yet another alternative, modeling discourse and discursive styles might be used to allow perceivers to selectively filter out undesired language from their social media feeds. At the platform level, this raises the potential for serious privacy and surveillance concerns which must be considered. However, even at the level of individual interactions, work in NLP has shown it is possible to identify aspects of interpersonal communication in chat contexts, such as whether a relation is cooperative (Rashid et al., 2020).

Operationalizing offensiveness in terms of specific ends also allows developers to focus on particular harms and, for content moderation, add specificity to whether individual or symbolic harms may be at stake. On platforms where individual interactions may be visible to many, such as Twitter, there are murky questions about how to prioritize impacts on targets in comparison to impacts on perceivers if and when they diverge. For example, a digital passerby (perceiver) who is unfamiliar with queer mock impoliteness may take offense based on language used within a tweet, even if the tweet producer and receiver are mutually engaging in mock impoliteness. More broadly, misunderstandings of mock impoliteness might normalize offensive language use for those who do not recognize its contextual nature. Platforms must consider if and in which circumstances impacts to perceivers, who may interpret a message as earnest, warrant consideration over the target of the message.

These considerations are particularly salient in regard to platforms that allow one-to-many communication, however they are also relevant for platforms or spaces limited to private or one-on-one interactions. Certain kinds of language that we have not discussed here, for example antisemitic utterances, may be harmful even if the recipient is not offended and no third party reads the content (e.g., if the content is shared in a private message). As such messages can incite violence or hate by asserting that some groups or individuals are of lower value than others, these messages can cause harm. This may warrant their detection and prohibition on a given platform.

4.3 Limits to Modeling Context

Identifying context and the ends of offensiveness as key components for defining offensiveness raises challenges and illustrates limits to developing automated classification tasks. One major difficulty lies in inferring or recording contextual data.

Social identity has been a through line in our examples of the role context plays in both how offensiveness operates as well as in machine learning annotation. However, annotating or documenting social identity, in particular, becomes challenging and ethically dubious, as Scheuerman et al. (2020) discuss with regard to gender and race annotation for computer vision. NLP techniques that have been used to infer or extract demographic characteristics such as age (Hovy and Søgaard, 2015), can provide helpful approximations; however they are limited by similar ethical concerns to annotation. Moreover, identifying social characteristics of an individual or group targeted in, receiving, or perceiving an utterance may be impossible to determine. Documenting demographic information of data annotators and explicitly inviting reflection on identity to broaden the sociological norms a rater pool is able to recognize may be a promising alternative. Importantly, this requires limits to protect the privacy of workers, particularly if workers with marginalized identities are repeatedly sought out for their ability to recognize how people in their communities communicate. This is to say that evaluating the social identities of actors involved in an online interaction, as well as the social identities of those perceiving or annotating the interaction, is a hurdle. Indeed, social media platforms often allow degrees of anonymity that make such a task impossible to do with any reliability.

Importantly, we cannot rely on social identity alone to determine whether a person will be offended by language or not. Social identity groups are not monolithic and identity likely has varying ability to predict dynamics in different geographic regions or for members new to group sociality. In addition, social identity is fluid across contexts and time. An obvious example is a change in one's age over time, but even at the same age, one may identify as young or old relative to the individuals they are with. It may make sense to consider social identity in relation to the specific temporal context of an utterance, yet headline news stories about prominent individuals who have lied about their social identities, such as Rachel Dolezal[3], offer a clear example of cases where social interactions once considered innocuous undergo re-evaluation. In other words, what is the identity that should be annotated or documented, and what bearing should this have on future classification of this language? More broadly, there are hard limits to inferring cultural context on the global web, which introduces challenges to identifying potential harms of offensive language, and adds difficulty to observing or measuring these ends compared with those of individual harms. For these reasons, user interface components that allow users to provide direct input on potentially offensive content remain valuable.

Detection and moderation practices that are unable to distinguish sociological patterns underpinning mock impoliteness stand to target it as well as underlying practices of reclaiming language. Indeed, Oliva et al. (2020) precisely raise censorship of drag queens' mock impoliteness as motivation for their work. Evidence of racial biases in offensive language classification and reports of the negative impacts of 'race-blind' approaches to content moderation also suggest that poorly targeted detection approaches may disproportionately impact marginalized communities. Due to the limits introduced by detecting social identity and observing platform behavior, language models are unlikely to identify mock impoliteness language in all cases. In practice, selecting a set of annotators aligned with the communities and sociological norms represented in data is nontrivial. There are also limits to the types and amounts of sociodemographic information that can or should be collected about data annotators and users. However, as offensive language classification improves, insights into providing context in annotation can also serve to shape content moderation processes, for example, by incorporating similar context for human review of content. In this respect, our work contributes to the development of frameworks of analysis attuned to sociological and historical modes of discourse that are critical for the responsible deployment of offensive language classification tasks.

5 Conclusion

Contrary to common understandings of offensive language as negative and harmful, we show that offensive speech can function as a practice of resistance to unjust social norms and, in specific cases, can serve a socially beneficial role. In doing so we highlight three necessary criteria for evaluating offensive language, 1) the subject of an offensive utterance and their social position, 2) the outcomes of offensive language, and 3) the sociological role that offensiveness and offense serves. Queer mock impoliteness specifically illustrates that, although sarcasm, humor, and irony pose significant challenges to existing classification tasks, there is an ethical and social need to account for subversive uses of denotatively offensive language. This type of reappropriated speech serves to solidify a collective identity, protect ingroup members from outgroup abuse, and resist exclusionary and restrictive social norms. The practice finds its historical emergence in a different yet related practice of training for adversity put forward by the Cynics in which offensive discourse works as a way to challenge unreflective societal norms. Although operationalizing a relational definition of offensiveness comes with challenges, such as practical and ethical limits to observing social identity and user behavior, we point to promising research directions to better account for the expressly beneficial sociological role that offensiveness can play in social discourse.

References

Hannah Arendt. 2013. *The human condition*. University of Chicago press.

[3]https://www.theguardian.com/us-news/2017/feb/25/rachel-dolezal-not-going-stoop-apologise-grovel

A Ashwitha, G Shruthi, HR Shruthi, Makarand Upadhyaya, Abhra Pratip Ray, and TC Manjunath. 2021. Sarcasm detection in natural language processing. *Materials Today: Proceedings*, 37:3324–3331.

Agathe Balayn, Jie Yang, Zoltan Szlavik, and Alessandro Bozzon. 2021. Automatic Identification of Harmful, Aggressive, Abusive, and Offensive Language on the Web: A Survey of Technical Biases Informed by Psychology Literature. *ACM Transactions on Social Computing*, 4(3):1–56.

Valerio Basile, Cristina Bosco, Elisabetta Fersini, Nozza Debora, Viviana Patti, Francisco Manuel Rangel Pardo, Paolo Rosso, Manuela Sanguinetti, et al. 2019. Semeval-2019 task 5: Multilingual detection of hate speech against immigrants and women in twitter. In *13th International Workshop on Semantic Evaluation*, pages 54–63. Association for Computational Linguistics.

Abeba Birhane. 2021. Algorithmic injustice: a relational ethics approach. *Patterns*, 2(2):100205.

Justin Cheng, Michael Bernstein, Cristian Danescu-Niculescu-Mizil, and Jure Leskovec. 2017. Anyone can become a troll: Causes of trolling behavior in online discussions. In *Proceedings of the 2017 ACM conference on computer supported cooperative work and social computing*, pages 1217–1230.

Elanor Colleoni, Alessandro Rozza, and Adam Arvidsson. 2014. Echo chamber or public sphere? predicting political orientation and measuring political homophily in twitter using big data. *Journal of communication*, 64(2):317–332.

Patricia Hill Collins. 2002. *Black feminist thought: Knowledge, consciousness, and the politics of empowerment*. routledge.

A Feder Cooper, Benjamin Laufer, Emanuel Moss, and Helen Nissenbaum. 2022. Accountability in an algorithmic society: Relationality, responsibility, and robustness in machine learning. *arXiv preprint arXiv:2202.05338*.

Jonathan Culpeper. 2011. *Impoliteness: Using language to cause offence*, volume 28. Cambridge University Press.

Aida Mostafazadeh Davani, Mark Díaz, and Vinodkumar Prabhakaran. 2021. Dealing with disagreements: Looking beyond the majority vote in subjective annotations. *arXiv preprint arXiv:2110.05719*.

Mark Díaz, Ian Kivlichan, Rachel Rosen, Dylan K. Baker, Razvan Amironesei, Vinodkumar Prabhakaran, and Emily Denton. 2022. Crowdworksheets: Accounting for individual and collective identities underlying crowdsourced dataset annotation. In *Proceedings of the 2022 ACM Conference on Fairness, Accountability, and Transparency*, FAccT '22. Association for Computing Machinery.

Michel Foucault. 1982. The subject and power. *Critical inquiry*, 8(4):777–795.

Michel Foucault. 2012. *Discipline and punish: The birth of the prison*. Vintage.

Michel Foucault and Michel Foucault. 2012. *The courage of the truth: (the government of self and others II). Lectures at the collège de France, 1983 - 1984*. Palgrave Macmillan, Basingstoke.

Danielle Gaucher, Brianna Hunt, and Lisa Sinclair. 2015. Can pejorative terms ever lead to positive social consequences? The case of SlutWalk. *Language Sciences*, 52:121–130.

Pierre Hadot. 2002. *What is ancient philosophy?* Harvard University Press.

Dirk Hovy. 2015. Demographic factors improve classification performance. In *Proceedings of the 53rd annual meeting of the Association for Computational Linguistics and the 7th international joint conference on natural language processing (volume 1: Long papers)*, pages 752–762.

Dirk Hovy and Anders Søgaard. 2015. Tagging performance correlates with author age. In *Proceedings of the 53rd annual meeting of the Association for Computational Linguistics and the 7th international joint conference on natural language processing (volume 2: Short papers)*, pages 483–488.

Dirk Hovy and Diyi Yang. 2021. The Importance of Modeling Social Factors of Language: Theory and Practice. In *Proceedings of the 2021 Conference of the North American Chapter of the Association for Computational Linguistics: Human Language Technologies*, pages 588–602, Online. Association for Computational Linguistics.

Alice E Marwick and Danah Boyd. 2011. I tweet honestly, i tweet passionately: Twitter users, context collapse, and the imagined audience. *New media & society*, 13(1):114–133.

Sean McKinnon. 2017. "Building a thick skin for each other": The use of 'reading'as an interactional practice of mock impoliteness in drag queen backstage talk. *Journal of Language and Sexuality*, 6(1):90–127.

Pushkar Mishra, Marco Del Tredici, Helen Yannakoudakis, and Ekaterina Shutova. 2019. Author profiling for hate speech detection. *arXiv preprint arXiv:1902.06734*.

Stephen O Murray. 1979. The art of gay insulting. *Anthropological Linguistics*, 21(5):211–223.

Thiago Dias Oliva, Dennys Marcelo Antonialli, and Alessandra Gomes. 2021. Fighting hate speech, silencing drag queens? artificial intelligence in content moderation and risks to lgbtq voices online. *Sexuality & Culture*, 25(2):700–732.

Desmond Patton, Philipp Blandfort, William Frey, Michael Gaskell, and Svebor Karaman. 2019. Annotating social media data from vulnerable populations: Evaluating disagreement between domain experts and graduate student annotators. In *Proceedings of the 52nd Hawaii International Conference on System Sciences*.

John Pavlopoulos, Jeffrey Sorensen, Lucas Dixon, Nithum Thain, and Ion Androutsopoulos. 2020. Toxicity Detection: Does Context Really Matter? In *Proceedings of the 58th Annual Meeting of the Association for Computational Linguistics*, pages 4296–4305, Online. Association for Computational Linguistics.

Vinodkumar Prabhakaran, Aida Mostafazadeh Davani, and Mark Diaz. 2021. On Releasing Annotator-Level Labels and Information in Datasets. In *Proceedings of The Joint 15th Linguistic Annotation Workshop (LAW) and 3rd Designing Meaning Representations (DMR) Workshop*, pages 133–138, Punta Cana, Dominican Republic. Association for Computational Linguistics.

Farzana Rashid, Tommaso Fornaciari, Dirk Hovy, Eduardo Blanco, and Fernando Vega-Redondo. 2020. Helpful or hierarchical? predicting the communicative strategies of chat participants, and their impact on success. In *EMNLP| Findings*. Association for Computational Linguistics.

Maarten Sap, Dallas Card, Saadia Gabriel, Yejin Choi, and Noah A. Smith. 2019. The Risk of Racial Bias in Hate Speech Detection. In *Proceedings of the 57th Annual Meeting of the Association for Computational Linguistics*, pages 1668–1678, Florence, Italy. Association for Computational Linguistics.

Maarten Sap, Swabha Swayamdipta, Laura Vianna, Xuhui Zhou, Yejin Choi, and Noah A Smith. 2021. Annotators with Attitudes: How Annotator Beliefs And Identities Bias Toxic Language Detection. *arXiv preprint arXiv:2111.07997*.

Morgan Klaus Scheuerman, Kandrea Wade, Caitlin Lustig, and Jed R Brubaker. 2020. How We've Taught Algorithms to See Identity: Constructing Race and Gender in Image Databases for Facial Analysis. *Proceedings of the ACM on Human-Computer Interaction*, 4(CSCW1):1–35.

Tones Smith. 2012. Pathology, bias and queer diagnosis: a crip queer consciousness.

Yujian Sun, Ying Li, and Tingxuan Zhao. 2021. The improved neural network model in humor detection with traditional humor theory. In *2021 International Conference on Communications, Information System and Computer Engineering (CISCE)*, pages 549–554. IEEE.

Salome Viljoen. 2021. A relational theory of data governance. *Yale LJ*, 131:573.

Zeerak Waseem, Thomas Davidson, Dana Warmsley, and Ingmar Weber. 2017. Understanding Abuse: A Typology of Abusive Language Detection Subtasks. In *Proceedings of the First Workshop on Abusive Language Online*, pages 78–84, Vancouver, BC, Canada. Association for Computational Linguistics.

Max Weber. 2019. Economy and society. In *Economy and society*. Harvard University Press.

Leila Weitzel, Ronaldo Cristiano Prati, and Raul Freire Aguiar. 2016. The comprehension of figurative language: What is the influence of irony and sarcasm on NLP techniques? In *Sentiment analysis and ontology engineering*, pages 49–74. Springer.

Towards a Multi-Entity Aspect-Based Sentiment Analysis for Characterizing Directed Social Regard in Online Messaging

Joan Zheng, Scott Friedman, Sonja Schmer-Galunder, Ian Magnusson, Ruta Wheelock, Jeremy Gottlieb, Diana Gomez, Christopher Miller
SIFT
19 N 1st Ave., Suite 400, Minneapolis, MN 55401
{jzheng, friedman, sgalunder, imagnusson, rwheelock, jgottlieb, dgomez, cmiller}@sift.net

Abstract

Online messaging is dynamic, influential, and highly contextual, and a single post may contain contrasting sentiments towards multiple entities, such as dehumanizing one actor while empathizing with another in the same message. These complexities are important to capture for understanding the systematic abuse voiced within an online community, or for determining whether individuals are advocating for abuse, opposing abuse, or simply reporting abuse. In this work, we describe a formulation of directed social regard (DSR) as a problem of multi-entity aspect-based sentiment analysis (ME-ABSA), which models the degree of intensity of multiple sentiments that are associated with entities described by a text document. Our DSR schema is informed by Bandura's psychosocial theory of moral disengagement and by recent work in ABSA. We present a dataset of over 2,900 posts and sentences, comprising over 24,000 entities annotated for DSR over nine psychosocial dimensions by three annotators. We present a novel transformer-based ME-ABSA model for DSR, achieving favorable preliminary results on this dataset.

1 Introduction

The social media landscape is a complex, dynamic information environment where actors express advocacy, opposition, empathy, dehumanization, and various moralistic signals, with the intent—or sometimes the side-effect—of influencing others. A single message may also express multiple sentiments in one sentence, e.g., opposing one political candidate and endorsing another, or blaming one party for harming another, or dehumanizing one party and empathizing with another.

The complexity of multiple sentiments—which may comprise multiple strategies of influence—in a single message means that classifying an entire tweet's sentiment (Da Silva et al., 2014), or even quantifying it (Gao and Sebastiani, 2016), along a single dimension, is both at too high a granularity (i.e., we want to assess the author's perspective *on multiple topics*) and at too few dimensions (i.e., we want to assess the author's perspective *along multiple dimensions*).

Aspect-based sentiment analysis (ABSA) (Yang et al., 2018), allowing multiple dimensions of sentiment on a message, gets us part-way to a solution. Multi-entity ABSA (ME-ABSA) (Tao and Fang, 2020) gets us further in this direction by classifying along multiple dimensions across entities, but these models are frequently expressed as classification problems (e.g., **positive**, **neutral**, and **negative** predictions), and we desire a finer-grained numerical approach.

In the present work, we present a novel multi-entity transformer-based ABSA regression implementation of *directed social regard* (DSR), the prediction of social attitudes directed toward various actors and topics mentioned in the text. Social attitudes are modelled along nine continously-valued sentiment aspects: advocate, oppose, dehumanization, empathy, violent, condemn, justified, responsible, and harmed. Masked language modelling methods are utilized to support sets of aspects associated with each unique entity type. In the present work, DSR is computed for each *character* (i.e., human individual, human group, or ideology) in a message and each event that harms characters within a message. Also in the present work, the DSR dimensions are informed in part by Bandura's psychosocial theory of moral disengagement (Bandura, 1999, 2016), which we describe below.

To implement and validate our approach, three labelers rated nine dimensions of social regard for each character and event in a dataset of English-language social media posts sourced from curated Twitter datasets. To model DSR, we desitned a transformer-based regression architecture designed specifically for fine-grained sentiment analysis of

Proceedings of the Sixth Workshop on Online Abuse and Harms (WOAH), pages 203 - 208
July 14, 2022 ©2022 Association for Computational Linguistics

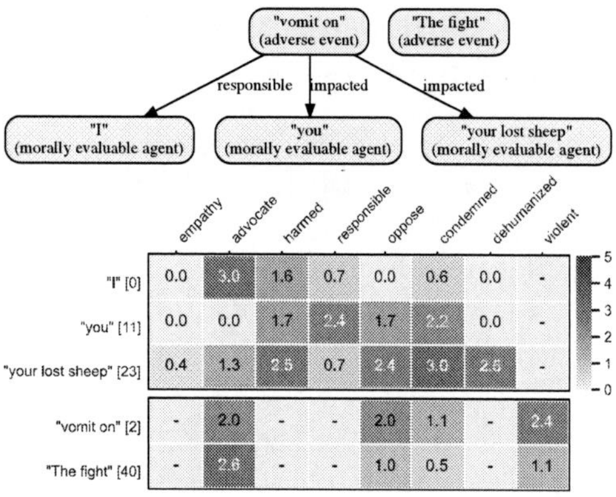

Figure 1: NLP output from "I vomit on you and your lost sheep. The fight is not over and never will be." adapted from a Kaggle social media dataset.

multiple entities.

We next describe the psychosocial theory of moral disengagement. We then describe our approach and empirical results, closing with a discussion of limitations and future work.

1.1 Moral Disengagement

People have the capacity for compassion and cruelty toward others—and both at the same time—depending on their moral values and on whom they include and exclude in their category of humanity (Bandura, 1999, 2016). These are matters of *moral disengagement*, the psychosocial mechanisms of selectively disengaging self-sanctions from inhumane or detrimental conduct.

Evidence of moral disengagement is present in modern hate speech: social media contains calls to violence against outsiders (Kennedy et al., 2018; Hoover et al., 2020); online forums dehumanize girls and women (Ging, 2019; Hoffman et al., 2020); and the manifestos of violent actors justify their actions by dehumanizing and blaming others (Peters et al., 2019). We have evidence that hate speech with these indicators increases prejudice through desensitization (Soral et al., 2018)—and that the frequency of this language is related to the frequency of violent acts in the world (Olteanu et al., 2018)—so understanding moral disengagement has real-world importance.

2 Approach

We describe our knowlege graph and attibute schema, sources of textual data, annotation process, and our architecture for representing and scoring attributes of social regard.

2.1 DSR Schema

Our DSR schema for a single social media post includes (1) a simple knowledge graph representation adapted from previous work in social media NLP (withheld for review), and (2) nine numerical intensity ratings on said characters and events to capture the directed social regard of the author, which is the primary focus of this work. An example of the system's output for a public Kaggle dataset tweet is shown in Figure 1. This was not part of our training dataset, so this is a novel machine prediction. We use this example to describe our schema.

The knowledge graph contains two types of *entities*, each comprising a span (i.e., contiguous span of tokens) in the text: (1) **characters**, also known as **morally evaluable agents**, comprising the author, human individuals, ethnicities, organizations, religions, ideologies, and geopolitical entities, and (2) **adverse events** that may cause harm or be morally questionable as described by the author. In Figure 1, the characters are "I," "you," and "your lost sheep," since the latter was inferred to refer to people in this context. The events include "vomit on" and "the fight."

The DSR values capture sentiment according to dimensions of moral disengagement described above, in addition to sentiment analysis, as expressed by the author of the text. For each dimension we describe whether it was motivated by Bandura's (1999, 2016) moral disengagement theory ^{B} or by sentiment analysis ^{S} and whether it applies to characters ^{c} or events ^{e} or both.

1. **Advocate**: Endorsement or support of an entity by the author.^{S,c,e}
2. **Oppose**: Opposition or adversarial attitude to an entity by the author.^{S,c,e}
3. **Dehumanization**: Actor described with non-human or lesser-than-human attributes, diminishing their agency or humanity.^{B,c}
4. **Empathy**: Actor described with empathy, compassion, humanity.^{B,c}
5. **Violent**: Event described as having literal or metaphorical physical or sexual violence.^{B,e}
6. **Condemn**: Entity morally condemned.^{B,c,e}
7. **Justified**: Entity morally justified.^{B,c,e}
8. **Responsible (for harm)**: Actor described as causing harm to others or to themselves.^{B,c}
9. **Harmed**: Actor described as being harmed by themselves or others.^{B,c}

Each of the Bandura-motivated dimensions captures a factor of moral disengagement: diminishing or accentuating humanity indicates whether the author might include the target in their circle of humanity; descriptions of violence and responsibility for harm are indicators of blame or advocacy for violence; mention of harmed individuals (including oneself) is an indicator of victimization and potential justification of subsequent action; and moral condemnation and justification indicate a moral standpoint for adverse events.

The heat-map in Figure 1 shows the nine moral dimensions across all of the characters and events from this example, where "your lost sheep" are the ony ones dehumanized.

2.2 Dataset and Annotation Methodology

Documents were selected from text posts known to contain online abuse or hate speech, including the Moral Foundations Twitter Corpus (Hoover et al., 2020); the Gab Hate Corpus (Kennedy et al., 2018); *How ISIS Uses Twitter* dataset from Kaggle (Khuram, 2017); and Manosphere community text posts (Ribeiro et al., 2020).

To optimize for content eligible for fine-grained sentiment analysis, documents were considered only if they met three criteria: (1) written in 280 or fewer characters; (2) written in English words or emoticons; and (3) contained more content than user mentions, URLs, or links to images.

Three English speakers were hired on the Prolific survey platform (Palan and Schitter, 2018) to score entities for DSR attributes. Out of our collected documents, 2,907 documents that met our criteria were annotated by at least two of our human annotators. These annotations contain a total of 24,425 unique entities. Annotators were asked to rate entities for each sentiment using a scale ranging from zero (not present) to five (most intense).

To measure inter-annotator agreement between our three human raters, we compute Krippendorff's α (Krippendorff, 2011) for each of the nine aspects, as shown in Table 1.

For drawing tentative conclusions, Krippendorff recommends using variables with reliabilities above $\alpha = 0.667$ (Krippendorff, 2018), which are achieved by our aspects **violent** and **oppose**. Both these aspects were labeled with intensity 4-5 more frequently compared to other aspects. For training and testing purposes, we identified annotations with high agreement as those where annotators

Aspect	A1	A2	A3	α
advocate	21.4%	16.1%	18.0%	0.366
condemned	20.4%	8.0%	10.5%	0.477
dehumanized	2.7%	3.8%	5.4%	0.591
empathy	1.0%	12.6%	3.2%	-0.065
harmed	7.9%	10.8%	9.2%	0.580
justified	7.3%	4.1%	1.5%	0.171
oppose	24.0%	25.4%	36.2%	0.672
responsible	11.2%	13.6%	8.0%	0.607
violent	4.1%	5.6%	8.0%	0.753

Table 1: Nonzero label usage comparision across our three annotators (A1-3) across 24,245 entities and nine aspect labels, along a five point intensity scale. Also includes Krippendorff's α.

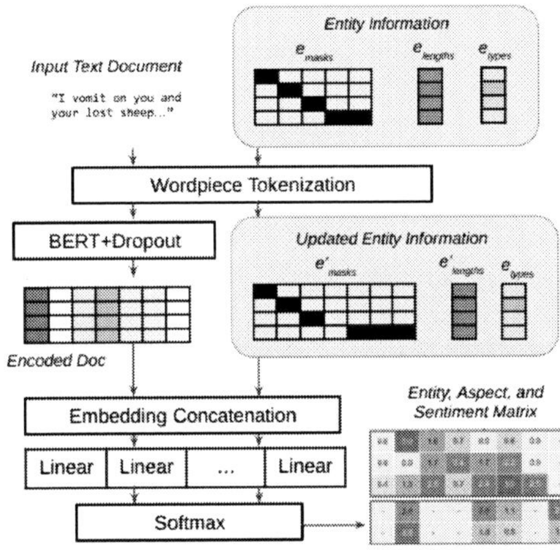

Figure 2: An overview of the ABSA architecture optimized for the DSR task.

falling within two standard units of each other, and with a maximum difference of two intensity units. These selection criteria limit disagreements while maintaining moderate-intensity aspects.

2.3 Architecture

We used two transformer-based NLP models: (1) an entity- and relation-extractor based on the SpERT architecture (Eberts and Ulges, 2020) to extract characters and entities comprising one or more continuous tokens in the text and (2) a novel ABSA-based model that scores each character or entity for the applicable DSR dimensions.

Importantly, for training and testing the DSR performance, we only use the human-annotated characters and events; we do not train or test the DSR model on machine-predicted entities, but this is how we envision applying the model on novel texts. We focus on the ABSA/DSR in this paper.

ABSA/DSR Architecture. The input for the DSR ABSA model is a text with entities annotated with (1) token start/end indices and (2) entity type (i.e., **character** or **event**). These may be either manually annotated (as we have done in our evaluation) or automatically predicted from a entity recognition system, e.g., (Eberts and Ulges, 2020; Friedman et al., 2021).

As shown in Figure 2, the text document is processed by a pre-trained BERT (Devlin et al., 2019) embedding layer using wordpiece tokenization. An interaction layer creates a fixed-dimentional pooled matrix, which contains a concatenation of BERT-encoded document and its entities represented as masked token sequences, the collection of masks for each entity type, and the lengths of each token span. These separate sequences are concatenated together as a matrix to support batch evaluation along multiple entities by the linear aspect classifiers.

This matrix representation feeds into a separate linear layers for each DSR aspect. Which entity gets graded by each linear layer is determined by the type of entity (e.g., as shown in Figure 1, an **event** entity does not have a **dehumanized** DSR aspect). This is implemented when multiplying the concatenated input matrix by the entity mask, which creates a matrix with nonzero inputs at the same indices as the linear layers it is eligible to be scored by. A softmax activation function calcuates the prediction associated with each aspect.

3 Experiment

We evaluated the DSR/ABSA architecture on the above dataset with the above DSR schema. We used human-labeled characters and events as inputs for this experiment in order to focus the evaluation on the DSR rather than the span extraction, but we report that on a 90/10 train/test split, the entity extractor scored F1 scores of 0.95 and 0.73 for extracting characters and events, allowing determiner mismatch, e.g., an event "the airstrikes" is allowed to match to "airstrikes."

We use the pre-trained, case-sensitive BERT-base model for fine-tuning (12 transformer blocks, 768-size hidden layer, 12 attention heads, and 110M total parameters). We fine-tuned with dropout probability 0.1 for 3 epochs, and we trained with learning rate 2e-5. Train, evaluation, and test splits were generated from our social media dataset using by creating 60/20/20 splits.

Aspect	R^2	RMSE
advocate	0.257	1.285
condemned	0.259	1.293
dehumanized	0.130	0.649
empathy	0.150	0.752
harmed	0.194	0.968
justified	0.207	1.037
oppose	0.284	1.419
responsible	0.207	1.037
violent	0.114	0.572

Table 2: ABSA/DSR model performance: R^2 measures correlation between human and machine ratings and RMSE measures prediction error. Averaged RMSE is 1.00 out of five units of intensity.

Results. Results are shown in Table 2, with lowest error (i.e., RMSE) on **violent**, **dehumanized**, and **empathy** dimensions. As mentioned above, **violent** was one of the more intensely-rated aspects and had highest α score, so we believe this contributed to successful learning. The aspect **dehumanized**—and its dual, **empathy**—are central to Bandura's theory of moral disengagement.

The average RMSE across aspects was 1.00 of a 5-point intensity scale, and all R^2 results directly correlated, explaining between 11-29% of variance in annotators' intensity scores across aspects. We regard these results as preliminary but encouraging for continued work in this domain.

4 Discussion and Future Work

We have described an approach to encoding the directed social regard (DSR) of authors toward events and actors in their posts, informed by Bandura's (1999, 2016) psychosocial theory of moral disengagement. This helps characterize abuse and harm in online messaging, including the advocacy and opposition to said abuse and harm, by highlighting entities that are associated with aspects associated with moral disengagement.

Our transformer-based approach uses a multi-entity aspect-based sentiment analysis (ME-ABSA) treatment to represent and predict DSR across nine psychosocial dimensions. We provide empirical evidence that transformer-based architectures can detect relevant actors and events and then predict human DSR ratings within reasonable preliminary error bounds.

Limitations and Future Work. One factor likely reducing the performance of our DSR model is the imbalanced representation of sentiment labels in our dataset. There is a scarcity of examples in our dataset of entities that are associated with some sentiments, particularly moderate to positive sentiments labels and sentiments with low to moderate degrees of intensity. As shown in Table 1, annotators used aspect labels **empathy** and **justified** less frequently than other sentiment aspects in our schema, and was not able to reach a reliably high degree of agreement when annotating these sentiments. To improve the capability of our directed social regard model for applications outside of the domain of online abuse and hate, it would be beneficial to learn from examples that contain a more diverse selection of sentiments expressed, such as examples associated with positive to neutral sentiments as well as examples that contain a balanced range of low, moderate, and high degrees of intensity.

Acknowledgements

This material is based upon work supported by the Defense Advanced Research Projects Agency (DARPA) under Contract No. HR001121C0186 and Contract No. FA86650-19-6017. Any opinions, findings and conclusions or recommendations expressed in this material are those of the authors and do not necessarily reflect the views of the Defense Advanced Research Projects Agency (DARPA).

References

Albert Bandura. 1999. Moral disengagement in the perpetration of inhumanities. *Personality and social psychology review*, 3(3):193–209.

Albert Bandura. 2016. *Moral disengagement: How people do harm and live with themselves*. Worth publishers.

Nadia FF Da Silva, Eduardo R Hruschka, and Estevam R Hruschka Jr. 2014. Tweet sentiment analysis with classifier ensembles. *Decision support systems*, 66:170–179.

Jacob Devlin, Ming-Wei Chang, Kenton Lee, and Kristina Toutanova. 2019. BERT: Pre-training of deep bidirectional transformers for language understanding. In *Proceedings of NAACL-HLT 2019*, pages 4171–4186, Minneapolis, Minnesota. Association for Computational Linguistics.

Markus Eberts and Adrian Ulges. 2020. Span-based joint entity and relation extraction with transformer pre-training. *24th European Conference on Artificial Intelligence*.

Scott Friedman, Ian Magnusson, Vasanth Sarathy, and Sonja Schmer-Galunder. 2021. From unstructured text to causal knowledge graphs: A transformer-based approach. In *Proceedings of the 2021 Conference on Advances in Cognitive Systems*.

Wei Gao and Fabrizio Sebastiani. 2016. From classification to quantification in tweet sentiment analysis. *Social Network Analysis and Mining*, 6(1):1–22.

Debbie Ging. 2019. Alphas, betas, and incels: Theorizing the masculinities of the manosphere. *Men and Masculinities*, 22(4):638–657.

Bruce Hoffman, Jacob Ware, and Ezra Shapiro. 2020. Assessing the threat of incel violence. *Studies in Conflict & Terrorism*, 43(7):565–587.

Joe Hoover, Gwenyth Portillo-Wightman, Leigh Yeh, Shreya Havaldar, Aida Mostafazadeh Davani, Ying Lin, Brendan Kennedy, Mohammad Atari, Zahra Kamel, Madelyn Mendlen, et al. 2020. Moral foundations twitter corpus: A collection of 35k tweets annotated for moral sentiment. *Social Psychological and Personality Science*, 11(8):1057–1071.

Brendan Kennedy, Mohammad Atari, Aida Mostafazadeh Davani, Leigh Yeh, Ali Omrani, Yehsong Kim, Kris Coombs, Shreya Havaldar, Gwenyth Portillo-Wightman, Elaine Gonzalez, et al. 2018. The gab hate corpus: A collection of 27k posts annotated for hate speech.

Zaman Khuram. 2017. How isis uses twitter.

Klaus Krippendorff. 2011. Computing krippendorff's alpha-reliability.

Klaus Krippendorff. 2018. *Content analysis: An introduction to its methodology*. Sage publications.

Alexandra Olteanu, Carlos Castillo, Jeremy Boy, and Kush Varshney. 2018. The effect of extremist violence on hateful speech online. In *Proceedings of the International AAAI Conference on Web and Social Media*.

Stefan Palan and Christian Schitter. 2018. Prolific. ac—a subject pool for online experiments. *Journal of Behavioral and Experimental Finance*, 17:22–27.

Jeremy Peters, Michael Grynbaum, Keith Collins, Rich Harris, and Rumsey Taylor. 2019. How the El Paso Killer Echoed the Incendiary Words of Conservative Media Stars.

Manoel Horta Ribeiro, Jeremy Blackburn, Barry Bradlyn, Emiliano De Cristofaro, Gianluca Stringhini, Summer Long, Stephanie Greenberg, and Savvas Zannettou. 2020. From pick-up artists to incels: a data-driven sketch of the manosphere. *arXiv preprint arXiv:2001.07600*.

Wiktor Soral, Michał Bilewicz, and Mikołaj Winiewski. 2018. Exposure to hate speech increases prejudice through desensitization. *Aggressive behavior*, 44(2):136–146.

Jie Tao and Xing Fang. 2020. Toward multi-label sentiment analysis: a transfer learning based approach. *Journal of Big Data*, 7(1):1–26.

Jun Yang, Runqi Yang, Chongjun Wang, and Junyuan Xie. 2018. Multi-entity aspect-based sentiment analysis with context, entity and aspect memory. In *Proceedings of the AAAI Conference on Artificial Intelligence*, volume 32.

Flexible text generation for counterfactual fairness probing

Zee Fryer* **Vera Axelrod** **Ben Packer** **Alex Beutel** **Jilin Chen** **Kellie Webster**
Google Research
{zeef, vaxelrod, bpacker, alexbeutel, jilinc, websterk}@google.com

Abstract

A common approach for testing fairness issues in text-based classifiers is through the use of counterfactuals: does the classifier output change if a sensitive attribute in the input is changed? Existing counterfactual generation methods typically rely on wordlists or templates, producing simple counterfactuals that don't take into account grammar, context, or subtle sensitive attribute references, and could miss issues that the wordlist creators had not considered. In this paper, we introduce a task for generating counterfactuals that overcomes these shortcomings, and demonstrate how large language models (LLMs) can be leveraged to make progress on this task. We show that this LLM-based method can produce complex counterfactuals that existing methods cannot, comparing the performance of various counterfactual generation methods on the Civil Comments dataset and showing their value in evaluating a toxicity classifier.

Original: True and the same goes with [headscarves]. Its not religious requirement but a cultural choice. Simple otherwise there would be no [Muslim woman] that don't wear them and clearly there are.

Counterfactual: True and the same goes with [yarmulkes]. Its not [a] religious requirement but a cultural choice. Simple otherwise there would be no [Jewish man] that don't wear them and clearly there are.

Figure 1: Counterfactual generated by our LLM-based method, given the original text and the prompt "make this not about Muslims".

1 Introduction

It is well known that classifiers (such as toxicity detectors) can pick up negative associations about marginalized groups from their training data, e.g. due to under-representation of those groups in the training data, or the higher levels of toxicity in the text data referring to these groups (Sap et al., 2019; Dixon et al., 2018; Zhou et al., 2021).

One common method of testing classifier models for these unwanted associations is by comparing the classifier's outputs on a particular type of counterfactual text pair: specifically, text pairs which are as similar as possible in format and meaning, but such that one text references a particular sensitive attribute and the other does not (Figure 1; here the sensitive attribute is Islam). If the classifier exhibits a large number of "flips" (changes in prediction from original to counterfactual) on these pairs, this indicates a potential problem that may be addressed through mitigations such as dataset augmentation (Dixon et al., 2018) or counterfactual logit pairing (Garg et al., 2019).

Here we focus on counterfactual generation, and specifically the following questions: 1) How can we efficiently generate large datasets of counterfactual pairs? 2) While preserving the diversity, fluency and complexity of real-world inputs? 3) To probe for subtle or previously-unknown issues?

One approach is to ask humans to create counterfactual counterparts by editing existing examples, but this can be both costly and slow (see e.g. §3 in Kaushik et al. (2020)). Another method is to use human-curated wordlists to generate counterfactuals: for example to apply ablation or substitution on existing texts or to fill in preset templates (Garg et al., 2019; Dixon et al., 2018; Rudinger et al., 2018; Sheng et al., 2019a). While these approaches can efficiently generate large datasets (excluding the time required to create the initial wordlists), the results often fail to be fluent, diverse or complex (as we show in Section 5) and are not likely to uncover novel issues that the wordlist creators had not considered.

We suspect that as it becomes more common to use large language models (LLMs) as the base for

*Work done as a Google AI Resident.

Proceedings of the Sixth Workshop on Online Abuse and Harms (WOAH), pages 209 - 229
July 14, 2022 ©2022 Association for Computational Linguistics

classifier models (such as toxicity classifiers), these classifiers will become more sensitive to factors such as fluency, word order, and context, and counterfactual generation methods will need to evolve correspondingly to keep up.

With this in mind, we define a new counterfactual generation task (Section 3.1) and demonstrate the potential of existing LLM techniques to address this problem (Section 3.2). Specifically, we show how ideas from Reif et al. (2021) can be used to generate natural, diverse, and complex counterfactuals from real-world text examples (as in Figure 1) and combine this with both automated and human evaluation methods (Section 3.3) to ensure that the resulting counterfactuals are of high quality and suited to the task at hand. This human-in-the-loop component also helps to mitigate the risks introduced by using an LLM to generate the text (Section 3.4). Finally, we compare the performance of our method with existing counterfactual generation methods (Section 5), and show that existing methods may not capture certain subtle issues in toxicity classifiers, and that our method addresses some of these deficiencies (Section 5.3).

We use toxicity detection as a testbed in this work, and focus on generating counterfactuals to probe for false positives – that is, non-toxic text which is misclassified as toxic due to identity references. While we focus on this particular application to demonstrate one way in which our framework can be useful, it could also be applied in other contexts: for example, probing for false negatives, applications other than toxicity detection, and counterfactual perturbations other than removing the presence of a sensitive attribute.

2 Related Work

2.1 Counterfactual generation

Two common types of counterfactual text pair generation are 1) rule-based methods using templates and/or wordlists, and 2) controlled text generation using deep learning-based language models.

Template-based counterfactual datasets are often built from short, simple sentences: for example, the Jigsaw Sentence Templates dataset consists of templates such as "I am a ⟨adjective⟩ ⟨identity-label⟩" and "I hate ⟨identity-label⟩".[1] Other examples include Rudinger et al. (2018); Sheng et al. (2019a). While this approach provides fine-grained control over identity references and toxicity balance, it also has disadvantages: for example, the resulting text is often not natural and looks quite different from the actual task data. Works such as Prabhakaran et al. (2019) and Hutchinson et al. (2020) partially mitigate this by using real-world data and targeting specific syntactic slots for substitution, but this can yield incoherent or contradictory text when there are multiple entities referenced in a sentence. Finally, recent works with templates such as Röttger et al. (2021) and Kirk et al. (2021) have been effective at detailing problems with modern toxicity classifiers, by investing significant targeted effort into probing task-specific functionality, and employing human validation for generated examples.

There have also been attempts to use deep learning to build more general-purpose counterfactual generators. One example is Polyjuice (Wu et al., 2021), which combines a finetuned GPT-2 model with control codes to generate diverse natural perturbations. But, as we show below, it is difficult to use Polyjuice to modify references to a pre-specified topic. Another example is CAT-Gen (Wang et al., 2020), which trains an RNN-based encoder-decoder model, using a separate attribute classifier to guide the decoder towards the modifying the desired attribute. However, both of these require large training sets labeled by sentence permutation type (Polyjuice) or attribute (CAT-Gen).

Other methods combine a pretrained language model with a task-specific classifier, e.g. Dathathri et al. (2020) and Madaan et al. (2020) which both leverage Bayes' rule to guide text generation while avoiding the need to retrain or finetune the language model itself, and Davani et al. (2021) which uses GPT-2 to generate text and uses wordlists and likelihood thresholds to identify valid counterfactuals. ToxiGen (Hartvigsen et al., 2022) uses GPT-3 with and without an adversarial classifier-in-the-loop method to generate a large set of challenging examples for toxicity detection, employing identity-specific engineered prompts. Our method is most similar to these approaches, though we rely less on task-specific classifiers and use generic prompts.

2.2 Counterfactual evaluation

While most counterfactual generation work includes a definition of what constitutes a "good" counterfactual and some method of measuring success relative to these desiderata, the definitions and methods vary depending on factors such as the intended downstream use of the counterfactuals.

[1] `https://github.com/conversationai/unintended-ml-bias-analysis`

Attribute	Original	LLM-D **rewrite**
LGBQ+	How is "embracing and accepting" their *homosexuality* not a lifestyle choice?	How is "embracing and accepting" their **love** not a lifestyle choice?
transgender	Some people are born *transgender*. That appears to be a verifiable fact. Why is this a question of "left" or "right"?	Some people are born **left-handed**. That appears to be a verifiable fact. Why is this a question of "left" or "right"?
Judaism	Get *JPFO* up here. If anyone has anything to say about guns it is that organization. For those that do not know. *JPFO is Jews for the Preservation of Firearms.*	Get **the NRA** up here. If anyone has anything to say about guns it is that organization. For those that do not know. **NRA is for National Rifle Association**.
Islam	If its *Muslim* he's all over it.... I can't figure this guy's loyalty. Who is influencing this guy..... Is it the *Muslim Brotherhood, Saudi Arabia, Qatar*??	If it's **American** he's all over it.... I can't figure this guy's loyalty. Who is influencing this guy..... Is it the **Democrats, Republicans, Supreme court**??

Table 1: Examples of LLM-D-generated counterfactuals, demonstrating LLM-D's ability to make neutral context-aware substitutions or multiple consistent substitutions to remove explicit and implicit references.

Many methods prize counterfactuals with minimal edits relative to the original text and measure success using distance, e.g. Ross et al. (2021a) Madaan et al. (2020). However, this is not well suited for evaluating counterfactuals generated from longer or complex original texts, as these often require multiple edits to remove all references to the sensitive attribute. Some methods reward grammaticality but do not require the text to make semantic sense (Sheng et al., 2020), while others require both fluency and consistency (Ross et al., 2021b; Reif et al., 2021; Madaan et al., 2020); some use automated metrics such as perplexity (Wang et al., 2020) and masked language model loss (Ross et al., 2021a) while others use human raters to evaluate fluency (Reif et al., 2021; Wu et al., 2021).

Building on these prior results, we combine several automated metrics to filter out poor quality counterfactuals (e.g. ones with large additions/deletions beyond those required to remove the sensitive attribute). We also develop a human evaluation framework to rate the quality of the counterfactuals that pass automated filtering, with a view to making it easy for human annotators to rate examples quickly and consistently while also rewarding diverse and non-obvious counterfactual generation (e.g. rows 1 and 2 of Table 1).

2.3 Toxicity detection

It is well documented (Davidson et al., 2019; Dixon et al., 2018) that toxicity and hate speech classifiers often pick up on correlations (that are not causations) between references to certain identities and toxic speech: that is, these models incorrectly learn that sensitive attributes such as certain sexual orientations, gender identities, races, religions, etc. are themselves indications of toxicity.

Recent work has gone further and explored the effect of *indirect* toxic examples on classifiers (Sap et al., 2020; Lees et al., 2021; Han and Tsvetkov, 2020), finding that many datasets do not adequately represent this form of toxicity (Breitfeller et al., 2019) and that classifiers are ineffective at identifying it (Han and Tsvetkov, 2020). Based on this, we conjecture that toxicity classifiers may also associate *indirect* references to sensitive attributes with toxicity, which is consistent with (Hartvigsen et al., 2022). We focus on exploring this facet of counterfactual probing.

3 Methodology

Our goal is to detect when a model produces a different score for two examples (original and counterfactual) that differ only by changing a sensitive attribute and that have the same groundtruth label. Ideally the dataset of counterfactual pairs used in this testing should be both large in size and diverse in topic in order to maximise the chances of identifying issues with the model, including issues that the dataset creators may not have considered.

3.1 Task Definition

We define our task as follows:

Given a corpus of text examples that reference a specific sensitive attribute (e.g. a particular religion, LGBQ+ identity, transgender identity), generate a counterfactual text for each original text that preserves both the original label and the original meaning (as far as possible) while removing all references to the chosen sensitive attribute.

Taken as a set, the counterfactuals should be:

- **Complex**: *The texts should reflect the complexity of expected real-world inputs.*
- **Diverse**: *The counterfactual edits should*

cover a range of topics, both within the attribute's category (e.g. replacing one religion with another) and more generally (replacing specific references with neutral words such as "person", "religion", etc).

- **Fluent and consistent**: *The generated text should match the style and phrasing of the input text, should be internally consistent (e.g. no changing topic part way through), and should read like plausible natural language.*

3.2 Counterfactual Generation with LLMs

To generate our counterfactuals we build on the results of Reif et al. (2021), which accomplishes a wide range of style transfers using a Transformer-based large language model combined with prompting. Inputs to the LLM consist of three parts: a small fixed set of prompts that demonstrate the rewriting task, the piece of text to be rewritten, and an instruction such as "make this more descriptive" or "make this include a metaphor". The LLM returns up to 16 attempts at rewriting the input text according to the given instruction.

In order to use this method for counterfactual generation, we retain the prompts used in Reif et al. (2021) (see Table 8 for the full prompt text) but replace the style transfer instruction with ones specific to our task, e.g. "make this not about Muslims" or "make this not about transgender people" (see Appendix A.2 for details). This is one of the few parts of our pipeline that uses the sensitive attribute, and this generalises easily to other attributes simply by changing the instruction.

We use LaMDA (Thoppilan et al., 2022) as the underlying LLM for text generation in this paper, which belongs to the family of decoder-only Transformer-based dialog models. The LaMDA model used here, which we refer to as LLM-D, is described in §6 of Thoppilan et al. (2022): it has 137B parameters, and was pretrained as a general language model (GLM) on 1.97B public web documents and finetuned into a dialog model on an additional dataset of curated dialog examples.

For the experiments reported here, we exclusively used the finetuned dialog model: both for safety reasons (LLM-D's finetuning includes a focus on reducing toxic text generation (Thoppilan et al., 2022)) and technical reasons (it could generate longer passages of text than other models available to us). However, we also achieved success using our method with the underlying GLM model (referred to as "PT" in Thoppilan et al. (2022)), and since prompting techniques have achieved success on multiple different language models (Reif et al., 2021; Brown et al., 2020) we expect that our method would generalise to other LLMs.

3.3 Counterfactual Evaluation

We evaluate counterfactuals in two phases: an automated phase using a combination of standard metrics and a simple two-layer classifier, and a human evaluation phase based on criteria we developed for rating complex counterfactuals. A key consideration here is that while counterfactuals should be as similar as possible to the originals, they must also remove sensitive attribute references; thus we cannot be *too* strict in enforcing similarity, especially via automated methods.

LLM-D was configured to generate up to 16 responses for each input, so we use a combination of automated metrics to identify potential good counterfactuals to pass to human raters. In addition to some simple filtering rules (e.g. to catch examples where LLM-D simply regurgitates its prompt) we use three main metrics:

- BLEU score (Papineni et al., 2002),
- BERTScore (Zhang et al., 2020), and
- a prediction of whether the sensitive attribute is still referenced (described below).

A high BLEU score relative to the original text indicates high lexical similarity (Reif et al., 2021, Appendix B), while a high BERTScore indicates semantic similarity; based on early (separate) tuning experiments, we found that requiring both scores to be above 0.5 was a good trade-off between producing plausible counterfactuals while also allowing some diversity of responses.

The sensitive attribute predictor is a two-layer fully connected classifier trained for this purpose; full training details are given in Appendix A.3. We imposed a threshold of 0.5 on this classifier as well, although the results in this paper suggest that this would benefit from further tuning.

Our human evaluation criteria evaluate the (original, counterfactual) pair along four axes:

1. fluency/consistency,
2. presence of sensitive attribute,
3. similarity of label, and
4. similarity of meaning.

Raters are asked whether the proposed counterfactual is fluent and consistent (yes/no/unsure), whether it references the sensitive attribute (explicitly/implicitly/not at all), whether it should be assigned the same label as the original (yes/no/unsure),[2] and whether it is similar in meaning and format to the original (scale of 0 to 4). The full rater instructions are given in Appendix C.

We use majority vote to consolidate annotator ratings for each example, discarding ties. For our purposes, a counterfactual is deemed "good" if it is fluent, does not reference the sensitive attribute, has the same label as the original, and scores at least 2 (out of 4) on similarity of meaning. Thus examples where the majority vote resulted in a rating of "unsure" were treated as if they had been rated "no" when reporting results in Section 5.

Quantifying "similarity of meaning" "Similarity of meaning" was the hardest metric to define, since removing references to the sensitive attribute often required major edits to the input text. Thus, our score buckets split the counterfactuals in a way that captures both type and severity of edit. This allows us to identify a more diverse pool of good counterfactuals, while also making it easy for users to select a stricter subset if required.

A score of 4 indicates a perfect ablation counterfactual with no unnecessary changes or new information, 3 means that the counterfactual contains substitutions to similar or neutral words (e.g. "Muslim" $\rightarrow$ "Christian", "Judaism" $\rightarrow$ "religion"; useful for comparing classifier predictions among identities within a category), while 2 allows for more diverse edits such as minor additions/deletions or substitutions to other topics (useful for initial fairness probing of a model). 1 indicates an example that is reasonably similar to the original but too different to be a useful counterfactual, and a 0 indicates that the text is changed beyond recognition. See Appendix C for full guidelines and examples.

3.4 Safety

Large language models come with safety and toxicity issues (Bender et al., 2021; Abid et al., 2021), which is of particular concern when using them to generate text for the purpose of counterfactual fairness probing in other models. The LLM-D model has been finetuned by its creators to help mitigate some of these safety concerns (Thoppilan et al., 2022, §6), and we also built safeguards into our pipeline to reduce the chances of our method producing problematic or toxic counterfactuals. Even with human-in-the-loop, it is still possible for our method to produce some problematic examples, e.g. ones that perpetuate negative stereotypes, but we aim to reduce this risk.

First, we only aim to generate counterfactuals in the sensitive $\rightarrow$ neutral direction. That is, we choose input texts that reference the sensitive attribute, and ask LLM-D to remove these references; we do NOT ask the model to generate text about marginalized groups starting from neutral texts (though in practice it can sometimes substitute one identity group for another). Additionally, our evaluation setup ensures that all generated text is checked by at least one human, specifically includes a criteria checking for *implicit* references to the identity as well as explicit ones, and includes a "reject for other reason" box to allow raters to remove examples if either the original or counterfactual text contains negative stereotypes or hate speech. This provides a second line of defence against any toxic text that might slip through.

4 Implementation

4.1 Data

The CivilComments dataset (Borkan et al., 2019) is a set of approximately 2 million English-language internet comments from 2015-2017, with crowdsourced toxicity annotations. CivilComments-Identities (CC-I) is a 450k subset of CivilComments where each text has additional crowdsourced labels for references to various identities, such as gender,[3] sexual orientation, religion, and race.

Our experiments focus on four identity subcategories in CC-I, namely `muslim`, `jewish`, `transgender`, and `homosexual_gay_and_lesbian`,[4] which for simplicity we refer to as `LGBQ+`. These categories were chosen because they are all groups that have faced high levels of online toxicity that may have bled through into classifier models (e.g. Abid et al. (2021); Borkan et al. (2019)), and because the annotators we used for our experiments were sufficiently familiar with these categories to evaluate our generated counterfactuals effectively.

[2]Note that this criteria is task-dependent; in our case the labels were toxic/nontoxic.

[3]The available labels in this category are `male`, `female`, `transgender`, and `other_gender`, which should always be used with extreme care to avoid any implication that "male"/"female" and "transgender" refer to disjoint sets (see e.g. Larson (2017)); for this work we use only the `transgender` label.

[4]Despite the name, this category appears to have been more broadly interpreted by crowd raters as referring to all non-straight sexual orientations, and therefore we continued to treat it as such in our experiments.

Method	Text	F	A	L	M
Original	*So you are saying it's OK? Not enough? Long way to go? An apologist for Islamic terrorism?*	-	-	-	-
Ablation	so you are saying it's ok? not enough? long way to go? an apologist for **terrorism**?	✓	✓	✓	4
Substitution	so you are saying it's ok? not enough? long way to go? an apologist for **christian** terrorism?	✓	✓	✓	3
Polyjuice	So you are saying it's OK? Not enough? Long way to go? An apologist for **secular enlightenment**?	✓	✓	✓	2
LLM-D	So you are saying it's OK? Not enough? Long way to go? An apologist for **terrorism**?	✓	✓	✓	4
Original	*Shocking that this article didn't once mention "islam", "islamic" or "Muslim".*	-	-	-	-
Ablation	shocking that this article didn't once mention "", "" or "".	✗	✓	-	-
Substitution	shocking that this article didn't once mention "**christianity**", "**christian**" or "**christian**".	✓	✓	✓	3
Polyjuice	**Waving** that this article didn't once mention "islam", "islamic" or "**islandic**".	✗	✗	-	-
LLM-D	Shocking that this article didn't once mention "**christian**", "**christians**" or "**Christ**".	✓	✓	✓	3

Table 2: Civil Comments examples referencing Islam, with generated counterfactuals and human annotations (**F**luent, doesn't reference **A**ttribute, similarity of **L**abel, and similarity of **M**eaning). In the top example all methods produced a reasonable counterfactual; in the second, only LLM-D and substitution generated good counterfactuals.

We restrict our dataset to texts between 10 and 45 words long that do not contain URLs, for ease of analysis by human raters. We further require that texts have a score of at least 0.8 for the relevant attribute, and a toxicity score of at most 0.1: i.e. least 80% of the CC-I annotators agreed that the text referenced the specified attribute/identity, and at most 10% of them viewed the comment as toxic.

We chose to focus on only non-toxic examples (as rated by the CC-I annotators) in our experiments, because toxic examples can introduce an unwanted confounding factor: there are many examples in the dataset that are only toxic because they contain a slur, and removing or substituting the slur often renders the resulting text non-toxic. Since we are focused on the ability to generate counterfactuals with the same label as the original, we excluded these examples from our dataset. Note that this a choice we make in the context of this particular application, but the general methodology described here could also be used to investigate toxic original examples if deemed appropriate.

4.2 Counterfactual generation

We compare our LLM-D-based generation method to three other methods: ablation, substitution, and the Polyjuice counterfactual generator (Wu et al., 2021). We summarise each of these methods here, and full details are given in Appendix B.

We generate a list of keywords relevant to each topic using frequency analysis on the entire CC-I corpus, followed by manual curation to remove words that often co-occur with a sensitive attribute but are not specific to that topic (e.g. "discriminating" and "surgery" for transgender identity).

To generate ablation counterfactuals, we replace any occurrence of the keywords in our input examples with the empty string. For substitution, we replace all religion-based keywords with a corresponding concept from Christianity, and all sexuality/gender words with their "opposite", e.g. "gay" → "straight", "transgender" → "cisgender". Keywords with no obvious replacement (e.g. "transition", or "Israel") are left unchanged. Note that this can make the substitution method appear artificially good at performing multiple consistent substitutions within a sentence, something that can usually only be achieved with complex rule-based systems (e.g. Lohia (2022)), and comes at the cost of limited counterfactual diversity. This is discussed further in Section 5 when comparing the results of substitution and LLM-D counterfactuals.

In order to fairly compare our LLM-D method with Polyjuice, we generated 16 Polyjuice counterfactuals per input: 8 with no constraints on generation, and 8 where we first used our ablation keyword list to replace all topic-specific keywords in the input sentence with the token `[BLANK]`. These 16 results were then filtered and ranked in the same way as with LLM-D, and the top result returned.

Examples for each method are given in Table 2.

4.3 Counterfactual evaluation

All human annotation of our generated counterfactuals were performed by three of the authors. Each annotator initially rated a subset of the examples, divided to ensure that every counterfactual received at least two ratings, and any examples with non-unanimous scores were passed to the third rater (with scores hidden) for a tiebreaker vote. Examples that received three distinct ratings for a category (yes/unsure/no) were discarded; the only

Method	# examples	Fluent	Attribute ref	Label	FAL and... Meaning 4	Meaning 3+	**Meaning 2+**
Ablation	200	46.6	87.6	99.5	33.0	33.0	33.0
Substitution	200	96.5	88.7	100.0	0.0	84.0	84.5
Polyjuice	162	71.2	15.4	88.8	2.5	4.9	10.5
LLM-D	191	95.7	71.1	96.3	14.1	39.3	62.3

Table 3: Percentage of counterfactuals (generated from Islam-referencing texts) that were labeled by annotators as being fluent, not referencing the sensitive attribute, and having the same label as the original, respectively. "FAL and Meaning n+" lists the percentage of examples that satisfied all of these criteria *and* were given a score of n or higher by annotators for similarity of meaning.

exception to this was the Similarity of Meaning category, where we averaged the raters' scores.

In order to ensure rating consistency and refine the clarity of the instructions, we performed two smaller rounds of test annotation first (50-100 examples) followed by a review session to discuss examples with divergent scores or "unsure" ratings. While the annotators were of diverse genders (male, female, non-binary) and moderately to extremely familiar with the sensitive attributes chosen for our experiments, we also note that they were all white citizens of Western countries and that this could have informed their interpretation of the toxicity task and what substitutions are "neutral".

4.4 Toxicity detection

We use our generated counterfactuals to evaluate the robustness of the Perspective API toxicity classifier to counterfactual perturbations.[5] Perspective API defines toxicity as "a rude, disrespectful, or unreasonable comment that is likely to make you leave a discussion"; the toxicity score is the predicted probability of a reader perceiving the input as toxic.

We focus on the change in predicted toxicity score from original to counterfactual. This is both because any toxicity cut-off threshold will likely vary by use-case, and because we expect that large changes in score will provide interesting and useful information about the classifier even if they do not happen to straddle the toxicity threshold.

5 Results

5.1 Comparison of generation methods

We sample 200 examples that reference Islam from our curated subset of CivilComments-Identities and generate a counterfactual with each of four methods: ablation, substitution, Polyjuice, and our LLM-D-based method. The resulting 753 counterfactuals were shuffled and split between the three annotators for rating;[6] annotators had access to the sensitive attribute label but not the generation method for each example. The results are given in Table 3. Recall that for our purposes, a counterfactual is "good" if it is fluent, does not reference the sensitive attribute, has the same label as the original, and scores at least 2 on similarity of meaning (bolded column in Table 3).

In Table 3 we see that ablation counterfactuals are often not fluent, but that when the input text can be ablated successfully (e.g. sentences where the keywords are used as adjectives, such as "The Muslim woman...") the resulting counterfactuals all receive the maximum score for Similarity of Meaning. Polyjuice was generally unsuccessful at removing references to the sensitive attribute, despite the use of `[BLANK]` tokens to direct the model to the portions of the sentence requiring editing. While substitution achieved higher success rates than LLM-D in this experiment, we show in Section 5.2 below that this may partly have been due to the choice of topic and/or wordlist; this breakdown also does not capture the diversity of topics in the generated counterfactuals.

Finally, we note that the subset of input texts for which ablation produced a good counterfactual tended to be the "easy" examples, in that substitution produced a good counterfactual for 98.5% of this subset, and LLM-D 75%.

5.2 Generation on multiple topics

We sample 100 examples from our curated subset of CivilComments-Identities for each of the attributes Judaism, LGBQ+, and transgender, along with a subset of 100 examples referencing Islam from the set used above. Annotators had access to

[5] www.perspectiveapi.com

[6] Neither LLM-D nor Polyjuice always successfully generated valid counterfactuals, resulting in 191 LLM-D counterfactuals and 162 Polyjuice counterfactuals.

Method	Topic	# examples	Fluent	Attribute ref	Label	FAL and... Meaning 3+	FAL and... **Meaning 2+**
LLM-D	LGBQ+	99	100.0	54.6	98.6	24.2	48.5
	transgender	99	97.9	43.9	98.5	22.2	36.4
	Judaism	95	96.7	58.4	96.2	41.1	50.5
	Islam	94	95.6	67.0	97.5	35.1	58.5
substitution	LGBQ+	20	93.8	92.3	100.0	50.0	50.0
	transgender	20	95.0	42.1	100.0	35.0	35.0
	Judaism	20	89.5	57.9	100.0	50.0	50.0
	Islam	20	100.0	80.0	100.0	80.0	80.0

Table 4: Percentage of examples satisfying each rating criteria, split by topic. Columns are similar to Table 3.

the sensitive attribute label for each example while rating. Results are given in Table 4.

The key observation here is that our LLM-D-based method generalises easily to multiple topics. We also see further evidence (e.g. attribute reference in Table 4) that our pipeline's automated ranking requires further finetuning, in particular for identifying counterfactuals which have successfully removed all references to the sensitive attribute. In examining discarded LLM-D responses we found that of the 200 examples where the top-ranked LLM-D response did not pass human rating, 105 of these examples (52.5%) had a plausible counterfactual further down the ranking (as judged by one annotator); including these in our evaluation would have raised LLM-D's overall success rate to 75%.

We also generate substitution counterfactuals for a subset of 20 randomly selected examples for each topic, and find that substitution performs almost identically to LLM-D at generating good counterfactuals for each of the non-Islam topics. For the LGBQ+ and transgender categories in particular, this may be due to the fact that explicit labels are most commonly used only to refer to minority groups: one talks about "same-sex marriage" and "transgender athletes", but simply "marriage" and "athletes" when referring to the majority group. Thus a reference to e.g. "cisgender atheletes" still carries an implicit reference to transgender issues. This highlights the need for more complex and diverse counterfactual generation techniques that do not rely solely on substitutions and wordlists.

5.3 Toxicity detection

Throughout this section we restrict our attention only to the "good" counterfactuals (as rated by the human annotators) because poor-quality ones can produce artificially high or low swings in toxicity (due to changing the text too much relative to the original, or by failing to remove the sensitive attribute, respectively); we omit Polyjuice because it produced too few good examples to analyse.

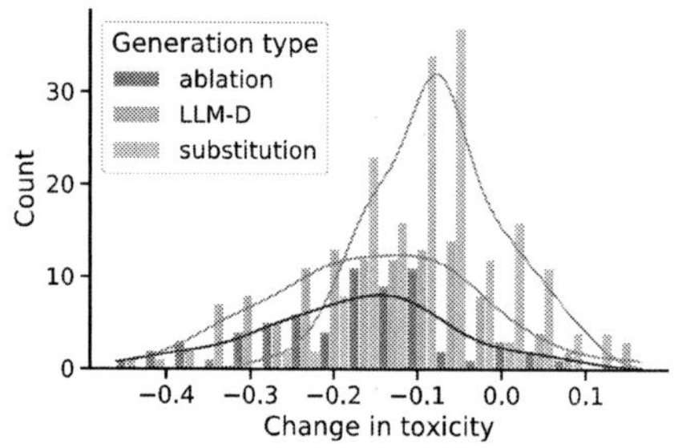

Figure 2: Differences in toxicity score from original texts to their counterfactuals; negative scores indicate that Perspective API rated the counterfactual *less likely* to be viewed as toxic than the original.

Counterfactuals generated by all methods have lower predicted toxicity scores on average than the original Islam-referencing texts, as shown in Figure 2; see also Figure 3 in the appendix for a more detailed breakdown. Substitution produce the smallest change in toxicity scores: an average difference of -0.08, compared to -0.15 for LLM-D and -0.17 for ablation. This suggests that counterfactuals generated by LLM-D and other methods may be producing more challenging examples for the classifier than substitution is, possibly because substitution (by design!) produces text that stays within the same broad topic, and this lack of diversity can make it harder to uncover unexpected negative associations in the classifier.

We also look at the average change in toxicity score across the four topics for both LLM-D and substitution-generated counterfactuals (Table 5). While the sample sizes are too small to draw concrete conclusions, the small average change in toxicity for religion-referencing substitution counter-

Method	Topic	# ex	Avg tox diff
LLM-D	LGBQ+	48	-0.25
	transgender	36	-0.10
	Judaism	48	-0.11
	Islam	55	-0.15
substitution	LGBQ+	10	-0.28
	transgender	7	-0.15
	Judaism	10	-0.04
	Islam	16	- 0.05

Table 5: Average difference in toxicity from original to counterfactual, measured on the good counterfactual pairs generated in Section 5.2. A negative value indicates that the Perspective API classifier found the counterfactual *less* toxic than the original.

factuals compared both to other topics and to LLM-D-generated counterfactuals reinforces the conjecture that the toxicity classifier may view all references to religion as similarly toxic. This suggests that more diverse counterfactuals are indeed necessary to effectively probe a model for subtle counterfactual fairness issues.

Note that the average change in toxicity score is not necessarily meaningful to an end-user. For example, if Perspective API is used to remove comments online with scores above a certain threshold, only score changes around that threshold will have a noticeable end-user impact. Figures 3 and 4 in the appendix provide a more detailed breakdown of how these score changes were distributed, which can help to place the above results in context. However, for the purposes of counterfactual fairness probing we believe it is still important to look at all score changes, not only those near the cut-off point, as this can help to identify areas of potential bias *before* end-users are affected.

6 Conclusion

Our Contributions We have defined a new counterfactual generation task for fairness probing of text classifier models, and have shown that several common types of methods fail to satisfy the requirements of this task and that these failures may limit the effectiveness of the resulting counterfactuals in probing these classifier models. We further show that our LLM-D-based approach combined with automated and human rating can generate high quality, diverse, and complex counterfactual pairs from real-world text examples.

Usage and Limitations Counterfactuals generated via our LLM-D-based approaches could used both to test for undesired behaviour in classifiers and potentially to mitigate that behaviour via methods such as dataset augmentation, as has been found useful in various settings, e.g. Dinan et al. (2020), Hall Maudslay et al. (2019).

However, we emphasise that this is not without risk. Language models are known to produce toxic text (Wallace et al., 2019) and reflect or amplify biases from their training data (Sheng et al., 2019b), among other problems (Bommasani et al., 2021, §5); we always recommend human review on at least a subset of the data when using potentially sensitive generated text. Language is contextual, and there is a great deal of social context that must be accounted for when attempting to evaluate the behaviours and biases of machine learning models and generated text, so it is important for human review to be performed by a diverse pool of reviewers knowledgeable about the downstream task and the social issues at play (in contrast to the small set of annotators for this illustrative study).

Using text generated from methods such as ours is also not appropriate in all situations. For example, we emphasise that this generated data should be used to *augment* other forms of data, not replace it. Similarly, while this study sought to generate diverse texts for analysis, a more restrictive definition of counterfactual may be appropriate when using generated text to *mitigate* classifier issues, e.g. by using a stricter cut-off for the "Similarity of Meaning" evaluation criteria.

Future Research There are several areas of future research to highlight. Most generally, for this investigation we focused on one way this framework can be useful, and made several narrowing choices; however, our framework can be useful in other contexts and applications such as investigating false negatives (by considering original examples that are toxic), probing other types of classifiers than toxicity models, or generating other types of counterfactuals than simply removing the sensitive attribute (e.g. rewording text to explore model robustness). Furthermore, our method would benefit from improved control over the LLM-generated text through e.g. prompt tuning (Lester et al., 2021), demonstration-based prompt-engineering and adversarial decoding (Hartvigsen et al., 2022), or fine-tuning (Wei et al., 2021), as well as more effective filtering of counterfactuals that still reference the sensitive attribute.

Acknowledgements

We would like to thank Vinodkumar Prabhakaran, Ian Tenney, Emily Reif, Ian Kivlichan, Lucy Vasserman, Blake Lemoine, Alyssa Chvasta, and Kathy Meier-Hellstern for helpful discussions and feedback at every stage of this project.

References

Abubakar Abid, Maheen Farooqi, and James Zou. 2021. *Persistent Anti-Muslim Bias in Large Language Models*, page 298–306. Association for Computing Machinery, New York, NY, USA.

Emily M. Bender, Timnit Gebru, Angelina McMillan-Major, and Shmargaret Shmitchell. 2021. On the dangers of stochastic parrots: Can language models be too big? In *Proceedings of the 2021 ACM Conference on Fairness, Accountability, and Transparency*, FAccT '21, page 610–623, New York, NY, USA. Association for Computing Machinery.

Rishi Bommasani, Drew A. Hudson, Ehsan Adeli, Russ Altman, Simran Arora, Sydney von Arx, Michael S. Bernstein, Jeannette Bohg, Antoine Bosselut, Emma Brunskill, Erik Brynjolfsson, Shyamal Buch, Dallas Card, Rodrigo Castellon, Niladri Chatterji, Annie Chen, Kathleen Creel, Jared Quincy Davis, Dora Demszky, Chris Donahue, Moussa Doumbouya, Esin Durmus, Stefano Ermon, John Etchemendy, Kawin Ethayarajh, Li Fei-Fei, Chelsea Finn, Trevor Gale, Lauren Gillespie, Karan Goel, Noah Goodman, Shelby Grossman, Neel Guha, Tatsunori Hashimoto, Peter Henderson, John Hewitt, Daniel E. Ho, Jenny Hong, Kyle Hsu, Jing Huang, Thomas Icard, Saahil Jain, Dan Jurafsky, Pratyusha Kalluri, Siddharth Karamcheti, Geoff Keeling, Fereshte Khani, Omar Khattab, Pang Wei Koh, Mark Krass, Ranjay Krishna, Rohith Kuditipudi, Ananya Kumar, Faisal Ladhak, Mina Lee, Tony Lee, Jure Leskovec, Isabelle Levent, Xiang Lisa Li, Xuechen Li, Tengyu Ma, Ali Malik, Christopher D. Manning, Suvir Mirchandani, Eric Mitchell, Zanele Munyikwa, Suraj Nair, Avanika Narayan, Deepak Narayanan, Ben Newman, Allen Nie, Juan Carlos Niebles, Hamed Nilforoshan, Julian Nyarko, Giray Ogut, Laurel Orr, Isabel Papadimitriou, Joon Sung Park, Chris Piech, Eva Portelance, Christopher Potts, Aditi Raghunathan, Rob Reich, Hongyu Ren, Frieda Rong, Yusuf Roohani, Camilo Ruiz, Jack Ryan, Christopher Ré, Dorsa Sadigh, Shiori Sagawa, Keshav Santhanam, Andy Shih, Krishnan Srinivasan, Alex Tamkin, Rohan Taori, Armin W. Thomas, Florian Tramèr, Rose E. Wang, William Wang, Bohan Wu, Jiajun Wu, Yuhuai Wu, Sang Michael Xie, Michihiro Yasunaga, Jiaxuan You, Matei Zaharia, Michael Zhang, Tianyi Zhang, Xikun Zhang, Yuhui Zhang, Lucia Zheng, Kaitlyn Zhou, and Percy Liang. 2021. On the opportunities and risks of foundation models.

Daniel Borkan, Lucas Dixon, Jeffrey Sorensen, Nithum Thain, and Lucy Vasserman. 2019. Nuanced metrics for measuring unintended bias with real data for text classification. *CoRR*, abs/1903.04561.

Luke Breitfeller, Emily Ahn, David Jurgens, and Yulia Tsvetkov. 2019. Finding microaggressions in the wild: A case for locating elusive phenomena in social media posts. In *Proceedings of the 2019 Conference on Empirical Methods in Natural Language Processing and the 9th International Joint Conference on Natural Language Processing (EMNLP-IJCNLP)*, pages 1664–1674, Hong Kong, China. Association for Computational Linguistics.

Tom Brown, Benjamin Mann, Nick Ryder, Melanie Subbiah, Jared D Kaplan, Prafulla Dhariwal, Arvind Neelakantan, Pranav Shyam, Girish Sastry, Amanda Askell, Sandhini Agarwal, Ariel Herbert-Voss, Gretchen Krueger, Tom Henighan, Rewon Child, Aditya Ramesh, Daniel Ziegler, Jeffrey Wu, Clemens Winter, Chris Hesse, Mark Chen, Eric Sigler, Mateusz Litwin, Scott Gray, Benjamin Chess, Jack Clark, Christopher Berner, Sam McCandlish, Alec Radford, Ilya Sutskever, and Dario Amodei. 2020. Language models are few-shot learners. In *Advances in Neural Information Processing Systems*, volume 33, pages 1877–1901. Curran Associates, Inc.

Boxing Chen and Colin Cherry. 2014. A systematic comparison of smoothing techniques for sentence-level BLEU. In *Proceedings of the Ninth Workshop on Statistical Machine Translation*, pages 362–367, Baltimore, Maryland, USA. Association for Computational Linguistics.

Sumanth Dathathri, Andrea Madotto, Janice Lan, Jane Hung, Eric Frank, Piero Molino, Jason Yosinski, and Rosanne Liu. 2020. Plug and play language models: A simple approach to controlled text generation. In *International Conference on Learning Representations*.

Aida Mostafazadeh Davani, Ali Omrani, Brendan Kennedy, Mohammad Atari, Xiang Ren, and Morteza Dehghani. 2021. Improving counterfactual generation for fair hate speech detection. In *Proceedings of the 5th Workshop on Online Abuse and Harms (WOAH 2021)*, pages 92–101, Online. Association for Computational Linguistics.

Thomas Davidson, Debasmita Bhattacharya, and Ingmar Weber. 2019. Racial bias in hate speech and abusive language detection datasets. In *Proceedings of the Third Workshop on Abusive Language Online*, pages 25–35, Florence, Italy. Association for Computational Linguistics.

Jacob Devlin, Ming-Wei Chang, Kenton Lee, and Kristina Toutanova. 2019. BERT: Pre-training of deep bidirectional transformers for language understanding. In *Proceedings of the 2019 Conference of the North American Chapter of the Association for Computational Linguistics: Human Language*

Technologies, Volume 1 (Long and Short Papers), pages 4171–4186, Minneapolis, Minnesota. Association for Computational Linguistics.

Emily Dinan, Angela Fan, Adina Williams, Jack Urbanek, Douwe Kiela, and Jason Weston. 2020. Queens are powerful too: Mitigating gender bias in dialogue generation. In *Proceedings of the 2020 Conference on Empirical Methods in Natural Language Processing (EMNLP)*, pages 8173–8188, Online. Association for Computational Linguistics.

Lucas Dixon, John Li, Jeffrey Sorensen, Nithum Thain, and Lucy Vasserman. 2018. Measuring and mitigating unintended bias in text classification. In *Proceedings of the 2018 AAAI/ACM Conference on AI, Ethics, and Society*, AIES '18, page 67–73, New York, NY, USA. Association for Computing Machinery.

Sahaj Garg, Vincent Perot, Nicole Limtiaco, Ankur Taly, Ed H Chi, and Alex Beutel. 2019. Counterfactual fairness in text classification through robustness. In *Proceedings of the 2019 AAAI/ACM Conference on AI, Ethics, and Society*, pages 219–226.

Rowan Hall Maudslay, Hila Gonen, Ryan Cotterell, and Simone Teufel. 2019. It's all in the name: Mitigating gender bias with name-based counterfactual data substitution. In *Proceedings of the 2019 Conference on Empirical Methods in Natural Language Processing and the 9th International Joint Conference on Natural Language Processing (EMNLP-IJCNLP)*, pages 5267–5275, Hong Kong, China. Association for Computational Linguistics.

Xiaochuang Han and Yulia Tsvetkov. 2020. Fortifying toxic speech detectors against veiled toxicity. In *Proceedings of the 2020 Conference on Empirical Methods in Natural Language Processing (EMNLP)*, pages 7732–7739, Online. Association for Computational Linguistics.

Thomas Hartvigsen, Saadia Gabriel, Hamid Palangi, Maarten Sap, Dipankar Ray, and Ece Kamar. 2022. Toxigen: Controlling language models to generate implied and adversarial toxicity. In *ACL*.

Ben Hutchinson, Vinodkumar Prabhakaran, Emily Denton, Kellie Webster, Yu Zhong, and Stephen Denuyl. 2020. Social biases in NLP models as barriers for persons with disabilities. In *Proceedings of the 58th Annual Meeting of the Association for Computational Linguistics*, pages 5491–5501, Online. Association for Computational Linguistics.

Divyansh Kaushik, Eduard Hovy, and Zachary Lipton. 2020. Learning the difference that makes a difference with counterfactually-augmented data. In *International Conference on Learning Representations*.

Hannah Rose Kirk, Bertram Vidgen, Paul Röttger, Tristan Thrush, and Scott A. Hale. 2021. Hatemoji: A test suite and adversarially-generated dataset for benchmarking and detecting emoji-based hate. *CoRR*, abs/2108.05921.

Brian Larson. 2017. Gender as a variable in natural-language processing: Ethical considerations. In *Proceedings of the First ACL Workshop on Ethics in Natural Language Processing*, pages 1–11, Valencia, Spain. Association for Computational Linguistics.

Alyssa Lees, Daniel Borkan, Ian Kivlichan, Jorge Nario, and Tesh Goyal. 2021. Capturing covertly toxic speech via crowdsourcing. In *Proceedings of the First Workshop on Bridging Human–Computer Interaction and Natural Language Processing*, pages 14–20, Online. Association for Computational Linguistics.

Brian Lester, Rami Al-Rfou, and Noah Constant. 2021. The power of scale for parameter-efficient prompt tuning. In *Proceedings of the 2021 Conference on Empirical Methods in Natural Language Processing*, pages 3045–3059, Online and Punta Cana, Dominican Republic. Association for Computational Linguistics.

Pranay Lohia. 2022. Counterfactual multi-token fairness in text classification. *arXiv preprint arXiv:2202.03792*.

Ilya Loshchilov and Frank Hutter. 2018. Decoupled weight decay regularization. In *International Conference on Learning Representations*.

Nishtha Madaan, Inkit Padhi, Naveen Panwar, and Diptikalyan Saha. 2020. Generate your counterfactuals: Towards controlled counterfactual generation for text. *arXiv preprint arXiv:2012.04698*.

Kishore Papineni, Salim Roukos, Todd Ward, and Wei-Jing Zhu. 2002. Bleu: a method for automatic evaluation of machine translation. In *Proceedings of the 40th Annual Meeting of the Association for Computational Linguistics*, pages 311–318, Philadelphia, Pennsylvania, USA. Association for Computational Linguistics.

Vinodkumar Prabhakaran, Ben Hutchinson, and Margaret Mitchell. 2019. Perturbation sensitivity analysis to detect unintended model biases. In *Proceedings of the 2019 Conference on Empirical Methods in Natural Language Processing and the 9th International Joint Conference on Natural Language Processing (EMNLP-IJCNLP)*, pages 5740–5745, Hong Kong, China. Association for Computational Linguistics.

Emily Reif, Daphne Ippolito, Ann Yuan, Andy Coenen, Chris Callison-Burch, and Jason Wei. 2021. A recipe for arbitrary text style transfer with large language models. *arXiv e-prints*, pages arXiv–2109.

Alexis Ross, Ana Marasović, and Matthew E Peters. 2021a. Explaining nlp models via minimal contrastive editing (mice). In *Findings of the Association for Computational Linguistics: ACL-IJCNLP 2021*, pages 3840–3852.

Alexis Ross, Tongshuang Wu, Hao Peng, Matthew E Peters, and Matt Gardner. 2021b. Tailor: Generating and perturbing text with semantic controls. *arXiv preprint arXiv:2107.07150*.

Paul Röttger, Bertie Vidgen, Dong Nguyen, Zeerak Waseem, Helen Margetts, and Janet Pierrehumbert. 2021. HateCheck: Functional tests for hate speech detection models. In *Proceedings of the 59th Annual Meeting of the Association for Computational Linguistics and the 11th International Joint Conference on Natural Language Processing (Volume 1: Long Papers)*, pages 41–58, Online. Association for Computational Linguistics.

Rachel Rudinger, Jason Naradowsky, Brian Leonard, and Benjamin Van Durme. 2018. Gender bias in coreference resolution. In *Proceedings of NAACL-HLT*, pages 8–14.

Maarten Sap, Dallas Card, Saadia Gabriel, Yejin Choi, and Noah A. Smith. 2019. The risk of racial bias in hate speech detection. In *Proceedings of the 57th Annual Meeting of the Association for Computational Linguistics*, pages 1668–1678, Florence, Italy. Association for Computational Linguistics.

Maarten Sap, Saadia Gabriel, Lianhui Qin, Dan Jurafsky, Noah A. Smith, and Yejin Choi. 2020. Social bias frames: Reasoning about social and power implications of language. In *Proceedings of the 58th Annual Meeting of the Association for Computational Linguistics*, pages 5477–5490, Online. Association for Computational Linguistics.

Emily Sheng, Kai-Wei Chang, Prem Natarajan, and Nanyun Peng. 2019a. The woman worked as a babysitter: On biases in language generation. In *Proceedings of the 2019 Conference on Empirical Methods in Natural Language Processing and the 9th International Joint Conference on Natural Language Processing (EMNLP-IJCNLP)*, pages 3407–3412.

Emily Sheng, Kai-Wei Chang, Prem Natarajan, and Nanyun Peng. 2020. Towards controllable biases in language generation. In *Findings of the Association for Computational Linguistics: EMNLP 2020*, pages 3239–3254.

Emily Sheng, Kai-Wei Chang, Premkumar Natarajan, and Nanyun Peng. 2019b. The woman worked as a babysitter: On biases in language generation. In *Proceedings of the 2019 Conference on Empirical Methods in Natural Language Processing and the 9th International Joint Conference on Natural Language Processing (EMNLP-IJCNLP)*, pages 3407–3412, Hong Kong, China. Association for Computational Linguistics.

Romal Thoppilan, Daniel De Freitas, Jamie Hall, Noam Shazeer, Apoorv Kulshreshtha, Heng-Tze Cheng, Alicia Jin, Taylor Bos, Leslie Baker, Yu Du, et al. 2022. Lamda: Language models for dialog applications. *arXiv preprint arXiv:2201.08239*.

Eric Wallace, Shi Feng, Nikhil Kandpal, Matt Gardner, and Sameer Singh. 2019. Universal adversarial triggers for attacking and analyzing NLP. In *Proceedings of the 2019 Conference on Empirical Methods in Natural Language Processing and the 9th International Joint Conference on Natural Language Processing (EMNLP-IJCNLP)*, pages 2153–2162, Hong Kong, China. Association for Computational Linguistics.

Tianlu Wang, Xuezhi Wang, Yao Qin, Ben Packer, Kang Li, Jilin Chen, Alex Beutel, and Ed Chi. 2020. Cat-gen: Improving robustness in nlp models via controlled adversarial text generation. In *Proceedings of the 2020 Conference on Empirical Methods in Natural Language Processing (EMNLP)*, pages 5141–5146.

Jason Wei, Maarten Bosma, Vincent Y Zhao, Kelvin Guu, Adams Wei Yu, Brian Lester, Nan Du, Andrew M Dai, and Quoc V Le. 2021. Finetuned language models are zero-shot learners. *arXiv preprint arXiv:2109.01652*.

Tongshuang Wu, Marco Tulio Ribeiro, Jeffrey Heer, and Daniel S Weld. 2021. Polyjuice: Generating counterfactuals for explaining, evaluating, and improving models. In *Proceedings of the 59th Annual Meeting of the Association for Computational Linguistics and the 11th International Joint Conference on Natural Language Processing (Volume 1: Long Papers)*, pages 6707–6723.

Tianyi Zhang, Varsha Kishore, Felix Wu, Kilian Q. Weinberger, and Yoav Artzi. 2020. Bertscore: Evaluating text generation with bert. In *International Conference on Learning Representations*.

Xuhui Zhou, Maarten Sap, Swabha Swayamdipta, Yejin Choi, and Noah Smith. 2021. Challenges in automated debiasing for toxic language detection. In *Proceedings of the 16th Conference of the European Chapter of the Association for Computational Linguistics: Main Volume*, pages 3143–3155, Online. Association for Computational Linguistics.

A LLM-D counterfactual text generation

A.1 Setup

Following Reif et al. (2021), we use "{" and "}" delimiters in the formatting of the prompt to encourage LLM-D to provide its response in a similar format, and automatically discard any text outside of the first set of delimiters in each response. The prompts are formatted in a second-person conversational style, as this is the style of data that LLM-D was finetuned on; for a template suitable for standard next-token language models, see (Reif et al., 2021, Table 7).

While our initial experiments used the underlying General Language Model (GLM) part of LLM-D, all results in this paper were generated using

LLM-D. We used a temperature of 1 and $k = 40$ for the top-k next token sampling, and we did not discard responses regardless of the "safety" score LLM-D assigned to them, as we found that this too severely curtailed the diversity of responses. We mitigated the safety risks of this by ensuring that we had a robust human evaluation step in place later in the pipeline.

We also filter out responses with failure modes observed often in early experiments, including responses that were just a string of punctuation or the "shrug emoji" ¯_(ツ)_/¯, verbatim repetitions of the input text, and responses that regurgitated part of the prompt ("here is a rewrite...", "here is some text..."). These filters were applied to the initial set of 16 responses from the model.

A.2 Prompt and instruction selection

The full set of prompts used in all of our experiments are listed in Table 8; these are the same prompts used in Reif et al. (2021).

We experimented with different prompts, but found that more task-specific prompts did not produce measurably better results, and in fact found that LLM-D tended to overfit much more strongly to the final few prompts when the prompts specifically referenced the sensitive attribute. For example, using a set of 7 prompts demonstrating examples of counterfactual generation specifically for transgender identity, where the last two prompts referenced beauty pageants and Kiwi transgender weightlifter Laurel Hubbard respectively, the (unfiltered) LLM-D responses to the 100 transgender-referencing examples used in Section 5.2 included 22 references to New Zealand, 31 references to weight lifters, and 5 references to beauty queens / beauty pageants. By comparison, using the prompts in Table 8 generated 0 results involving any of these keywords, and a total of 7 results referencing bells/snow/trees (see the final two prompts in Table 8).

For the rewriting instruction, we found that "make this not about [sensitive attribute]" helped to focus the language model's attention on the desired parts of the sentence (as opposed to Polyjuice, which would often produce permutations that were completely unrelated to the sensitive attribute reference in the sentence) but that this did not reliably translate into *removing* the reference to the sensitive attribute. However, the fact that LLM-D produces 16 independent responses meant that there was consistently at least one response that did satisfy the criteria to be a good counterfactual, and one direction of future work is to automatically identify these responses more effectively.

A.3 Automated metrics

We used the implementation of BLEU score provided by the `sacrebleu` package, using the NIST smoothing method as described in Chen and Cherry (2014) to mitigate the fact that we are using a corpus-level metric to compute scores on individual pairs of sentences.

The implementation of BERTScore is the one provided by the authors (Zhang et al., 2020), modified to accept a Flax-based BERT model. BERTScore computes both a recall score (which rewards text pairs where everything in the original sentence is also represented in the counterfactual) and a precision score (rewards pairs where everything in the counterfactual is also represented in the original).[7] We use the resulting F1 score as our metric since we want our counterfactuals to neither add too much nor delete too much compared to the original text.

The attribute classifier is also JAX/Flax-based, and comprises a 2-layer fully connected network (hidden dimension 2048), using the first token of the input text's BERT representation (Devlin et al., 2019) as the embedding function. It was trained on a subset of CivilComments-Identities (all texts, regardless of toxicity, that referenced at least one attribute of interest with a score > 0.5, along with 20k negative examples that referenced none of the attributes of interest) using the AdamW optimizer (Loshchilov and Hutter, 2018) (with learning rate 0.001, weight decay 0.002) for 36k steps with a batch size 256, using a binary cross-entropy loss function to allow for multi-label predictions.

B Counterfactual generation methods

B.1 Ablation

For ablation, we generate a list of key terms per identity and simply remove those terms from each text. The lists for each attribute are in Table 6.

The term list was generated by fitting a unigram naive bayes classifier to the non-toxic subset of Civil Comments data (toxicity < 0.1), separating texts labeled with the given identity group (attribute score > 0.5) from a random sample of the rest. The

[7]Note that these are not symmetric: for example, a counterfactual that simply repeats the original text but adds an extra detail to the end would score more highly on recall than precision.

20 features (unigrams) most strongly associated with the identity class were used as the candidate wordlist, and were filtered by hand to remove irrelevant terms.

We emphasise that these wordlists are *not* complete representations of the corresponding attributes and that our ablation counterfactuals were generated purely to provide a baseline score for comparison to other methods.

B.2 Substitution

To generate counterfactuals using substitution, we take the ablation wordlists and (where possible) assign each one a corresponding word from another identity in the same broad category, e.g. replacing one religion with another. For examples with no plausible substitution (e.g. "transition" in the transgender category) we leave the word unchanged. See Table 7 for the full set of word pairs.

As with the ablation wordlists above, we emphasise that these are not necessarily complete representations of the corresponding attributes. They were generated purely for the purposes of providing a baseline for comparison in our experiments, and should not be used as-is to generate counterfactuals for fairness probing in real world settings.

B.3 LLM-D

We use the same fixed set of prompts for every input text (see Appendix A.2 and Table 8), and the instruction "make this not about X", where X is the sensitive attribute referenced in the input text. LLM-D generates up to 16 responses per input, which are filtered as described in Appendix A.3 and then ranked by taking the average of their BLEU score and BERTScore F1 score. Only the top-ranked example is returned for rating.

For some inputs, it can happen that none of LLM-D's responses are of sufficient quality to pass the filtering step. We rerun the generation pipeline on each of these failed inputs until a counterfactual is returned, up to a maximum of 5 attempts.

B.4 Polyjuice

Polyjuice (Wu et al., 2021) is a general-purpose counterfactual generator that uses a finetuned LM (GPT-2) along with control-codes to generate diverse permutations of sentences. To our knowledge, Polyjuice has not been evaluated for fairness probing, but its flexible generation abilities make it a promising approach to compare with.

A Polyjuice user can choose from various types of permutation (negation, shuffle, deletion, etc) and can even specify where in the sentence the edit should be made by replacing words or phrases with the `[BLANK]` token.

For each input text, we generate 16 potential counterfactuals: 8 where we allow Polyjuice to choose which parts of the text to modify, and 8 where we direct its attention to the sensitive attribute reference(s) by replacing all keywords from the corresponding ablation list with the `[BLANK]` token. These 16 examples are then filtered and ranked by the same criteria as the LLM-D examples, and the top-scoring one is returned for rating.

As with the LLM-D counterfactuals, we rerun the Polyjuice generation pipeline on inputs that failed to return a valid counterfactual, up to 5 times per example.

We found that some of the generated Polyjuice counterfactuals still contained tokens such as `BLANK` or `EMPTY`, which we replaced with the empty string before rating the examples.

C Human rater guidelines

We rate each (original, counterfactual) pair on four criteria:

- fluency
- presence of sensitive attribute
- similarity of meaning
- similarity of label

Precise definitions of each criteria (along with examples) are given in the rater instructions below. For our purposes, we required an (original, counterfactual) pair to be rated "yes" for fluency, "no reference" for presence of sensitive attribute, "yes" for similarity of label, and at least 2 (out of 4) for similarity of meaning.

These guidelines are designed to be flexible and easily modifiable to apply to multiple text formats (internet comments, video titles, etc) and downstream tasks (toxicity detection, sentiment analysis, etc). We highlight the parts that are specific to our task by [bracketing and underlining] them.

C.1 Rater instructions

1. ***Fluency/consistency***
   Is the text fluent and consistent, and does it make sense? (yes/no/unsure)
   Ignore any extraneous punctuation marks at the beginning or end of the text. You should also ignore capitalisation / lack thereof unless

it makes a significant difference to the fluency. Evaluate the fluency relative to the original text and in the context of the domain: these examples are [internet comments], so they need not adhere to perfect spelling and grammar to be realistic examples.

Examples of sufficiently fluent sentences:

- "islam is great, its just a fact" [fine: minor incorrect grammar but not unrealistic for internet speech]
- "Some folks are born white... just accept it." [fine: awkward phrasing but not inconsistent]

Examples of sentences that are not consistent or do not make sense:

- "*Christians* want to impose *sharia law* on the country." [inconsistent: Sharia law is associated with Islam]
- "The problem with on violence is it harms" [does not make sense]
- "—!!!!!–,,,,,,xxxxz" [gibberish]

2. ***Presence of sensitive attribute***
   Does the text:
   - **explicitly reference the attribute?**
   - **implicitly reference the attribute?**
   - **not reference the attribute?**

   The targeted attribute will be specified for each example; references to other sensitive attributes (e.g. references to other religions when the specified attribute is Islam) do not count.

   An *implicit reference* is a group or identity referenced but not stated explicitly. For example:
   - "Jack went on a date with his boyfriend" implicitly references the fact that Jack is queer but does not state it explicitly.
   - "Our state is trying to pass a bathroom bill, this sucks" implicitly references transgender identity, since "bathroom bill" is commonly understood to be a type of law that targets trans and non-binary people.
   - "She wore a hijab on stage" is an implicit reference to Islam, since the hijab is a common marker of Muslim identity.

   If the text contains an explicit reference to the attribute, there's no need to evaluate it for implicit references as well.

3. ***Similarity of meaning***
   Taking into account both the changes made to remove references to the sensitive attribute and any other changes in the sentence, how similar is the text to the original? (scale of 0 to 4)
   - **Score of 4**: Retains the same grammatical structure and overall meaning as the original, and changes only the parts of the sentence required to remove the sensitive attribute (no other changes or deletions).
   - **Score of 3**: Substitutes or removes the sensitive attribute, only differing from the original in ways that don't materially affect the meaning of the example, e.g. minor grammatical changes, use of synonyms, substitutions to similar or semantically neutral concepts ("BLM" $\rightarrow$ "environmental protestors", "Allah" $\rightarrow$ "God" are examples of similar substitution, "Muslims" $\rightarrow$ "people", "Antifa" $\rightarrow$ "protest movement" are examples of neutral substitution).
     Note that here "neutral" means words like "people" ,"citizens", "protest movement", "religion" etc. Non-toxic substitutions that change the meaning of the sentence should be assigned a score of 2 (see below).
   - **Score of 2**: Makes an additional change (addition or removal) beyond the minimal changes required to remove the sensitive attribute, and/or makes edits that change the meaning of the sentence.
   - **Score of 1**: Bears some resemblance to the original sentence, but has major changes beyond those necessary to remove the sensitive attribute.
   - **Score of 0**: Is completely unrelated to the original sentence.

Here are some example texts for each score.

- Original:
  - How would you feel about opening a meeting with a Muslim prayer to Allah?
- Score of 4:
  - How would you feel about opening a meeting with a prayer? [no changes beyond minimal necessary]
  - How would you feel about opening a meeting with prayers?
- Score of 3:
  - How would you feel about opening a

meeting with a *Christian* prayer to *God*? [substitution to similar concept]
  - How would you feel about opening a meeting with a *religious reading*? [substitution to neutral concept]
  - How would you feel about opening *this event* with a prayer? [minor extra rewording beyond minimum necessary]
- Score of 2:
  - *Since we're in Portland*, how would you feel about opening this meeting with a prayer? [addition of extra detail in addition to necessary chances]
  - How would you feel about opening a meeting with a *brief political statement*? [substitution that changes the meaning of the sentence]
  - How would you feel about opening a meeting? [removal of extra detail that changes the meaning in a non-trivial way]
- Score of 1:
  - What's all this about meetings and prayers? [similar topic but major changes to original beyond those necessary to remove attribute]
- Score of 0:
  - By the banks of the Seine. [no resemblance to original]

4. ***Similarity of label***
Should this example be assigned the same ground-truth [toxicity] label as the original text? (yes/no/unsure)
Note: you are not trying to determine whether the two texts are equivalent or whether the concepts referenced in either text are comparable or even true: *your answer should depend only on whether you would think it would cause harm if a [toxicity] classifier model treated the two texts differently.*
[For the purposes of this question, we define toxicity to mean "a rude, disrespectful, or unreasonable comment that is likely to make you leave a discussion".][8]
The following are examples where both texts *should* be assigned the same label, because a [toxicity] classifier model should treat them the same way:
   - Text: Miss Nevada (2021) is a beauty queen.
   Original: Miss Nevada (2021) is a transgender woman.
   (both non-toxic)
   - Text: Maybe the lead scientist is a woman.
   Original: Maybe the lead scientist is gay.
   (both non-toxic)
   - Text: I hate white people.
   Original: I hate straight people.
   (both toxic)

   The following are examples where the example should *not* be assigned the same label as the original text, because a [toxicity] classifier model should *not* treat them the same way:
   - Text: All white men are dangerous. (toxic)
   Original: All white men think cats are great. (non-toxic)
   - Text: Can't trust a velociraptor, they don't have morals. (non-toxic)
   Original: Can't trust a Christian, they don't have morals. (toxic)
5. ***Reject for other reason? (yes/leave blank)***
Use this field to flag examples that pass all of the other criteria but seem inappropriate for use as counterfactuals.

C.2 Example

Text: He was a baker? I did not see that in the story.
Original: He was Muslim? I did not see that in the story.
Sensitive attribute: Islam

1. Is the text fluent and consistent, and does it make sense? (yes/no/unsure)
`Yes`
2. Does the text: explicitly reference the attribute? implicitly reference the attribute? not reference the attribute?
`Not reference the attribute`
3. Taking into account both the changes made to remove references to the sensitive attribute and any other changes in the sentence, how similar is the text to the original? (scale of 0 to 4)
2

[8]This is the definition of toxicity used by Perspective API; `https://developers.perspectiveapi.com/s/about-the-api-key-concepts`

4. Should this example be assigned the same ground-truth toxicity label as the original text? (yes/no/unsure)
   `Yes`
5. Reject for other reason? (yes or ⟨leave blank⟩)
   `⟨leave blank⟩`

Attribute	Ablation unigrams
LGBQ+	gay, gays, homosexual, homosexuality, homosexuals, lesbian, lesbians, lgbt, lgbtq, sexuality
transgender	bathroom, bathrooms, hormones, lgbt, lgbtq, testosterone, trans, transgender, transgendered, transition
Judaism	holocaust, israel, israeli, israelis, jew, jewish, jews, judaism, semitic, semitism, zionist
Islam	allah, hijab, islam, islamic, islamist, islamists, islamophobia, koran, mosque, mosques, muslim, muslims, quran, sharia, sunni

Table 6: Ablation Wordlists, generated as described in Appendix B.1. Note that these are not intended to be comprehensive wordlists for each topic, nor are all of the words direct references to the attribute itself (e.g. "Israel" or "bathroom"); we chose to retain these indirect references if they appeared in the top 20 unigrams produced by the naive Bayes classifier since we were evaluating the resulting counterfactuals on implicit references to the attribute as well as explicit ones.

Attribute	Replacement category	Substitution wordpairs
LGBQ+	heterosexual	(gay, straight), (gays, straights), (homosexual, heterosexual), (homosexuality, heterosexuality), (homosexuals, heterosexuals), (lesbian, straight), (lesbians, straights), (lgbt, straight), (lgbtq, straight)
transgender	cisgender	(lgbt, cis), (lgbtq, cis), (trans, cis), (transgender, cisgender), (transgendered, cisgendered)
Judaism	Christianity	(jew, christian), (jewish, christian), (jews, christians), (judaism, christianity)
Islam	Christianity	(allah, god), (hijab, cross), (islam, christianity), (islamic, christian), (islamist, fundamentalist), (islamists, fundamentalists), (islamophobia, anti-christian bias), (koran, bible), (mosque, church), (mosques, churches), (muslim, christian), (muslims, christians), (quran, bible), (sharia, canon law), (sunni, catholic)

Table 7: Substitution Wordlists. Note that while some of the pairings are direct analogs (e.g. "gay" → "straight", "Muslim" → "Christian"), others were chosen to maximise the chances of generating valid counterfactuals while retaining the general meaning of the sentence (e.g. "LGBTQ" → "straight"/"cis", "hijab" → "cross"); we are *not* implying that all of these pairings are completely analogous.

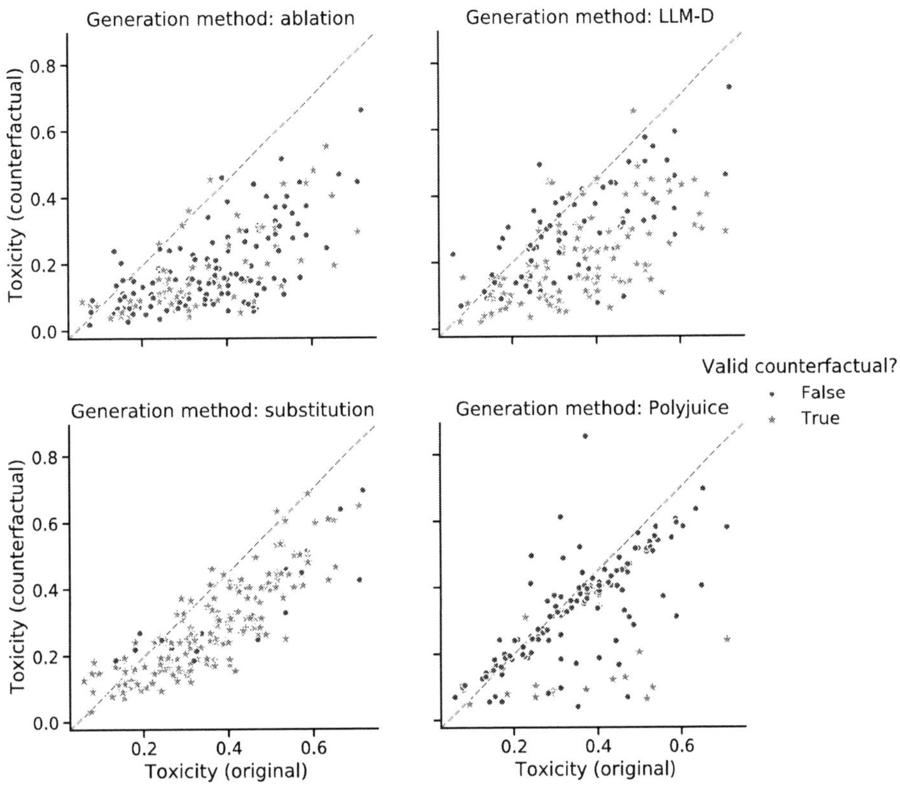

Figure 3: Toxicity scores of counterfactuals (generated from the Islam-referencing texts in Section 5.1) plotted against the toxicity scores of their original text; points in the lower right portion of each graph correspond to examples where Perspective API rated the counterfactual as *less* likely to be toxic than the original. We include the counterfactuals that did not pass the human rating step in order to illustrate the effects of different counterfactual generation methods on toxicity detection: for example, ablation failed mostly on the fluency criteria so its "poor" counterfactuals still exhibit a drop in toxicity here, whereas Polyjuice failed mostly on removing references to the sensitive attribute so its "poor" counterfactuals tend to cluster around the $y = x$ line.

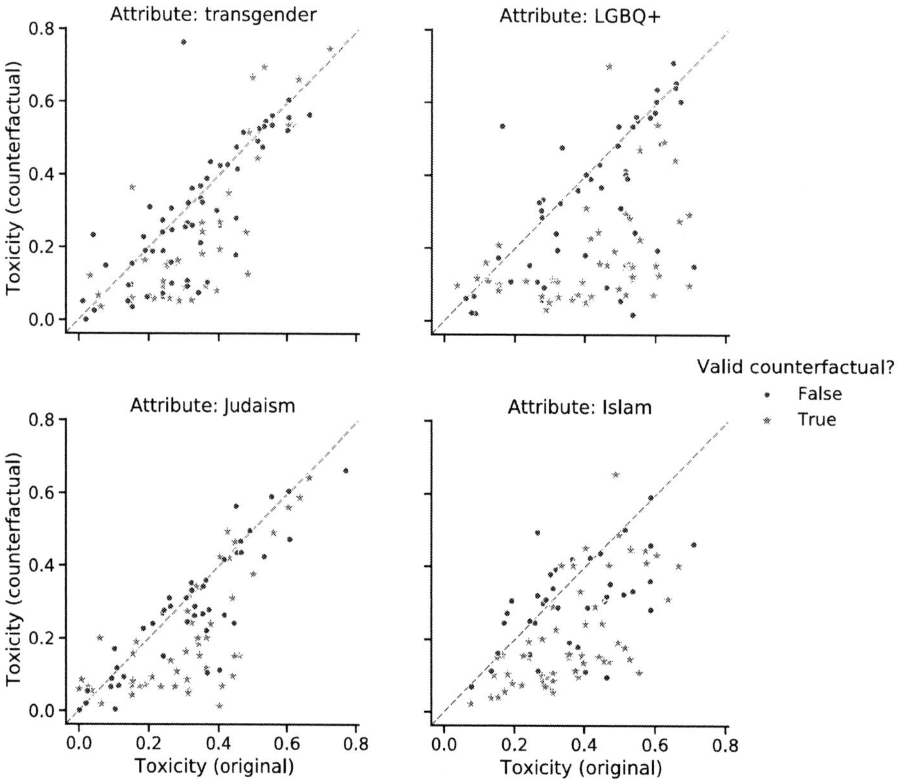

Figure 4: Toxicity scores of LLM-D counterfactuals (from Section 5.2) plotted against the toxicity scores of their original text; points in the lower right portion of the graph correspond to examples where Perspective API rated the counterfactual as *less* likely to be toxic than the original. Observe that the LGBQ+ category sees some swings in toxicity score that could result in a label flip (represented by the points closest to the bottom right corner), a phenomenon which is much less common with the other three topics.

```
0: Here is some text: {When the doctor asked Linda to take the medicine, he smiled and gave her a lollipop.}. Rewrite it to be more scary.

1: {When the doctor told Linda to take the medicine, there had been a malicious gleam in her eye that Linda didn't like at all.}

0: Here is some text: {they asked loudly, over the sound of the train.}. Rewrite it to be more intense.

1: {they yelled aggressively, over the clanging of the train.}

0: Here is some text: {When Mohammed left the theatre, it was already dark out}. Rewrite it to be more about the movie itself.

1: {The movie was longer than Mohammed had expected, and despite the excellent ratings he was a bit disappointed when he left the theatre.}

0: Here is some text: {next to the path}. Rewrite it to be about France.

1: {next to la Siene}

0: Here is some text: {The man stood outside the grocery store, ringing the bell.}. Rewrite it to be about clowns.

1: {The man stood outside the circus, holding a bunch of balloons.}

0: Here is some text: {the bell ringing}. Rewrite it to be more flowery.

1: {the peales of the jangling bell}

0: Here is some text: {against the tree}. Rewrite it to be include the word "snow".

1: {against the snow-covered bark of the tree}'
```

0: Here is some text: {**input text here**}. Rewrite it to be **instruction here**.

Table 8: The full prompt text used to generate counterfactuals with LLM-D. The "0" and "1" indicate two speakers, since LLM-D expects inputs formatted in turns of conversation. The text to be rewritten and the corresponding instruction (e.g. "not about transgender people") are inserted in the last line (blue, boldface).

A Appendix

In this appendix, we present the search space used for grid search for each of our classical machine learning models.

Logistic Regression

- solver: liblinear
- penalty: l1, l2
- C: 0.0001, 0.001, 0.01, 0.1, 1, 10, 100

Random Forest

- bootstrap: True
- max_depth: 10, 50, 100, None
- max_features: auto
- min_samples leaf: 1, 2, 4
- min_samples_split: 2, 5, 10
- n_estimators: 5, 10, 100

Support Vector Machines

- kernel: linear, rbf
- C: 0.001, 0.01, 0.1, 1, 10, 100
- gamma: 0.0001, 0.001, 0.01, 0.1

Proceedings of the Sixth Workshop on Online Abuse and Harms (WOAH), pages 230 - 230
July 14, 2022

Targeted Identity Group Prediction in Hate Speech Corpora

Pratik S. Sachdeva
D-Lab
University of California, Berkeley
pratik.sachdeva@berkeley.edu

Renata Barreto
School of Law
University of California, Berkeley
rbarreto@berkeley.edu

Claudia von Vacano
D-Lab
University of California, Berkeley
cvacano@berkeley.edu

Chris J. Kennedy
Center for Precision Psychiatry
Harvard Medical School
chris_kennedy@hms.harvard.edu

Abstract

The past decade has seen an abundance of work seeking to detect, characterize, and measure online hate speech. A related, but less studied problem, is the specification of identity groups targeted by that hate speech. Predictive accuracy on this task can supplement additional analyses beyond hate speech detection, motivating its study. Using the *Measuring Hate Speech* corpus, which provided annotations for targeted identity groups on roughly 50,000 social media comments, we create neural network models to perform multi-label binary prediction of identity groups targeted by a social media comment. Specifically, we study 8 broad identity groups and 12 identity sub-groups within race and gender identity. We find that these networks exhibited good predictive performance, achieving ROC AUCs of greater than 0.9 and PR AUCs of greater than 0.7 on several identity groups. At the same time, we find performance suffered on identity groups less represented in the dataset. We validate model performance on the HateCheck and Gab Hate Corpora, finding that predictive performance generalizes in most settings. We additionally examine the performance of the model on comments targeting multiple identity groups. Lastly, we discuss issues with a standardized conceptualization of a "target" in hate speech corpora, and its relation to intersectionality. Our results demonstrate the feasibility of simultaneously detecting a broad range of targeted groups in social media comments, and offer suggestions for future work on modeling and dataset annotation for this task.

1 Introduction

The proliferation of hate speech on online platforms continues to be a significant human rights issue, associated with a host a negative consequences (Tsesis, 2002; Wilson, 2017). Hate speech distinguishes itself from other types of toxic or offensive content in that it specifically targets an individual or group on the basis of their membership in an identity group, such as race, religion, gender, sexual orientation, etc. (Sellars, 2016). Thus, developing methods that can identify and characterize hate speech, and its targets, is of paramount importance.

Given the scale of online hate speech, much effort has been made toward the development of automated approaches to classify or measure it given raw text (Fortuna and Nunes, 2018; Tontodimamma et al., 2021). While initial efforts used binary labels, subsequent work has introduced additional labels that more finely characterize or measure hate speech (Kennedy et al., 2020; Davidson et al., 2017; Kennedy et al., 2022). These include studies that implicitly specify the targeted identity group, such as labeling speech as racism or sexism (Waseem and Hovy, 2016).

Predicting the identity group targeted by social media content is useful beyond hate speech detection. Such algorithms could identify comments that target groups of interest for secondary analyses. These analyses include evaluating the impacts, such as adverse health outcomes, of social media targeting specific communities (Nguyen et al., 2021). Furthermore, leveraging knowledge of the target identity can better inform interventions or moderation of hateful content (Tekiroglu et al., 2020). Thus, automated approaches to targeted identity prediction could serve these analyses by streamlining the process of labeling new corpora for study.

While some efforts have been made to develop algorithms that predict targeted identity groups, they have largely focused on classifying individual vs. group targets (Zampieri et al., 2019) or implicitly

Proceedings of the Sixth Workshop on Online Abuse and Harms (WOAH), pages 231 - 244
July 14, 2022 ©2022 Association for Computational Linguistics

characterizing the target (Waseem and Hovy, 2016). Predictive models capable of identifying a broad range of targeted protected classes have been less studied (Chiril et al., 2022). Hate speech corpora that include the requisite range of targeted identity annotations have been limited until recently, opening the door to a full examination of this problem (Kennedy et al., 2020; Mathew et al., 2020; Kennedy et al., 2022).

In this work, we developed models to predict identity groups targeted by social media comments. Using the *Measuring Hate Speech* (MHS) corpus (Kennedy et al., 2020), we trained neural networks to predict 8 identity group and 12 sub-group targets of hate speech. We demonstrated that these models exhibited good predictive performance, validating them within the MHS corpus and on external datasets. Lastly, we examined model performance on comments with multiple targets, finding that performance depended highly on those targets.

2 Related Work

Hate Speech Detection and Measurement. This work builds on the long line of work investigating automated hate speech detection (Waseem and Hovy, 2016; Waseem, 2016; Davidson et al., 2017; Del Vigna et al., 2017). Currently, the state-of-the-art approaches utilize large-scale transformer models with transfer learning to detect hate speech (Koufakou et al., 2020; Tran et al., 2020). We use similar approaches in this work.

Targeted Identity Detection. Most work investigating the identification of identity targets in hate speech has viewed it as a sub-task of hate speech detection (Waseem et al., 2017). Several works focused on hate speech detection have implicitly considered target identity via labels that contain information about the target of the speech, such as "racism", "sexism", and others (Kwok and Wang, 2013; Waseem and Hovy, 2016; Indurthi et al., 2019; Grimminger and Klinger, 2021). Other work has considered hate speech targets in the context of "single" or "group" targets. Notably, the shared task OffensEval 2019 (Zampieri et al., 2019) included single vs. group target identification, which has been used in subsequent multi-task frameworks (Plaza-del Arco et al., 2021). Lastly, Mossie and Wang (2020) consider the identification of ethnic groups in Ehtiopian social media comments.

Several works have sought to define the notion of "targeting" while providing analysis on what groups are targeted (ElSherief et al., 2018; Silva et al., 2016). These works largely used rules or lexica based approaches for detection. Shvets et al. (2021) explicitly define a "target" and corresponding "aspects", while developing neural networks to extract text matching these concepts in comments.

The creation of corpora that provide labels on targeted identity groups have allowed further analysis of targeted identity prediction (Mathew et al., 2020; Kennedy et al., 2020, 2022). Most relevant to this work is an analysis by Chiril et al. (2022) examining multi-task target identity prediction on a wide range of past corpora. Our study builds on these works by examining the performance on a thorough range of both broad target identity groups and more specific sub-groups.

3 Methods

All code used in this work is available on the `hate_measure` repository[1], which contains a codebase of various models applicable to the MHS dataset, and the `hate_target` repository[2], which contains the code used for the analyses and figures described in this paper. All datasets were obtained as described by their corresponding entries on the Hate Speech Data website (Vidgen and Derczynski, 2020).

3.1 Datasets

We trained and evaluated all models on the Measuring Hate Speech (MHS) corpus created by Kennedy et al. (2020). We performed additional generalization evaluations on two other corpora: the HateCheck Corpus (Röttger et al., 2021) and Gab Hate Corpus (GHS) (Kennedy et al., 2022). We chose to train on the MHS corpus because it was the largest dataset that covered a diverse range of platforms.

Measuring Hate Speech. The MHS corpus was constructed to facilitate the measurement of hate speech with item response theory. It consists of 50,070 hate speech comments obtained from Reddit, Youtube, and Twitter, labeled by 11,143 annotators. Annotations consisted of 10 survey items spanning a theorized spectrum of hatefulness. Additional annotations, of main interest for this work, included the target of the comment. Specifically, annotators were asked *"Is the [comment] directed at or about any individuals or groups based on..."*,

[1] `https://github.com/dlab-projects/hate_measure`

[2] `https://github.com/dlab-projects/hate_target`

with the option to select among the following eight identity groups: race/ethnicity, religion, national origin or citizenship status, gender, sexual orientation, age, disability status, political identity; or "none of the above". Annotators could select more than one identity group. We note that the MHS corpus allows target identity annotations to include those that are the subject of supportive speech. Thus, "target" within the scope of this dataset can be understood to mean the identity group a comment speaks to, whether it is hateful or supportive.

For each identity group selected (if any), the annotator was prompted to select identity sub-groups. For example, if the annotator indicated a target based on race/ethnicity, they were asked to specify racial/ethnic sub-group identities, including: Black/African American, Hispanic/Latino, Asian, Middle Eastern, Native American or Alaska Native, Pacific Islander, Non-hispanic White, or an "Other" category with the option to provide written text. As another example, the possible sub-groups for gender identity included Men, Women, Non-binary, Transgender Men, Transgender Women, or Transgender unspecified (along with an "Other" category allowing for annotator specification). See Appendix B for all identity sub-groups.

HateCheck Corpus. The HateCheck Corpus is comprised of a set of functional tests for hate speech detection models. The samples in HateCheck are synthetically constructed to allow diagnostic assessment of model performance. These synthetic expressions generally make apparent who the target is, e.g., "I hate [IDENTITY GROUP]". Thus, they serve as a useful sanity check for validating the performance of a model.

The HateCheck Corpus contains 3,901 comments, of which 3,606 have a labeled target. These targets are specifically labeled as "gay people", "women", "disabled people", "Muslims", "black people", "trans people", and "immigrants". To evaluate generalization performance, we recast these labels as follows: "gay people"$\rightarrow$ Sexual Orientation, "women" $\rightarrow$ Gender Identity, "disabled people" $\rightarrow$ Disability, "Muslims" $\rightarrow$ Religion, "black people" $\rightarrow$ Race, "trans people" $\rightarrow$ Gender Identity, and "immigrants" $\rightarrow$ National Origin.

Gab Hate Corpus. The Gab Hate Corpus (GHC) is comprised of 27,665 posts from the social media platform Gab (Kennedy et al., 2022). Using a hierarchical coding typology, The posts were annotated for "the presence of hate-based rhetoric." The corresponding identity group targets include nationality/regionalism, race/ethnicity, gender identity, religious/spiritual identity, sexual orientation, ideology, political identification, and mental/physical health status. We recast the ideology and political identification labels as a single "political ideology" label and map the remaining groups directly onto those of the MHS corpus.

The GHC only includes target identity labels if the comment expressed hate toward those target identities. Since the MHS corpus includes target identity labels for either hateful or supportive speech, we omitted samples in the GHC which lacked target identity labels, resulting in a subcorpus of 7,801 comments. We did this since a model trained on the MHS may predict targets for the GHC that would have no corresponding label, since annotators would not have identified targets if they did not deem the comment hateful.

3.2 Data Preparation

We performed minimal preprocessing on each data sample, including normalizing blank space and replacing URLs, phone numbers, and emails with respective tokens. We then passed each comment through a tokenizer corresponding to the base model architecture being trained.

We formulated the task of predicting targeted identities as a multi-label binary prediction. However, each comment was annotated by more than one annotator. Annotators expressed moderate agreement on identifying the targeted groups, with Krippendorff's alphas ranging from $0.6 - 0.75$ (see Appendix C). We used soft labeling for training, where the proportion of annotators identifying an identity group as a target served as the "label". When calculating evaluation metrics, we only used binary labels by majority voting.

Following Kennedy et al. (2020), we removed annotators according to two quality checks revolving around the infit mean-square statistic (Linacre et al., 2002), and satisfactory identification of target identities. Filtering annotators according to these quality checks resulted in 8,472 annotators remaining, with 39,565 accompanying comments.

3.3 Model Architecture

We tested various pre-trained transformer architectures in predicting the multi-label binary outcome. Specifically, we used Universal Sentence Encoder (Cer et al., 2018), BERT (Devlin et al., 2018), and RoBERTa (Liu et al., 2019) as base models. We

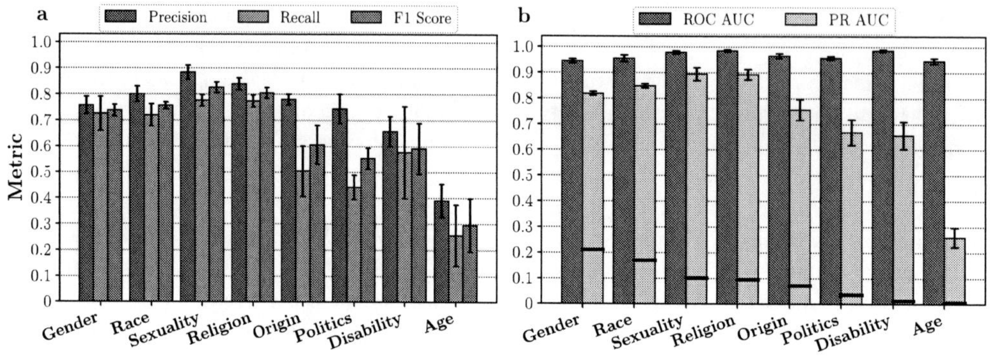

Figure 1: **Transformer models are predictive of target identity groups.** The performance on target group identity prediction across test folds of the MHS corpus as quantified by threshold-dependent and threshold-agnostic metrics. Error bars denote the standard deviation across the test folds. **a.** Precision, recall, and F1 score on test set data according to a 0.5 threshold, for each target group identity. **b.** ROC and PR AUC on test set data. Black lines denote the incidence rate (proportion of positive labels) of the corresponding target identity group. Identity groups are sorted in order of decreasing incidence rate.

stacked a feedforward layer on top of the model embeddings, and then placed M binary output layers, where M is the number of output groups under consideration. We applied dropout to the feedforward layer, with the specific rate chosen as a hyperparameter. We used pre-trained models obtained from HuggingFace (Wolf et al., 2020).

3.4 Training Procedure

We considered a variety of hyperparameter configurations when training models, varying the size of the dense layer, the batch size, and the dropout rate. The full set of configurations is listed in Appendix A. We used a validation set to determine the number of epochs to train on, as described below. We additionally weighted each sample by the square root of the number of annotators. Lastly, we used cross-entropy as the loss function for each output, and used the sum of individual losses as the loss for the entire network.

We performed 5-fold cross validation to train and evaluate models. After shuffling the data across samples, we split the dataset into 5 folds. For each architecture, we trained 5 models, each using 4 folds for training and the remaining fold for evaluation. Each training fold was further split into training and validation sets. We then trained the model using the training set data with early stopping on the validation loss. When validation performance decreased past epoch E, we halted training, and retrained the model on the entire training fold for E epochs. We then evaluated the model performance on the test fold. Model evaluation metrics were reported across the 5 test folds. For out-of-corpus generalization tasks, we applied a model trained on the entire dataset, using the average number of epochs across folds during cross-validation.

3.5 Evaluation Metrics

Since most labels we considered were imbalanced, we evaluated an array of complementary metrics. As is commonly done, we focused on a set of threshold-dependent metrics (precision, recall, F1 score) and threshold-agnostic metrics (ROC AUC and PR AUC) in the main text. We report two additional metrics–the accuracy over chance and log-odds difference–in the Appendix.

We used traditional threshold-dependent metrics capturing false positive/false negative rates, including the *precision*, *recall*, and *F1 score*. We calculated these metrics using predictions at a threshold of 0.5, unless otherwise specified. We supplement the traditional metrics with threshold-agnostic metrics, including the area under the receiver operater characteristic curve (ROC AUC), and the area under the precision-recall curve (PR AUC). Importantly, we use the PR AUC in addition to ROC AUC as it may be more informative in imbalanced datasets (Davis and Goadrich, 2006). We used macro-averaging to summarize a metric across labels. This process consisted of weighting each label's performance metric by their incidence rate when calculating an overall average.

We considered two additional metrics: *accu-*

racy over chance and the *log-odds difference*. For brevity, we describe them here, but report their values in Appendix A. We considered accuracy divided by chance performance in order to confirm that models did in fact generalize beyond that of a naive classifier which could artificially achieve high accuracy in imbalanced settings. In *highly* imbalanced settings (i.e., fewer than 1% of the labels in the positive class), accuracy over chance may not sufficiently capture the performance of a predictive model. This stems from the difficulty in improving performance in highly accurate regimes (e.g., it is more difficult to improve from 99% to 99.5% than 90% to 90.5% accuracy). Thus, we additionally turn to the log-odds difference:

$$\text{LOD} = \log\left(\frac{a}{1-a}\right) - \log\left(\frac{b}{1-b}\right) \quad (1)$$

where a is the test set accuracy and b is the baseline accuracy (e.g., chance). The log-odds difference more effectively weights the difficulty in achieving performance gains when the dataset is heavily imbalanced (e.g., the second term is very large).

4 Results

Our main goal was the multi-label binary prediction of target identity groups. We first trained and evaluated models to predict the targeting of the broad identity groups. We repeated these experiments, but on identity sub-group predictions. We then evaluated the performance of the model on two additional datasets: the HateCheck and Gab Hate Corpora. Lastly, we evaluated the performance of the model on samples which had multiple targets.

4.1 Targeted Identity Group Prediction

We first considered the task of predicting the identity group(s) targeted by a comment. We constructed a multi-label binary prediction task, with the binary outcomes corresponding to gender, race/ethnicity, sexual orientation, religion, national origin, politics, disability, and age (ordered in decreasing incidence rate). We then trained a variety of transformer-based neural networks to predict the targeting of each identity group in parallel. Each model consisted of a base network (pre-trained transformer model) stacked with a dense layer mapping onto the 8 identity groups, with variations on the hyperparameter configuration and data preparation. The full set of experiments and architectures, along with their performance, is listed in Appendix A. For brevity, we show results using a RoBERTa-Large base network with soft labels and training samples weighted by number of annotators (see Methods), which exhibited the best performance of the models we considered.

We found that the model generally excelled at predicting the target of the comment, with performance varying according to the incidence rate of the label. We first evaluated model performance using threshold-dependent metrics such as precision, recall, and the F1 score (Fig. 1a). At a threshold of 0.5, the model achieved F1 scores from $0.7 - 0.85$ for the gender, race, sexual orientation, and religion labels. For national origin, politics, disability, and age, the F1 score decreased. This likely corresponds to the decrease in incidence rate for these labels (Fig. 1b: black lines). Additionally, precision generally exceeded recall, indicating that the model generally suffered from false negatives more often than false positives. This implies that the model could fail to identify comments which targeted identity groups, particularly for the national origin and political ideology labels.

We examined the threshold-agnostic labels–ROC AUC and PR AUC–similarly finding that they indicated high predictive accuracy (Fig. 1b). The ROC AUC values for all identity groups were above 0.90. Meanwhile, PR AUC values were above 0.80 for the gender, race, sexual orientation, and religion labels, above 0.60 for the politics and disability labels, and below 0.30 for age. The performance of the PR AUC roughly tracked with the incidence rate (Fig. 1b), as we might expect. We note that the PR AUC may be a better indicator of performance than the ROC AUC due to the imabalanced nature of the dataset (Davis and Goadrich, 2006). Together, these results demonstrate that the model can simultaneously predict several targeted identity groups. However, this performance suffers on identity groups that are less represented in the dataset (e.g., age and disability).

4.2 Targeted Identity Sub-Group Prediction

We next considered the prediction of specific identity sub-groups. For example, secondary analyses on social media comments may be interested in comments targeting a specific gender identity (e.g., comments targeting women). To this end, we evaluated the performance of a similar task–multi-label binary prediction–but the identity sub-groups. We specifically focus on racial/ethnic iden-

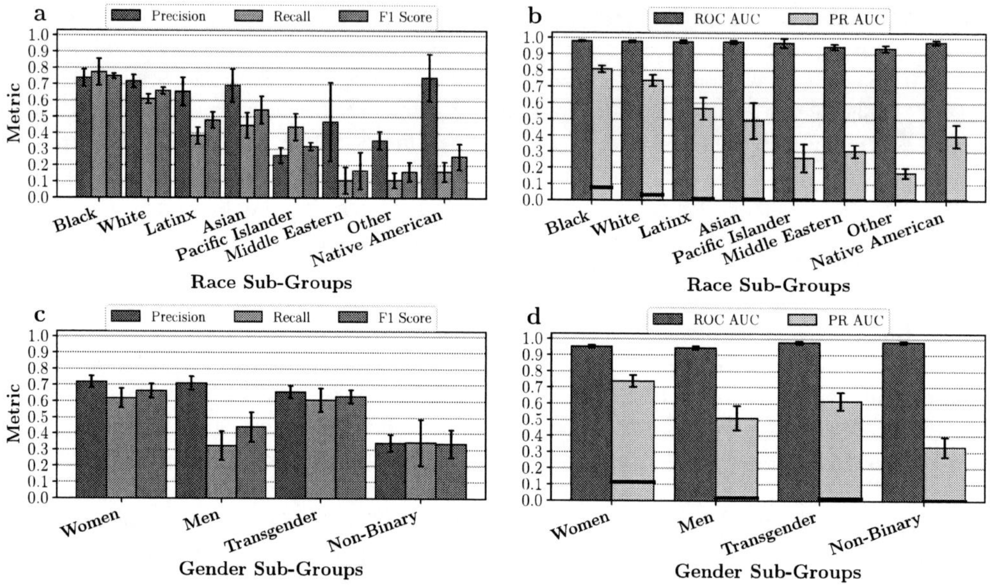

Figure 2: **Model performance on identity sub-groups varies strongly across sub-groups.** The performance on target sub-group identity prediction across test folds of the MHS corpus as quantified by threshold-dependent and threshold-agnostic metrics. **a-b.** Precision, recall, and F1 score on the test set data according to a 0.5 threshold (**a**) and ROC/PR AUCs (**b**) for the racial sub-groups. **c-d.** Same as top row, but for the gender identity groups. Black lines denote the incidence rate (number of positive labels) of the corresponding target identity group. Identity groups are sorted in order of decreasing incidence rate.

tity sub-groups (Black, White, Latinx, Asian, Middle Eastern, Pacific Islander, Native American, or some other group; listed in decreasing order of incidence rate) and gender identity sub-groups (women, men, non-binary; listed in decreasing order of incidence rate) because these groups were the most well-represented in the corpus. Within the gender identity sub-group task, we added an additional transgender label. As in the case of the broader identity groups, we found that the best performing model was a network with a RoBERTa-Large base with soft labels and weighted samples.

We found that the best performing model exhibited high predictive performance on some racial identities (Fig. 2). However, predictive performance was generally lower than that of the group identity prediction. We first evaluated threshold-dependent metrics, finding that the model exhibited the best performance on Black-targeting speech, a median F1 score of 0.72. Similar to the target identity models, precision generally exceeded that of recall, implying the presence of false negatives. These discrepancies were most strongly observed in the racial groups which had the lowest incidence rate, including Middle Eastern, Pacific Islander, Native American, and the Other category (Fig. 2b: black lines). Among the threshold-agnostic metrics, ROC AUC generally indicated superior predictive performance, though this may be a product of label imbalance (Davis and Goadrich, 2006). PR AUC generally tracked with the F1 score (and the incidence rate). A notable exception is Asian identity, which exhibited higher PR AUC than Latinx identity, despite having a lower indicidence rate.

Meanwhile, for the gender sub-groups, we observed worse performance relative to race. The best predictive performance was observed on identifying comments targeting women, with an F1 score of roughly 0.65. Interestingly, we observed substantially better predictive performance in identifying comments targeting transgender people compared to men, despite comparable incidence rates. Overall, we found that the reduced number of samples resulted in decreased predictive performance for many identity sub-groups.

4.3 Models Generalize to External Corpora

Thus far, we have examined model performance on held-out data within the MHS corpus, which consists of comments from Reddit, Twitter, and

HateCheck Corpus

Identity Group	Accuracy (Chance)	F1 Score	ROC AUC	PR AUC
Disability	0.989 (0.869)	0.957	0.996	0.986
Gender	0.978 (0.739)	0.954	0.994	0.990
National Origin	0.986 (0.875)	0.941	0.990	0.972
Race	0.981 (0.871)	0.926	0.990	0.972
Religion	0.984 (0.869)	0.935	0.967	0.951
Sexual Orientation	0.993 (0.852)	0.974	0.991	0.981

Gab Hate Corpus

Identity Group	Accuracy (Chance)	F1 Score	ROC AUC	PR AUC
Disability	0.972 (0.969)	0.237	0.857	0.408
Gender	0.954 (0.927)	0.636	0.939	0.721
National Origin	0.868 (0.846)	0.402	0.821	0.523
Politics	0.788 (0.710)	0.557	0.826	0.667
Race	0.873 (0.781)	0.622	0.880	0.778
Religion	0.924 (0.827)	0.773	0.916	0.763
Sexual Orientation	0.981 (0.954)	0.780	0.948	0.784

Table 1: **Target identity models generalize to out-of-corpus, out-of-platform comments.** The test performance of the target identity model (specifically, the model corresponding to Fig. 1) on the HateCheck (top table) and Gab Hate Corpus (bottom table). The labels provided by each corpus were reassigned to align with the model's outputs (see Methods). Model predictions for identity groups without a corresponding label (age and political affiliation for HateCheck; age for GHC) were discarded. F1 score is calculated with a threshold of 0.5.

YouTube. However, past work has found that hate speech models exhibit a drop in performance on external corpora, particularly when those corpora are sourced from other platforms (Koufakou et al., 2020; Arango et al., 2019). Therefore, we sought to assess out-of-corpus/platform performance of the trained model by evaluating it on two corpora: the HateCheck corpus and Gab Hate Corpus (GHC).

We first considered the HateCheck corpus because it served as a sanity check for model validation. The HateCheck corpus consists of functional tests for hate speech, which often clearly make apparent the targeted identity group (Röttger et al., 2021). Due to the relatively simple syntactic structure, we should expect a trained model to perform well at identifying targeted identities. We relabeled the HateCheck identity groups to align with the trained model, matching to 6 of its 8 identity groups (see Methods). We applied our model to all samples in the corpus and evaluated the performance.

We found that the model exhibited superior predictive performance on the HateCheck corpus (Table 1: top). We obtained accuracies ranging from $0.97 - 0.99$ for each identity group, greatly exceeding that of chance, which ranged from $0.7 - 0.86$. At a threshold of 0.5, F1 scores were all above 0.90. Meanwhile, AUC scores were well above 0.95 for all identity groups, implying tight control of false positives and false negatives.

We supplemented the above generalization check with the Gab Hate Corpus (GHC), consisting of comments extracted from the social media platform Gab (Kennedy et al., 2022). The GHC covers a wide range of target group identities that match closely with those of the MHS corpus. Furthermore, it presents a useful test case to evaluate the extent to which the target identity model generalizes to a new distribution of comments. We applied our model to the subset of comments on which the annotators specified a hateful target (see Methods).

We found that the model generally performed well on the GHC, but exhibited a slight drop in predictive performance relative to the MHS corpus (Table 1: bottom). The model achieved accuracies ranging from $0.78 - 0.98$, well above chance. The model exhibited wide ranging F1 scores, with poor or average performance on the disability, national origin, and political affiliation groups. The ROC AUC and PR AUC scores similarly suggested good predictive performance, but were lower than those on the MHS corpus. Tracking with incidence rate, the model exhibited the best performance on the gender, race, religion, and sexual orientation categories. Overall, these results demonstrate that the

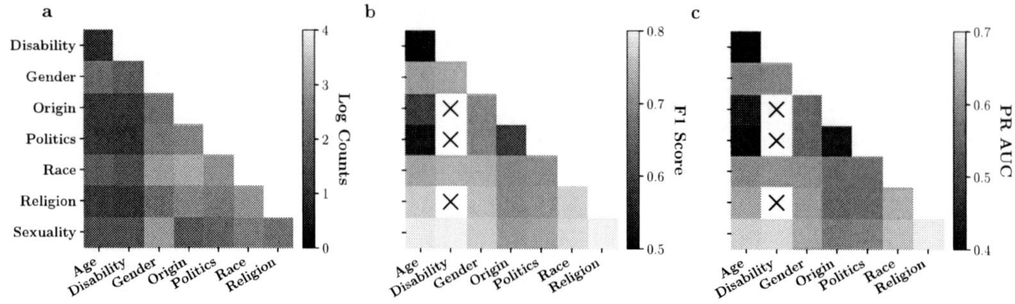

Figure 3: **Models exhibit diverse performance on multi-target samples. a.** The log-count of samples for each pair of identity groups in the MHS corpus. **b.** The macro-F1 score evaluated on sub-corpora containing samples in which each pair of identity groups was targeted (according to annotators) or predicted to be targeted by the classifier. **c.** The PR AUC on the same sub-corpora, across identity group pairs.

predictive models generalize fairly well to novel, out-of-platform data.

4.4 Model Performance on Multiple Targets

Hate speech can target multiple identity groups, either referencing them as separate targets (e.g., referencing a Black person and woman separately) or as a single, intersectional target (e.g. referencing a Black woman, a single subject with racial and gender identity components). We sought to examine how well the classifier performed in scenarios where two identities were targeted in the same comment, either by annotation or prediction.

We first examined the number of comments for each pair of target identity groups in the corpus. We assigned binary labels based on annotator majority voting for each target. Then, for each pair of identity groups, we calculated the number of comments which targeted both identity groups. The distribution of log-counts for each pair of identity groups is shown in Figure 3a. These counts generally aligned with the number of samples for each identity group. For example, (gender, race), the two largest identity groups in the corpus, had among the highest log-counts. However, the relationship between the identity groups also played a role in the observed counts. For example, (race/ethnicity, national origin) and (gender identity, sexual orientation) were the two combinations with the largest number of samples. This likely stems from the topic overlap within each pair.

We might expect a classifier to perform well on identity group pairs with a large number of samples. The classifier could, however, produce errors on these pairs by mistaking one identity group for another. Furthermore, the classifier may predict multiple targets when only one target is present. In order to evaluate the performance of the model in these settings, we consolidated a sub-corpus of comments for which (i) annotators identified two targeted identity groups or (ii) the classifier identified two targeted identity groups. Thus, the sub-corpus could contain either false negatives (classifier failed to predict both identity groups) or false positives (classifier mistakenly identified multiple identity groups). For each pair of identity groups, we calculated the average F1 score and PR AUC across the pair of labels (weighted by incidence rate). We note that we could only calculate these metrics when the classifier exhibited some false positives. If this did not occur, the F1 score and PR AUC would be undefined. We denote these rare instances with an X in Figure 3.

We examined the distribution of the F1 score and PR AUC across the pairs of identity groups (Fig. 3b-c). We found that, generally, the model exhibited worse performance on identity pairs which had the least number of samples, such as (age, disability) and (age, politics). On the other hand, the model generally performed well in cases where there were an abundance of samples, such as (race, gender). However, we observed other interesting relationships. For example, the model exhibited the best performance for identity pairs that were less related to each other, such as (age, sexual orientation), despite these pairs having lower counts. Notably, (origin, politics) exhibited markedly lower predictive performance, despite having more samples than other pairs. Together, these results highlight that performance on samples with multiple identity groups is modulated by the identity group pair under consideration.

5 Discussion

We have demonstrated that transformer-based neural network models can achieve good predictive performance on classifying multiple targeted identity groups or sub-groups simultaneously. We additionally validated the models on out-of-corpus data, finding that the results indicated some degree of generalizability. These results largely serve to benchmark this task for future studies, but also raise additional questions on the definition and conceptual framing of "targeting" in hate speech corpora.

We evaluated the performance of the model on multiple targets. However, the survey question prompting for identity targets did not distinguish between a *single* target with multiple identities, or *multiple* distinct targets. For example, a secondary analysis may be interested in comments that target Black women (at the intersection of racial and gender identity sub-groups), which are distinct from comments that separately target a Black person and a woman, but would be indistinguishable under the labeling scheme. The distinction is important, as the former setting corresponds to intersectional identity (Crenshaw, 2018), on which datasets and machine learning algorithms have been demonstrated to exhibit biased coverage or performance (Kim et al., 2020). Thus, the development of new labeling instruments that ask annotators to make the distinction between intersectional and multiple targets is of interest for future work. For example, Fortuna et al. (2019) developed a hierarchical labeling scheme which allowed for the the identification of intersectional targets in a Portugese dataset.

In this work, we considered multi-label networks designed to simultaneously predict either identity groups or sub-groups. However, constructing networks that can simultaneously predict multiple *sets* of sub-groups is of interest, particularly for identifying intersectional targets in social media content. This can be viewed as *multi-task* problem, which may require adjustment to network architectures in order to achieve desirable performance (Crawshaw, 2020; Talat et al., 2018). The development of multi-task networks with identity group specific sub-networks is of interest for future work (Plaza-del Arco et al., 2021). Such networks could, for example, contain sub-networks predicting racial identity sub-groups, gender identity sub-groups, and others, in parallel.

We relied on synthesizing annotator responses into a single label for each comment, while incorporating some knowledge of their disagreement. This approach generally falls in line with the weak perspectivist approach in predictive computing (Basile et al., 2021). However, annotator disagreement on the identity group targets (Appendix C) indicates that there is some subjectivity in identifying targeted groups. Data perspectivist approaches more strongly incorporating different annotator responses are a viable path forward (Basile et al., 2021; Sudre et al., 2019; Uma et al., 2020). At the same time, continued improvement in labeling instruments could further ameliorate these issues. For example, instruments that allow annotators to explain their reasoning in a structured fashion could shed light on why annotator disagreement is present. Qualitative examination of comments could support additional theorization of the the concept of "targeting". In this vein, following Kennedy et al. (2020), it may be possible to develop a measurement scale for "targeting" to facilitate item response theory approaches on this task.

Extensions to this work could facilitate parsing of the sentence to better elucidate the manner in which hateful comments refer to targets. For example, Shvets (2021) develop extraction networks to identify the text corresponding to both the "target" of a comment and its "aspect", or the characteristic attributed to the target. Such work could facilitate additional qualitative examination of comments.

While hate speech is understood to "target" a person or group based on a characteristic, the notion of "targeting" is slightly different across datasets. For example, we used "target" to mean the identity group that a comment is directed toward, whether the comment exhibited positive or negative valence. This was framed in the context of a measurement scale spanning supportive and hateful speech (Kennedy et al., 2020). However, other corpora limit their definition to content that is strictly hateful. These subtle distinctions limit the ability of out-of-corpus validation on datasets. For example, in this context, we could only use a subset of the GHC for generalization, since many comments were deemed not hateful (and thus did not have targeted identity annotations), despite referencing an identity group. Datasets may also reference the manner in which "targeting" occurs, such as calls to violence, usage of profanity, or implicit rhetoric (e.g., sarcasm or irony). Further work is needed to standardize these definitions to better inform the curation of future corpora.

Acknowledgements

We thank members of the D-Lab for useful feedback and discussions.

References

Aymé Arango, Jorge Pérez, and Barbara Poblete. 2019. Hate speech detection is not as easy as you may think: A closer look at model validation. In *Proceedings of the 42nd international acm sigir conference on research and development in information retrieval*, pages 45–54.

Valerio Basile, Federico Cabitza, Andrea Campagner, and Michael Fell. 2021. Toward a perspectivist turn in ground truthing for predictive computing. *arXiv preprint arXiv:2109.04270*.

Daniel Cer, Yinfei Yang, Sheng-yi Kong, Nan Hua, Nicole Limtiaco, Rhomni St John, Noah Constant, Mario Guajardo-Cespedes, Steve Yuan, Chris Tar, et al. 2018. Universal sentence encoder. *arXiv preprint arXiv:1803.11175*.

Patricia Chiril, Endang Wahyu Pamungkas, Farah Benamara, Véronique Moriceau, and Viviana Patti. 2022. Emotionally informed hate speech detection: a multi-target perspective. *Cognitive Computation*, 14(1):322–352.

Michael Crawshaw. 2020. Multi-task learning with deep neural networks: A survey. *arXiv preprint arXiv:2009.09796*.

Kimberlé Crenshaw. 2018. Demarginalizing the intersection of race and sex: A black feminist critique of antidiscrimination doctrine, feminist theory, and antiracist politics [1989]. In *Feminist legal theory*, pages 57–80. Routledge.

Thomas Davidson, Dana Warmsley, Michael Macy, and Ingmar Weber. 2017. Automated hate speech detection and the problem of offensive language. In *Proceedings of the International AAAI Conference on Web and Social Media*, volume 11.

Jesse Davis and Mark Goadrich. 2006. The relationship between precision-recall and roc curves. In *Proceedings of the 23rd international conference on Machine learning*, pages 233–240.

Fabio Del Vigna, Andrea Cimino, Felice Dell'Orletta, Marinella Petrocchi, and Maurizio Tesconi. 2017. Hate me, hate me not: Hate speech detection on facebook. In *Proceedings of the First Italian Conference on Cybersecurity (ITASEC17)*, pages 86–95.

Jacob Devlin, Ming-Wei Chang, Kenton Lee, and Kristina Toutanova. 2018. Bert: Pre-training of deep bidirectional transformers for language understanding. *arXiv preprint arXiv:1810.04805*.

Mai ElSherief, Vivek Kulkarni, Dana Nguyen, William Yang Wang, and Elizabeth Belding. 2018. Hate lingo: A target-based linguistic analysis of hate speech in social media. In *Proceedings of the International AAAI Conference on Web and Social Media*, volume 12.

Paula Fortuna, Joao Rocha da Silva, Leo Wanner, Sérgio Nunes, et al. 2019. A hierarchically-labeled portuguese hate speech dataset. In *Proceedings of the Third Workshop on Abusive Language Online*, pages 94–104.

Paula Fortuna and Sérgio Nunes. 2018. A survey on automatic detection of hate speech in text. *ACM Comput. Surv.*, 51(4).

Lara Grimminger and Roman Klinger. 2021. Hate towards the political opponent: A Twitter corpus study of the 2020 US elections on the basis of offensive speech and stance detection. In *Proceedings of the Eleventh Workshop on Computational Approaches to Subjectivity, Sentiment and Social Media Analysis*, pages 171–180, Online. Association for Computational Linguistics.

Vijayasaradhi Indurthi, Bakhtiyar Syed, Manish Shrivastava, Nikhil Chakravartula, Manish Gupta, and Vasudeva Varma. 2019. FERMI at SemEval-2019 task 5: Using sentence embeddings to identify hate speech against immigrants and women in Twitter. In *Proceedings of the 13th International Workshop on Semantic Evaluation*, pages 70–74, Minneapolis, Minnesota, USA. Association for Computational Linguistics.

Brendan Kennedy, Mohammad Atari, Aida Mostafazadeh Davani, Leigh Yeh, Ali Omrani, Yehsong Kim, Kris Coombs, Shreya Havaldar, Gwenyth Portillo-Wightman, Elaine Gonzalez, et al. 2022. Introducing the gab hate corpus: defining and applying hate-based rhetoric to social media posts at scale. *Language Resources and Evaluation*, pages 1–30.

Chris J Kennedy, Geoff Bacon, Alexander Sahn, and Claudia von Vacano. 2020. Constructing interval variables via faceted rasch measurement and multitask deep learning: a hate speech application. *arXiv preprint arXiv:2009.10277*.

Jae Yeon Kim, Carlos Ortiz, Sarah Nam, Sarah Santiago, and Vivek Datta. 2020. Intersectional bias in hate speech and abusive language datasets. *arXiv preprint arXiv:2005.05921*.

Anna Koufakou, Endang Wahyu Pamungkas, Valerio Basile, Viviana Patti, et al. 2020. Hurtbert: incorporating lexical features with bert for the detection of abusive language. In *Fourth Workshop on Online Abuse and Harms*, pages 34–43. Association for Computational Linguistics.

Irene Kwok and Yuzhou Wang. 2013. Locate the hate: Detecting tweets against blacks. In *Twenty-seventh AAAI conference on artificial intelligence*.

John M Linacre et al. 2002. What do infit and outfit, mean-square and standardized mean. *Rasch measurement transactions*, 16(2):878.

Yinhan Liu, Myle Ott, Naman Goyal, Jingfei Du, Mandar Joshi, Danqi Chen, Omer Levy, Mike Lewis, Luke Zettlemoyer, and Veselin Stoyanov. 2019. Roberta: A robustly optimized bert pretraining approach. *arXiv preprint arXiv:1907.11692*.

Binny Mathew, Punyajoy Saha, Seid Muhie Yimam, Chris Biemann, Pawan Goyal, and Animesh Mukherjee. 2020. Hatexplain: A benchmark dataset for explainable hate speech detection. *arXiv preprint arXiv:2012.10289*.

Zewdie Mossie and Jenq-Haur Wang. 2020. Vulnerable community identification using hate speech detection on social media. *Information Processing & Management*, 57(3):102087.

Thu T Nguyen, Shaniece Criss, Eli K Michaels, Rebekah I Cross, Jackson S Michaels, Pallavi Dwivedi, Dina Huang, Erica Hsu, Krishay Mukhija, Leah H Nguyen, et al. 2021. Progress and push-back: How the killings of ahmaud arbery, breonna taylor, and george floyd impacted public discourse on race and racism on twitter. *SSM-population health*, 15:100922.

Flor Miriam Plaza-del Arco, Sercan Halat, Sebastian Padó, and Roman Klinger. 2021. Multi-task learning with sentiment, emotion, and target detection to recognize hate speech and offensive language. *arXiv preprint arXiv:2109.10255*.

Paul Röttger, Bertie Vidgen, Dong Nguyen, Zeerak Waseem, Helen Margetts, and Janet Pierrehumbert. 2021. HateCheck: Functional tests for hate speech detection models. In *Proceedings of the 59th Annual Meeting of the Association for Computational Linguistics and the 11th International Joint Conference on Natural Language Processing (Volume 1: Long Papers)*, pages 41–58, Online. Association for Computational Linguistics.

Andrew Sellars. 2016. Defining hate speech. *Berkman Klein Center Research Publication*, 2016(20):16–48.

Alexander Shvets, Paula Fortuna, Juan Soler, and Leo Wanner. 2021. Targets and aspects in social media hate speech. In *Proceedings of the 5th Workshop on Online Abuse and Harms (WOAH 2021)*, pages 179–190, Online. Association for Computational Linguistics.

Anna Shvets. 2021. System description for the CommonGen task with the POINTER model. In *Proceedings of the 1st Workshop on Natural Language Generation, Evaluation, and Metrics (GEM 2021)*, pages 161–165, Online. Association for Computational Linguistics.

Leandro Silva, Mainack Mondal, Denzil Correa, Fabrício Benevenuto, and Ingmar Weber. 2016. Analyzing the targets of hate in online social media. In *Tenth international AAAI conference on web and social media*.

Carole H Sudre, Beatriz Gomez Anson, Silvia Ingala, Chris D Lane, Daniel Jimenez, Lukas Haider, Thomas Varsavsky, Ryutaro Tanno, Lorna Smith, Sébastien Ourselin, et al. 2019. Let's agree to disagree: Learning highly debatable multirater labelling. In *International Conference on Medical Image Computing and Computer-Assisted Intervention*, pages 665–673. Springer.

Zeerak Talat, James Thorne, and Joachim Bingel. 2018. Bridging the gaps: Multi task learning for domain transfer of hate speech detection. In *Online harassment*, pages 29–55. Springer.

Serra Sinem Tekiroglu, Yi-Ling Chung, and Marco Guerini. 2020. Generating counter narratives against online hate speech: Data and strategies. *arXiv preprint arXiv:2004.04216*.

Alice Tontodimamma, Eugenia Nissi, Annalina Sarra, and Lara Fontanella. 2021. Thirty years of research into hate speech: topics of interest and their evolution. *Scientometrics*, 126(1):157–179.

Thanh Tran, Yifan Hu, Changwei Hu, Kevin Yen, Fei Tan, Kyumin Lee, and Se Rim Park. 2020. HABERTOR: An efficient and effective deep hatespeech detector. In *Proceedings of the 2020 Conference on Empirical Methods in Natural Language Processing (EMNLP)*, pages 7486–7502, Online. Association for Computational Linguistics.

Alexander Tsesis. 2002. *Destructive messages: How hate speech paves the way for harmful social movements*, volume 27. NYU Press.

Alexandra Uma, Tommaso Fornaciari, Dirk Hovy, Silviu Paun, Barbara Plank, and Massimo Poesio. 2020. A case for soft loss functions. In *Proceedings of the AAAI Conference on Human Computation and Crowdsourcing*, volume 8, pages 173–177.

Bertie Vidgen and Leon Derczynski. 2020. Directions in abusive language training data, a systematic review: Garbage in, garbage out. *Plos one*, 15(12):e0243300.

Zeerak Waseem. 2016. Are you a racist or am i seeing things? annotator influence on hate speech detection on twitter. In *Proceedings of the first workshop on NLP and computational social science*, pages 138–142.

Zeerak Waseem, Thomas Davidson, Dana Warmsley, and Ingmar Weber. 2017. Understanding abuse: A typology of abusive language detection subtasks. *arXiv preprint arXiv:1705.09899*.

Zeerak Waseem and Dirk Hovy. 2016. Hateful symbols or hateful people? predictive features for hate speech detection on twitter. In *Proceedings of the NAACL student research workshop*, pages 88–93.

Richard Ashby Wilson. 2017. *Incitement on trial: Prosecuting international speech crimes.* Cambridge University Press.

Thomas Wolf, Lysandre Debut, Victor Sanh, Julien Chaumond, Clement Delangue, Anthony Moi, Pierric Cistac, Tim Rault, Remi Louf, Morgan Funtowicz, Joe Davison, Sam Shleifer, Patrick von Platen, Clara Ma, Yacine Jernite, Julien Plu, Canwen Xu, Teven Le Scao, Sylvain Gugger, Mariama Drame, Quentin Lhoest, and Alexander Rush. 2020. Transformers: State-of-the-art natural language processing. In *Proceedings of the 2020 Conference on Empirical Methods in Natural Language Processing: System Demonstrations*, pages 38–45, Online. Association for Computational Linguistics.

Marcos Zampieri, Shervin Malmasi, Preslav Nakov, Sara Rosenthal, Noura Farra, and Ritesh Kumar. 2019. Predicting the type and target of offensive posts in social media. In *Proceedings of the 2019 Conference of the North American Chapter of the Association for Computational Linguistics: Human Language Technologies, Volume 1 (Long and Short Papers)*, pages 1415–1420, Minneapolis, Minnesota. Association for Computational Linguistics.

A Extended Experiment Results

Base Model	Hyperparams	Acc/Chance	LOD	AUC ROC	PR ROC	F1 Score
USE V4	Binary Labels H256 B32 D0.1	1.062	0.941	0.949	0.498	0.428
USE V4	Soft Labels H256 B128 D0.1	1.130	1.131	0.938	0.607	0.529
DistilBERT	Binary Labels H256 B64 D0.1	1.135	1.179	0.942	0.648	0.597
DistilBERT	Binary Labels H128 B64 D0.1	1.136	1.203	0.940	0.650	0.584
BERT Base	Binary Labels H128 B32 D0.1	1.137	1.215	0.942	0.667	0.610
BERT Base	Soft Labels H128 B32 D0.1	1.138	1.243	0.952	0.681	0.594
BERT Base	Soft Labels Weighted Samples H128 B32 D0.1	1.139	1.259	0.952	0.682	0.597
RoBERTa Base	Binary Labels H128 B32 D0.1	1.137	1.202	0.947	0.660	0.609
RoBERTa Base	Soft Labels Weighted Samples H128 B32 D0.1	1.139	1.231	0.952	0.673	0.593
RoBERTa Large	Soft Labels Weighted Samples H256 B8 D0.05	1.164	1.343	0.964	0.724	0.647

Table 2: Full experimental results. LOD denotes "log-odds difference". USE denotes "Universal Sentence Encoder". "H" denotes the size of the hidden layer. "B" denotes batch size. "D" denotes dropout rate. Metrics are calculated by averaging across identity groups.

B Annotator Identity Groups and Sub-Groups

Identity Group	Identity Subgroups
Race or ethnicity	Black or African American, Latino or non-white Hispanic, Asian, Middle Eastern, Native American or Alaska Native, Pacific Islander, Non-hispanic white
Religion	Jews, Christians, Buddhists, Hindus, Mormons, Atheists, Muslims
National origin	A specific country, immigrant, migrant worker, undocumented person
Gender identity	Women, men, non-binary or third gender, transgender women, transgender men, transgender (unspecified)
Sexual orientation	Bisexual, gay, lesbian, heterosexual
Age	Children (0 - 12 years old), adolescents / teenagers (13 - 17), young adults / adults (18 - 39), middle-aged (40 - 64), seniors (65 or older)
Disability status	People with physical disabilities (e.g., use of wheelchair), people with cognitive disorders (e.g., autism) or learning disabilities (e.g., Down syndrome), people with mental health problems (e.g., depression, addiction), visually impaired people, hearing impaired people, no specific disability

Table 3: Identity group and corresponding subgroups annotators were asked to identify as targets of comments.

C Annotator Agreement on Targeted Identity Groups

Identity Group	Krippendorff's Alpha
Age	0.341
Disability	0.744
Gender Identity	0.712
National Origin	0.571
Race	0.672
Religion	0.797
Sexual Orientation	0.718

Table 4: Annotator agreement on target identity group labels, calculated across samples with Krippendorff's alpha.

Revisiting Queer Minorities in Lexicons

Krithika Ramesh[♣] **Sumeet Kumar**[♡] **Ashiqur R. KhudaBukhsh**[♠*]
[♣]Manipal University
[♡]Indian School of Business
[♠]Rochester Institute of Technology
kramesh.tlw@gmail.com, Sumeet_Kumar@isb.edu, axkvse@rit.edu

Abstract

⚠ This paper contains words that are offensive.

Lexicons play an important role in content moderation, often being the first line of defense. However, little or no literature exists in analyzing the representation of queer-related words in them. In this paper, we consider twelve well-known English lexicons containing inappropriate words and analyze how gender and sexual minorities are represented in these lexicons. Our analyses reveal that several of these lexicons barely make any distinction between pejorative and non-pejorative queer-related words. We express concern that such unfettered usage of non-pejorative queer-related words may impact queer presence in mainstream discourse. Our analyses further reveal that the lexicons have poor overlap in queer-related words. We finally present a quantifiable measure of consistency and show that several of these lexicons are not consistent in how they include (or omit) queer-related words.

1 Introduction

On August 23, 2013, the online version of the Oxford English Dictionary updated the meaning of a word. Updates to this dictionary are not uncommon. However, the updates typically include new words in the latest edition. For instance, `Bollywood`, the notorious name for the Mumbai film industry, made its way into the dictionary in 2004. Or, for example, the ongoing pandemic forced a slew of vaccine-related words – `vaccine passport`, `vaccine hesitancy`, and `vaxxed` – into the 2021 edition. Every new edition introduces several such words reflecting the ever-changing world with intermixing cultures and acknowledging the fluid and expansive nature of English – one of the most popular, pluricentric world languages (Leitner, 1992).

What was remarkable about the August 23, 2013, online update was that this word had its first known usage in the 14th century, and its primary meaning remained unaltered since its inclusion in the very first edition of the Oxford dictionary! `Marriage`, previously defined as the *formal union of a man and a woman, typically as recognized by law, by which they become husband and wife*, received an inclusive definition in the dictionary following the legalization of gay marriage in the UK. The new definition dispensed with the gender restriction and defined marriage as a union between two persons.

Words and their meanings exist in a continuum (Hamilton et al., 2016; Xie et al., 2019), often shifted and shaped by evolving social norms, hard-fought legal acceptances, and new world events. Lexicons proposed to aid content moderation, in turn, exhibit a rather static nature and a much narrower scope, representing a collection of words deemed as potentially hateful/harmful/abusive/toxic/offensive by a group of annotators (possibly exhibiting limited diversity and/or with under-specified expertise) at a given point of time. In this paper, we focus on twelve such lexicons aimed at aiding content moderation. A varied collection of words have been used to describe them, including being termed as abusive, offensive, profane, toxic, and hate speech lexicons. We use an umbrella term *inappropriate* to refer to any of these descriptions. In this paper, we focus on twelve inappropriate lexicons and analyze the presence (and absence) of words related to gender and sexual minorities (we call these words queer-related words) in them [1].

Our paper seeks to attract the attention of the

* Ashiqur R. KhudaBukhsh is the corresponding author.

[1]Code and additional resources are available at `https://github.com/stolenpyjak/revisiting-queer-lexicons`.

Proceedings of the Sixth Workshop on Online Abuse and Harms (WOAH), pages 245 - 251
July 14, 2022

broader community of psycho-linguistic experts and ethicists on the following issues.

First, our study reveals that these lexicons have limited overlap, and many of these under-specify how they were obtained. While data sets have received considerable attention for audits (Gebru et al., 2021), inappropriate lexicons have received little or no attention for quality control. Given that such lexicons often serve as the first line of defense against inappropriate content, certain omissions and inclusions can significantly influence what gets flagged as inappropriate and may impact minorities to get their voices heard. As we seek to move towards more transparent, responsible, and ethical AI systems, we need to build stronger guardrails for methods and resources that are used for content moderation/filtering.

We see our work as a voice in the scientific conversation focusing on the treatment of the queer community in language technologies (Dev et al., 2021; Nozza et al., 2022; Dodge et al., 2021). Among these recent prominent studies, Dev et al. (2021) discuss the potential erasure of non-binary identities due to stereotypical harms propagated by language models; Nozza et al. (2022) reveal that large language models exhibit discriminative behavior by producing harmful text completions for subjects from the queer community; and Dodge et al. (2021) demonstrate how blocklist-based filters have been shown to remove content related to the queer community, particularly when it contains terms related to sexual orientation. Our work focusing on queer-related terms in inappropriate lexicons complements these aforementioned important studies.

Second, our study raises a question that we believe is timely and important. We observe that several non-pejorative words representing gender and sexual minorities (e.g., `gay`, `queer`, `lesbian`, `trans`) are present in these inappropriate lexicons. However, these lexicons often do not make any clear distinction between the targets for harm and targeted harms. We worry that unfettered use of `gay`, `lesbian` or `trans` along with their pejorative versions (e.g., `faggot` [2]) within the same lexicon may hinder the inclusion of sexual minorities into mainstream discourse. Thus we seek guidance from true experts on this issue that may significantly influence how a safe web may look like for sexual minorities in the future.

Third, continuing the same thread of discussion surrounding the inclusion or omission of non-pejorative versions representing gender and sexual minorities, we present a first step towards quantifying inconsistencies in lexicons with respect to queer-related words. Our study reveals that these lexicons exhibit inconsistencies that can potentially influence content moderation outcomes if these lexicons are used as an aid.

2 Design Considerations

2.1 Classification of Lexicons into Abusive, Offensive, and Hate Speech

As mentioned in Davidson et al. (2017), the difference between hate speech, offensive language, and abusive language is that hate speech tends to be directed toward specific communities so as to disparage or disadvantage them. Davidson et al. (2017) also state that their definition of hate speech may not include all instances of offensive language, as it is possible that these derogatory terms that target certain communities may be used in a manner that is not necessarily motivated by the intention to deride the said community. This includes words that have been reclaimed by the very same groups they were meant to stigmatize. This distinction is important as the resulting lexicon used in offensive/abusive language detection may vary from those used in hate speech detection, as the latter may contain more relevant pejoratives targeted at specific demographics. Caselli et al. (2020) explore the distinction between abusive language and offensive language. According to Caselli et al. (2020), abusive language focuses more on the intention of the message conveyed, and offensive language emphasizes more on the target's sentiment and the profanity in the message. However, profane language is shown to fall under both these categories. Additionally, we find that the source for some of our lexicons uses the terms *profane*, *abusive* and *offensive* interchangeably. The term *toxicity* is also used for one of these lexicons, which Mohan et al. (2017) use to refer to various forms of harassment, such as hate speech, cyber threats, cyberbullying, etc. As our lexicons are obtained from multiple sources with various such classifications and definitions of their own, we thereby deem it necessary to classify all these words as *inappropriate words*

[2]In this paper, we have not censored any of these historically charged words. There is a broad range of opinions and practices on censoring (or not censoring) historically charged words (Cannon, 2005; Stephens-Davidowitz and Pabon, 2017; Sap et al., 2020; Schick et al., 2021).

that cover a broad taxonomy of potentially harmful language.

2.2 Development of Queer Lexicon

In order to carry out our analysis across these English lexicons, we survey several web sources to identify terms that are commonly used among the queer community. We compile terms based on both gender and sexuality (including any pejorative terms encountered) from multiple online resources [3].

The non-pejorative version of the lexicon was obtained by eliminating terms that are considered pejorative from multiple sources, including [4]. Overall, our list of queer-specific words, $\mathcal{L}^Q$, consists of 115 terms. Of this, we identify 28 as pejorative (denoted as $\mathcal{L}_p^Q$) and 87 as non-pejorative terms (denoted as $\mathcal{L}_{np}^Q$). These 115 terms have consensus labels from two annotators, one cis-female and one cis-male, of whom one identifies as a queer.

We acknowledge that our list is not comprehensive and may (inadvertently) fail to include terms pertaining to several sexualities and genders across the spectrum. We further note that some of the terms in this non-pejorative version of the lexicon (such as gay) can be considered derogatory based on context. Similarly, as mentioned in Section 2.1, some of the terms not present in the non-pejorative version of this lexicon have been reclaimed by some parts of the queer community and, therefore, may not be considered derogatory in a given context. Ideally, we feel that studies that aim to construct and utilize lexicons should provide information regarding the same (see, e.g., Pamungkas et al. (2022)), as opposed to imposing a blanket statement (via their lexicon) that dictates that terms like gay are considered offensive language or hate speech.

Overall, we use 12 well-known lexicons listed in Table 1. In addition, we also present the overlap of individual lexicons with $\mathcal{L}^Q$, $\mathcal{L}_{np}^Q$ and $\mathcal{L}_p^Q$ along with any publicly available annotation details.

[3]https://www.smcgov.org/lgbtq/lgbtq-glossary
https://www.itspronouncedmetrosexual.com/2013/01/a-comprehensive-list-of-lgbtq-term-definitions/
https://www.healthline.com/health/different-types-of-sexuality#takeaway

[4]https://www.advocate.com/arts-entertainment/2017/8/02/21-words-queer-community-has-reclaimed-and-some-we-havent

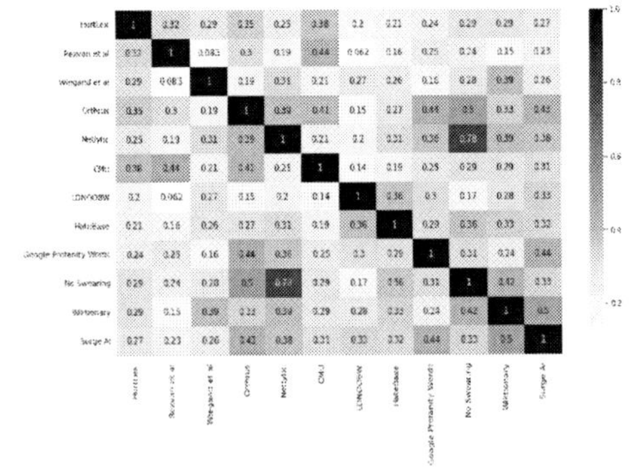

Figure 1: Jaccard similarity of all queer-related words in the inappropriate lexicons. Jaccard similarity is a statistic to gauge similarity between two sets, $\mathcal{A}, \mathcal{B}$, expressed as $\frac{|\mathcal{A}\cap\mathcal{B}|}{|\mathcal{A}\cup\mathcal{B}|}$.

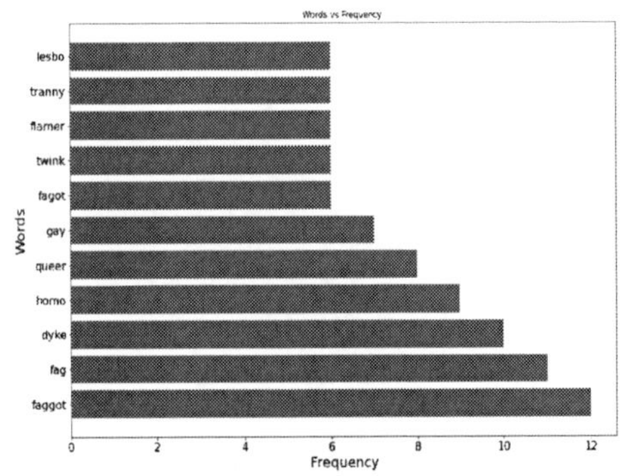

Figure 2: Some of the most frequently occurring queer-related words in the English lexicons.

3 Analysis

We now present an analysis of these lexicons considering the following aspects.

Coverage: We first note that the overlap between $\mathcal{L}^Q$ and the twelve inappropriate lexicons is minimal, with the CMU Lexicon achieving the highest overlap (23.48%), indicating that a vast majority of the queer lexicon is not incorporated into any of the well-known lexicons. When we combine all lexicons, the resulting lexicon has a slightly higher overlap of 40.87%. As shown in Figure 1, within the lexicons, limited overlap of these queer-related terms exists. These findings point to the following observations. First, lexicons can benefit from further inclusive efforts in identifying pejorative (if the sole intended purpose is to detect harm) and non-pejorative (if the purpose also involves detecting targets of harm) queer-related terms. Second, given that there is poor overlap within lexicons with

Name	Year	Size	Annotation Method	Overlap with $\mathcal{L}^Q$	Overlap with $\mathcal{L}^Q_{np}$	Overlap with $\mathcal{L}^Q_p$	Classification
HurtLex	2019	5,963	Experts	11.3%	6.9%	25%	Offensive, aggressive, and hateful words
Rezvan et al. (2018)	2018	700	Crowdsourced sources, compiled by a Native English speaker	10.43%	8.05%	17.86%	Offensive/Profane words
Wiegand et al. (2018)	2018	7,049	Experts	12.17%	4.6%	35.71%	Abusive words
Palomino et al. (2021)	2021	1,924	Compiled from multiple lexicon sources	15.65%	9.2%	35.71%	Toxic/Profane words
Kwon and Gruzd (2017)	2017	426	Crowdsourced with custom expert additions	6.09%	1.15%	21.43%	Offensive words
CMU Lexicon	Not specified	1,383	Not specified	23.48%	16.09%	46.43%	Offensive/Profane words
LDNOOBW	2019	403	Not specified	4.35%	0%	17.86%	Offensive/Profane words
HateBase	2019	1,522	Crowdsourced	8.7%	2.3%	28.57%	Hate speech lexicon
Google Profanity Words	2022	451	Not specified	6.96%	0%	28.57%	Offensive/Profane words
NoSwearing	2022	361	Partially crowdsourced list	7.83%	3.45%	21.43%	Offensive/Profane words
Wiktionary	2022	4,738	Crowdsourced	15.65%	3.45%	53.57%	Offensive/Profane words
Surge AI	Not specified	1,598	Not specified	13.04%	1.15%	50%	Offensive/Profane words

Table 1: Details about English lexicons and their overlap with $\mathcal{L}^Q$ and $\mathcal{L}^Q_p$.

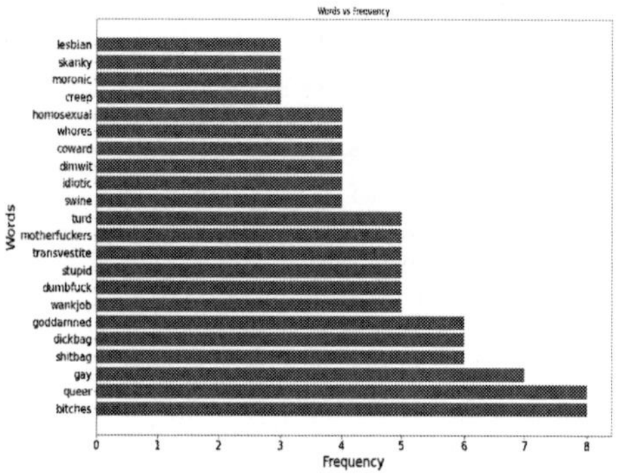

Figure 3: Most frequently occurring queer-related words juxtaposed with similarly frequently occurring slurs from the lexicons.

Name	Consistency %
(Bassignana et al., 2018)	55.56
(Rezvan et al., 2018)	66.67
(Wiegand et al., 2018)	100.0
(Palomino et al., 2021)	66.67
(Kwon and Gruzd, 2017)	88.89
CMU Lexicon	88.89
LDNOOBW	88.89
HateBase	77.78
Google Profanity Words	88.89
NoSwearing	77.78
Wiktionary	77.78
Surge AI	100.0

Table 2: Consistency % of the English Lexicons

respect to queer-related terms, consulting multiple lexicons can improve coverage.

***Annotation*:** We note that four lexicons have not specified how they are annotated. Of the remaining, only three are vetted by experts. Existing lexicons with an unspecified annotation that can potentially decide the content outcome for minorities is a major concern, and we identify this as an area where future lexicons can substantially improve.

***Presence of pejorative and non-pejorative terms*:** We note that ten lexicons have more pejorative queer-related words than non-pejorative queer-related words (in terms of absolute value). We argue that putting the pejorative and non-pejorative terms together in the same lexicon potentially conflates between targets of harm and words to inflict harm. As shown in Figure 2, among the most-frequent queer-related words in the lexicon, `gay` and `queer` are present. To emphasize our point further, Figure 3 juxtaposes a few words from $\mathcal{L}^Q_{np}$ along with other similarly frequent words across the lexicons. We note that words like `motherfuckers` or `whores` have appeared less frequently than `queer` or `gay`! We believe that unless these lexicons present concrete examples distinguishing between pejorative and non-pejorative usage of `gay` as presented in Pamungkas et al. (2022), unfettered use of non-pejorative queer-related terms can seriously limit queer presence in mainstream discourse.

***Consistency*:** If a lexicon contains both `dyke` and `faggot` in it yet omits `tranny`, content moderation outcomes (that considers this lexicon) could affect the transgender minority. Similarly, notwithstanding our earlier point that speculates if non-pejorative queer specific words should be at all present in an inappropriate lexicon, presence of `gay` in the lexicon but absence of `lesbian` could potentially trigger differential content moderation treatment for the two communities. In what follows, we develop simple constraints and quantify how consistent published lexicons are. We acknowledge that our choice of lexicon subsets and defined constraints are somewhat over-simplified and a far more nuanced treatment is possible, our primary goal in this experiment is to attract the research community's attention about addressing these potential inconsistencies that can pave the way towards better practices in future lexicons.

Let $\mathcal{L}_{np}$ and $\mathcal{L}_p$ denote two disjoint lexicon subsets where $\mathcal{L}_{np}$ contains non-pejorative queer-related words and $\mathcal{L}_p$ contains pejorative queer-related words; i.e., $\mathcal{L}_{np} \cap \mathcal{L}_p = \emptyset$. Further, let a bijective mapping f from $\mathcal{L}_{np}$ to $\mathcal{L}_p$ exist, i.e., for each element in $\mathcal{L}_{np}$, a corresponding unique element in $\mathcal{L}_p$ exists and vice versa. Let the function, f, returns the corresponding pejorative word.

We define $\mathcal{L}_{np} = \{\texttt{gay}, \texttt{lesbian}, \texttt{trans}\}$ and $\mathcal{L}_p = \{\texttt{faggot}, \texttt{dyke}, \texttt{tranny}\}$. Next, we define the following constraints with respect to a lexicon $\mathcal{L}$:

1. $\forall w_1, w_2 \in \mathcal{L}_{np}$, if $w_1 \in \mathcal{L}$ then $w_2 \in \mathcal{L}$
2. $\forall w_1, w_2 \in \mathcal{L}_p$, if $w_1 \in \mathcal{L}$ then $w_2 \in \mathcal{L}$
3. $\forall w \in \mathcal{L}_{np}$, if $w \in \mathcal{L}$ then $f(w) \in \mathcal{L}$. If $f(w) \notin \mathcal{L}$, we impose a penalty of equal weight. That is, if `gay` exists in the lexicon, but its pejorative counterpart `faggot` does not, we penalize the consistency score by the same weight awarded to a lexicon with both the pejorative and non-pejorative versions.

The consistency of these lexicons based on these constraints are depicted in Table 2, with lexicons that contain neither words from $\mathcal{L}_p$ or $\mathcal{L}_{np}$ being declared completely consistent as well. The lexicons from Wiegand et al. (2018) and the Surge AI profanity lexicon[5] do not fall under this category, and are the most consistent. It is worth noting that neither of these lexicons contains words from the non-pejorative set $\mathcal{L}_{np}$.

[5]https://www.surgehq.ai/datasets/profanity-dataset

4 Conclusions and Discussions

In this paper, we analyze the presence of queer-related words in several well-known inappropriate English language lexicons. Our analysis identifies possible avenues to provide stronger guardrails against potential harm through (1) expanding lexicons with additional terms; (2) setting more transparent annotation guidelines; (3) distinguishing between pejorative and non-pejorative queer related terms; and (4) improving lexicon consistency concerning queer-related terms.

We believe our most important contribution is raising the question of whether non-pejorative queer-related terms should appear in inappropriate lexicons to begin with. With the current disturbing situation in US politics, where six states are considering passing what the proponents of minority rights dub as the *Don't say gay* bill [6], we strongly feel that including non-pejorative queer-related words merits serious discussion. We believe our paper will motivate a scientific dialogue by setting better guidelines to encourage queer presence in mainstream discourse.

Our work raises several important points to ponder.

***Grounding Other Research Efforts*:** Apart from aiding content moderation, inappropriate lexicons can lend grounding to other research efforts. For example, a recent paper (Ramesh et al., 2022) has consulted the CMU Lexicon and another lexicon listing *taboo-words* for kids (Jay, 1992) to construct a set of inappropriate words for kids. Ramesh et al. (2022) take a rather passive stance in their treatment of queer-related words. Ramesh et al. (2022) state that the authors extensively debated whether non-pejorative queer-related words such as `gay` or `queer` should be in the lexicon, but since these words were already present in both lexicons, they retain them, seeking more inputs from developmental psychologists. Unless the research community takes a more definitive stance on when and how non-pejorative queer-related words should be included in these inappropriate language lexicons, we may see more research efforts sidestepping this important issue.

***Cultural Effect*:** Our study is limited to English lexicons. We notice the non-uniform presence of queer-related words across lexicons even within

[6]https://www.npr.org/2022/04/10/1091543359/15-states-dont-say-gay-anti-transgender-bills

that. Different countries and cultures have varying degrees of legal, social, and cultural acceptance of the queer community. We believe our study will open the gates for a multi-lingual, multi-cultural analysis of queer presence in inappropriate lexicons.

In-The-Wild Impact Assessment: We hypothesize that lexicon variations can influence content outcome when deployed in the wild to decide the moderation fate of web users. While some anecdotal evidence already exists[7], an extensive in-the-wild impact assessment of how different lexicons can affect content moderation outcomes can further strengthen our findings.

A List To Criticize Other Lists: Regardless of how well-meaning our intentions are, the 115 queer-related terms chosen by our annotators affect our analyses. Nonetheless, we point out that several of our findings are unaffected (or minimally affected) by $\mathcal{L}^Q$. For example, the annotation details (or lack thereof) of the inappropriate lexicons have nothing to do with $\mathcal{L}^Q$. Second, our consistency analysis focuses on a handful of pejorative and non-pejorative queer-related words that are well-recognized by the community. Finally, using well-recognized non-pejorative words such as `gay` and `queer` to substantiate our argument, we show that certain non-pejorative queer-related words are more frequently listed than unambiguously inappropriate non-queer-related words.

5 Acknowledgements

We thank the anonymous reviewers for their thoughtful suggestions. We thank Joseph W. Hostetler for his valuable input.

References

Elisa Bassignana, Valerio Basile, and Viviana Patti. 2018. Hurtlex: A multilingual lexicon of words to hurt. In *CLiC-it*.

Kevin D Cannon. 2005. "ain't no faggot gonna rob me!": Anti-gay attitudes of criminal justice undergraduate majors. *Journal of Criminal Justice Education*, 16(2):226–243.

Tommaso Caselli, Valerio Basile, Jelena Mitrović, Inga Kartoziya, and Michael Granitzer. 2020. I feel offended, don't be abusive! implicit/explicit messages in offensive and abusive language.

Thomas Davidson, Dana Warmsley, Michael Macy, and Ingmar Weber. 2017. Automated hate speech detection and the problem of offensive language.

Sunipa Dev, Masoud Monajatipoor, Anaelia Ovalle, Arjun Subramonian, Jeff Phillips, and Kai-Wei Chang. 2021. Harms of gender exclusivity and challenges in non-binary representation in language technologies. In *Proceedings of the 2021 Conference on Empirical Methods in Natural Language Processing*, pages 1968–1994, Online and Punta Cana, Dominican Republic. Association for Computational Linguistics.

Jesse Dodge, Maarten Sap, Ana Marasović, William Agnew, Gabriel Ilharco, Dirk Groeneveld, Margaret Mitchell, and Matt Gardner. 2021. Documenting large webtext corpora: A case study on the colossal clean crawled corpus. In *Proceedings of the 2021 Conference on Empirical Methods in Natural Language Processing*, pages 1286–1305, Online and Punta Cana, Dominican Republic. Association for Computational Linguistics.

Timnit Gebru, Jamie Morgenstern, Briana Vecchione, Jennifer Wortman Vaughan, Hanna Wallach, Hal Daumé Iii, and Kate Crawford. 2021. Datasheets for datasets. *Communications of the ACM*, 64(12):86–92.

William L. Hamilton, Kevin Clark, Jure Leskovec, and Dan Jurafsky. 2016. Inducing domain-specific sentiment lexicons from unlabeled corpora. In *Proceedings of the 2016 Conference on Empirical Methods in Natural Language Processing*, pages 595–605, Austin, Texas. Association for Computational Linguistics.

Timothy Jay. 1992. *Cursing in America*, volume 10. Philadelphia: John Benjamins.

K. Hazel Kwon and Anatoliy Gruzd. 2017. Interpersonal swearing dictionary.

Gerhard Leitner. 1992. English as a pluricentric language. *Pluricentric languages: Differing norms in different nations*, 62:178–237.

Shruthi Mohan, Apala Guha, Michael Harris, Fred Popowich, Ashley Schuster, and Chris Priebe. 2017. The impact of toxic language on the health of reddit communities. pages 51–56.

Debora Nozza, Federico Bianchi, Anne Lauscher, and Dirk Hovy. 2022. Measuring harmful sentence completion in language models for LGBTQIA+ individuals. In *Proceedings of the Second Workshop on Language Technology for Equality, Diversity and Inclusion*, pages 26–34, Dublin, Ireland. Association for Computational Linguistics.

Marco Palomino, Dawid Grad, and James Bedwell. 2021. GoldenWind at SemEval-2021 task 5: Orthrus - an ensemble approach to identify toxicity. In *Proceedings of the 15th International Workshop on Semantic Evaluation (SemEval-2021)*, pages 860–864, Online. Association for Computational Linguistics.

[7]`https://www.wired.com/story/ai-list-dirty-naughty-obscene-bad-words/`

Endang Wahyu Pamungkas, Valerio Basile, and Viviana Patti. 2022. Investigating the role of swear words in abusive language detection tasks. *Language Resources and Evaluation*, pages 1–34.

Krithika Ramesh, Ashiqur R. KhudaBukhsh, and Sumeet Kumar. 2022. "Beach" to "Bitch": Inadvertent Unsafe Transcription of Kids' Content on YouTube. In *The Thirty-Sixth AAAI Conference on Artificial Intelligence, AAAI 2022*, page to appear. AAAI Press.

Mohammadreza Rezvan, Saeedeh Shekarpour, Lakshika Balasuriya, Krishnaprasad Thirunarayan, Valerie Shalin, and Amit Sheth. 2018. Publishing a quality context-aware annotated corpus and lexicon for harassment research.

Maarten Sap, Saadia Gabriel, Lianhui Qin, Dan Jurafsky, Noah A. Smith, and Yejin Choi. 2020. Social bias frames: Reasoning about social and power implications of language. In *Proceedings of the 58th Annual Meeting of the Association for Computational Linguistics, ACL 2020, Online, July 5-10, 2020*, pages 5477–5490. Association for Computational Linguistics.

Timo Schick, Sahana Udupa, and Hinrich Schütze. 2021. Self-diagnosis and self-debiasing: A proposal for reducing corpus-based bias in nlp. *Transactions of the Association for Computational Linguistics*, 9:1408–1424.

Seth Stephens-Davidowitz and Andrés Pabon. 2017. *Everybody lies: Big data, new data, and what the internet can tell us about who we really are.* HarperCollins New York.

Michael Wiegand, Josef Ruppenhofer, Anna Schmidt, and Clayton Greenberg. 2018. Inducing a lexicon of abusive words – a feature-based approach. In *Proceedings of the 2018 Conference of the North American Chapter of the Association for Computational Linguistics: Human Language Technologies, Volume 1 (Long Papers)*, pages 1046–1056, New Orleans, Louisiana. Association for Computational Linguistics.

Jing Yi Xie, Renato Ferreira Pinto Junior, Graeme Hirst, and Yang Xu. 2019. Text-based inference of moral sentiment change. In *Proceedings of the 2019 Conference on Empirical Methods in Natural Language Processing and the 9th International Joint Conference on Natural Language Processing (EMNLP-IJCNLP)*, pages 4654–4663, Hong Kong, China. Association for Computational Linguistics.

HATE-ITA: Hate Speech Detection in Italian Social Media Text

Debora Nozza, Federico Bianchi, Giuseppe Attanasio
Bocconi University
Via Sarfatti 25
Milan, Italy
{debora.nozza,f.bianchi,giuseppe.attanasio3}@unibocconi.it

Abstract

Warning: This paper contains examples of language that some people may find offensive.

Online hate speech is a dangerous phenomenon that can (and should) be promptly counteracted properly. While Natural Language Processing has been successfully used for the purpose, many of the research efforts are directed toward the English language. This choice severely limits the classification power in non-English languages. In this paper, we test several learning frameworks for identifying hate speech in Italian text. We release HATE-ITA, a set of multi-language models trained on a large set of English data and available Italian datasets. HATE-ITA performs better than mono-lingual models and seems to adapt well also on language-specific slurs. We believe our findings will encourage research in other mid-to-low resource communities and provide a valuable benchmarking tool for the Italian community.

1 Introduction

Online hate speech is a dangerous phenomenon that can (and should) be promptly counteracted properly. While Natural Language Processing supplies algorithms to achieve that, most research efforts are directed toward the English language. Indeed, there is now a plethora of approaches and corpora (Indurthi et al., 2019; Kennedy et al., 2020b; D'Sa et al., 2020; Mollas et al., 2022; Kiela et al., 2021, inter alia), that can be adopted for addressing English hate speech detection.

However, this choice strongly limits the classification power in other languages where fewer resources are available, like Italian. Researchers have put a great effort into improving Italian models (Fersini et al., 2018; Bosco et al., 2018; Sanguinetti et al., 2018, 2020). However, previous work does not address the task systematically, resulting in no clear evidence of the performance of these models. Consider also that a competitive baseline for hate speech detection in Italian does not yet exist. Current datasets are not broad enough to cover all the protected categories and are generally based on a few thousand samples. Data annotation is a costly process, and annotating hate speech requires tremendous care.

Multi-lingual models give a possible way out of this issue. Nozza (2021) shows that combining multiple languages in training can help overcome the apparent limitations of hate speech detection models. We start from those conclusions to build up our work by collecting a large dataset of English hate speech data that we combine with some data in Italian. We use this new collection to train multi-lingual models and show the performance and examples across different Italian datasets.

The contribution of this short workshop paper is thus straightforward: we thoroughly evaluate and release to the community a set of models for Italian hate speech detection obtained through fine-tuning of multi-lingual models (HATE-ITA).[1] These models are wrapped in high-level API that will allow the community to access and use these models for future research easily. These models set a new baseline on two state-of-the-art hate speech detection datasets in Italian. To the best of our knowledge, this is the first paper that showcases the use of a large English dataset in combination with a small portion of Italian to create a robust resource for hate speech detection in Italian.

Contribution **1)** our experiments show that multi-lingual models can effectively be used to cover missing ground in some mid-to-low resource languages; **2)** while providing researchers with strong baselines, our models can also be used to study which areas and targets are still not yet covered, thus guiding directions for future research (see Section 4.4). We release HATE-ITA as an open-source Python library[2].

[1] https://huggingface.co/MilaNLProc

[2] https://github.com/MilaNLProc/hate-ita

Proceedings of the Sixth Workshop on Online Abuse and Harms (WOAH), pages 252 - 260
July 14, 2022

2 Datasets

2.1 Background

In this work, we consider the task of hate speech as binary (*hate/non-hate*). To control the number of samples for each protected group in the training data, we consider the target of the hateful messages. We select six target attributes based on the type of discrimination, namely origin, gender identity, sexual orientation, religious affiliation, and disability. We consider these targets as the superset of classes able to cover the majority of dataset-specific labels. We discarded the *other* and *none* class from all the datasets because they might represent other classes.

2.2 State-of-the-art Corpora

We describe the datasets we included in the training set in this work. The English corpora have been selected by filtering the ones covering our desired targets from a public list[3].

Italian For Italian, we consider two different corpora proposed for Evalita shared tasks (Caselli et al., 2018): the automatic misogyny identification challenge (AMI18) (Fersini et al., 2018) for hate speech towards women and the hate speech detection shared task (HaSpeeDe18) (Bosco et al., 2018) for the part related to hate speech towards immigrants proposed in (Sanguinetti et al., 2018). Both datasets comprise 2,500 instances for training, 500 for validation, and 1,000 for testing.

English Ousidhoum et al. (2019) present MlMa, a multi-lingual multi-aspect hate speech analysis dataset in Arabic, English, and French. The dataset consists of tweets collected by querying language-specific keywords.

Mollas et al. (2022) propose ETHOS, a multi-label English hate speech detection dataset of Reddit posts. They employ an automatic pre-annotation process where the posts are first labeled with a machine learning classifier. Only the uncertain ones (within the [.4, .6] probability range) are manually labeled using a crowdsourcing platform. Following the authors, we binarise the values of each label (if value $\geq 0.5 \rightarrow 1$ else value $\rightarrow 0$). The targets are identified only when the post is hateful, so we discard the non-hateful ones. Here, we map the targets *national_origin* and *race* to *origin*.

Kennedy et al. (2020c) collected a large set of comments from different social media sources (YouTube, Twitter, and Reddit). The annotation process has been performed via a crowdsourcing platform where each comment receives four ratings. The authors further ensured that every annotator received comments across all the hate speech scale. Since the dataset is annotated with a continuous hate score, we used a threshold set to binarise the problem: if value $< -1 \rightarrow 0$ and if value $> 0.5 \rightarrow 1$. We merged *origin* and *race* classes into the *origin* class.

Mathew et al. (2021) collected English posts from the social media platforms Twitter and Gab. Then, they used a crowdsourcing platform for annotating each post as hate, offensive, or normal speech; annotators also have to select the target communities mentioned in the posts. Labels are aggregated, and the final one is obtained through majority voting. We discard the instance when there is no majority (i.e., the three annotators have assigned a different label). Here, we binarise the targets as suggested by the authors into toxic (*hate-speech* or *offensive*) and non-toxic (*normal*). We also map the targets based on the grouping made in the paper (see Table 3 in (Mathew et al., 2021)), with the only exception of *Indigenous* and *Refugee* that we assign to *origin* class.

Kennedy et al. (2020a) presented the Gab Hate Corpus (GHC), a multi-label English corpus of posts from the social network `gab.com`. Comments were annotated by at least three trained annotators with the following classes: *Call for Violence*, *Assault on Human Dignity*, or *Not Hateful*. Following Kennedy et al. (2020b), we aggregate the first two for obtaining the hateful class. We selected only the targets used in our study (removing *political*) and merged *nationality/regionalism* and *race or ethnicity* classes into the *origin* class.

Kiela et al. (2021) introduced a novel framework for dynamically creating benchmark corpora. The annotators are asked to find adversarial examples, i.e., hard examples that a target model would misclassify. The obtained dataset also provides the target group.[4] Here, we mapped their targets to ours, removing the ones not covered.

Table 1 shows the size of the dataset created by combining all the afore-mentioned English corpora.

[3] `https://hatespeechdata.com/`

[4] `https://github.com/bvidgen/Dynamically-Generated-Hate-Speech-Dataset`

	Hate	Non-hate	Total
Disability	3,128	1,488	4,526
Gender	22,655	24,182	46,829
Origin	44,047	31,211	75,327
Religion	17,010	10,840	27,864
Sex. Orientation	9,980	12,312	22,313
Total	97,014	80,729	177,749

Table 1: Statistics of the English dataset.

Model	MONO	MULTI	ZERO
XLM-Large	59.25	**81.23**	57.27
XLM-Base	52.36	**80.74**	54.47
XLM-Twitter	63.52	**83.34**	56.45
mBERT	66.93	**80.48**	51.87
ITA-Base-XXL	61.20	-	-
ITA-Base	40.45	-	-

Table 2: Macro-F1 results. The most frequent class classifier has a Macro-F1 of 36.85.

3 Experimental Methodology

Our experimental setup illustrates three aspects: 1) the performance of the different models on a train, validation, and test setup that we construct on our data, 2) the performance on different datasets (also considering two new additional datasets that we take as *out-of-domain*) and 3) a qualitative evaluation section in which we use explainability methods to assess which words are contributing more to the prediction.

3.1 Models

In this paper, we tested different pretrained language models. As multi-lingual models: the XLM Roberta base and large models from (Conneau et al., 2020) (XLM-Base, XLM-Large), multilingualBERT[5] (mBERT), and a model pre-trained on multi-lingual twitter data (XLM-Twitter) (Barbieri et al., 2021). As mono-lingual models for Italian: *dbmdz/bert-base-italian-xxl-cased* (ITA-Base-XXL) and *dbmdz/bert-base-italian-cased* (ITA-Base).[6] In addition, we used DeHateBert (Aluru et al., 2020), a fine-tuned mBERT model trained on (Sanguinetti et al., 2018).

For the models we train, we run three different experimental frameworks: 1) *mono-lingual* (MONO), in which we train our models only on Italian data; 2) *multi-lingual* (MULTI), in which we combine the Italian and the English data for training; 3) *zero shot, cross-lingual* (ZERO), in which we train a model only with English data. All the models are tested on the Italian test data (Fersini et al., 2018; Sanguinetti et al., 2018).

3.2 Data Setup

We used the splits provided by the associated shared tasks for the Italian dataset. This setup ensures performance comparability. For Sanguinetti et al. (2018), we isolated 500 instances from the training to be used as the validation set. For the combined English data, we isolate 20% with stratified sampling to be used as the validation set. The details of the parameters used to fine-tune the models can be found in the Appendix A. Models are trained for 5 epochs and evaluated every 50 steps, and we select the best checkpoint considering the validation loss.

[5]`https://github.com/google-research/bert/blob/master/multilingual.md`

[6]`https://huggingface.co/dbmdz`

4 Results

4.1 Overall Results

Table 2 shows the results only for the models that we trained by testing on the official splits of each Italian dataset (see Section 2.2). We have found two crucial takeaways. First, the best multi-lingual model (XLM-Large) performs sensibly better than the best model trained only on mono-lingual data (mBERT). Second, models subject to multi-lingual training **always** outperforms mono-lingual ones. Recent research (Nozza et al., 2020) has shown that language-specific datasets are more effective when used to fine-tune language-specific models; this research suggests that training only on the small set of Italian data is not enough even when using a language-specific model: joint fine-tuning with larger datasets is an effective way of obtaining more accurate hate speech classifiers. This is a very interesting result: considering the small amount of Italian data used by the multi-lingual model, this opens future applications of multi-lingual pipelines to low-resource languages. Finally, the increase in performance of the multi-lingual framework comes directly from the Italian data we added to the training since the performance of the purely zero-shot cross-lingual models is much worse than the mono-lingual one.

Model	AMI18	AMI20	Sanguinetti et al. (2018)	HaSpeeDe18	HaSpeeDe20
XLM-Twitter	**82.10**	72.73	78.53	74.59	72.68
XLM-Base	79.88	66.47	79.64	76.40	72.57
XLM-Large	80.37	**73.75**	**79.96**	**78.13**	**75.86**
DeHateBert	42.66	53.97	-	-	70.79

Table 3: Results on different benchmark datasets for the multi-lingual models.

4.2 Results by Dataset

This section shows the results split by datasets for our multi-lingual best models and for DeHateBert. We show the results on the test sets of Sanguinetti et al. (2018) and AMI18 (Fersini et al., 2018). Moreover, we also test on the complete test set of HaSpeeDe18, Bosco et al. (2018) and the shared task re-runs HaSpeeDe20 (Sanguinetti et al., 2020) and AMI20 (Fersini et al., 2020b). Unfortunately, DeHateBert was not fine-tuned following the guidelines described in (Bosco et al., 2018) as the authors used different splits. For this reason, we cannot evaluate the performance of this model on HaSpeeDe18 and (Sanguinetti et al., 2018) (some examples of the examples in the test sets are used for training).

Table 3 shows the results for each dataset. We do not show results for Italian models as they perform much worse (see Table 2). These results show that our models have consistent performance over most categories. Indeed, XLM-Twitter, beats DeHateBert by 39 and 19 points in F1 on AMI18 and AMI20 respectively. This outcome further demonstrates the need for protected group coverage in the training set.

4.3 Results on Multi-Lingual HateCheck

We also use the recently introduced Multi-Lingual HateCheck (MHC) (Röttger et al., 2022). MHC is a suite of functional tests for multi-lingual hate speech detection models that extend the original English HateCheck (Röttger et al., 2021). MHC tests several functionalities that can affect hate prediction (e.g., counterspeech, spelling variations, use of slurs). Here, we used only the Italian subset. MHC should serve as an external testbed to validate our models.

Results in Table 4 show the consistent performance of our models. XLM-Twitter and XLM-Large strongly outperform the results of the original baseline proposed by Röttger et al. (2022).

Model	F1-h	F1-nh	Macro-F1
XLM-Twitter	84.74	61.17	72.96
XLM-Base	82.71	55.10	68.90
XLM-Large	**88.63**	**65.88**	**77.26**
Röttger et al.	81.50	57.80	69.60

Table 4: Results on different MULTILINGUAL HATECHECK. We report F1 score the for **h**ateful and **non-h**ateful cases, and the overall macro-F1 score.

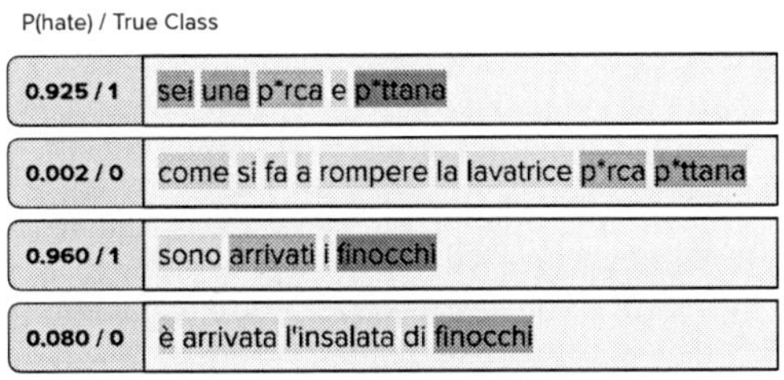

Figure 1: Examples of predictions with SHAP (Lundberg and Lee, 2017) contributions on a color scale; color scale: blue (not-hate), red (hate). Translation available in Appendix B.

4.4 Qualitative Evaluation

Figure 1 reports token contribution explanations of four correct predictions from our multi-lingual XLM-Large. The texts are complex examples in Italian, as standard models usually misclassify them (Nozza, 2021). We extracted token contributions using the interpretability suite provided in Attanasio et al. (2022b). The first two examples regard the taboo Italian expression *p*rca p*ttana* (literally *p*rca* (*pig*) + *p*ttana* (*sl*t*)). When used separately (*porca e puttana* (*pig and slut*)), they should be considered literally; when used together, the two words form taboo expressions that do not have a misogynistic connotation. The latter two examples regard the ambiguous Italian term *finocchi*. The word means *fennels* in a food-related context, but can also be translated to *f*ggots* when refereed to individuals.

5 Related Work

National evaluation campaigns and shared tasks played a significant role in releasing non-English corpora for hate speech detection (Wiegand et al., 2018; Mulki and Ghanem, 2021; Basile et al., 2019; Ptaszynski et al., 2019). Indeed, the research of hate speech detection in Italian in mono-lingual settings mainly revolves around the datasets (Fersini et al., 2018; Bosco et al., 2018; Sanguinetti et al., 2020; Fersini et al., 2020b) released for shared tasks (Bakarov, 2018; Cimino et al., 2018; Attanasio and Pastor, 2020; Lees et al., 2020; Lavergne et al., 2020; Fersini et al., 2020a; Attanasio et al., 2022a, inter alia).

In NLP, the scarcity of data in languages beyond English has generated an interest in zero-shot learning (Srivastava et al., 2018; Ponti et al., 2019; Pfeiffer et al., 2020; Wu et al., 2020; Bianchi et al., 2021, 2022, inter alia) and the application of this to hate speech detection methods (Corazza et al., 2020; Stappen et al., 2020; Aluru et al., 2020; Leite et al., 2020; Rodríguez et al., 2021; Feng et al., 2020; Pelicon et al., 2021). In particular, Aluru et al. (2020) exploited several deep learning models and multi-lingual embeddings for performing an extensive analysis on 16 datasets in 9 different languages in few- and zero-shot learning settings. Rodríguez et al. (2021) use the pre-trained Language Agnostic BERT Sentence Embeddings (Feng et al., 2020) obtaining good results. Other research efforts focused on translating English data to enrich data availability in other languages with mixed results: Ibrohim and Budi (2019) shows that translations do not bring good results using traditional machine learning classifiers. However, more sophisticated pipelines of translation and pre-training can indeed provide some improvement over standard benchmarks (Pamungkas et al., 2021; Wang and Banko, 2021).

6 Conclusion

This paper presents a novel resource for Italian hate speech detection on social media text, HATE-ITA. Researchers can use this new set of models to assess the quality of new systems by providing a more reliable benchmark. However, this is just the first step. Indeed, we do not claim to have released the final model for Italian hate speech detection; HATE-ITA requires careful benchmarking to understand if it can accurately capture hate speech on other targets.

Acknowledgements

This project has partially received funding from the European Research Council (ERC) under the European Union's Horizon 2020 research and innovation program (grant agreement No. 949944, INTEGRATOR), and by Fondazione Cariplo (grant No. 2020-4288, MONICA). Debora Nozza, Federico Bianchi, and Giuseppe Attanasio are members of the MilaNLP group and the Data and Marketing Insights Unit of the Bocconi Institute for Data Science and Analysis.

Ethical Statement

While promising, the results in this work should not be interpreted as a definitive assessment of the performance of hate speech detection in Italian. We are unsure if our model can maintain a stable and fair precision across the different targets and categories. HATE-ITA might overlook some sensible details, which practitioners should treat with care.

References

Sai Saketh Aluru, Binny Mathew, Punyajoy Saha, and Animesh Mukherjee. 2020. A deep dive into multilingual hate speech classification. In *Machine Learning and Knowledge Discovery in Databases. Applied Data Science and Demo Track: European Conference, ECML PKDD 2020, Ghent, Belgium, September 14–18, 2020, Proceedings, Part V*, page 423–439, Berlin, Heidelberg. Springer-Verlag.

Giuseppe Attanasio, Debora Nozza, Dirk Hovy, and Elena Baralis. 2022a. Entropy-based attention regularization frees unintended bias mitigation from lists. In *Findings of the Association for Computational Linguistics: ACL2022 (Forthcoming)*. Association for Computational Linguistics.

Giuseppe Attanasio, Debora Nozza, Eliana Pastor, and Dirk Hovy. 2022b. Benchmarking post-hoc interpretability approaches for transformer-based misogyny detection. In *Proceedings of the First Workshop on Efficient Benchmarking in NLP*. Association for Computational Linguistics.

Giuseppe Attanasio and Eliana Pastor. 2020. PoliTeam @ AMI: Improving sentence embedding similarity with misogyny lexicons for automatic misogyny identificationin italian tweets. In Valerio Basile, Danilo Croce, Maria Maro, and Lucia C. Passaro, editors, *EVALITA Evaluation of NLP and Speech Tools for Italian - December 17th, 2020*, pages 48–54. Accademia University Press.

Amir Bakarov. 2018. Vector space models for automatic misogyny identification (short paper). In *Proceedings of the Sixth Evaluation Campaign of Natural*

Language Processing and Speech Tools for Italian. Final Workshop (EVALITA 2018) co-located with the Fifth Italian Conference on Computational Linguistics (CLiC-it 2018), Turin, Italy, December 12-13, 2018, volume 2263 of *CEUR Workshop Proceedings*. CEUR-WS.org.

Francesco Barbieri, Luis Espinosa Anke, and Jose Camacho-Collados. 2021. Xlm-t: A multilingual language model toolkit for twitter. *arXiv preprint arXiv:2104.12250*.

Valerio Basile, Cristina Bosco, Elisabetta Fersini, Nozza Debora, Viviana Patti, Francisco Manuel Rangel Pardo, Paolo Rosso, Manuela Sanguinetti, et al. 2019. Semeval-2019 task 5: Multilingual detection of hate speech against immigrants and women in twitter. In *13th International Workshop on Semantic Evaluation*, pages 54–63. Association for Computational Linguistics.

Federico Bianchi, Debora Nozza, and Dirk Hovy. 2022. XLM-EMO: Multilingual emotion prediction in social media text. In *Proceedings of the 12th Workshop on Computational Approaches to Subjectivity, Sentiment and Social Media Analysis*. Association for Computational Linguistics.

Federico Bianchi, Silvia Terragni, Dirk Hovy, Debora Nozza, and Elisabetta Fersini. 2021. Cross-lingual contextualized topic models with zero-shot learning. In *Proceedings of the 16th Conference of the European Chapter of the Association for Computational Linguistics: Main Volume*, pages 1676–1683, Online. Association for Computational Linguistics.

Cristina Bosco, Dell'Orletta Felice, Fabio Poletto, Manuela Sanguinetti, and Tesconi Maurizio. 2018. Overview of the EVALITA 2018 hate speech detection task. In *Proceedings of the Sixth Evaluation Campaign of Natural Language Processing and Speech Tools for Italian. Final Workshop (EVALITA 2018)*, volume 2263, pages 1–9, Turin, Italy. CEUR.org.

Tommaso Caselli, Nicole Novielli, Viviana Patti, and Paolo Rosso. 2018. EVALITA 2018: Overview of the 6th Evaluation Campaign of Natural Language Processing and Speech Tools for Italian. In *Proceedings of Sixth Evaluation Campaign of Natural Language Processing and Speech Tools for Italian. Final Workshop (EVALITA 2018)*, Turin, Italy. CEUR.org.

Andrea Cimino, Lorenzo De Mattei, and Felice Dell'Orletta. 2018. Multi-task learning in deep neural networks at EVALITA 2018. In *Proceedings of the Sixth Evaluation Campaign of Natural Language Processing and Speech Tools for Italian. Final Workshop (EVALITA 2018) co-located with the Fifth Italian Conference on Computational Linguistics (CLiC-it 2018), Turin, Italy, December 12-13, 2018*, volume 2263 of *CEUR Workshop Proceedings*. CEUR-WS.org.

Alexis Conneau, Kartikay Khandelwal, Naman Goyal, Vishrav Chaudhary, Guillaume Wenzek, Francisco Guzmán, Edouard Grave, Myle Ott, Luke Zettlemoyer, and Veselin Stoyanov. 2020. Unsupervised cross-lingual representation learning at scale. In *Proceedings of the 58th Annual Meeting of the Association for Computational Linguistics*, pages 8440–8451, Online. Association for Computational Linguistics.

Michele Corazza, Stefano Menini, Elena Cabrio, Sara Tonelli, and Serena Villata. 2020. Hybrid Emoji-Based Masked Language Models for Zero-Shot Abusive Language Detection. In *Findings of the Association for Computational Linguistics: EMNLP 2020*, pages 943–949, Online. Association for Computational Linguistics.

Ashwin Geet D'Sa, Irina Illina, Dominique Fohr, Dietrich Klakow, and Dana Ruiter. 2020. Label propagation-based semi-supervised learning for hate speech classification. In *Proceedings of the First Workshop on Insights from Negative Results in NLP*, pages 54–59, Online. Association for Computational Linguistics.

Fangxiaoyu Feng, Yinfei Yang, Daniel Cer, Naveen Arivazhagan, and Wei Wang. 2020. Language-agnostic bert sentence embedding.

Elisabetta Fersini, Debora Nozza, and Giulia Boifava. 2020a. Profiling Italian misogynist: An empirical study. In *Proceedings of the Workshop on Resources and Techniques for User and Author Profiling in Abusive Language*, pages 9–13, Marseille, France. European Language Resources Association (ELRA).

Elisabetta Fersini, Debora Nozza, and Paolo Rosso. 2018. Overview of the EVALITA 2018 task on automatic misogyny identification (AMI). *Proceedings of the 6th evaluation campaign of Natural Language Processing and Speech tools for Italian (EVALITA 2018)*, 12:59.

Elisabetta Fersini, Debora Nozza, and Paolo Rosso. 2020b. AMI @ EVALITA2020: Automatic misogyny identification. In *Proceedings of the 7th evaluation campaign of Natural Language Processing and Speech tools for Italian (EVALITA 2020)*, Online. CEUR.org.

Muhammad Okky Ibrohim and Indra Budi. 2019. Translated vs non-translated method for multilingual hate speech identification in twitter. *International Journal on Advanced Science, Engineering and Information Technology*, 9(4):1116–1123.

Vijayasaradhi Indurthi, Bakhtiyar Syed, Manish Shrivastava, Nikhil Chakravartula, Manish Gupta, and Vasudeva Varma. 2019. FERMI at SemEval-2019 task 5: Using sentence embeddings to identify hate speech against immigrants and women in Twitter. In *Proceedings of the 13th International Workshop on Semantic Evaluation*, pages 70–74, Minneapolis, Minnesota, USA. Association for Computational Linguistics.

Brendan Kennedy, Mohammad Atari, Aida Mostafazadeh Davani, Leigh Yeh, Ali Omrani, Yehsong Kim, Kris Coombs Jr., Shreya Havaldar, Gwenyth Portillo-Wightman, Elaine Gonzalez, Joe Hoover, Aida Azatian*, Gabriel Cardenas*, Alyzeh Hussain*, Austin Lara*, Adam Omary*, Christina Park*, Xin Wang*, Clarisa Wijaya*, Yong Zhang*, Beth Meyerowitz, and Morteza Dehghani. 2020a. The Gab Hate Corpus: A Collection of 27k Posts Annotated for Hate Speech.

Brendan Kennedy, Xisen Jin, Aida Mostafazadeh Davani, Morteza Dehghani, and Xiang Ren. 2020b. Contextualizing hate speech classifiers with post-hoc explanation. In *Proceedings of the 58th Annual Meeting of the Association for Computational Linguistics*, pages 5435–5442, Online. Association for Computational Linguistics.

Chris J Kennedy, Geoff Bacon, Alexander Sahn, and Claudia von Vacano. 2020c. Constructing interval variables via faceted rasch measurement and multitask deep learning: a hate speech application. *arXiv preprint arXiv:2009.10277*.

Douwe Kiela, Max Bartolo, Yixin Nie, Divyansh Kaushik, Atticus Geiger, Zhengxuan Wu, Bertie Vidgen, Grusha Prasad, Amanpreet Singh, Pratik Ringshia, Zhiyi Ma, Tristan Thrush, Sebastian Riedel, Zeerak Waseem, Pontus Stenetorp, Robin Jia, Mohit Bansal, Christopher Potts, and Adina Williams. 2021. Dynabench: Rethinking benchmarking in NLP. In *Proceedings of the 2021 Conference of the North American Chapter of the Association for Computational Linguistics: Human Language Technologies*, pages 4110–4124, Online. Association for Computational Linguistics.

Eric Lavergne, Rajkumar Saini, György Kovács, and Killian Murphy. 2020. Thenorth @ haspeede 2: Bert-based language model fine-tuning for italian hate speech detection (short paper). In *Proceedings of the Seventh Evaluation Campaign of Natural Language Processing and Speech Tools for Italian. Final Workshop (EVALITA 2020), Online event, December 17th, 2020*, volume 2765 of *CEUR Workshop Proceedings*. CEUR-WS.org.

Alyssa Lees, Jeffrey Sorensen, and Ian Kivlichan. 2020. Jigsaw @ AMI and haspeede2: Fine-tuning a pre-trained comment-domain BERT model. In *Proceedings of the Seventh Evaluation Campaign of Natural Language Processing and Speech Tools for Italian. Final Workshop (EVALITA 2020), Online event, December 17th, 2020*, volume 2765 of *CEUR Workshop Proceedings*. CEUR-WS.org.

João Augusto Leite, Diego Silva, Kalina Bontcheva, and Carolina Scarton. 2020. Toxic language detection in social media for Brazilian Portuguese: New dataset and multilingual analysis. In *Proceedings of the 1st Conference of the Asia-Pacific Chapter of the Association for Computational Linguistics and the 10th International Joint Conference on Natural Language Processing*, pages 914–924, Suzhou, China. Association for Computational Linguistics.

Scott M Lundberg and Su-In Lee. 2017. A unified approach to interpreting model predictions. In *Advances in Neural Information Processing Systems*, volume 30. Curran Associates, Inc.

Binny Mathew, Punyajoy Saha, Seid Muhie Yimam, Chris Biemann, Pawan Goyal, and Animesh Mukherjee. 2021. Hatexplain: A benchmark dataset for explainable hate speech detection. In *Proceedings of the AAAI Conference on Artificial Intelligence*, volume 35, pages 14867–14875.

Ioannis Mollas, Zoe Chrysopoulou, Stamatis Karlos, and Grigorios Tsoumakas. 2022. Ethos: a multi-label hate speech detection dataset. *Complex & Intelligent Systems*, pages 1–16.

Hala Mulki and Bilal Ghanem. 2021. Working notes of the workshop arabic misogyny identification (armi-2021). In *Forum for Information Retrieval Evaluation*, FIRE 2021, page 7–8, New York, NY, USA. Association for Computing Machinery.

Debora Nozza. 2021. Exposing the limits of zero-shot cross-lingual hate speech detection. In *Proceedings of the 59th Annual Meeting of the Association for Computational Linguistics and the 11th International Joint Conference on Natural Language Processing (Volume 2: Short Papers)*, pages 907–914, Online. Association for Computational Linguistics.

Debora Nozza, Federico Bianchi, and Dirk Hovy. 2020. What the [MASK]? Making sense of language-specific BERT models. *arXiv preprint arXiv:2003.02912*.

Nedjma Ousidhoum, Zizheng Lin, Hongming Zhang, Yangqiu Song, and Dit-Yan Yeung. 2019. Multilingual and multi-aspect hate speech analysis. In *Proceedings of the 2019 Conference on Empirical Methods in Natural Language Processing and the 9th International Joint Conference on Natural Language Processing (EMNLP-IJCNLP)*, pages 4675–4684, Hong Kong, China. Association for Computational Linguistics.

Endang Wahyu Pamungkas, Valerio Basile, and Viviana Patti. 2021. A joint learning approach with knowledge injection for zero-shot cross-lingual hate speech detection. *Information Processing & Management*, 58(4):102544.

Andraž Pelicon, Ravi Shekhar, Blaž Škrlj, Matthew Purver, and Senja Pollak. 2021. Investigating cross-lingual training for offensive language detection. *PeerJ Computer Science*, 7:e559. Publisher: PeerJ Inc.

Jonas Pfeiffer, Ivan Vulić, Iryna Gurevych, and Sebastian Ruder. 2020. MAD-X: An Adapter-Based Framework for Multi-Task Cross-Lingual Transfer. In *Proceedings of the 2020 Conference on Empirical Methods in Natural Language Processing (EMNLP)*, pages 7654–7673, Online. Association for Computational Linguistics.

Edoardo Maria Ponti, Ivan Vulić, Ryan Cotterell, Roi Reichart, and Anna Korhonen. 2019. Towards zero-shot language modeling. In *Proceedings of the 2019 Conference on Empirical Methods in Natural Language Processing and the 9th International Joint Conference on Natural Language Processing (EMNLP-IJCNLP)*, pages 2900–2910, Hong Kong, China. Association for Computational Linguistics.

Michal Ptaszynski, Agata Pieciukiewicz, and Paweł Dybała. 2019. Results of the PolEval 2019 shared task 6: First dataset and open shared task for automatic cyberbullying detection in Polish Twitter. *Proceedings of the PolEval 2019 Workshop*, page 89.

Sebastián E. Rodríguez, Héctor Allende-Cid, and Héctor Allende. 2021. Detecting Hate Speech in Cross-Lingual and Multi-lingual Settings Using Language Agnostic Representations. In *Progress in Pattern Recognition, Image Analysis, Computer Vision, and Applications*, pages 77–87, Cham. Springer International Publishing.

Paul Röttger, Haitham Seelawi, Debora Nozza, Zeerak Talat, and Bertie Vidgen. 2022. Multilingual HateCheck: Functional tests for multilingual hate speech detection models. In *Proceedings of the 6th Workshop on Online Abuse and Harms (WOAH 2022)*. Association for Computational Linguistics.

Paul Röttger, Bertie Vidgen, Dong Nguyen, Zeerak Waseem, Helen Margetts, and Janet Pierrehumbert. 2021. HateCheck: Functional tests for hate speech detection models. In *Proceedings of the 59th Annual Meeting of the Association for Computational Linguistics and the 11th International Joint Conference on Natural Language Processing (Volume 1: Long Papers)*, pages 41–58, Online. Association for Computational Linguistics.

Manuela Sanguinetti, Gloria Comandini, Elisa Di Nuovo, Simona Frenda, Marco Stranisci, Cristina Bosco, Tommaso Caselli, Viviana Patti, and Irene Russo. 2020. Haspeede 2 @ EVALITA2020: overview of the EVALITA 2020 hate speech detection task. In *Proceedings of the Seventh Evaluation Campaign of Natural Language Processing and Speech Tools for Italian. Final Workshop (EVALITA 2020), Online event, December 17th, 2020*, volume 2765 of *CEUR Workshop Proceedings*. CEUR-WS.org.

Manuela Sanguinetti, Fabio Poletto, Cristina Bosco, Viviana Patti, and Marco Stranisci. 2018. An Italian Twitter corpus of hate speech against immigrants. In *Proceedings of the Eleventh International Conference on Language Resources and Evaluation (LREC 2018)*, Miyazaki, Japan. European Language Resources Association (ELRA).

Shashank Srivastava, Igor Labutov, and Tom Mitchell. 2018. Zero-shot learning of classifiers from natural language quantification. In *Proceedings of the 56th Annual Meeting of the Association for Computational Linguistics (Volume 1: Long Papers)*, pages 306–316, Melbourne, Australia. Association for Computational Linguistics.

Lukas Stappen, Fabian Brunn, and Björn W. Schuller. 2020. Cross-lingual zero- and few-shot hate speech detection utilising frozen transformer language models and AXEL. *CoRR*, abs/2004.13850.

Cindy Wang and Michele Banko. 2021. Practical transformer-based multilingual text classification. In *Proceedings of the 2021 Conference of the North American Chapter of the Association for Computational Linguistics: Human Language Technologies: Industry Papers*, pages 121–129, Online. Association for Computational Linguistics.

Michael Wiegand, Melanie Siegel, and Josef Ruppenhofer. 2018. Overview of the GermEval 2018 Shared Task on the Identification of Offensive Language. In *Proceedings of GermEval 2018, 14th Conference on Natural Language Processing (KONVENS 2018)*.

Ledell Wu, Fabio Petroni, Martin Josifoski, Sebastian Riedel, and Luke Zettlemoyer. 2020. Scalable zero-shot entity linking with dense entity retrieval. In *Proceedings of the 2020 Conference on Empirical Methods in Natural Language Processing (EMNLP)*, pages 6397–6407, Online. Association for Computational Linguistics.

A Model Training

All the models are trained with the same pipeline. We report the shared parameters in Table 5. As mentioned in the table we fix the maximum number of epochs, but we evaluate the models during training and eventually select the model with the best validation loss. All the experiments are run 5 times and we take the average of the results.

Param	**Value**
Batch Size	64
Warm Up Steps	50
Learning Rate	1e-3
Learning Epochs*	5
Optimizer	AdamW
Betas	0.9 and 0.999
Max Length	100

Table 5: The main parameters we used to run the models. *While epochs are 5, we remark that we are running a step-wise evaluation.

B Examples Translation

We provide as literal as possible translations.

- IT: *Sei una p*rca e p*ttana*
- EN: *you are pig and sl*t*

- IT: *Come si fa a rompere la lavatrice p*rca p*ttana*
- EN: *How the hell can you break the washing machine*

- IT: *Sono arrivati i finocchi*
- EN: *Here come the f*ggots*

- IT: *È arrivata l'insalata di finocchi*
- EN: *Here it comes the fennel salad*

Author Index